NETWORKING
The First Report and Directory

NETWORKING

The First Report and Directory

Jessica Lipnack and Jeffrey Stamps

A DOLPHIN BOOK
Doubleday & Company, Inc., Garden City, New York
1982

Copyright © 1982 by Jessica Lipnack and Jeffrey Stamps
Library of Congress Cataloging in Publication Data
Lipnack, Jessica
Networking.
"A Dolphin Book"
Includes indexes.
1. Associations, institutions, etc.–United States–Directories.
2. Self-help groups–United States Directories.
I. Stamps, Jeffrey. II. Title. III. Title: Networking.
AS29.5.L56 061'.3 81-43292
Hardcover edition ISBN 0-385-18121-3
Paperback edition ISBN 0-385-17772-0 AACR2
Dolphin Books
Doubleday & Company, Inc.
All rights reserved
Printed in the United States of America
First Edition

These copyrighted works have been quoted with permission:
Itzhak Bentov, *Stalking the Wild Pendulum: On the Mechanics of Consciousness,* © 1977 (E. P. Dutton). Marilyn Ferguson, *The Aquarian Conspiracy: Personal and Social Transformation in the 1980s,* © 1980 (J. P. Tarcher, Inc.). Hazel Henderson, *Creating Alternative Futures: The End of Economics,* © 1980 (Berkley). *Rain Magazine,* "Raindrops," January 1980, © 1980 (Rain Umbrella). Leif Smith and Patricia Wagner, *The Networking Game,* © 1980 (Network Research). David Spangler, editor, *Conversations With John,* © 1980 (Lorian Association).

Typography by Typesetting Service Corp., Providence, RI

Designed by Marilyn Schulman

To Eliza and Miranda

Contents

The Art of Networking

GUIDE BY GUIDE/WHY THE NETWORKS THAT ARE HERE ARE HERE/
ON NETWORKING WELL

Acknowledgments

A book like this comes about because it is needed and because many people want it to happen. Every name that appears in this book is here because someone took the time to gather information, put it in an envelope, and mail it. The list of these names goes on for pages—represented, in fact, by the very pages that appear as the directory for this book. We thank everyone who has contributed in that way.

Two people, above all, have supported our effort from the very beginning. One, Ron Bernstein, suggested the original idea, found us a publisher, and read our drafts. When we began working on this book, Ron was our literary agent; now he is our friend. The other, Robert A. Smith, III, is our networking mentor. The first letter that we ever wrote asking for help in formulating a book about networking went to Bob. He was the original source for every connection reflected in the directory.

Two of the people Bob pointed us toward have become important teachers for us: Virginia Hine and Robert Muller. We thank them for their help and encouragement. We are also grateful to Bill Ellis, Michelle Harrison, Hazel Henderson, Steve Johnson, Phil Kreitner, Lisa Marlin, Olivia and Hob Hoblitzelle, Mark Satin, and Fred von Dreger for reading chapters.

Our family and friends have helped in invisible, indispensable ways: Mirtala Bentov, Jane Carpineto, Priscilla Harmel, Gus Jaccaci, Erwin and Marianne Jaffe, Peter and Trudy Johnson-Lenz, Robin King, Emily LaMont, Eric Lipnack, Ethel Lipnack, Bob McAndrews, Jimmy Morris, Judy Smith, Ann Stamps, David Stamps, Susan Stamps, and Ben and Kate Taylor. Marylois Brick Bing, Analee Keenan, Ferial and Behnaz Majzoobi, June Mullen, and Susan Rochette made it possible for us to constructively combine work and home.

The third member of our writing team is our workhorse computer, a Wang 2200, a marvel of flexibility, reliability, and indefatigability. Every aspect of our research, writing, and production process—from contacting people to compiling and cross-indexing the directory to writing the chapters to providing the electronic final copy for typesetting—has passed through our computer. We are grateful to Bob Carr and Howie Finn, of Wang Laboratories, for their considerable help in the experimental process that enabled us to translate our original manuscript into the type you are now reading. And thanks to Jay Higgins, of Typesetting Service, for his cooperation.

We thank Lindy Hess, our senior editor, for understanding and supporting the book and for being willing to take risks. We appreciate the editorial work of Gerry Helferich, Kathy Tiddens, and Roy Wandelmaier, and are grateful for the design work of Marilyn Schulman.

Eliza and Miranda helped too.

Jessica Lipnack

Jeffrey Stamps

West Newton, Massachusetts

December 1981

Introduction

Networking: The First Report and Directory is two books in one: It is a report on networking and it is a directory of networks. The *report* is divided into twelve chapters. The *directory* is divided into five guides. All directory pages are indicated by a shaded corner, as on this page.

Each group whose name appears in this book has its own letter/number code that enables you to cross-reference the group within the various parts of the directory. The code consists of a letter–**H**, **S**, **U**, **V**, **L**, **G**, or **E**–and a number. The letter tells you which chapter of the book contains the contact information for the group. Thus, the networks listed in Chapter 3, Healing Networks, are coded **H**, while the networks listed in Chapter 4, Sharing Networks, are coded **S**. The listings of networks that follow Chapters 3 through 9 are collectively known as the *Topic Guide*.

All the networks listed in the seven topical areas are indexed together in the four guides that follow Chapter 12.

- The *Organization Guide* is an alphabetical listing of every group in the book.

- The *Location Guide* is a geographical listing of the networks.

- The *Keyword Guide* provides a sampling of the issues, interests, and values of the networks.

- The *Title Guide* provides a sampling of the publications and materials the networks produce.

The 1526 names that appear here are among about 1600 groups that responded to the 4000 letters we sent out over an 18-month period. These names are not endorsements or recommendations: They are examples of what people are doing with their time. In one way or another, all the groups whose names appear here identify with the idea of networking–people connecting with people.

NETWORKING
The First Report and Directory

1

Discovering Another America

This book is about networks and networking. Networks are the links that bind us together, making it possible for us to share work, aspirations, and ideals. Networking is a process of making connections with other people. This book is specifically concerned with the networking that creates the universe we call Another America.

WHAT IS ANOTHER AMERICA?

Another America is not a place but a state of mind. Touching every area of our lives, there is Another America, not often seen on television or read about in newspapers. It is an Emerald City of ideas and visions and practical enterprises that people move in and out of depending on their moods and needs, a domain that is very new, and at the same time, very old.

In this special universe, health is perceived as the natural state of the body, cooperation is regarded as an effective way to meet basic needs, nature's ecological orchestra is revered as one unified instrument, inner development is valued as a correlate to social involvement, and the planet is understood to be an interconnected whole.

Another America answers the questions "Whatever happened to the 1960s?" and "Where did people go in the 1970s?" There is Another America and it is pulsating and expanding and unfolding through *networking*, an organic communications process that threads across interests, through problems, and around solutions. Networks are the meeting grounds for the inhabitants of this invisible domain. These flexible, vibrant organizations often exist without boundaries, bylaws, or officers. Networks are the lines of communication, the alternative express highways that people use to get things done. In crisis and in opportunity, the word spreads quickly through these people-power lines.

Another America and its networks are complements. Another America represents the ideas and the values. Networks and networking are the structures and processes through which the ideas and values come alive.

Fueled in large part by the sweat equity of the survivors of the 1960s and inspired by a vision of a peaceful yet dynamic planet, an entirely new culture is emerging in our land. It is connected by casual, ever-changing links among millions of people with shared needs, values, and aspirations. As short-lived, self-camouflaging, a-disciplinary crosshatches of activity, networks are invisible, uncountable, and unpollable. Networks can be highly active one day, and totally defunct the next. Every time a network comes to life its form is a little different.

Networks are stages on which dissonance is not only tolerated but encouraged, yet consensus is a common goal. They are the experimental seedbeds in which people risk stretching their creativity. Networks are efficient and effective; feedback is as spontaneous as telephones, mailings, and meetings permit. Networks are often personal and friendly, supportive and affirming, critical and energizing. Networks can be intimate and immediate—at times they serve as our extended families, bonding people together as strongly as bloodlines.

Networks are the connections that make us all one people on one small planet near one small star. They are our newest and probably our oldest social invention. They are our gift to our children who are natural networkers on the day they are born.

There are spokespeople in Another America, but there are few exalted leaders, presidents, or boards of directors. There are people who serve as models, but there are few figureheads whose lives are to be cloned. There are entry points and connections—nodes and links—but there are few hierarchical structures along which individuals can advance. Another America exists everywhere, from the smallest towns to the largest cities, offering anyone who shares the vision the opportunity to participate.

There is nothing to be "won" in Another America: There are only problems to solve, using personal resourcefulness as the source of solutions. There are goods that are produced to be used but not consumed, and obsolence refers to an antiquated value system that calls for winners and losers. Even the language people use is different: From a litany of overused clichés, people are finding novel ways to express themselves in optimistic, hope-filled phrases that help to create the reality toward which people are striving.

• Outside the cement-block walls of the high-technology medical profession is a world in which people are learning to heal themselves and are reclaiming the two poles of the life cycle by bringing birth and death back into their homes.

• In contrast to the high-speed, competitive, militaristic America that we all know, there is Another America, which is measured, cooperative, and peaceful, yet alive with the promise of what life could be like if war were simply not a possibility.

• Beyond the periphery of the fossil-fuel and nuclear-fission-intensive America, which threatens to expire within our lifetime and contaminate our offspring for generations to come, is a wellspring of ever-renewable energy resources that are heating people's homes and generating their electricity.

• As the conventional politics and marketplaces of the machine age continue to break down, a value system is emerging in Another America that reflects deep concern with individual and collective human needs.

• Sidestepping the stifling regimentation of rote learning that typifies much of education is a school without school in which people are learning from one another and teaching their children at home.

• Meeting outside the temples and churches of organized religion is an ever-present chapel without walls in which people are growing from within, without paying obeisance to the patriarchal hierarchy or rigid dogma of established religions.

• Alongside the official pronouncements that evolution happens over many, many lifetimes and is only a series of random mutations anyway is Another America, which knows in its heart that humanity is evolving very quickly, right now, and that we all are responsible for the outcome.

It is possible to live in both Americas at once and people are doing so all the time. Another America knows no national boundaries: It recognizes the interconnectedness of the entire planet, yet this important new networking movement has its seeds well planted in U.S. soil. The networks that offer a different eventuality for us all are firmly grounded in America, and their impact is slowly being felt around the globe, sidestepping the nation-state model that has dominated the earth for the past 400 years.

While the 1970s have been characterized as the age of narcissism, a more careful reading of the times reveals quite a different picture. People did turn inward, and in self-reflection they discovered precisely what they had been yearning for a few years earlier. By looking within themselves–at their skills, their talents, and their local needs–people found a gigantic reservoir of untapped resources that could be applied to remaking our civilization. By focusing in on hundreds of small issues, people discovered thousands of imaginative solutions.

For every problem that is tossed up before us in newspapers and on television, someone–if not ten, twenty, or thirty someones–somewhere in the country is working on a solution. While the cameras have been turned in another direction and reporters have been preoccupied with following the multiple trails of disaster and corruption, the survivors of the 1960s have worked to create Another America, which is hidden to some and highly visible to others.

The 1970s, we can now see, were a time of hard work, experimentation, and bridge building. It was during the 1970s that networks came into their own, offering a strong counterpoint to the centralized bureaucracies that now dominate people's lives.

Networkers in various areas seem all to be saying the same thing: If you don't like what is, create something you do like. Regardless of whether they are designing programs for the elderly, initiating community alliances with prisons, exchanging information about home schooling, supporting options within holistic health, organizing against nuclear power, raising money to save an endangered species, creating a computerized community bulletin board, structuring a local skills-bank, forging a mountain commune, establishing a food co-op, starting a growth center, or building a windmill, all are verbalizing similar messages based on the same underlying values.

- Although a women's health network may appear to have nothing to do with saving the whales, the declarations, functions, and styles of both groups indicate that they are operating out of the same, mutualistic concerns for a world in which honor and protection are accorded to all living beings.

- While a group working to prevent the construction of a nuclear power plant may appear to have nothing in common with an organic-seed exchange, these two vital networks are both working to engage people in re-creating the world around them.

- Even though there is no formal connection between a Native American sovereignty network and a guild for individual artisans, they share some deep conceptual connections and a value system that honors individual choice and cultural pluralism.

- Whereas a housing cooperative may think it has nothing to say to a hospice, on closer examination it is apparent that both cherish values that support people's control over their own lives.

- Although a utility rate-reform network might not feel it has any similarity to a home-birth group, both networks are posing similar challenges to monopolistic institutions–in one case to power companies, in the other case to hospitals.

These connections cross categories, transcending individual issues. It is a shared value system that defines the pattern of a "metanetwork," a network of networks, an immense subculture, an America within America.

Another America exists as a pattern of connections and values, a complex lattice-work of hope and despair, anger and love, fantasy and reality, descriptions of problems, and examples of solutions. While some might say that optimism is unrealistic at this point in history, networkers counter with the belief that the future we create together is a matter of attitude and that while the doomsayers are important beacons, they spotlight only a portion of reality. Every day, every new situation, every new problem is a challenge and a potential for beneficial change.

Another America is entered by taking another look at what is going on around us and recognizing the connections and nascent links among all the little islands of hope. If the idea of Another America seems remote, if not a fantasy, here in Chapter 1, reconsider this feeling after wandering through the hundreds of networking examples in this book. Look closely at the networks working in areas you know something about and imagine the simple links that would carry you into the nearest conceptual neighborhoods of this country of the mind.

MAPPING THE NETWORKS

In contacting people for our networking directory (see Chapter 12), we asked them to tell us which of seven categories best described their work: health and the life cycle, communities and cooperatives, energy and ecology, politics and economics, education and communications, personal and spiritual growth, or global and futures-oriented networks.

Each of the categories represents a process: Networks in health and the life cycle are concerned with *healing*, networks in communities and cooperatives are concerned with *sharing* lives and goods, networks in energy and ecology are concerned with *using* resources, networks in politics and economics are concerned with *valuing* people and things, networks in education and communications are concerned with *learning*, networks in personal and spiritual growth are concerned with *growing* within, and networks in global and futures issues are concerned with the planet-as-a-whole *evolving*.

Networks coalesce because people are prepared to surpass the status quo in each of the areas. Networkers are activists who create something else if what exists falls short of their needs. Networkers begin their work by talking with other people, exploring to find common points of agreement, then settling on mutually satisfying plans for action. People use networking to solve small individual problems such as organizing play groups for babies as well as to tackle huge planetary problems such as nuclear proliferation. People network alone and they network together. When a few people get together to network, they usually form a group.

The directory portion of our book is primarily a compendium of *groups that network*. Each of these groups does work that falls into one of the seven process/value categories described above. Within each of the seven areas, all the groups are linked loosely together as a metanetwork working in that area. Although many of the groups have formed coalitions from time to time, the groups themselves remain autonomous and independent. There is no metamembership organization that these groups belong to. These networks are related to one another through mutuality of interests and similarity of concerns largely without formal connections.

Networks are forming in each of the seven categories because people perceive *another* way of meeting their needs and of organizing the country. Networks often identify themselves by appending the sometimes overused word "alternative" to their areas: alternative education, alternative energy, alternative health, alternative economics. In truth, these new networks precisely fit the definition of alternative offered by the dictionary and the "sense" of the word offered by the thesaurus. Webster's defines alternative as "providing or necessitating a choice between two things," and Roget's suggests synonyms such as "horns of a dilemma," "options," and "preferences."

Networkers clearly state that they are grappling with very real "horns of dilemmas"; they feel that our planetary predicament "necessitates a choice between two ways," and they are working to find more suitable "options" that better suit their "preferences."

Healing (health and the life cycle) networks have formed because people want to be well.

Sharing (communities and cooperatives) networks have formed because people are happiest when they are actively working within their communities—whether geographic or conceptual.

Using (ecology and energy) networks have formed because people want to benefit from the earth's bounty without harming it.

Valuing (politics and economics) networks have formed because people want a sane politics and a fair economic system.

Learning (education and communications) networks have formed because people want to learn and they want to communicate—two interrelated human drives.

Growing (personal and spiritual growth) networks have formed because people quest for inner peace and for an understanding of the nature of the universe.

Evolving (global and futures) networks have formed because people have come to understand that nationalism, limitless growth, and political hegemony are antiquated ideas that ignore the reality that we are four and a half billion still-primitive people living on ten percent of the surface area of one small planet in one remote solar system of one of billions of galaxies dancing through space.

It is indeed a spider's web that reaches from healing to sharing to using to valuing to learning to growing to evolving. Seven chapters of this book (Chapter 3 through Chapter 9) are organized according to these topic areas. Each of the topical chapters elaborates upon some of the reasons that networks have formed in that area, then examines a few networks related to the area, amplifying on how networks differ and how they are the same. A topical guide to the networks associated with the chapter theme, including contact information and, in some cases, short descriptions, follows each of the seven chapters (see Chapter 12 for more about the directory guides).

Just as it is impossible to accurately count every cell in your body—by the time you are done counting, the number and relationships would have already changed—so it is impossible to catalog every beneficial network. The very nature of networks is that they are short-lived and constantly reconfiguring. The lists included here constitute *a* directory of constructive networks, not *the* directory of constructive networks. These networks represent starting points; if the network you are looking for is not listed here, contact another that is similar and you'll find your way.

WHAT ARE NETWORKS?

Network. We hear the word every day. A television network. A telephone network. Networks of pathways, roadways, railways, and waterways. Or simply *Network*, the Hollywood film.

The word has come to describe all types of people associations: a friendship network, a neighborhood network, a women's network, a support network, a self-help network, an old-boy network, a scuba-diving network, a knitter's network.

Seymour Saranson, a sociologist at Yale University, has written extensively about "human resource networks." Psychologists Ross Speck and Carolyn Attneave have developed a psychotherapeutic model called "network therapy." The academic discipline of social-network analysis publishes a scholarly journal called *Social Networks*.

The Oxford Universal Dictionary cites the first use of the word in 1560, meaning "a work in which threads, wires, or the like are arranged in the form of a net," or later "a complex structure of rivers, canals, railways, or wireless transmitting stations."

A network in the modern sense, in the sense we are using in this book, has no dictionary definition...yet. The word itself has evolved not as jargon, but to mean something new, something that can be regarded as being similar to, yet quite different from, its earlier meanings. Its more complex meaning has extended the word into additional grammatical forms. The noun is "a network." The verb is "to network." The gerundive form is "networking." A person who networks is a "networker."

This new meaning of "network" includes but is not limited to these images:

- a physical system that looks like a tree or a grid;

- a system of nodes and links;

- a map of lines between points;

- a persisting identity of relationships;

- a "badly knotted fishnet";

- a structure that knows no bounds;

- a nongeographic community;

- a support system;

- a lifeline;

- everybody you know;

- everybody you know who . . .
  also swims;
  also grows tomatoes;
  also loves folk dancing;
  also burns wood;
  also reads Teilhard de Chardin.

In this book, we are describing and documenting networks spontaneously created by people to address problems and offer possibilities primarily *outside* of established institutions. Thus our concern with defining terms has been to understand how networks differ from other social structures that people have created.

From the moment we began thinking about this book, we puzzled over the distinction between a network and an organization. How, we asked ourselves, will we know if this or that group of people is networking or organizing? Later, after our concept of networks had jelled, another question arose: Out of all the networks we are finding, how do we select among them for inclusion in our book?

We did not begin by trying to answer these questions. We did not attempt to define networks and then search for those groups that fit our preconceptions. Rather, we used the process of networking itself to lead us to an understanding of what networking is all about (see Chapter 12). We contacted one person whom we knew to be a networker and followed his lead to all the others. Eventually we sifted through more than 50,000 names culled from the suggestions, publications, directories, and mailing lists of people or groups already contacted, and wrote 4000 letters of inquiry.

Using one "standard" letter to explain our work to our 4000 primary contacts, we posed several questions about networking:

- Are you a network or do you perform a significant networking function?
- Do you consider yourself part of a larger network?
- Who else participates in the larger network?

Out of the massive (40 percent) response to our relatively naive question "Are you networking?" some patterns began to emerge. We discovered that a network, like the moon before the Apollo space flights, has a visible face and an invisible face. A *network*, our networker friends taught us, has a visible face that delineates an organizational *structure* whose features may include a title, a legal form, governing plans, personnel, offices, members, publications, and other attributes of an organized group of people doing some focused work together, or it may include none of these things. Regardless, the networkers stressed, a network also has an invisible face, which can be seen only by looking at the *process* of *networking*.

Eventually we realized that it was not useful to distinguish between networks and organizations. Rather, we came to regard the network as a *type* of organization, one that is significantly different from other types of organizations such as bureaucracies or hierarchies. We have identified ten aspects of networks that differentiate the free form, adaptive nature of networks from the beadledom of bureaucracies and the rigidity of hierarchies.

The Structure of Networks

   (1) Wholeparts
   (2) Levels
   (3) Distributed
   (4) Fly-eyed
   (5) Hydra-headed

In contrast to bureaucracies, whose existence hinges on members who perform highly specialized tasks and who are totally dependent on one another, networks are composed of self-reliant and autonomous participants–people and organizations who simultaneously function as independent "wholes" and as interdependent "parts." We have coined the word *wholeparts* to describe this fundamental feature of networks.

Unlike hierarchies, in which lower-level people (such as secretaries) have considerably less importance and power than those above them (such as managers), networks operate because of the integrated importance of all *levels* of structure and function. The person who types the newsletter performs as necessary a function as the person who writes it. Indeed, in a network, this is often the same person, a person who on another day may be licking stamps, answering the phone, or forming new goals.

Contrasting with the bureaucratic tendency to centralize control and decision making, in networks power and responsibility are *distributed*. Whereas bureaucracies seek to bring people and power into the hands of a dominant authority, networks deliberately create a decentralized pattern of power with many people accountable for the work of a network. Similarly, while bureaucracies function along vertical lines, with information flowing up and orders flowing down, networks function along horizontal lines with information and ideas passing from person to person and group to group. Within the groups constituting a network, however, traditional authority lines may well be operative.

While bureaucracies tend to adopt single standards and policies, networks tolerate—and even encourage—many perspectives about goals and means. Although it may appear that the network "sees" only one point of view, on closer inspection the network has one apparent eye that embodies a plethora of others. Like its transparent, two-winged, flight-born relative, the network is *fly-eyed*.

While hierarchies are rigidly constructed with steps up a pyramid of ranks to a pinnacle that houses and exalts one revered leader or board of directors, networks have many leaders and few, if any, rungs of power. Like the Hydra, the nine-headed serpent which grew two heads each time one was cut off by Hercules, a network is *hydra-headed*, speaking with many equivalent but different voices at the same time.

To see the invisible face of a network requires a really different way of looking at organizations. Instead of focusing on offices, officers, and products, look at the purposes, roles, and connections. Instead of seeing the President in the Oval Office, look for the role of the presidency and consider the process of the executive function. A house may be appreciated for its visible detail, but there is an invisible house revealed in the designer's blueprint that describes the relationships that hold the house together and make it one integrated whole. Looking at relationships rather than the entities that enact the relationships is akin to being able to see the cartoon outline of Wonder Woman's "invisible" airplane. It is through the perspective of process that the essence of networking really comes alive.

The Process of Networking

    (6) Relationships
    (7) Fuzziness
    (8) Nodes and Links
    (9) Me and We
  (10) Values

While bureaucrats are obsessively concerned with concrete and quantifiable things—such as memos, products, or the number of pencils in the supply room—networkers are concerned with abstract and qualitative *relationships* between people. In a network, a person is always more highly valued than the paper s/he creates or files.

Unlike a hierarchy, whose internal parts and external boundaries can be crisply mapped on a flow chart, a network has few clear inner divisions and has indistinct borderlines. A network makes a virtue out of its characteristic *fuzziness*, frustrating outside observers determined to figure out where a network begins and ends.

Contrasting with bureaucrats, who scrupulously define their own specialized tasks and those of each underling, networkers play multiple roles, sometimes defying definition. In communicating, which is the main business of networks, a networker may in one moment serve as a *node*-an entry point or an end recipient—and in another moment serve as a *link*-a connector between nodes and conveyor of information.

Whereas hierarchies regard social organizations as more important than their human members, networks accord equal importance to the individual and the group. In the network, *me and we* reflects the balanced integrity of personal worth and collective purposes.

While bureaucracies bind their members though mechanisms of reward and punishment (promotions and demotions), networks cohere through the shared *values* of their members. If a network could be drawn on paper, its lines of coherence would consist of the ideas that the participants agree upon, manifested in commitments to similar ideals.

A clique that runs city hall from a booth at Joe's Diner is networking in the same way as an environmental coalition that plans strategy and trades information at a rotating potluck supper. An old-boy network that gathers at a country club is based on the same peer relationships and horizontal connections as a floating seminar of holistic health practitioners. The difference lies in the values that bind the networks. The tenth aspect of networking–values–ultimately enabled us to answer our last question, to make choices about which networks belong in this book.

By immersing ourselves in the words and deeds of Another America, we have identified a canvas of values that both are and are not our own. While we stood on the foundation of our personal values to make our initial inquiries, we now find that our value horizons have been extended and the meanings have deepened through the contributions of countless souls, some known to us and some not.

We set out on our journey looking for networks in seven topical categories, roughly representing the scope of our interests. We soon found ourselves being guided by the values that networkers were expressing in conversation and in print. In the end, we decided to organize the book according to the spectrum of seven values that bind together the disparate pieces of Another America into a network of networks.

In Another America, an approach of *healing* people contrasts sharply with the attitude of fixing bodies. *Sharing* is emphasized over competing. *Using* resources thoughtfully is an honored idea that stands in opposition to abusing resources. The orientation of *valuing* is itself regarded as an inescapable part of being human. *Learning* is revered as a lifelong process that significantly differs from being taught to conform to institutional standards. Looking inward, we see ourselves as *growing* throughout our lives rather than decaying with age. Finally, we behold a planet and people *evolving* and transforming, a vision of joy that contrasts with the prevailing vision of sorrow, one that sees a wretched earth and huddled masses retreating and stagnating.

Chapter 2, which follows, provides a brief glimpse of one small working network. The seven topical/value areas are described in Chapter 3 through Chapter 9, including the primary directory entries for each area. Chapter 10 and Chapter 11 constitute the theory section, extending the ideas outlined above. Chapter 12 describes the directory and then concludes the text with some thoughts on the art of networking. It is followed by four extensive guides that cross-reference the networks included after the topical chapters.

2

One Very Special Network: The Boston Women's Health Book Collective

The Boston Women's Health Book Collective office, housed in the basement of an Armenian church in Watertown, Massachusetts, is bubbling with activity on a Friday afternoon in October 1980.

A DAY IN THE LIFE

Judy Norsigian, a Collective member and networker extraordinaire, is seated at her desk, flooded with light for her television interview. A *Newsweek Television* reporter, a woman in her thirties (not much older than Judy), is questioning the women's-health activist about the newly released study that links tampon use to toxic shock syndrome. Speaking carefully and articulately, with the casual ease of someone who has done hundreds of interviews, Judy explains the problem that tampon use poses and offers some alternatives that women can consider.

Just a few feet away, Pamela Morgan, one of four salaried employees of the Collective, is typing a letter that will be sent to scores of women who are being asked to participate in the revision of the group's best-selling book, *Our Bodies, Ourselves.*

Less than a desk's distance from Pamela, Jane Pincus, a Collective member who has just moved back to Boston after five years in northern New England, is on the telephone with a woman who is trained in shiatsu—the Japanese pressure point massage technique that releases blocks, aches, and spasms in the body. Jane is inviting the masseuse to give a demonstration at the upcoming meeting of the Rising Sun Feminist Health Alliance, the network of northeast women's health activists that meets semiannually as a support group and a retreat from the hectic, stressful pace that these women maintain.

Behind Jane, two more members of the Collective—Vilunya Diskin, who has just arrived from a day of classes at the Harvard School of Public Health, where she is studying for a Ph.D. in population studies, and Norma Swenson, who with Judy has returned just two days earlier from speaking at a women's health conference in Alberta, Canada—are absorbed in a planning meeting in the office's conference space, reviewing their ideas about children's nutrition in preparation for a meeting with two people from a large New York foundation.

Within a few moments, Judy's television interview is finished and she switches places with Jane. Now Jane is on camera, explaining the traps that women have been led into by the pharmaceutical manufacturers who market products without sufficiently testing them. Judy, in the meantime, is answering a call from a woman in Lexington, Kentucky, who needs information about the harmful side effects of taking phenobarbital while on the Pill. As Judy cites the *New England Journal of Medicine* study that documents the potentially toxic effects of combining these two prescription drugs, the telephone on which she is talking rings again; she excuses herself, momentarily putting the first caller on hold while she answers the incoming call from an Ann Arbor woman who needs help in preparing public testimony on an out-of-hospital birth center bill before the Michigan legislature.

Until January 1980, the group had no office, operating for the previous ten years out of the women's homes. The new office is furnished with a collection of donated chairs, couches, filing cabinets, shelves, and desks. All available space is being used to good effect: hanging plants frame posters on women's rights; directories of women's action groups are heaped next to stacks of the Collective's latest book, *Ourselves and Our Children*; and literature racks are filled with articles, pamphlets and reports about menopause, cervical caps, Depo-Provera, DES, sterilization, breast cancer, hysterectomy, and numerous other topics. Cartons packed with copies of *Nuestros Cuerpos, Nuestras Vidas*, the Spanish-language edition of *Our Bodies, Ourselves*, which the Collective publishes and distributes itself, are draped with antique silk scarves, making an aesthetic virtue of the reality of limited space. Information—the raw material, the energy resource, and the finished product of networking—has transformed a one-time classroom into a living, breathing, encyclopedia on women's health.

No sooner are television interviews, telephone calls, and planning sessions complete than the foundation visitors arrive, two of scores of people who pass through the Collective's doors each month. In the past few weeks alone, women from Québec, Senegal, Bangladesh, Ireland, and Brazil have visited, reporting on the women's movement in their countries while gathering more data for use at home.

"We all have the same issues," Judy explains to the foundation people, stuffing envelopes while she talks. "Women abroad have the same concern about empowerment as we do, the same interest in gaining control over their lives, the same problems with violence against women. Even though they may manifest differently, the central issues are really the same: In India, brides are burned to death if their dowries are too small; here in the United States, violence takes the form of rape and battering."

What are the women's credentials for doing this work? the foundation people ask in a curious, rather than confronting, manner.

In the classical academic/professional sense, the women really have no "credentials" other than a number of undergraduate and postgraduate degrees. "That's precisely the point," explains Norma, who obtained a master's degree in public health at Harvard *after* participating in the initial rewrite of the original edition of *Our Bodies, Ourselves*, first issued under the title *Women and Their Bodies* in 1970. "We're not medical people; we're simply a group of women who wanted to understand more about ourselves."

The telephone rings again as the foundation people pursue more specific information, trying to understand how a group of "uncredentialed" women could have written a best-selling book (now in its 19th printing with sales exceeding two million copies and translations into a dozen languages), then gone on to write another popular book, *Ourselves and Our Children*, while fulfilling speaking engagements, which average about one per week, participating in numerous projects and special-interest groups, and managing to maintain long-term marriages, weather family traumas, and raise more than a dozen children among themselves.

Norma answers the phone, agreeing to do a 10-minute interview with a feminist from Holland, who arrives at the office 20 minutes later to take pictures of the Collective in action.

WHY A WOMEN'S HEALTH MOVEMENT?

The Boston Women's Health Book Collective serves as an unparalleled entry point into the international women's health network. While the group and its work are not responsible for the meteoric growth of the women's health movement in the 1970s, that has certainly been one of the Collective's triumphs, serving as the standard-bearer for women's challenges to the prevailing high-technology, pathological approach to human health that typifies modern medicine.

Why would a group of women feel the need to write a book about women's health? Why would the response from other women be so overwhelming? What was the need that the Collective addressed that was not being met in established America?

The American medical profession has strayed far from its honored lineage as an offspring of the healing arts, a gigantic soup of timeworn natural remedies from many traditions, passed along in elaborate rituals from shaman to shaman, from mid-wife to midwife, from healer to healer. Whereas once healing was revered as an innate gift, today medicine is a prestigious profession whose perks increase as doctors advance higher on the medical ladder. Although understanding the "person as a whole" was once an unquestioned assumption of healers, today subspecialists have cropped up to minister to every minute subdivision of the body.

We can see this principle in action by following the pregnancy of a woman, who could see as many as six doctors if she chose the prevailing medical approach to giving birth. An obstetrician is no longer really a pregnancy specialist; s/he is the "general practitioner" of parturition, making referrals to an endocrinologist (if the woman has had any history of infertility), a radiologist (if the woman agrees to the now routine practice of prenatal ultrasound and amniocentesis testing), a neurologist (if the woman is bothered by the frequent symptom of tingling in her extremities), an orthopedist (if the woman has wrist pain and/or tendonitis—another common symptom), and finally a neonatologist, the successor to the pediatrician, for once the baby emerges from the womb, the obstetrician is officially off the case.

In order to even understand her course of treatment for the "disease of giving birth," a pregnant woman has to become conversant with a whole new language of medical "technese." As the traditional testing ground for medications and anesthesias to be used in other forms of surgery, obstetrics is not a fixed science. Routines and methods come in and go out of fashion; today's universal use of epidural anesthesia is just as quickly replaced by tomorrow's new order to attach every woman and baby in labor to a fetal-heart monitor.

However, to regard these impermanent routines as fads fails to recognize the true seriousness and long-term harmfulness of using pregnant women as guinea pigs. We have only to recall the recent thalidomide tragedy, in which an untested drug was prescribed for pregnant women as a sedative in the early 1960s, causing severely disfiguring birth defects in their children, or the diethylstilbestrol (DES) catastrophe of the 1950s, 1960s, and early 1970s, in which millions of babies were exposed to this dangerous hormone before birth, resulting in an unusually high rate of a rare form of vaginal cancer in the girls and testicular abnormalities and sterility in the boys.

Every natural stage of women's physical maturation has been medicalized, objectified as an illness that must be treated—beginning with menarche, continuing through pregnancy and childbirth, and ending with menopause. Pain-killers and mood elevators are routinely prescribed for menstruation; cesarean delivery—birth by surgery—is fast becoming the preferred treatment of many obstetricians, with the number of surgical births having tripled from 1970 to 1980; and hormones, tranquilizers, and routine hysterectomies have become the standardized treatment for women in menopause.

The tampon fiasco, which has received so much publicity, is only the tip of the medical-malfeasance iceberg in regard to women's health:

• Intrauterine devices (IUDs), widely prescribed in the late 1960s and early 1970s and currently being marketed in Third World countries, have been found to induce many harmful side effects, from intense pain and excessive bleeding to permanent uterine damage and infertility.

• In Puerto Rico, more than one third of the women of childbearing age have been sterilized. According to the Committee to End Sterilization Abuse in New York, most of the women consented to the operation without knowing that surgical sterilization is rarely, if ever, reversible.

• Hysterectomies have become the second-most-frequently performed operation in the United States, with 25 percent of all women over 50 having had one, in spite of the fact that the operation is major surgery and has been estimated to be unnecessary in as many as 30 to 50 percent of all cases.

• About 20-30 percent of all births in the United States are now performed by surgery, accompanied by an alarmingly high postoperative infection rate of about 25 percent. While the overall maternal death rate in childbirth has dropped since the turn of the century due to public health advances, the maternal death rate from cesareans remains much higher than that of vaginal deliveries.

• Radical mastectomy remains the treatment of choice of many surgeons for breast cancer, despite the fact that other less traumatic and less mutilating methods have been found to produce equal or better survival rates.

Over the past 20 years, many women have begun to recognize this unhealthful pattern and have responded in many ways: They have developed their own networks, through which they can meet their own health needs; they have critiqued the existing system of care and worked to change it; and they have created the field of "women's health for women," with its own research, books, conferences, and ultimately, philosophy. Where the medical community, in which 90 percent of the doctors are men, has regarded women's bodies as "other" and their physical maturation as disease, the women's health movement has advanced a model of women as "ourselves," as healthy people whose life changes are moments of opportunity and awakening.

MAKING HISTORY

The history of the Collective offers a valuable insight into how networks form, jell, and persist over time without elaborate planning, self-conscious statements of purpose, or long-term goals. The Boston Women's Health Book Collective, one of the oldest and most successful of the networks we have learned about, just happened.

"We never set out to *do* anything," Vilunya recalls. "You don't plan to bring a group of twelve women together, enlist the help of hundreds of others, write a book that sells 250,000 copies over 2 years through 'underground' distribution with a price that is *lowered* from $.75 to $.30, face the choice of *which* major publisher to sign with, and then find your book on the New York *Times* best-seller list for 3 years."

"Everything flowed organically from one thing to another," she says. "And it's still growing."

Indeed, in 1982, eleven of the twelve original members of the group (the twelfth moved to Canada in the early 1970s) are still actively involved, representing a cross-section of middle- and upper-middle-class, college-educated white women ranging in age from 34 to 50.

"We've seen one another through four new babies (making sixteen children in all), three divorces and a wedding, one case of the hot flashes, some dramatic long affairs, one child going off to college and four entering adolescence," writes Collective member Wendy Coppedge Sanford in *Heresies* magazine.

The Collective got its start when Nancy Hawley, an antiwar activist involved in the first informal women's liberation group in Boston, gave a workshop on "Women and Their Bodies" at a women's conference in Boston in May 1969.

"We decided to have the conference because our weekly women's meetings at MIT, where several of our husbands studied or worked, were too limiting. Every week, more and more women showed up, all by word of mouth," Nancy remembers.

"It was a very exciting time," Jane reflects. "The air was full of rhetoric—even karate was in the air."

Nancy's workshop was the catalytic event that set everything else in motion: The sign-up sheet at the workshop became the mailing list for a group that gathered over the summer with the task of making a list of "good" obstetricians and gynecologists. Calling themselves "The Doctor's Group," they consisted of ten women, five of whom are still in the Collective: Jane, Nancy, and Vilunya (all friends previously), and Esther Rome and Paula Doress, both of whom had attended the conference where Nancy gave her workshop.

By the fall, the "good" doctors list was abandoned, and the women had begun to research topics of interest to them, unconsciously creating the chapters that would ultimately appear in *Our Bodies, Ourselves*. "I was very interested in the postpartum experience," Esther says, "because my mother had had a very serious depression after I was born. So I went to the library and found that practically nothing had been written about it. All of us were having the same experience in the libraries: There was no information to be found. That was when we started piping up with our own experiences and our own knowledge. We never set out to 'discover' anything—we only wanted to learn more to evaluate what the doctors were saying."

The topics of interest created so much new information—and so much excitement—that the women decided to offer the material in the form of a course for other women.

"I was in a very serious postpartum depression when I went to the first meeting, and I vividly remember every moment of that night," Wendy says 10 years later. She had been prodded to attend the course by Esther; they knew each other because their husbands were in architecture school together. "We broke up into small groups, and a woman started talking about postpartum depression. It was an extraordinary moment of release for me when I realized that I was not to *blame* for my depression. I took that energy and poured it back into the group for the next 10 years."

The MIT course was also the entry point for three other Collective members: Pamela Berger, Joan Ditzion, and Ruth Bell, who maintains her ties to the Boston group even though she now lives in Los Angeles. (Ruth is also the major author of *Changing Bodies, Changing Lives*, modeled after *Our Bodies, Ourselves*, and geared for teens.) Out of this core working group of nine (and literally scores of other women who dropped in and out over the next year or so), the "topics" were expanded to fill a book called *Women and Their Bodies*, including chapters on anatomy and physiology, socialization, venereal disease, pregnancy, abortion, postpartum depression, sexuality, birth control, and political analysis of medical institutions. For the first time in history, a group of women had written a book about themselves, for themselves, a fact that was later translated into the subtitle of their book (*By and for Women*). *Women and Their Bodies*, run off on newsprint by a local "movement" printer (the New England Free Press), and stapled together, was an overnight success. By the time of the second printing, the women had unequivocally claimed their work as their own by retitling their book *Our Bodies, Ourselves*.

"Every day orders flooded the office of the Free Press," Judy (who joined the group with Norma, as the last two members, in the fall of 1971) told *New Roots* magazine. "Women in the Boston area sent it to their friends all over the country who sent it to their friends, and within 2 years, 250,000 were sold without spending a cent on advertising." In addition to the friendship network, thousands of books were sold through the burgeoning women's movement on college campuses.

·It seemed that everyone was talking about this $.30 book, including New York publishers who proceeded to contact the group and make increasingly attractive offers to republish it–offers that threw the group into 6 months of soul-searching. While they knew that mass distribution would mean that the book would reach even more women, they were very wary of having a huge corporation profit from their work. Setting out very clear and unusual demands to the publisher–including final control over the cover and all promotional advertising as well as unlimited discount copies for distribution at nonprofit women's clinics–the group was pleased to find Simon and Schuster agreeing to its terms. In order to sign the contract, the group had to be an "entity." They formed a nonprofit corporation and called themselves the "Boston Women's Health Book Collective."

"We never had a solemn moment when we said, 'We are us,'" Wendy remarks, demonstrating how a network may close off a part of itself naturally and become a formal organization. "We never needed to say to anyone, 'You can't join,'" Jane adds. "We were simply making our book, and who we were was obvious."

The group has met weekly ever since–through one major revision of the 1973 Simon and Schuster edition (issued in 1976), a Spanish-language version of the book, one update of the book in 1979, and the conception and creation of *Ourselves and Our Children*, published in 1978 by Random House (the original competitor with Simon and Schuster). In addition, the group has also published two basic pamphlets of current concern: *Sexually Transmitted Diseases and How to Avoid Them* and *Menstruation*, and has coauthored the *International Women and Health Resource Guide*. In 1982, the group is hard at work once again with a completely new revision of the first book, a new subgroup, The Parenting Group, including three new women working solely on the projects that have developed out of *Ourselves and Our Children*, and a score of other projects of concern to women, funded by the royalties from their books. The royalties have also served to help fund many other women's initiatives, including a women's health center, journal, film, and news service.

It is astonishing to realize that this enormous web of connections began when one woman gave a workshop attended by thirty other women on a sunny day in May, 1969, three weeks to the day after her second child was born. Yet this is precisely how networks coalesce: An individual makes a small gesture in a larger environment of people who are thinking along the same lines. The context allows the network to emerge naturally among the people involved. No one person is responsible; rather, everyone is.

3

Healing Networks:
Health and the Life Cycle

The *women's health* movement is one strand of three compelling new approaches to health. Along with the *holistic health* movement and the *consumer/medical self-care* movement, the women's health movement has served as a titanic magnet, attracting millions of medically disenfranchised Americans out of doctors' offices and hospitals in the past decade.

While the women's health movement has propounded the most comprehensive critique of the social and political aspects of the medical industry, both the holistic health and consumer health movements also offer constructive pathways out of the omnipotent-doctor/powerless-patient/drug-and-surgery model that dominates the medical world. The holistic health movement, comprising primarily individual care providers loosely connected to one another, is the network within which a substantial array of nontraditional therapies congregate. The consumer health movement tackles the dollars-and-cents issues of the largest industry in the United States—the health industry—which employs more people and processes more dollars than any other sector of the American civilian economy. Its subsidiary branch, the medical self-care movement, shows people how they can become more self-reliant in meeting their health needs.

The networking model is invaluable to people seeking replacements for routinized and institutionalized health care. Medicine, with its hospitals, credentialed specialists and subspecialists, trade associations, drug manufacturers, insurance companies, high-technology research institutes, and equipment suppliers, is the archetypical functioning old-boy network, which in 1980 included only four percentage points (6 percent to 10 percent) more female physicians than it did in 1910. Belita Cowan, executive director of the National Women's Health Network, points out, "The American Medical Association has the largest and most powerful lobby in Washington."

In storefronts, borrowed offices, spare bedrooms, converted basements, and newly insulated attics, these alternatives in health care are surviving and growing outside institutional bases. Working with little capital, these new health networks operate on the currency of information, providing people with access to another way of dealing with cancer, curing ulcers, lowering blood pressure, coping with hot flashes, giving birth to babies, and dying with dignity.

At the very core of this new attitude toward medicine is the belief in health, both for the individual and for the planet. Without a healthy planet there can be no healthy people. Without a healthy people, there can be no healthy planet. For all our doctors, hospitals, and drugs, Americans are not healthy.

Whereas doctors have for the past century been seen as those who could cure us, the image of health emanating from Another America implies that we are primarily responsible for healing ourselves. Without repudiating the enormous skill and resources that medicine can offer in the appropriate context, such as the extraordinary contribution to health that antibiotics have given us, as well as the medical community's unparalleled skill in dealing with body trauma, the new outlooks on health draw on the vast body of healing knowledge that has survived for thousands of years. Instead of seeing health as something that happens to us, the new healing networks enable us to see that being healthy is something we do ourselves everyday, all the time, throughout our whole lives.

WOMEN'S HEALTH

The women's health movement is the daughter of the women's liberation movement, a massive networking effort of the late 1960s and early 1970s, in which women shared their personal life stories in the earliest forms of the now-popular support groups. Within their personal support groups, women risked revealing the inner reaches of their minds and feelings. Calling this newfound intimacy "consciousness raising," women discovered similar patterns, regardless of their background, location, or current circumstances. In a rare instance of self-anthropology, in which the explorers investigated the cultural patterning of their own lives, these women brushed away the dust from the covert patriarchal power structure that their forebears in the 19th century had begun to unearth.

Like a newly born galaxy, the women's movement burst into a myriad tiny pieces, reformulating in thousands of groups, working on hundreds of issues, threaded together by the physics of networking. The women's health movement is the one aspect of the women's movement that touches all women, regardless of who they are, where they live, or what they have done with their lives. There is barely a woman alive in the country who has not seen a doctor for what the medical profession has called "women's complaints."

In 1975, five feminist activists laid out the plan to create a national voice for women's health. Calling itself initially the National Women's Health Lobby, the group had its seeds in a long-distance telephone conversation between author Barbara Seaman, whose books *The Doctors' Case Against the Pill* and *Women and the Crisis in Sex Hormones* had already alerted many women to the need for more research in the field of birth control, and Belita Cowan, a women's activist then based in Ann Arbor, Michigan, where she served as editor of *Her-self*, a feminist newspaper.

In the mutual recognition that women's health could not change without a presence in the nation's capital, Cowan and Seaman then enlisted the help of three other well-known feminists (Phyllis Chesler, author of *Women and Madness*, Mary Howell, M.D., author of *Helping Ourselves* and *Healing at Home*, and Alice Wolfson, a Washington, D.C., area women's health activist). Together, the group staged its first action: a memorial service attended by 500 people on the steps of the Food and Drug Administration (FDA) to commemorate the "thousands of women who had died needlessly from the Pill." In one of those great coincidences of the calendar, the memorial service took place the day before the U.S. House of Representatives' Subcommittee on Health and the Environment was to conduct hearings on the controversial hormone diethylstilbestrol (DES). With the impetus to present its concerns on Capitol Hill, the new women's health lobby mobilized its forces quickly and kicked off its new campaign with great vitality.

Beginning with one of the smallest seed grants in network history ($15 from a group of lawyers representing a woman who had been injured by a Dalkon Shield IUD, later removed from the market as a result of pressure brought to bear by the women's lobby-network and other groups), the group put even this minute amount of money to work. Belita Cowan used it to purchase postage stamps that she distributed to other members of the network for a nationwide letter-writing campaign about women's health.

Realizing that its work reached beyond lobbying efforts normally directed at legislative bodies, which have had less influence on women's health than regulatory bodies such as the FDA and government agencies such as the Department of Health and Human Services, the group decided to drop the word lobby from its title, thus becoming the National Women's Health Network (NWHN).

"A network implies a grass-roots group," explains Cowan, now executive director of the group in Washington. "Unlike other women's organizations, we started from the bottom up. Our goal was to have a constituency from all over the country with women of different ages, ethnic and racial backgrounds, consumers and providers." Today, the staff operates under the mandate of a working board of directors, each of whom nominates herself. The membership as a whole elects the board.

For the first 3 years of its existence, NWHN operated out of a post-office box, with its income deriving from membership fees and all its work being performed on a volunteer basis. In 1978, grants from two women's foundations bolstered the coffers to $17,000, half of which was allocated as a salary for an executive director.

"It was a risky step, investing such a high proportion of our money in one person," explains Cowan, who was selected for the job.

Apparently, it was a well-calculated risk, because one of Cowan's principal charges was to raise money, and by the end of the year she had raised $72,000. With this kind of funds, a trifle in the world of business but a windfall in the shoestring world of network finances, NWHN was mobilized.

Today, NWHN represents the most significant national force in the women's health movement. NWHN monitors FDA meetings, helps to provide expert witnesses at regulatory hearings, submits oral and written testimony to Congress, runs a speakers bureau, issues timely news alerts on critical women's health issues, and disseminates women's health information through its publication *Network News*. Early in 1980, the group published nine resource guides covering various aspects of women's health, including birth control, sterilization, childbirth, breast cancer, menopause, hysterectomy, self-help, abortion, and DES.

Many other networks concerned with specific issues in women's health crisscross at one time or another through NWHN. Each of these groups represents a strong network of its own that often includes organizations that are not networks themselves. Speaking to this point, Roberta Young, staff coordinator for the California-based Coalition for the Medical Rights of Women (CMRW) says, "We do not see ourselves so much as a 'network' as we do a 'coalition.' Our purpose is to organize women around particular issues, which they address through individual committees, working together as a 'coalition' to improve the quality, accessibility, and responsiveness of health care to women's needs. We have, however, established a *network*, the California Women's Health Network, to begin to coordinate the efforts of various and sundry women's health activists and groups around the state by helping them to form a network to share information and resources with one another and to provide a strong base for organizing and educating women on health related issues."

The California Women's Health Network is one of a number of regionally based alliances that spread the word about women's health–using, variously, newsletters, newspapers, journals, and even letter-writing chains to keep information flowing.

One such network has evolved out of the New Hampshire Feminist Health Center, one of the two dozen facilities that provide direct health services to women, through the publication of its quarterly newspaper-journal *WomenWise*. Editor Alice Downey explains:

This publication exists as both a network and as part of larger networks, i.e., the women's health movement, the women's movement, and feminism. Early on we delineated the purposes of the paper. While we did not use the term "network" or "networking," I feel the goals we set forth are well defined by the "network" concept: To promote a greater political awareness on the part of women and, ideally, more political activity on their own behalf . . . and to show the "relevancy" of the women's health movement to New Hampshire.

WomenWise sees itself as contributing to women's history (we are a record-keeper of sorts) and to feminist journalism and here are more networks we feel a part of. Losing our history—as has happened over and over again—is counteracted by the existence of publications such as WomenWise and, in consequence, it is fair to say that WomenWise is part of a feminist communications network seeking to stake out a place for women's issues in the media and in our lives.

WomenWise staff members are also a part of the Rising Sun Feminist Health Alliance, to which the Boston Women's Health Book Collective belongs, "a group formed just a couple of years ago for the specific purpose of networking feminist health activists from the eastern seaboard. NHFHC was a founder of this organization, which meets twice a year, providing a time and place for analysis, planning and mutual support among women's health activists," Downey explains.

As a closed network, Rising Sun does not advertise its meetings, hold conferences, or distribute literature. Its purpose is solely to support people working on similar issues; the larger alliance of such people has no goals of its own to further. As such, this closed network is an invaluable semiannual exchange and check-in point for its members.

From time to time, other women's health networks have developed around particular issues: to alert women to a danger or to inform them of a new option. For example, an informal unnamed network exists around passing information about the cervical cap, the barrier method of birth control that has been in use in other countries for the past 50 years but which has been little used in the United States. There is no central clearinghouse on information about the cap, nor is there a newsletter or group formed around it. Rather, the health-care practitioners who are fitting caps and those who are using them engage in an informal dialogue and information exchange that is quietly resulting in a shift away from use of the diaphragm to use of the cap. Similar networks of support have arisen out of the use of natural birth control, which combines monitoring daily temperature readings with cervical mucus discharges, thus allowing women to determine their times of maximum fertility. Again, the information is passed primarily by word of mouth, supported in some circles by The Natural Birth Control Book, by Margaret Nofziger, who researched and wrote the book from her base at The Farm, in Tennessee (see Chapter 4, Sharing).

Though the roots of the movement for choices in childbirth go back to the late 1940s and many of its organizations have passed far beyond the simple shoestring network stage, the natural-childbirth movement comprises a network of its own. Beginning with the first childbirth education group, formed in Minneapolis in 1948, the natural-childbirth movement had a renaissance in the late 1970s as increasing numbers of families chose to have their babies at home, many assisted by midwives, rather than doctors. The strongest network of support for this exodus from traditional hospital practices has been the National Association of Parents and Professionals for Safe Alternatives in Childbirth. Known by its catchy acronym, NAPSAC, the group is a meeting ground for doctors, nurses, midwives, childbirth educators, and parents concerned with preserving freedom of choice in childbearing.

Such networks are likely to attract more adherents, including increasing numbers of professionals, as the options offered in the independent world of women's health multiply, replacing a greater portion of services currently offered by established medicine.

HOLISTIC HEALTH

It's a hot summer afternoon when the telephone rings. Our friend Judy in New York is calling for leads into the branch of the holistic health tree that addresses cancer. A friend of Judy's has just been told that she has breast cancer and Judy is contacting us in order to supply her friend with some starting points that can lead her to supplements and/or alternatives to surgery and radiation. Flipping through our files, we rapidly locate three departure points in New York: a holistic health center that combines traditional Western medicine with nonallopathic techniques, a health research group that has recently published a report on cancer therapies, and a counseling center that teaches mental techniques that help mobilize the body's own immune system to eliminate cancerous cells.

While the term "holistic" has suffered from overuse, the concept of holistic health vibrates with fresh meaning. Integrating psyche (mind) and soma (body), the holistic health movement derives from two separate disciplines, one very old and one very new—the medical fraternity itself and the human potential movement—whose union has yielded invaluable insights into human health.

Holistic health recognizes the connection between emotional experiences and physical consequences, the individual parts of the body and the body as a whole, and the person as a subsystem within the system of the planet. Holistic health offers remedies that employ the best aspects of modern medicine and the exquisite model of the healing properties of the world around us, unifying Eastern practices such as acupuncture and shiatsu with therapies such as herbs and touch. Reversing the assumptions of psychosomatic medicine (a subspecialty that holds the mind accountable for making the body ill), holistic health accentuates the power of the mind in making the body well. It's the difference between a negative and a positive approach. For some people, holistic health even reaches into the realms of spiritual or psychic healing similar to the kinds of spontaneous remissions described in the Old and New Testaments.

In the past 10 years, many unusual forms of therapy have been loosely grouped under the title of "holistic health," offering promising new correctives to everything from catastrophic illness to chronic back pain. The very nature of the word "holistic"—meaning something that "overarches the summation of its individual parts"—constructs an umbrella for homeopathy, yoga, Alexander technique, relaxation, rolfing, biofeedback, touch healing, postural integration, polarity therapy, herbology, t'ai chi, massage, chiropractic, Bach flower remedies, fresh-food and vegetarian diets, hair analysis, hot springs, and even running.

Perhaps because its principal spokespeople are providers rather than consumers of health care, the holistic health movement is ironically a collection of individuals each espousing his or her own particular brand of "holism," yet in contact with many others in other holistic "specialities." Thus, within holistic health, networking happens by referral—like our friend in New York who called us for cancer therapy leads. The telephone lines of Another America are abuzz with people seeking help with problems that the medical community cannot solve: A 40-year-old doctor with a muscle spasm in his back is referred to a Feldenkrais-trained therapist; an infertile couple follow up on a suggestion to consult a dietary analyst; a dancer with a pinched nerve in her neck follows the recommendation that she see a muscular therapist.

By plugging into a local care provider, one can get access to practitioners in other parts of the country. For example, the Association for Research and Enlightenment (A.R.E.) Clinic, in Phoenix, Arizona, maintains a national referral file of holistic-health-care providers, while the Center for Integral Medicine, in Los Angeles, has established a computerized referral service.

Similar networks exist among the more established disciplines within holistic health such as homeopathy and chiropractic, as well as among such vital ancillary-care providers as cancer counselors (cf. the Cancer Counseling and Research Center, in Fort Worth, Texas) whose services help people with cancer who are also receiving traditional treatment.

Likewise, a number of networks have grown up around specific cancer therapies that have yet to be accepted into established medicine, including metabolic, mega-vitamin, and laetrile therapies, used in conjunction with or as replacements for sur-gery, radiation, and chemotherapy. With extensive support among people in refuge from the cancer establishment, these networks mobilize in times of crisis, most vis-ibly recently during the lifetime of Chad Green, the young child with leukemia whose parents chose to confront the state on the issue of who should determine the type of care given to children with cancer.

Yet another array of networks have formed out of concern for people who are dying. The hospice (literally "a way station for travelers") movement simulates the kinship systems that have supported families during times of birth and death throughout most of human history. Today the hospice movement has two aspects: the application of hospice ideas in hospitals and in dying people's homes, and the physical establishment of separate dying centers for terminally ill people.

Serving a similar support need are a number of mutual self-help groups, leaderless peer support systems, which recognize the intensely personal and unraveling effects of catastrophic illness and death: Widow-to-widow programs, programs for parents of children who have died, and families-of-suicides programs have all grown out of hospice work, offering compassionate refuges among people who intuitively under-stand each other's problems.

The hospice-inspired support groups constitute a small fraction of the hundreds of mutual self-help groups that have developed to deal with everything from phobias (cf. Terrap, a network for agoraphobics) to allergies (cf. the Human Ecology Action League, a network for people with allergic responses to chemicals and other prod-ucts of industrialization) to addictions (cf. Alcoholics Anonymous, one of the oldest networks supporting people addicted to alcohol). The National Self-Help Clear-inghouse, a New York-based center that is the collection and distribution hub for information about the self-help movement, estimates that some 500,000 self-help groups exist—involving more than 10,000,000 Americans.

Even the virtues of love and sharing are called upon as healing agents by self-help groups. The Center for Attitudinal Healing, in Tiburon, California, organizes support groups for children with catastrophic illnesses and their families. Using the motto "As we help others, we help ourselves," the Center has attracted considerable notice, having been featured on "60 Minutes," the "Phil Donahue Show," and Fred Rogers' "Old Friends, New Friends." The Center coordinates a Pen/Phone Pal serv-ice, which uses a network approach to introduce geographically separated people to each other. "Before any two people are brought together," the Center's newsletter explains, "a staff member or volunteer talks with each of them to establish areas of mutual interest and their willingness to be supportive of each other. Children are usually matched by illness or age. Mothers and fathers often want to talk to other parents facing similar crises."

Expanding the definition of illness far beyond the physical changes in the body, these new networks are gaining increasing validity within more mainstream institutions. The establishment of professional societies such as the American Holistic Medical Association and the American Holistic Nurses Association and the granting of third-party insurance payments to chiropractors in some states indicate that holistic health can coexist and flourish alongside the existing medical system.

Holistic health and women's health, two supposedly obvious allies in the search for a new workable model of human health, have remained separate, and in some instances, at loggerheads. Sometimes trapped in ideological constraints, other times imprisoned by concerns of the moment that necessitate the blocking out of other considerations, these two important movements have not always shared information sufficiently to jointly address some of the most important issues facing us.

For example, while the holistic health movement has paid some attention to childbirth, encouraging women to decline the medical community's high-technology, pathological model of birth, holistic health research has not addressed itself to the hazards of the increasing battery of procedures that are routinely being performed on pregnant women. By keeping its focus largely on providing therapies for stress-related conditions, the holistic health movement has not served women's routine health needs.

The women's health movement, on the other hand, has been primarily focused on the critique of existing practices within the medical profession. Although there is a commendably long and invaluable list of hazards that the women's health movement has identified and publicized, ranging from calling for the regulation of intrauterine devices (IUDs) to having mercury removed from spermicides, to questioning the universal use of mammography for breast-cancer screening, relatively few other suggestions for treating women with immediate health needs have been proposed thus far.

There is an immediate and pressing need for a strong network of mutual support to be created out of these two movements. Each operates within a world of its own with impressive connections that already reach around the globe. As the holistic health movement matures and becomes more confident, its ability to move into the politics of health will become more refined. Similarly, as the women's health movement becomes more focused on individual issues, its battery of cures and remedies will flower, bringing these two natural friends into alignment.

CONSUMER HEALTH

A simple true story illustrates how a health-care consumer is born: Ethel, a 70-year-old former schoolteacher, trips on the sidewalk and crashes to the cement pavement, breaking her shoulder blade. In the emergency room of the hospital, an orthopedist, whom Ethel has neither seen before nor asked to have brought on the case, walks in, looks at an X-ray, mumbles something to the attending physician, and walks out. A week later, Ethel receives a bill for $100 from the orthopedist. In that moment, Ethel drops her self-image as an injured patient and becomes an angry consumer of health-care services.

At the same time as the holistic health and women's health movements were incubating, another important new network of concern was congealing among people who regard medicine as a model of commerce. The consumer health movement has redefined doctors as merchants, patients as consumers, and medical institutions as big business. Although these monikers sit uneasily on doctors and hospitals, they carry with them a substantial truth about the medical world.

Among the first to take cognizance of the high cost of medicine was the Public Citizen Health Research Group, one of the many nodes in the Ralph Nader network of public-interest research groups. Working both with balance sheets and law suits, the Health Research Group has been producing material that substantiates the concept that patients should be informed consumers. Today the group copublishes *Consumer Health Action Network* with the Consumer Coalition for Health (CCH), a national alliance of labor, civil-rights, and public-interest organizations working to increase consumer control over the health-care system.

"We believe that weak and confused bureaucracies have failed," says CCH, "and that only through broad-based citizens' movements can we achieve the goals of lowered costs, increased access, and the redirection of resources towards prevention and primary care. To this end, we work to support and strengthen local consumer groups—and to give individual consumers the information they need to help improve our health-care system."

Since 1976, the Center for Medical Consumers and Health Care Information (CMCHCI) has been providing consumers with a source of health information that is independent of the medical community. CMCHCI operates from four basic principles:

(1) The medical care system is overutilized, often to the detriment of health;

(2) Health care will be improved once consumers have access to information doctors have traditionally kept to themselves;

(3) Information on nonmedical alternatives to health problems should be readily available to consumers; and

(4) Consumers should be as fully informed of the risks of a given drug or medical procedure as they are of the benefits.

Toward that end, the Center publishes a bimonthly consumer newsletter, *Health Facts*, with each issue devoted to a specific health or medical topic. The newsletters are primers on topics such as antibiotics, nutrition, annual physical examinations, depression, low back pain, hypertension, cancer, and exercise. Although, according to staff member Deborah Moody, the Center performs no networking function other than "to bring information to people across the country via the newsletter," it serves to supply many networks with the information they need to carry out their work.

A similar service is performed by the Health Policy Advisory Council, which focuses on the workings and policy implications of the health-care delivery system itself. Since 1970, Health/PAC has offered an activist voice for changes in the health care system, including the publication of two major books, *The American Health Empire* and *Prognosis Negative*. Health/PAC also provides an institutional base for health-care professionals seeking to change their professions from the inside: the Health Planners Network, which holds monthly forums for people studying and working in the field, and the Nurses Network, which is the mechanism by which activist nurses around the country remain in contact with one another.

In the same way, Nurses in Transition, based in San Francisco, also provides a channel for nurses to exchange their insights about where their profession is going. These professional networks are avenues through which people trained within the medical system are transforming their field.

One such application of change from within can be seen in the medical self-care world, a medical adaptation of the feminist self-help movement in which women learn how to do self-examinations and perform simple laboratory tests previously executed only by doctors. Using the same idea, some physicians have applied the concept to consumers. Calling his publication *Medical Self-Care*, Tom Ferguson got the idea for the magazine while trying to come up with a thesis topic at Yale Medical School.

> During my first year on the hospital wards, I was continually amazed at how little responsibility most patients took for their own health.

> About half the patients I saw that year had a preventable illness. Every time I saw a smoker with lung cancer or emphysema, a heavy drinker with liver disease, a fat sedentary middle-aged man with a heart attack, or someone who'd "gone crazy" because that was the only way they'd learned to deal with stress, I realized that medical care is not something to be left to doctors and other health workers.

> It was not that these people lacked good medical care. Most of them had excellent physicians. But somehow there was a whole area of health maintenance and preventive medicine that neither the doctor nor the patient was taking responsibility for.

> I got to feeling like a mechanic working on cars wrecked by people who had never learned to drive. What we needed was not more mechanics but a little drivers' education.

With these ideas in mind, Ferguson created his excellent quarterly journal that includes articles on how to take care of yourself in a healthful way as well as on how to understand medical literature. While *Medical Self-Care* is not directly challenging the basic model of medicine, it is offering consumers another way to work with their doctors in a more responsible fashion. When combined with the concepts emanating from holistic health and women's health, the self-care movement holds promise for changing the way in which people perceive their own states of health.

Taken as a whole, the three vital healing networks elaborated here—women's health, holistic health, and consumer health—constitute a comprehensive complement and challenge to the medical monopoly of doctor/hospital/insurance company/drug industry. Every group mentioned here has at least one counterpart, if not many, in other areas of the country, working on other aspects of the same issues, informing people about their medical choices. No one knows for sure how *many* people avail themselves of these other solutions, yet the number increases daily—as more training centers for midwifery, homeopathy, chiropractic, and the healing arts open their doors, and as people become more physically fit.

HEALTH and the LIFE CYCLE

Healing Guide

H

The Healing Guide includes groups that are primarily concerned with health and the life cycle. Many of these groups also work on other issues.

Each group is identified by a letter/number code. The letter **H** stands for Healing. Every group whose code begins with **H** is listed in the Healing Guide.

The entry for each network whose code is lower than 100 includes a brief description. These representative networks are a cross-section of the initial groups we contacted in our research. Each network whose code is greater than 100 is listed with complete contact information. If the ✳ symbol, for publications, or ◆ symbol, for materials, appears with a listing, consult the Title Guide under Healing Titles.

The Healing Guide includes groups that are concerned with aging, allergies, body therapies, childbirth, children, death and dying, the disabled, health as a consumer issue, health research, the health professions, holistic health, hospices, mental health, parents, pregnancy, self-care, self-help, women's health . . . and a few others.

H001
Alternative Medical Association
7915 Southeast Stark
Portland, OR 97215
503/253-4031   ✳◆

✳ *Journal of the Alternative Medical Association ($7 year)*
◆ *People's Desk Reference: Traditional Herbal Formulas ($74)*

Holistic health center focusing around herbal remedies. Circulates self-diagnosing medical form; mail-order herbal remedy services. Distributes holistic/natural health home-study course.

H002
Center for Attitudinal Healing
19 Main Street
Tiburon, CA 94920
415/435-5022   ◆◆◆

◆ *There is a Rainbow Behind Every Cloud ($5.95)*
◆ *Love Is Letting Go of Fear (Jampolsky, $4.95)*
◆ *To Give Is to Receive (Jampolsky, $5.95)*

Unique health education center for seriously ill children and their families. Program organized around network of peer support in person, by mail, and by telephone. Conducts workshops, distributes tapes, and connects people.

H003
Center for Integral Medicine
1515 Palisades Drive, Suite L
Pacific Palisades, CA 90272
213/459-3373

Health education center exploring new approaches to treatment of chronic and catastrophic illness. Sponsors conferences and research projects. Maintains computer-based national referral network. Has direct-care arm.

H004
Center for Medical Consumers and Health Care Information
237 Thompson Street
New York, NY 10012
212/674-7105   ✳◆◆

✳ *Health Facts (bimonthly/$8.50)*
◆ *Cancer Therapies ($1.50)*
◆ *Medical X-Rays ($1.50)*

Excellent resource that helps people become informed, critical consumers of medical care. Maintains free library for lay people, phone-in audiotape service on 150 subjects, issue-oriented newsletter, and workshop program.

H005
Center for Science in the Public Interest
1755 S Street, N.W.
Washington, DC 20009
202/332-9110   ✳

✳ *Nutrition Action (monthly/$15)*

Research/education group that provides easy-to-understand information about food, the food industry, and government regulations. Publishes "how-to" manuals, posters, books, reports, monthly magazine, and T-shirts.

H006
Cesarean Connection
P.O. Box 11
Westmont, IL 60509
312/968-8877   ✳◆◆

✳ *The Bulletin (12 issues/$12 year)*
◆ *Mother's Guide to Cesarean Childbirth*
◆ *How to Start a Cesarean Support Group ($1)*

National clearinghouse for information on cesarean births. Maintains national referral file, distributes educational materials, and organizes support groups.

H007
Coalition for the Medical Rights of Women
1638-B Haight Street
San Francisco, CA 94117
415/621-8030   ✳✳

✳ *Coalition News (bimonthly/$10)*
✳ *Second Opinion (bimonthly)*

Effective activist organization that forms coalitions to address women's health needs. Organizers of the California Women's Health Network. Sponsors conferences, workshops, and public actions; many educational materials.

H008
Committee for Abortion Rights and Against Sterilization Abuse
386 Park Avenue South, Room 1502
New York, NY 10016
212/532-6685   ✳

✳ *CARASA News (monthly/$5)*

Key node in movement to protect women's reproductive rights that formed when Hyde Amendment cut off Medicaid abortions. Research, education, and organization around topics like birth control, sterilization, health care, welfare, others.

H009
Consumer Coalition for Health
P.O. Box 50088
Washington, DC 20004
202/638-5828   ✳

✳ *CHAN–Consumer Health Action Network (bimonthly/$15)*

National alliance of labor, civil rights, and public-interest groups concerned with consumer control of health care system. Home base for network of consumer health advocates, organizers, and planners.

H010
East West Journal
17 Station Street
Brookline, MA 02146
617/232-1000   ✳

✳ *East West Journal (monthly/$12)*

Monthly magazine that evolved out of macrobiotic community in Boston. Articles about food, diet, gardening, nutrition, natural healing remedies, and spiritual issues.

H011
Gray Panthers
3635 Chestnut Street
Philadelphia, PA 19104
215/EV2-3300   ✳◆◆

✳ *Gray Panther Network (bimonthly/$5)*
◆ *Paying Through the Ear: Report on Hearing Health Care*
◆ *Nursing Homes: A Citizen's Action Guide*

First group to draw attention to "agism," linking it to broad social critique. Activist groups in 40 states hold educational progams, petition drives, rallies, other events. Nonhierarchically organized; excellent materials.

H012
Health Policy Advisory Council
17 Murray Street
New York, NY 10007
212/267-8890   ✳◆◆

✳ *Health/PAC Bulletin (6 issues/$14)*
◆ *American Health Empire: Power, Profits and Politics*
◆ *Prognosis Negative: Crisis in the Health Care System*

Significant, long-standing node in network of activists concerned with health policy. Clearinghouse for Nurses' Network and Health Planners Network. Publishes bulletin, educational materials, and maintains resource center.

H013
Hospice Institute for Education Training and Research
765 Prospect Street
New Haven, CT 06511
203/787-5871   ✳

✳ *Kharis (3 issues)*

Outgrowth of first hospice (center for people who are dying) in U.S. Primary purpose is to offer training in work with terminally ill people and their families to health care professionals.

H014
Human Ecology Action League
505 North Lake Shore Drive
Chicago, IL 60611   ✳

✳ *Human Ecologist (monthly/$12)*

Information and support on ecologically induced illnesses. Lifeline for people suffering from allergies arising out of high-tech world (additives, preservatives, pesticides, odors). Referral services.

H015
Huxley Institute for Biosocial Research
1114 First Avenue
New York, NY 10021
212/759-9554

Key source of information on treatment of mental illness through nutrition and other biochemical therapies. Sponsors physician training and conferences, distributes materials, maintains library, and does referrals.

H016
La Leche League International
9616 Minneapolis Avenue
Franklin Park, IL 60131
312/455-7730   ✳◆◆

✳ *La Leche League News (6 issues/$3)*
◆ *Womanly Art of Breastfeeding ($3.95)*
◆ *Mother's in the Kitchen ($4.95)*

Key source of information and support on breast-feeding. Nursing mothers volunteer to help other nursing mothers. Organizes breast-feeding support groups, conferences, and professional seminars. Distributes research.

H017
Lesbian Mothers National Defense Fund
P.O. Box 21567
Seattle, WA 98111
206/325-2643

Network of support and help for lesbian mothers.

H018
Madness Network News
P.O. Box 684
San Francisco, CA 94101
415/548-2980   ✳

✳ *Madness Network News ($5)*

Newspaper of the psychiatric inmates/anti-psychiatry movement. Publishes national and international news, has a directory of groups and list of doctors administering shock treatments.

H019
Mothering Magazine
P.O. Box 2046
Albuquerque, NM 87103
505/897-1432   ✳

✳ *Mothering ($8 year)*

The only magazine of its kind, providing alternative approaches to pregnancy, childbirth, child rearing, and education. First-person articles abound. Contains poetry, photographs, and information for "new age" mothers.

H020
NAPSAC: Safe Alternatives in Childbirth
P.O. Box 267
Marble Hill, MO 63764   ✳◆◆

✳ *NAPSAC News (4 issues/$8)*
◆ *Directory of Alternative Birth Services ($3.50)*
◆ *NAPSAC Conference Proceedings ($6)*

National Association of Parents and Professionals for Safe Alternatives in Childbirth. Serves as key node in childbirth movement. Publishes research on safety of out-of-hospital birth and national directory.

H021
National Alliance for Optional Parenthood
2010 Massachusetts Avenue, N.W.
Washington, DC 20036
202/296-7474   ✳

✳ *Optional Parenthood Today (6 issues/$20)*

Membership group supporting people who choose not to have children in "pronatalist" society. Sponsors teen pregnancy education project and maintains a library and a referral system.

H022
National Citizens Coalition for Nursing Home Reform
1424 16th Street, N.W.
Washington, DC 20036
202/797-8227   ✳

✳ *Collation (8 issues/$15)*

Advocacy group that monitors and does public education around quality of care in nursing homes, organizes projects for residents, provides training, maintains complaint hot lines, and promotes consumer involvement.

H023
National Women's Health Network
2025 I Street, N.W., Suite 105
Washington, DC 20006
212/223-6886   ✳◆

✳ *Network News (bimonthly/$25)*
◆ *Health Resource Guides*

Key node in women's health movement. Connects 500 member groups and individuals. Publishes newsletter and news alerts, provides speakers and witnesses, and serves as clearinghouse. Monitors federal women's health policy.

H024
New Directions in Psychology
c/o State and Mind
P.O. Box 89
Somerville, MA 02144
617/623-9804   ✳

✳ *State and Mind (4 issues/$4)*

One of earliest groups of mental health workers, patients, and students challenging the psychiatric establishment. Sponsors lectures, forms self-help groups, and does referrals.

H025
New Hampshire Feminist Health Center
38 South Main Street
Concord, NH 03301
603/225-2739   ✳

✳ *WomenWise (quarterly/$5)*

Nonprofit clinic providing health services in feminist tradition of informed "well-woman" care. Publishes a superb newspaper of national interest that provides helpful news items, book reviews, survey articles, legal updates.

H026
Parent Support-Group Project
294 Washington Street, Suite 630
Boston, MA 02108
617/426-2022

Network-building project among support groups for expectant and existing parents in Boston area including visually impaired parents, teen mothers, single fathers, isolated families. Publishes directory for referrals.

H027
Survival Foundation
OMangod Press
P.O. Box 77
Woodstock Valley, CT 06282
203/974-2440   ◆◆◆

◆ *New Age Directory ($4.95)*
◆ *Survival into the 21st Century ($12.95)*
◆ *Love Your Body (recipes, $2.50)*

Produces directory of 2500 people, groups, and businesses dedicated to the "organic" life. Includes 40 categories of back-to-the-land, vegetarian, consciousness, and healing groups. Special emphasis on raw ("living") food sources.

H028
Tallahassee Feminist Women's Health Center
540 West Brevard Street
Tallahassee, FL 32303
904/224-9600   ✳

✳ *The Examiner*

Feminist health care center run by women for women. Services include self-help clinics, abortions, pregnancy screening, gynecologic clinic, telephone counseling, and referral service.

H029
Terrap: Network for Agoraphobics
1010 Doyle Street
Menlo Park, CA 94025
415/329-1233   ✳◆

✳ *Terrap Times (bimonthly/$10)*
◆ *Agoraphobia: Symptoms, Causes, and Treatment ($3)*

Information and clinical resource for people with phobias, particularly agoraphobia. Offers various clinical services throughout the country and serves as link-up for agoraphobic pen-pal network.

H030
Touch for Health Foundation
1174 North Lake Avenue
Pasadena, CA 91104
213/794-1181   ✳

✳ *TFH Newsletter (monthly)*

Conducts research and sponsors training in touch healing. Combines acupuncture, acupressure, and Western techniques. Organizes conferences, distributes books and papers.

H031
Women's Health Services
316 East Marcy Street
Santa Fe, NM 87501
505/988-8869   ✳

✳ *Hot Flash ($5)*

Unique clinic combining women's health care with holistic health principles. Key feminist educational resource in Southwest. Provides direct care, maintains library, organizes events, and publishes excellent newsletter.

H101
Academy of Orthomolecular Psychiatry
P.O. Box 372
Manhasset, NY 11030

H102
Action Coalition for Retirement with Dignity
257 East Onondaga Street
Syracuse, NY 13202
315/422-2331

H103
Acupressure School of Massage Therapy
1533 Shattuck Avenue
Berkeley, CA 94709
415/845-1059

H104
Advocates for Freedom in Mental Health
4448 Francis
Kansas City, KS 66103
913/236-9312

H105
Aletheia Psycho-Physical Foundation
515 Northeast 8th
Grants Pass, OR 97526
503/479-4855   ◆◆

H106
Alliance for Perinatal Research and Services
321 South Pitt Street
Alexandria, VA 22314   ◆

H107
Alliance for the Liberation of Mental Patients
1427 Walnut Street, 4th Floor
Philadelphia, PA 19102
215/LO3-3828

H108
American Academy of Husband-Coached Childbirth
P.O. Box 5224
Sherman Oaks, CA 91413

H109
American Alliance for Health and Physical Education
1900 Association Drive
Reston, VA 22091
703/476-3400   ✳

H110
American Conference of Therapeutic Selfhelp/Selfhealth
710 Lodi Street
Syracuse, NY 13203
315/471-4644   ✳

H111
American Healing Association
Yucca Street, Box 6311
Los Angeles, CA 90028
213/320-2907

H112
American Holistic Medical Association
Rural Route #2, Welsh Coulee
La Crosse, WI 54601
608/786-2660

H113
American Holistic Nurses' Association
4106 Bluebonnet
Houston, TX 77025
713/666-0610   ✳

H114
Association for Childbirth at Home International
P.O. Box 1219
Cerritos, CA 90701
213/668-1132   ✳

H115
Association for Research and Enlightenment Clinic
4018 North 40th Street
Phoenix, AZ 85018
602/955-0551   ✳

H116
Association for the Preservation of Anti-Psychiatric Artifacts
P.O. Box 9
Bayside, NY 11361   ✳

H117
Austin Lay Midwives Association
82 East 47th Street
Austin, TX 78751
512/452-7340

H118
Bay Area Coalition on Occupational Safety and Health
439 42nd Street
Oakland, CA 94609

H119
Bay Area Committee for Alternatives to Psychiatry
944 Market Street, Room 701
San Francisco, CA 94102
415/982-7799   ✳

H120
Beauty Without Cruelty
175 West 12th Street
New York, NY 10012

H121
Being Thin
12 Orchard Street
Newton, MA 02158
617/527-2959

H122
Birth and Life Bookstore
P.O. Box 70625
Seattle, WA 98107
206/789-4444

H123
Birthing Monthly Newsletter
P.O. Box 415
Winona Lake, IN 46590   ✳

H124
Boston Area Childbirth Education
333 Concord Avenue
Lexington, MA 02173
617/862-0954

H125
Boston Center for Psychosynthesis
93 Union Street, Suite 400
Newton Centre, MA 02159
617/965-3255

H126
Boston Self-Help
18 Williston Road
Brookline, MA 02146
617/227-0080

H127
Boston Women's Health Book Collective
P.O. Box 192
West Somerville, MA 02144
617/924-0271   ◆◆◆

H128
Bread & Roses Women's Health Center
238 West Wisconsin Avenue, #700
Milwaukee, WI 53203
414/278-0260   ✳

H129
California School of Herbal Studies
P.O. Box 350
Guerneville, CA 95446
707/869-0972

H130
Canadian Coordinating Council on Deafness
55 Parkdale Avenue
Ottawa, Ontario
CANADA K1Y 1E5
613/728-0936   ✳

H131
Canadian Holistic Healing Association
308 East 23rd Avenue
Vancouver, British Columbia
CANADA V4V 1X5
606/876-5955   ✳

H132
Cancer Counseling Center
29 Quentin Road
Scarsdale, NY 10583
914/723-8534

H133
Cancer Counseling and Research Center
1300 Summit, Suite 710
Fort Worth, TX 76102
817/335-4823   ✦✦

H134
Cape Cod Health Care Coalition
148 A Cedar Street
Hyannis, MA 02601
617/771-2636

H135
Carolina Brown Lung Association
P.O. Box 1101
Roanoke Rapids, NC 27870
919/537-1858

H136
Center for Early Adolescence
University of North Carolina
Carr Mill Mall, Suite 223
Carrboro, NC 27510
919/966-1148   ✳

H137
Center for Humane Options in the Childbirth Experience
1300 Morse Road, #200
Columbus, OH 43229
614/436-2191   ✳

H138
Cesareans/Support Education and Concern (C/SEC)
66 Christopher Road
Waltham, MA 02154
617/547-7188   ✳✦

H139
Child Care Information Exchange
70 Oakley Road
Belmont, MA 02178
617/484-5696   ✳

H140
Children in Hospitals
31 Wilshire Park
Needham, MA 02192

H141
Children's Defense Fund
1520 New Hampshire Avenue, N.W.
Washington, DC 20036
800/424-9602   ✳

H142
Children's Holistic Institute for Life Development
172 West 79th Street
New York, NY 10024
212/580-1622

H143
Choosing Healthy Options in Changing Environments
6550 Indiana
Golden, CO 80401
303/420-7213   ✳

H144
Chrysalis
1052 West 6th Street
Los Angeles, CA 90017
                                               ✳

H145
Cinema Medica
2335 West Foster Avenue
Chicago, IL 60625
800/621-5147   ✦✦✦

H146
Clearing Community and School of the Healing Arts
525 Oakland Avenue
Iowa City, IA 52240
319/337-5405

H147
Club SeneX
P.O. Box 450147
Miami, FL 33145
305/856-5064

H148
Committee to End Violence Against the Next Generation
977 Keeler Avenue
Berkeley, CA 94708
415/527-0454 ✳

H149
Community Network Development Project
Florida Mental Health Institute
13301 North 30th Street
Tampa, FL 33612
813/974-4672

H150
Coping with the Overall Pregnancy/Parenting Experience
37 Clarendon Street
Boston, MA 02116
617/357-5588

H151
Do It Now Foundation
Drug Survival News
P.O. Box 5115
Phoenix, AZ 85010 ✳

H152
Doctors Ought to Care
924 West Webster Street
Chicago, IL 60614
312/348-8427

H153
East West Academy of Healing Arts
P.O. Box 31211
San Francisco, CA 94131
415/285-9400

H154
East/West Center for Holistic Health
141 Fifth Avenue & 21st Street
New York, NY 10010
212/673-8200

H155
Endometriosis Association
c/o Bread & Roses
238 West Wisconsin Avenue, #700
Milwaukee, WI 53203
414/278-0260 ✳

H156
Flower Essence Society
P.O. Box 586
Nevada City, CA 95959
906/265-9163 ✳

H157
Hawaii Health Network
1487 Hiikala Place, #17
Honolulu, HI 96816 ✳

H158
Health Activation Network
P.O. Box 923
Vienna, VA 22180
703/938-5426 ✳

H159
Health Link
Family Health Center
Toledo, IA 52342
515/484-4953 ◆

H160
Health Policy Council
56 East 11th Street
New York, NY 10003 ✳

H161
Health Writers
306 North Brooks Street
Madison, WI 53715
608/255-2255 ✳

H162
Health for the New Age
1a Addison Crescent
London, W14 8JP
ENGLAND
01-603 7751 ✳

H163
Herbal Education Center
6 Crescent Road
Burlington, VT 05401

H164
Hippocrates Health Institute
25 Exeter Street
Boston, MA 02116
617/267-9525 ◆

H165
Holistic Health Organizing Committee
P.O. Box 688
Berkeley, CA 94701
415/841-6500

H166
Holistic Health Practitioners' Association
396 Euclid Avenue
Oakland, CA 94610
415/835-5018 ✳

H167
Holistic Health Referrals
1 Brattle Circle
Cambridge, MA 02138
617/661-3732 ◆

H168
Holistic Health Review
Human Sciences Press
72 Fifth Avenue
New York, NY 10011

H169
Holistic Psychotherapy and Medical Group
1749 Vine Street
Berkeley, CA 94703
415/843-2766 ✦

H170
Holmes Center for Research in Holistic Healing
P.O. Box 75127
Los Angeles, CA 90075
213/380-6176 ✳

H171
Home-Oriented Maternity Experience
511 New York Avenue
Washington, DC 20012
301/587-4664 ✳

H172
Homebirth
P.O. Box 355
Boston, MA 02215 ✳

H173
Homeopathic Educational Services
5916 Chabot Crest
Oakland, CA 94618
415/658-4325 ✦

H174
Hot Springs Information Network
P.O. Box 370
Edgewood, TX 75117
214/896-4002 ✳

H175
Informed Homebirth
P.O. Box 788
Boulder, CO 80306
303/484-8337 ✳

H176
Institute for Family Research and Education
760 Ostrom Avenue
Syracuse, NY 13210
315/423-4584 ✦

H177
Integral Health Services
245 School Street
Putnam, CT 06260
203/928-7729

H178
Interface Foundation
230 Central Street
Newton, MA 02166
617/964-7140

H179
International Childbirth Education Association
P.O. Box 20048
Minneapolis, MN 55420
612/854-8660

H180
International College of Applied Nutrition
P.O. Box 386
La Habra, CA 90631

H181
**International Foundation for the Promotion of
   Homeopathy**
76 Lee Street
Mill Valley, CA 94941
415/383-5343 ✳

H182
Journal of the Nutritional Academy
1238 Hayes
Eugene, OR 97402 ✳

H183
Ken Dychtwald & Associates
1023 Amito Avenue
Berkeley, CA 94705
415/845-4519 ✦

H184
Life-Force Cancer Project
2210 Wilshire Boulevard, Box 281
Santa Monica, CA 90403
213/450-5005

H185
Long Island Childbirth Alternatives
12 New York Avenue
Shoreham, NY 11786
516/689-8229 ✳

H186
**Macrobiotic Health Information Center of New
   Jersey**
300 Washington Avenue
Belleville, NJ 07109
201/751-3303

H187
Macrobiotic: A Guide for Natural Living
East West Foundation
506-A York Road
Towson, MD 21204
301/828-1066 ✳

H188
Marion County Community Mental Health Center
3180 Center Street, N.E.
Salem, OR 97214 ◆

H189
Massachusetts Coalition of Battered Women Service Groups
120 Boylston Street
Boston, MA 02116
617/426-8492

H190
Massage and Bodywork
P.O. Box 2215
Leucadia, CA 92024 ◆

H191
Maternal and Child Health Center
Physical Therapy Services
2362 Massachusetts Avenue
Cambridge, MA 02140
617/964-9343 ◆

H192
Maternity Center
1119 East San Antonio
El Paso, TX 79901
915/533-8142

H193
Medical Self-Care Magazine
P.O. Box 718
Inverness, CA 94937 ✳

H194
Mental Patients Association
2146 Yew Street
Vancouver, British Columbia
CANADA V6K 3G7
604/738-1422 ✳

H195
Mid-Hudson Area Maternity Alternatives
Red Top Road, Box 26a
Wallkill, NY 12589 ✳

H196
National Alliance for the Mentally Ill
1234 Massachusetts Avenue, N.W.
Washington, DC 20005
202/783-6393 ✳

H197
National Coalition Against Domestic Violence
1728 N Street, N.W.
Washington, DC 20036
202/347-7015 ◆◆

H198
National College of Naturopathic Medicine
510 Southwest Third Avenue
Portland, OR 97204
503/226-3745 ✳

H199
National Committee for Prevention of Child Abuse
332 South Michigan Avenue
Chicago, IL 60604
312/663-3520 ✳◆

H200
National Council on Alternative Health Care Policy
P.O. Box 1183
San Jose, CA 95108
408/287-0643

H201
National Feminist Therapists Association
5030 Del Monte Avenue, #14
San Diego, CA 92107
714/233-8984 ✳

H202
National Health Federation
P.O. Box 688
Monrovia, CA 91016
213/358-1155 ✳

H203
National Hospice Organization
301 Maple Avenue West, Suite 506
Vienna, VA 22180
703/938-4449

H204
Network Against Psychiatric Assault
1744 University Avenue
Berkeley, CA 94703
415/548-2980

H205
New Age Wellness Center
9000 Southwest 87th Court, #201
Miami, FL 33176
305/279-0850

H206
New Age in Austin
Rural Route #1, Box 183
Dale, TX 78616
512/559-2063 ✳

H207
New Beginnings Birth Center
450 Tollgate Road
Warwick, RI 02886
401/737-1599

H208
Newtrition Outreach: Whole Foods Information
402 South Glendale
Ann Arbor, MI 48103
313/668-8084

H209
North Carolina Occupational Safety and Health Project
P.O. Box 2514
Durham, NC 27705
919/286-2276 ✶

H210
Northern Pines: A Wholistic Health Retreat
Route 85, Box 279
Raymond, ME 04071
207/655-7624

H211
Nurse Healers/Professional Associates Cooperative
70 Shelley Avenue, Box 7
Port Chester, NY 10573 ✶

H212
Nurses in Transition
P.O. Box 14472
San Francisco, CA 94114
415/282-7999 ✶

H213
Nutritional and Preventive Medical Clinic
99 Avenue Road, Suite 306
Toronto, Ontario
CANADA M5R 2G5
416/923-0716

H214
Omega: Program of Grief Assistance
270 Washington Street
Somerville, MA 02143
617/776-6369 ✶

H215
On Our Own Network
c/o Second Congregational Church
395 High Street
Holyoke, MA 01040

H216
Ontario Patients' Self-Help Association
P.O. Box 7251, Station A
Toronto, Ontario
CANADA M5W 1X9
416/362-3193 ✶

H217
Parents Without Partners
P.O. Box 81
Brookline, MA 02146

H218
Pavillion Newsletter: Advocacy for the Disabled
114 Floral Street
Newton Highlands, MA 02161 ✶

H219
People's Doctor: Medical Newsletter for Consumers
664 North Michigan Avenue
Chicago, IL 60611 ✶

H220
Planned Parenthood
810 Seventh Avenue
New York, NY 10019
212/541-7800

H221
Psychiatric Inmates' Rights Collective
P.O. Box 299
Santa Cruz, CA 95061 ✶

H222
Public Citizen Health Research Group
2000 P Street, N.W.
Washington, DC 20036
202/872-0320

H223
Pumpkin Hollow Farm
Rural Route #1, Box 135
Craryville, NY 12521

H224
Pyramid: Resource Sharing Network for Drug Abuse Prevention
3746 Mt. Diablo Boulevard, #200
Lafayette, CA 94549
415/284-5300 ✶

H225
Renaissance House
P.O. Box 292, Village Sta.
New York, NY 10014
212/929-7720 ◆

H226
San Francisco Young Adult Network
944 Market, #603
San Francisco, CA 94109
415/989-6097 ✶

H227
Sarasota School of Natural Healing Arts
290 Cocoanut Avenue
Sarasota, FL 33577
813/957-1097

H228
Self Care Associates
P.O. Box 161
Boulder Creek, CA 95006
408/338-6108 ✶

H229
Seminars on Sexuality
8845 West Olympic Boulevard
Beverly Hills, CA 90211
213/659-3487

H230
Society for Occupational and Environmental
Health
2914 M Street, N.W.
Washington, DC 20007
202/965-6633 ✦✦

H231
Society for the Protection of the Unborn Through
Nutrition
17 North Wabash Avenue, 603
Chicago, IL 60602
312/332-2334 ✳

H232
Soundiscoveries
P.O. Box 194, Back Bay Sta.
Boston, MA 02117 ✦✦✦

H233
Spring Hill: Community, Retreat and Counseling
Center
P.O. Box 124
Ashby, MA 01431
617/386-5622

H234
Statewide Comprehensive Health Education
Coalition
P.O. Box 1132
Jefferson City, MO 65102

H235
Tri-Self Clinic
510-14 Cornwall Avenue
Cheshire, CT 06410
203/272-1330

H236
Turtle Island Holistic Health Community
569-71 Selby Avenue
St. Paul, MN 55102
612/291-7637

H237
Vanier Institute of the Family
151 Slater Street, #207
Ottawa, Ontario
CANADA K1P 5H3
613/232-7115 ✳✦✦

H238
Vegetarian Times
41 East 42nd Street, Suite 921
New York, NY 10017
212/490-3999 ✳

H239
Washington State Midwifery Council
1512 Langridge Avenue
Olympia, WA 98502
206/943-8607

H240
Well-Being Magazine
41 East 42nd Street, #921
New York, NY 10017
212/490-3999 ✳

H241
Wellness Associates
42 Miller Avenue
Mill Valley, CA 94941
415/383-3806 ✦

H242
Wellness Institute
P.O. Box 132
Sloatsburg, NY 10974
914/753-2787 ✳

H243
Wholistic Health and Nutrition Institute
150 Shoreline Highway, #31
Mill Valley, CA 94941
415/332-2933

H244
Womancare: A Feminist Women's Health Center
424 Pennsylvania Avenue
San Diego, CA 92103
714/298-9352

H245
Women Healthsharing
P.O. Box 230, Station M
Toronto, Ontario
CANADA M6S 4T3
416/968-1363 ✳

H246
Women and Health Roundtable
200 P Street, N.W., #403
Washington, DC 20036
202/466-3545 ✳

H247
Working on Wife Abuse
46 Pleasant Street
Cambridge, MA 02139 ✦

4

Sharing Networks:
Communities and Cooperatives

When the Pilgrims landed at Plymouth Harbor in 1620, they disembarked with a sense of community, with a desire to create an egalitarian life for themselves, and with a commitment to sharing their goods and resources. For the people already there, sharing was a basic, unquestioned value: Among the Native Americans, the tribal imperative of working for the good of all has always been regarded as fundamental to human coexistence.

Today, the concept of sharing is experiencing a renaissance whose manifestations cut across economic, social, sexual, ethnic, and religious lines, a rebirth reflected in myriad formal and informal cooperatives. Similarly, neighborhoods and communities are in the midst of a revival. Threatened with extermination by gentrification (the country "gentry" moving back into the cities), local people are re-creating their sense of community in what author Harry Boyte has called *The Backyard Revolution*.

In many places, the supermarket has been replaced by the basement food co-op, and families have organized themselves into baby-sitting arrangements in which time, not money, is the currency. Other groups have formed to purchase everything from cordwood (such as People's Community Enterprises, in Duluth, Minnesota) to weatherproofing materials (such as the Boston Building Materials Cooperative, in Jamaica Plain, Massachusetts) to prefabricated, energy-efficient, low-cost houses (such as Family Homes Cooperative, in Crab Orchard, West Virginia). Even some lawyers have broken out of corporate law offices and reestablished themselves in more than 3000 legal co-ops.

In neighborhoods and communities, people are organizing to shape for themselves what local governments have failed to give them. The Neighborhood Information Sharing Exchange has profiled more than 2000 local groups that are working on everything from reusing abandoned school buildings to converting vacant city lots into lush urban gardens. "Local" is an idea that grabs people—and propels them to work.

In this chapter, the cooperative movement is chronicled with sections on *food and shelter*, illustrating the diversity of the cooperative form applied to the basics of life; communities are discussed in terms of both *cities and neighborhoods*; and *self-reliance and barter* bring the idea of sharing back around to individual responsibility.

The cooperative spirit is as old as the country itself. According to the U.S. Department of Agriculture's *Cooperative Facts*, the first formal co-op in the country predates the American Revolution, formed in 1752 as an insurance hedge against fire loss. The Philadelphia Contributorship for the Insurance of Homes from Loss of Fire, a brainchild of that master of innovative ideas, Benjamin Franklin, still exists today, its more than two-century history a validation of the value, adaptability, and longevity of the cooperative form.

Cooperatives are grounded in local needs and in the communities that they serve, and they arise from a heritage of resource sharing, which saw its largest growth from the mid 1850s to the early 1900s. By the turn of the century, tobacco, hogs, grain, butter, cheese, fruit, cattle, wool, eggs, poultry, rice, beans, pecans, and even cranberries were all being produced and sold through cooperatives. By the time of the Depression of the 1930s, credit unions, the cooperative equivalent of banks, were serving millions of people, while hundreds of thousands more were being hooked up to electricity and telephone service through utility cooperatives.

Taken as a whole, these pre-1970 consumer and farmer-producer cooperatives constitute what is now known as the cooperative movement's "Old Wave," fittingly separate and distinguishable from the "New Wave," primarily consumer co-ops that arose in the 1970s. While producer co-ops continue to attract new members and to form in new areas (such as organic food production), it is the consumer co-ops, organized to purchase everything from books to clothes to houses, that are attracting the greatest number of people. Cooperative buying offers pocketbook relief when prices are rising.

Kirkpatrick Sale's book *Human Scale* includes evidence of how rapidly the cooperative movement has grown during the 1970s, with nearly every kind of co-op almost doubling in size in the past 10 years. He writes: "Credit unions have grown from 17 million members in 1965 to 32 million in 1977; health co-ops from 3.4 million to 6.1 million; electricity co-ops from 4.9 million to 6.6 million."

Co-ops may sound like a utopian scheme of some idealistic commune in the woods. But, in fact, they are enduring organizations, growing larger, and reaching a broader range of people as we move toward the year 2000. While the double spiral of soaring prices and crime rates in the 1970s distracted many of us from what author Mark Satin calls the "appropriate" (rather than "alternative") structures right under our noses, practical people in tens of thousands of communities have worked to build a cooperative economy.

The co-op movement took a big leap forward in 1980 with the opening of the National Consumer Cooperative Bank, created by an act of Congress as the first piece of consumer legislation to be enacted in more than a decade. Initially funded by the government, the Bank is designed to eventually be owned by its co-op borrowers who buy into the bank as voting shareholders as they repay their loans. Historically, co-ops have encountered difficulty in obtaining loans from traditional lending institutions, particularly in a tight money market. The Co-op Bank was designed to lend money either through its own channels or through the Bank's Self-Help Development Fund, set up to aid new co-ops with no financial track record. The Bank also provides technical assistance to its borrowers, sometimes requiring such professional backup as a stipulation to making loans.

In a spring 1980 interview with *Co-op* magazine, Ralph Nader describes the links between the consumer and cooperative movements:

> The consumer movement is the cooperative movement, and the cooperative movement is the consumer movement. But co-ops are not where it starts. It starts with developing a consumer perspective that is very rigorous in a most theoretical and empirical sense.

> The consumer movement is the foundation—it helps people get more information, more legal rights, more representation in government. It is followed up by a much more command-oriented consumer power system, namely housing co-ops, food co-ops, auto repair co-ops, insurance co-ops, baking co-ops, and other co-ops all over the country controlled by the people who pay all the bills in this country—the consumers.

Co-ops are a very important alternative form of private enterprise that is much more consistent with American democratic values of community power, of information, of responsibility for present and future generations.

Is the cooperative solution easy? Not at all, says Phil Kreitner, whose research on co-ops led to his doctoral dissertation on the subject, "The Theory of Economic Cooperation, U.S. New Generation Food Co-ops and the Cooperative Dilemma." Kreitner sees a basic contradiction in co-op life–community-scale co-op development is "undertaken in a predominantly multinational-scale economic institutional environment"–which pushes co-ops toward either "collapse or cooptation." For Kreitner, the solution lies in co-ops teaching their members "not only *how* to work by collective (i.e., cooperative) *means*, but *why* to work for collective (i.e., community) ends."

Thus, establishing local cooperatives leads to community building. Cooperative and community movements are together celebrating and renewing neighborhoods and creating powerful new resource and information exchanges that serve the needs of communities in the here and now, projects that have grown among the realities of violent crime and urban decay.

The cooperative movement creates momentum for community work. A small local buying group soon realizes there is strength in numbers, that it has the power to address other problems, needs, and issues. At that point, the original network that formed the cooperative reconfigures: New people are drawn in and a new network is formed. Very subtly, these two movements are reinfusing the country with a basic value on which America was nurtured: sharing.

FOOD AND SHELTER

The supermarket is the measuring rod that most Americans use as their own economic indicator. Shoppers need not consult the Dow Jones average, the financial page, or the commodities market to know that last week's price on a pound of hamburger is this week's price on a pound of potatoes. Like scholars who know the intricate political machinations of feudal Europe, dollar-conscious supermarket savants can recite the detailed price-rise history of many products.

The food co-op is an economic alternative to the supermarket. The best known of the 1970s co-ops are the 10,000 food co-ops, ranging in size from a few families to the 96,000-member Berkeley Food Co-op, in California. The *Food Co-op Directory* reports that co-ops grossed an incredible half billion dollars in sales in 1979. Writing in *The Guide to Cooperative Alternatives*, Ann Evans, editor of *Jam Today: California Journal of Cooperation*, explains how food co-ops developed and how their organizational form affects the larger social fabric:

At first, common sense caused people to wonder about the foods they ate; later national health problems confirmed their suspicions. "Vote with your stomach" became the slogan as more people turned from a synthetic diet toward natural foods. Concern over the quality and cost of food increased the constituency looking for an alternative. Less meat, less fat, and fewer food additives brought a new sense of health and self to many Americans. Frances Moore Lappé's *Diet for a Small Planet* appeared in the kitchen, as the zen of eating blossomed in the American consciousness.

Rejecting the kind of packaging which merely "depicts" nature and costs more than its contents, people sought simple, cheap methods of packaging (generic labels like "Honey"). Others sought foods sold in bulk bins which required no packaging at all. This was made possible by foods now more popular such as dry beans and whole grains, which, unlike heavily processed foods, do not spoil on direct contact with the environment. Model legislation such as California's Bulk Foods Act (1978) ensured the consumer's right to buy food in bulk. Enough demand exists for less packaging to effect a change in the wasteful practices used today. At last, even the food marketing chains are responding.

As the newer cooperatives searched for appropriate models, they looked to the remnants of American cooperative heritage in search of their roots. Cooperatives such as Hyde Park in Chicago, Greenbelt in Washington, D.C., and Eau Claire in Wisconsin, all formed in the thirties, provide a legacy of managerial experience in participatory structures. Organizations such as the National Consumer Cooperative Alliance, the Cooperative League of the USA, and conferences such as Wind through the Pines in Austin, Texas (1977) bring the old and the new together. The old rekindle the spirit while the young choose those elements of the thirties' experience they wish to preserve and build upon. While cooperatives of both eras incorporated democracy in the ownership and control of the business, the newer cooperatives also carried democracy into the marketplace.

If increased use of capital provides the lifeblood of a cooperative, its heart is voluntary member involvement. Such members are the public entrepreneurs of the cooperative movement; their motivation is largely dependent on a shared sense of its cornerstones, the personal experience of members who involve themselves in the cooperative's decision-making process. If frustration and inefficiency result from this process, the sense of community will be eroded. Alternatively, through skillful use of the democratic process, member involvement becomes a productive, positive experience. The enhanced strength and legitimacy of the group and the process it uses helps to create a strong community within the cooperative, and a strong cooperative within the community.

Gaining control over food cost and food quality is a fundamental way to reempower our lives. A family consuming the typical American diet ingests 45 chemicals in a day's eating, including some that leach into our foods through the plastic and other synthetic wrapping materials designed to grab our attention. The food co-op is the antithesis of the football-field sized American supermarket, which has grown so big that the aisles are marked with one way signs. The vast network of people and groups that give us access to purer foods at more reasonable prices have done far more than saved us money. They are moving us closer to the land, reuniting us in a very fundamental way with nature, bringing us back into the flow of the seasons and the natural bounty of the earth.

Summer is usually the lean time for food co-op participation. During the spring, 33 million Americans take spade in hand, turn over a little bit of earth—whether in their backyard, on their windowsill, atop their apartment building, or around the corner in what was once an abandoned lot—drop in a few seeds, and sit back to reap an amazing $13 billion worth of food each year, having saved an average of $367 in food bills in 1979 for the 42 percent of all American families who grow some of their own vegetables.

Gardening is perhaps the most universally loved pastime, and its invention is simultaneous with the settling of the first towns, 12,000 years ago. Imagining a network of early gardeners exchanging their discoveries of organic growth, making one another privy to the tips and tools of the earth, tingles ancient pathways in our collective memory banks. Today, the gardening network is thriving, serving as perhaps the greatest ongoing advertisement for clean air, clean water, and peace that human beings have ever unconsciously created.

"Gardeners are very happy people," Robert Muller (see Chapter 9) points out. Gardeners naturally form networks as an outgrowth of their hobby. Gardening brings people in touch with the earth, and the networks that they form out of their love of growing things bring them in touch with one another. The title of the newspaper of the National Association for Gardening sums up the spirit of the home-grown-food movement: *Gardens for All.*

Like food, shelter is a basic human necessity, and cooperatives have emerged in this area to meet a variety of needs and life-styles. As most urban Americans know, the housing crisis is acute and immediate. Expressed by such words as gentrification and displacement, the fact is that less housing is available, at higher prices, while more people need to be housed. Multiple-family dwellings are being taken over as upper-middle-class people return to the cities, where three run-down apartments are turned into one townhouse. Developers are tearing down whole blocks of buildings at a time, replacing them with high-rise multiple units at much higher rents, or more frequently, converting existing or new apartments to condominiums, pricing the large majority of people right out of the housing market. In 1980, mortgage money all but evaporated and what little lending was done cost the borrower an exorbitant interest rate, which excluded nearly all potential home buyers from the market.

A number of networks have developed around the housing issue, some to work against the shrinking housing market, others to propose other options. *Shelterforce* is the national publication of the housing movement, which in June 1980 held a conference to bring tenant groups together into an active nationwide network. The newspaper addresses the current concerns in shaping a national policy, including such issues as the "upgrading of public housing into luxury housing," the "sweep-out of tenants to make way for hotel development," condominium conversion, and tenants-rights to purchase buildings.

"Housing cooperatives are one strategy for dealing with the problem of providing housing," says the National Association of Housing Cooperatives (NAHC), a 30-year old group now representing more than 100,000 families living in 425 cooperatives in the United States. "Cooperative housing is not a stop-gap solution, applied to displacement and the housing shortage until the crisis is over," NAHC says. "Housing cooperatives are a more permanent, stabilizing tool for dealing with displacement. . . Cooperatives complement other forms of housing, including rental, condominium, and single-family home ownership."

Like condominiums, cooperatives allow everyone living in a building to own part of it, each member paying a monthly fee that covers the operating costs of the cooperative. Unlike condominiums, however, there is no third-party owner who derives a profit from the overall living space. All cooperative members have an equal vote in decisions affecting the property, thus locating the decision making about the cooperative solely with the members.

The housing co-op idea has broad-based appeal, and it has been applied at every income level, from the luxurious Manhattan townhouse cooperative that vetoed prospective member Richard Nixon, to the economical Co-Op City, in the Bronx, which houses thousands of low-income families. NAHC believes that the cooperative idea fosters the idea of a "strong community," since members remain in charge of their housing.

Americans have been drawn to the idea of establishing independent, self-sufficient communities for the past 400 years, from the religious Puritans and

Shakers in the 17th and 18th centuries, to the Transcendentalists' Brook Farm in the 19th century, to the counterculture/middle-class-idealist communards of the 20th century.

"In order to be in control of our lives, we must control the networks providing those things essential to our lives," writes Steve Washam, a networker based in Washington State. "To this end a number of spiritual and social change groups have attempted to establish small and organic self-sufficient communities. Most of these experiments have ended in what one veteran of several communes has termed 'all kinds of far-out lessons,' or continue with only partial success."

For most 1960s activists and 1970s seekers, an "alternative life-style" (meaning living with a group, in a community, on a farm, and/or in a commune), has been one of the stepping-stones along the path. Yet, with a few notable exceptions, most of these experiments have disintegrated over time. "Whether there are more problems getting a community together or keeping it together is hard to say, but there are lots of problems on both ends that need answers," writes John West, who has participated in and studied the intentional-community movement since the late 1960s.

West names two primary obstacles to successfully sustaining communities:

> (1) The main theme of the communes [of the 1960s] was "do your own thing." This attitude is completely anti-community . . . and was carried into the intentional communities and contributed heavily to the failure rate; and (2) The Madison Avenue syndrome which is an abbreviation of the business and political philosophy of the last 30 to 40 years that has sold individualism and competitiveness because individuals make safer constituents than do groups and they certainly make better consumers. However, both individualism and competitiveness can cause a great deal of trouble in a community situation.

Although born into nuclear families, many of which were enjoying some degree of post-World War II/pre-Vietnam War affluence, these later communards nonetheless persisted in their attempts to live together. To date, the most successful experiments in living have been formed around a shared spiritual quest, headed by a charismatic leader, notably the 1100-member Farm, in Tennessee, and the 250-member Love Family in Oregon. Even so, since the 1978 mass suicide in Guyana, the idea of a "commune" has become frightening to many people, the concept having become hopelessly entwined with the idea of a "brainwashed cult."

The Farm is an inspiring example of what a community with common purpose can accomplish. From its base in Summertown, The Farm has reached around the world. Through its PLENTY Project ("towards a world of plenty for everyone"), The Farm is building the Motsemocha Village Technology Center, an energy-efficient rural development experiment in Lesotho, Africa, is operating a free ambulance service in the South Bronx, New York, is constructing solar water purifiers in an arid section of Tijuana, Mexico, is the guiding force behind the establishment of a village-scale soy dairy in San Bartolo, Guatemala, and has delivered more than 1000 babies at home, trained scores of midwives, and authored a book that has served as one of the bibles of the home birth movement: *Spiritual Midwifery*.

In spite of practical and political problems, the commune movement has managed to survive, greatly aided by the support network that keeps communes in touch with one another. Like nuclear families, individual communes have suffered from alienation, a problem that is being addressed by The Grapevine, in California (a clearinghouse for the communal movement), and its older relative, the New Community

Project (NCP), in Boston. Every Sunday night since 1970, NCP has been holding a potluck dinner after which people meet to deal with problems that arise in group living. "Eating together is the focal point of communal life," explains NCP volunteer Janet Fillion. "After our meal, we have a discussion group, which is followed by a clearinghouse time in which groups needing people can meet people needing groups."

NCP also maintains a series of "referral books," loose-leaf binders that offer people a "humane, low-key, friendly" alternative to placing ads in newspapers. In addition to the Boston, Cambridge, Suburban, and Rural Commune books, NCP also keeps up to date what it calls "The Women's Looking Book," "The Men's Looking Book," and "The Couples' Looking Book," further broken down into such fine distinctions as "Women with Kids," "Women Without Kids," "Women Who Want to Live with Kids," and "Women Who Don't Want to Live with Kids." This service has been of particular help to single parents who, Fillion points out, have an especially difficult time finding places to live.

One network of the 1960s intentional communities that has survived intact and offers a utopian model for others to observe and learn from is the Federation of Egalitarian Communities (FEC), whose first community, Twin Oaks, in Virginia, was inspired by B. F. Skinner's book *Walden Two*. FEC is an example of how "small homestead-oriented groups and village-like communities similar to the Israeli kibbutz" can become viable alternatives for a broad range of people. FEC is a network that links six intentional communities (four in the United States, one in Canada, and one in Mexico) that subscribe to a set of core principles.

Each of the Federation communities:

(1) Holds its land, labor and other resources in common;

(2) Assumes responsibility for the needs of its members, receiving the products of their labors and distributing these and all other goods equally or according to need;

(3) Practices non-violence;

(4) Uses a participatory form of government in which the members have either a direct vote, the right of impeachment or overrule;

(5) Does not deny membership nor promote inequality among its members through discrimination on grounds of race, creed, age or sex; and

(6) Assumes responsibility for maintaining the availability of natural resources for present and future generations through ecologically sound production and consumption.

One of the principal ways in which FEC maintains its network is through the joint publication of a magazine, *Communities: A Journal of Cooperative Living*, which includes regular sections on "Reach" and "Resources," in which people looking for communities, as well as those communities looking for people, can find out about one another. Summing up its 8 years of publishing, *Communities* published *A Guide to Cooperative Alternatives* in 1979, which lists and describes nearly 400 projects and experiments in the United States in the areas of community organizing, health and well-being, economics and work, food, housing, communications and networking, family life and relationships, and energy and environment. *GCA* offers a handy thumbnail sketch of each cooperative/alternative group community and contains a directory listing some 85 intentional communities in North America.

CITIES AND NEIGHBORHOODS

In the past 10 years, cities and citizens have found themselves faced with multiple crises—ranging from bankrupting budgets to failing services. While the causes of these problems have filled many tomes of literature and have given rise to the professional specialty of urban planning, these academic analyses have failed to provide immediate options that can make a difference in people's lives. The Model Cities programs of the early 1970s are long-gone, replaced by grass-roots efforts that address current needs.

A number of network-minded people throughout the country have begun to develop and implement solutions. The very easiest "thing" to network is information. Hence, the information-sharing network has sprung up in many cities, providing both *local* resources and the basis for a *national* exchange of ideas.

The Portland Book, an astounding compilation of material about Portland, Oregon, is an example of how much information people can have access to if someone is willing to do the hard work of bringing it all together in one place. In 1978, Steve Johnson, a cofounder and editor of *Rain Magazine*, the first appropriate technology newsletter in the country, retreated to the country. Johnson was suffering from the networker's special malady: information overload. After a year of waking up to the sounds of birds chirping rather than the thud of the mountain of mail that daily poured through the *Rain* mailbox, Johnson regrouped his energies, returned to the city where he had lived all his life, and began to compile *The Portland Book*.

For 4 months all Johnson did was gather information, a passion he feels may have its roots in his childhood, when, as an 8-year-old, he spent much of his time reading almanacs. Like many other networkers, Johnson has been called an "information junkie." Indeed, collecting information can become an addiction, but like all such inexplicable human drives, when combined with discipline and purpose, the information junkie may become a true artist. Using no technology higher than a questionnaire, 3x5 index cards, and a typewriter, Johnson created an encyclopedia of Portland, skillfully organizing 2000 organizations and government agencies, 1000 publications, and a series of chapters on topics ranging from lifelong learning to the history of the area, into one easy-to-read, 200-page, "Part of the Whole Earth," large-format paperback.

When he was done, the idea for a local information center that would provide networking services was an obvious follow-up. Joining with several others, he created the Portland Community Resource Center, which uses a variety of computer and paper research tools to track down information that clients need. In 1981, Johnson closed his circle when the resource center merged with Rain Magazine, becoming the Rain Community Resource Center (RCRC). RCRC is the kind of local information facility that could benefit every community, and indeed the Portland effort is an important node in a much larger national network based in Washington, D.C.: the Neighborhood Information Sharing Exchange (see below).

The community information resource center is one of many ways in which local groups can become more efficient. One of the oldest and strongest community networks is the Community Congress of San Diego (CCSD), a powerful coalition of community groups that got its start in the late 1960s. CCSD, now representing 150 local community groups in the political arena, is a superb example of network evolution. Begun originally as a support system for six social workers providing alternative human services at a time when teenage runaways and crash pads were two of the most compelling problems in the country, the tiny network grew to attract the interest of other providers of alternative human services.

Although CCSD is more than a "network" today, it still uses its early networking concepts to guide its decision making and to create consensus around specific issues within the greater San Diego community. CCSD now receives grants and runs training sessions and conducts a college of "community learning," where community workers can earn academic degrees without leaving their jobs. CCSD is a potent voice in the San Diego community. For example, it blocked the construction of a juvenile detention center and worked instead to funnel those available funds into programs within the community for the rehabilitation of juvenile offenders.

While the network model has been used to galvanize action for a particular kind of city service such as human services, it has also been used to help a city as a whole. At a time when the New York City budget was deeply in the red and local services were being cut, the Citizens Committee for New York City (CCNYC) was formed, in late 1975, to provide technical assistance to neighborhood-based organizations and block associations in the city's five boroughs.

"Are we a network? I suppose the answer to that is yes, if being a network means facilitating communication between disparate groups," says Sandra Silverman, the group's executive director. "Our conferences, for example, bring together people from all walks of life, of all races, all classes, and all neighborhoods, who can share ideas with one another based on common experiences relating to their own neighborhoods."

In 1977, CCNYC published *The New York Self-Help Handbook: A Step-by-step Guide to Neighborhood Improvement Projects*, which offers New Yorkers the information they need to revitalize their city. Each section, from "Sidewalk Sweeps" to "Playlots" to "Street Olympics" to "Friendly Visiting," includes a description, a series of basic steps, a reference for technical assistance, and examples of successful models. The "Bench Painting" section, for example, contains the kind of basic one, two, three information that people need in order to get things done:

Organize your group to paint the benches in your local park or minipark, or your street or street mall.

BASIC STEPS

(1) Contact the Parks Department to obtain permission to paint benches . . . the Department has guidelines for paint types and colors.

(2) Publicize the event with flyers, posters, and through community newsletters to attract more volunteers.

(3) Obtain donations or discounts on paints, brushes and other equipment from local paint stores or other merchants. Use a good quality outdoor paint.

(4) Paint the benches. Don't forget "Wet Paint" signs!

TECHNICAL ASSISTANCE

Contact the Citizens Committee for New York City to apply for an incentive grant under the Parks Preservation Program. Paint for benches is an acceptable item for a grant of up to $100.

MODELS

The 181st Street Block Association, Manhattan, repainted benches in a local minipark. The Port Authority, which has jurisdiction over the park, granted them permission to beautify the park and also provided all the materials the block association needed (paint, brushes, etc.). The group advertised around the neighborhood with posters announcing the "paint-in" ten days before the date of the project. Neighborhood residents contributed refreshments for the event.

The painting group consisted of about twenty school children and three or four adults. Many people in the neighborhood had felt that the children were being destructive to the area; this beautification project also served as a tool for educating the young people to take pride in their work.

Clearly, networking can be used within large urban areas to address many kinds of problems. In the same way, the network model can be brought down to the neighborhood level, where many highly effective networks have gotten their start.

It is in the streets of American cities that our extraordinary variety of backgrounds is evident and, although our history reveals tremendous tensions among the various immigrant communities, America's neighborhoods have always been very special. Today an interest in neighborhood life is on the rise again, particularly as local communities have lost power to centralized government. There exists no support system so strong as the people who live nearby, who can join together to solve local problems and to help one another out in times of crisis.

We live in a neighborhood that exists on two sides of a very heavily traveled street complicated by a sharp bend in the road that over the years has resulted in many accidents and a number of deaths. When two very serious accidents occurred in 2 weeks, the neighbors said, "Enough!" and decided to take action. A petition was circulated calling on the city officials to respond quickly. Within a few months—after we had attended numerous confusing, frustrating meetings, written letters, then rewritten them as "someone" lost copy after copy, filled out repetitive and contradictory forms that one official after another proclaimed as "required," and placed countless phone calls to our local lawmakers and civil servants—the city appropriated money and constructed guard rails along the sharp curve.

The neighborhood network formed quickly, operated smoothly, and disbanded as soon as the problem appeared solved. Other than a few dollars spent on copying letters, a few pitchers of iced tea provided for the hot summer evening meetings, and a considerable amount of time spent trying to make sense out of a confused bureaucracy that even its officials could not explain to us, our summertime networking effort required no money. No time was wasted on organizational details, such as coming up with a statement of purpose or bylaws or officers or even assigning a recording secretary—all necessary functions in other contexts but completely irrelevant to a local neighborhood campaign to have guardrails installed.

It is situations such as ours that have given birth to literally hundreds of thousands of local neighborhood networks that have formed to remedy immediate problems. These local problem-solving networks have tackled everything from simple issues such as having guardrails, stop signs, and streetlights installed to much more complicated undertakings such as developing a commercial-scale windmill for providing electricity to a tenement in New York.

In the effort to help people benefit from one another's local experience, the Neighborhood Information Sharing Exchange (NISE) has created a working network of active neighborhood organizations whose purpose is to put people in touch to share information.

"I love neighborhood work because you can really see things change," says Susan Hyatt, who works as the community information specialist at NISE. "Neighborhood work engenders a sense of being able to do something. For example, someone calls NISE and says they're having a problem with Hispanic housing displacement. Drawing on our data base of more than 2000 local groups we are able to give them referrals to pursue and books to read. The rest of the work is left up to them."

NISE maintains a networking service for local groups that operates under the following provisos:

You must:

(1) Be a neighborhood organization.

(2) Tell us about your group's history, successful projects, current issues, technical expertise, etc., by filling out one of our neighborhood organization profile forms.

(3) Be willing to share your expertise with other neighborhood organizations should they contact you.

(4) Keep NISE up to date as you develop solutions and strategies.

One inspiring example of a local group that makes use of NISE's networking services is the National Congress of Neighborhood Women (NCNW), which coalesced in 1974 after a year of local networking among women in working-class neighborhoods in Brooklyn, New York. NCNW was started because its founders' concerns fell between the existing cracks of the early 1970s groups: "The women's movement was not reaching our sisters in working-class neighborhoods and especially those women who are full-time homemakers and . . . the 'neighborhood' and 'ethnic' movements were not taking into consideration the special needs of women."

NCNW has its roots in an Italian neighborhood where women had already been active in a block association and had organized a children's summer program—indicating that these women had the skills for getting things done. Eventually, they saw the need to develop a national coalition around the needs of neighborhood women. Working from an initial CETA grant that provided salaries but no money for rent, telephone, equipment, or supplies, the group piggybacked along until it persuaded three foundations to fund a neighborhood-based college program for women. Today, NCNW has 28 affiliated organizations in 19 cities and works on such diverse issues as redlining and jobs, as well as maintaining a community college where neighborhood women can earn degrees.

Neighborhood networks overlap and cooperate on issues but form according to differing constituencies and emphases. At the same time as NCNW was forming, so was another federation of neighborhood organizations, the National Association of Neighborhoods (NAN), which got its start in 1975. At its national meeting during the Bicentennial Year, appropriately held in Philadelphia, NAN drafted and adopted the Neighborhood Bill of Responsibilities and Rights, which succinctly states a vision of democratic decentralization.

With its goal of returning power to local people, NAN is blazing a trail of neighborhood action whose implications at higher levels of government are obvious. In 1979, NAN took its Bill of Responsibilities and Rights to another level: It convened local platform committees throughout the country to hammer out and adopt a National Neighborhood Platform Gathering in 47 different local meetings, NAN participants totalled 10,000 people, who in turn chose 700 delegates to the National Neighborhood Platform Convention, which developed an agenda for action in the 1980s.

At the core of the neighborhood movement is a desire to decentralize decision making—one of the key changes in our social structure that is the goal of all the networks of Another America. Local power means local responsibility and local creativity, making the best use of local resources and skills. Each neighborhood, every social hamlet and hollow, that thrives by democratic decentralization creates a stream of change that eventually joins the larger river of social reorganization.

Another America is being constructed at many levels at once, but day-to-day change is always "local" to someone. Still, the community and neighborhood networks face their greatest challenge ever with the enormous cuts in the federal budget in 1981. With little government funding of any sort available, local groups must truly be self-reliant.

SELF-RELIANCE AND BARTER

Counterposed against the centralist mechanisms that have removed food-growing from local farms to distant agribusiness production centers thousands of miles away and have resulted in the creation of supertankers that travel halfway around the globe to carry U.S. oil back to the United States, *local self-reliance* is the handy phrase that sums up the idea of putting locally available resources to work in satisfying basic human needs. While people sometimes choose to move to new neighborhoods to find a more appropriate life-style, increasingly people are remaining where they are, making a transformation in place.

The Community Self-Reliance Center, in Ithaca, New York, summarizes the need for local solutions this way: "The faraway energy sources we have grown dependent on are becoming scarce, uncertain and expensive. The energy crisis has far-reaching implications for transportation, housing, and agriculture. Our society is geared toward private automobiles, our buildings are poorly insulated, and our food comes from distant places, grown on soil fertilized by petrochemicals."

The local self-reliance movement has outposts everywhere working on myriad programs that, taken as a whole, could potentially supply much of people's material needs with a minimum of imports from distant sources. Like the neighborhood movement, local self-reliance cuts across class, economic, ethnic, religious, and sexual divisions: The proverbial American pie has always been baked at home from apples grown out back.

Although the term self-reliance can be confused with a brand of "me-first" selfishness that once resulted in the build-your-own bomb shelter/lay-away-your-guns mentality of the early 1960s and is known again in the 1980s as survivalism, self-reliance has quite a different meaning for networkers. Self-reliant living implies a taking of responsibility at the local level *within* the context of community.

Drawing on this implicit understanding, *The Whole Earth Catalog* and its successor journal *CoEvolution Quarterly*, first published in 1973, had an immediate and far-reaching audience who soon made the book the bible of the self-reliant living movement. *The Whole Earth Catalog* (updated, revised, and reissued in 1980 as *The Next Whole Earth Catalog*) has been an invaluable resource to the many networks that it has interacted with and reported on over the years. It would be hard to imagine a library on self-reliant living without a copy of the book on its shelves.

Among the technical assistance providers to the local self-reliance network is the Institute for Local Self-Reliance, a nonprofit research company founded in 1974 to "help cities and neighborhoods put their wealth to work—and then keep the benefits in their own communities." Defining community wealth as the availability of local resources, the Institute has developed a number of fascinating solutions to local problems, including drafting a blueprint for an energy-self-reliant city, developing a waste utilization system that processes recycled material, and designing an alcohol fuel plant that uses supermarket and produce-center wastes. Much of the Institute's work has been collected in a series of short papers on subjects such as cottage industries, urban agriculture, and energy self-reliance, some of which have been published in its ongoing bimonthly magazine, *Self-Reliance*.

Using the self-reliant-living concept at the local community level, Community Self-Reliance (CSR), in Northampton, Massachusetts, is a plug-in point for a number of networks in western Massachusetts. "The goal of CSR is the rebuilding of a local food system based on the New England tradition of individual and community self-reliance," says its literature. "Whereas 19th century New England produced nearly all of its own food, Massachusetts now produces only 15 percent of the food it consumes. The region's loss of control over one of its basic needs–food–is one facet of the general loss of individual and community control."

Toward this end, CSR is undertaking a number of projects simultaneously, including: a public education program on the importance of a local food system, with special effort directed at outreach among low-income, minority, elderly, and school-aged people; the development of a community resource center with materials related to food, agriculture, and nutrition, as well as community economics; the development of a locally controlled community food system model; and the building of a community group coalition to work toward local self-reliance.

One of the vehicles that CSR is using is a classic example of a closed local network. "The Thursday Morning Breakfast Group," explains CSR Resource Developer John Taylor, "is purely a networking group with representations from various valley community groups. We meet every Thursday morning in the town of Sunderland to exchange information and ideas. The group has no officers per se, but a rotating steering committee. We also have no set mailing address since we occasionally change meeting places. The best way to correspond with this group is through a member, who then corresponds with the whole group on Thursday morning." This modern-day networking equivalent of the quilting bee is a convenient method for busy people to get together and trade ideas without becoming slaves to endless meetings. All share a meal, one of the oldest forms of human cooperation, and get their business done rapidly before getting on with the work of the day.

As local self-reliance echoes the values of early American settlers, other lessons from the same heritage are stimulating new economic models. Chief among these is the resurgence of interest in barter, the oldest form of human commerce.

Barter is one of the principal modes of commerce among multinational corporations, the modern extensions of the Dutch and other European trading companies. Contrasting such large-scale transactions with the informal child-care co-ops that families organize, Steve Washam writes as follows: "At the other end of the spectrum [from co-ops] are the multinational corporations which swap fleets of airplanes for banana plantations, ships for inventories, and prime mass media time for travel and accommodations for their executives. These companies can amass fortunes without paying a penny of tax."

According to the Barter Research Project, conducted at the University of Wisconsin in 1978, barter is used by 60 percent of all companies on the New York Stock Exchange who manufacture consumer goods. In 1977, barter accounted for more than $12 billion in goods and services.

Whatever the corporate motives may be in using barter, tax evasion is hardly the reason people set up barter networks in their communities. Since barter was the principal mode of commerce in the precivilization period when small-group network skills developed, long before urbanization and the invention of money, the reasons for its reappearance at this time in history may have as much to do with social evolution as with dollars and cents. As Washam comments: "More and more, I am coming to equate barter with cooperation. We find ways of exchanging which are mutually beneficial and practice them. We share goods, services, information, and concerns."

Barter inherently uses the network form: Each member of the exchange is a node offering services in return for those provided by another node. A *barter exchange* allows large numbers of people to participate in the system, trading diverse skills and services over relatively long time periods. Thus, people exchange in *kind*, rather than in *like*. In other words, we will take care of your children every Wednesday afternoon, while you repair our neighbor's roof, who in turn teaches piano once a week to our daughter.

One of the most successful barter networks has been Skillsbank in Ashland, Oregon, begun in 1975. While Ashland is an atypical American community–having a homogeneous, largely middle-class, rural population–its model may be helpful to other communities considering barter. Gaea Laughingbird, who works at Skillsbank, explains how the system developed:

> Skillsbank began five years ago when community organizer Kathy Ging first set it up in a small corner of the community food store. Through the years, it has changed and grown. Now we are housed in a beautifully rustic lodge in the midst of verdant Lithia Park. Skillsbank members contributed 3000 hours of labor to transform the building from an abandoned eyesore to a showcase for what people can do when they get together on a commonly benefitting project.

Skillsbank director Marilyn Shargel explains how the system works:

> All skills and services offered by members are classified, coded, recorded and held in reserve. When a member provides a service, his/her card shows a deposit of work credit hours. When a member receives a service his/her account shows a withdrawal of work credit hours. All work credit hours are of equal value.

> We presently have approximately 500 members who exchange over 450 skills and services with no money whatsoever. Some of the services offered include accounting, bookkeeping, child care, gardening, construction, plumbing, gourmet cooking, sports and games, tutoring, legal and medical consultation and musical instruction.

Informal barter doubtless has always existed among humans. Formal barter, originally trade–trading caravans, trading ships, trading posts–has historically provided the early links and interfaces between cultures. Can the new barter forms serve to create new links among people in a community? For David Tobin, director of The Barter Project, in Washington, D.C., which serves as technical assistance provider to developing barter networks, the real promise of a barter exchange lies in its ability to provide survival goods and services to poor people. "The real question," he says, "is whether barter can be used at the grass-roots level–not in middle-class communities or campus towns. Is barter useful at the survival level? What we really need to know is whether it is a viable community-wide idea."

From an individual's point of view, sharing is a value oriented outward to other people, a reflection of the human need to cooperate and form group associations. But, like the spacetime traveler who sets out across the curved universe and without changing course finally returns to the point of origin, the practice of sharing returns to the individual and the inwardly oriented value of personal autonomy and survival. True sharing involves exchanges among peers and thus is an intrinsically democratic value. Exchanges between kings and peasants, the powerful and the powerless, are not sharing exchanges. Sharing builds community, and healthy sharing is based on self-reliant people and groups.

In this age of awakening globalism, we are beginning to understand that, at this point in our evolution, we must be self-reliant as one planet. Billions of sharing people add up to one planet with integrity, a mighty metaphor for how we are each strengthened ourselves as we share with others.

Sharing Guide

S

The Sharing Guide includes groups that are primarily concerned with communities and cooperatives. Many of these groups also work on other issues.

Each group is identified by a letter/number code. The letter **S** stands for Sharing. Every group whose code begins with **S** is listed in the Sharing Guide.

The entry for each network whose code is lower than 100 includes a brief description. These representative networks are a cross-section of the initial groups we contacted in our research. Each network whose code is greater than 100 is listed with complete contact information. If the ✳ symbol, for publications, or ✦ symbol, for materials, appears with a listing, consult the Title Guide under Sharing Titles.

The Sharing Guide includes groups that are concerned with agriculture, bicycles, citizen action, communes, community resources, cooperatives, food, homesteading, housing, intentional communities, local self-reliance, rural affairs . . . and a few others.

S001
Citizens Committee for New York City
3 West 29th Street, 6th Floor
New York, NY 10001
21278-4747 ✳◆◆

✳ *Citizens Report (quarterly)*
◆ *New York Self Help Handbook ($4.95)*
◆ *Lend a Hand ($.25)*

Self-help program started in response to New York's fiscal crisis. Provides technical assistance to neighborhood groups, conducts conferences, recruits volunteers, and gives out grants, prizes, and brooms!

S002
Civic Action Institute
1010 16th Street, N.W.
Washington, DC 20036
202/293-1461 ✳◆◆

✳ *Neighborhood Ideas (10 issues/$25)*
◆ *Neighborhood Action Guides ($1 each)*
◆ *Citizen Participation in Community Development ($3)*

Technical assistance and training center for civic-minded people and groups. Convenes annual national conferences, produces practical written materials.

S003
CoEvolution Quarterly
P.O. Box 428
Sausalito, CA 94965
415/332-1716 ✳◆◆

✳ *CoEvolution Quarterly (4 issues/$12)*
◆ *Next Whole Earth Catalog ($14)*
◆ *One Million Galaxies (map, $5)*

Magazine that evolved out of The Whole Earth Catalog. Contains smorgasbord of information—from fiction and cartoons to book and product reviews to interviews and timely articles. Crossroads for many networks.

S004
Communities: Journal of Cooperative Living
P.O. Box 426
Louisa, VA 23093
703/894-5126 ✳◆

✳ *Communities: Journal of Cooperative Living (5 issues/$7.50)*
◆ *Guide to Cooperative Living ($5.95)*

Voice of the cooperative living movement. Many resources for cooperative and communal living. Publishers of a resource guide to "almost anything ... hopeful in America." Based at the Twin Oaks (Virginia) Community.

S005
Community Congress of San Diego
1172 Morena Boulevard
San Diego, CA 92110
714/275-1700 ✳✳✳

✳ *C/O: Journal of Alternative Human Services (quarterly)*
✳ *The Bulletin (weekly)*
✳ *Congressional Record (monthly)*

Inspiring alliance of 150 community organizations that developed from small network of alternative social-service agencies. Networking is intrinsic to its mode of operation. Conducts fund raising, advocacy, and political action.

S006
Community Self-Reliance
16 Armory Street
Northampton, MA 01060
413/586-0543 ◆

◆ *Consumers Directory of Local Farmers ($1.50)*

Focus of several networking activities in Massachusetts around issues of food, agriculture, nutrition, economic development, and energy. Working to rebuild New England's local food-supply system. Community resource center.

S007
Community Service
P.O. Box 243
Yellow Springs, OH 45387
513/767-2161 ✳

✳ *Community Service Newsletter (bimonthly/$10)*

One of the oldest groups in the U.S. concerned with idea of "community." Excellent book service; helped start Communities magazine. Conferences for ongoing projects in small towns, neighborhoods, land trusts, and other topics.

S008
Cooperative Directory Association
P.O. Box 4218
Albuquerque, NM 87196
505/247-3278 ◆

◆ *Food Co-Op Directory ($5)*

Publishers of the Food Co-op Directory, listing 4600 co-ops in U.S. and Canada. Contains pertinent information about the cooperative movement.

S009
Federation of Egalitarian Communities
P.O. Box 6B2
Tecumseh, MO 65760
417/679-4682

Umbrella organization for 6 successful intentional communities in Canada, U.S., and Mexico. Based on principles of cooperation, equality, and nonviolence. Magazine, conferences, and handmade products.

S010
Food Learning Center
114 ½ East Second Street
Winona, MN 55097
507/452-1815   ✦

✦ *Co-op Food Facts*

Publishes "Co-op Food Facts," a series of 10 packets explaining the derivation, use, storage, and some recipes for food sold in co-ops. Project of the Minnesota-area All Cooperating Assembly.

S011
Institute for Local Self-Reliance
1717 18th Street, N.W.
Washington, DC 20009
202/232-4108   ✳✦✦

✳ *Self-Reliance (bimonthly/$8)*
✦ *Cities, Energy and Self-Reliance ($2)*
✦ *Urban Gardener (poster, $3)*

Vital node in urban self-reliance movement. Concerns include economics, technology, food, energy, and community organization. Conducts projects, issues reports. Informative newsletter contains many resources.

S012
Institute for Non-Violent Education, Research, and Training
R.F.D.   1
Newport, ME 04953   ✳

✳ *Maine Statewide Newsletter (12 issues/$4)*

Crossroads for information on social action in Maine. Produces and distributes information on nonviolence, food, health, and consensus-making.

S013
Institute on Man and Science
Rensselaerville, NY 12147
518/797-3783   ✦

✦ *Small Towns and Small Towners*

Conference and research center focusing on economic viability and environmental quality in rural areas and small towns. Involved in building an energy-efficient "new town" in Pennsylvania.

S014
Kerista Village
P.O. Box 1174
San Francisco, CA 94101
405/566-6502   ✳✳

✳ *Utopian Eyes: A Journal of Visionary Arts (quarterly/$6)*
✳ *Storefront Classroom: A Utopian Newspaper (bimonthly/free)*

Imaginative utopian community experimenting with new ideas in health, community living, education, ecology, and spirituality. Holds retreats and workshops.

S015
National Association of Housing Cooperatives
1012 14th Street, N.W., #805
Washington, DC 20005
202/628-6242   ✳

✳ *Cooperative Housing Bulletin (monthly)*

Key membership group for housing co-ops, representing 100,000 families in U.S. Monitors government actions, sponsors conferences and education, distributes materials, offers consulting, and conducts research.

S016
National Association of Neighborhoods
1612 20th Street, N.W.
Washington, DC 20009
202/332-7766   ✳✳✦

✳ *NAN Bulletin ($10 year)*
✳ *National Neighborhood Platform ($2)*
✦ *Neighborhood Economic Enterprises ($3.50)*

National focus of neighborhood movement. Coordinates information-sharing among local groups and offers technical assistance in housing, economic development, environmental issues. Developed National Neighborhood Platform.

S017
National Catholic Rural Life Conference
4625 Northwest Beaver Drive
Des Moines, IA 50322
515/270-2634   ✳

✳ *Catholic Rural Life (monthly)*

Fifty-year-old group. Disseminates educational materials about the decline in American farms and attendant problems, including natural resources and food policy, rural development, and rural ministry.

S018
National Center for Citizen Involvement
1214 16th Street, N.W.
Washington, DC 20036
202/467-5560   ✳✳✦

✳ *Newsline (bimonthly)*
✳ *Voluntary Action Leadership (quarterly/$9)*
✦ *Nonprofit Organization Handbook ($29.95)*

Key node in volunteer community. Resource center for volunteer programs at local, state, and national levels. Gathers information on volunteerism, organizes training sessions and conferences, and distributes materials.

S019
National Commission on Resources for Youth, Inc.
36 West 44th Street
New York, NY 10036
212/840-2844   ✳✦✦

✳ *Resources for Youth (quarterly)*
✦ *What Kids Can Do: Forty Projects by Kids ($6)*
✦ *Youth Counsels Youth Manual ($5)*

Collects, catalogues, and validates information on more than 1500 youth participation programs in U.S. Free newsletter reports on projects. Distributes films and publications.

S020
National Congress of Neighborhood Women
11-29 Catherine Street
Brooklyn, NY 11211
212/388-6666   ✳

✳ *Neighborhood Woman*

Exemplary group of local women working on everyday community survival issues: housing, community development, education, jobs, and family services. Voice for low- and moderate-income working-class women.

S021
National Family Farm Coalition
918 F Street, N.W., 2nd Floor
Washington, DC 20004
202/638-6848

Coalition lobbying for Family Farm Development Act, redirecting federal policies in support of small and moderate-sized family farms.

S022
National Hispanic Coalition for Better Housing
810 18th Street, N.W., Suite 705
Washington, DC 20006
202/783-1478   ✳

✳ *Housing and Community Development Monthly Report*

Federally funded program to improve housing and aid community development for 12 million Hispanic Americans. Issues monthly report, maintains public research files, and develops housing policies.

S023
National Neighbors
815 15th Street, N.W., Suite 611
Washington, DC 20005
202/347-6501   ✳

✳ *Neighbors: A Publication on Interracial Living ($5 year)*

Only national federation of multiracial neighborhood groups. Working to foster integrated communities through single housing market, improvement of schools, and economic mixing within neighborhoods.

S024
National Network of Runaway and Youth Services
1705 De Sales Street, N.W.
Washington, DC 20036
202/466-4212   ✳✦✦

✳ *Network News (6 issues/$10)*
✦ *Network of Runaway Services: A Nationwide Guide ($4.75)*
✦ *Community Response to Community Problems ($5.50)*

Key node in national alliance of youth centers, runaway programs, free clinics, and other human-service agencies. Uses networking to link isolated members to larger support group.

S025
National Self-Help Clearinghouse
New Human Services Institute
33 West 42nd Street, Room 1227
New York, NY 10036
212/840-7606   ✳✦✳

✳ *Self-Help Reporter (bimonthly/free)*
✦ *How to Organize a Self-Help Group ($3)*
✳ *Social Policy (5 issues/$15)*

Central node for contacting and learning about self-help and mutual-aid groups. Provides referrals, conducts research, publishes reports and newsletter, and offers professional training in working with self-help groups.

S026
National Self-Help Resource Center
2000 S Street, N.W.
Washington, DC 20009
202/338-5704   ✳✦✦

✳ *Network Notes (monthly/$10)*
✦ *Uplift: What People Themselves Can Do ($6)*
✦ *Community Resource Centers: The Notebook ($8)*

Washington-based center offering technical assistance to local communities. Developers of National Community Resource Centers Network, which relies heavily on local information networking. Workshops in community building.

S027
National Training and Information Center
1123 West Washington Boulevard
Chicago, IL 60607
312/243-3035   ✳

✳ *Disclosure ($9 year)*

Energetic resource for the neighborhood movement. Offers research and training in community organizing skills. Particularly concerned with insurance and mortgage redlining, community reinvestment, and utilities.

S028
Natural Helping Networks Project
Regional Research Institute
P.O. Box 751
Portland, OR 97207   ✦

✦ *Networks for Helping ($5)*

Research project focusing on social-support and personal networks, investigating the idea that "who you know" does make a difference in terms of mental health.

S029
Neighborhood Information Sharing Exchange
1725 K Street, N.W., Suite 1212
Washington, DC 20006
202/293-2813   ✳

✳ *Neighborhood Information Sharing Exchange*

Federally funded working network of neighborhood groups. Exchanges information about successful local programs in community planning, housing rehabilitation, energy conservation, and commercial revitalization.

S030
New York Urban Coalition
1515 Broadway
New York, NY 10036
212/921-3500   ✳

✳ *Neighborhoods: The Journal for City Preservation (4/$12 yr)*

Focal point for many local community self-help projects for minorities and poor people. Created in wake of 1967 riots. Conducts programs in housing, education, jobs, and drug abuse.

S031
North American Students of Cooperation
P.O. Box 7293
Ann Arbor, MI 48107
313/663-0889   ✳✦✦

✳ *Co-op Magazine (bimonthly/$10.50)*
✦ *Food Co-op Handbook ($5.95)*
✦ *Wind Through the Pines: Co-op Slide Show ($30 rental)*

Vital source of information on cooperative movement (food, housing, work, crafts, daily care, etc.). Offers consulting and training to co-ops. Publishes magazine, distributes slide show and range of "how-to-co-op" publications.

S032
Project for Kibbutz Studies
Center for Jewish Studies, 108 Vansberg Hall
10 Divinity Avenue
Cambridge, MA 02138
617/495-3436   ✦✦

✦ *Communal Future: The Kibbutz and the Utopian Dilemma ($28)*
✦ *Project for Kibbutz Studies Monographs*

Ongoing research project on the nature, meaning, and implications of the kibbutz, the cooperative living community indigenous to Israel. Offers courses, lectures, consultations, and publications.

S033
Riptide/University Services Agency
310 Locust Street
Santa Cruz, CA 95060
408/425-7478

Coalition of 15 community-oriented businesses providing basic goods and services (e.g., food, child care, trucking).

S034
Rural America
1346 Connecticut Avenue, N.W.
Washington, DC 20036
202/659-2800   ✳✳✳

✳ *RuralAmerica (monthly/$15)*
✳ *Rural CDBG Monitor (bimonthly)*
✳ *RWA Reporter*

National voice for people in small towns and rural areas. Provides advocacy, technical assistance, and other support on housing, rural energy, ecology, health, transportation, and farming. Reports, films, and slide shows.

S035
School of Living: Publishers of Green Revolution
P.O. Box 3233
York, PA 17402
717/755-1561   ✳✦✦

✳ *Green Revolution (monthly/$8)*
◆ *Decentralism (Loomis, $5)*
◆ *Education and Living (Borsodi, $5)*

Affectionately known as the grandparent organization of the new age. Has been offering "work-study-action" programs in social change for 40 years. Offers courses, workshops, and year-long trainings. Distributes literature.

S036
Shelterforce Collective
380 Main Street
East Orange, NJ 07018
201/678-6778   ✳

✳ *Shelterforce ($5)*

Voice of the national housing movement, interested in housing policy, rent control, condominium conversion, and tenants rights. Contains "Resources for Organizers" column. Must reading for housing activists.

S037
Small Towns Institute
P.O. Box 517
Ellensburg, WA 98926
509/925-1830   ✳

✳ *Small Town (bimonthly/$15)*

Publishes a long-standing magazine on small-town life and development. Includes Community Forum column, where small-towners exchange information.

S038
Urban Alternatives Group
3475 Margarita Avenue
Oakland, CA 94605
415/562-9936

Eclectic network builders in areas such as limited equity housing, single parents, and skill sharing. Publish monthly newsletter as part of Green Revolution. West Coast branch of group that began in Columbus, Ohio.

S039
Urban Alternatives Group/Columbus
5268 Rush Avenue
Columbus, OH 43214
614/888-4858

Sponsors workshops (called Choices and Change) that help people through life transitions (such as loneliness, depression, being single again, etc.). Helps support growth of personal networks.

S040
Warmlines: A Parent Network and Resource Center
306 Franklin Street
Newton, MA 02158
617/244-6843   ✳

✳ *Local Connections ($5)*

Excellent example of local, low-cost information-sharing network. Maintains baby-sitter file, organizes discussion groups, keeps up to date on local children's resources, and publishes newsletter. All-volunteer staff and donations.

S101
Acres, U.S.A: A Voice for Eco-Agriculture
P.O. Box 9547
Raytown, MO 64133
816/737-0064   ✳

S102
Agricultural Marketing Project
2606 Westwood Drive
Nashville, TN 37204
615/297-4088   ✳

S103
Alaska Youth Advocates
204 East 5th Avenue, #211
Anchorage, AK 99501
907/274-6541

S104
Alliance of Warehouse Federations
P.O. Box 14440
Minneapolis, MN 55414
612/376-2478   ✳

S105
American Association for State and Local History
1400 Eighth Avenue South
Nashville, TN 37203   ✳◆

S106
American Homebrewers Association
P.O. Box 287
Boulder, CO 80306
303/447-0816   ✳

S107
Antahkarana Circle
Star Route Box 82-D
Oroville, WA 98844

S108
Architecture 2001
60 Union Street
Newark, NJ 07105
201/645-4993

S109
Arts Services Associates
P.O. Box 92222
Milwaukee, WI 53202
414/276-5599

S110
Associated Cooperatives
4801 Central Avenue
P.O. Box 4006
Richmond, CA 94804
415/526-0440   ✦

S111
Basement Alliance
348 West 20th Street
New York, NY 10011   ✳

S112
Bicyclist Federation of Pennsylvania
445 Dreshertown Road
Fort Washington, PA 19034
215/646-7879

S113
Bikeways in Buffalo
309 Highland Avenue
Buffalo, NY 14222

S114
Birdsong Farm
P.O. Box 143
North Berwick, ME 03906
207/676-4038

S115
Blooming Prairie Warehouse
1223 South Riverside Drive
Iowa City, IA 52240

S116
Bloomington Free Ryder: Biweekly Newspaper
104½ East Kirkwood
Bloomington, IN 47401   ✳

S117
Boston Building Materials Cooperative
52 Plympton Street
Boston, MA 02118
617/542-5842

S118
Boston Urban Gardens
66 Hereford Street
Boston, MA 02115
617/267-4825

S119
Boulder Women's Network
3575 9th Street
Boulder, CO 80302
303/443-2619

S120
Briarpatch Network
330 Ellis Street
San Francisco, CA 94102

S121
Butterbrooke Farm Seed Co-op
78 Barry Road
Oxford, CT 06483   ✳

S122
California Cooperative Federation
P.O. Box 195
Davis, CA 95616   ✳

S123
California Institute for Rural Studies
P.O. Box 530
Davis, CA 95616
916/756-6555

S124
Carousel Press: Books for Parents
P.O. Box 6061
Albany, CA 94706
415/527-5849   ✦✦

S125
Carrier Pigeon/Alyson Publications
P.O. Box 2783
Boston, MA 02208
617/542-5679

S126
Center for Community Change
1000 Wisconsin Avenue, N.W.
Washington, DC 20007
202/338-3565   ✳✦

S127
Center for Community Economic Development
1320 19th Street, N.W.
Washington, DC 20036
202/659-3986   ✳

S128
Center for Neighborhood Development
Park College School for Community Education
818 Grand
Kansas City, MO 64106
816/842-6182

S129
Chicago Association of Neighborhood
  Development Organizations
122 South Michigan, Room 2001
Chicago, IL 60603
312/461-1015 ✳

S130
Chicago Men's Gathering Newsletter
P.O. Box 11076
Chicago, IL 60611 ✳

S131
Circle Pines Center
Delton, MI 49046
616/623-5555

S132
Circle of Light/Findhorn
P.O. Box 1486
Kihei, HI 96753
800/367-6030

S133
City Miner: Community/Personal
  Adventure/Aesthetics
P.O. Box 176
Berkeley, CA 94701 ◆

S134
Cleareye Natural Foods
Rural Route #1
Savannah, NY 13146
315/365-2895

S135
Common Health Warehouse
810 Clough Avenue
Superior, WI 54880
715/392-9862 ✳

S136
Community Economics
1904 Franklin Street, Suite 900
Oakland, CA 94612
415/832-8300 ✳

S137
Community Jobs
1704 R Street, N.W.
Washington, DC 20009
202/387-7702 ✳

S138
Community Produce
1426 Alaskan Way
Seattle, WA 98101
206/624-1681

S139
Community Self-Reliance Center
140 West State Street
Ithaca, NY 14850
607/272-3040 ✳

S140
Community Service Restitution
320 Washington Street, Room 300
Brookline, MA 02146
617/734-8800

S141
Connecticut Citizen Action Group
P.O. Box G
Hartford, CT 06106
203/527-7191 ✳

S142
Consortium for Youth of South Central
  Connecticut
One State Street
New Haven, CT 06511
203/789-8113

S143
Consumer Coop Press Service
P.O. Box 7271, Powderhorn Sta.
Minneapolis, MN 55407

S144
Cooperative League of the USA
1828 L Street, N.W., Suite 1100
Washington, DC 20036
202/872-0550 ✳

S145
Cooperative and Communal Living Network
P.O. Box 5446
Berkeley, CA 94705
415/849-1835 ✳

S146
Council on Foundations
1828 L Street, N.W.
Washington, DC 20036
202/466-6512

S147
Country Journal
P.O. Box 870
Manchester Center, VT 05255
802/362-1022 ✳

S148
Countryside: The Magazine for Serious
  Homesteaders
312 Portland Road
Waterloo, WI 53594 ✳

S149
Crafts Fair Guide
152 Buena Vista, Box 262
Mill Valley, CA 94941   ✦

S150
Creative Loafing in Atlanta
P.O. Box 8006
Atlanta, GA 30306
404/843-5623   ✳

S151
Dandelion Community Co-op
Rural Route #1
Enterprise, Ontario
CANADA K0K 1Z0
613/358-2304   ✳

S152
Delaware Friends of Bikecology
108 Wayland Road
Wilmington, DE 19807

S153
Densmore Discoveries
P.O. Box 18-X
Denver, CO 80218   ✳

S154
Distributing Alliance of the Northcountry
   Cooperatives
510 Kasota Avenue, S.E,
Minneapolis, MN 55414
612/378-9774   ✳

S155
Dovetail Press: Design for the Owner-Involved
   Builder
P.O. Box 1496
Boulder, CO 80306
303/449-2681   ✦✦✦

S156
Draft Horse Journal
P.O. Box 670
Waverly, IA 50677
319/352-5342   ✳

S157
F.A.R.O.G. Forum: Journal Bilingue
208 maison Fernald
University of Maine
Orono, ME 04469
207/581-7082   ✳✦

S158
Family Connection
4256 Washington Street
Roslindale, MA 02131
617/323-0300

S159
Family of New Age Networkers
P.O. Box 5577
Eugene, OR 97405   ✦

S160
Fed-Up Coop
304 East First Avenue
Vancouver, British Columbia
CANADA V5T 1A9   ✳

S161
Federation of Co-ops
P.O. Box 236, Bridge Street
North Vassalboro, ME 04962   ✳

S162
Federation of Ohio River Cooperatives
723 College Avenue
Morgantown, WV 26505   ✳

S163
Federation of Southern Cooperatives
P.O. Box 95
Epes, AL 35460
205/652-9676

S164
Fellowship House Farm
Rural Route #3, Sanatoga Road
Pottstown, PA 19464
215/326-3008

S165
Film-Makers Cooperative
175 Lexington Avenue
New York, NY 10016   ✦

S166
Food Conspiracy Cooperative
412 North 4th Avenue
Tucson, AZ 85705   ✳

S167
Free Venice Beachhead
P.O. Box 504
Venice, CA 90291
213/823-5092   ✳

S168
Gay Community News
22 Bromfield Street
Boston, MA 02108
617/426-4469   ✳

S169
Gay Sunshine Press
P.O. Box 40397
San Francisco, CA 94140
415/824-3184   ✳

S170
Gentle Strength Cooperative
P.O. Box 890
Tempe, AZ 85281   ✳

S171
Goodfellow Catalog of Wonderful Things
P.O. Box 4520
Berkeley, CA 94704
415/845-7645

S172
Greater Illinois People's Cooperative
719 West O'Brien Street
Chicago, IL 60607
317/226-5931

S173
Grindstone Island Centre
P.O. Box 564, Station P
Toronto, Ontario
CANADA M5S 2T1
416/923-4215

S174
Hanover Consumer Cooperative Society
45 South Park Street
Hanover, NH 03755   ✳

S175
Harmony Community
820 Dorchester
Winnepeg, Manitoba
CANADA R3M 0R7   ✳

S176
Hartford Food System
2550 Main Street
Hartford, CT 06120
203/249-9325   ◆

S177
**Home Front: For Young Pregnant Women and
    their Families**
23 Beacon Street
Boston, MA 02108
617/227-7395

S178
Home Ownership Development Program
Baltimore Housing and Community
Development
222 East Saratoga Street
Baltimore, MD 21202
301/396-3124   ◆

S179
Homesteaders News
R.D. #2, Box 151
Addison, NY 14801
607/359-3985   ✳

S180
Indianapolis Mayor's Bicycle Task Force
1426 West 29th Street
Indianapolis, IN 46208
317/924-9151   ◆

S181
Information Tree/San Francisco
P.O. Box 4094
San Francisco, CA 94101
415/665-5338

S182
Institute for Community Economics
120 Boylston Street
Boston, MA 02116
617/542-1058

S183
Interest File
18 Laurel Street
Cambridge, MA 02139
617/661-7835   ✳

S184
International Cooperative Community
P.O. Box 35
Bodega, CA 94922   ◆

S185
Intra-Community Cooperative
1335 Gilson Street
Madison, WI 53715
608/257-6633   ✳

S186
Lancaster Independent Press
P.O. Box 275
Lancaster, PA 17604
717/394-9841   ✳

S187
Living Free: Personal Journal of Self-Liberation
P.O. Box 29, Hiler Branch
Kenmore, NY 14223   ✳

S188
**Logical Connection: Skillsharing for Private
    Practitioners**
2444 Carmel Street
Oakland, CA 94602
415/482-1226

S189
Los Angeles Men's Collective
P.O. Box 25836
Los Angeles, CA 90025

S190
Love Family
617 West McGraw
Seattle, WA 98119
206/285-4646

S191
Magnolia: Southeastern Confederation for
Cooperation
P.O. Box 20293
Tallahassee, FL 32304

S192
Maine Bicycle Coalition
P.O. Box 4544
Portland, ME 04112

S193
Maine Times
41 Main Street
Topsham, ME 04086   ✳

S194
Mediaworks
P.O. Box 4494
Boulder, CO 80306
303/494-1439   ◆

S195
Men's Program Unit
University YMCA
1001 South Wright Street
Champaign, IL 60820
217/337-1517   ✳

S196
Men's Resource Center
3534 Southeast Main Street
Portland, OR 97214
503/235-3433

S197
Message Post
P.O. Box 190
Philomath, OR 97370   ✳

S198
Michigan Federation of Food Cooperatives
209 South 4th Avenue, Upstairs B
Ann Arbor, MI 48104
313/663-3111   ✳✳

S199
Midwest Academy
600 West Fullerton Avenue
Chicago, IL 60614
312/975-3670

S200
Mothers and Others
24 Vernon Street
Framingham, MA 01701

S201
Mutual Aid Project
17 Murray Street
New York, NY 10007
212/349-8155   ◆

S202
National Hook-up of Black Women
1100 Sixth Street, N.W.
Washington, DC 20001
202/667-6993

S203
National Runaway Switchboard
2210 North Halstead Street
Chicago, IL 60614
312/929-5854

S204
National Trust for Historic Preservation
1785 Massachusetts Avenue, N.W.
Washington, DC 20036
202/673-4000   ✳✳✳

S205
Neighborhood Organization Research Group
814 East Third Street
Indiana University
Bloomington, IN 47401
812/337-0441   ✳

S206
Network Exchange News Service
P.O. Box 1906
Eugene, OR 97440
503/345-2667   ✳

S207
New Age Chicago
2930 North Lincoln
Chicago, IL 60657
312/348-8578   ◆

S208
New Community Project
449 Cambridge Street
Allston, MA 02134
617/783-3060   ◆

S209
New England Food Cooperative Organization
129 Franklin Street
Cambridge, MA 02139   ✳

S210
New Seeds Information Service
Rural Route #1
Winlaw, British Columbia
CANADA V0G 2J0   ◆

S211
New West Trails
1145 East Sixth Street
Tucson, AZ 85719
602/623-2003   ◆

S212
New York State Coalition for Local Self Reliance
P.O. Box 6222
Syracuse, NY 13217   ✳

S213
North Carolina Anvil
P.O. Box 1148
Durham, NC 27702
919/688-9544   ✳

S214
North Oak Street Chowder and Marching Society
112 North Oak Street
London, OH 43140

S215
Northwest Organic Herb Cooperative
Rural Route #1, Box 355
Trout Lake, WA 98650
509/395-2025   ✳

S216
Northwest Provender Alliance
1515 10th Avenue
Seattle, WA 98122

S217
Northwest Regional Foundation
North 910 Washington
Spokane, WA 99201
509/327-5596

S218
Old House Journal
69A Seventh Avenue
Brooklyn, NY 11217
212/636-4514   ✳◆

S219
Older Women's Network
P.O. Box 6647
Santa Barbara, CA 93111   ✳

S220
Organize Training Center
1208 Market Street
San Francisco, CA 94102
415/552-8990   ◆

S221
Owner-Builder Publications
P.O. Box 817
North Fork, CA 93643   ◆◆

S222
Ozark Area Community Congress
Route A, Box 67
Caulfield, MO 65626

S223
Parents Anonymous
120 Boylston Street
Boston, MA 02116
617/727-0067

S224
Personal Freedom Network
P.O. Box 9801
Colorado Springs, CO 80932

S225
**Plexus: San Francisco Bay Area Women's
  Newspaper**
545 Athol Avenue
Oakland, CA 94606
415/451-2585   ✳

S226
**Project SHARE: Improving the Management of
  Human Services**
P.O. Box 2309
Rockville, MD 20852
301/251-5170

S227
RFD: Country Journal for Gay Men Everywhere
Rural Route #1, Box 127
Bakersville, NC 28705   ✳

S228
Raisin Consciousness
1218 4th Avenue
Los Angeles, CA 90019   ✳

S229
Regional Young Adult Project
944 Market Street, Room 705
San Francisco, CA 94102
415/543-0890   ◆◆

S230
Rural American Women
1522 K Street, N.W., Suite 700
Washington, DC 20005
202/785-4700   ✳

S231
Santa Clara Valley Bicycle Association
P.O. Box 662
Los Gatos, CA 95030   ✳

S232
Sealand: The Cheap Land Catalogue
Ashenbottom Farm
Ewoodbridge, BB4 6JY
ENGLAND   ✳

S233
Share Foundation/Television Network
39737 Paseo Padre Parkway
P.O. Box 1958
Fremont, CA 94538
415/651-2447

S234
Society of Ontario Nut Growers
Rural Route #1
Niagara-on-the-Lake, Ontario
CANADA L0S 1J0   ✳

S235
Southern Appalachian Resource Catalog
P.O. Box 71-A
Warne, NC 28909
704/389-8323   ◆

S236
Southern Neighborhoods
P.O. Box 36250
Decatur, GA 30032
404/284-7454   ✳

S237
Southern Rural Development Center
P.O. Box 5406
Mississippi State University
Mississippi State, MS 39762
601/325-3207

S238
**Spectrum: Cooperative Newspaper for the
   Tallahassee Community**
2105 Autumn Lane
Tallahassee, FL 32304   ✳

S239
Star Root: Fortnightly Newspaper
P.O. Box 773
Redway, CA 95560   ✳

S240
**Support Center: Management Assistance to Non-
   Profit Groups**
1709 New Hampshire Avenue, N.W.
Washington, DC 20009

S241
Techqua Ikachi: Traditional Hopi Viewpoint
P.O. Box 174
Hotevilla, AZ 86030   ✳

S242
Texas Observer: A Journal of Free Voices
600 West Seventh
Austin, TX 78701
512/477-0746   ✳

S243
**The Smallholder: Ideas and Information for
   Country People**
Argenta, British Columbia
CANADA V0G 1B0   ✳

S244
Transportation Alternatives
600 Lexington Avenue, Suite 572
New York, NY 10022
212/759-9066   ✳

S245
Trust for Public Land
82 Second Street
San Francisco, CA 94105
415/495-4014

S246
United Neighborhood Centers of America
232 Madison Avenue
New York, NY 10016
212/679-6110

S247
Urban Planning Aid
120 Boylston Street, Room 523
Boston, MA 02116
617/482-6695   ✳

S248
Vegetarian Society of D.C.
1455 Harvard Street, N.W.
Washington, DC 20009
202/232-VEGE   ✳

S249
Village of Anything Is Possible
7288 North Sherman
Liberal, KS 67901

S250
Washington Area Bicyclist Association
1332 Eye Street, N.W.
Washington, DC 20005
202/393-2555   ✳

S251
**Washington Blade: Gay Newspaper of the
   Nation's Capital**
930 F Street, N.W., Suite 315
Washington, DC 20004
202/347-2038   ✳

S252
Whiteaker Community Council
21 North Grand
Eugene, OR 97402
503/687-3556   ✳

S253
Winds of Change
P.O. Box 1004
Winters, CA 95694   ✳

S254
Wishing Well
P.O. Box 117
Novato, CA 94948   ✳

S255
Woman's Place
Athol, NY 12810
518/623-9970

S256
**Women's Information, Referral and Education
    Service**
c/o Junior League of Boston
117 Newbury Street
Boston, MA 02116
617/247-4078   ✳

S257
Wool Gathering
Elizabeth Zimmerman Ltd.
Babcock, WI 54413   ✳

S258
Yestermorrow: Design/Builder School
P.O. Box 344
Warren, VT 05674
802/496-3437

CHAPTER

5

Using Networks: Ecology and Energy

Human beings are now confronted with the fact
that we share a planet together . . . No matter what
else we may be, we are also *planet people,* part of
the Earth's living biosphere.

Planet Drum Foundation

In the landmark film *The Powers of Ten,* one of the finest attempts to help people
understand the levels of natural organization, the viewer is taken on a journey that
begins with a person lying on a beach, continues outward up a series of steps
through the solar system to the theoretical edge of the universe, returns to the person
lying on the beach again, and then proceeds on a descending staircase through the
body to the lilliputian world of the electron.

It is absolutely mind-boggling to try to grasp the ideas of the vastness of the universe and the minuteness of the electron at the same time. In the middle of the
macro/microcosm is the person, the zero point for all human-comprehensible scales
of large and small. Complementing the unique perspective of one person is the singular whole that encompasses us all, our one earth. The meaning that author
Theodore Roszak has telescoped into the phrase "person/planet" (the title of one of
his books) is represented in the 1980s by the image of an astronaut circling the moon
and emotionally exclaiming, "I can hold the earth in the palm of my hand." Each of
us does, indeed, hold that fragile jewel in the cup of our hands.

From our perspective here at the typewriter, we find it difficult to remember that
we are just tiny specks on the planet, two of the now four and a half billion people
who populate the 10 percent of the earth on which people live (about a person for
each year of our planet's evolution). Yet, that recognition of the interconnectedness
of everything, an ancient truth found in many religions, has given rise to the ecology
and energy movements, along with the problem-solving networks in appropriate
technology.

Ever since the 1962 publication of Rachel Carson's terrifying book *Silent Spring,*
which revealed the impact of chemical pollution on our rivers, streams, and oceans,
networks have been forming around the ideas of clean environments, ecological balance, the responsible use of the earth's resources, and the creation of technologies
that are life-enhancing and in proportion to what author Kirkpatrick Sale has identified as *human scale* in his book by that name. These networks appear to be singu-
larly adept at holding together and celebrating the incredible powers of the earth to
provide us with everything from grapes and electricity to yurts and flight to whales
and rainbows.

Were it not for the oddly forgettable fact that everything *is* interconnected, the
exploitation of natural resources might have been relegated to a list of concerns that
could be dealt with later. However, what environmentalists have been telling us is
that we have to change our patterns of resource consumption or be prepared to die
on a desolate, barren, spoiled planet. We cannot strip the Black Hills of South Dakota

without changing the ecology of the entire region and ultimately the world. Nor can we ignore the question: What is nature's response to the decimation of whole species, whether tiny snail darters or gargantuan whales?

One dramatic display of the current irresponsible use of natural resources is today seen in Pennsylvania, the state where both oil and coal were first extracted in the United States. At the fourth point of a polygon that touches Scranton, the capital of the anthracite coal region, Titusville, where the first oil well was drilled, and Pittsburgh (whose football team is called the Steelers), is Three Mile Island, Metropolitan Edison's nuclear power plant run amuck.

The disaster at Three Mile Island marked a turning point in the ecology/energy movements. For the first time in the nuclear era, a large and random segment of the population, ordinary middle-class working people who had hardly given nuclear power a second thought, awoke to a real-life nightmare that forced them out of their homes. Like the horror-stricken face of the 14-year-old runaway bent over the dead body of one of the four students killed at Kent State University on May 4, 1970, the photo of the mother covering her baby's head with a blanket in Middletown, Pennsylvania, to protect her child from the invisible, untouchable, deadly radiation emanating from the nuclear power plant, is a symbol of Three Mile Island.

Three Mile Island, which remains a radioactive hotspot, may have moved off the front pages of the newspapers, but it has moved into center consciousness of others faced with nuclear power plants in their communities. Less than sixty miles from Middletown, the residents of Pottstown, Pennsylvania, are embroiled in controversy over the construction of the Limerick Nuclear Power plant, scheduled for activation in 1985, which dwarfs the magnificent farmlands of the Pennsylvania Dutch northeast of Philadelphia. At the same time, thousands of people find themselves out of work due to the closing of the longtime employer Firestone Tire and Rubber, whose plant has been sold to the Hooker Chemical Company, the corporation primarily responsible for the disaster in Love Canal, New York.

In the face of such dubious technological "progress," hopelessness and despair are being transmuted into resolute thought and action through four interrelated webs of networks: the *environmentalists*, whose concern is for the preservation of our land, sea, and air–and the protection of all species and forms of life therein; the *antinuclear* activists, who can be found in every profession, including nuclear scientists and some who have chosen to identify themselves with our primordial beginnings by such names as the Clamshell and Abalone Alliances; *renewable energy* pioneers, who are taking the "soft path" to future energy needs and sources; and the *appropriate technology* groups, who are rediscovering old tools and inventing new ones that work in harmony with nature.

Chroniclers throughout history have documented the development of humanity's mastery over resources–from the Prometheus legend that describes him stealing fire from the gods, to matriarchical studies (such as that of Elizabeth Gould Davis), which credit women with the discovery of tools and fire. Fire, one of nature's gifts, illustrates how such gifts may be *used* or *abused*. Fire can be used constructively for cooking, heating, and lighting, but it can also be awesomely destructive. As entrepreneurs dig and drill into the earth to build vast industrial empires around the exploitation of oil, gas, and coal, dismantling whole mountain ranges in order to turn shale into coal and coal into gas, the abuse of gifts hundreds of millions of years in the making seems staggering.

Because the term "using" itself has a connotative tinge of exploitation, it reminds us that virtually all ecological/energy choices have side effects harmful or restricting to someone or something. As "*sapiens*," we are not yet wise enough to fully grasp the ramifications of our personal and social choices as they relate to the bioplanet. As Another Americans, we strive to do the best we can, acting more like "caretakers" than "visitors"–which is how the Community Congress of San Diego describes itself:

> "Caretaker" is a term used by Edward E. Sampson to describe those individuals who value and care for the earth they live on, the people they live with, and the other life forms which surround them. Sampson contrasts "caretakers" with "visitors" who when visiting different locations stop long enough to exploit the territory, taking things of value and leaving their cast-off debris and garbage. It is the caretaker value base which is at the core of Community Congress and which most closely defines the "essence" of this network.

ENVIRONMENT

The current environmental movement got its start in the 1950s and 1960s when outdoor adventurers slowly caught wind of the fact that developers were moving in on their territory. Born principally as a network of concern among mountain climbers, backpackers, bird watchers, and other nature lovers, these people began to coordinate their efforts and eventually joined long-standing outdoor recreation organizations such as the Sierra Club to work around conservation issues.

With roots reaching back to the turn of the century, the Sierra Club is the grandparent of the early conservation movement. (The Sierra Club headquarters in San Francisco was one of only two buildings to survive that city's 1906 earthquake.) During the Depression, the Sierra Club was the leader in a number of conservation battles, opposing such outrageous plans as a federal government scheme to flood the Grand Canyon and turn it into a lake!

Before long, conservation became too narrow a term to describe the problem: The issues went much deeper than the selling of the redwoods for the purpose of building highways. As the conservation movement was gathering steam, so was a parallel group concerned with the quality of air. "In 1964," writes futurist Hazel Henderson in her book *Creating Alternative Futures: The End of Economics*, "I joined with some other worried citizens and mothers of small children in New York City to form an organization called Citizens for Clean Air. I soon learned that if the air was to remain breathable and the environment life-sustaining for my infant daughter during her lifetime, I and other citizens would have to commit ourselves to a process of learning about the complex, interdependent, urban industrial societies in which we lived and about the basic assumptions on which their technical and economic systems were founded."

Yet, for a number of years, the two branches of the movement remained separate. Henderson recalls writing to conservation-oriented environmentalists in the early 1960s, asking if they were concerned with urban environmental issues such as air pollution and lead contamination. She was shocked when the reply came back: "We see no connection."

Eventually, however, the rural conservationists and the urban environmentalists did meet, and over the next few years Henderson-type thinking attracted a large, committed following that worked on many local environmental issues, culminating in the first national environmental action, in 1970. On April 22 of that year of Cambodia and Kent State and Jackson State, people with these broader environmental concerns came together to celebrate Earth Day in Washington, D.C., and sites throughout the nation. Earth Day attracted tremendous media attention: The image of the earth as a brilliant blue-and-white-swirled ball hanging in black space became a widely recognized symbol, and before long, "ecology," a word previously reserved for biology classes, became commonly used.

Ecology and a clean environment have great appeal. It's difficult to find anyone who will consciously speak against clean air or clean rivers. Yet, being in favor of clean air—and doing something about it—are two quite different matters. Out of the large inactive network of implicit environmental concerns have arisen a number of action-oriented groups working in different ways to preserve the planet and its many levels of physical, biological, and human complexity.

Breaking off from the Sierra Club in the late 1960s, Friends of the Earth (FOE) has served as a cornerstone of the environmentalist movement. One of the largest groups currently active in the movement, FOE has evolved into an activist environmental lobby, working on legislation and mounting public campaigns around such issues as nuclear power, clean energy, clean air, wild lands, and wildlife. FOE also maintains contacts with independent sister groups in twenty-three other countries.

FOE's greatest impact may be a few years in the future, as the innovative ideas of physicist Amory Lovins, FOE's London representative, receive wider publicity and are actively applied. Lovins is the author of a comprehensive plan for a sustainable future called the "Soft Energy Path," which has become a rallying point and document for agreement among a broad range of environmental activists. Lovins' plan "is a route to reliance half a century from now based solely on renewable energy sources—solar energy and its derivatives, including wind and water power, and the conversion of organic matter into fuels. Energy conservation and frugal use of fossil fuels will get us through the transition period," Friends of the Earth literature explains.

One of Lovins' greatest achievements may be in persuading people who are deeply committed to preserving "wilderness" to recognize the interconnectedness of open space and the greater issues of how we are going to use all our resources.

"Wilderness is a strictly civilized concept," says Roger Dunsmore in *Wild Idea ... Wild Hope*, a pamphlet published by Planet Drum Foundation. "The fact that we see natural areas as 'wild' and call them wilderness is an indication of the extent to which we are removed from our own natural state. It must be completely unimaginable to indigenous people that we could call their life-sphere a 'wild' place. Wilderness is a home. It's a home for whatever species are there and it's the original human home."

Planet Drum has published a variety of innovative materials about different regions of the planet. Unrestricted by form or content, Planet Drum gathers together whatever it needs in the way of material to understand a region of the earth, transforms it into resplendently designed media—which include, variously, maps, charts, poems, diaries, newsletters, and essays—calls it a "bundle," and mails it off to members.

A bundle from Planet Drum on the Rocky Mountains called "Backbone—The Rockies" includes a conversation between the group's review (*Raise the Stakes!*) editor, Peter Berg, and geohistorian Robert Curry; "Rockies—The Source," a study compiled by residents of the Slocan Valley, in British Columbia; "Rocky Mountain Lifetime," an amazing information wheel about the region; "A House at 8000'," a journal excerpt about life in a solar-heated house in the Rockies; *Wild Idea ... Wild Hope*, the pamphlet mentioned above; and "The Eye in the Rock," a poem celebrating the beauty and spirit of the Rockies. A beautiful map delineates the spine of the Rockies from north of the Peace River and east of Slave Lake, in the Canadian Northwest Territories, to the valley carved out in the southwestern United States between the Colorado and the Rio Grande and carries this description:

Think of the Rocky Mountains as a sunburst or a star. Its rays are patterns of water and soil moving across North America. Soil fertility from the cornfields of Indiana to the delta of the Columbia in Oregon is owed to nutrients eroded from the Rockies by wind and water.

People in the Rockies live in the heart of the star. People living in the Mississippi Delta, on the edges of the Bering Sea and the Gulf of California, around the Hudson Bay, people at the far reaches of the rays, all watch Rockies water go by.

When we saw the Rockies in this pattern, we knew that we had yet another image of a network to add to our mental collection.

Eco-consciousness (ecological consciousness), such as that purveyed by Planet Drum, is mind-expanding; it transcends national borders, legislative actions, and economic gaming. "There is adequate new evidence for considering the Rockies as a whole and continuous biotic province or biogeographical province: A neutral natural zone whose real survival is based on biological and geological processes rather than on the priorities of nations, states, or provinces, and corporations whose boundaries and self-interests run willy-nilly throughout the region."

Whereas one stream of the environmental movement works at the legislative and regulatory level (such as FOE and Environmental Action) and a second stream works to network information (such as Planet Drum), yet a third stream of the movement is focused on action.

Greenpeace, an international direct action environmental organization, has engaged in some of the most dramatic and effective campaigns to protect the planet and its denizens in this century. "We attempt to spotlight ecological atrocities by nonviolent physical protest at the scene," says San Francisco Greenpeace Director Tom Falvey. "Thus we have placed our bodies between harpoons and endangered whales every year since 1975 in the Pacific, the Atlantic, off Australia and Japan. We go up to the Newfoundland ice floes every March (since 1976) and confront the sealers who club newborn seals to death for their pelts.

"In 1971, 1972, and 1973 we sent ships into both the American and French nuclear weapon test zones during the actual explosions (!) to interfere with, and provoke public protest against, these test runs for Armageddon."

Traveling in their oceangoing vessel *Rainbow Warrior*, Greenpeace members have risked their lives to carry out their actions. Greenpeace is a no-frills organization, distributing only that information that is directly relevant to what it is doing. Its one-page information sheets on topics such as "Of Whales and Whaling," "Nuclear Energy: There Are Alternatives," and "Harp Seal Fact Sheet" are succinct, fact-filled statements about these problems.

The poignant image of Greenpeacers in their rubber dinghies rolling over ocean waves as they protect sea mammals from their would-be executioners is the stuff of which myths are created, material sufficient for the awe-inspiring book *Warriors of the Rainbow*, by Robert Hunter. Even the names they have chosen, Greenpeace for the movement and *Rainbow Warrior* for the vessel, carry a planetary survival message. While soldiers have for 40 centuries identified themselves with minute, arbitrarily defined patches of the earth's surface, fighting humans to "protect" humans, these terrestrial guerrillas identify with the planet as a whole, indeed, with existence as a whole, transcending human chauvinism. Greenpeace lives the belief that the planet and all its creatures are one.

NO NUKES

Greenpeace is one of many environmentally active groups that cross the line into the antinuclear movement. It is not surprising, since the generation of power for war and peace by splitting the atom has proved to be strategically nerve-wracking, environmentally disastrous, economically inefficient, technologically oversold, and widely unpopular–and quite likely the greatest threat we pose to our own survival. Opponents of nuclear power and nuclear weapons can now be found in every quarter, from the hallowed halls of medical schools where doctors such as those in Physicians for Social Responsibility have documented the potentially fatal consequences of nuclear technology, to the pristine research laboratories out of which come such groups as the Union of Concerned Scientists (see below), to Mobilization for Survival, a coalition of some 130 groups concerned with peace, justice, and human needs.

There is a vast network of concern about nuclear power and nuclear weapons (see Chapter 6, Valuing, for more on nuclear weapons) that cuts straight across the population. No other action movement documented in this book has attracted such a broad-based constituency, transcending color, sex, economics, and life-style. The reason is simple: Radioactive fallout, whether generated by a nuclear weapon or a nuclear power plant, knows none of the artificial barriers (geography, class, wealth, race) that we use to separate ourselves from each other. German citizens simplified this point for all the world to see at an antinuclear march following the 1979 debacle at Three Mile Island: "We all live in Pennsylvania," their banners read. In 1981, millions of Europeans marched against nuclear weapons. Well-informed scientists, beginning with Albert Einstein (whose theoretical insight on the nature of matter/energy led inexorably to the realization of the fantastic power locked in the little atom), and continuing with the work of scientists such as biochemist Linus Pauling and, more recently, pediatrician Helen Caldicott, have long been issuing ominous warnings about the dangers of this technology.

The current American antinuclear-power movement can trace one of its lineages to a fateful night in February of 1974. On Washington's birthday of that year, a western Massachusetts farmer single-handedly knocked down a weather tower that the local utility company, anticipating the possibility of system failure and wishing to determine the direction of the prevailing winds in the event of an accident, had built on the site slated for construction of a nuclear power plant.

Sam Lovejoy, at that time 27 years old, followed his act of conscience with a trip to the local police station, where he turned himself in. Lovejoy's experience and subsequent trial became the subject of a documentary, by Green Mountain Post Films, entitled *Lovejoy's Nuclear War*, which, much to the film makers' surprise, was soon requested for bookings all over the world. Green Mountain Post Films was itself set off on a new journey, and by 1980, the group was distributing some 25 films about nuclear power, alternative energy, and nonviolent protest.

Lovejoy's story is inspiring, because it demonstrates how one person can make a difference, and how, in this case, a man could make his influence felt through his network of contacts, beginning with his local community and ultimately reaching around the globe.

Today, the antinuclear movement is like a gigantic octopus with tentacles reaching into every profession. One of the central meeting grounds for professionals has been the Union of Concerned Scientists (UCS) "an independent, nonprofit group of scientists, engineers, and other professionals who have spent a decade conducting research into nuclear power safety questions." On the 30th anniversary of the atomic bombing of Hiroshima, UCS issued its Scientists' Declaration on Nuclear Power, signed by more than 2000 biologists, chemists, engineers and other scientists from such prestigious institutions as Princeton, the National Institutes of Health, UCLA, Brandeis, MIT, Stanford, Harvard, Dartmouth, and Rockefeller University:

> The country must recognize that it now appears imprudent to move forward with a rapidly expanding nuclear power plant construction program. The risks of doing so are altogether too great. We therefore urge a drastic reduction in new nuclear power plant construction starts before major progress is achieved in the required research and in resolving present controversies about safety, waste disposal, and plutonium safeguards. For similar reasons, we urge the nation to suspend its program of exporting nuclear plants to other countries pending resolution of the national security questions associated with the use by these countries of the by-product plutonium from United States nuclear reactors.

UCS and other organizations (such as the Task Force Against Nuclear Pollution, which lobbies at the congressional level by using a petition that calls for a moratorium on the construction of new plants) play an inestimable role in lending credibility to the antinuclear movement. Their most visible activies are the year-in and year-out demonstrations held at the existing and proposed sites of nuclear power plants such as Seabrook, New Hampshire, and Diablo Canyon, California.

Among the research and information groups in this area is the Nuclear Information and Resource Service (NIRS), which helps new antinuclear groups get started, as well as keep existing groups informed about new developments in this country and abroad. NIRS maintains lists of local groups and serves a networking function by connecting people to existing groups in their local area. The group distributes fact sheets on nuclear power, summing up the major problems, and provides handy short guides on how to raise money and get publicity.

The antinuclear movement has structured itself naturally on the network model by forming local "affinity groups" as independent nodes in a larger network. With outposts in every state and most of the Canadian provinces, and sister organizations in nearly every country, the antinuclear network is among the largest in the world. Yet this enormous network of individuals and groups has no leader, no hierarchy, no management. Should its work be done, the antinuclear network will disintegrate as quickly as it appeared.

While one impulse in Another America is "anti" about the gamut of established energy policies, another impulse is "pro" about other energy options. Following the 1960s politics of protest, Another America began striking positive notes about alternative futures along with the challenges to past practices. People active in or sympathetic to the antinuclear movement are apt to be simultaneously involved in some sort of renewable-energy option.

RENEWABLE ENERGY

Nowhere is the concept of "opportunity in crisis" so clear as in the energy field. Renewable (also called "alternative") energy is the summary title for a number of initiatives–what Amory Lovins calls "the soft energy path" (see his 1977 book by that title)–or what could simply be called "the soft solar network," since all energy sources ultimately derive from the sun. For practical purposes, it is helpful to make some distinctions within the soft energy field, since each of the "paths" encompasses its own network of people and projects that interweave and exchange resources. Some of these paths are:

- The (specifically) *solar* network, the largest, best-known, and most universally applicable of our available energy options;

- The *wood* network, growing primarily in the forest-rich, generally northern and mountainous regions;

- The *wind* network, appropriately positioned chiefly at water's edge;

- The *water* network, tapping the available power coursing by our two ocean coasts, by scores of mighty rivers, and by thousands of backwater streams that already have dams.

Along with the groups that stress the values of conservation, cogeneration (using energy ordinarily wasted in energy-conversion processes, such as drying clothes in wood-stove-warmed rooms), and waste conversion (such as is involved in the production of methane gas), these organic, noninvasive, self-renewing energy networks stand in sharp contrast to the fossil-fuel industries, which were born of a worldview in which more is better, waste creates profit, side effects are trivialized, and the past (fossil) and future be damned. Even the names of these abundant resource net-works-sun, wood, wind, and water-have an elemental poetry about them.

Obtaining our energy by deliberately digging into the earth with mines and wells instead of receiving it with open arms directly from the sun makes us look like ridiculous energy ostriches. What could be more obvious than obtaining our energy from the sun—our boundless, inexhaustible, everlasting, completely free local furnace? Perhaps the greatest obstacle to solar energy exists not in the technology to tap it, which ranges from absolutely nothing to sophisticated photovoltaic storage cells, but rather, in the fact that no one can own the sun. Unlike the moon that America hesitated not a moment to plant Old Glory upon, the sun eludes ownership. What could be more preposterous than the idea of affixing the American flag, or as has been done with most of our other natural resources, a corporate logo, to the sun?

Solar

The solar network has been by far the most effective, even though precariously balanced and potentially threatened, of all the grids in the renewable-energy field. Perhaps because solar-generated heat and power are so potentially competitive with their fossil-fuel rivals, the solar solution has been back-burnered, budget-cut, and research-reported nearly to death. Yet solar energy is a practical, economical, available technology that could be put into place almost overnight. Indeed, the mendacious slogan of the nuclear power industry, "safe, clean, and cheap," by rights belongs to the sun. In three stunning pages in *Human Scale*, Kirkpatrick Sale summarizes the solar argument. Using such concepts as economical, conservational, democratic, decentralized, efficient, and adaptable, Sale demonstrates that solar technology is the appropriate energy source for now and the future, consistent with the needs and values of Another America. Just a few of Sale's 13 points make the case:

- The sun's rays fall in roughly equal proportion, given polar and equatorial variations, on every man, woman, and child around the globe. . . . Sunshine falls at an average of 17 thermal watts per square foot all over the United States—varying only by a factor of two between sunny Arizona and cloudy Washington.

• Solar energy . . . would take different forms in different regions: direct sunlight in the Southwest and Southeast, wind power on ocean and lake coastlines and in higher altitudes, water and wood power particularly in the Northeast and Northwest, methane production in rural areas of the South and the Plains states.

• Solar energy [loses]. . . very little energy through conversion, and even less through transmission . . . in contrast to a normal electric utility that loses 50-65 percent in conversion and transmission.

These sorts of facts have not been lost on solar advocates, whose extensive network has managed to grow in spite of government research funds being chopped from budgets and the ever-growing encroachment of the multinational corporations into the field. More than 1000 firms manufacture solar equipment, many of them guided by one brilliant inventor who has seen yet another way to convert the sun's rays into long-lasting heat, light, or power. The greater solar network includes such diverse groups as the Western Solar Utilization Network (Western SUN) that links state solar offices and promotes the use of passive and active solar energy designs, the *Solar Living and Solar Greenhouse Digest*, a publication based in Arizona (which calls itself the "solar energy state"), and the Solar Energy Research Institute that publishes the *Solar Law Reporter*.

The sun was once worshipped as a god and later acknowledged as the ruling body of the solar system. Yet, in recent times, the sun has been out of favor with the human "powers that be." Hoping to change this situation, the Solar Lobby, the outgrowth of Sun Day (following the 1970 tradition established by Earth Day), speaks for the sun on Capitol Hill and keeps tabs on federal machinations with energy. Following the devastating budget cuts of 1981, this lobby will need even more strength and support.

Another America has recruited the sun as the standard bearer of our dawning energy era, as exemplified by the monthly magazine *Solar Age*, an offshoot of Total Environmental Action, a solar education, research, and design firm in southern New Hampshire, whose founder, Bruce Anderson, author of *The Solar Home Book*, has served as chair of the Solar Lobby board.

Wood

The use of wood for energy began hundreds of thousands of years ago and has continued unabated to the present. In Third and Fourth World countries, wood is at the basis of both survival and ritual. A typical family in western Africa spends 20-30 percent of its income on firewood; in Thailand, a father's role at his child's birth is to keep the fire burning with special wood he has gathered during the ninth month of pregnancy.

Wood may have lost some of this traditional magic in America, but its use is on the rise, with about 1.5 million households having converted to wood in the 1980 season alone and an estimated 15 million households projected to be heating with wood by 1985. If federal funding of research and development in the solar field has been skimpy, funding in the field of small-scale direct combustion can only be described as ludicrous. Writing in *Alternative Sources of Energy*, Andrew Shapiro, founder of the Wood Energy Research Corporation, in Camden, Maine, reports that "to date, the Federal Government has spent less than $1 million [on] research [and] development."

So people are taking matters into their own hands, and the wood network has birthed its own mythic heroes and heroines, such as the bands of people who roam the northern forests planting trees for hire. The Northwest Forest Workers Association, a federation of worker-owned, democratically managed tree-planting collectives, supports research and education in ecological forestry and promotes use of logging wastes for the production of energy. The collectives operate independently, moving from potential forest to potential forest, planting trees.   The smell of burning apple wood and the quiet heat of the fire, coupled with independence from expensive and noisy oil-powered systems, are drawing increasing numbers of people to heating with wood. Publications such as *Wood N' Energy*, the newsletter of the Society for the Protection of New Hampshire Forests, and the *Wood Burning Quarterly*, in Minnesota, are keeping wood burners up to date on the latest tips and developments. However, one of the more sobering developments was the quick realization by wood-stove manufacturers and users that this form of combustion is a heavy pollutant itself. Hazel Henderson states the problem frankly:

> Wood-burning is becoming a significant air pollution problem releasing many carcinogens, particulates, *and* Dioxin (as in Agent Orange). New England wood-stove romanticism is about finished. All stoves are polluters and will have to be redesigned or retrofitted.

Redesign is underway by many woodstove manufacturers, such as Franklin Industries, in Providence, Rhode Island, which has developed a catalytic combustion system for wood stoves to reduce emissions and increase efficiency.

At the same time, informal groups are meeting to attempt to gain an overview of what wood can mean to a region as a whole, as both an economic and an energy resource. For example, the New England Wood Energy Advisory Council, an informal group of wood energy researchers, bureaucrats, entrepreneurs, and promoters from federal and state agencies, universities, private industry, and nonprofit organizations, meets to explore the management and exploitation of resources in New England.

Wood may seem to be a home heating option primarily for the hale and hearty. However, the growing field of small-scale combustion promises to attract larger numbers of users in multiple housing units as well as institutions by, for example, using wood pellets that can be automatically fed into a combustion system. Due to supply management, handling, and air-quality problems, wood is not likely to be a total energy solution for any community in America, but used together with other energy forms, it is making an important contribution to the comfort and budgets of many people.

Wind

Similarly, wind power is hardly a universal panacea for energy generation; yet, in the appropriate location, wind is both sensible and economical. On Cuttyhunk Island, off the southern coast of Massachusetts, for example, a single windmill is supplying half the electric requirements for the island, not an inconsiderable reduction in a community dependent on the importation of diesel fuel by barge that has driven the local utility rates 20 percent higher than those of New York City. But even that unlikely spot, New York City, is the home of a commercial scale windmill, built by local teenagers, and now supplying all the electricity to an apartment building on the city's Lower East Side.

Clearly, windpower is on the upswing, and although the U.S. wind industry is a distant relative of our travelogue image of Holland's windmills, "the winds, they are a'blowing" with the promise of locally generated power. Although both the government (particularly through NASA) and such large corporations as Boeing are moving into wind power, the bulk of interest and activity rests with local inventors who are developing into manufacturers, many of whom cross paths as members of the American Wind Energy Association.

Intrinsic to these new inventors seems to be a social conscience that is a striking departure from their Industrial Age forebears. The "wind people" seem to approach their work with a sense of environmental protection and planetary zeal. "Windy," the sole proprietor of the Windlight Workshop, in Santa Fe, New Mexico, closes his newsletter (how many sole proprietors in any field publish newsletters?) with the words "I like to help people (that's why I'm in this business) but the benefit must be mutual . . . please enclose a self-addressed stamped envelope for response. Respect in return, Windy."

Water

The potential in America for hydroelectric power generation is great and widespread. Dams need not be the size of the gargantuan Bonneville Dam, in Washington, or require bureaucracies the size of the Tennessee Valley Authority, to generate electricity. Literally thousands of rural river runs are rushing water past people blind to the power available to them. In New England alone, more than 250 sites were under consideration for development of hydro-generated power in 1981.

Recognizing the potential in our riverways, as well as in the oceans themselves, water-generated-power groups have been spreading the word about this non-polluting form of energy. "Most of the nation's water potential is unused, but enough unused back-country dams exist in the U.S. *right now*, according to the Federal Power Commission, to supply the entire annual electrical needs for a population of 40 million people—more than the Rocky Mountain and Pacific regions combined—if only they were equipped with generators," writes Sale. While most of the projects are being developed by renewable-resource-minded entrepreneurs, support for water power comes through conservation groups concerned with other issues, as well as from industry groups such as the National Alliance for Hydroelectric Energy, based in Washington.

Sun, wood, wind, water—the sources of power for human civilization since its origin. An inventive spirit motivates the reclaiming of these power sources for future human civilization, a spirit which merges often with the creative forces behind appropriate technology.

APPROPRIATE TECHNOLOGY

Small Cat, a wise old creature, sits on the windowsill, basking in the sun. "But she's not small," people say when they ask her name. "She may not be small," we reply, "but she is beautiful."

Our cat's name is one of many fanciful, affectionate uses to which the name of the famous book by E. F. Schumacher has been put. *Small Is Beautiful* introduced people to the idea of the human side of technology, of tools that could be seen as *appropriate* to living in harmonious balance with the earth.

Appropriate technology has had as many descriptions as it has had applications, ranging from very fuzzy notions of sometimes-crazy-looking contraptions to more-generalized, value-oriented definitions such as the one offered by the Southern Unity Network/Renewable Energy Project (SUN/REP): "Appropriate technology is any technology—old or new—which is decentralized, labor-intensive, small-scale, accessible to rich and poor, and safe."

Appropriate technology conjures up images of windmills, waterwheels, compost heaps, organic gardens, wood stoves, solar panels, and bicycles. For those who have made the study and invention of appropriate technologies their life work, the concept embraces many kinds of tools that people can use on a human scale. Appropriate technology has broad appeal in a world in which people are overwhelmed by buildings that are so tall that they sway in the wind, by planes that fly so far overhead that we only hear them, and by traffic that becomes so jammed at the end of the workday that people can actually *save* time by *waiting* to leave until rush hour is over. Appropriate technology is based on the decentralized use of tools in contrast to that overapplied informing principle of industrial civilization: centralization. Centralization has rendered many institutions, services, and approaches ineffective, frustrating, unresponsive, and alienating, by making them too big and too abusive of critical balances.

With the awareness that locally-originated and point-to-point services are often the most sensible means of solving local technical problems, the appropriate technology movement has been strongly attracted to the idea of networking. Indeed, among the first groups to create networks in the 1970s were the A.T. centers, and, unlike other networks that have chosen words such as "movement," "group," "association" and sundry other nouns to sum up their collectivity, nearly all the A.T. groups have at some time called themselves or one of their offshoots a "network." Other social-change groups are deeply indebted to the A.T. movement for its very articulate theory and practice of the network idea.

One of the first and longest-standing A.T. initiatives is *Rain Magazine* (see Chapter 4, Sharing), which calls itself "the journal of appropriate technology." Begun in 1974 as a newsletter for sharing A.T. information in the Pacific Northwest, the Portland-based publication now enjoys wide national readership. The magazine quickly brings the reader up to date on what's happening in A.T.; each issue includes book reviews, how to's, excerpts from reports, interviews, essays, and short new blurbs. *Rain* has also given birth to several books (notably *The Rainbook*) and to primers on various subjects.

By the mid-1970s, *Rain* had become one of the highlights of the A.T. circuit, attracting everyone from college students doing term papers on A.T. to governors and corporate executives adopting, and in some cases co-opting, A.T. ideas for political power and economic profit. As success is often measured in notoriety, it could be said that A.T. efforts had met with tremendous success. This success produced an identity crisis of sorts in the A.T. community, one that is still being deliberated and debated. A January 1980 essay in the "Raindrops" column of *Rain* sums up the predicament:

Appropriate technology, whether called that or not, has been receiving increased recognition and gaining national and international prominence as a key component in the transition to a more ecologically and socially balanced world. At the same time, the recent whirlwind of attention has precipitated a kind of "growth" in appropriate technology not unlike the "growth" we've been discussing the limits of for so many years—an undifferentiated, somewhat out-of-control growth that's happening so far and so wide and so fast it seems nearly impossible to keep track of until it's already become history.

One thing we've learned from the "limits of growth" debate is that "growth," like "development," is a word with many connotations. As far as the growth of appropriate technology, we have to ask *what kind of growth* are we working toward? And further, *what kind of movement* should the appropriate technology movement become?

There are hard questions to be answered. What does it mean after being on the outside for all these years to find ourselves on the inside? What does it mean to have a surge of public attention, corporate interest and government support (though still a piddling amount when compared to things like nuclear power and defense) on our work toward local self-reliance? Some pretty important distinctions are getting blurred—do we need to draw the line?

We're sermonizing we admit—but we're getting impatient. We can define our terms, or have them defined for us. A remark by Jim Parker at a recent talk at AERO (Alternative Energy Resources Organization—Montana) crystallized our concern. "Waiting for the old order to collapse of its own weight," he said, "just doesn't seem as appealing anymore. It might fall on me."

The A.T. network is not just waiting for the old order to collapse. A.T. projects are numerous and inspiring, and visits to some experimental centers are like time-travel into Utopia. New implementations of R. Buckminster Fuller's famous phrase "doing more with less" are being developed at locations such as the Farallones Integral Urban House, in Berkeley, California—where lawn mowers have been replaced by rabbits, and garbage disposals take the form of sawdust buckets. At the New Alchemy Institute, in Falmouth, Massachusetts, fish are being farmed in indoor solar-heated pools. Such sophisticated and beautiful projects could be called appropriate *art*. Adaptations of these ideas are being tried elsewhere as the A.T. network reaches from the high-tech United States to the jungles of Guatemala to the food-short nation of Bangladesh.

Within the United States, A.T. groups have also formed networks at the regional level. Since 1977, the Cascadian Regional Library (CAREL) has been networking information and organizing events in the Pacific Northwest. Developed as an outgrowth of the 1976 Leap Year Conference on Regional Federation, at which an Information Access Committee took responsibility for providing the important and usually overlooked function of disseminating information about the conference *as it was happening*, CAREL went on to establish outposts in eight cities in the Northwest. The network's office in Eugene, Oregon, gathers information from these eight nodes, then compiles it into a publication, *Cascade: Journal of the Northwest*, sometimes in tabloid, sometimes in magazine, format.

Cascade employs a well-organized style—a cross between an encyclopedia and the want ads, providing a large amount of information in a small amount of space. Every organization, book, product, and/or person mentioned in *Cascade* is printed in bold-faced type, followed by an address. Thus, *Cascade* offers access as well as information simultaneously, a method that is used in some other publications as well. In essence, *Cascade* is a regional trade journal for a new way of life, offering resources in many areas, including A.T., land use and shelter, arts and crafts, education, economics, human services, and transportation.

The real potential of A.T. has yet to be realized as the network, by definition, is experimental. In locations as different as New York City, where the Energy Task Force has built its apartment-building-top windmill; western Massachusetts, where the Northeast Appropriate Technology Network (NEATNET) houses three ongoing projects—a self-reliant energy project, a community resource center, and the publication of *New Roots* magazine; and Butte, Montana, where the U.S. Government-funded National Center for Appropriate Technology serves as a clearinghouse and funding source for local A.T. projects, appropriate technologies are being discussed, developed, and evaluated.

Perhaps no network mentioned in this book is as promising and as inherently "American" as the A.T. movement. A.T. is about invention and innovation, about experimentation and equipment. In the gadget-happy, do-it-yourself world of America's dreams, the A.T. movement is at once a blend of tinkering and imagination and the spawning ground for technological contributions with a social conscience (which the high-tech explosion of the past 40 years has sorely lacked). A.T. gives rise to lovely reveries in which streets are quiet and clean, houses are warm and efficient, and obsolescence and waste are remnants of a history that we've left behind us like our primordial tails.

Reveries for some, but for other early advocates A.T. has become something of a nightmare. "The term A.T. has now been fully co-opted," writes Hazel Henderson. "Articles in *Science* describe nukes as 'appropriate technology.' Even A.T.'s in other cultural settings turn into disasters."

Phil Kreitner (see Chapter 4), who spent much of his time in the late 1970s traveling the United States talking with people involved in A.T., writes that the A.T. movement has two major weaknesses:

> [A.T.] is preoccupied with alternative technology to the neglect of alternative institutions. The American passion for tinkering with mechanical gadgets and concepts ignores the need to do some heavy tinkering with the ways in which those gadgets are produced, distributed, and used.

> It serves born-poor people very poorly. Non-poor, or "nouveau pauvre," inventors come up with technologies much more adaptable to the owner-occupied home than to the renter-occupied apartment building. And once corporations get their high-tech (i.e., high profit) hands on the technology, we end up with the expensive chrome-plated parodies that grace A.T. expositions.

Yet the very fact that people like Henderson and Kreitner have continued to explore and critique the development of appropriate technology is an encouraging sign. The *appropriateness* of technology is one core issue of our age. To create tools that aid us, rather than control us, is a formidable challenge.

Using Guide

U

The Using Guide includes groups that are primarily concerned with ecology and energy. Many of these groups also work on other issues.

Each group is identified by a letter/number code. The letter U stands for Using. Every group whose code begins with U is listed in the Using Guide.

The entry for each network whose code is lower than 100 includes a brief description. These representative networks are a cross-section of the initial groups we contacted in our research. Each network whose code is greater than 100 is listed with complete contact information. If the ✳ symbol, for publications, or ◆ symbol, for materials, appears with a listing, consult the Title Guide under Using Titles.

The Using Guide includes groups that are concerned with appropriate technology, bicycles, forests, generating power, natural resources, nuclear power and weapons, the oceans, pesticides, pollution, recycling, renewable resources, seals, solar, utilities, water, wilderness, wind . . . and a few others.

U001
Alternative Sources of Energy
107 South Central Avenue
Milaca, MN 56353
Researchers and publishers concerned with practical applications of alternative technologies. Bibliographic searches, information requests, and consulting available through Energy Information and Referral Service (EIRS).

U002
Anvil Press
P.O. Box 37
Millville, MN 55957
507/798-2361 ◆

◆ *Primer on Nuclear Power ($2.50)*

Publishers of books and booklets on self-reliant living, radical politics, and ecological struggles. Among these is an excellent primer on nuclear power that explains the problems and dangers in simple language.

U003
Bicycle Network
P.O. Box 8194
Philadelphia, PA 19101
215/236-4439 ◆◆

◆ *Man Who Loved Bicycles ($7)*
◆ *Cycle and Recycle (wall calendar/$3)*

Key information hub for bicycle activists. Crossroads for 80 "two-wheeled transit authorities" in 20 countries working to increase safety and viability of bicycling as means of public transportation.

U004
Cascadian Regional Library
1 West Fifth Avenue, #1492
Eugene, OR 97440
503/485-0366 ✳

✳ *Cascade: Journal of the Northwest (10 issues/$10)*

Clearinghouse for information on innovative projects in Pacific Northwest. Publishes bimonthly journal and organizes conferences. Defines networking as "facilitating cooperation among people." Sells national mailing list.

U005
Center for Neighborhood Technology
570 West Randolph Street
Chicago, IL 60606
312/454-0126 ✳

✳ *Neighborhood News (biweekly/$25)*

Innovative research and technical assistance group that nurtures successful thrifty neighborhood projects and jobs in housing, food, energy, recycling, others. Helps build urban solar greenhouses and year-around gardens.

U006
Citizen/Labor Energy Coalition
600 West Fullerton
Chicago, IL 60614
312/975-3680

Coalition of 200 groups in 35 states working for energy policies reflecting needs of poor and moderate-income people. Successful campaigns in prohibiting utility cutoffs, rate reforms, and model conservation plans.

U007
Citizens for a Better Environment
59 East Van Buren, Suite 1600
Chicago, IL 60605
312/939-1984 ✳◆

✳ *CBE Environmental Review (6 issues/$15)*
◆ *Solar Water Heating in Chicago*

Environmental research and education group working on toxic substances, water and air pollution, utility rates, nuclear power, and energy use. Won landmark U.S. Supreme Court suit ensuring public-interest groups' right to canvass.

U008
Committee for Nuclear Responsibility
P.O. Box 11207
San Francisco, CA 94101 ◆

◆ *Irrevy: An Irreverent View of Nuclear Power ($3.95)*

Excellent information source, chaired by "father of the antinuclear movement" John W. Gofman, M.D., former nuclear physicist and codiscoverer of Uranium 233, a nuclear fuel. Opposes nuclear power on human-rights grounds.

U009
Commonweal
P.O. Box 316
Bolinas, CA 94924 ✳

✳ *Common Knowledge (quarterly/$10)*

Unusual clinical and research center concerned with effect of toxic substances on human health. Research includes Genotoxin Survey (mapping polluted areas of California) and growing quality, uncontaminated food. Planning community.

U010
Critical Mass Energy Project
P.O. Box 1538
Washington, DC 20013
202/546-4790   ✻

✻ *Critical Mass Journal (monthly/$7.50)*

Nuclear watchdog group that does research on dangers, accidents, costs, and legislation on nuclear power. Documents congressional voting records on energy issues. Consumer orientation. Nader group.

U011
Environmental Action Foundation
724 Dupont Circle Building
Washington, DC 20036
202/659-1130   ✻◆

✻ *Power Line (monthly/$15)*
◆ *Utility Action Guide*

Information clearinghouse on utility reform and alternative energy groups. Very active in linking local groups with like needs. Evolved out of Earth Day in 1970. Variety of useful publications.

U012
Environmental Action Inc.
1436 Connecticut Avenue, N.W.
Washington, DC 20036
202/833-1845   ✻

✻ *Environmental Action (monthly/$15)*

Membership group that lobbies for environmentally sound legislation and keeps eye on how members of Congress vote and how corporations behave ecologically. Conducts imaginative public campaigns. Non-hierarchical staff.

U013
Environmental Defense Fund
475 Park Avenue South
New York, NY 10016
212/686-4191   ✻

✻ *EDF Letter ($20 year)*

Environmental group working at legal and regulatory levels to maintain and clean up our bioplanet. Files lawsuits concerned with wildlife protection, energy, toxic chemicals, and water resources.

U014
Food Monitor
P.O. Box 1975
Garden City, NY 11530
516/742-3704   ✻

✻ *Food Monitor (bimonthly/$10)*

Excellent source of information about food, land, and hunger on the planet. Founded by singer Harry Chapin and food writer/activists Frances Moore Lappe and Joseph Collins.

U015
Friends of the Earth
124 Spear Street
San Francisco, CA 94105
415/495-4770   ✻✻◆

✻ *Not Man Apart (monthly/$25)*
✻ *Soft Energy Notes (bimonthly/$25)*
◆ *Soft Energy Paths (Lovins, $3.95)*

Long-standing international environmental lobby concerned with "soft energy," clean air, wild lands, wildlife, and nuclear power. Provides expert testimony, brings lawsuits, organizes campaigns. The publications are beautiful.

U016
Friends of the Trees
Star Route Box 82-D
Oroville, WA 98844   ✻◆

✻ *Tree Leaflet ($3)*
◆ *True Fairy Tale ($4)*

Key source of information on tree- and shrub-seed saving. Maintains mail order seed business and tree-seed exchange. Also serves as information switchpoint for annual Northeast Washington Barter Fairs.

U017
Green Mountain Post Films
P.O. Box 229
Turners Falls, MA 01376
413/863-4754   ◆◆◆

◆ *No Nukes: Everyone's Guide to Nuclear Power ($9)*
◆ *Energy War: Reports from the Front ($6.95)*
◆ *Lovejoy's Nuclear War ($65 rental)*

Award-winning documentary filmmakers and distributors of films on the antinuclear and environmental movements. Best-known film is Lovejoy's Nuclear War. Also distributes books, videotapes, and occasional bulletins.

U018
Greenpeace Foundation
Fort Mason, Building E
San Francisco, CA 94123
415/474-6767   ◆◆◆

◆ *To Save a Whale ($6.95)*
◆ *Mind in the Waters ($9.95)*
◆ *Whale Jewelry ($5)*

International direct-action environmental organization. Spotlights ecological atrocities by on-site nonviolent physical protest. Very daring efforts. Excellent fact sheets.

U019
National Center for Appropriate Technology
P.O. Box 3838
Butte, MT 59701
406/494-4572   ✳

✳ *Appropriate Technology (A.T.) Times*

Federally funded program that develops and applies appropriate technology for low-income people. Conducts research, awards small experimental grants, promotes decentralized networking, and provides technical assistance.

U020
Natural Resources Defense Council
122 East 42nd Street
New York, NY 10017
212/949-0049   ✳

✳ *NRDC Newsletter (bimonthly/$7)*

Unusual public-interest law firm and research group working on environmental protection issues including energy, toxic substances, air and water pollution, transportation, and land. Reports and testimony. Has a large membership.

U021
Nuclear Information and Resource Service
1536 16th Street, N.W.
Washington, DC 20036
202/483-0045   ✳◆

✳ *Groundswell: An Energy Resource Journal (monthly/$15)*
◆ *Nuclear Information Resource Guide ($3)*

Excellent resource on nuclear power. Supplies hard information and materials. Good starting point for new antinuclear groups. Basic packet contains overview of problems, tips for organizing, maps, and resources ($3).

U022
Planet Drum Foundation
P.O. Box 31251
San Francisco, CA 94131
415/282-2550   ✳◆◆

✳ *Raise the Stakes! The Planet Drum Review ($10)*
◆ *Reinhabiting a Separate Country ($7)*
◆ *Backbone: The Rockies ($3.50)*

Unusual ecology group producing magnificent materials. Operates from idea that earth is a network of delicately balanced bioregions. Creates "bundles" of research, art, poetry, maps, and drawings.

U023
Rain Community Resource Center
2270 Northwest Irving
Portland, OR 97210   ◆◆◆

◆ *Portland Book: A Guide to Community Resources*
◆ *Rainbook: Resources for Appropriate Technology ($7.95)*
◆ *Consumer Guide to Woodstoves ($2)*

Excellent example of a community information center. Uses networking concepts to conduct research, compile directories, and foster community building. Maintains extensive library and skills-bank file.

U024
Scientists' Institute for Public Information
355 Lexington Avenue
New York, NY 10007
212/661-9110   ✳✳

✳ *SIPIscope (6 issues/$25)*
✳ *Environment (monthly/$12.75)*

Center that connects reporters with over 2000 scientists who can answer technical questions. Founded in 1963 by Margaret Mead and others. Also sponsors occasional seminars and public meetings; copublishes Environment magazine.

U025
Southern Unity Network/Renewable Energy Project
3110 Maple Drive, Suite 412
Atlanta, GA 30305
404/261-1764   ✳

✳ *SUN/REP (monthly)*

Coalition of individuals and organizations in 12 southern states which serves as advocacy/clearinghouse on appropriate technology. Provides technical assistance in grant writing and project start-up. Maintains resource file.

U026
Task Force Against Nuclear Pollution
P.O. Box 1817
Washington, DC 20013
202/547-6661   ✳✳

✳ *Task Force Against Nuclear Pollution Progress Report*
✳ *Clean Energy Petition*

Works at the legislative level against nuclear power. Sponsors of the Clean Energy Petition, already signed by 750,000 people, calling for government to promote solar and wind power and phase out nuclear power plants.

U027
Total Environmental Action
Church Hill
Harrisville, NH 03450   ✳◆◆

✳ *Solar Age ($20 year)*
◆ *Solar Home Book ($9.50)*
◆ *Solar Age Resource Book ($9.95)*

Solar and renewable energy consulting and educational firm started by Bruce Anderson. In addition to technical work, sponsors energy workshops and seminars, and distributes slide shows, building plans, manuals, and books.

U028
Washington Small Farm Resources Network
c/o Blue Mountain Action
19 East Poplar
Walla Walla, WA 99362   ✳

✳ *WSFRN News Release*

Information switch point for small-scale farmers in Washington State. Organizes meetings, conducts research, distributes material, and provides speakers on issues of interest to small-scale farmers. Follows legislation.

U029
Wind-Light Workshop
Rural Route #2, Box 271
Santa Fe, NM 87501
505/471-2573   ◆◆

◆ *Wind and Windspinners: A Nuts 'n Bolts Approach ($8)*
◆ *Homebuilt, Wind-Generated Electricity Handbook ($8)*

Wind and solar electrical service, manufacturer and how-to-do-it clearinghouse. "New wave" sole proprietorship. Send SASE for information.

U101
Abalone Alliance
944 Market Street, Room 307
San Francisco, CA 94102
415/543-3910   ✳

U102
Alabama Solar Coalition
P.O. Box 5714
Birmingham, AL 35209

U103
Alaska Center for the Environment
1069 West Sixth Avenue
Anchorage, AK 99501
907/274-3621   ✳

U104
Alaskan Conservation Foundation
308 G Street, Room 301
Anchorage, AK 99501
907/276-1917   ◆

U105
Alliance for Environmental Education
1619 Massachusetts Avenue, N.W.
Washington, DC 20036
202/797-4530

U106
Alternate Currents/SolarCity
156 Fifth Avenue, Suite 432
New York, NY 10010
212/924-7888   ✳

U107
Alternate Energy Institute
P.O. Box 3100
Estes Park, CO 80517   ✳

U108
Alternative Directions in Energy and Economics
502 Precita Avenue
San Francisco, CA 94110

U109
Alternatives: Journal of Friends of the Earth, Canada
Trent University
Peterborough, Ontario
CANADA K9J 7B8   ✳

U110
American Forestry Association
1319 18th Street, N.W.
Washington, DC 20036

U111
American Rivers Conservation Council
317 Pennsylvania Avenue, S.E.
Washington, DC 20003
202/547-6900   ✳

U112
American Wind Energy Association
1609 Connecticut Avenue, N.W.
Washington, DC 20009

U113
Animal Welfare Institute
P.O. Box 3650
Washington, DC 20007   ✳◆

U114
Appalachia Science in the Public Interest
180 Market Street
Lexington, KY 40507
606/254-1425   ✳

U115
Applewood Journal
P.O. Box 848
Point Reyes, CA 94956   ✳

U116
Aprovecho Institute
359 Polk Street
Eugene, OR 97402
503/929-6925

U117
Arcosanti
Cosanti Foundation
6433 Doubletree Road
Scottsdale, AZ 85253
602/948-6145   ◆◆✳

U118
Arkansas Solar Action Coalition
1145 West Hearn
Blytheville, AR 72315
501/762-2769

U119
Banyan Tree Books
1963 El Dorado Avenue
Berkeley, CA 94707   ◆

U120
Boston Clamshell Coalition
595 Massachusetts Avenue
Cambridge, MA 02139
617/661-6204   ✳

U121
British Columbia Energy Coalition
Galena Bay via Revelstoke
British Columbia
CANADA V0E 1X0

U122
Bullfrog Films
Oley, PA 19547
215/779-8226   ◆◆

U123
By Hand and Foot: Tools Dependent on Human Energy
P.O. Box 611
Brattleboro, VT 05301   ◆◆

U124
Canadian Coalition for Nuclear Responsibility
P.O. Box 236, Snowdon Post Office
Montreal, Quebec
CANADA H3X 3T4
514/842-1471   ✳

U125
Canadian Renewable Energy News
P.O. Box 4869, Station E
Ottawa, Ontario
CANADA K1S 5B4   ✳

U126
Catfish Alliance
P.O. Box 20049
Tallahassee, FL 32304

U127
Center for Community Technology
1121 University Avenue
Madison, WI 53715
608/251-2207   ✳

U128
Center for Environmental Problem Solving
5500 Central Avenue, Suite A
Boulder, CO 80301
303/444-5080   ✳

U129
Center for the Biology of Natural Systems
Department of Earth and Environmental Sciences
Queens College, C.U.N.Y.
Flushing, NY 11367

U130
Charles Stewart Mott Foundation
500 Mott Foundation Building
Flint, MI 48502

U131
Chesapeake Energy Alliance
2230 North Calvert Street
Baltimore, MD 21218   ✳

U132
Citizens Energy Council
P.O. Box 285
Allendale, NJ 07401
201/327-3914   ✳

U133
Citizens United for Responsible Energy
3115 Harvey Parkway
Oklahoma City, OK 73118
405/525-9004

U134
Citizens for Safe Power Transmission
P.O. Box 351
Red Hook, NY 12571   ✳

U135
Citizens' Energy Project
1110 Sixth Street, N.W., #300
Washington, DC 20001   ✦

U136
Clippings in Ecotopia
P.O. Box 43, Gravesend Sta.
Brooklyn, NY 11223

U137
Coalition for Direct Action at Seabrook
c/o Boston Clamshell Alliance
595 Massachusetts Avenue
Cambridge, MA 02139   ✦

U138
Community Energy Action Network
P.O. Box 33686
San Diego, CA 92103
714/236-1684   ✦

U139
**Community Network for Appropriate
  Technologies**
1321 Cleveland Avenue
Santa Rosa, CA 95401
707/528-6543   ✳

U140
Compost Science/Land Utilization
P.O. Box 351
Emmaus, PA 18049
215/967-4135   ✳

U141
Conservation Foundation
1717 Massachusetts Avenue, N.W.
Washington, DC 20036
202/797-4326   ✳

U142
**Conservation and Renewable Energy Inquiry and
  Referral Service**
P.O. Box 1607
Rockville, MD 20850
800/523-2929   ✦

U143
Consumer Action Now
355 Lexington Avenue
New York, NY 10017   ✦

U144
Continued Action on Transportation in the U.S.
128 First Street
Troy, NY 12180
518/274-6915   ✳

U145
Cornerstones: Energy Efficient Housebuilding
54 Cumberland Street
Brunswick, ME 04011
207/729-0540   ✦

U146
Dakota Resource Council
P.O. Box 254
Dickinson, ND 58601
701/227-1851   ✳

U147
Design Alternatives
3515 North 14th Street
Arlington, VA 22201
703/528-5179   ✦

U148
Documentary Guild
Shearer Road
Colrain, MA 01340
413/625-2402   ✦

U149
Earth Cyclers
Rural Route #1, Box 9
Edwall, WA 99008
509/236-2353

U150
Earth Lab Institute
1523 4th Street
Berkeley, CA 94710
415/526-2093

U151
**Earthmind: Energy Research, Education and
  Books**
4844 Hirsch Road
Mariposa, CA 95338   ✦

U152
Earthtone: For People Tuned to the Earth
P.O. Box 23383
Portland, OR 97223
503/620-3917   ✳

U153
Ecology Action of the Midpeninsula
2225 El Camino Real
Palo Alto, CA 94306
415/328-6752   ✦✦

U154
Energy Consumer
DOE Office of Consumer Affairs
Washington, DC 20585   ✳

U155
Energy People
120 31st Avenue North
Nashville, TN 37203
615/269-6786

U156
Energy Probe
43 Queens Park Crescent
Toronto, Ontario
CANADA M5S 2C3
416/778-7014   ◆

U157
Energy Task Force
156 Fifth Avenue
New York, NY 10010
212/675-1920   ◆

U158
Environmental Action Reprint Service
P.O. Box 545
La Veta, CO 81055
303/742-3221

U159
Environmental Policy Institute
317 Pennsylvania Avenue, S.E.
Washington, DC 20003
202/544-2600   ✳◆

U160
Farallones Institute: Integral Urban House
1516 Fifth Street
Berkeley, CA 94701
415/524-1150   ◆

U161
Farallones Institute: Rural Center
15290 Coleman Valley Road
Occidental, CA 95465

U162
**Farming Uncle: For Natural People and Mother
   Nature Lovers**
P.O. Box 91
Liberty, NY 12754   ✳

U163
Feminist Resources on Energy and Ecology
P.O. Box 6098, Teall Sta.
Syracuse, NY 13217

U164
Food Research and Action Center
2011 Eye Street, N.W.
Washington, DC 20006
202/452-8250   ◆

U165
Friends of the Parks
Lenox Hill
P.O. Box 610
New York, NY 10021

U166
Fund for Animals
140 West 57th Street
New York, NY 10019
212/246-2096

U167
General Assembly to Stop the Powerline
P.O. Box 5
Lowry, MN 56349
612/283-5439   ✳

U168
General Whale
1829 Versailles Avenue
Alameda, CA 94501
415/865-5550   ◆◆

U169
Georgia Solar Coalition
3110 Maple Drive, N.E., #403a
Atlanta, GA 30305
404/525-7657   ✳

U170
Geothermal World Info Center
5762 Firebird Court
Mission Oaks
Camarillo, CA 93010
805/482-6288   ◆

U171
Greenpeace Alaska
551 L Street
Anchorage, AK 99501
907/277-5922

U172
Greenpeace Examiner
P.O. Box 6677
Portland, OR 97228   ✳

U173
Greenpeace Seattle
4534½ University Way, N.E.
Seattle, WA 98105
206/632-4326   ✳

U174
Greenpeace/Vancouver
P.O. Box 34307
Vancouver, British Columbia
CANADA V6K 1P8
604/736-0321   ✳

U175
Hands-On: Guidebook to Appropriate
  Technology in Massachusetts
P.O. Box 302
North Amherst, MA 01059

U176
Harrowsmith Magazine/Canada
Camden East
Ontario
CANADA K0K 1J0
613/378-6661   ✳

U177
Health and Energy Learning Project
236 Massachusetts Avenue, N.E.
Washington, DC 20002
202/543-1070

U178
Herb Quarterly
c/o Uphill Press
P.O. Box 576
Wilmington, VT 05363   ✳

U179
High Country News: Natural Resources of the
  Rockies
P.O. Box K
Lander, WY 82520
307/332-4877   ✳

U180
Hudson Valley Green
P.O. Box 208
Red Hook, NY 12571   ✳

U181
Human Environment Center
1302 18th Street, N.W.
Washington, DC 20036
202/466-6040   ◆

U182
Humane Society of the United States
2100 L Street, N.W.
Washington, DC 20037
202/452-1100   ✳✳✳

U183
Illinois South Project
701 North Park
Herrin, IL 62948
618/942-6613   ✳

U184
Infinite Energy
P.O. Box 17945
Denver, CO 80217
303/629-0203

U185
Inland Regional Council
2737 25A Street
Clarkson, WA 99403
509/758-5796   ◆

U186
Institute for Ecological Policies
9208 Christopher Street
Fairfax, VA 22031
703/691-1271

U187
Intermediate Technology
556 Santa Cruz Avenue
Menlo Park, CA 94025
415/328-1730   ◆

U188
International Biomass Institute
1522 K Street, N.W., Suite 600
Washington, DC 20005
202/783-1133   ✳

U189
International Federation of Organic Agricultural
  Movements
P.O. Box 124
Hallowell, ME 04347   ✳

U190
International Solar Energy Society
Research Institute for Advanced Technology
U.S. Highway 190 West
Killeen, TX 76541
817/526-1300

U191
International Tree Crops Institute U.S.A.
P.O. Box 1272
Winters, CA 95694
916/795-2440   ◆

U192
Izaak Walton League of America
180 North Kent Street, #806
Arlington, VA 22209
703/528-1818   ✳

U193
Lamoureux Foundation: Home Energy
  Workshops
196 Morton Avenue
Albany, NY 12202
518/472-9760   ✳

U194
League of Michigan Bicyclists
P.O. Box 13001
Lansing, MI 48901   ✳

U195
Maine Audubon Society
Gilsland Farm
118 Old Route One
Falmouth, ME 04105
207/781-2330   ✳

U196
Maine Organic Farmers and Gardeners
    Association
P.O. Box 187
Hallowell, ME 04347
207/622-3118   ✳

U197
Mississippi Solar Coalition
887 Briarwood Drive
Jackson, MS 39211
601/956-4868

U198
Modern Energy & Technology Alternatives
P.O. Box 128
Marblemount, WA 98267
206/853-6851

U199
Mountain Bicyclists' Association
1200 Williams Street
Denver, CO 80218
303/333-2453   ✳◆

U200
Mudsharks Co-op
P.O. Box 584
Cottage Grove, OR 97424

U201
Musicians United for Safe Energy
72 Fifth Avenue
New York, NY 10011
212/691-5422

U202
National Association for Gardening
180 Flynn Avenue
Burlington, VT 05401
802/863-1308   ✳

U203
National Association of Railroad Passengers
417 New Jersey Avenue, S.E.
Washington, DC 20003
202/546-1550   ✳

U204
National Audubon Society
950 Third Avenue
New York, NY 10022   ✳✳

U205
National Coalition Against the Misuse of
    Pesticides
P.O. Box 50088
Washington, DC 20004
202/638-5828   ✳

U206
National Intervenors
236 Massachusetts Avenue, N.E.
Washington, DC 20002   ◆

U207
National Recycling Coalition
45 Rockefeller Plaza, #2350
New York, NY 10111
212/765-1054   ✳

U208
Nationwide Forest Planning Clearinghouse
P.O. Box 3479
Eugene, OR 97403
503/686-4073   ✳

U209
Natural Food Associates
P.O. Box 210
Atlanta, TX 75551
214/796-4136   ✳

U210
Nature Conservancy
1800 North Kent Street
Arlington, VA 22209
703/841-5300   ✳

U211
Needmor Fund
136 North Summit Street
Toledo, OH 43603
419/244-4981

U212
New Alchemy Institute
237 Hatchville Road
East Falmouth, MA 02536   ✳◆✳

U213
New England Coalition on Nuclear Pollution
P.O. Box 637
Brattleboro, VT 05301
802/257-0336   ✳

U214
New England Regional Energy Project
P.O. Box 514
Burlington, VT 05402
802/863-3408

U215
New England Solar Energy Association
P.O. Box 541, 22 High Street
Brattleboro, VT 05301
802/254-2386 ✳

U216
New Environment Association
270 Fenway Drive
Syracuse, NY 13224 ✳

U217
New Life Farm
Drury, MO 65638 ✳

U218
New Mexico Solar Energy Association
P.O. Box 2004
Santa Fe, NM 87501
505/983-2861 ✳◆

U219
New Times Films
1501 Broadway, Suite 1904
New York, NY 10036
212/921-7020 ◆◆

U220
Non Nuclear Network
427 Bloor Street West
Toronto, Ontario
CANADA M5S 1X7
416/922-3011

U221
North American Mycological Association
4245 Redinger Road
Portsmouth, OH 45662
614/354-2018 ✳

U222
North Carolina Coalition for Renewable Energy Resources
708 McCulloch
Raleigh, NC 27603
919/833-6940 ✳

U223
Northcoast Environmental Center
1091 H Street
Arcata, CA 95521
707/822-6918 ✳

U224
Northeast Appropriate Technology Network
P.O. Box 548
Greenfield, MA 01302
413/774-2257 ✳

U225
Northern Rockies Action Group
9 Placer Street
Helena, MT 59601
406/442-6615

U226
Northern Sun Alliance
1513 East Franklin Avenue
Minneapolis, MN 55404
616/874-1540 ✳

U227
Northwest Coalition for Alternatives to Pesticides
P.O. Box 375
Eugene, OR 97440
503/344-5044 ✳

U228
Ocean Education Project
245 Second Street, N.E.
Washington, DC 20002
202/544-2312 ✳

U229
Office of Appropriate Technology
State of California
1530 10th Street
Sacramento, CA 95814
916/445-1803 ◆

U230
Olympic Peninsula Citizens against Toxic Spray
P.O. Box 86
Beaver, WA 98305
206/327-3345

U231
Ozark Institute
P.O. Box 549
Eureka Springs, AR 72632
501/253-7384 ◆◆

U232
Pacific Northwest Research Center
P.O. Box 3708, University Sta.
Eugene, OR 97403 ◆

U233
Personal Mobility Committee
Transportation Building, Suite 702
Fourth and Sycamore Streets
Cincinnati, OH 45202

U234
Pollution Probe Foundation
12 Madison Avenue
Toronto, Ontario
CANADA M5R 2S1
416/967-0577 ✳

U235
Potomac Alliance
Natural Guard Fund
P.O. Box 9306
Washington, DC 20005
202/483-4284   ✳

U236
Prairie Alliance
P.O. Box 2424, Station A
Champaign, IL 61820
217/337-1510   ✳◆◆

U237
Project Jonah
P.O. Box 40280
San Francisco, CA 94140

U238
Rachel Carson Trust Fund for the Living
   Environment
8940 Jones Mill Road
Washington, DC 20015
301/625-1877

U239
Redwood City Seed Company
P.O. Box 361
Redwood City, CA 94064
415/325-7333   ◆

U240
Resource Center Network
Office to Coordinate Energy Research &
Education
Graduate Research Center
Amherst, MA 01003   ◆

U241
Resources for the Future
1755 Massachusetts Avenue, N.W.
Washington, DC 20036
202/328-5000   ✳

U242
Safe Energy Alternatives Alliance
324 Bloomfield Avenue
Montclair, NJ 07042
201/744-3358   ✳

U243
Safe Energy Resources
179 Orchard Street
Belchertown, MA 01007
413/256-6267

U244
Saginaw Valley Nuclear Study Group
5711 Summerset Drive
Midland, MI 48640

U245
San Diego Center for Appropriate Technology
5863 Hardy Avenue
San Diego, CA 92115
714/286-4301   ✳

U246
San Luis Valley Solar Energy Association
512 Ross Avenue
Alamosa, CO 81101
303/589-2233   ✳

U247
Saskatoon Environmental Society
P.O. Box 1372
Saskatoon, Saskatchewan
CANADA S7K 3N9   ✳

U248
Science for the People
897 Maine Street
Cambridge, MA 02139
617/547-0370   ✳◆

U249
Sea Shepherd Conservation Society
19265 West 4th Avenue
Vancouver, British Columbia
CANADA V6J 1M5   ◆

U250
Seed Savers Exchange
Rural Route #2
Princeton, MO 64673   ◆

U251
Sierra Club
530 Bush Street
San Francisco, CA 94108
415/981-8634   ✳

U252
Sierra Club Radioactive Waste Campaign
3164 Main Street
Buffalo, NY 14214
716/832-9100   ✳

U253
Small Farm Energy Project
Center for Rural Affairs
P.O. Box 736
Hartington, NB 68739
402/254-6893   ✳

U254
Society for Animal Rights
421 South State Street
Clarks Summit, PA 18411
717/586-2200   ✳

U255
Solar Business Office
Business and Transportation Agency
921 Tenth Street
Sacramento, CA 95814
916/445-0970

U256
Solar Energy Association of Northeast Colorado
425 North 15th Avenue
Greeley, CO 80631
303/356-4000 ✳

U257
Solar Energy Digest
P.O. Box 17776
San Diego, CA 92117
714/277-2980 ✳

U258
Solar Energy Research Institute
1536 Cole Boulevard
Golden, CO 80401
303/234-7380

U259
Solar Greenhouse Digest
P.O. Box 2626
Flagstaff, AZ 86003
602/526-4874 ✳

U260
Solar Lobby
1001 Connecticut Avenue, N.W.
Washington, DC 20036
202/466-6880 ✳

U261
Solar Times: News of the Solar Energy Industry
3 Old Post Road
Madison, CT 06443
203/245-9680 ✳

U262
Southern Oregon Citizens Against Toxic Sprays
P.O. Box 325
Grants Pass, OR 97526

U263
Southern Oregon Living Lightly Association
c/o Rainbow Bridge
117 Nob Hill
Ashland, OR 97520

U264
Stock Seed Farms
P.O. Box 112
Murdock, NB 68407
402/867-3771

U265
Sudbury 2001
P.O. Box 1313
Sudbury, Ontario
CANADA P3E 4S7
705/674-2001 ◆

U266
Summit Coalition for Alternatives to Pesticides
Summit Star Route, Box 94
Blodgett, OR 97326

U267
Synerjy: Directory of Energy Alternatives
P.O. Box 4790
New York, NY 10017 ✳

U268
Texas Solar Energy Coalition
516 Terrace Drive
Austin, TX 78704
512/447-9274

U269
The Plan: Community Food Tree Nurseries
P.O. Box 872
Santa Cruz, CA 95061 ✳

U270
The Sproutletter: Sprouts, Raw Foods, and Nutrition
P.O. Box 10985
Eugene, OR 97440 ✳

U271
Three Mile Island Alert
315 Peffer Street
Harrisburg, PA 17102 ✳

U272
Tilth: Biological Agriculture in the Northwest
13217 Mattson Road
Arlington, WA 98223 ✳

U273
Tree People
California Conservation Project
12601 Mulholland Drive
Beverly Hills, CA 90210
213/769-CONE ✳

U274
Trojan Decommissioning Alliance
310 Cheshire
Eugene, OR 97401

U275
Underground Space Center
11 Mines & Metallurgy
221 Church Street, S.E.
Minneapolis, MN 55455
612/376-1200 ✳

U276
Urban Solar Energy Association
277 Broadway
Somerville, MA 02145
617/623-3552 ✳

U277
Valley Watch
P.O. Box 2002
Evansville, IN 47714
812/464-5663 ✳

U278
Velo Quebec
1415 rue Jarry est
Montreal, Quebec
CANADA H2E 2Z7
514/374-4700 ✳

U279
Vermont Yankee Decommissioning Alliance
43 State Street, Box 1117
Montpelier, VT 05602
802/223-7222

U280
Waste Watch
1346 Connecticut Avenue, N.W.
Washington, DC 20036
202/466-2954 ◆

U281
Waterloo Public Interest Research Group
University of Waterloo
Waterloo, Ontario
CANADA N2L 3G1
519/884-9020 ◆

U282
Western Massachusetts Resource Network
P.O. Box 464
Williamsburg, MA 01096
413/268-7138

U283
Western Massachusetts Solar Energy Association
University of Massachusetts
Amherst, MA 01003 ◆

U284
Wilderness Society
1901 Pennsylvania Avenue, N.W.
Washington, DC 20006
202/828-6600 ✳

U285
Wind Power Digest: Access to Wind Energy Information
115 East Lexington
Elkhart, IN 46516
219/294-2023 ✳

U286
Windstar Foundation: Educational, Research and Retreat Center
P.O. Box 286
Snowmass, CO 81654
303/927-3402 ◆

U287
Women and Life on Earth
P.O. Box 580
Amherst, MA 01004
413/549-6136 ◆◆

U288
Women and Technology Project
315 South 4th East
Missoula, MT 59801
406/728-3041 ◆◆◆

U289
Women in Solar Energy
P.O. Box 778
Brattleboro, VT 05301
413/545-3450

U290
Wood 'n Energy
5 South State Street
Concord, NH 03301
603/224-9945 ✳

U291
World Association for Solid-Waste Transfer and Exchange
130 Freight Street
Waterbury, CT 06702
203/574-2463

U292
World Information Service on Energy
1536 16th Street, N.W.
Washington, DC 20036
202/387-0818 ✳

U293
Zero Population Growth
1346 Connecticut Avenue, N.W.
Washington, DC 20036
202/785-0100 ✳

6

Valuing Networks:
Politics and Economics

Almost 300 years ago, local groups calling themselves Committees of Correspondence formed a network, a communications forum where homespun political and economic thinkers hammered out their ideological differences, sculpting the form of a separate and independent country in North America. Writing to one another and sharing letters with neighbors, this revolutionary generation nurtured its adolescent ideas into a mature politics. Both men and women participated in the debate over independence from England and the desirable shape of the American future. It was in one of these letters that Abigail Adams first mentioned the idea of enfranchisement for women, while another of her friends, the playwright Mercy Otis Warren, used ideas from the letters to create her popular political satires about the British.

During the years in which the American Revolution was percolating, letters, newssheets, and pamphlets carried from one village to another were the means by which ideas about democracy were refined. Eventually, the correspondents agreed that the next step in their idea exchange was to hold a face-to-face meeting. The ideas of independence and government had been debated, discussed, discarded, and reformulated literally hundreds of times by the time people in the revolutionary network met in Philadelphia.

Thus, a network of correspondence and printed broadsides led to the formation of an organization after the writers met in a series of conferences and worked out a statement of purpose—which they called a "Declaration of Independence." Little did our early networking grandparents realize that the result of their youthful idealism, less than two centuries later, would be a global superpower with an unparalleled ability to influence the survival of life on the planet.

Like stars and people, governments are born, grow, and die. Their life cycles are punctuated by transitions and upheavals, patterns found in the development of all complex physical, biological, and human entities. Just as we humans are evolving, so are our politics—our social forms, our collective associations—evolving. As we evolve, so do our ideas about possible political structures. There is no name for it yet, this politics of the future, but all around us we see the seeds of a potent and growing grass-roots movement for fundamental change.

There is a need for a new politics and a new economics—now. Networkers working on politics and economics are weaving the hopes within our hearts together with our everyday concerns into a new social fabric that makes sense. The conditions that a new politics and economics must reckon with are like these: thousands of nuclear weapons poised to strike distant targets; many people over 65 living below the poverty level; few people controlling most of the wealth; foreshortened life expectancy for the American Indian; massive black unemployment; and women earning 59 cents for each dollar earned by men doing the same job.

Is it possible to build a political structure that interconnects with psychology, with art, with other cultures, with cosmology? Is it possible to create an economic system that is just, one that serves people rather than causing people to serve it? Yes. Although the political and economic landscape of Another America is in many ways the least developed of the areas we have surveyed, it is the area in which the problems are best understood. Realism is a word that crops up often when people talk economics and politics. Is the prospect of making decisions by consensus realistic? Based on our survey, yes. Does it exist now? No. Is there a political fire blazing, an economic windstorm blowing, commingling hope and hopelessness? Emphatically, yes.

Amid the mess that is causing Americans such great despair, there is the basis for resolving our predicament. We are all in this together. Hazel Henderson's simple slogan "We can't grow on like this" makes sense to every one of the 95 percent of us who do not control the wealth.

Politics and economics are about values, about the social processes of defining, using, and struggling over value.

Power and money are completely entwined in America, and both politics and economics relate to how we process differences in values. American capitalism is based on the assumption that profit is the single motivating economic value and that "realistic" power is devoid of human value beyond the jungle law of survival and dominance. But Another America understands that all power and wealth have a value context and that the evolutionary spectrum of human values is ignored only at the peril of civilization and now, perhaps, the very survival of humankind and the planet.

Organized networking is most evident among people who have the least power. Powerlessness is relative, and ultimately the politics/economics of "some have it, some don't" renders us all victims. In representing the range of *struggles for the basics*, we begin with a relatively small minority and gradually broaden the concept: American Indians to blacks to poor people to women to human beings everywhere threatened with species death by global catastrophe. Heading away from Armageddon are some representative *new visions* of new social orders, and at the end–under the title "1984"–we offer some of the signals of change that may be harbingers of a fundamental shift in American politics.

STRUGGLES FOR THE BASICS

Indians

Words written in 1843 by the great philosophical visionary Margaret Fuller call for recognition of American Indians without dishonoring their heritage. Fuller recorded her thoughts in her book *Summer on the Lake*, about a visit to Mackinaw Island, where the Chippewa and Ottawa tribes had convened to collect their annual recompense from the American Government:

> Let the missionary, instead of preaching to the Indian, preach to the trader who ruins him. . . . Let every legislator take the subject to heart, and, if he cannot undo the effects of past sin, try for that clear view and right sense that may save us from sinning still more deeply. And let every man and every woman, in their private dealings with the subjugated race, avoid all share in embittering, by insult or unfeeling prejudice, the captivity of Israel.

Fuller's words, with a modernization of usage, could be drawn from the newsletters of the many networks concerned with individual and group rights. Acknowledging our interconnectedness leads us to see that each of the struggles for individual and human rights is our own struggle.

Within the United States, the oldest struggle for group rights is that of the American Indian, a summary name that does a disservice to the true breadth and diversity of these peoples, now comprised in 482 recognized tribes living on 266 reservations even after centuries of *de facto* genocide. The American Government's treatment of the Indians is embarrassing, deplorable, *and* consistent with the raw industrial worldview in which might overrules right. White people were visitors on the land of Native Americans: Had these primitive European-born capitalists observed their own rules concerning ownership during those early years, our history would be very different.

As it was, the Indian people were "reserved" into small areas of land, mere fractions of the territory that various treaties promised. Now even that land is being threatened by the proponents of further development. Today the struggle of the Indian peoples revolves around the land on which they live and its resources: oil, coal, uranium, gas, and water—all in rich abundance on many Indian reservations. Without land, the survival of the traditional tribal way is impossible.

Contrasted with the magnificent respect for the land ("our mother, the earth") which is synonymous with the Native Way, the further exploitation of Native land by large corporations for the sake of extracting more energy resources is an abomination of almost unspeakable dimensions. The factors of high alcohol and suicide rates, severely depressed income and educational levels, continuing attacks on reservations, and the jailing of many leaders of the Indian movement have brought Native people to the verge of extinction. A strong network of support, largely invisible, exists to reverse these realities and to celebrate the great heritage of the American Indian and pave the way for another future.

One of the oldest and most visible support groups within the movement is the National Indian Youth Council (NIYC), which addresses such issues as land and resources, tribal government, health care, and anti-Indian backlash, and sponsors programs in employment, appropriate technology, youth recreation, environmental education, paralegal training, voter registration, and litigation. NIYC was born as an informal network and grew by consciously understanding itself as a *process*, thereby illustrating the profound contribution that American Indian culture and philosophy have to offer to the worldview of all Americans.

In history and principle, the National Indian Youth Council is a process, not an event. The process began in 1952 when Indian clubs at various universities began to form regional associations. It came to fruition during the Conference on American Indians (Chicago, 1960) when non-Indian scholars discussing Indian problems invited Indians for the first time to participate in their deliberations. The well-known "Chicago Conference" had two effects: it demonstrated the absurdity of white scholars trying to define Indian problems; and the necessity for a national Indian organization to define their own problems and offer solutions consistent with Indian culture and tradition.

NIYC was created in Gallup, New Mexico, in 1961, by ten college-educated Indians who had met at the Conference and envisioned that NIYC would become an organization of service to Indian People based upon the Indian system of agreement. . . . Each tribe has a distinct history; thus each tribe has different priorities in dealing with their problems and needs. What works for one tribe does not necessarily work for another tribe. NIYC approaches and responds to the variety of problems so differently that it may appear to the uninitiated that NIYC does not have a consistent philosophy or specific direction; but to NIYC this direction is as logical as the growth of a tree.

While NIYC is among the most visible of the native networks, there are many more which operate without public notice. Although the efforts of many Indian networks have been largely occupied with the legal defense of political prisoners, other groups have addressed issues of immediate daily concern. Many of these networks came together in the summer of 1980 under the umbrella of the Black Hills Alliance, which organized a 10-day meeting to plan actions on how to save a million acres of land in the Black Hills that was under seige by more than 25 multinational corporations prospecting for uranium, oil, natural gas, coal, and iron ore.

Concerned with the preservation and sensible use of this magnificent expanse of the American West, the people who gathered in the Black Hills sought to demonstrate the interconnectedness of Indian concerns with those of many others, including environmentalists, family ranchers, farmers (40,000 of whom gave up their land to prospecting in 1979 alone), health workers, and renewable energy proponents.

Blacks

Movements for social and political change in the United States began in the very process of birth of the country. In the 1800s, the focus was on the abolition of slavery, then enfranchisement for men, while the turn of the century saw the focus shift to concern with workers' rights, immigrant problems, and woman suffrage. By the 1950s, a new era concerned with civil rights for black people was heralded, a massive effort that spawned a number of other movements, including the black power movement, the antiwar movement, and the women's movement. By 1970, a large segment of this movement regrouped around the issue of welfare rights. Judy Meredith, an organizer for the Institute for Social Justice, in Boston, Massachusetts, sees two strands emanating from the antiwar movement, "one concerned with welfare rights and the concerns of poor people in the neighborhoods and the other concerned with citizen action and the issues of the 'upper' working class."

But what ever happened to the civil rights movement and later the black power movement? As we see it, the civil rights movement did not disintegrate with the silencing of some its leaders by imprisonment and by death, but rather, was diffused by its own internal shifting concerns. When Martin Luther King was gunned down in Memphis, he was there to lead a march about jobs; the drive for black employment is one of many issue-related efforts that continue in the 1980s.

The theory of networking suggests that the people-to-people links that were at the basis of the black power movement reached deep into the community, reinfusing the culture with a sense of identity. The slogan "Black is beautiful" became reality as black Americans reclaimed a feeling of pride in their heritage.

A personal story brought this point home to us: Lucrecy Johnson is a 60-year-old black woman, born in Creedmoor, North Carolina, who came North in the great migration of southern blacks at the tail end of the Depression. She raised her four children mostly alone and has had a hand in raising nearly all of her eleven grandchildren. She has worked all of her life, buying everything on time—even her indoor bathroom, which in 1970 was finally installed in her small wood frame house on the only unpaved street in her segregated Pennsylvania town.

Johnson eschewed the black power movement at its most media-visible height, firmly stating that she was not "black." Yet the ideas of the movement reached her. When "Roots," a second-generation offshoot of black cultural pride, was first aired on television in the mid-1970s, Johnson was ready: Her response was to dig into an old box in her attic and pull out the only existing photo of her grandmother. "I was always ashamed of this picture," she said, "because my grandmother was a slave. But now I realize who she was and that I can be proud of her." The picture now sits in her living room alongside that of her children's graduation and wedding pictures.

The black power movement separated into myriad small local action projects that have touched many aspects of people's daily lives. While the large national organizations—such as the Urban League, NAACP, and PUSH—appear to be at the "head" of the black movement, a much larger, largely invisible infrastructure exists which is setting up day-care centers, forming local community alliances, establishing cultural associations, involving people in tenants-rights activities, and providing access to inner-city-gardening plots.

Networking is the key to survival for all minority groups in the 1980s. At a time when the voices of division grow loud—pitting Black against Jew, Haitian against Cuban, Vietnamese against Chicano—it is doubly important that we work from our sense of interconnectedness as a species. Since greed and hate can never be the basis of lasting associations, those without power and resources must share and love. We know all too well what the resurgence of the Ku Klux Klan and the rise again of the American Nazi Party means for minority groups. Now is a crucial time for the networks among caring people to work together.

Poor People

A salary of $10,000 in 1970 was by no means large, but it could be adequate. In the 1980s, $10,000 barely pays the rent. With inflation soaring, prices rising literally overnight, and more and more people out of jobs or barely able to meet their bills even while working, the networks that are advocates for poor people must form alliances among themselves, setting aside tactical and ideological differences for the sake of advancing mutual causes.

Perhaps the largest organization concerned with poor people's rights is the Association of Community Organizations for Reform Now, universally known by its pithy acronym, ACORN. "ACORN doesn't ordinarily consider itself a 'network,'" says Seth Borgos, director of research. "The reason is that 'network' implies a fairly loose bond of affiliation, while ACORN is centralized in terms of financial management, staff, board structure, organizing standards, and other criteria. However, I recognize that by some definitions ACORN is a 'network' on account of its geographical scope and the large measure of autonomy which our organizations enjoy."

By any standards, ACORN is a large organization, with 28,000 member families (55 percent black, 40 percent white, and 5 percent chicano) organized in 19 states with offices in 45 cities. ACORN's philosophy is based on six key ideas: (1) All issues (consumer, environmental, and economic) in the United States are "mere manifestations of a much more fundamental issue: the distribution of power"; (2) the organization's constituency comprises all those people who are excluded from that power (traditionally low- to moderate-income people), whom the group has dubbed the "majority constituency"; (3) the organization is multi-issued; (4) involvement in electoral politics is necessary; (5) the organization must be internally financed; and (6) the organization must be geographically based, rooted in the neighborhood.

Working from these principles, ACORN has amassed an impressive list of bread-and-butter victories:

- abolishing the sales tax on medicine in Arkansas and Missouri;

- securing passage of a bill outlawing insurance redlining in Missouri;

- increasing the school exemption for senior citizens in Houston;

- winning lifeline telephone rates in Texas;

- establishing strict regulations on utility shut-offs and other utility consumer rights in Colorado, Arkansas, Georgia, Iowa, and Tennessee;

- winning a new $2 million youth job program in Philadelphia;

- getting the Public Utilities Commission to revoke the phone company's franchise in Redfield, Arkansas;

- blocking the investment of $8 million of city funds in a downtown parking garage in Des Moines; and

- beating a sales-tax increase in Tulsa, Oklahoma.

Putting its philosophy and experience together, ACORN has developed a nine-point People's Platform, which, with ACORN's characteristic no-nonsense candor, begins with the words: "We stand for a People's Platform, as old as our country, and as young as our dreams. We come before our nation, not to petition with hat in hand, but to rise as one people and demand." The Platform then proceeds to enumerate changes in energy, health care, housing, jobs and income, rural issues, community development, banking, taxes, and representation.

Ranging from the Emergency Land Fund, in the South, organized as a counterpoint to black "land drain" (Blacks owned 15 million acres of land in 1910, 3 million acres in 1980), to the Midwest Academy, in Chicago, which trains neighborhood organizers on vital community issues, to Massachusetts Fair Share, which has a broad membership base working on consumer issues, the networks concerned with pocketbook politics are thriving in the 1980s. As inflation soars, so do their constituencies.

Women

The women's movement, while working on group issues, represents deep concern for the preservation of individual rights. The women's movement is about dignity and justice—ultimately about the power each woman must assume over her destiny. The struggle encompasses global issues: how humanity should proceed, what values will inform our decision making, and how our decisions will be made.

One of the early recognitions of the second wave of feminism in the United States was that our language itself would become an issue. Historically, most women have been defined by their domestic identities and by their relationships to men: The use of gender-specific words like "mankind" (used when "humankind" is meant) makes it difficult to dispel old ideas about sex roles and to avoid passing stereotypes on to our children.

Early misinterpretations of the second wave of feminism led people to believe that women "wanted to be men." While many women may choose to perform tasks traditionally reserved for men, such as firefighting, construction, and plumbing (just as men may be choosing professions traditionally reserved for women, such as nursing, child care, and secretarial jobs), these role changes are not the point of the women's movement; they are merely its by-product.

At issue to the women's movement is a much more fundamental change in the way men and women understand one another and cooperate in the world. The women's movement is about the integrity of individuals. The symbols that have been seized upon to trivialize women's concerns have only served to retard progress toward a more humane world.

The heart and soul of the women's movement rests in networking: women making connections among women. Indeed, the entire genesis of the 1960s-born women's

movement can be traced to myriad networks that spontaneously developed throughout North America and abroad. Meeting in small groups—"consciousness raising"
sessions (a term later borrowed by the human-potential movement)—the women
made individual personal discoveries, experienced dramatic flashes of awareness of
the *Gestalt* in which they lived. These "clicks," as writer Jane O'Reilly has called
them, were the architecture that framed the larger worldview, the personal proofs
that isolated women share many problems in patriarchical society. Unlike many
other groups concerned with human rights, the women's movement grew out of a
personal awareness, which was then applied to political issues.

The women's movement is about awareness and about consciousness, concerns
with profound implications for our developing human species. Its most expansive
thinkers are talking about an integration of political and economic issues with new
ways of knowing, integrating the right brain (typically described as the "feminine"
hemisphere, where intuition and creativity are generated) with the left brain (typically described as the "masculine" hemisphere, where logic and reason are generated) and are challenging the 1970s idea that women are more "intuitive" than men,
that men are more "rational" than women. More than anything else, the women's
movement is reminding us of how much more lies within our grasp as human
beings, how much more creative we can be by dropping away our role restrictions in
favor of integrating both sides of our brain and behavior. But large evolutionary
jumps, such as that suggested by the women's movement, can never develop without
the long, slow, day-to-day work of confronting the inequities that exist for women in
the workplace, in the media, and in the home.

One very successful women's network that reflects the 1980s realities of women
on the job is Working Women: The National Association of Office Workers, which, as
a national membership organization, links women office workers into a support and
advocacy network. Working Women got its start in 1972, when a group of ten women
employed in downtown Boston offices met to discuss the quality of their work
experiences.

Using the name "9 to 5," the women began to organize and to dig out the facts of
life for women office workers. What they found was that over 20 million women,
about 10 percent of the entire U.S. population, are employed as office workers, with
an average salary for clerical workers of $8128 per year; and that 95 percent of all
working women earn less than $10,000 annually. Using this information as their
catalyst, the women in 9 to 5 went on to set up Working Women, with chapters in 40
states and 12 local affiliated groups, of which 9 to 5 is now one. Working Women has
been highly effective in drawing attention to the concerns of its constituency, having
secured raises, promotions, and back-pay settlements for thousands of women. More
than anything else, Working Women has identified a large, unorganized constituency, translating hunches and feelings about women's office experiences into
dollars-and-cents facts around which they can organize.

Working Women is a vital lifeline to its members, providing practical support for
documentable problems; it serves an entirely different function from the "new girl"
(aping "old boy") networks that are sweeping through the upper echelons of the
same offices where women on the rise are facing job discrimination. Whereas networking in the business world has come to be seen as the *sine qua non* of women getting ahead, Working Women takes quite a different approach, encouraging women to
work together to change the overall situation, rather than to learn the ropes of existing corporate life—the difference between a cooperative and a competitive approach.
As if to underscore this point, one of the "new girl" business networks in Boston
meets at the Harvard Club (which until the 1970s did not even admit women) and

operates with three basic ground rules: "no talking about husbands, kids, or feelings," a curious proviso from a group that uses the nickname "girl" rather than
"woman." This women's new wine in men's old bottles may ultimately serve to
advance the status of a few individual women but will do little to change the lives of
the vast number of working women in this country.

Thus the women's movement comprises many networks, working on many issues,
including such concerns as passage of the Equal Rights Amendment (ERAmerica),
sterilization abuse (Committee to End Sterilization Abuse), creating a library of
women's history (Women's History Research Center), establishing a women's media
network (The Women's Institute for Freedom of the Press), monitoring federal
actions regarding women (Women USA), working to eliminate violence against
women (simply named, Women Against Violence Against Women), identifying shel-
ters for battered women (Working on Wife Abuse), supporting displaced homemakers (Displaced Homemakers Network), and establishing networks of peer support
among professional women (National Hook-up of Black Women), just to name a few
of the thousands of women's groups. (See *Women's Action Alliance*, edited by Jane
Williamson et al., and *Women's Networks*, by Carol Kleiman, for extensive listings).

While no one of the networks *is* the women's movement, each is a hologram,
reflecting the larger women's movement; taken as a whole, they constitute an
immense metanetwork of shared perspectives, and they are moving us all toward a
new understanding of what women, and men, can be.

Human Survival

In war, almost everyone becomes powerless and subject to rule by a few. In nuclear
war, absolutely everyone becomes powerless after the first explosions.

Movements for peace in America are as old as America itself, waxing and waning
in visibility and strength depending upon the involvements of the U.S. military at
any moment. During the late 1960s, the peace movement (better known as the antiwar movement), had a tremendous impact on American foreign policy, and the dramatic consequences of that era still reverberate in the 1980s. Vietnam provided the
collective political baptism for the largest generation in American history.

The image of the world at peace is beautiful—and totally unknown in our recorded
history. History, as the books read, is rarely more than an accounting of one war after
another, with countries and borders changing before new maps could even be
drawn.

But now the stakes are higher than ever before, so high that the question can no
longer be framed as a choice between war and peace. Rather, since August 6, 1945,
the choice is between planetary survival and utter destruction. Despite the deeply
disturbing comments of politicians who make mindless statements such as "Nuclear
war is winnable," it is clear to anyone who has seriously studied the effects of
nuclear war and its aftermath that no one can win a nuclear war.

Thus in the 1980s, with less than two crucial decades before the new millennium,
the peace movement appears as a beacon of sanity, a sorely needed voice of reason
and compassion which offers a powerful counterpoint to the suicidal war cries of the
military establishment. As with the other extensive networks that are working to
achieve a more livable world, the peace network is vast and diverse, with groups
working at many social levels on many issues. Their work ranges from campaigns to
remove funding and approval for the MX missile system, the Air Force's massive,
idiotic shell game planned to occupy more than 20,000 square miles of western land
and to cost at least $50 billion, according to SANE, to a news alert network to defeat
repressive legislation (National Committee Against Repressive Legislation), to the
reactivation of the network opposing the draft (Committee Against Registration and

the Draft), to a media network that produces radio programs about issues in peace and justice (Great Atlantic Radio Conspiracy).

Now entering its third decade, SANE: A Citizen's Organization for a Sane World, got its start in the early 1960s with the first ban-the-bomb campaigns in the United States. Today SANE is focusing its efforts on lobbying for arms control and disarmament measures, developing plans for converting the vast military apparatus to productive civilian use, opposing development of the neutron bomb and the MX missile system, and building a network among the many existing groups concerned with the same issues.

SANE takes a very optimistic approach to problems, encouraging people to see that their actions can be effective. SANE has been effective; indeed, the organization was instrumental in the passage of the Limited Test Ban Treaty, has worked for the defeat of the ABM system in 1970, and was one of the cornerstones of the anti-Vietnam War movement. In proposing a course of action to stop the development of the MX missile, SANE developed the following guidelines, which are applicable to many other issues:

- Inform your community with "Letters to the Editor" of your local newspaper.

- Send messages to your Senators and Representatives in Congress.

- Press electoral candidates to take a stand against the mobile missile.

If you live in a possible deployment area:

- Urge your local officials to oppose this "weapon in the backyard."

- Organize a group of local citizens to campaign against the mobile missile.

- Join forces with environmentalist, religious and human needs organizations.

Clearly, SANE sees a solution to problems through a process of education and activism, spreading the word as widely as possible, working from a local base. In a very real way, SANE is saying that we can avert Armageddon by beginning at home in our own communities. It's an encouraging message for discouraged and disheartened people, and a message that is being echoed by such dedicated groups as the National Peace Academy Campaign, the Institute for World Order, and the Consortium on Peace Research, Education, and Development.

Similarly, the reactivation of the registration-and-draft-resistance networks, less than 15 years after their dramatic beginnings in the 1960s, indicates both how clear the threat of war is and how committed people are to peace. With its roots in the conscientious objection of the Quaker pacifists, the registration movement of the 1980s has refined the "Hell no, we won't go" message of the Vietnam era into a political and economic critique of the U.S. military-industrial complex. To register for war, these new resisters are telling us, is to fight for OPEC; the options are Exxon and existence: They are choosing life over oil.

Confronting the possibility of nuclear war is so awful to most of us that we want to shrink away from the thought. The escapist within us would like to live our own lives well–and possibly quickly–so as to avoid being around for the ever more possible holocaust. But deep inside we know that silence is no solution to the threat of nuclear war.

NEW VISIONS

There is an alternative to the headlong plunge toward nuclear war that seems to be preoccupying the thoughts of strategists in Washington and Moscow. Networks here and abroad are blending theory and practice, inventing a new politics to challenge the liberal and conservative industrial politics.

A new politics begins locally, spreads horizontally by networking, and integrates vertically through channels connecting autonomous organizations at all levels. It is naive and premature to assert that the basis for a new political party exists, though many nonmainstream political parties and independent candidacies have begun to reflect little pieces of what the new politics may be. Using adjectives such as participatory, anticipatory, appropriate, and transformative, the proposals for restructuring how we govern ourselves are numerous and growing and do not always cancel each other out. Those advocating redefining our borders along biotic regions are in harmony with the advocates of decentralism, who in turn have much in common with those calling for a personal politics.

The new politics is experimental, and some of it has already failed. Self-Determination, a self-consciously structured network in California, was started by veterans of the human-potential movement wishing to fuse the "personal/political"–an idea that in 1976 was both too visionary and too vague for Californians. But no single failure or success can represent the very broad basis on which the new politics is coming together. As Mark Satin writes in *New Age Politics: Healing Self and Society*:

> The new politics is arising out of the work and ideas of the people in many of the social movements of our time: the feminist, environmental, spiritual, and human potential movements; the appropriate technology, simple living, decentralist, and "world order" movements; the business-for-learning-and-pleasure movement and the humanistic-transformational educational movement. . . . Their contributions come together like the pieces of an intricate jigsaw puzzle.

Two little pieces of the puzzle illustrate the importance of networking in the new politics of the future.

Born out of Quaker activism of the 1960s (which included such dramatic efforts as sailing the ship *Phoenix* into North and South Vietnam ports to deliver medical supplies), the Movement for a New Society (MNS) is a "*network* of autonomous groups committed to radical nonviolent social change." Today the MNS office in Philadelphia serves as a switchboard for 30 groups throughout the country that are working on such issues as food, health, housing, nonviolent training, alternative institutions, and liberation.

Central to the MNS philosophy is the development of patterns for living consistent with its evolving political thinking. Toward that end, the Philadelphia office is also the crossroads for some 100 people of all ages living in 20 cooperatively shared houses in the western part of the city.

MNS walks a thin line between traditional leftist political groups and the counterculture. "We are attracting people who are interested in personal support and in living in community," explains MNS member Nancy Brigham. "This is different from the left, which traditionally has ignored people's personal lives, and different from the counterculture that ignores politics."

The group sustains itself on an amazingly low budget, $20,000 per year, which is raised from newsletter subscriptions, a literature service, and from the contributions of MNS collective members who have chosen to donate the wages of one hour per month to sustain the group.

"No one gets paid for doing MNS work," says Brigham. "So we don't have to spend a lot of time raising money. We live simply and most people have part-time work–based on Gandhi's idea of 'bread labor.'"

In fact, much of the group's philosophy is derived from the teachings of Gandhi, including the idea of a collective living-structure.

"When Gandhi returned to India from his travels abroad, the first thing he did was to set up an ashram, a safe space," explains MNS member David Albert. "He did no political work for three years until the ashram was firmly established. We started the Philadelphia Life Center [the name for the collective living units] to emulate this ideal, to create safe spaces within our culture where adults could live and also raise children if they wanted to."

With a belief in fundamental social change through nonviolent action, MNS has nurtured a "closely knit network of people working on very different social problems," says Albert. "One of our earliest and most important realizations was that everyone doesn't have to do everything. People can make different choices about what they want to work on."

MNS also operates without titles, without a hierarchical structure, and by rotating all jobs that are rotatable (recognizing that some, of course, are impractical to rotate, such as bookkeeping). One of MNS's greatest accomplishments has been to record and share its experiences with its various living/working/organizing experiments; they have published pamphlets on how to run meetings, how to conduct egalitarian study seminars, and how to resolve conflict. Major summaries of MNS thinking can be found in the network's two books, *Moving Toward a New Society* and *Building Social Change Communities*.

Addressing itself to the issue of a fractionalized movement, the MNS network offers these thoughts about the advantages of "many groups, one movement":

> There is certainly room in "the movement" for a multiplicity of small economic and political groups, linked with each other. Though people involved in collective farming may not always be able to take part in demonstrations–and people active in confrontation politics may not be able to farm collectively–the two *can* be associated, have a common understanding of the problems which underlie both politics and economics, and keep in close touch with each other, knowing that they are each part of a larger struggle to bring about a truly new society.

The New World Alliance (NWA) is a conscious attempt to create a national political movement based on values that have traditionally stood outside politics. NWA is the brainchild of Mark Satin, whose book *New Age Politics: Healing Self and Society* was one of the first attempts to break out of habitual right/left critiques of American politics. A draft resister, he lived in Canada for 11 years (1967-78) where he wrote, typeset, and self-distributed his book. When Satin returned to the United States under Carter's Vietnam amnesty program, he decided to take a cross-country bus trip to assess the mood of "new age" activists, to learn from them what was needed to start a new national political organization.

"I went systematically to 24 cities and regions from coast to coast, not just the 'hip' cities and regions like Cambridge, Massachusetts, and Colorado but also the more representative places like Detroit, Maine, Atlanta," he wrote to us in a letter. "I stopped when I found 500 people who said they'd answer a questionaire . . . on what a New Age-oriented political organization should be like–what its politics should be, what its projects should be, and how its first directors should be chosen." Twenty-one pages long in its final form, Satin's questionnaire plumbed people's political and philosophical beliefs with wide-ranging queries like "How should we respond to the Bakke decision?" "How should we, as a society, deal with the future?" "How can we make small or family farming more of an option for Americans?" "How large should the Board of Directors be?" and "Which, of 16 colors, should the new organization use for its stationery, emblems, and flag?"

Of the original 500 people to whom the questionnaire was sent, 350 responded, indicating that the time was ripe to start a new political organization. Satin returned the questionnaire tabulations to the respondents, asking them to nominate themselves for the governing council—89 people did, from whom 39 were chosen for the council by an unusual selection process developed from the questionnaire response itself: 40 percent by mail ballot, 30 percent by lottery, 20 percent by Satin himself, and 10 percent by four women.

In December 1979, the NWA held its first governing council meeting in New York, bringing together an eclectic blend of people whose most universal characteristic appears to be that many of them have written books. While a number clearly come out of counterculture backgrounds, an equal number have backgrounds in government and academia.

NWA is nonhierarchically structured, working in decentralized committees. NWA has also developed a political "living" platform that defines its positions on global policy, crime and justice, economics, science and technology, energy, health, and the environment. NWA also sponsors "Political Awareness Seminars" designed "to give people confidence that each one of us can have a significant impact on changing the world," and it is affiliated with a monthly newsletter, *Renewal*, edited by Satin, intended to take a "critical" and "constructive" look at "New Age/synergistic/transformational/politics of reconceptualization/politics as if people mattered."

1984

In a letter to Samuel Kercheval written on July 12, 1816, Thomas Jefferson expressed his long-held belief that each generation has a right and a duty to re-agree upon the fundamental laws by which it is governed, to reassess the laws of nature as they are presently understood.

> Some men look at constitutions with sanctimonious reverence and deem them like the ark of the covenant, too sacred to be touched. . . . But I know that laws and institutions must go hand in hand with the progress of the human mind. As [the mind] becomes more developed, more enlightened, as new discoveries are made, new truths disclosed, and manners and opinions change with the change of circumstances, institutions must advance also and keep pace with the times. . . . Let us [not] weakly believe that one generation is not as capable as another of taking care of itself and of ordering its own affairs. . . . Each generation is as independent of the one preceding as that was of all which had gone before. It has then, like them, a right to choose for itself the form of government it believes most promotive of its own happiness, consequently, to accommodate to the circumstances in which it finds itself that received from its predecessors.

Not only constitutions but also our declarations about the fundamental laws of nature are not sacred absolutes of human knowledge. Our covenants about what is real and how reality works have already undergone radical revisions a number of times in human history. To paraphrase Jefferson's view: Every generation has the right and the duty to reassess and re-agree upon the perceived laws of nature by which its worldview is governed. We believe that the way to our vision of a peaceful and humane planet will be by means of a substantial reordering of our shared world-view, of our shared basic assumptions and values. Only if millions of people, in their daily lives and work, use a new worldview to create new approaches and new solutions will we survive and evolve.

Pallas Athena, the Greek goddess of wisdom, is said to have sprung fully armed and fully grown from the brow of Zeus. Proponents of gradual change have some-times used this myth to disparage proponents of radical change, arguing that Athena's story is surely a myth, because, they assert, change starts gradually and accumulates, rather than appearing full-blown overnight. Yet there is an important truth in the Athena story that is particularly applicable to changes in politics, eco-nomics, and ways of knowing. Gradualists are correct in stating that social change starts with brief flickers and flashes of anomalies, exceptions, crises, and lonely pro-testing voices that slowly gather strength and influence, but when the shift to a new worldview comes, it does so swiftly and suddenly. Since most people are blind to the precursors of fundamental change, the new wisdom will seem to burst forth sud-denly, fully formed and ready to address the myriad crises of the present.

In our present collective drama, this moment has not yet occurred, nor is it pre-ordained in our script of the future. None of us need be reminded of the gloomy fore-casts for tomorrow's social health and personal welfare and for the planet's headlong plunge toward ecological catastrophe. Nor can we deny the dominant American sen-timent as expressed by Ronald Reagan's remarkable electoral landslide in 1980. However, scattered among the daily doomsday reports, there are unmistakable sig-nals of hidden trends that suggest the possibility of a future large-scale shift in worldviews.

One chronicler of these social signals is Alvin Toffler, who asserts that the indus-trial worldview reached its zenith in the mid-1950s and that a "third wave" of human civilization has been building for the past 25 years. That is, right now the world is undergoing a transformation as significant as the shifts from hunting to agri-culture at the dawn of human civilization ("first wave") and from agriculture to industry four centuries ago ("second wave"). Toffler characterizes the "hidden code" of industrial-age thought in terms of six assumptions:

Standardization

Specialization

Synchronization

Concentration

Maximization

Centralization.

As an astute reporter of the-future-right-under-our-noses, Toffler describes the emerging third wave of civilization in terms that complement the waning industrial assumptions. *Decentralized* structures are replacing centralized forms, values of *appropriateness* are challenging maximization, power and resources are being *dis-persed* to counter concentration, *flexible* time patterns are encroaching on the linear synchronization of tasks, *autonomy* and self-reliance are breaking the narrow bonds of specialization, and creative processes expressing *uniqueness* are contrasting with the frozen ruts of standardization.

Another signal of change has been documented by John Naisbitt, of the polling firm of Yankelovich, Skelly, and White, who monitored reports of social changes in 200 U.S. newspapers in the belief that widespread indicators of change would be reflected in local behavior. Emerging trends he identified include (in order):

FROM	TO
Industrial Society	Information Society
Centralization	Decentralization
Party Politics	Issue Politics
Machines	Human Technology
Racism/sexism	Equality
Top-down Management	Bottom-up Management
Equal Education/Health	Equal Access to Capital
Bigness	Appropriate Scale
Company Board of Directors	Independent Board
Representative Democracy	Participatory Democracy.

As though to underline the meaning of the most widely reported trend, the shift from an industrial to an information society, we ran across Naisbitt's report while using our computer to browse through the "Community News Conference" of the Electronic Information Exchange System (see Chapter 7, Learning).

In its "Values and Lifestyles" study for corporate clients, SRI International reports that there is a clear shift of values taking place in a small but key segment of the population (this according to an article in the charter issue of *Leading Edge Bulletin*, itself a harbinger of change as the follow-up newsletter to Marilyn Ferguson's popular book *The Aquarian Conspiracy*). Summarizing trends in terms of evolving symbols of success, the article reports that, for a significant group of people, values are shifting "from quantity toward quality, from the group toward the individual, from abundance toward sufficiency and from waste toward conservation."

Past symbols: fame, being in Who's Who, five-figure salary, college degree, splendid home, executive position, live-in servants, new car every year, club membership.

Present symbols: unlisted phone number, Swiss bank account, connections with celebrities, deskless office, second and third home, rare foreign car, being a vice president, being published, frequent and unpredictable world travel.

Future symbols: free time any time, recognition as a creative person, oneness of work and play, rewarded less by money than by honor and affection, major social commitments, easy laughter and unembarrassed tears, wide-ranging interests and actions, philosophical independence, loving, being in touch with oneself.

To these reports of change percolating beneath the crumbling facade of the industrial worldview can be added our own study of networks. Networks are not only the carriers of a new paradigm, they are a reflection of it: a segmented, decentralized, nonhierarchical, fuzzy, value-identified form of organization that is emerging at every social level from neighborhood to globe. The vast, vibrant, still-inchoate meta-network of people and organizations we are calling Another America is coalescing in every area of personal and social life, motivated by and bonding through shared values. Nascent therein is a great power for change.

When Americans next go to the polls to elect a President, it will be 1984. 1984—this year is a fixture in our recent collective consciousness, the year in which we measure ourselves and our society against George Orwell's 1949 vision of a closed, total-itarian, technocratic society 35 years in the future. Now that time-mark is rapidly approaching when we compare reality to the three governing slogans of the ruling Orwellian Party:

War Is Peace.

Freedom Is Slavery.

Ignorance Is Strength.

In a rough and premature way, the ingredients for a paradigm shift, a sudden wide-spread change in worldviews, are present even now. There is a vital movement for constructive, change and there is as well a potentially unifying scientific philosophy forming at the frontiers of knowledge (see Chapter 11). Ironically, the Ronald Reagan years may inadvertently help the people on these paths to find one another and bond into networks, generating an internal cohesion that finally creates an apparently sudden paradigm shift.

Liberalism and conservatism define the two poles of industrial politics, the former representing the layers of sophisticated patches that hold together revisionist indus-trialism, and the latter representing the earlier, simpler verities of classical industri-alism. As long as the dynamic of decision making was locked into this pattern, only industrial alternatives could appear in the public arena. Since Reagan swept away the liberal leadership that had dominated American politics since Franklin Roose-velt, there may now be an opportunity for postindustrial alternatives to arise in counterpoint to conservative rule, generating a new, sharply defined, com-plementary dynamic that makes a paradigm shift possible.

Often considered the *greatest* of the colonial Puritan preachers, Cotton Mather was also the *last*. A paradigm shift is sometimes preceded by what might be called "the Cotton Mather effect," the appearance of a powerful and persuasive representative of a worldview just as it is about to be displaced. Furthermore, in evolutionary transi-tions, there is frequently a distinct "step-back-to-leap-forward," a reversion to earlier ideas and behaviors before a leap to a new synthesis (see Chapter 11). Ronald Reagan may be the "Cotton Mather" of the industrial worldview, and his administration may be a conspicuous "stepping back" before transformation in the late 1980s.

Following his sizable mandate, the "honeymoon" customarily offered to the new President, and some early political successes, Reagan's administration is likely to have some problems as the novelty wears off and the industrial crises of economics, energy, ecology, and nationalistic warfare remain intractable. Since these crises are fueled by trends that are unstoppable within the industrial context, the need for a new paradigm may suddenly become intense. If a suitable conceptual vehicle is ready, then for the first time the long-submerged struggle between the old worldview and the new could burst into public consciousness.

While engaged in the minutiae of life and work, it is frequently hard to hold onto the vision of an optimistic future. Synchronicity, the apparently inexplicable coincidence of events, which we all experience, generates subtle signs that we are not alone.

On the day we were completing this chapter, two letters arrived from Robert A. Smith, III (see Chapter 12). We started to read ". . . as Jefferson stated so eloquently . . . ." and found ourselves staring at the same passage we had just used to begin this section. There are ideas and energies loose in America and the world that offer hope for a peaceful transition to a new level of human civilization, and Bob Smith is one of millions of people committed to that possibility. This is what Bob had to say:

> As Jefferson stated so eloquently, "laws and institutions must go hand in hand with progress of the human mind." The human mind is now being extended through networks and communications and the prosthetic brain being created becomes as important as our biological brain. We communicate democratic principles through networking but the networks themselves (they have a life of their own) must be living examples of the democracy they espouse. . . . Perhaps one of the key considerations for networking in the 1980s and helping Another America to realize its dreams is something Gore Vidal suggested—a Constitutional Convention. Certainly, in the nearly 200 years since America adopted its then extremely radical and still radical constitution many things have taken place which call for a revision to keep this document or covenant malleable as Jefferson envisioned it. . . . Akin to the heterogeneity of the 13 original bodies which unified under one document, networks could find a common focus to amend (1) our own Constitution and (2) amend all national constitutions so as to reflect the organic interdependence which is the world today and thereby overcome the forced fits of mechanical interdependence.

Valuing Guide

V

The Valuing Guide includes groups that are primarily concerned with politics and economics. Many of these groups also work on other issues.

Each group is identified by a letter/number code. The letter **V** stands for Valuing. Every group whose code begins with **V** is listed in the Valuing Guide.

The entry for each network whose code is lower than 100 includes a brief description. These representative networks are a cross-section of the initial groups we contacted in our research. Each network whose code is greater than 100 is listed with complete contact information. If the ✳ symbol, for publications, or ◆ symbol, for materials, appears with a listing, consult the Title Guide under Valuing Titles.

The Valuing Guide includes groups that are concerned with barter, blacks, business, corporations, economics, government, human rights, Indians, jobs, nuclear holocaust, peace, politics, prisons, public-interest campaigns, registration and the draft, self-management, surveillance, veterans rights, women . . . and a few others.

V001
Alliance Against Sexual Coercion
P.O. Box 1
Cambridge, MA 02139 ✦

✦ *Fighting Sexual Harassment: An Advocacy Handbook ($3.50)*

National clearinghouse for information on sexual harassment and other forms of violence against women. Evolved out of rape crisis-center work. Provides direct support services, job and legal referrals.

V002
Alternative Fund Federal Credit Union
102 West State Street
Ithaca, NY 14850
607/273-4611 ✦

✦ *Ithaca People's Yellow Pages ($.75)*

Not-for-profit cooperative financial institution espousing community self-reliance. Makes loans for "provident or productive purposes," including business and personal loans.

V003
Association of Community Organizations for Reform Now
628 Baronne Street
New Orleans, LA 70113
504/523-1691 ✷

✷ *USA–United States of Acorn ($6)*

Effective activist organization representing needs of low- and moderate-income people. Membership of 27,000 in 19 states. Works on taxes, housing, jobs, agriculture, health care, community development, and representation.

V004
Barter Project
1214 16th Street, N.W.
Washington, DC 20036
202/467-5560

New national support project for burgeoning neighborhood bartering groups. Crossroads for information exchange and technical assistance to local groups. Planning workshops and newsletter.

V005
California Newsreel
630 Natoma Street
San Francisco, CA 94103
415/621-6196 ✦✦✦

✦ *Planning Work: Resources for Labor Education ($3)*
✦ *Goodbye Rhodesia ($40 rental)*
✦ *Controlling Interest: The Multinational Corporation*

Film production and distribution company that concentrates on southern Africa and work-related issues (including unemployment, unions, and ownership). Produces "learning kits" to accompany films. Low-cost rentals available.

V006
Cambridge Documentary Films
P.O. Box 385
Cambridge, MA 02139
617/354-3677 ✦✦✦

✦ *Killing Us Softly: Advertising's Image of Women ($46 rental)*
✦ *Barefoot Doctors of China ($80 rental)*
✦ *Taking Our Bodies Back: The Women's Health Movement*

Produces excellent social-change films on women and advertising, violence and the media, women's health, and labor. Also distributes The Barefoot Doctors of China. Provides printed materials to accompany rentals/purchases.

V007
Campaign for Economic Democracy
409 Santa Monica Boulevard, #214
Santa Monica, CA 90401
213/393-3701 ✷

✷ *CED News ($15)*

Political organization based on idea of "economic democracy" and three key issues: renewable energy, public control of corporations, and controlling inflation in energy, housing, food, and health care.

V008
Central Committee for Conscientious Objectors
2208 South Street
Philadelphia, PA 19146
215/545-4626 ✷

✷ *Counter Pentagon (bimonthly)*

Key source of information and activity on conscientious objection, registration, the draft, and military recruiting. Started in 1948; highly visible during Vietnam War and increasingly active due to reinstitution of registration.

V009
Citizens Involvement Training Project
University of Massachusetts
138 Hasbrouck Laboratory
Amherst, MA 01003
413/545-2038 ✦✦✦

✦ *The Rich Get Richer and the Poor Write Proposals ($6)*
✦ *Power: A Repossession Manual ($6)*
✦ *Planning for a Change ($6)*

Project aimed at making citizens and groups more effective. Offers practical training sessions at nominal fee on vital issues such as funding, membership, and organizing. Publishes excellent series of handbooks.

VO10
Commission for the Advancement of Public Interest Organizations
1875 Connecticut Avenue, N.W.
Washington, DC 20009
202/462-0505　　　　　　　　　　◆

◆ *Periodicals of Public Interest Organizations ($5)*

Publishers of useful booklet describing the publications of about 100 active public-interest organizations. Nothing else like it in print. Also sponsors workshops and conferences.

VO11
Committee Against Registration and the Draft
245 Second Street, N.E.
Washington, DC 20002
202/547-4340　　　　　　　　　　✳

✳ *Anti-Draft (6 issues/$10)*

Coalition of 54 national organizations opposed to the draft. Organizes local and national activities and provides information on registration and military conscription.

VO12
Council on Economic Priorities
84 Fifth Avenue
New York, NY 10011
212/691-8550　　　　　　　　　　✳◆

✳ *CEP Newsletter (monthly/$15)*
◆ *Jobs and Energy*

Research group that disseminates information on activities of U.S. corporations. Ranks firms' social responsibility as a counterpoint to profit measures. Produces and updates reports. Can be costly but valuable.

VO13
Emergency Land Fund
564 Lee Street, S.W.
Atlanta, GA 30310
404/758-5506　　　　　　　　　　✳

✳ *Forty Acres and a Mule (monthly/$4)*

Key catalyst in movement to protect ownership of land by blacks in South. Offers legal, financial, educational, and technical assistance to minority and low-income landowners and farmers to counteract "land drain" by big business.

VO14
Grantsmanship Center
1031 South Grand Avenue
Los Angeles, CA 90015
213/749-4721　　　　　　　　　　✳

✳ *Grantsmanship Center News (bimonthly/$20)*

Resource for networks seeking funding. Offers five-day training sessions focusing on program planning and development, identification of funding sources, and proposal writing. Expensive, but some scholarships available.

VO15
Henry George School of Social Science
833 Market Street
San Francisco, CA 94103
415/362-7944　　　　　　　　　　◆

◆ *Foundation of Economic Freedom*

Teaching the work of Henry George–a 19th-century economist and proponent of "land value tax" to eliminate speculation on land–the school offers courses in economics and related subjects. Part of worldwide "Georgist" network.

VO16
Illinois Women's Agenda
53 West Jackson Boulevard, #623
Chicago, IL 60604
312/922-8530　　　　　　　　　　✳

✳ *Illinois Women's Agenda Newsletter ($25 year)*

Largest multi-issue state coalition of women's organizations in the U.S. Convened as part of national effort to address the National Women's Agenda. Develop programs, provide technical assistance, organize events, and publish.

VO17
Indian Rights Association
1505 Race Street
Philadelphia, PA 19102
215/563-8349　　　　　　　　　　✳

✳ *Indian Truth (bimonthly/$15)*

Educational organization that supports Indian programs and brings information about Native people to non-Indians. One of the oldest Native American support groups, founded in 1882.

VO18
Institute for Social Justice
628 Baronne Street
New Orleans, LA 70113
504/524-5034　　　　　　　　　　◆◆

✦ *Community Organizing Handbook ($2.50)*
✦ *Grassroots Fundraising Book ($4.75)*

Training and technical assistance for community organizers. Offers workshops, internships, and consulting. Publishes excellent handbooks. An outgrowth of ACORN.

V019
Institute for Southern Studies
P.O. Box 230
Chapel Hill, NC 27514
919/929-2141   ✳✳

✳ *Southern Exposure (quarterly/$10)*
✳ *Facing South (syndicated news column)*

Energetic action/research center providing the progressive voice of the New South. Tackles range of timely issues such as utility rate cuts, strip mining, brown lung disease, and prison reform. High-quality journal.

V020
Interfaith Center on Corporate Responsibility
475 Riverside Drive, #566
New York, NY 10027
212/870-2293   ✳

✳ *Corporate Examiner (12 issues/$25 year)*

Organization of church investors concerned with corporate social responsibility. Provides information on shareholder resolutions, public testimony, litigation, and on-site research. Organizes and participates in boycotts.

V021
Know Feminist Publishers
P.O. Box 86031
Pittsburgh, PA 15221
412/241-4844   ✳✦✦

✳ *KNOW News ($6 year)*
✦ *Women, Menopause and Middle Age ($5)*
✦ *I'm Running Away from Home But . . . ($5)*

One of the oldest feminist collectives in the U.S. Offshoot of NOW. Publishers of feminist books and study courses. Fact-filled newsletter contains many otherwise-hard-to-find resources, news summaries, and book reviews.

V022
Mobilization for Survival
3601 Locust Walk
Philadelphia, PA 19104
215/386-4875   ✳✦

✳ *The Mobilizer (monthly/$10)*
✦ *Peace Resource Packet ($4)*

Coalition of 150 peace groups in U.S., including student, environmental, religious, social-justice, and labor groups. Organizes teach-ins, local actions, and rallies.

V023
Movement for Economic Justice
1605 Connecticut Avenue, N.W.
Washington, DC 20009
202/462-4200   ✳

✳ *Just Economics (bimonthly/$12)*

Publishes magazine (with Institute for Social Justice) about poor people's issues with good suggestions for organizing. Campaigns on timely issues of poor; outgrowth of welfare rights movement. Current focus on jobs and justice.

V024
Movement for a New Society
4722 Baltimore Avenue
Philadelphia, PA 19143
215/SA9-3276   ✳✦✦

✳ *Dandelion (quarterly/$3.50)*
✦ *Moving Toward a New Society*
✦ *New Society Packet ($.70)*

Switchboard for oldest national network of autonomous local groups dedicated to non-violent social change. Collectives form around issues such as nuclear power, feminism, global justice, and nonviolence training. Publishes extensively.

V025
National Association of Office Workers
1224 Huron Road
Cleveland, OH 44115
216/566-9308   ✳

✳ *Working Women Newsletter (bimonthly/$5)*

Key node in the movement to gain equal rights for women office workers. Successful actions in many cities for back pay, pay raises, and promotion. Developing policy and influencing public opinion on needs of working women.

V026
National Committee Against Repressive Legislation
510 C Street, N.E.
Washington, DC 20002
202/543-7659

Activist group that keeps tabs on repressive legislation. Worked for repeal of Emergency Detention Act and "No Knock Laws." Shares mailing list. Successor to Committee to Abolish the House Un-American Activities Committee (HUAC).

V027
National Indian Youth Council
201 Hermosa, N.E.
Albuquerque, NM 87108
505/266-7966   ✳

✳ *Americans Before Columbus (monthly/$8)*

Long-standing service organization based on preservation and enrichment of traditional tribal communities. Works to prevent coal gasification and strip mining on Native land. Education and action against uranium mining; job training.

V028
New American Movement
3244 North Clark Street
Chicago, IL 60657
312/871-7700 ✳✳

✳ *Moving On (bimonthly/$5)*
✳ *Reproductive Rights Newsletter (4 issues/$3)*

National focus for local chapters of organization that blends feminism and socialism. Concerned with reproductive rights, energy, housing, employment, and international issues. Magazine, working papers, and newsletter.

V029
New England Human Rights Network
c/o American Friends Service Committee
2161 Massachusetts Avenue
Cambridge, MA 02140
617/661-6130 ✳

✳ *New England Human Rights Newsletter (12 issues/$5 year)*

Crossroads for human-rights issues in New England. Coalition of 25 local groups. Exchanges information, works for passage of human-rights legislation, and organizes actions. Maintains speaker and resource file.

V030
New Ways to Work
457 Kingsley Avenue
Palo Alto, CA 94301
415/321-9675 ✳

✳ *New Ways to Work (4 issues/$5)*

Entry point to San Francisco Bay Area world of "alternative work." Offers job-related counseling, job listings, and workshops. Maintains resource library, conducts Job Sharing Project, and publishes reports on workplace innovations.

V031
Peacework
c/o American Friends Service Committee
2161 Massachusetts Avenue
Cambridge, MA 02140
617/661-6130 ✳

✳ *Peacework (monthly/$5)*

Newsletter of the New England peace movement. Informative, interesting, and provocative news and political commentary. Many listings. Begun in 1972 as antidraft and war-tax-resistance newsletter.

V032
Planner's Network
360 Elizabeth Street
San Francisco, CA 94114
415/282-1249 ✳

✳ *Planners Network (bimonthly)*

Network of professionals primarily interested in urban planning and decentralization. Excellent example of progressive support network within a profession, focusing on issues, trading ideas, and reporting on local action.

V033
Project Work
490 Riverside Drive, Room 517
New York, NY 10027
212/777-0200 ✳◆

✳ *Project Work Newsletter (6 issues/$5)*
◆ *Alternative Work in New York City*

Entry point to New York City world of "alternative work." Technical assistance on cooperatives, job sharing, collectives, and democratic management. Serves as clearinghouse for workplace democracy movement.

V034
Renewal Newsletter: New Values, New Politics
P.O. Box 3242
Winchester, VA 22601 ✳◆

✳ *Renewal: New Values, New Politics (triweekly/$15)*
◆ *New Age Politics (Satin, $5)*

Unusual and informative newsletter concerned with politics and social transformation. Contains otherwise hard-to-find international news, book reviews, short first-person stories, and conference reports.

V035
SANE
514 C Street, N.E.
Washington, DC 20002
202/546-4868 ✳

✳ *SANE World (monthly/$4)*

Grandparent of the ban-the-bomb peace groups. Lobbies and educates on arms control, nuclear disarmament, the MX missile, conversion of defense facilities to peaceful purposes, and opposition to the new draft.

V036
SkillsBank
340 South Pioneer Street
Ashland, OR 97520
503/482-2265   ✳

✳ *SkillsBank Newsletter (6 issues/$10)*

Successful exchange network in which 500
people share about 450 skills including
accounting, child care, plumbing, tutoring,
and music. Maintains tool library and publishes newsletter.

V037
Vocations for Social Change
P.O. Box 211, Essex Sta.
Boston, MA 02112
617/423-1621   ◆✳◆

◆ *Boston People's Yellow Pages ($4.95)*
✳ *What's Left in Boston (monthly/$5)*
◆ *Your Rights as a Worker ($2)*

Inventors of the Boston People's Yellow
Pages, now in 5th edition. Publish and distribute 12 titles dealing with work and economics. Provide referrals for workers'
problems and for people seeking jobs.

V038
We-Know-Now Free Trade Exchange
122 East 2nd Street
Winona, MN 55987
507/454-2474   ✳

✳ *Free Trade: News 'n Views (biweekly)*

Meeting ground for many "sane alternatives"
groups in Minnesota. Storefront for free trade
exchange, an alternative to barter.

V039
Women U.S.A.
76 Beaver Street
New York, NY 10005
212/422-1414

National communications network that links
women on basic political and economic
issues. Organizes petition drives, distributes
timely news alerts, and maintains 800 telephone numbers with taped 90-second messages by prominent women.

V040
Women's Action Alliance
370 Lexington Avenue, #603
New York, NY 10017
212/532-8330   ◆

◆ *Women's Action Almanac ($7.95)*

First national clearinghouse on women's
issues and programs. Ongoing services
include development of National Women's
Agenda (Women's Bill of Rights), nonsexist
child development, and technical assistance.

V101
Abortion Fund
1801 K Street, N.W., Suite 200
Washington, DC 20006

V102
Accion/Micro Enterprise Development
  Corporation
P.O. Box 147
Pittsfield, ME 04967
207/487-3195

V103
Agape Foundation: Fund for Nonviolent Social
  Change
944 Market Street, Room 510
San Francisco, CA 94102
415/391-4196

V104
Akwesasne Notes: For Native and Natural
  Peoples
Mohawk Nation
Via Rooseveltown, NY 13683
518/358-9531   ✳◆◆

V105
Alternatives to Violence Project
15 Rutherford Place
New York, NY 10003
212/677-2593   ✳

V106
American Town Meetings Project
611 Longshore Drive
Ann Arbor, MI 48105
313/665-5579

V107
Amnesty International
National Office
304 West 58th Street
New York, NY 10019

V108
Anarchist Association of the Americas
P.O. Box 840, Ben Franklin Sta.
Washington, DC 20044   ✳

V109
Animal Rights Network
P.O. Box 5234
Westport, CT 06880   ✦

V110
Another Mother for Peace
407 North Maple Drive
Beverly Hills, CA 90210

V111
Armistice/Live Without Trident
P.O. Box 12007
Seattle, WA 98102
206/324-1489   ✳

V112
Association for Self-Management
1747 Connecticut Avenue, N.W.
Washington, DC 20009
202/265-7727   ✳

V113
Association of Libertarian Feminists
15 West 38th Street, #201
New York, NY 10018
212/274-5059   ✳

V114
Association on American Indian Affairs
432 Park Avenue South
New York, NY 10016   ✳

V115
Back to the People: New Age Goods
Long Corner Road
Mt. Airy, MD 21771
301/831-7726

V116
Bay Area Lawyers for the Arts
Fort Mason, Building 310
San Francisco, CA 94123
415/775-7200   ✳

V117
Black Law Journal
Dodd Hall, #A2
University of California
Los Angeles, CA 90024
213/825-7941   ✳

V118
Boston INFACT
c/o University Christian Movement
11 Garden Street
Cambridge, MA 02138
617/491-5314

V119
Boston Study Group
P.O. Box 198
Chestnut Hill, MA 02167   ✦

V120
Brown Committee
630 Shatto Place
Los Angeles, CA 90005
213/385-1982   ✳

V121
Bulletin of the Atomic Scientists
1020-24 East 58th Street
Chicago, IL 60637
312/363-5225   ✳

V122
California Agrarian Action Project
P.O. Box 464
Davis, CA 95616
916/756-8518   ✳

V123
California Housing Information and Action Network
2936 West 8th Street
Los Angeles, CA 90005

V124
California Tax Reform Association
1228½ H Street
Sacramento, CA 95814
916/446-0145   ✳

V125
Campaign for Political Rights
201 Massachusetts Avenue, N.E.
Washington, DC 20002
202/547-4705   ✳✦

V126
Catalyst National Network
14 East 60th Street
New York, NY 10022
212/759-9700   ✦

V127
Caucus for a New Political Science
420 West 118th Street, #733
New York, NY 10027   ✳

V128
Center for Auto Safety
1346 Connecticut Avenue, N.W.
Washington, DC 20036
202/659-1126   ✳✦

V129
Center for Conflict Resolution
731 State Street
Madison, WI 53703
608/255-4079   ✳

V130
Center for Conflict Resolution
George Mason University
4400 University Drive
Fairfax, VA 22030
703/323-2038

V131
Center for Defense Information
122 Maryland Avenue, N.E.
Washington, DC 20002
202/543-0400   ✳◆◆

V132
Center for National Security Studies
P.O. Box 423
Lawrence, KS 66044
202/544-5380   ✳

V133
Center for New National Security
1768 Lanier Place, N.W.
Washington, D.C. 20005
202/232-5103

V134
Center for Non-Profit Organization
155 West 72nd Street, Suite #604
New York, NY 10023
212/873-7580   ◆

V135
Center for Nonviolent Persuasion
3229 Bordeaux
Sherman, TX 75090
214/893-3886   ✳◆

V136
Center for Popular Economics
P.O. Box 785
Amherst, MA 01002

V137
Center for Public Representation
520 University Avenue
Madison, WI 53703
608/251-4008   ✳

V138
Center for Research on Criminal Justice
P.O. Box 4373
Berkeley, CA 94704

V139
Center for Women in Government
SUNY Albany, Draper Hall, Room 302
1400 Washington Avenue
Albany, NY 12222
518/455-6211   ✳

V140
Center for a Woman's Own Name
261 Kimberly Street
Barrington, IL 60010
312/381-2113   ◆

V141
Center for the Study of Responsive Law
P.O. Box 19367
Washington, DC 20036   ✳✳◆

V142
Center on Law and Pacifism
P.O. Box 1584
Colorado Springs, CO 80901
303/635-0041   ✳

V143
**Children's Legal Rights Information and Training
   Program**
2008 Hillyer Place, N.W.
Washington, DC 20009
202/332-6575   ✳

V144
Citizen Action
336 Chester - 12th Building
Cleveland, OH 44114
216/861-5200   ✳

V145
Citizen Alert
P.O. Box 5391
Reno, NV 89513
702/786-4220

V146
Citizen Soldier
175 Fifth Avenue, #1010
New York, NY 10010
212/777-3470   ✳◆

V147
Citizens Commission on Police Repression
633 South Shatto Place, #200
Los Angeles, CA 90005
213/387-3937   ✳

V148
Citizens Party
1605 Connecticut Avenue, N.W.
Washington, DC 20009
202/232-3996

V149
Civilian Congress
2361 Mission Street
San Francisco, CA 94110
415/673-7638   ◆

V150
Coalition to End Grand Jury Abuse
105 2nd Street, N.W.
Washington, DC 20002
202/547-0138   ✦

V151
Come Unity: An Alternative Independent Journal
7419 Third Avenue
St. Petersburg, FL 33710   ✳

V152
**Committee for Action Research on the
    Intelligence Community**
P.O. Box 647, Ben Franklin Sta.
Washington, DC 20044   ✳

V153
Committee on Native American Struggles
National Lawyers Guild
P.O. Box 6401
Albuquerque, NM 87197   ✳

V154
Common Cause
2030 M Street, N.W.
Washington, DC 20036
202/833-1200   ✳

V155
Conscience and Military Tax Campaign
44 Bellhaven Road
Bellhaven, NY 11713
516/286-8824

V156
Constructive Citizen Participation
P.O. Box 1016
Oakville, Ontario
CANADA L6J 1B8
416/845-4714   ✳

V157
Consumer Education Research Group
17 Freeman Street
West Orange, NJ 07052   ✳

V158
Consumer Information Center
Pueblo, CO 81009   ✦

V159
**Crafts Report: Marketing and Management for
    Crafts Professionals**
700 Orange Street
Wilmington, DE 19899
302/656-2209   ✳

V160
Cultural Correspondence
c/o Dorrwar Bookstore
107½ Hope Street
Providence, RI 02906

V161
Custody Action for Lesbian Mothers
P.O. Box 281
Narberth, PA 19072
215/667-7508

V162
Democratic Socialist Organizing Committee
853 Broadway, #801
New York, NY 10003
212/260-3270   ✳

V163
Disability Rights Center
1346 Connecticut Avenue, N.W.
Washington, DC 20036
202/223-3304   ✦✦

V164
Displaced Homemakers Network
755 8th Street, N.W.
Washington, DC 20001
202/347-0522   ✳✦

V165
ERAmerica
1525 M Street, N.W.
Washington, DC 20005

V166
Engage/Social Action
United Methodist Church
100 Maryland Avenue, N.E.
Washington, DC 20002
202/546-6924   ✳

V167
**Equal Times: Boston's Newspaper for Working
    Women**
235 Park Square Building
Boston, MA 02116
617/426-1981   ✳

V168
Eschaton Foundation: Community Spirit Fund
P.O. Box 2324
Santa Cruz, CA 95063

V169
Exploratory Project for Economic Alternatives
2000 P Street, N.W.
Washington, DC 20036
202/833-3208   ✦✦✦

V170
Federal Laboratory Consortium
c/o National Science Foundation
Washington, DC 20550
202/634-7996

V171
Feminist Alliance Against Rape
P.O. Box 21033
Washington, DC 20009
202/466-8629 ✳

V172
Focus/Midwest
928a North McKnight
St. Louis, MO 63132 ✳

V173
Free For All
1623 Granville Avenue, #11
Los Angeles, CA 90025
213/826-9665

V174
Freedom of Information Clearinghouse
P.O. Box 19367
Washington, DC 20036 ◆

V175
Friends Peace Committee
1515 Cherry Street
Philadelphia, PA 19102
215/241-7230 ◆◆

V176
Give and Take Bartering Center
135 Church Street
Burlington, VT 05401
802/864-0449

V177
Government Institutes
4733 Bethesda Avenue, N.W.
Washington, DC 20014
301/656-1090

V178
Greensboro Justice Fund
853 Broadway, Room 1912
New York, NY 10003 ✳

V179
Halt: Americans for Legal Reform
201 Massachusetts Avenue, N.E.
Washington, DC 20002

V180
Harvest Publications
907 Santa Barbara Street
Santa Barbara, CA 93101 ◆

V181
Home Equity Conversion Project
110 East Main Street, Room 1020
Madison, WI 53703
608/266-8103

V182
Homemakers Organized for More Employment
P.O. Box 408
Orland, ME 04472 ◆

V183
Human Economy Center
P.O. Box 551
Amherst, MA 01004
413/253-5428 ✳◆

V184
Indochina Curriculum Group
11 Garden Street
Cambridge, MA 02138
617/354-6583 ◆

V185
Inform, Incorporated
25 Broad Street
New York, NY 10004
212/425-3550 ✳

V186
Inmate Legal Association
Third & Federal Street
Trenton, NJ 08625

V187
Institute for Labor Education and Research
853 Broadway #2007
New York, NY 10003
212/674-3322 ✳◆

V188
Institute for Peace and Justice
2913 Locust Street
St. Louis, MO 63103
314/533-4445 ✳

V189
Institute for Social Justice/Eastern Office
100 Massachusetts Avenue
Boston, MA 02115
617/266-7130

V190
Institute for Social Service Alternatives
P.O. Box 1144, Cathedral Sta.
New York, NY 10025 ✳

V191
**International Seminars in Training for
   Nonviolent Action**
P.O. Box 38
South Boston, MA 02127
617/926-6015 ✳

V192
Jewish Peace Fellowship
P.O. Box 271
Nyack, NY 10960
914/EL8-4601 ✳

V193
Joint Center for Political Studies
1301 Pennsylvania Avenue, N.W.
Washington, DC 20004
202/626-3500   ◆

V194
**Kapitalistate: Working Papers on the Capitalist
    State**
P.O. Box 5138
Berkley, CA 94705   ✳

V195
King City Senior Barter Bank
400 King City Courthouse
Seattle, WA 98104
206/344-7394

V196
League for Ecological Democracy
P.O. Box 1858
San Pedro, CA 90733
213/833-2633   ✳

V197
Legal Services Corporation
733 15th Street, N.W.
Washington, DC 20005
202/272-4000

V198
Libertarian Review
1404 Franklin Street
Oakland, CA 94612
415/832-5093

V199
Looking Left
State University of New York
Binghamton, NY 13901
607/798-2484   ✳✳

V200
**Los Angeles Commission on Assaults Against
    Women**
543 North Fairfax Avenue
Los Angeles, CA 90036
213/392-8381   ◆◆

V201
**Making It Legal: Primer for Craftmaker, Artist
    and Writer**
P.O. Box 463
Flagstaff, AZ 86002   ◆

V202
Maryland Food Committee
105 West Monument Street
Baltimore, MD 21201
301/837-5667   ✳

V203
Massachusetts Public Interest Research Group
120 Boylston Street
Boston, MA 02116
617/423-1796   ✳

V204
Mental Health Law Project
1220 19th Street, N.W., #300
Washington, DC 20036
202/467-5730

V205
**Mexican American Legal Defense and
    Educational Fund**
28 Geary Street
San Francisco, CA 94108
415/981-5800   ✳

V206
Midwest Committee for Military Counseling
59 East Van Buren Street, #809
Chicago, IL 60605
312/939-3349   ◆

V207
Mother Jones
625 Third Street
San Francisco, CA 94107
415/495-6326   ✳

V208
National Abortion Federation
110 East 59th Street
New York, NY 10022
212/688-8516   ✳

V209
**National Action Committee on the Status of
    Women**
40 St. Clair Avenue East, Suite 306
Toronto, Ontario
CANADA M4T 1M9
416/922-3246   ✳

V210
**National Action/Research on the Military
    Industrial Complex**
c/o American Friends Service Committee
1501 Cherry Street
Philadelphia, PA 19102
215/241-7175   ◆

V211
National Committee for Responsive Philanthropy
810 18th Street, N.W., #408
Washington, DC 20006
202/347-5340   ✳

V212
National Consumer Cooperative Bank
2001 S Street, N.W.
Washington, DC 20009
800/424-2481

V213
National Council of La Raza
1725 Eye Street, N.W., #200
Washington, DC 20006
202/923-4680 ✳

V214
National Economic Development and Law
    Center
2150 Shattuck Avenue
Berkeley, CA 94704
415/548-2600 ✳

V215
National Gay Task Force
80 Fifth Avenue
New York, NY 10011
212/741-5800 ✳

V216
National Lawyers Guild
853 Broadway, #1705
New York, NY 10003
212/260-1360 ✳

V217
National Network of Grantmakers
919 North Michigan Avenue
Chicago, IL 60611 ◆

V218
National Organization for Women
P.O. Box 7813
Washington, DC 20044
202/347-2279 ✳

V219
National Organization for an American
    Revolution
P.O. Box 2617
Philadelphia, PA 19142

V220
National Organization for the Reform of
    Marijuana Laws
530 Eighth Street, S.E.
Washington, DC 20003
202/223-3170 ✳

V221
National Prison Project
1346 Connecticut Avenue, N.W.
Washington, DC 20036
202/331-0500 ◆

V222
National Resistance Committee
P.O. Box 42488
San Francisco, CA 94101
415/524-4778

V223
Network: A Catholic Social Justice Lobby
806 Rhode Island Avenue, N.E.
Washington, DC 20018
202/526-4070 ✳

V224
Nevada Elected Women's Network
P.O. Box 218
McDermitt, NV 89421 ✳

V225
New Age Caucus
11771 Santa Monica Boulevard
Santa Monica, CA 90025
213/473-2219 ✳

V226
New Directions for Women
223 Old Hook Road
Westwood, NJ 07675
201/666-4677 ✳

V227
New Directions for Young Women
376 South Stone Avenue
Tucson, AZ 85701
602/623-3677

V228
New England Cooperative Training Institute
216 Crown Street, Room 404
New Haven, CT 06510
203/562-3551

V229
New England Free Press
60 Union Square
Somerville, MA 02143
617/628-2450 ◆

V230
New Seed Press Feminist Collective
P.O. Box 3016
Stanford, CA 94305 ◆◆◆

V231
New World Alliance
733 15th Street, N.W., #1131
Washington, DC 20005
202/347-6082 ✳

V232
New World Review
156 Fifth Avenue, #308
New York, NY 10010
212/243-0666 ✳◆

V233
New York Public Interest Research Group
5 Beekman Street
New York, NY 10038
212/349-6460   ✳

V234
Nine to Five (9 to 5)
140 Clarendon Street
Boston, MA 02116
617/536-6003

V235
North Country M.N.S. Organizing Collective
2412 University Avenue, S.E.
Minneapolis, MN 55414
612/373-8351

V236
Off Our Backs: A Women's News Journal
1724 20th Street, N.W.
Washington, DC 20009
202/234-8072   ✳

V237
Ohio Public Interest Campaign
340 Chester - 12th Building
Cleveland, OH 44114

V238
One Less Bomb Committee
551 Hayward Mill Road
Concord, MA 01742
617/369-8751

V239
Open Road
P.O. Box 6135, Station G
Vancouver, British Columbia
CANADA V6R 4G5   ✳

V240
Organization Resource Associates
106 East Bridge Street
Berea, OH 44017
216/243-3740

V241
Peace Project
1290D Maunakea Street, #244
Honolulu, HI 96817

V242
People's Business Commission
1346 Connecticut Avenue, N.W.
Washington, DC 20036
202/466-2823   ◆◆◆

V243
Physicians for Social Responsibility
P.O. Box 144
56 North Beacon Street
Watertown, MA 02172
617/924-3468   ✳

V244
Popular Economics Press
P.O. Box 221
Somerville, MA 02143
617/628-2450   ◆

V245
Powder River Basin Resource Council
48 North Main Street
Sheridan, WY 82801
307/672-5809   ✳

V246
Prisoners Union
1315 18th Street
San Francisco, CA 94107
415/648-2880   ✳

V247
Privacy Journal
P.O. Box 8844
Washington, DC 20003
202/547-2865

V248
Productivity Group
5103 Beverly Skyline
Austin, TX 78731

V249
Project Equality
4049 Pennsylvania, 2nd Floor
Kansas City, MO 64111
816/561-0811   ◆

V250
Public Eye: A Journal Concerning Repression in America
343 South Dearborn, #918
Chicago, IL 60604   ✳

V251
Radical Alliance of Social Service Workers
P.O. Box 70
New York, NY 10028

V252
Radical America
38 Union Square
Somerville, MA 02143
617/628-6585   ✳

V253
Recon Publications
P.O. Box 14602
Philadelphia, PA 19134   ◆◆

V254
Robert's Think Tank
P.O. Box 2161
Bellingham, WA 98227   ✳

V255
Rocky Flats Nuclear Weapons Facilities Project
American Friends Service Committee
1660 Lafayette Street, Suite D
Denver, CO 80218
303/832-4508   ◆

V256
Sanity Now!
P.O. Box 261
La Puente, CA 91747   ✳

V257
Second Wave: Magazine of the New Feminism
P.O. Box 344
Cambridge, MA 02139   ✳

V258
Sister Courage: Radical Feminist Newspaper
P.O. Box 296
Allston, MA 02134   ✳

V259
Social Advocates for Youth
975 North Point Street
San Francisco, CA 94109
415/928-3222   ✳

V260
**Sojourner: Northeast Women's Journal of News
    and the Arts**
143 Albany Street
Cambridge, MA 02139
617/661-3567   ✳

V261
South Carolina Committee Against Hunger
1726 Hampton Street
Columbia, SC 29201
803/254-0183

V262
South Carolina Libertarian Party
P.O. Box 50115
Columbia, SC 29503
803/254-VOTE   ✳

V263
Southern Coalition on Jails and Prisons
P.O. Box 120044
Nashville, TN 37212   ✳

V264
Southern Poverty Law Center
1001 South Hull Street
Montgomery, AL 36101

V265
Syracuse Peace Council
924 Burnet Avenue
Syracuse, NY 13203
315/472-5478   ✳

V266
Tarrytown Group
Tarrytown Conference Center
East Sunnyside Lane
Tarrytown, NY 10591
914/591-8200   ✳

V267
Tax Reform Research Group
215 Pennsylvania Avenue, S.E.
Washington, DC 20003
202/544-1710   ✳◆

V268
Taxation With Representation
6830 North Fairfax Drive
Arlington, VA 22213
703/532-1850   ✳✳

V269
Team for Justice
1035 St. Antoine
Detroit, MI 48226
313/965-3242   ✳

V270
The Militant: Socialist Newsweekly
14 Charles Lane
New York, NY 10014
212/929-3486   ✳

V271
The Spokeswoman: Feminist News Digest
53 West Jackson Street, #525
Chicago, IL 60604   ✳

V272
Toolbox Training and Skills-sharing Collective
337 17th Avenue East
Seattle, WA 98112
206/322-4962

V273
Toronto Association for Peace
P.O. Box 37, Station E
Toronto, Ontario
CANADA M6H 4E1
416/245-7408   ◆

V274
Transaction Periodicals Consortium
Rutgers–The State University
New Brunswick, NJ 08903
201/932-2280   ✳

V275
Tribal Sovereignty Program
P.O. Box 10
Forestville, CA 95436
707/887-7256   ✳

V276
Union Women's Alliance to Gain Equality
P.O. Box 40904
San Francisco, CA 94140
415/282-6777   ✳

V277
Union for Radical Political Economics
41 Union Square, #901
New York, NY 10003   ✳

V278
Union of Concerned Scientists
1384 Massachusetts Avenue
Cambridge, MA 02138
617/547-5552   ✳

V279
Vanguard Public Foundation
4111 24th Street
San Francisco, CA 94114
415/285-2005   ◆

V280
Vermont Alliance
5 State Street
Montpelier, VT 05602
802/229-9104

V281
Veterans Education Project
American Civil Liberties Union Foundation
1346 Connecticut Avenue, N.W.
Washington, DC 20036
202/466-2244   ✳

V282
Vietnam Veterans Against the War
P.O. Box 20184
Chicago, IL 60620
312/651-1583   ✳

V283
Washington Monthly
2712 Ontario Road, N.W.
Washington, DC 20009
202/462-0128   ✳

V284
Washington Spectator & Between the Lines
P.O. Box 442
Merrifield, VA 22116   ✳

V285
Wisconsin Women's Network
625 West Washington Street
Madison, WI 53703
608/255-9809   ✳◆

V286
Woman Activist: Action Bulletin for Women's Rights
2310 Barbour Road
Falls Church, VA 22043
703/573-8716   ✳

V287
Women Against Violence Against Women
543 North Fairfax Avenue
Los Angeles, CA 90036
213/223-8771   ✳

V288
Women Against Violence in Pornography and Media
P.O. Box 14614
San Francisco, CA 94114
415/552-2709   ✳

V289
Women's Enterprises of Boston
739 Boylston Street
Boston, MA 02116
617/266-2243   ✳

V290
Women's Equity Action League
805 15th Street, N.W., Suite 822
Washington, DC 20005
202/638-4560   ✳✳◆

V291
Women's Legal Defense Fund
2000 P Street, N.W., Suite 400
Washington, DC 20036
202/887-0346   ✳◆

V292
Women's Party for Survival
7 Gilmore Street
Everett, MA 01249

V293
Women's Work Force Network
1511 K Street, N.W.
Washington, DC 20006
202/628-3143   ✳

V294
Working Papers for a New Society
186 Hampshire Street
Cambridge, MA 02139   ✳

V295
Working Women's Institute
593 Park Avenue
New York, NY 10021
212/838-4420

V296
Youth International Party
P.O. Box 392, Canal Street Sta.
New York, NY 10013
212/533-5028

V297
Youth Project
1555 Connecticut Avenue, N.W.
Washington, DC 20036
202/483-0030

7

Learning Networks:
Education and Communications

Home schools, alternative schools, community schools, learning exchanges, experiential learning and universities without walls are but a few of the courses that people are using to keep education consistent with their values and with the larger patterns of their lives. Newsletters, magazines, journals, handbooks, radio programs, audio tapes, films, video cassettes, computer conferences, and satellites are examples of the media people are using to communicate. Educating and communicating are natural to networking.

To illustrate how networking can work, we retrace one of the journeys we made in exploring Another America: specifically, the pathway that led us to the experiential education network.

In the past decade, experiential education has been incorporated into American education from kindergarten to the postgraduate level. Students acquire practical experience while learning: Sixth-graders spend a week on a farm, high school students work part time in a day-care center, college nursing students work in hospitals, graduate students receive course credit for the "real-life" experience of working in mental-health clinics.

Our networking journey illustrates both how we mapped the territory in various areas and how networks function by forming links along lines of tenuous and tangential connections and related interests. Our odyssey is also a multileveled tale in the spirit of psychologist Stanley Milgram, who found that anyone in America can reach anyone else by going through a statistical average of no more than 5.5 other people. In this example, we reached the universe of experiential education at our fourth "stop" of inquiry. Along the path of this particular itinerary within our larger networking junket, we passed by more than 1500 other groups and individuals.

Our tour begins at Stop 0, in Newton, Massachusetts, where we sent our very first letter of inquiry for the book to Robert A. Smith, III at Stop 1, then living in Huntsville, Alabama (see Chapter 12). Two of the nine referrals that Smith sent to us were Peter and Trudy Johnson-Lenz (see below) at Stop 2, in Lake Oswego, Oregon, and Robert Theobald at Stop 2A, in Wickenburg, Arizona. Both referred us on to Leif Smith at Stop 3, at the "office for Open Network" (described later in this chapter), in Colorado, but in two very different ways: The Johnson-Lenzes wrote us a note suggesting three contacts, the first of which was Leif Smith; Theobald's referral came, in characteristic networking fashion, indirectly.

At the time that Theobald received our letter, both he and the Johnson-Lenzes were members of the Electronic Information Exchange System (EIES), a computer conferencing system (described later in this chapter) based in Newark, New Jersey. Theobald sent a copy of our letter to a group of people participating in a conference called the TRANSFORM Exchange on the EIES computer system. Among the people receiving the letter was Charlton Price at Stop 2B, in Tacoma, Washington, who was then serving as the editor of the EIES newsletter, *Chimo*. Price published our letter to Theobald in the electronic newsletter available to everyone on the computer system (which we subsequently learned about when Price sent us a copy of the newsletter item in the mail). Another user of the computer conferencing system, David

Voremberg, at Stop 2C, in Somerville, Massachusetts (about 15 minutes from our home), saw the same message in the electronic newsletter, called us on the phone and, among other suggestions, mentioned that we should contact Smith in Denver.

So we wrote to Smith at Stop 3. He and his coworker, Patricia Wagner, responded first with a telephone call and then with a follow-up packet of materials that included two years' of their tabloid newspaper (no longer being published) containing several hundred more references, which we then combed looking for people and groups that seemed relevant and/or intriguing. Among those names was that of Maria Snyder, who became Stop 4, at the Association for Experiential Education, located in Denver, which publishes the *Journal of Experiential Education*. In contacting Snyder, we had reached an entry point into the experiential-education metanetwork.

Snyder responded quickly and fully, providing us with yet another list of names, including that of the Council for Advancement of Experiential Learning (CAEL), at Stop 5, in Columbia, Maryland. CAEL is both a node point for research in experiential education, and one of twelve participating links in the Coalition for Alternatives in Postsecondary Education (CAPE), at Stop 6, in Frankfort, Kentucky. CAPE's General Secretary, Robert Sexton, responded to our inquiry, incidentally telling us that our letter "arrived after having been shredded by some kind of postal machine." Apparently, the letter remained sufficiently legible for him to understand what we were looking for, because he sent a pile of documents explaining that CAPE works on policy issues affecting teachers, administrators, institutions, and students involved in nontraditional higher-education programs.

Sexton referred us on to each of CAPE's twelve members; eventually, we received a response from the Free University Network (FUN), at Stop 7, whose headquarters in Manhattan, Kansas, serves as the exchange point for 247 participating groups in 40 states and Canada. FUN's universe includes both course-offering groups and learning exchanges, which operate through telephone referrals and information banks. The Kansas office sponsors conferences and workshops, provides technical assistance, and publishes a directory of its member organizations, one of which is at Boston College, in Newton, Massachusetts, where our search for information began.

In this chapter, we explore the education and communications channels of Another America: *educational choices* matching every grade level of the traditional institutions; *learning resources*, including learning exchanges, clearinghouses, and resource centers (which cross the ever-shifting line between education and communication); *inspirational journalism*; and *computer-aided networking*, which may soon become commonplace as access to decentralized small-scale computers spreads.

EDUCATIONAL CHOICES

Like many people reading this book, we have spent a lot of time in schools, all together 45 years–representing more than 60 percent of our lives. We have experienced most of what Western education offers: public and private schools; Ivy League, state-supported, and experimental colleges and universities; and the refined bulwark of Western erudition where students still wear black gowns to classes and evening meals: Oxford University. In our experience, learning has as little to do with schools as healing has to do with hospitals or spirituality has to do with churches. Like all centralized establishments, schools are good for our mechanical brains and bad for our creative minds.

American education itself became an issue in the 1960s: among college students and some teachers who were reacting both to external political events and to the internal regimentation that had come to typify the modern American diploma mill, and among educators struggling with the structural problems of elementary, secondary, and postsecondary education. Some titles of books written in this period tell the story: *Death at an Early Age*, *Compulsory MisEducation*, *Deschooling Society*, *How Children Fail*, and *Instead of Education*.

With these titles as beginning points for developing a new philosophy of education, a movement grew up, one anticipated by the turn-of-the-century American philosopher John Dewey, the originator of the concept of progressive education. By the beginning of the 1970s, many alternative schools for youngsters had been opened and, by the end of the 1970s, "adult education" had expanded to include everything from auto repair to building a solar greenhouse. From home schools to alternative schools, from the university without walls to the learning exchange, people have been carving the many pieces that create an innovative educational mosaic for life-long learning.

One of the first people to have offered a broad critique of the American educational system is John Holt, whose book *How Children Fail* makes the clear point that schools, not children, are responsible for the failure syndrome, which is created through the performance/reward model that schools employ. Holt sums up the problems in our existing educational system, and provides the explanation for the various educational alternatives that have developed in the past two decades in the March 1978 issue of *Radcliffe Quarterly*, where he elaborates seven basic assumptions which he believes describe the dominant educational philosophy in America.

The educational networks started in the 1960s and 1970s, and continuing into the 1980s, can be regarded as reversals of or alternatives to one or more of Holt's seven points.

(1) Learning is an activity separate from the rest of life, done best when one is not doing anything else, and best of all in places where nothing else is done.

(2) Important learning is, must be, and can only be the result and product of teaching. What we learn for ourselves, from the experience of our daily lives, can only be trivial or untrue.

(3) Teaching is best done, and most often can only be done, by specialists who do no other work.

(4) Children cannot be trusted to learn about the world around them. They must be made to learn, told what to learn, and shown how.

(5) Education is a people-improving process; the more of it we have done to us, the better we are.

(6) People are raw material, bad in their original state, but almost infinitely processable and improvable.

(7) People have no right to refuse any processing or treatment that their betters believe will improve them.

Antioch College, the first institution of higher learning to use the now-popular work/study model, underscores the first two of Holt's points. The alternative education movement of the 1960s drew heavily on the complements to Holt's third and fourth criticisms when it broke down classroom walls and allowed children to

explore for themselves in natural environments. Finally, the anti-education movement and the resultant flight from the automatic B.A./M.A./Ph.D. route, characterized by the high percentage of college dropouts and decreasing enrollment in
graduate schools, were largely in reaction to Holt's final three points.

"Innovators network spontaneously," says Allen Parker, director of the Center on
Technology and Society and author of a book on networking in alternative education. Parker has made a study of some 28 educational networks, examining how they
get started, how they operate, and what they do with their work.

Through his study, Parker has identified three aspects of the alternative schools
movement operating in independent elementary and secondary schools, public elementary and secondary schools, and universities.

Within the elementary and secondary levels, two challenges to standardized public education exist: alternative schools and home schools, the latter perhaps the most
hotly debated subject within education today. Inspired by A. S. Neill's experimental
English school, Summerhill, alternative schools have their information gathering
point in the National Coalition of Alternative Community Schools, which publishes
a directory including more than 100 resources and describes the schools as follows:

> The schools are small, frequently serving fewer than fifty students total; they
> maintain low student-teacher ratios. They offer a wide variety of activities to
> learners as part of the everyday fare—open learning environments, apprentice-
> ship programs, overnight trips away from the school, the use of the community
> as the classroom, and more. They are alternatives to conventional schooling.

Alternative-school students are offered approaches such as the Montessori method,
which stresses a utilitarian approach to learning, the Steiner method, which encourages learning through the use of music, dance, and art, and many other, more eclectic
educational philosophies.

The home schooling movement has been significantly influenced by Holt, who,
along with author Ivan Illich, questions the value of institutionalized learning of any
sort—whether standard or alternative—all of which Holt calls "compulsory schooling," an accurate term to describe the once-lauded attempt to provide education for
the masses. In 1978, Holt began publication of *Growing Without Schooling* (GWS), a
newsletter that reports and exchanges information about teaching children at home.

Holt's newsletter includes reports on home schooling from parents, summaries of
legal cases in various states (parents frequently must fight for the right to educate
their children at home), how-to tips, news from abroad, and an occasional directory
listing of home schoolers by state. GWS is one of the best networking tools in print
and a good model for other networks: it is simply designed, easy to read, and
inexpensive to produce, as almost all of the copy is typed.

Working directly on the legal issue in alternative schooling is the National Association for the Legal Support of Alternative Schools, based in Santa Fe, New Mexico,
and headed by Ed Nagel, an imaginative educator who describes himself as
"teacher/lawyer/janitor" at the Santa Fe Community School, founded in 1970.
Despite the trials that have beleaguered him and other alternative schoolers, Nagel
manages to maintain a sense of humor that shines through both his chatty newsletter, *Tidbits*, and his book, *Cheez! Uncle Sam*.

It is difficult to anticipate what will become of the alternative school movement as
public-school budgets are cut, teachers are laid off, and the federal funding for education is diminished. Networks often flourish when established institutions go dormant or turn their attention elsewhere. Similarly, local networks are often the

precursors to the development of new social structures better able to meet people's needs. California's Proposition 13 and its companions in other states (such as Proposition 2-1/2 in Massachusetts) may ultimately create the conditions supporting an even greater flowering of the alternative education movement.

Within the many debates of the 1960s were some fundamental areas of agreement—at least among those who were truly concerned with learning (in contrast to those who were truly concerned with preserving the structure of the institution). They agreed that courses and credits and degrees were only the mechanics of learning, not the process. As the 1970s wore on, even the disciplines themselves split open as the outcry against specialism reached into every field of study (see Chapter 11).

Many have experimented with expanding the boundaries of traditional education. The new college movement of the late 1960s, for example, proliferated into a carnival of experiments in higher education. Poet Judson Jerome's Inner (within Antioch) College was one of the original seedbeds for testing ideas with a committed core group of several dozen students and teachers, in which participant/observation was used to keep roles fluid and processes dynamic. The Inner College was its own laboratory, closed to the larger college.

Networkers in higher education have pushed beyond the brick and mortar, creating universities without walls, setting education a-sail in floating colleges, and decentralizing it completely into community learning centers. Here students are older, more experienced, and committed by life choice to learning.

In the past decade, new institutions of high academic quality have been created that work from the assumption that competent people can direct their own learning sufficiently to complete an advanced-degree program without the ritual of classes and weekly lectures. For self-motivated people, noncampus academic programs combine academic rigor and flexibility in a process that enables them to successfully integrate learning into both their personal lives and their work lives.

Robert McAndrews, an anthropologist and one of the original Peace Corps volunteers, received his Ph.D. from the Humanistic Psychology Institute (HPI), a non-residential graduate program based in San Francisco, while living and teaching in Colorado Springs, Colorado. McAndrews describes the experience as "exactly right for me. I was always a maverick student. I simply couldn't thrive in the traditional institutions, but at a place like HPI, I was able to develop my own course of study—and have it mentored by the ideal person in my field: Gregory Bateson."

HPI faculty communicate with students (whose average age is 36), by mail, telephone, occasional visits, and annual all-institute meetings. Nonresidential institutions such as HPI, the Union Graduate School, and others are moving toward the network form, paying close attention to the essence of education: communicating and sharing intellectual resources. While they were only a peripheral innovation on the educational landscape of 1980, noncampus forms of education may be expected to dramatically increase over the next decade as energy costs cause the shutdown of centralized educational plants. Moreover, even as energy costs escalate, information costs plummet, offering new options for the information-intensive models such as HPI, which by 1981 was studying the possibility of using computer conferencing (see below) to help create a nongeographic academic community.

Clearly, Ivan Illich's idea of "learning webs . . . readily available to the public and designed to spread equal opportunity for learning and teaching" delineates the appropriate educational form for the energy-poor, information-rich world of the 1980s and beyond.

LEARNING RESOURCES

While educational alternatives are being developed to supplement or replace the traditional educational institutions, new forms of educational organization are also serving the learning needs of an information age never envisioned by America's founding generations.

Learning exchanges, for example, offer a powerful tool for diversifying and redefining the nature of learning as a lifelong process. A learning exchange is the educational counterpart of the barter exchange (see Chapter 4). Within the exchange, all offerings are of equal value—and diverse beyond the modern educator's wildest imagination. Link, a learning network based at the University of Iowa, whose goal, according to comanager Brian Shaw "is to bring people together to share the knowledge each has with the other," features among its several hundred offerings model rocketry, Norwegian, old-time Irish fiddle, medieval arts, psychology of color and music, transcribing audio tapes, beekeeping, raspberry gardening, railroad history, lipreading, and general systems theory. This educational smorgasbord is a networker's dream of interest-specific offerings. Democratizing education through networking leads both to the decentralization of centers of learning and the decredentialization of expertise.

At the same time as the learning exchange has matured, so has an entirely new educational concept which is dependent upon the distillation, clarification, indexing, and dissemination of information from a wide variety of sources: the clearinghouse. Two clearinghouse networks that have made their mark within the world of education are the Educational Resources Information Center (generally known by its acronym, ERIC), a department within the National Institute of Education, and the National Diffusion Network, funded by the U.S. Office of Education.

"The ERIC system is a decentralized network involving 15 clearinghouses," explains Judi Conrad, Information Specialist for Rural, Small School and Outdoor Education. "Each clearinghouse covers a scope or scopes of interest in education. The Clearinghouse on Rural Education and Small Schools covers, in addition to rural and small school education, American Indian education, Mexican-American education, migrant education, and outdoor education."

ERIC clearinghouses gather educational literature (in such areas as adult, career, and vocational education, educational management, elementary and childhood education, education of handicapped and gifted children, and higher education), select for quality and relevance, catalog, index, and abstract the material, then enter it into the computer data base. ERIC's data are accessible both through computer searches, a process that needs further explanation to the user, provided by a 20-page booklet called "How to Use ERIC," and through books of ERIC abstracts, microfiche, and hardcopy services.

The National Diffusion Network (NDN), the largest network operating within the field of education, got its start in the early 1970s, when the budget for the Office of Education, which until that time had funded similar projects, was severely cut. After the budget cut, determined educators marshaled their forces to lobby Congress to reinstate the funding. They were successful, and as a result, some $8-10 million annually is now allocated to NDN, which spends the money on packaging existing programs and involving new people in learning about those programs. Operated out of the Far West Laboratory for Educational Research and Development, in San Francisco, NDN is organized around state facilitators who catalogue programs, which are then publicized and in some cases made available elsewhere by NDN.

While ERIC and NDN represent one end of the clearinghouse spectrum, operating by government sanction with government funds, still other groups are using the

clearinghouse concept to considerable effect with no government support and minimal funding. The Southwest Research and Information Center (SRIC), in Albuquerque, New Mexico, with no goal other than to make information available, offers
a new model for learning. This network-based learning model is unique, the product
of the information explosion as filtered through the worldview of people who are
deeply concerned about humanity's future.

Kenneth Schultz, a research associate at SRIC, describes how the group got its
start, as well as how its impressive publication, *The Workbook*, was begun:

> Networking information among people and groups around the country was a
> prime objective of Katherine and Peter Montague, founders of SRIC, from the
> beginning of the organization in 1971. Utilizing past contacts with people and
> groups around the nation, information exchanges were established. Through
> reading newsletters and journals, new people were identified. Much of the
> initial contact was with national organizations working in various
> fields—environmental issues, health and public interest concerns.

> Originally *The Workbook* was conceived as a book to network public interest
> groups around the nation. In 1974, however, it was decided to start publication
> of a magazine annotating sources of information on many issues. Additional
> groups were then contacted about information on their work and com-
> plimentary issues were sent to national and local organizations. Exchange sub-
> scriptions were established with other magazines as well as with organizations
> with newsletters.

> Today, SRIC receives over 250 publications. These publications are read or
> skimmed, with publications or activities of interest noted. Generally letters are
> then sent to the publisher or organization asking for sample copies or other
> information. Newsletters and publications are housed in our library, which is
> open to the public for reference use.

> *The Workbook* has annotated over 1500 sources of information from about
> 1000 different organizations. Despite the diversity of groups mentioned, there
> are constantly new groups starting, new ideas being tried and thereby many new
> sources of information for each issue.

SRIC also takes part in the environmental and energy movements, key issues in
New Mexico, rich in uranium and other natural resources. Thus, SRIC has been
actively involved in studying nuclear waste problems, uranium mining and milling
operations, and utility issues. The results of this research have been published in a
variety of media including pamphlets, booklets, slide shows, papers, testimonies,
and legal briefs.

The Workbook contains sections on agriculture, business/corporations, consumer
affairs, economy/taxes, energy, food/nutrition, government, military, health care,
housing, information, land use, mental institutions, minorities, the Third World,
natural resources, pollution/environment, regions, rural life, transportation, urban life,
and women. Subtitled "access to information," *The Workbook* describes its credo
this way: " *The Workbook* staff believes that war, racism, sexism, poverty, crime and
environmental destruction are all parts of the same problem. Solutions to the problem will require action on many fronts. We hope *The Workbook* can serve this vast,
nameless movement for change."

Fragmenting knowledge, seeing myriad isolated problems rather than connecting
patterns of problems and solutions, is inherent in the very structure of our academic

disciplines. The prevailing scientific dogmas underlying the ways in which people have been taught for the past several hundred years is reductionism, the "break it down" approach to learning. Thus, like the natural sciences, the physical sciences, and medicine, education has become an assemblage of little pigeonholes neatly stacked together in buildings and along corridors, yet woefully isolated one from another.

This critique of specialization in education is not new; indeed, the movement to create cross-disciplinary majors at the college level evolved precisely out of this recognition. However, the solution to specialism is not to do more of it. In other words, the problems inherent in the specialist approach to sociology, for example, cannot be resolved by also studying the specialties of anthropology, early American literature, and Florentine art. At best, this approach produces a multispecialist (a bio-physio-neuro-linguist) but does not produce a competent generalist who searches for "the patterns which connect," which Bateson perceived.

Some of the earliest theoretical work on networks emerged out of the recognition that ideas in academia grow in "invisible colleges"–veiled lines of communication that cross disciplines and institutions–an idea developed in the 1972 book, by sociologist Diana Crane, *Invisible Colleges: Diffusion of Knowledge in Scientific Communities*. Responding to the construct of intellectual fragmentation, networks have evolved in each of the disciplines, offering new and enlightening perspectives on the specialties, often breaking out of academia altogether. Within some disciplines, experts are working from the inside out, pushing back the boundaries of their knowledge and even redefining what they are looking for. One group that developed out of the narrow confines of its discipline is the Anthropology Resource Center (ARC), which challenges the traditional anthropologist's approach as too clinical and dispassionate to make the kind of valuable contribution inherent in the grand idea of a temporal study of human behavior.

Most anthropologists have observed and recorded, counted and categorized, then sorted and analyzed how various groups of people, traditionally preindustrial people, live and behave. Using the very simple but hitherto rarely implemented method of "co-researchers," ARC makes its "findings available to the people they have studied." With this philosophy, ARC poses some powerful questions to others in its profession:

> Since its inception as a profession, anthropology has looked upon the poor nations of the world with the inquisitive gaze of the colonizer. Today, as applied anthropologists ponder the nutritional and medical problems that accompany development, the field is undergoing a renaissance as a practical science. Has the new anthropology anything more than the old to offer those whom Fanon called "the wretched of the earth"?

> Would not anthropologists–and other professionals–be more useful to the cause of humanity and truth if they worked for a new structure of inquiry in which the practices and culture of the wealthy and powerful and not those of the starving, were the subject of investigation?

To turn the camera around, the group created the first public-interest anthropology resource center in 1975, which Shelton H. Davis and Robert O. Mathews, two of its founders, describe in a 1979 issue of *Practicing Anthropology*:

> Public interest anthropology differs from traditional applied anthropology in what is considered the object of study, whose interests the researcher represents, and what the researcher does with the results of his or her work. Public

interest anthropology grows out of the democratic traditions of citizen activism rather than the bureacratic needs of management and control. It is based on the premise that social problems—war, poverty, racism, sexism, environmental degradation, misuse of technology—are deeply rooted in social structure, and that the role of the intellectual is to work with citizens in promoting fundamental social change.

These new academic networks are the beacons of hope in our professions—new, invisible colleges forming around concern for the future and respect for the reality of the past, new, invisible learning networks revolving around communities of concern, rather than the career advancements and glorification of individual scholars. There are no Nobel prizes for the breakthrough thinkers in these invisible networks, yet their work may ultimately serve as the foundation upon which our future will rest.

INSPIRATIONAL JOURNALISM

Early on in the conception of this book, an editor remarked that all networks seem to share one common characteristic: They produce newsletters. While many networks do not have newsletters and other networks publish newspapers and magazines, or use another medium—there is nevertheless a substantial truth embedded in this editor's comment.

Newsletters. Hundreds of them pack our file drawers and everybody probably has at least one or two lying around.

At first glance, we might assume that "newsletter" is a new word, one of those new-fangled technoterms designed not to inform but merely to grab attention. But "newsletter" is quite an old word, really, whose first recorded mention, in 1674 appeared barely two centuries after the death of Gutenberg. According to The Oxford Universal Dictionary, the newsletter is "a letter specially written to communicate news of the day . . . also, a printed account of the news, sometimes with blanks left for private additions."

Newsletters are concise, pithy, pertinent, friendly, and foster interaction. Devoid, for the most part, of advertising and often no more than two-to-four pages in length, newsletters are our running commentaries on the state of the art in each of Another America's areas of interest. Just a random flip through our files turns up *Black Bart*, an irregular newsletter with an eclectic perspective on current events, spirituality, and human interaction; *Peacework*, the newsletter of the New England Peace Movement; *Exchange Networks*, the newsletter of the National Center for Citizen Involvement; *Plenty News*, the newsletter of the Plenty Project, in Tennessee; *FOCUSCreativity*, a newsletter about creativity; and *Birthing*, a newsletter about childbirth, from Illinois.

Much of the communication within networks is informal and extemporaneous. A networker in Maryland makes 20 copies of an article that he finds useful and sends it around to 20 friends. A networker in Rhode Island learns of a magazine planning a special issue on evolving ideas within academic disciplines and calls seven people who might have something to contribute. A group of visual artists concerned with human survival in the nuclear age decide to do a show together, then invite participation from several hundred others through a form letter. All these "networkings" are means of communication; they speak directly to people where they are—and move them to action.

Futurist Hazel Henderson believes that a network's integrity is reflected in its newsletter. "If it's tacky looking and mimeo, the network is probably OK," she told us in a telephone interview from her Florida home. "If it's printed on glossy paper with two colors, watch out."

Henderson's simple characterization of newsletters is a good rule of thumb. In the main, newsletters produced by the networks cateloged in this book display more content than form. There is often mininum attention paid to design, or paper quality, or print style, or headline size. Getting the word out is the purpose of these periodicals; they digest and distill the essence of the network's interests, without frills. Written in a style which, some 300 years after its invention, remains personal, the newsletter is still intrinsically a communication from one person to another, complete with the affective quality that letters contain. Traveling from author to reader with an absolute minimum of editorial interference, the newsletter's articles have a clear point of view. Fear of stepping on toes, whether advertisers' or readers', is left for commercial publications; the newsletter is provocative, challenging, stimulating, and sometimes outrageous.

Erasing the distinction between "professional" writers and amateurs, the newsletter values the author's opinions and experience over literary skill in allowing a piece to qualify for publication. Newsletters represent the balkanization of the press, the opening up of the channels of communication to everyone. Children write *Hostex*, the newsletter of the home school exchange; mental patients write the untitled newsletter of the Alliance for the Liberation of Mental Patients; midwives write *The Practicing Midwife*, a newsletter of the home birth movement. Another America's newsletters contain as much vital, relevant information as the big city newspapers.

A new breed of journalist is cutting its teeth in newsletters, expanding into little-heard-of journals, and eventually bringing their work to the more established channels of communication. However, unlike journalists trained in the objective, "5-W" (who, what, where, when, why) tradition of the established media, Another America's reporters work from subjective conviction, from their own beliefs in how we can uncover, create, and celebrate a better world around us.

These new journalists are the kids who wrote the *Foxfire* books, the "new age" poets whose verse is found from time to time in print, the therapists who write honestly and insightfully about our emotional lives, the spiritual seekers who pass along the great teachings of the ages. They are anyone who picks up a pen or a paintbrush or a microphone in an inspired, impassioned moment and speaks honestly, from the heart, about what the world means. Guided by integrity and by a search for the ennobling projects that engage human beings, inspirational journalists are bringing us the news that Margaret Mead was looking for. "Why can't we celebrate human achievement on the evening news," she asked, "rather than reinforcing war, disease, and disasters?"

Why not, indeed?

Good news, yes, but inspirational journalism also has its practical side. "Newspapers might get you all excited about a new project," Steve Johnson (see Chapter 4), cofounder of *Rain Magazine*, in Portland, Oregon, remarks. "But they never provide an address. So you read the article, become interested, and stop dead in your tracks." The inseparable corollary of this new brand of journalism, then, is practicality. Why inform only partially?

Inspirational journalism provides the tools for action. The inclusion of names, addresses, and telephone numbers is equally as important as the explanatory material in the article or the radio program or the cable television show. Words like "resources," "access," and "tools" headline sidebars that refer people to the plug-in points that allow readers, listeners, and viewers to become engaged.

Ultimately, the purpose of all communication is to inform. Journalists are the pioneers on the frontiers of the information age, scouting for those projects, approaches, ideas, and exemplary individuals whose work reflects widely held values. While exposing the wrongs, the corruption, the deception, and the charlatans is an invaluable journalistic service, it is incomplete without its complement of positive news and comment. There is a wealth of encouraging, enlightening, elevating, and ennobling news in the world. The thousands of groups that we have reached in our networking journey are merely the tip of the iceberg.

We live in the Global Village of Marshall McLuhan. If anything is plentiful, it is raw information. Radio has spread to nearly every hamlet on the globe, and television has reached most small towns. In the United States alone, 40,000 new books are published each year, more than 100 new books per day. Magazines, journals, broadsheets, video discs, tape cassettes, cable television, and satellites are transforming humanity.

In a December 1980 meeting at a Boston television station where he had come to tape a Christmas Eve program, Robert Muller (see Chapter 9) said, "The time has come for us to bring together all the knowledge of all the encyclopedias of the world with all their great diversity of viewpoints." Like the gargantuan library at Alexandria, in which all the knowledge of the ancient world was brought together in one place, so there is a need now to interweave all the knowledge on the planet. This concept represents the ideal of all networking: to collect, synthesize, and distribute, freely and widely, meaningful information.

Imagine, for a moment, the utopian global community where people are literate both in the written word and the video image, where use of print and electronic technology, including television, radio, and computers, is taught much the way people learn to drive today. Using a TV camera or a computer is no more complicated, and certainly a lot less dangerous, than driving a car. Indeed, children are learning to navigate the channels of electronic communication all the time. At the age of three, our daughter Miranda was able to call up routines on our small computer–then, in a flash, she would leap off the chair to play with her blocks.

Networking, of the sort we are familiar with today, seems pretty old-fashioned when placed side by side with the futuristic image of the Global Village. Yet, these two worlds are already coming together. We could not have written this book without the daily visits of Dick Ryan, our postman, and we could not have written this book without our computer.

COMPUTER-AIDED NETWORKING

The emergence of inexpensive, decentralized computer capability in the past five years offers networkers a friendly and flexible assistant when used to augment traditional networking resources and skills. While the argument against computers has been sagely presented and sorely experienced by nearly everyone living in overindustrialized societies, the decentralized small computer is one of the most powerful tools ever to become available to networkers.

Mark Cherniack, director of the Franklin County Energy Project, in western Massachusetts, pinpoints the nub of the problem that plagues many networkers, one that is potentially solvable with the use of a small computer: "I was doing networking in the seven northeastern states on appropriate technology, which means everything, and I got burned out. I found that my brain was simply not evolved enough to keep track of everything. In order to be an effective networker, you have to keep information at the tips of your fingers all the time, and before long, there's too much to keep track of."

For people who are working within specific topic areas, trying to keep track of new developments, resources, references, titles, names, and addresses, there is no tool so perfectly suited to the task as the computer. Drawing on the value of this technology, two experimental networks have formed in recent years, each providing a different insight into what computers can add to the networking process.

One experiment that is actively providing people with services in their everyday lives is the "office for Open Network," in Denver, the only organization of its kind in the United States. Neither a "group" nor a movement, the office for Open Network is a communication medium through which people can find others whose services or interests may match or complement their own. As the designers of the process put it:

> Everyone has his/her own personal networks–business, family, social, etc. Personal networks, however, have their limitations. Suppose you are an attorney with an interest in Russian icons or in designing a City of the Future. Where do you go? The odds are against your finding someone in your personal networks with such interests. The best way to extend your personal networks is to use the process called the open network to put you in touch with others conducting similar explorations, thereby enabling you to collaborate to mutual advantage as you so wish.

> In effect, the office for Open Network complements your personal networks. However, unlike traditional organizations, it has no social, political, religious, or educational entry requirements nor does it endorse any ideology.

Designed by Leif Smith, the office for Open Network uses a computer for storing, searching, and producing information. When a person opens an account with the office, information is entered into the computer in a standardized format. With current users interested in categories as diverse as pottery, gold investments, poetry, water systems, archaeology, food, children, and mountain climbing, the information network makes available a variety of resources to its users.

When we contacted the office run by Smith and Patricia Wagner, their enthusiastic response to our request for information came in the form of a 34-page computer printout that Wagner had generated by having the computer make "a search" using the words ("pattern of keys") *network*, *learning*, and *tools*. She then chose what she thought would be useful to our needs and sent that to us. Smith explains: "The good guessing of human beings is more important to our work than computer searches." Whereas a 34-page printout is often a writer's nightmare, a haystack of information bits with only a few needles to reward a diligent review, in this case it proved to be a highly succinct list of resources specifically useful to us.

For an annual connection fee, people have access to computer and paper files, a telephone network, a designated amount of space in both the computer and paper files, and the chance to expand their personal networks through what Smith and Wagner call "access to the unexpected."

Since its inception, in 1975, the office for Open Network has grown to include some 850 scientists, artists, mathematicians, crafts people, writers, entrepreneurs, politicians, investors, bankers, theologians, educators, engineers, architects, consultants, city planners, philosophers, poets, and inventors. The youngest user of the network is a "precocious 10-year-old," according to Wagner, "who paid for her own membership and then told her school about what she'd done. Then the school itself became a user of the network."

What sets the office for Open Network totally apart from other information-sharing networks is both its level of sophistication and its commitment to "a deliberate policy of nonexclusion–there is no censorship." Devoid of ideology, the office for Open

Network is clearly not a new age/counterculture organization. Yet, its users include such people as well as those predominantly more mainstream. Three examples of network connections make this point:

- An immunologist at the National Asthma Center found a new mathematical model which enabled him to continue his research.

- An inventor designed and tested a self-contained water system for a house—no pipes, no sewage. He needed capital investment to start production and was put in touch with another user who introduced his plans to investors.

- Open Network users organized and raised capital for visits to Denver by E. F. Schumacher, economist, and Nathaniel Branden, psychologist.

Leif Smith explains how the office for Open Network differs from other networks in a fascinating interview with Thomas James appearing in the *Journal of Experiential Education*'s Fall 1980 issue (and reprinted in the Spring 1981 issue of *CoEvolution Quarterly*), "Networks: An Exploration in Education":

Most networks that we know about are what I call focused networks: There is a worldview that governs them, such as the network of professional engineers in Denver, the network of people interested in West Coast Indian art—it goes on and on, all the definably different ways a network can be focused. The office for Open Network is perhaps a first. I've never seen anything like it, where a deliberate attempt was made to avoid all focus. Not because we think focus is bad, but because we think there is something else that needs to be done. People are like artists in their explorations, but instead of a palette with colors of paint they have a palette of focused networks. Give them an open network and the palette increases manyfold. Successful connections through the Open Network process number in the thousands. They are the sort that happen in a matter of thirty seconds and are gone. We never hear any more about them. We did our job and that's that.

In 1981, Smith and Wagner published *The Networking Game*, a small handbook that offers some profound insights into the art of networking (see Chapter 12). Thus, the office for Open Network is being networked to people beyond the network itself.

Computer conferencing, the use of a computer to mediate exchanges among large numbers of people in widely scattered places, is a second representative computer application that holds promise as a networking tool. While there are several commercial computer conferencing systems in existence, the one that has received the widest notice is the nonprofit Electronic Information Exchange System (EIES, pronounced "eyes") designed by Murray Turoff. For the first three years of its development, EIES was supported by grants from the National Science Foundation. Thus a large amount of the early experimentation involved professionals from a number of disciplines who used computer conferencing as a way to exchange information within their fields of study. "Communities" were formed in such areas as devices for the disabled, social-network analysis, office automation, medical applications, and legislative research.

EIES began experimentally in 1976, expanded greatly with increased NSF funding in 1977, and went through yet another change in spring 1980, when the NSF-funded operational trials were over and the system had to become self-supporting. Using computer terminals in their homes or offices, members of the system are able to hold "conferences," over long periods of time, that simulate but do not duplicate "in-person" conferences. Each conference has its own moderator, and participants are able to add comments, references, papers, and any other information that is pertinent to the topic of discussion. Overall, the effect is something like an open microphone at a conference that never ends—a microphone that picks up both formal and informal presentations and discussions. Using a computer makes it easy to store, organize, search for, and retrieve all this information.

In addition to providing computerized conferencing facilities, EIES is also an electronic mail service, allowing users to send private messages to one another. Since everything that happens on EIES is stored in the computer, physically situated at the New Jersey Institute of Technology, in Newark, messages can be sent at one time and received whenever the addressee next signs on to the system. Communication can be synchronous, when both parties are using the system at the same time, or asynchronous, when messages are sent and retrieved at different times.

When we "signed on" to the system for the first time, we perused the list of others who were using EIES at that moment and noticed the name of Steve Johnson, one of our postal and telephone friends whom we met through the network book, so we sent him a message: "Hello, Steve. Here we are on EIES. How are you and what did you have for breakfast?" A few minutes later a response headlined "How About Them Cookies?" came back to our bold first message. Johnson welcomed us to EIES and invited us to participate in an EIES conference he was planning a few weeks thence in Seattle. With the Neighborhood Information Sharing Exchange, also a member of EIES, Johnson was planning a demonstration of the system at the Seattle CityFair, a huge exposition on urban alternatives. A number of EIES participants were forewarned, and the demonstration happened over a period of days. Each day, Johnson sent a report of what was happening at the CityFair to the group he had invited to participate in the temporary conference on EIES. Johnson introduced a new comment into the conference whenever people came by his booth at the fair requesting information that the disembodied EIES participants might have. EIES members then responded with information.

As the communities on EIES have developed and expanded, and people have moved in and out of the system, the EIES world has also grown and changed, much as a geographically based community might, complete with old-timers, newcomers, and visitors. One "conference" on EIES is called "The Poetry Corner," an ongoing scroll for people to inscribe their thoughts in verse. Another conference is called simply "Graffiti" and contains various bits of wall-written wit, as well as jokes, riddles, and rhymes. Often when EIES members have the opportunity, they take their terminals to "real life" conferences and demonstrate the system to those who are interested.

While some people use EIES to explore their immediate professional interests in narrow disciplines, others use the system in a more generalized manner, moving in and out of conferences, developing new ideas as they go. Among these explorers have been Peter and Trudy Johnson-Lenz, communications consultants whose work on EIES has been both practical, in the form of contributing some of the most advanced computer software tools, and philosophical. The Johnson-Lenzes have developed a number of structured communications processes on EIES, notably: the FUTURES TOUR, developed with futurist Robert Theobald for the U.S. Department of Agriculture to help individuals explore alternative futures; VISIONS&TOOLS, a process for envisioning positive futures and the tools to make them a reality; COMMUNITY NEWS, an ongoing exchange on topics of interest to neighborhoods and communities; and ATTUNE, a process for universal meditation, where members come to reflect, read quotations from the world's spiritual literature, and share their inspirations with others in the group.

EIES cannot replace face-to-face meetings or telephone calls, nor is it meant to. Rather, EIES-like systems offer yet another means for people who are widely separated to know one another and to work together. Much to our delight, when we joined EIES we found many people whom we knew already and we have made a number of new friends. The reason? EIES is an excellent medium for people who like to network, especially for the computer-oriented types who are dealing with the experimental, emergent forms of communication. "Electronic cottages," Toffler's phrase for the decentralized computer/telecommunications-based home/workplace of the future, have already made their appearance as nodes in the proliferating webs of networks.

A 1980 survey published in *The Wall Street Journal* reported that, within most bureaucratic organizations, only about one in ten people is willing to use a computer. Among the generation that has seen computers develop in two brief decades from multimillion-dollar vacuum-tube behemoths that filled large rooms to powerful "computers-on-a-chip" so small that dozens can be held in the hand, this attitude toward computer use is readily understandable. We wonder what a survey done in 1910 would have indicated about the automobile? Would more than one in ten people have said they could envision themselves driving a car as a daily necessity? Similarly, we wonder what a *Wall Street Journal* like survey would indicate if taken in the year 2000, when today's children, who have grown up with computers and "intelligent toys" all around them, come of age.

We think of our own children. For the first three months of her life, our baby daughter, Eliza, took all her naps in the office-computer room of our house, where we were compiling the research for this book. And our older daughter, Miranda, still a preschooler, knows which piece of equipment is the computer and which is simply the typewriter, distinctions that to a less astute observer would appear meaningless since the two pieces of equipment have similar keyboards. Miranda knows that "run" is a word that makes the computer go, as well as being a description of one of her favorite activities.

Our children have been born into a world totally different from that which we were born into during the years in and around the dropping of the first atomic bombs. Our generation seems to have been born to be connected together in this world, with each of us bearing the responsibility for what to do in this awesome moment of transition, predicament, and potential that faces us.

Learning Guide

L

The Learning Guide includes groups that are primarily concerned with education and communications. Many of these groups also work on other issues.

Each group is identified by a letter/number code. The letter **L** stands for Learning. Every group whose code begins with **L** is listed in the Learning Guide.

The entry for each network whose code is lower than 100 includes a brief description. These representative networks are a cross-section of the initial groups we contacted in our research. Each network whose code is greater than 100 is listed with complete contact information. If the ✷ symbol, for publications, or the ✦ symbol, for materials, appears with a listing, consult the Title Guide under Learning Titles.

The Learning Guide includes groups that are concerned with adult education, alternative schools, book publishing and distribution, computers, experiential education, film production and distribution, free universities, holistic advertisments, home schools, information collection, lifelong learning, literary and poetic journals, open networks, postsecondary educational programs, radio tapes, television . . . and a few others.

L001
Alternatives in Education
Rural Route #3, Box 171
Spencer, WV 27276   ✳

✳ *Alternatives in Education ($2)*

Voice of the home schooling movement in West Virginia. Informal, first-person articles on issues of interest to parents: music, arts, and "lessons." Reports on legal aspects of home schooling.

L002
Another America Networking
P.O. Box 66
West Newton, MA 02165   ✦✦

✦ *Networking: The First Report and Directory*
✦ *Holonomy: A Human Systems Theory (Stamps, $14)*

We are the people who wrote this book. Please send additions, corrections, updates, and suggestions about listings to us at this address.

L003
Anthropology Resource Center
59 Temple Place, Suite 444
Boston, MA 02111
617/491-3261   ✳

✳ *ARC Newsletter ($5)*

Anthropology with a social conscience. First public-interest anthropology resource center. Returns research results to those studied. Establishing Public Scholars Research Bank; has information center.

L004
Association for Experiential Education
P.O. Box 4625
Denver, CO 80204
303/837-8633   ✳✳

✳ *Jobs Clearinghouse Bulletin ($4 year)*
✳ *Journal of Experiential Education (semiannual)*

International network of individuals, schools, and groups interested in experience-based teaching and learning. Sponsors conferences, publications, and popular Jobs Clearinghouse Bulletin. Subgroups on special issues.

L005
Center on Technology and Society
P.O. Box 38-206
Cambridge, MA 02138
617/491-1112   ✦

✦ *Managing Our World: The United Nations in the 1980s*

Research- and project-oriented group that stresses pluralism and diversity in its work. Instrumental in organizing farmers' market in Boston. Uses networking concepts in education and appropriate technology studies.

L006
Coalition for Alternatives in Postsecondary Education
c/o Council on Higher Education
1050 U.S. Route 127 South
Frankfort, KY 40601
502/564-3553

Coalition of groups, institutions, and individuals concerned with alternative approaches to higher education. Members include many postsecondary educational experiments. Prepares and delivers congressional testimony.

L007
Committee of Small Magazine Editors and Publishers
P.O. Box 703
San Francisco, CA 94101   ✳

✳ *Independent Publisher (monthly/$35)*

Only national association of independent publishers. Sponsors annual conferences and seminars, provides mailing lists, and exhibits new titles. Newsletter is excellent resource for writers, editors, and publishers.

L008
Community Memory Project
916 Parker Street
Berkeley, CA 94703
415/841-1114   ✳

✳ *Journal of Community Communications (quarterly/$9)*

Fascinating service which extends idea of individual memory to community level with computers. Probably first computer network designed for use "in the streets." Calls itself a "shared community filing cabinet." Still formative.

L009
Council for the Advancement of Experiential Learning
American City Building, #212
Columbia, MD 21044
301/997-3535   ✳✦

✳ *CAEL Newsletter (bimonthly)*
✦ *New Directions Sourcebooks in Experiential Learning*

Association of 300 educational institutions concerned with "hands-on" learning outside traditional classrooms. Provides support to members through annual meetings, materials, research, consulting, and workshops.

L010
Education Exploration Center
P.O. Box 7339, Powderhorn Sta.
Minneapolis, MN 55407
612/722-6613   ◆◈

◆ *Teaching Human Dignity ($8.95)*
◆ *Teaching the Vietnam War ($7.50)*

Disseminates books, curricula, and audiotapes on social-change issues, little-known
resources, and examples of successful educa-
tional-political work. Topics include nuclear
power, oral history, and the Vietnam War.

L011
Education for Freedom of Choice in Ohio
439 The Arcade
Cleveland, OH 44114
216/621-8224

Provides education to community and professional groups on medical, psychological,
legal, and ethical issues of abortion. Maintains
speakers bureau and resource library and
offers in-service training for workshops.

L012
Electronic Information Exchange System
New Jersey Institute of Technology
323 High Street
Newark, NJ 07102
201/645-5503   ✳◆

✳ *Chimo: Electronic Newsletter of EIES*
◆ *The Network Nation: Human Communication via Computer*

Computer conferencing system which allows
people on system to communicate instan-
taneously. A future experiment ongoing in the
present. "Communities" include general systems, futures, social nets, and devices for the
disabled.

L013
Feminist Writers' Guild
P.O. Box 9396
Berkeley, CA 94709   ✳

✳ *Feminist Writers' Guild Newsletter
(quarterly/$10)*

National network of women writers providing
mutual support. Reports on chapter news,
provides practical tips on writing, organizes
mutual critiques, and publishes reviews.

L014
Feminist Writers' Guild/New York
P.O. Box 184, Village Sta.
New York, NY 10014

Local chapter of national FWG. Sponsors
poetry readings, film showings, fiction,
poetry, playwriting workshops, and writers
support groups.

L015
FocusCreativity
Dudley Lynch & Associátes
827 Westwood Drive
Richardson, TX 75080   ✳

✳ *FOCUSCreativity (triweekly/$35)*

Reports on many aspects of creativity, especially practical applications for education,
business, and government. Organizes seminars and workshops.

L016
Folk-School Association of America
C.P.O. Box 287
Berea, KY 40408
606/986-9341   ✳

✳ *Options (quarterly/$3)*

Unique concept of education which fosters
"moments of awakening" in students of all
ages. Based on Danish Folk-Schools. Seeks to
instill sense of "connectedness to the world."
Newsletter, but no schools as yet.

L017
Free University Network
1221 Thurston
Manhattan, KS 66502
913/532-5866   ✳◆

✳ *Learning Connection (4 issues/$15)*
◆ *Directory of Free Universities and Learning
Networks ($1)*

Association of 200 groups offering ungraded,
unaccredited classes to public. Provides technical assistance to new groups, maintains contact file, sponsors conferences, and has
directory of free universities and learning
exchanges.

L018
Great Atlantic Radio Conspiracy
2743 Maryland Avenue
Baltimore, MD 21218
301/243-6987   ◆

◆ *Great Atlantic Radio Series (tapes, $5)*

Collective that produces and distributes
award-winning broadcast-quality audiotapes
on politics, protest, media, the arts, liberation
stuggles abroad, women, men, radicalism, the
professions, holidays, food, health, etc.

L019
Guild Communications Network
2724 Pall Mall
Sterling Heights, MI 48077   ✳

✳ *Networkers Package ($10)*

Clearinghouse and key node for transformation-oriented information in Great Lakes region. Distributes useful packets on networking and communications. Organizes mailing lists and directories.

L020
Holt Associates
308 Boylston Street
Boston, MA 02116 ✳◆◆

* *Growing Without Schooling*
  (bimonthly/$10)
◆ *How Children Learn (Holt, $1)*
◆ *Instead of Education (Holt, $3.50)*

Central node in the "unschooling" movement linking home schoolers and others interested in learning outside institutions. Lively newsletter packed with news, resources, and personal experiences.

L021
Humanistic Psychology Institute
1772 Vallejo Street
San Francisco, CA 94123
415/441-5034 ✳✳

* *Perspectives (3 issues/$5)*
* *Humanistic Psychology Institute Review*
  ($4 copy)

Nonresidential external-degree masters and Ph.D. programs. Uses network model to link students with faculty. Most students work while earning degree. Degrees in psychology and human sciences.

L022
Intercommunity Center for Justice and Peace
20 Washington Square North
New York, NY 10011
212/475-6677 ✳

* *Justice in the Schools*

Coalition of 25 Roman Catholic religious congregations concerned with human rights, alcoholism, disarmament, prisons, theology, education, corporate responsibility, and sexual preference. Sponsors workshops and newsletter.

L023
Liberation News Service
17 West 17th Street
New York, NY 10011
212/989-3555 ✳

* *LNS ($240 year)*

Press service that carries stories overlooked by straight wire services. Distributes packets of news copy and graphics. Excellent source for other publications. Began in 1967 in order to provide alternative Vietnam views.

L024
National Association of Legal Services to Alternative Schools
P.O. Box 2823
Santa Fe, NM 87501 ✳◆

* *Tidbits (4 issues/$20)*
◆ *Cheez! Uncle Sam ($8.95)*

Focus for movement to protect alternative schools. Conducts research and coordinates and supports legal action. Publishes humorous newsletter containing reports, news summaries, and extensive resource listings.

L025
National Center for Service-Learning
ACTION
606 Connecticut Avenue, N.W.
Washington, DC 20525
800/424-8580 ✳

* *Synergist*

Federal program that provides technical assistance and resource materials on "service-training" programs, in which students volunteer as tutors, counselors, companions to the elderly, and consumer advocates.

L026
National Federation of Community Broadcasters
1000 11th Street, N.W.
Washington, DC 20001
202/789-1200 ✳✳◆

* *NFCB Newsletter (monthly/$15)*
* *Fast Forward (quarterly)*
◆ *SOURCETAP: Directory of Program*
  Resources for Radio ($35)

Key switchboard for noncommercial radio stations, which collectively reach 20% of U.S. public. Assists existing and new radio, as well as other media projects. Monitors regulation, sponsors program sharing, and has co-op.

L027
National Society for Internships and Experiential Education
1735 Eye Street, N.W., Suite 601
Washington, DC 20006
202/331-1516 ✳

* *Experiential Education*

Important node in the experiential learning movement. Clearinghouse, technical assistance, conferences, and research on off-campus learning opportunities. Formed by merger of two earlier organizations.

L028
New Jersey Unschoolers
2 Smith Street
Farmingdale, NJ 07727
201/928-2473 ✳

＊ *New Jersey Unschoolers Newsletter*

Key link in home schooling movement in New Jersey, where it is legal. Informal support network in which parents exchange ideas and resources. Newsletter contains valuable information on unschooling.

L029
Northwest Regional Educational Laboratory
710 Southwest Second Avenue
Portland, OR 97204
503/248-6800

Educational research and development center in Pacific Northwest. Crossroads of 820 agencies and organizations. Develops, conducts, produces, and evaluates educational programs and materials. Largely government-funded.

L030
Ohio Coalition for Educational Alternatives Now
66 Jefferson Avenue
Columbus, OH 43215
614/469-9066 ＊

＊ *OCEAN News ($10)*

Network of home-study and alternative-school people. Maintains library, organizes meetings, and has a newsletter section on "children at home."

L031
Open Network
P.O. Box 18666
Denver, CO 80218
303/832-9764 ◆◆

◆ *Open Network Information Packet ($4)*
◆ *Networking Game (Wagner & Smith, $1.50)*

Unique, unparalleled network which exists as a "pure" form of a network without a central issue or ideology. Speaks its own language, which becomes clear with use of system. "Weaves" connections, computer-aided.

L032
Organizational Development Network
1011 Park Avenue
Plainfield, NJ 07060
201/561-8677 ＊

＊ *OD Practitioner ($30)*

National membership group for people working in the profession of organizational development.

L033
Southwest Educational Development Laboratory
211 East 7th Street
Austin, TX 78701
512/476-6861

One of eight educational laboratories in U.S., serving the six-state southwest region. Conducts research, offers educational programs, provides technical assistance, and publishes numerous papers and reports.

L034
Southwest Research and Information Center
P.O. Box 4524
Albuquerque, NM 87106
505/242-4766 ＊＊＊

＊ *The Workbook: Environmental, Social and Consumer (8/$10)*
＊ *Mine Talk (bimonthly/$18)*
＊ *Nuclear Waste News (bimonthly/$5)*

Major networking resource, bringing scientific, writing, and legal expertise to bear on environmental and social problems. Publishers of The Workbook, a gold mine of indexed information about new groups, projects, and ideas.

L035
Student Press Law Center
917 G Place, N.W.
Washington, DC 20001
202/347-7154 ＊

＊ *SPLC Report (3 issues/$10)*

Collects, organizes, and distributes information on First Amendment rights of high school and college journalists. Provides legal assistance to students and faculty advisers experiencing censorship. Distributes manual and journal.

L036
Union for Experimenting Colleges and Universities
P.O. Box 85315
Cincinnati, OH 45201
513/621-6444

Both a degree-granting institution and a consortium of other institutions committed to change and experimentation in higher education. Undergrad program is "University Without Walls"; graduate is known as "Union Graduate School."

L101
Academy for Educational Development
680 Fifth Avenue
New York, NY 10019
212/397-0040   ✳

L102
Action for Children's Television
46 Austin Street
Newtonville, MA 02160
617/527-7870   ✳

L103
**Adult Education Association of the United States
   of America**
810 18th Street, N.W.
Washington, DC 20006
202/347-9574   ✳

L104
Alliance for Citizen Education
401 North Broad Street, #810
Philadelphia, PA 19108
215/WA2-8960   ✳

L105
Alliance of Information and Referral Services
P.O. Box 10705
Phoenix, AZ 85064   ✳

L106
Alternate Media Center
New York University
144 Bleecker Street
New York, NY 10012
212/598-3338

L107
**Alternative America: Directory of 5000 Groups
   and Organizations**
P.O. Box 134
Cambridge, MA 02138
617/876-2789   ◆✳

L108
Alternative Press Center
P.O. Box 7229
Baltimore, MD 21218
301/243-2471   ◆

L109
Alternative Press Syndicate
P.O. Box 774
New York, NY 10010
212/481-0120   ✳

L110
Alternative Schools Network
1105 West Lawrence Avenue, #210
Chicago, IL 60640
312/728-4030   ◆

L111
Amateur Radio Research and Development
1524 Springvale Avenue
McLean, VA 22101   ✳◆

L112
American Association of University Women
2401 Virginia Avenue, N.W.
Washington, DC 20037
202/785-7727   ✳

L113
American Historical Association
400 A Street, S.E.
Washington, DC 20003
202/544-2422

L114
American Society for Training and Development
One Dupont Circle
Washington, DC 20036
202/659-1085   ✳

L115
Antioch University West
650 Pine
San Francisco, CA 94108
413/856-1688

L116
Appalachia Educational Laboratory
P.O. Box 1348
Charleston, WV 25325
304/344-8371

L117
Appalachian Journal
132 Sanford Hall
Appalachian State University
Boone, NC 28608

L118
Appalshop Films
P.O. Box 743
Whitesburg, KY 41858
606/633-5708   ◆◆◆

L119
Arton's Publishing: Fuse Magazine
31 Dupont
Toronto, Ontario
CANADA M5R 1V3
416/967-9309   ✳

L120
Aspen Institute for Humanistic Studies
717 Fifth Avenue
New York, NY 10022
212/759-1053   ✳◆

L121
Associated Information Managers
316 Pennsylvania Avenue, S.E.
Washington, DC 20003
202/544-1969 ✳

L122
Association for Humanistic Education
P.O. Box 13042
Gainesville, FL 32604 ✳

L123
Ateed Centre
P.O. Box 275, Station P
Toronto, Ontario
CANADA M5S 2S8
416/924-4878 ✳

L124
**Atlanta Network: Teaching, Learning and
   Interest Sharing**
P.O. Box 14432
Atlanta, GA 30324
404/876-8888

L125
Bear's Guide to Non-Traditional College Degrees
P.O. Box 646
Mendocino, CA 95460
707/937-0813 ◆

L126
Berkeley Outreach Recreation Program
605 Eshleman Hall
University of California
Berkeley, CA 94720
415/849-4662

L127
Book People
2940 7th Street
Berkeley, CA 94710
415/549-3030

L128
Both Sides Now
Rural Route #6, Box 166
Tyler, TX 75704

L129
Canadian Alliance of Home Schoolers
P.O. Box 640
Jarvis, Ontario
CANADA N0A 1J0 ✳✳

L130
Canadian Information Sharing Service
121 Avenue Road
Toronto, Ontario
CANADA M5R 2G3
416/960-3903 ✳

L131
Canyon Cinema Cooperative
2325 Third Street, Suite 338
San Francisco, CA 94107
415/626-2255 ◆

L132
Center for Black Studies
Wayne State University
Detroit, MI 48202
313/577-2321

L133
Center for Investigative Reporting
The Broadway Building
1419 Broadway, Room 600
Oakland, CA 94612
415/835-8525 ◆

L134
Center for New Schools
59 East Van Buren
Chicago, IL 60605
312/939-7025

L135
Center for the Study of Democratic Institutions
P.O. Box 4068
Santa Barbara, CA 93102

L136
Change in Liberal Education Network
912 East 63rd Street, #200
Kansas City, MO 64110 ◆

L137
**Children's Creative Response to Conflict
   Program**
Fellowship of Reconciliation
P.O. Box 271
Nyack, NY 10960
914/358-4601 ◆✳

L138
Church Street Center for Community Education
135 Church Street
Burlington, VT 05401
802/656-4221

L139
City Lights Journal
261 Columbus Avenue
San Francisco, CA 94133 ✳

L140
**Clearinghouse of Free-Standing Educational
   Institutions**
1806 Vernon Street, N.W.
Washington, DC 20009
202/462-6333 ✳◆

L141
Coalition to End Animal Suffering in Experiments
P.O. Box 27
Cambridge, MA 02238
617/825-6700   ◆

L142
College Media Journal
P.O. Box 258
Roslyn, NY 11576
516/248-9118   ✳

L143
Common Ground
1300 Sanchez Street
San Francisco, CA 94131
415/647-1776

L144
Community Education Cooperative
College of the Mainland
8001 Palmer Highway
Texas City, TX 77590
713/938-1211

L145
Community Information Center
College of Library and Information Services
University of Maryland
College Park, MD 20742
301/454-5441   ✳

L146
Conditions: Writing by Women
P.O. Box 56, Van Brunt Sta.
Brooklyn, NY 11215   ✳

L147
Consumer Educational Resource Network
Office of Consumer Education
1832 M Street, N.W., Room 807
Washington, DC 20036

L148
**Council for Educational Development and
   Research**
1518 K Street, N.W., #206
Washington, DC 20005
202/638-3193

L149
Council on Interracial Books for Children
1841 Broadway
New York, NY 10023   ✳

L150
Creative Women's Collective
236 West 27th Street, 12th Floor
New York, NY 10001
212/924-0665

L151
Cultural Survival
11 Divinity Avenue
Cambridge, MA 02138
617/495-2562   ✳◆◆

L152
D.C. Gazette
1739 Connecticut Avenue, N.W.
Washington, DC 20009
202/232-5544   ✳◆

L153
Denver Free University
P.O. Box 18455
Denver, CO 80218
303/832-6688   ✳

L154
Direct Cinema Limited
P.O. Box 69589
Los Angeles, CA 90069
213/656-4700   ◆◆

L155
Double Helix: Community Media
4219 Laclede Avenue
St. Louis, MO 63108
314/534-9117

L156
Downtown Community Television Center
87 Lafayette Street
New York, NY 10013
212/966-4510

L157
Earthbooks Lending Library/Allegheny Branch
P.O. Box 556
Harmony, PA 16037
412/452-6434

L158
Earthenergy Media
P.O. Box 188
Santa Barbara, CA 93102   ◆

L159
Educational Film Library Association
43 West 61st Street
New York, NY 10023
212/246-4533   ✳◆

L160
Educational Futures
2118 Spruce Street
Philadelphia, PA 19103
215/735-2118   ✳

L161
Educational Resources Information Center
Office of Dissemination and Resources
National Institute of Education
Washington, DC 20208
202/254-5555 ✳◆

L162
Educomics
P.O. Box 40246
San Francisco, CA 94140 ✳✳✳

L163
Far West Laboratory
1855 Folsom Street
San Francisco, CA 94103
415/565-3000

L164
Feminary: A Feminist Journal for the South
P.O. Box 954
Chapel Hill, NC 27514 ✳

L165
Ferity: Hawaii's Feminist Newsjournal
University YWCA
1820 University Avenue
Honolulu, HI 96822 ✳

L166
Fine Print: A Review for the Arts of the Book
P.O. Box 7741
San Francisco, CA 94120
415/776-1530 ✳

L167
**Fireworks: Feminist Journal of the John Dewey
    High School**
John Dewey High School
50 Avenue X
Brooklyn, NY 11223
212/373-6400 ✳

L168
Flower Films
10341 San Pablo Avenue
El Cerrito, CA 95430
415/525-0942 ◆◆

L169
Food for Thought Books
325 Main Street
Amherst, MA 01002
413/253-5432 ◆◆

L170
Gifted Children Newsletter
530 University Avenue
Palo Alto, CA 94301
415/321-1770 ✳

L171
Guild Books and Periodicals
1118 West Armitage
Chicago, IL 60614
312/525-3667

L172
Gulf of Maine Bookstore
61 Main Street
Brunswick, ME 04011
207/729-5083

L173
Hagborn: A Radical Feminist News Journal
P.O. Box 894
Albany, NY 12201 ✳

L174
Holistic Life University
1627 Tenth Avenue
San Francisco, CA 94122
415/665-3200

L175
Home Study Exchange
P.O. Box 2241
Santa Fe, NM 87501 ✳

L176
Homosexual Information Center
6758 Hollywood Boulevard, #208
Los Angeles, CA 90028 ◆

L177
Hydra Book Company
P.O. Box 813
Forest Grove, OR 97116
503/357-0327

L178
Information for People
P.O. Box 3763
Spokane, WA 99220
509/535-3256

L179
Institute for Responsive Education
704 Commonwealth Avenue
Boston, MA 02215
617/353-3309 ✳

L180
Institute for Wholistic Education
P.O. Box 575
Amherst, MA 01002
413/549-0886

L181
International Society for General Semantics
P.O. Box 2469
San Francisco, CA 94126
415/543-1747 ✳

L182
Kartemquin Films
1901 West Wellington
Chicago, IL 60657
312/472-4366   ✦✦

L183
Latino Institute
1760 Reston Avenue, Suite 101
Reston, VA 22090
703/471-4527   ✶

L184
Learning Connection
900 Jerusalem Avenue
Uniondale, NY 11553
516/538-9100

L185
Learning Exchange
P.O. Box 920
Evanston, IL 60204
312/273-3383   ✶

L186
Learning Tools
1359 Gaylord
Denver, CO 80206
303/321-3597

L187
Learning Web
318 Anabel Taylor Hall
Cornell University
Ithaca, NY 14850
607/256-5026   ✦

L188
Link Learning Network
Activities Center
University of Iowa
Iowa City, IA 52240
319/353-5465   ✶

L189
Manas: Journal of Independent Inquiry
P.O. Box 32112, El Sereno Sta.
Los Angeles, CA 90032
213/283-8838   ✶

L190
Martha Stuart Communications
66 Bank Street
New York, NY 10014
212/255-2718   ✦

L191
Math Science Network
Math Science Resource Center
Mills College
Oakland, CA 94613
415/635-5074   ✶

L192
Media Access Project
1609 Connecticut Avenue, N.W.
Washington, DC 20009
202/232-4300   ✦✦

L193
Media Alliance
Fort Mason, Building D
San Francisco, CA 94123
415/441-2557   ✶

L194
MediaSense
3232 Sixth Street
Boulder, CO 80302
303/449-0211

L195
Mix Recording Publications
2608 9th Street
Berkeley, CA 94710
415/843-7901   ✶

L196
Mother Earth News
P.O. Box 70
Hendersonville, NC 28739   ✶

L197
Ms. Magazine
370 Lexington Avenue
New York, NY 10017   ✶

L198
Museum of Holography
11 Mercer Street
New York, NY 10013
212/925-0526

L199
National Association for Gifted Children
2070 County Road H
St. Paul, MN 55112
612/784-3475

L200
**National Association for the Education of Young
   Children**
1834 Connecticut Avenue, N.W.
Washington, DC 20009
202/232-8777   ✶

L201
National Center for Educational Brokering
1211 Connecticut Avenue, N.W.
Washington, DC 20036
202/466-5530   ✶

L202
National Center for Research in Vocational Education
Ohio State University
1960 Kenny Road
Columbus, OH 43210
614/486-3655

L203
National Chicano Research Network
Institute for Social Research, #6073
University of Michigan
Ann Arbor, MI 48104
313/763-5432   ✳

L204
National Coalition of Alternative Community Schools
1289 Jewett Street
Ann Arbor, MI 48104   ✳◆

L205
National Committee for Citizens in Education
410 Wilde Lake Village Green
Columbia, MD 21044
301/997-9300   ✳

L206
National Diffusion Network
Far West Laboratory
1855 Folsom Street
San Francisco, CA 94103   ◆

L207
National Federation of Local Cable Programmers
3700 Far Hills Avenue
Kettering, OH 45429
513/298-7890   ✳

L208
National Home Study Council
1601 18th Street, N.W.
Washington, DC 20009
202/234-5100   ◆

L209
National News Bureau
262 South 12th Street
Philadelphia, PA 19107
215/985-1990

L210
National Organizations Advisory Council for Children
331 East 38th Street
New York, NY 10016
212/686-5522

L211
National Radio Club
P.O. Box 118
Poquonock, CT 06064

L212
National Technical Information Service
U.S. Department of Commerce
5285 Port Royal Road
Springfield, VA 22161
703/557-4600   ◆

L213
Network for Learning
56 East 11th Street, 9th floor
New York, NY 10003
212/473-3333

L214
Networking Group
P.O. Box 1
Baldwin, NY 11510
516/223-4117

L215
New England Training Center for Community Organizers
620 Potters Avenue
Providence, RI 02908
401/941-4840

L216
New Front Films
1409 Willow Street, Suite 505
Minneapolis, MN 55403
612/872-0805   ◆◆

L217
New Orleans Video Access Center
2010 Magazine Street
New Orleans, LA 70130
504/524-8626   ✳

L218
New Pages Press
4426 Belsay Road
Grand Blanc, MI 48439
313/742-9583   ✳◆

L219
Northern California Open Network
5012 Timbercreek Drive
Sacramento, CA 95841

L220
Northern California/Southern Oregon Resource Network
P.O. Box 869
Mt. Shasta, CA 96067
916/926-3192

L221
Northwest Women in Educational Administration
Department of Education
Eugene, OR 97401
503/686-5072

L222
Pacific Region Association of Alternative Schools
1119 Geary Boulevard
San Francisco, CA 94109
415/474-4344   ◆

L223
Packard Manse Media Project
P.O. Box 450
Stoughton, MA 02072   ◆◆

L224
Parents Union for Public Schools
401 North Broad Street, #1030
Philadelphia, PA 19108
215/574-0337

L225
Pioneer Productions
35 Saint Germain Street
Boston, MA 02115
617/266-9170

L226
Primary/Secondary Peace Education Network
20 Washington Square North
New York, NY 10011
212/475-6677

L227
**Process: Networking Forum for Citizen
    Participation**
P.O. Box 3405, Station D
Ottawa, Ontario
CANADA K1P 6H8   ✳

L228
Project on the Status and Education of Women
c/o Association of American Colleges
1818 R Street, N.W.
Washington, DC 20009
202/387-1300   ✳

L229
Providence Learning Connection
77 Ives Street, Box 66
Providence, RI 02906
401/274-9330

L230
Public Media Center
25 Scotland Street
San Francisco, CA 94133
415/885-0200   ◆

L231
Quest: A Feminist Quarterly
P.O. Box 8843
Washington, DC 20003   ✳

L232
Research for Better Schools
444 North Third Street
Philadelphia, PA 19123
215/574-9300

L233
Rodale Press
Organic Park
Emmaus, PA 18049
215/967-5171   ✳✳✳

L234
Sagamore Institute
110 Spring Street
Saratoga Springs, NY 12866
518/587-8770

L235
Salt Magazine
P.O. Box 302 A
Kennebunkport, ME 04046
207/967-3311   ✳

L236
San Francisco Bay Guardian
2700 19th Street
San Francisco, CA 94110
415/824-7660   ✳

L237
Sandy River School
R.F.D. #3
Farmington, ME 04938
207/778-2386

L238
Shambhala Publications
P.O. Box 271
Boulder, CO 80306
303/449-6111   ◆

L239
Shelter Publications
P.O. Box 279
Bolinas, CA 94924   ◆◆

L240
Signs: Journal of Women and Culture in Society
Barnard Hall
Barnard College
New York, NY 10027   ✳

L241
Sipapu: Newsletter for Librarians
Rural Route #1, Box 216
Winters, CA 95694   ✳

L242
Small Press Review
c/o Dustbooks
P.O. Box 100
Paradise, CA 95969   ✳◆◆

L243
Society of Scribes and Illuminators
43 Earlham Street
London, WC2H 9LD
ENGLAND

L244
Southern California Open Network
P.O. Box 1651
San Pedro, CA 90733
213/548-5709

L245
Southern Progressive Periodicals Directory
P.O. Box 120574
Nashville, TN 37212   ✦

L246
Stay Smart
Carbon-Lehigh Intermediate Unit
2370 Main Street
Schnecksville, PA 18078
215/799-4111

L247
**Stony Hills: New England Alternative Press
   Review**
Weeks Mills
New Sharon, ME 04955   ✳

L248
Teachers' Centers Exchange
Far West Laboratory
1855 Folsom Street
San Francisco, CA 94103
415/565-3095   ✦

L249
Telecommunications Cooperative Network
370 Lexington Avenue, Suite 715
New York, NY 10017
212/689-1321

L250
The Network: Educational Service and Research
290 South Main Street
Andover, MA 01810
617/470-1080   ✳

L251
The Progressive
408 West Gorham Street
Madison, WI 53703   ✳

L252
Today News Service
National Press Building
Washington, DC 20045
202/628-6999

L253
Uni-Ed Associates
P.O. Box 2343
Elberon, NJ 07740
201/870-0423   ✳

L254
Unifilm
419 Park Avenue South
New York, NY 10014
212/686-9890   ✦

L255
United Ministries in Education
925 Chestnut Street, 6th Floor
Philadelphia, PA 19107
215/928-2791   ✳

L256
Urban Scientific & Educational Research
P.O. Box 19112
Washington, DC 20036
202/483-9018

L257
Washington Community Video Center
P.O. Box 21068
Washington, DC 20009
202/387-0219   ✳

L258
Western Behavioral Sciences Institute
P.O. Box 2029
La Jolla, CA 92038
714/459-3811   ✳✦

L259
White Buffalo Multimedia
P.O. Box 73
Woodstock, NY 12498

L260
Womansplace Bookstore
2401 North 32nd Street
Phoenix, AZ 85008
602/956-0456   ✦

L261
**Women in Focus: Film Production and
   Distribution**
6-45 Kingsway
Vancouver, British Columbia
CANADA V5T 3H7
604/872-2250   ✦

L262
**Women's Educational Equity Communications
   Network**
Far West Laboratory
1855 Folsom Street
San Francisco, CA 94103
415/565-3000

L263
Women's History Research Center
2325 Oak Street
Berkeley, CA 94708
415/548-1770   ◆◆

L264
Women's Information Exchange
1195 Valencia Street
San Francisco, CA 94110

L265
Women's Institute for Freedom of the Press
3306 Ross Place, N.W.
Washington, DC 20008
202/966-7783   ✳◆

L266
Women's Press
P.O. Box 562
Eugene, OR 97440
503/485-4156   ✳

L267
Women's Referral Service
P.O. Box 3093
Van Nuys, CA 91407
213/995-6646

L268
Women: Journal of Liberation
3028 Greenmount Avenue
Baltimore, MD 21218
301/235-5245   ✳

L269
WomenSpace Women's Center
1258 Euclid Avenue, #200
Cleveland, OH 44115
216/696-3100   ✳

L270
Workshop for Learning Things
5 Bridge Street
Watertown, MA 02172

L271
Youth Liberation Press
P.O. Box 524
Brooklyn, NY 11215
212/783-2957   ◆

L272
Zipporah Films
54 Lewis Wharf
Boston, MA 02110   ◆◆◆

Growing Networks:
Personal and Spiritual Growth

In a vivid portrayal of the meaning of a personal search, one dancer in the Boston improvisational group called River darts from point to point, frantically asking which way to go, raving her need for external direction until she reaches a guide who says simply, "Go inside." The dancer folds down upon herself and that section of the dance is over.

SEARCHING

Go inside. It is a message that was received by millions of Americans in the 1970s.

Inner growth, personal change, evolution, transformation. Coming to grips with yourself, changing, growing. Running, practicing yoga and t'ai chi, meditating, sitting, chanting. Consulting astrology, numerology, and the *I Ching*. Reading the Seth material and the Don Juan books. Alan Watts and Ram Dass. Therapy: rolfing, psychodrama, Gestalt, psychosynthesis, bioenergetics, T-groups. A weekend workshop.

In the 1970s we rediscovered and crafted some special tools, honed to fulfill what psychologist Abraham Maslow simply called our "human potential"–a phrase that became the name tag for a movement without precedent in recent human history.

Something dramatic and unpredicted spilled out of the social upheavals of the 1960s. The quest for collective social change merged with the yearning for individual personal change.

While many critics have regarded this transition as a leap toward narcissism, self-absorption, and delusion (including journalists such as Tom Wolfe, who wrote the quintessential article with that theme, "The Me Decade and the Third Great Awakening," in an August 1976 issue of *New York* magazine), others, particularly those who took the leap themselves, have found that the difference between collective social work and individual personal work is illusory. We are all possessors of undesirable thoughts and impulses, characteristics which, when magnified to the social level, lead to racism, cultural insensitivity, economic exploitation, sexual chauvinism, jealousy, and violence. Rather than denying that these characteristics are real, the human-potential movement recognizes that they are real, with roots and shadows in each of us. If we truly do want to create a different society, one based on humane, equitable, loving principles, we have to also explore, alter, and reconfigure that part of the planet that we at once know best and least: ourselves.

So it was that, in the 1970s, many social activists also became personal seekers and spiritual aspirants and Americans embarked on a search for meaning. Even the born-again millions reflect a shadow of this same impulse. The drive for the better job, the next degree, the larger car was alchemized in the 1970s into the quest for meaning, for relevance, for coherence, for what Sufi leader Pir Vilayat Khan identifies as the "feeling that it all makes sense."

Whereas, once, the dominant intellectual perception was that if one really faced "true reality" one would see how awful things really are, a lighter, more optimistic outlook came to those who were willing to put pessimism aside. If we know from our own experience that we can mature beyond jealousy, allow hurts to dissipate, and convert anger into constructive action, then we can believe the same to be true of others.

This subtle but profound shift away from existential ennui, the dominant philosophical stance of the past several decades, and from the loneliness that had paralyzed so many Americans in the 20th century, was reflected in how people spent their time. Weekends at resorts were traded for weekends at retreats. Evening seminars replaced going to the movies. Individual alienation gave way to a sense of belonging. Words like meditation soon became modified by even more obscure terms such as transcendental, and practices like TM (Transcendental Meditation) became the American spiritual-fulfillment fast-food.

It was not an organization or an institution or even a philosophy that caused the 1970s to explode with workshops, weekends, trainings, courses, seminars, articles, tapes, speakers, and, yes, gurus. Rather, it was a confluence of historical happenstances that funneled into a moment in time:

• A generation with great cultural and social freedom — World War II babies– grew up.

• Religious, racial, ethnic, and sexual integration became a highly regarded value (though hardly a reality).

• Utopia Overnight was rendered an impractical vision.

• East did indeed meet West: Scores of Eastern teachers bearing ancient eastern traditions made pilgrimages not to Mecca or the Ganges but to Minneapolis and Galveston.

• California became a laboratory for new ideas and practices that was unlike anywhere else. Just the word "California" came to say quite a lot.

Many apparently new ideas were mixed with very old disciplines, as people sampled from a plentiful psychological menu. Emphases changed: t'ai chi and yoga replaced weight-lifting and sit-ups; the "health food" movement put the concept of dieting in new perspective. Theories abounded, some complementary, some contradictory: Our emotions, many said, are locked in our muscles, others said between our muscles, while still others said in our organs, while yet others said not in our bodies at all but, rather, in our minds, which merely reflect the sad state of our bodies. Meditate with a mantra (a special word or sound), meditate without a mantra. Watch the breath, hold the breath, breathe in, breathe out. Relax the back, hold the spine straight. Imagine a brilliant light in your mind, empty your mind of thought.

Out of this mélange of insights, theories, and conjectures arose centers and movements and disciplines too numerous to count, too varied to categorize, yet too meaningful to their participants to be ignored. Certainly there was much to criticize and even more to caricature in the fledgling attempts at ceremonializing and systematizing the process of self-understanding, and egregious mistakes were made–some by fools, others by well-intentioned if overzealous seekers–yet the basic message of the greater movement reflected the age-old quest of inner fulfillment as a complement to, not a contradiction of, earthly peace.

Still, the field was littered with charlatans and exploiters, some simply hungry for the buck, others twisted and demented, preying on the näiveté of the people around them–the most pitiful, ghastly example being the Reverend Jim Jones. It was easy to fixate on the dishonorable elements—which is largely what the media chose to do, sometimes pinpointing and exposing the snake-oil hawkers, but all too often lumping everything together.

As the 1980s rolled in, it became even easier to sort out which groups and ideas actually contributed to human evolution. Just as is the case with physical objects—some are beautiful and of rare quality, while others are shoddy and useless—so it is with nonphysical methods and disciplines: The personal- and spiritual-growth worlds are populated by the elegant and the authentic, as well as by the spurious, shabbily produced imitations. To grow within, we must be discriminating about the nourishment we choose to ingest. As the sages have told us, there is no neutral ground in the universe—either we contribute or we detract. It's as simple as that.

There is no single right plan for personal growth, nor is there a central synod for the new spirituality. This chapter points to some of the connecting points for these unique networks—unique because to pursue and nurture and accept these personal and spiritual practices is surely a very important way of manifesting love in the world.

PERSONAL GROWTH

It is difficult to separate the personal-growth (or human-potential or consciousness) movement from the many influences that created a revival of interest in spiritual practice in the 1970s. The two movements are intricately and inextricably involved: Unraveling the origins and evolution of one, we inevitably trip across the trail of the other; one discipline, the field of transpersonal psychology, seeks to describe these overlapping areas.

The human-potential movement, for all its well-earned parodies and embarrassing excesses, has served as a vital stepping-off point for millions of people otherwise locked into the drudgery of 9-to-5 existence. It is also the practical application of the field known as humanistic psychology, that development in psychological theory that acknowledges humans as something more than the sum of their physical reflexes (which is what behavioral psychology studies) and something greater than their unconscious sources of neuroses and psychoses (which is what Freudianism addresses).

Like the human-potential movement, humanistic psychology arose naturally, in part due to the writings of one classically trained psychologist, Abraham Maslow. Rather than looking at neurotic people and their problems, Maslow chose to study creative people and their possibilities. Maslow's 1962 book *Toward a Psychology of Being* popularized the concept of *self-actualization*, the process by which people motivate themselves to grow, evolve, and become more creative. Within his model, Maslow pinpointed the transformative moments that people live through—those *peak experiences* that metamorphose people's lives, making them more than they were before, propelling them toward the "farthest reaches of being human" (the title of one of his books, posthumously published).

Buttressed by the writings of Carl Rogers, Rollo May, and Fritz Perls, just to name a few, humanistic psychology made a fragile claim to a place on the academic map, formed its own professional organization, the Association for Humanistic Psychology (which soon sponsored annual meetings, appended in time to the yearly conferences of its more traditional parent, the American Psychological Association), began publication of a scholarly journal, *The Journal of Humanistic Psychology*, and over the next two decades served as one of the primary hatcheries for scores of new psychotherapeutic methods.

These psychotechnologies, as Marilyn Ferguson has fittingly labeled them, are a miscellany of instruments for coping with personal dilemmas. With them, we can become fluent in the language of our bodies, observe our birth experiences creeping into our behavior at the dinner table, train our minds to reduce blood pressure, mobilize our immune systems to reverse life-threatening illnesses, and design more-beautiful mental images of ourselves that will soon show on our faces, in our limbs, and in our lives, allowing us to work more effortlessly, run more lightly, sleep more soundly. There is a technology for every small hamlet nestled in our psyches: Some, like est, are expensive and known to millions; others, virtually unknown, are passed along without cost in moments of crisis—like the person who teaches a friend the principles of progressive relaxation in the midst of an anxious long-distance telephone call.

Countless networks have emanated from the cornucopia of techniques, many of them derived from ancient teachings. Americanized and popularized, offered not only to initiates but to lay people as well, the techniques are really new again. With thousands, perhaps millions of people practicing them, a new form of awareness is in the process of being born.

The human-potential movement is inseparably yoked to the establishment of meeting places, called centers, that were started in the 1960s and 1970s. Oldest and most famous of these is Esalen, a "center" that has no direct connection to any of the others yet by its very existence has served as a symbolic template. Unpretentiously snuggled into a cliff beneath Highway 1 on the spectacular continental edge of the Pacific, steamed by hot springs once frequented by the Esselen Indians, Esalen has both natural beauty as a distinction as well as the history of being the original "growth" center in the United States.

Esalen came about by an accident of birth. Michael Murphy, now an accomplished author (*Golf in the Kingdom*, *Jacob Atabet*, *The Psychic Side of Sports*), got the idea to establish a center to explore his consuming interest in philosophy and religion, particularly Eastern religion. One of the first 1960s seekers to travel to India (where he stayed for some time at the Sri Aurobindo Ashram in Pondicherry), Murphy returned with no clear plan for his life. He suggested to his grandmother that he might take over family property at the hot springs in Big Sur, and before long, Murphy and a few friends had opened an "institute"

Although it was originally conceived with a more intellectual orientation, Esalen soon became known as a place where people would go for "experiences" (now a very common word, like "relationships," both of which have collected a family of semantic innuendoes that simply did not obtain before the 1960s). Eminent and sometimes bizarre luminaries rising on the new psychological frontier came to deliver week-long and even month-long sessions, and people spent extraordinary amounts of money to listen to, take part in, and evaluate the presentations. All kinds of new techniques—from pummeling apart the connective tissue between the muscles (innocuously called rolfing, after its developer, Ida Rolf) to elaborating new models of the universe—were thrashed out in the Esalen bungalows. By the end of the 1970s, the personal orientation of the seminars had expanded to embrace social and scientific issues.

While growth centers have at times functioned as the staging ground for absurd and sometimes destructive ideas, these new centers for a new kind of learning have also served a powerful purpose in authenticating the value of inner knowledge, corroborating the magnitude of affective (emotional) learning. Further, the human-potential movement has proffered permissions that depart from the cultural norm: for men to cry, for women to be angry, for people to confront the dark underbelly of existence, to wrestle with it, and to ingest it, composting pain into wisdom and experience. The panic that comes with loss, the wounds of rejection, the terror of dying, the awesome fear of giving birth are the daily agendas of growth sessions.

People are attracted to the sessions because of needs that arise from traumas in their lives such as a serious illness, a divorce, or a death, or simply to enrich their lives. People travel great distances to attend specialized courses, and they meet locally or correspond by telephone and mail to explore their mutual interests further. Much of the message of the personal-growth world spreads through speakers and workshop leaders who travel from city to out-of-the-way retreat center and back to the city again.

The human-potential network is peculiarly American and very much the child of the postindustrial information age, in which an insight today can be a training session or a workshop or even a book tomorrow. No credentials, thank you, for the learning all ultimately returns to our sense of ourselves. Which makes it a bit scary. No one knows what the human potential really is. For every moment that we seem to fathom what humans can do, we do something else. The motivating question—Where does it all end?—seems to be eclipsed by the belief that it never does.

The workshops and lectures are merely one aspect of this imprecise realm known as personal growth. One may start with a "training," a jargonistic way of describing concentrated short courses such as Arica, Actualizations, Dimensional Mind Approach, Insight Training (or any of dozens of other programs, none of which would likely favor being included in the same sentence with the others), in which a particular way of looking at the world is espoused. While some "trainees" then become proselytes of that particular approach, volunteering or perhaps being paid to work for the organization, most people then move on to something else, perhaps to another training (yes, dilettantes appear here, too) or perhaps more selectively to learning about diet or exercise or meditation. A massage (or polarity or shiatsu or some other physical treatment or bodily reeducation such as Alexander method or Feldenkrais technique) may come next, possibly coincident with studying yoga or t'ai chi or aikido or inaugurating a daily program of running.

While there is no formal relationship between any two points in the network, an offhand remark or flyer on a desk or direct suggestion may guide someone from Point A to Point B. For example, two students in an Iyengar yoga group strike up a conversation after class, one mentions a dream, the other responds with an anecdote about a workshop she attended the weekend before, and within a few moments, the person who had the dream has decided to attend the Intensive Journal Workshop the next time it is offered. There is no explicit connection between B. K. S. Iyengar (who developed the yoga system) and Ira Progoff (who developed the Intensive Journal Method), yet their disciplines both are familiar stopping points on people's journeys inward. In a very large view, there is a *Gestalt* alliance among all the byways concerned with personal development, a coherence that ultimately links all the areas of networking addressed in this book. Anthropologist Virginia Hine puts it this way in her paper "How Do We Get from Here to There? The Conceptual Paradigm Shift":

Many a down to earth anti-nuke farmer, for example, has a beloved and therefore influential son or daughter involved in Zen. A worker in a local rent-control project of the consumer movement is also a follower of a Swami presiding over an international network of meditation centers. An est graduate lives in a commune that is tied into the holistic health movement and is currently serving as technical advisor to an ad hoc corporate task force. A teacher in an alternative school practices Silva Mind Control and devotes her spare time to fighting multinational corporations selling non-nutritious baby foods in Brazil.

Here we see the personal and the social in a productive interplay, enhancing one's ability to be active in the world. But the bias against self-exploration is deeply ingrained in our Western culture. (Try consulting a thesaurus for synonyms for words like self-exploration and prepare yourself for a deluge of unflattering terms, including: self-centered, self-important, self-seeking, and self-absorbed, as well as conceited, egotistical and smug.)

The journey within is very long indeed, frequently leading people to a new philosophical view, one that may stand alongside, absorb, or possibly replace one's religious beliefs. A concern with self coexists with a concern for the context within which the self exists, that vast amorphous unknown quantity (or is it quality?) called Universe. This is the point of departure for the spiritual-growth networks whose numbers have mushroomed in the past 20 years.

SPIRITUAL GROWTH

What is spiritual growth and why do people become involved, indeed engrossed, in it? Spiritual growth makes people happier and provides a framework for understanding the biggest questions of all: What is the nature of the universe? and Who is this "I" that asks this question?

Lisa Marlin, a high school teacher who eventually left education to become a therapist in the humanistic-psychology tradition and a student of meditation and other spiritual practices, explains her transition this way:

> No matter how much I worked on my personality, it wasn't enough. No matter how much I worked on my body, it wasn't enough. I was constantly plagued by my list of "if only's." If only I moved to Arizona, I would be happy. If only I had a good relationship with a man, I would be happy. If only it were a sunny day, I would be happy. I wanted to see my life making sense, to have a deeper sense of myself, to find a dependable source of happiness inside.

Like many other people, she turned to meditation, one of the basic ancient technologies that people use to further their spiritual development.

The development of the spiritual growth movement was helped by at least three apparently unrelated phenomena rooted in the 1960s: the space program, which gave us physical proof that our pearly blue planet spins in a sea that is mostly empty (mirroring both the reality being revealed beneath the lens of the powerful electron microscope and ancient Eastern cosmological wisdom, which speaks of "the void" and "the Absolute" as the same thing); the widespread availability of psychotropic (mind-altering) drugs such as marijuana, LSD, mescaline, and psilocybin, which reportedly enabled their users to briefly experience states of universal "oneness" that had long been described by religious seers and mystics; and jet travel and electronic communication, which greased the tracks for cross-cultural connections. Science, technology, and the marketplace made it easy to accept and have access to what theologian Harvey Cox has called the "turning east."

The connection between Eastern teachings and Western followings did not begin when the Beatles went to India to meet Maharishi Mahesh Yogi—the incident that many regard as the catalytic moment in the life of the new spirituality. The tradition of Indian masters, in particular, coming to the West can be traced to the late-19th century, when Swami Vivekananda, a 30-year-old classically trained Vedantic monk, a student of the Indian sage Ramakrishna, traveled at his own initiative to the Parliament of World Religions at the 1893 Chicago World's Fair. Vivekananda, then unknown to both the other speakers and the audience, is reported to have given an electrifying speech. His reputation spread quickly, and he decided to stay in the United States, where he was invited to travel from place to place, largely at the invitation of the unconventional intellectual/Bohemian community then in the making. During his time in the United States, he created the Ramakrishna Vedanta Society, which still exists today. (Vivekananda's visits to Boston, where he was particularly well received, were partially responsible for New England bluebloods being nicknamed "Boston Brahmins.")

In 1920, Paramahansa Yogananda came to the United States, helping to bring the practice of yoga to the West. Through Yogananda's organization, the Self-Realization Fellowship, some traditional Vedantic teachings (dating as far back as perhaps 4000 b.c.) were disseminated in the West through correspondence courses as well as meetings.

Over the next several decades, other classically trained Indian spiritual figures came to the United States, spreading knowledge previously locked in the East, and they attracted considerable followings. Among these people have been four important and very different figures who began their journeys in India.

Meher Baba, known to his followers as the Avatar (meaning the incarnation of God) and who lived most of his adult life in silence, made two visits to the United States before his death, in 1969. A quote from Meher Baba, "Don't worry, be happy," became something of a slogan in the 1960s, serving as a common point of reference for his following which neither proselytized nor actively sought converts.

Hazarat Inayat Khan was the vehicle for the Westernization of Sufism, a word thought to be derived from the Greek *sophia* (wisdom), a variegated tradition based on teachings originating in Hinduism, Buddhism, Zoroastrianism, the mystery schools of ancient Egypt and Greece, and Islam. Headed today by his son Pir Vilayat Khan, the Sufi order is a nondogmatic path that recognizes the common heritage of all religious traditions.

Krishnamurti, who ultimately broke ranks with the British Theosophists (who had identified him as the messiah while he was still a young boy in India), eventually established bases in California and Switzerland, where he continues to give talks. Krishnamurti's basic message of spiritual self-reliance is a pertinent complement to current thought in the fields of health (see Chapter 3), community life (see Chapter 4), and energy (see Chapter 5).

Maharishi Mahesh Yogi, perhaps the most visible of these teachers, has brought Transcendental Meditation to the West. Although the TM program separates itself from any overt spiritual connections (choosing instead the somewhat sanitized subtitle "the science of creative intelligence"), Maharishi is a Vedic scholar who has undertaken the task of translating many scriptures still locked in Sanskrit. TM reached its peak of public visibility in the mid-1970s, when Maharishi appeared on the "Merv Griffin" television show, resurfacing again in the late 1970s, when the press began to report on the TM Siddhis (literally meaning "perfection") program, an expensive and extensive training program in which meditators reportedly learn to bring the mind and body into a state of coherence and thus levitate.

The movement has also included American teachers schooled in Buddhist practice. Rick Fields, himself a student of Buddhism and documenter of what he has identified as American Buddhism, describes the phenomenon this way in *The Next Whole Earth Catalog*:

> It has taken about 2500 years for Buddhism to reach America. Thoreau . . . translated and published possibly the first mahayana sutra [scripture] in America (from the French in *The Dial*, 1854) and . . . realized what the Orientals mean

by contemplation as he sat in his sunny doorway one morning at Walden. . . . D. T. Suzuki, the first patriarch of American Zen, took an editing and translating job in La Salle, Illinois in 1897, and there have been Zen Buddhists of some sort here ever since. In the sixties, formal Zen practice became generally available, and in the seventies Americans trained in the forest monasteries of Southeast Asia returned home, while Tibetan exiles, having crossed the Himalayas on foot, arrived by jet.

[There are] three traditional subdevelopments of Buddhist development . . . the Theravadin school is the earliest . . . and now survives chiefly in Burma, Thailand, and Ceylon. Mahayana, a later development, based on the idea of the Bodhisattva, who postpones entry into Nirvana in order to work with others, is found in China, Japan, Korea, and Vietnam. Vajrayana, or Tantric Buddhism, developed in northern India [and] was practiced in Tibet, Mongolia, and Sikkim.

The now considerable network of Zen (Mahayana) Buddhist centers—from the famous Zen Center of San Francisco started by Shunruyu Suzuki Roshi (author of *Zen Mind, Beginner's Mind*), to the Zen Center in Rochester, New York, started by Roshi Philip Kapleau (author of *The Three Pillars of Zen*)—have reached many, many North Americans. Teachers coming out of Tibet, such as Chogyam Trungpa, Rinpoche, who founded the Naropa Institute, in Boulder, Colorado, have extended the Vajrayana tradition to the West. Americans Joseph Goldstein (who stumbled upon Buddhism while in the Peace Corps in Asia) and Jack Kornfield, among others, have imported the Theravadin tradition, now based at the Insight Meditation Center, in Barre, Massachusetts—formerly a Catholic monastery.

Among the most impressive people to come to the West in recent years is Tenzin Gyatso, His Holiness, the 14th Dalai Lama of Tibet. The Dalai Lama is the exiled spiritual and political leader of Tibet, a country occupied since 1959 by the Chinese. Recognized at the age of two as the "incarnation" of the previous (13th) Dalai Lama, he was subsequently given an intense course of study in Buddhist scripture and logic. The Dalai Lama is symbolic as a transitional figure between East and West, one who deals both with the personal and the social, the spiritual and the political realities of daily life.

Another significant teacher to emerge from the East is Swami Muktananda Paramahansa, who was initiated in India into the ancient Siddha Yoga lineage in 1947. Known to his followers as Baba, Muktananda has introduced a new element to the current spiritual diaspora: He initiates people into Siddha Yoga by a transmission of "energy," known as "Shaktipat," a tradition more customarily reserved for advanced spiritual students. Literally meaning "touch of energy," Shaktipat awakens what Eastern traditions call "kundalini," spiritual energy housed in the body at the base of the spine. Arriving for the first time in the United States, in 1970, Muktananda quickly attracted a following. Today there are Siddha Yoga centers in many large cities of the world, and Muktananda's base in Ganeshpuri, India, has grown to accommodate both the numbers and habits of the Western followers.

The growth of the following of people like Muktananda challenges the idea that spiritual seekers are innocent sheep who trudge along in their masters' footsteps, obeying orders and abdicating responsibility for their own decision making. Although weekend workshops (called intensives) and courses are offered for a fee, no one "joins" Siddha Yoga, and the boundaries of the Siddha Yoga universe are very fuzzy indeed. While some followers (who call themselves devotees) do consult Muktananda for advice on personal issues, there are no strict rules that require people to renounce their families, abandon their original religions, or wear strange garments. On the contrary, like many other practices, Siddha Yoga encourages people to bring spiritual practice and insight into their daily lives.

Speaking at Harvard Divinity School in February 1981 on the nature of the guru-disciple relationship, Pascal Kaplan, who studied seven spiritual groups and wrote his doctoral dissertation on this topic, drew the following distinction between cults, which he believes appeal to people's egos, and authentic spiritual practice, which he regards as aiding the dissolution of the ego, a step aspired to on many paths:

> A cult figure will orient his or her teaching and organization to the process of enhancing the ego life of those who come under that person's influence rather than enhancing the spiritual processes. Cults are very precise in defining membership—who's in and who's out. Whoever's in is good, right, and holy. Whoever's out is everything else. In cults, the emphasis is on hierarchy—my place and my role—with merit badges and Boy Scout ranks and knowing one's place and having one's role clearly defined.

In the many new spiritual networks, such distinctions as "who's in" and "who's out" are not only inappropriate but at cross-purposes with the desires of the aspirants. For every spiritual group member, there are dozens more people who participate autonomously in many spiritual disciplines, creating the links and thus the greater network of affiliated spiritual teachings. Even so, many people have been sucked into personality cults from which extrication is difficult.

One very useful self-help network, Sorting It Out, in Berkeley, California, provides assistance to people whom it calls "leave-takers." Founder Joshua Baran, a former Zen priest who lived in a monastery before starting the project, explains:

> We work with people who have left spiritual groups and gurus/teachers. Since the project was started, we've seen leave-takers from nearly one hundred different groups (like Zen, Tibetan Buddhism, The Farm, TM, 3HO, Rajneesh, est, Arica, Siddha Yoga, etc.).

This does not mean that any of these groups or methods is "bad" as such. It does mean, however, that leaving a close-knit community, particularly one based on shared spiritual bonds, is very difficult. The name itself—Sorting It Out—implies that people leaving groups have a lot of work to do, quite different from the highly publicized incidents of cult deprogramming.

Just as the East has spawned its own school of what has been called "freshwater spiritualism," so has the West. The new reformism in Christianity has been reported in the press primarily as the turn toward fundamentalism. Yet there is another strand with a typically Christian message, one that acknowledges a many-dimensional reality within which Jesus Christ is one, albeit central, figure. The Course in Miracles, two volumes reportedly dictated to an agnostic woman, then an assistant professor of medical psychology at Columbia University, from a "higher source," has been one of the documents for the transmission of this third force in Christianity. "Miracle" groups have sprung up in many places, with people taking the course (which offers a program of study for every one of 365 days) and meeting to discuss their studies. While many aspects of traditional Christianity come through the pages of The Course in Miracles, there is also information that is reminiscent of the Christian mystics (whose teachings have been largely overlooked or avoided by the Church) as well as what might be described as a "new age" message that encourages the use of affirmations (repetitions of positive thoughts) and visualizations (creating mental pictures). Although less formalized and without a central written doctrine, a parallel practice is evolving out of classical Judaism: In Berkeley, California, a group known as the Aquarian Minyan combines traditional religious practices with esoteric teachings from Judaism.

Any thorough discussion of the "consciousness movement" must acknowledge the considerable upsurge of interest in the psychic and the occult in the past several decades, tantalizing and potentially absorbing practices that are often confused with spiritual traditions. It is often the case that when people start meditating, or engage in some other spiritual practice in a disciplined way, their extrasensory faculties seem to become more finely honed, enabling them to see beyond the five senses, demonstrating such attributes as clairvoyance (the ability to perceive things that are out of visible range), clairaudience (the ability to hear beyond the immediate audio range), and other remarkable feats. (For some people, these "powers" appear to be innate.)

Westerners, long divorced from nonmaterial perceptions, are fascinated by such "impossible" abilities. However, ancient teachers and modern masters are adamant in stating that advanced "powers" are not the point, or the goal, or even a desirable objective of spiritual practice–they are merely its occasional by-product. While seeing an aura, the misty-colored halo around the body, may come with spiritual unfolding, it is really no different from being able to see the skin on people's faces. For every layer of reality we unfold, there is another and another and another. Seeing auras or having preknowledge of an event, or being able to hear across great distances, or being able to bend physical objects with the mind do not make people more spiritual than people who do not do these things.

For people within the cyclone of spiritual awakening, there is sometimes another little-discussed problem: the occurrence of strange physical symptoms (such as tingling sensations, pressures in the head, and numbness) as well as psychological side effects, such as disorientation, that apparently have no medical explanation. In his book *Stalking the Wild Pendulum: On the Mechanics of Consciousness*, Itzhak Bentov, who combined his practical scientific knowledge as a biomedical inventor with his spiritual experiences as a meditator, posited that these physical and mental side effects were caused by rapid spiritual development, called "kundalini rising":

> The psychological symptoms tend to mimic schizophrenia. It is very likely, therefore, that such individuals may be diagnosed as schizophrenics and be either institutionalized or given very drastic and unwarranted treatment. It is ironic that persons in whom the evolutionary processes of Nature have begun to operate more rapidly, and who can be considered as advanced mutants of the human race, are institutionalized as sub-normal by their "normal" peers. I dare to guess, on the basis of discussions with my psychiatrist-friends, that this process is not as exotic and rare as one would like to believe, and possibly 25 to 30 percent of all institutionalized schizophrenics belong to this category–a tremendous waste of human potential.

The little-researched area of physical and mental symptoms brought on by spiritual development begs for more consideration. One network addressing this issue is the Spiritual Emergency Network started by artist Christina Grof (who reports that she underwent such experiences), and her husband, Stanislav Grof, a psychiatrist known for his seminal work using hallucinogenic drugs in a therapeutic setting (*Realms of the Human Unconscious*).

Much of the life of the spiritual-growth networks blossoms because people read books like Bentov's and recognize experiences that they have not seen confirmed elsewhere, or because people hear the poetry and see the sculpture of Mirtala Bentov in her exquisite film *The Human Journey*, or because people pass along such powerful pamphlets as *Conversations with John*, edited by David Spangler (author of *Revelation: The Birth of A New Age*, cofounder of the Lorian Association, a spiritually-oriented group, and one of the early members of Findhorn, the spiritual community situated in Scotland).

In *Conversations with John*, which Spangler reports that he received while in meditation ("John is a being of spirit," he writes in the Preface), an overview of the difficult years we are facing is laid out. A tough-minded yet optimistic message for spiritually attuned people is presented, concluding with some practical advice on how people can acknowledge the existence of other levels of reality without abdicating responsibility for their own lives:

You do not need a spiritual force to tell you to seek peace, to nourish freedom, to embody these qualities, and to offer them as gifts to others. You do not need a spiritual force to tell you that many of the values of your society deal with elements of life which really have no value, which do not serve the overall well-being of the world in any way. You do not need a spiritual force to tell you to abandon these elements or at least to put them in a different perspective. You do not need a spiritual force to tell you that you should seek out different, more holistic and nourishing values. You do not need a spiritual force to tell you that you should live in harmony with each other, for if you don't, it is obvious your communities will be torn apart.

The decade that's ahead will challenge you as human beings on all fronts of your lives: physically, emotionally, mentally, spiritually, economically, socially, politically. Yet, in the midst of all of this, there will be an increasing number of people who will be essentially untouched, who will be sources of protection, security, and new vision, whose energy will go into exploring and creating alternatives.

. . . What is needed is precise, appropriate, skillful, wise, loving, and serene action, thought, and attunement filled with power and open to the true pain of your time and to the potentials of healing that pain.

. . . Be of good cheer. The future can be nothing but the shadow of your presence. Look to the moments of your lives right now, for here lives that spirit and that power which you seek. May the blessings of that spirit enrich your lives and your vision, and be the daily unfoldment of the worlds we share.

While spiritual practice sits at the core of many people's lives, for others the very idea of a spiritual dimension in life seems atavistic, primitive, and unenlightened. This perspective is shared by many intellectuals as well as by such groups as the American Humanist Association, who deplore talk of "other realities," imploring instead that people take full charge of their own powers and not abdicate responsibility to an unseen "greater force." There is a very loving and enriching quality to the Humanist message, one that satisfies many of the same yearnings that impel people toward spiritual practice.

Yet another dimension to the idea of spiritual growth is being explored from a feminist perspective. The work of 19th-century historians such as Bachofen documents a distinct heritage of humans worshiping a female, rather than a male, deity.

In the 20th-century, the scholar Erich Neumann continued this research, which is documented in his extensive work *The Great Mother*. The physician S. Esther

Harding followed with *Woman's Mysteries*. (Both Neumann and Harding were students of C. G. Jung.) Interest in this work was revived in the late 1960s with the publication of Elizabeth Gould Davis' widely read book, *The First Sex*, and by the end of the 1970s with the writings of theologian Mary Daly (*Beyond God the Father*), Anne Kent Rush's exquisitely designed and easy to read *Moon, Moon*, and art historian Merlin Stone's more scholarly works *When God Was a Woman* and *Ancient Mirrors of Womanhood*. Together, these works represent a new interpretation of religious history, one that encompasses the later patriarchal traditions that have inspired even the most modern of spiritual networks. Women are gathering for festivals connected with the moon, the spring and fall equinoxes, the summer and winter solstices, to honor these ancient traditions.

Carol P. Christ (yes, that's her real name), a theological scholar, forecasts the impact of this new trend in spirituality in her book *Diving Deep and Surfacing: Women Writers on Spiritual Quest*:

> Recently women have begun to write about the connections between spirituality and personal and spiritual change. They have pointed out that women's spiritual quest provides new visions of individual and shared power that can inspire a transformation of culture and society. . . . Women's spiritual quest is thus not an alternative to women's social quest, but rather is one dimension of the larger quest women have embarked upon to create a new world.

Ultimately, the purpose of spiritual development is to enrich daily life. By translating sometimes abstract and abstruse teachings into ordinary situations, we make spiritual development a real, concrete contribution to the everyday world.

ONE WORKING SPIRITUAL NETWORK

One very special network that appears to bridge the esoteric realms and the gut reality of everyday existence has emerged from the transformation of Ram Dass—in his previous life a psychologist at Harvard, named Richard Alpert, who catapulted to fame alongside Timothy Leary. Ram Dass was one of the first psychedelic experimenters to observe the transitory, ephemeral nature of "getting high." By the end of the 1960s, he had sloughed off his previous identity in favor of a spiritual path, which he pursued to India, where he became a student of a spiritual master, Neem Karoli Baba. Returning to an enthusiastic American reception, Ram Dass went on the first of many lecture tours on which he spoke humorously of his experiences with spiritual development. He convened gatherings, some of which took place at his family homestead on Webster Lake, in Franklin, New Hampshire, where interested people camped out for several days to meditate, chant, and listen to him speak.

Although people tried to become his disciples, Ram Dass did not accept the role of guru to a devoted following, and beyond that, his ability to poke fun at himself has kept him in touch with his own humanity. That quality, coupled with some embarrassing mistakes and rather substantial errors of judgement that he was willing to make public (in such classic essays as "Egg on My Beard"), have endeared the man to many who would otherwise have written him off.

What fewer people know is that Ram Dass has also created what amounts to a Spiritual Good Works Factory. In the mid-1970s, he established the Hanuman (after the Indian God-monkey by that name) Foundation (HF) as a nonprofit tax-exempt corporation to which he donated his earnings from his lectures and his books (notably *Be Here Now*, *The Only Dance There Is*, and *Grist for the Mill*, which he coauthored with Stephen Levine). Today the Hanuman Foundation comprises three separate, independent projects: the Prison-Ashram Project, the Dying Project, and the Hanuman Foundation Tape Library. "The Hanuman Foundation exists only through these three projects," explains Bo Lozoff, director of the Prison-Ashram Project. "There is no 'central office' or administrative arm. The three project directors operate autonomously, and we collaborate (other than friendships) only to do the books each year and report to the government. Donations and correspondence are made to the particular project one is interested in. HF has a board of directors which meets annually to discuss the projects and ideas for any new projects seeking support. HF has no 'members' or opportunities for such ties.

"Though we operate very nonexpansively (there are only about seven paid employees for all the projects), I consider HF and its projects to indeed be networks of sorts. We all agreed at the outset to have a healthy caution against empire building, so our position has been to encourage, advise and train thousands of people to set up their own local efforts in various ways. Each HF project has an extensive mailing list—our own is around 7500 people at any given time, with a turnover of at least 1500 each year. Over 3000 of these folks are not in prison, and many are involved in one way or another with mini-projects. Through our bimonthly newsletters, two or three lecture tours a year, and training seminars, we act as a networking agency to them."

Each project has its own mission:

[The Prison-Ashram Project] provides information and encouragement to prisoners who would like to use their time for spiritual training. As well as introducing them to meditation, yoga, and spiritual ideas (not religious), we also try to help people avoid getting caught or seduced into various traps or trips that often go along with these studies. Our emphasis is on a light, good-humored, non-preachy perspective.

We've been fortunate through the years to gain solid credibility with the American correctional establishment. These linkages have taught us a great deal about relating to the culture at large, since we have usually considered ourselves to be far outside that culture. It's really nice seeing how service tends to assimilate us into the mainstream and break down illusory walls which were our own creations in the first place.

When the originators first envisioned the Prison-Ashram Project, they expected that their constituency would be drawn largely from counterculture types who had been imprisoned for drug or political offenses. Much to their surprise, however, they found instead that "most of the thousands of prisoners who wrote to us were 35 to 45 years old and had been in prison up to 25 years already. Or they were people who had been sentenced to 200 years plus life; people who had less than an eighth grade education."

The response moved Lozoff to reexamine his original assumptions and to rethink how to present yoga and meditation within the prison walls. As a result, he developed what he calls "prison yoga." "We can help people convert their prison experience into a monastic one," he told Sufi Times, "but it's a very particular monastic environment—one lived within an atmosphere of hostility, hatred, and suspicion."

From its base in Santa Fe, New Mexico, the Dying Project, a second arm of the Hanuman Foundation, serves a different purpose, bringing a profound understanding to thinking about death. In an issue of the Dying Project Newsletter, Ram Dass proposes a rather unusual and expanded way of looking at death:

Do you remember 8:22 this morning? Do you remember that moment? It was just another sleepy moment, wasn't it? Just another sleepy minute. But if we experienced full awareness, then each moment, including 8:22, would be precious, yet nothing special. Just as if your consciousness could expand out far enough to include other lives and someone said, "Do you remember that death?" And you'd say, "Which one? I think I was eating breakfast." "No, you remember the one I'm talking about. You were on the toilet that time." "Oh, THAT time; oh yeah, right." "Can you imagine just remembering the sequence of deaths and birth as just more moments, just 8:22 in the flow of things?"

What we're exploring is the stretching of our being . . . out, out, out into time–and beyond time; into space, and beyond space. That stretching provides the change in perspective which takes each moment and makes it precious and clear and conscious, yet nothing special. And death is another of these moments, equally precious, yet nothing special.

"There's no unfinished business when you're in the moment," explains Dying Project director Stephen Levine, an early editor of the San Francisco Oracle, among the first underground newspapers in the country, and a teacher of Buddhist meditation. "We are trying to understand death as a means of spiritual awakening, Westernizing ideas that have been around for thousands of years. Death has to be a part of our lives. Gandhi was one of the many who have used their fearlessness of death as their strongest weapon."

With these ideas in mind, Levine organizes five-day Conscious Living/Conscious Dying seminars for people with terminal illnesses and for those in the helping professions who work with people who are dying.

Levine also spends a lot of time on the telephone counseling people long-distance. "When you are on the telephone and you close your eyes, there is nothing but you and the other person. You are inside the other being," he explains.

Along with this free phone consultation, the Dying Project is also involved in establishing a Dying Center, where people with terminal illnesses can come to die. "In the beginning, there will perhaps be only one or two patients who wish to die in an environment which affords a conscious use of their present situation as a means of coming to a deeper awareness of being. Eventually, we foresee perhaps as many as six patients living and learning and teaching with us at any one time. We also foresee implementing an intern program whereby those who wish to use death as a means of awakening may join us as volunteers for from two weeks to two months," the newsletter says.

For all the valuable work the Hanuman Foundation is doing, its approach remains low-key without requiring anything of the reader, participant, or listener. There is no doctrine to be swallowed, no tithe to be paid, no radical change in life-style to be effected. Rather, the message of this powerful little network is simply to become aware of who you are, where you are, as Levine puts it, "to become aware of the spaciousness."

The Hanuman Foundation's work is a consummate example of translating ancient Eastern wisdom into usable Western form, a true synthesis of two superficially alien partners. Prison yoga? Conscious dying? Contradictions in terms? No, partners in the cosmic dance.

Growing Guide

G

The Growing Guide includes groups that are primarily concerned with personal and spiritual growth. Many of these groups also work on other issues.

Each group is identified by a letter/number code. The letter **G** stands for Growing. Every group whose code begins with **G** is listed in the Growing Guide.

The entry for each network whose code is lower than 100 includes a brief description. These representative networks are a cross-section of the initial groups we contacted in our research. Each network whose code is greater than 100 is listed with complete contact information. If the ✳ symbol, for publications, or the ◆ symbol, for materials, appears with a listing, consult the Title Guide under Growing Titles.

The Growing Guide includes groups that are concerned with arts, body movement and awareness, consciousness, crafts, death and dying, holistic studies, humanistic psychology, meditation, music, outdoor activities, recreation, retreat centers, spiritual practice, theatre, transformation, travel . . . and a few others.

G001
American Humanist Association
7 Harwood Drive
Amherst, NY 14226   ✳✳

✳ *Free Mind (bimonthly/$15)*
✳ *Humanist (monthly/$12)*

Home base for national group that holds that human beings, not supernatural powers, shape destiny. Produces TV programs, sponsors conferences and institutes. Trains "counsellors" to officiate at marriage and memorial events.

G002
Another Place
Route 123
Greenville, NH 03048
603/878-1510

A conference and networking center that survived the 1970s with new plans and organization for the 1980s. Symbolic home for many New England social-change activists. Weekends on work, coops, healing arts, and education.

G003
Association for Humanistic Psychology
325 Ninth Street
San Francisco, CA 94103
415/626-2375   ✳✳◆

✳ *AHP Newsletter (monthly/$20)*
✳ *Journal of Humanistic Psychology
   (4 issues/$12)*
◆ *AHP Resource Directory ($6)*

International membership organization for people interested in nonbehavioral approaches to psychology. Lively annual conferences and regional meetings offer presenters and participants experimental meeting grounds for new ideas.

G004
Association for Transpersonal Psychology
4615 Paradise Drive, # 3049
Stanford, CA 94305
415/327-2066   ✳✳

✳ *Association for Transpersonal Psychology
   Newsletter (4/$25)*
✳ *Journal of Transpersonal Psychology
   (2 issues/$15)*

Membership organization for people interested in aspects of psychology that go beyond individuals. Includes consciousness research, meditation, transcendence, and spirituality topics. Conferences and publications.

G005
Bed & Breakfast League
20 Nassau Street
Princeton, NJ 08540
609/921-0440   ◆

◆ *Bed & Breakfast Directory*

Travelers' service that provides people with a place to sleep and breakfast–a "new, old-fashioned hospitality network"–in private homes. Members pay $45 annual fee. Nightly costs range from $12 (single) to $28 (double).

G006
Cambridge Zen Center
263 North Harvard Street
Allston, MA 02134
617/254-0363

Zen Buddhist meditation center. Offers intensives.

G007
Center for Leisure Guidance
P.O. Box 1980
Cambridge, MA 02139
617/266-4646

Clinical and educational facility offering alternatives to television as the #1 American leisure-time activity. Organizers of "Summerthing," bringing cultural events to neighborhoods. Programs, workshops, and counseling.

G008
Chimo: The Holistic Magazine for Our Times
79 Victoria Street
Toronto, Ontario
CANADA M5C 2B1
416/366-8897   ✳

✳ *Chimo: The Holistic Magazine of Our Times
   (monthly/$12)*

Insightful and well-designed Canadian monthly that deals with philosophy, spirituality, body therapies, healing practices, and ecology. Each issue contains annotated directory of groups and centers.

G009
Cooperative Communities of America
7501 Sebago Road
Bethesda, MD 20034
301/229-2802   ✳◆

✳ *News from CCA ($5 year)*
◆ *Travelers Network ($10 year)*

Optimistic, friendly referral service, which maintains the Travelers Network (for places to stay) and Communities Network (to build cooperation). Working to foster "sense of community" through collective purchasing.

G010
Dromenon: Journal of New Ways of Being
P.O. Box 2244
New York, NY 10001
212/675-3486   ✳

✳ *Dromenon: A Journal of New Ways of Being
   (4 issues/$9)*

New ideas about consciousness are the focus
of this journal founded by Jean Houston.
Maintains network of people who organize
groups "conducive to transformative growth."

G011
Dying Project
P.O. Box 1725
Santa Fe, NM 87501   ✳◆◆

✳ *Dying Project Newsletter (donation)*
◆ *Living/Dying Retreat (tape, $2.50)*
◆ *Grist for the Mill (Ram Dass & Levine, $3.95)*

Enlightening project of Hanuman Foundation.
Sponsors retreats, gives lectures, and counsels people around issue of dying. Informal
networks from among those attending
retreats. Distributes newsletters, audiotapes,
and books.

G012
Emissaries of Divine Light
P.O. Box 238
Loveland, CO 80537   ◆

◆ *Spirit of Sunrise (by Michael Cecil et al.)*

Network of 230 centers in North America
where people share eclectic approach to life
and spirituality. Some centers are communes.
Also known as "The Family" or "The Body."
"Integrity, honesty, and simplicity" are the
keys.

G013
Intimate Talk: Journal of Expression
P.O. Box 489
Berkeley, CA 94701
415/527-1900   ✳

✳ *Intimate Talk ($24 year)*

Unique magazine/newsletter drawing on personal experiences. Publisher Louise Lacey
coordinates theme issues; editorial meetings
consist of contributors discussing topics.
Unusual voice for inner experience–unlike
anything else.

G014
Lama Foundation
P.O. Box 444
San Cristobal, NM 87564

Eclectic spiritual community that sponsors
summer sessions, publishes books, and
makes silk-screen flags and other crafts.

G015
Matagiri Sri Aurobindo Center
Mount Tremper, NY 12457   ✳◆◆

✳ *Collaboration (quarterly/$2)*
◆ *Essential Aurobindo ($3.95)*
◆ *Practical Guide to Integral Yoga ($6)*

Residental center for dissemination of information about Indian masters Sri Aurobindo
and The Mother, whose teachings are being
followed in the utopian new community of
Auroville, India. Visitors welcome.

G016
New Age Information Service
P.O. Box 1043
Corvallis, OR 97330

We wrote to them and they sent us a huge
packet of information–brochures, mailing
lists, booklets, articles, newsletters–primarily
on spiritual issues.

G017
New Games Foundation
P.O. Box 7901
San Francisco, CA 94120
415/664-6900   ✳◆◆

✳ *New Games News/Letter (quarterly/$5)*
◆ *More New Games ($6.95)*
◆ *New Games Book ($4.95)*

One-of-a-kind membership group that promotes noncompetitive, "everyone wins" form
of play for adults and children. Organizes New
Games Days in cities, sponsors workshops,
and distributes books and toys on new games
theme.

G018
Omega Institute for Holistic Studies
P.O. Box 396
New Lebanon, NY 12125
518/794-8850

Summer programs in healing, physical fitness,
music, dance, drama, fine arts, and spirituality. Costs from $50 to $185. Experienced faculty organized by Sufi community.

G019
Prison Ashram Project
Rural Route #1, Box 201
Durham, NC 27705   ✳◆

✳ *Prison Ashram Project
   (bimonthly/donation)*
◆ *Inside/Out: A Spiritual Manual for Prison
   Life (free)*

Very creative and practical project that supports inmates in using the prison experience
for spiritual growth. Sponsors Prison/
Community Alliances–cultural and educational exchanges.

G020
Public Action Coalition on Toys
222 East 19th Street, #8a
New York, NY 10003　　　　　　　　◆

◆ *Guidelines on Choosing Toys for
Children ($1)*

Volunteer group working to encourage development of safe and sensible toys–a vitally
needed service. Organizes letter-writing campaigns and forums for parents. Publishes
excellent handbook on buying toys.

G021
Rites of Passage
857 Delong Avenue
Novato, CA 94947
415/892-5371　　　　　　　　　　◆

◆ *Basic Paradigm of a Future Socio-Cultural
System (Hine)*

One sparkling node in a network aimed at "re-
ritualizing" America. Creates relevant new rituals for life transitions, particularly from adolescence to adulthood, often utilizing
wilderness experiences.

G022
Sing Out! The Folk Song Magazine
505 Eighth Avenue
New York, NY 10018
212/594-8105　　　　　　　　　　✳

✳ *Sing Out! The Folk Song Magazine
(bimonthly/$8.50)*

One of the very few (and probably the oldest)
folk music networks in the U.S. Through Sing
Out! magazine, concerts, radio shows, and
workshops, indigenous American folk/
people's music is returned to its roots.

G023
Sphinx and Sword of Love Bookstore
111 Mt. Auburn Street
Cambridge, MA 02138
617/491-8788

Excellent source of books and music on personal, spiritual, and social transformation.
Mail-order catalog available.

G024
Spiritual Community Guide
P.O. Box 1080
San Rafael, CA 94902
415/863-4788　　　　　　　　　◆◆

◆ *Spiritual Community Guide ($5.95)*
◆ *Pilgrim's Guide to Planet Earth ($8.95)*

Publishes Spiritual Community Guide, first
comprehensive directory of resources in "new
age" community. Contains everything from
restaurants to schools to health. Rents mailing
lists and publishes other titles.

G025
Sri Chinmoy Centre
85-45 149th Street
Jamaica Hills, NY 11435　　　　✳✳✳

✳ *Anahata Nada (bimonthly)*
✳ *Jharna-Kala (art quarterly/$10 year)*
✳ *Aum Magazine (monthly/$5 year)*

Crossroads of international group following
the artist, musician, spiritual leader Sri
Chinmoy Ghose. Supports work of United
Nations. Organizes festivals, public medita-
tions, concerts, runners races, and lectures.

G026
The Sun: A Magazine of Ideas
412 West Rosemary Street
Chapel Hill, NC 27514
919/942-5282　　　　　　　　　　✳

✳ *The Sun (12 issues/$12)*

Lovely magazine combining features, interviews, poetry, fiction, photography, and
reviews. Abounds with first-person material;
lively reader-response section.

G027
Transformation Project
c/o Esalen Institute
P.O. Box 67
Mill Valley, CA 94941　　　　　　◆

◆ *Psychic Side of Sports (Murphy & White)*

Research project investigating the outer
reaches of the human body's abilities. Documenting instances of extraordinary mental and
physical functioning. Developing model of
psycho-physical transformation.

G028
Well Being: A Network for Spiritual Journeyors
P.O. Box 887
San Anselmo, CA 94960
415/461-2373　　　　　　　　　　✳

✳ *Spiritual Journeys (monthly/$12 year)*

Formal network of people on eclectic spiritual
paths. Puts "like-minded souls" in touch with
one another. Subtitled "A Network for Spiritual Journeyors."

G029
Women Outdoors
474 Boston Avenue
Medford, MA 02155
617/628-2525　　　　　　　　　　✳

✳ *Good News (monthly/$3)*

Unique network of women who use experiences in nature ("outdoor adventuring") to
better understand their lives. Publishes journal, organizes events and trips, and compiles
job-information newsletter.

G101
Actualizations
3632 Sacramento Street
San Francisco, 94118

G102
Alternative Resource Center
P.O. Box 1707
Forest Park, GA 30050
404/361-5823   ✦

G103
Alternatives: Tools for Holistic Living
Rural Route #1, Box 390
New Market, VA 22844   ✳

G104
American Astrology
2505 Alvernon Way
Tucson, AZ 85712   ✳

G105
American Institute of Buddhist Studies
86 College Street
Amherst, MA 01002
413/256-0281

G106
American Spiritual Healing Association
P.O. Box 23006
Washington, DC 20024

G107
Anima: An Experiential Journal
1053 Wilson Avenue
Chambersburg, PA 17201
717/263-8303   ✳

G108
Animal Town Cooperative Games
P.O. Box 2002
Santa Barbara, CA 93120

G109
Appalachian Mountain Club
5 Joy Street
Boston, MA 02108
617/523-0636

G110
Aquarian Minyan
2020 Essex Street
Berkeley, CA 94703
415/835-1208

G111
Aquarian Research Foundation
5620 Morton Street
Philadelphia, PA 19144
215/849-1259   ✳

G112
Arcana Workshops
407 North Maple Drive, Suite 214
Beverly Hills, CA 90210
231/273-5949   ✳

G113
Association for Moral Education
221 East 72nd Street
New York, NY 10021
212/734-6658   ✳

G114
Association for Research and Enlightenment
Atlantic Avenue and 67th Street
Virginia Beach, VA 23451
804/428-3588

G115
Association for Unity, Research, and Awareness
1548 Grace Street
Lincoln, NB 68503
402/466-0732   ✳

G116
**Association of National Non-Profit Artists'
  Centers**
217 Richmond Street
Toronto, Ontario
CANADA M5V 1W2
416/368-1756   ✳

G117
Astro*Carto*Graphy
P.O. Box 22293
San Francisco, CA 94122   ✦

G118
Auroville Association
212 Farley Drive
Aptos, CA 95003

G119
Baha'i International Community
345 East 46th Street
New York, NY 10017
212/867-2930

G120
Bear Tribe Medicine Society
P.O. Box 9167
Spokane, WA 99209
509/258-7755   ✳✦✦

G121
Black Bart Newsletter
P.O. Box 48
Canyon, CA 94516   ✳

G122
Black Hills Alliance
P.O. Box 2508
Rapid City, SD 57701
605/342-5127

G123
Blackberry Books
P.O. Box 186
Brunswick, ME 04011   ✳◆◆

G124
Boomerang Newsletter
1882 Columbia Road, N.W.
Washington, DC 20009   ✳

G125
Boston Visionary Cell
36 Bromfield Street, Room 200
Boston, MA 02108
617/482-9044

G126
Brain/Mind Bulletin
P.O. Box 42211
Los Angeles, CA 90042   ✳

G127
California Association of Bicycle Organizations
P.O. Box 2684
Dublin, CA 94566   ✳

G128
Camp Winnarainbow
P.O. Box 21
Fairfax, CA 94930

G129
Canada Quilts
360 Stewart Drive
Sudbury, Ontario
CANADA P3E 2R8   ✳

G130
Canadian Sport Parachuting Association
333 River Road
Ottawa, Ontario
CANADA K1L 8B9
613/749-0152   ✳

G131
Center for Arts Information
625 Broadway
New York, NY 10012
212/677-7548

G132
Center for Esoteric Studies
533 East Anapamu Street
Santa Barbara, CA 93103   ✳

G133
Center for Studies of the Person
1125 Torrey Pines Road
La Jolla, CA 92037

G134
Center for Women's Studies and Services
908 E Street
San Diego, CA 92101
714/233-8984   ✳✳◆

G135
Center for the History of American Needlework
Old Economy Village
14th and Church Streets
Ambridge, PA 15003
412/266-6440   ✳◆◆

G136
Center of the Light
P.O. Box 540
Great Barrington, MA 01230
413/229-2396

G137
Chautauqua Institution
Chautauqua, NY 14722
716/357-5635

G138
Cherry Creek: A Theatre Company
406 South Third Street
St. Peter, MN 56082
507/931-1690   ✳

G139
Chicago Mural Group
2261 North Lincoln Avenue
Chicago, IL 60614

G140
Children's Art Foundation
P.O. Box 83
Santa Cruz, CA 95063   ✳

G141
Churches Center for Theology and Public Policy
4500 Massachusetts Avenue, N.W.
Washington, DC 20016
202/363-3088   ✳

G142
Clown College
P.O. Box 1528
Venice, FL 33595
813/488-2226

G143
Coming Changes Newsletter
710 Reid Street
De Pere, WI 54115   ✳

G144
Committee for the Game
1460 Southwest A Street
Corvallis, OR 97330

G145
Community for Religious Research and Education
P.O. Box 9164
Berkley, CA 94709
415/836-0151 ✳

G146
Consciousness Synthesis Clearing House
305 Calle Miramar
Redondo Beach, CA 90277
213/375-8086

G147
Contact Quarterly: A Vehicle for Moving Ideas
P.O. Box 603
Northampton, MA 01061
413/586-8243 ✳

G148
Cosmic Awareness Communications
P.O. Box 115
Olympia, WA 98507 ✳

G149
Council on International Educational Exchange
205 East 42nd Street
New York, NY 10017
212/661-1414 ◆◆

G150
Creative Education Foundation
1300 Elmwood Avenue
Buffalo, NY 14222
716/862-6223 ✳

G151
Creative Yoga Studio
2 Summit Avenue
Brookline, MA 02146
617/277-0999

G152
Damage Magazine: Not for Everybody
P.O. Box 26178
San Francisco, CA 94126
415/861-7118 ✳

G153
Dialogue House Library
National Intensive Journal Program
80 East 11th Street
New York, NY 10003
212/673-5880 ◆◆

G154
Diamond Sangha Center: Zen Buddhist Society
Koko An Zendo
2119 Kaloa Way
Honolulu, HI 96822 ✳✳

G155
Different Worlds: Magazine of Adventure Role-Playing Games
Chaosium Incorporated
P.O. Box 6302
Albany, CA 94706 ✳

G156
Dimensional Mind Approach
P.O. Box 571
Cambridge, MA 02238
617/884-0902

G157
Dormant Brain Research and Development Laboratory
Laughing Coyote Mountain
Black Hawk, CO 80422

G158
Encounter Four: Adventure Course for Youth in Trouble
Butler County Community College
College Drive, Oak Hills
Butler, PA 16001
412/287-8711

G159
Esalen Institute
Big Sur, CA 93920
408/667-2335

G160
Essene Light Center
3427 Denson Place
Charlotte, NC 28215

G161
Essentia Films
Salina Star Route
Boulder, CO 80302
303/443-3484 ◆◆

G162
Faithist Journal
2324 Suffock Avenue
Kingman, AZ 86401
602/757-4569 ✳

G163
Family Pastimes
Rural Route #4
Perth, Ontario
CANADA K7H 3C6
613/267-4819 ◆

G164
Feathered Pipe Ranch
P.O. Box 1682
Helena, MT 59601
406/442-8196

G165
Fine Woodworking
The Taunton Press
P.O. Box 355
Newtown, CT 06470
203/426-8171   ✳✦

G166
Focusing Institute
5637 South Kenwood
Chicago, IL 60637   ✦

G167
Foundation for Inner Peace
P.O. Box 635
Tiburon, CA 94920   ✦

G168
Foundation of Light
399 Turkey Hill Road
Ithaca, NY 14850

G169
Friends Journal
152-A North Street
Philadelphia, PA 19102   ✳

G170
Front Range: Women in the Visual Arts
Valley Vista Lane
Jamestown Star Route
Boulder, CO 80302
303/443-6224   ✦

G171
Fund for Advancement of Camping
4502 North Tamiami Trail
Sarasota, FL 33578
312/322-0827   ✦

G172
Games
515 Madison Avenue
New York, NY 10022
212/421-5984   ✳

G173
Great Expeditions: Real Travellers and Explorers
P.O. Box 46499, Station G
Vancouver, British Columbia
CANADA V6R 4G7
604/224-7610   ✳

G174
Guild of American Luthiers
8222 South Park Avenue
Tacoma, WA 98408
206/472-8439

G175
Hanuman Foundation Tape Library
P.O. Box 61498
Santa Cruz, CA 95061   ✳

G176
**Hardscrabble Hill: Residential Retreat Center for
    Women**
Castine Road, Box 130
Orland, ME 04472
207/469-7112

G177
Hartley Productions: Films for a New Age
Cat Rock Road
Cos Cob, CT 06807
203/869-1818

G178
Healing Light Center
138 North Maryland
Glendale, CA 91206
213/244-8607

G179
High Times
17 West 60th Street
New York, NY 10023
212/974-1990   ✳

G180
Human Dimensions Institute and Center
Rural Route #1, Box 1420
Columbus, NC 28722

G181
I Ching Sangha
237 Chattanooga Street
San Francisco, CA 94114

G182
Illuminations
P.O. Box 1000
Cambridge, MA 02139
617/864-6180   ✦✦✦

G183
Infinite Odyssey: Wilderness Adventures
25 Huntington Avenue, #324
Boston, MA 02116
617/353-1793

G184
Inner Paths: Eastern and Western Spiritual Thought
80 East 11th Street
New York, NY 10003
212/533-0100   ✳

G185
Inner-Space Interpreters Services
P.O. Box 1133, Magnolia Park
Burbank, CA 91507
213/843-0476   ◆

G186
Insight Meditation Society
Barre, MA 01005   ◆◆

G187
Insight Training Seminars
215 Cherry Lane
Wynnewood, PA 19096

G188
Institute for Consciousness and Music
7027 Bellona Avenue
Baltimore, MD 21212
301/377-7525

G189
Institute for the Development of the Harmonious Human Being
P.O. Box 370
Nevada City, CA 95959   ◆◆◆

G190
Institute for the New Age
45 East 78th Street
New York, NY 10021
212/737-8808

G191
International Church of Ageless Wisdom
P.O. Box 101
Wyalusing, PA 18853
717/746-1864   ✳

G192
International Home Exchange Service
P.O. Box 3975
San Francisco, CA 94119
415/457-8474   ✳

G193
International New Thought Alliance
7314 East Stetson Drive
Scottsdale, AZ 85251
602/945-0744   ✳

G194
Jump Cut: A Review of Contemporary Cinema
P.O. Box 865
Berkeley, CA 94701   ✳

G195
Jungian-Senoi Dreamwork Institute
P.O. Box 9332
Berkeley, CA 94709
413/848-0311   ◆

G196
Karma Triyana Dharmachakra
Mountaintop Retreat Center
Mead Mountain Road
Woodstock, NY 12498   ✳

G197
Kite Lines
7106 Campfield Road
Baltimore, MD 21207
301/484-6287   ✳

G198
Kripalu Yoga Center
P.O. Box 106E
Summit Station, PA 17979
717/754-3051   ✳

G199
Kripalu Yoga Fellowship/Toronto
2428 Yonge Street
Toronto, Ontario
CANADA M4P 2H4
416/282-5600   ✳

G200
Kronos: Journal of Interdisciplinary Synthesis
Glassboro State College
Glassboro, NJ 08028   ✳

G201
Laughing Man Institute
P.O. Box 3680
Clearlake Highlands, CA 95422
707/994-9281   ✳◆◆

G202
League of American Wheelmen
P.O. Box 988
Baltimore, MD 21203
301/727-2022   ✳

G203
Life Systems Educational Foundation
219 First Avenue South
Seattle, WA 98104
206/447-9396

G204
Life Understanding Foundation
741 Rosarita Lane
Santa Barbara, CA 93105
805/682-5151   ✳

G205
Lilith: The Jewish Women's Magazine
250 West 57th Street, #1328
New York, NY 10019
212/757-0818   ✳

G206
Lindisfarne Association
The Lindisfarne Press
Rural Route #2
West Stockbridge, MA 01266
413/232-4377   ✳◆◆

G207
**Lorian Association: Serving the Spirit of
    Wholeness**
7146 Elderberry
Middleton, WI 53562   ◆◆

G208
Lost Music Network
P.O. Box 2391
Olympia, WA 98507
206/352-2391   ✳

G209
Love Project
P.O. Box 7601
San Diego, CA 92107
714/225-0133   ✳

G210
Love: A Journal
P.O. Box 9
Prospect Hill, NC 27314   ✳

G211
Lucis Trust
866 United Nations Plaza, #566
New York, NY 10017
212/421-1577

G212
M. Gentle Men for Gender Justice
306 North Brooks, Box 313
Madison, WI 53715   ✳

G213
Magical Blend: A Magazine of Synergy
P.O. Box 11303
San Francisco, CA 94101   ✳

G214
**Many Hands: Guide to Holistic Health and
    Awareness**
Beyond Words Bookshop
150 Main Street
Northampton, MA 01060
413/586-6304   ◆

G215
Maui Zendo
Rural Route #1, Box 220
Haiku, HI 96708

G216
Menorah: Sparks of Jewish Renewal
Public Resource Center
1747 Connecticut Avenue, N.W.
Washington, DC 20009
202/483-7902   ✳

G217
Metamorphoses: Development in Canada
483 MacLaren Street
Ottawa, Ontario
CANADA K1R 5K5   ✳

G218
Minnesota Zen Meditation Center
3343 East Calhoun Parkway
Minneapolis, MN 55808
612/822-5313   ✳

G219
Modern Haiku
P.O. Box 1752
Madison, WI 53701   ✳

G220
Monroe Institute of Applied Sciences
P.O. Box 175
Farber, VA 22938
804/361-1252   ✳

G221
Movement of Spiritual Inner Awareness
3500 West Adams Boulevard
Los Angeles, CA 90018
213/737-1134   ✳

G222
Muktananda Meditation Center
3815 Garrott
Houston, TX 77006
713/529-0006

G223
Naropa Institute
1111 Pearl Street
Boulder, CO 80302
303/444-0202

G224
National Outdoor Leadership School
P.O. Box AA
Lander, WY 82520
307/332-4381

G225
Nature Explorations
2253 Park Boulevard
Palo Alto, CA 94301
415/324-8737

G226
New Age Awareness Center
P.O. Box 6994
Tyler, TX 75711
214/581-1631

G227
New Age Gazette
P.O. Box 2145
Scottsdale, AZ 85252
602/833-2625 ✳

G228
New Age Government
P.O. Box 112
Newtown, CT 06470
203/748-4786

G229
New Age Magazine
244 Brighton Avenue
Allston, MA 02134
617/254-5400 ✳

G230
New Age Mating
Church of New World Religion
P.O. Box 5562
San Francisco, CA 94101
415/431-8790

G231
New Age Music Network
P.O. Box 9416
San Rafael, CA 94902 ✳

G232
New Age Network of Colorado Springs
P.O. Box 6647
Colorado Springs, CO 80934
303/634-1855 ✳

G233
New Age Resource Center
111 Racine Street
Memphis, TN 38111
901/458-2540

G234
**New Art Examiner: Independent Voice of the
    Visual Arts**
230 East Ohio, Room 207
Chicago, IL 60611
312/642-6236 ✳

G235
New Atlantean Research Society
5963 32nd Avenue North
St. Petersburg, FL 33710
813/347-1213 ✳

G236
New Dimensions Radio and Tapes
267 States Street
San Francisco, CA 94114
415/621-1126 ◆

G237
**New Life Foundation for Holistic Health and
    Research**
P.O. Box 355
Athens, ME 04912
207/654-2636 ✳

G238
New Options for a Vital United States (NOVUS)
Prospect House, Suite 817
1200 North Nash Street
Arlington, VA 22209 ✳

G239
**New Realities: Magazine of Body, Mind and
    Spirit**
680 Beach Street
San Francisco, CA 94109
415/776-2600

G240
New Trust Network
2030 Santa Cruz Avenue
Menlo Park, CA 94025
415/854-1308

G241
North American Network of Women Runners
P.O. Box 924
Shaker Heights, OH 44120
216/283-4916 ✳

G242
Omega Foundation
P.O. Box 300
Loveland, CO 80537
303/669-3336 ◆

G243
Ontario Zen Center
1 Hambly Avenue
Toronto, Ontario
CANADA M4E 2R5
416/691-0592

G244
Ottawa Psychic Study Centre
P.O. Box 3770, Station C
Ottawa, Ontario
CANADA K1Y 4J3

G245
Outdoor Education for the Handicapped Project
403 Bradley Hall
University of Kentucky
Lexington, KY 40506
606/258-2772

G246
Outside: Magazine of the Great Outdoors
3401 West Division Street
Chicago, IL 60651
312/342-7777   ✳

G247
Outward Bound
384 Field Point Road
Greenwich, CT 06830
800/243-8520   ◆

G248
Oz Projects: Retreat in the Redwoods
P.O. Box 147
Point Arena, CA 95468
707/882-2449

G249
Parabola: Myth and the Quest for Meaning
150 Fifth Avenue
New York, NY 10011
212/924-0004   ✳

G250
Pax Center
345 East 9th Street
Erie, PA 16503
814/459-8349   ✳

G251
PhenomeNEWS
1735 South Main, #7
Pleasant Ridge, MI 48069
313/548-7571   ✳

G252
Poetry Project
Saint Mark's Church in-the-Bowery
10th Street and 2nd Avenue
New York, NY 10003
212/674-0910   ✳

G253
Progressive Utilization Theory Universal (Prout)
922 South 48th Street
Philadelphia, PA 19143
215/726-6165   ✳

G254
Protestant Committee on Urban Ministry
3410 University Avenue, Room 200
Minneapolis, MN 55414
612/331-6210

G255
Providence Zen Center
R.F.D. #5, Pound Road
Cumberland, RI 02864
401/769-6464   ✳

G256
Quadrinity Center
2295 Palou Avenue
San Francisco, CA 94124
413/397-0466   ◆

G257
Rare Earth: Exotic Properties for Sale
P.O. Box 946
Sausalito, CA 94966
415/331-2700   ✳

G258
**ReVision: A Journal of Knowledge and
    Consciousness**
Rudi Foundation
P.O. Box 468
Cambridge, MA 02138
617/354-2390   ✳

G259
Roues Libres: Association Cycliste
Case Postale 666, Haute-Ville
Quebec, Quebec
CANADA G1R 4S2

G260
Rowan Tree: Publishers of The Unicorn
P.O. Box 8814
Minneapolis, MN 55408   ✳

G261
Rowe Conference Center
Kings Highway Road
Rowe, MA 01367
413/339-4216

G262
Rudrananda Ashram
316 North Washington Street
Bloomington, IN 47401
812/339-2353   ✳

G263
SYDA Foundation
P.O. Box 600
South Fallsburg, NY 12779

G264
Samisdat
P.O. Box 129
Richford, VT 05476
514/263-4439   ✳

G265
San Francisco Mime Troupe
855 Treat Street
San Francisco, CA 94110
415/285-1717

G266
Sanatana Dharma Foundation
3100 White Sulphur Springs Road
St. Helena, CA 94574
707/963-9487   ✳

G267
**Segue Foundation: Publishers of Books and
  Magazines**
300 Bowery
New York, NY 10012   ◆

G268
Shadybrook House
King Memorial Road
P.O. Box 98
Mentor, OH 44060
216/953-1050   ✳

G269
Shambhala Booksellers
2482 Telegraph Avenue
Berkeley, CA 94704
415/848-8443

G270
Shanti Nilaya
P.O. Box 2396
Escondido, CA 92025
714/749-2008   ◆◆◆

G271
Siddha Yoga Dham Ann Arbor
1520 Hill Street
Ann Arbor, MI 48104
313/994-5625

G272
Siddha Yoga Dham Boston
Fernwood Road/Manor House
Brookline, MA 02167
617/734-0137

G273
Sino-American Buddhist Association
City of 10,000 Buddhas
Talmage, CA 95481
707/462-0939   ✳

G274
Sirius Community
P.O. Box 388
Amherst, MA 01002
413/256-8015   ◆◆

G275
Sluggo: Journal of Disturbing Clues
P.O. Box 4862
San Francisco, CA 94101   ✳

G276
**Sobek Expeditions: Outdoor Adventure Rivers
  Specialists**
P.O. Box 67
Angels Camp, CA 95222
209/736-2661

G277
Society for Human and Spiritual Understanding
16 Monmouth Street
Brookline, MA 02146
617/566-7639   ✳

G278
Society of Folk Harpers and Craftsmen
Robinson's Harp Shop
P.O. Box 161
Mount Laguna, CA 92048   ✳

G279
Sojourners: Christian Renewal Community
1309 L Street, N.W.
Washington, DC 20005
202/737-2780   ✳

G280
Soluna: Creative Healing and Self-Exploration
159 George Street
London W1H 5LB
ENGLAND
01/723 7256   ✳

G281
Sorting It Out: Support for Spiritual Leavetakers
P.O. Box 9446
San Francisco, CA 94709
415/524-3200

G282
**Spirals: Bridging the Gap Between Science and
  Mysticism**
P.O Box 29472
San Francisco, CA 94129   ✳

G283
Spiritual Emergency Network
c/o Esalen Institute
Big Sur, CA 93920

G284
Spiritual Friends
P.O. Box 2067
San Diego, CA 92112
714/583-2314

G285
Spiritual Frontiers Fellowship
10819 Winner Road
Independence, MO 64052
816-254-8585

G286
Sproing: Science Fiction and Fantasy
1150 St. Paul Street
Denver, CO 80206   *

G287
Sri Aurobindo's Action Center
P.O. Box 1977
Boulder, CO 80306
303/499-3313   *

G288
St. Louis Unit of Service of World Goodwill
P.O. Box 11333
Clayton, MO 63105   *

G289
Stash
118 South Bedford Street
Madison, WI 53703
608/251-4200   *

G290
Sufi Order for the Esoteric Arts & Sciences
83 Elm Street, P.O. Box 135
Jamaica Plain, MA 02130
617/522-0800   *

G291
Summit Lighthouse
P.O. Box 7000
Pasadena, CA 91109

G292
Survival Cards
P.O. Box 1805
Bloomington, IN 47402
812/336-8206   ◆

G293
Synergic Power Institute
P.O. Box 9096
Berkeley, CA 94709
415/549-0839   ◆

G294
T'ai Chi
P.O. Box 26156
Los Angeles, CA 90026
213/665-7773   *

G295
Taeria Foundation Spiritual Community
P.O. Box 782
Carrizozo, NM 88301   *

G296
Tayu Institute
P.O. Box 42555
San Francisco, CA 94101   *

G297
Temple of Understanding
Wainwright House
Stuyvesant Avenue
Rye, NY 10580
914/WO7-6080   *◆

G298
Textile Artists' Newsletter: Review of Fiber Arts
5533 College Avenue
Oakland, CA 94618   *

G299
The Awakeners
P.O. Box 966
East Brunswick, NJ 08816

G300
The Churchman
1074 23rd Avenue North
St. Petersburg, FL 33704   *

G301
The Farm
156 Drakes Lane
Summertown, TN 38383

G302
The Loving Brotherhood
P.O. Box 556
Sussex, NJ 07461
201/875-4710   *

G303
Theatre-Action
C.P.O. 358
Ottawa, Ontario
CANADA K1N 8V3
613/236-3133   *

G304
Theosophical Society of America
P.O. Box 270
Wheaton, IL 60187
312/668-1571   *

G305
Three-H-O Foundation (3HO)
1306 Massachusetts Avenue
Cambridge, MA 02138
617/864-3636

G306
Trailhead Ventures
P.O. Box CC
Buena Vista, CO 81211
303/395-8001

G307
Travelers' Directory
6224 Baynton Street
Philadelphia, PA 19144   ✳◆

G308
Unified States of Awareness Communications
3760 Wesson
Detroit, MI 48210
313/895-5981

G309
United States Parachute Association
806 15th Street, N.W., Suite 444
Washington, DC 20005
202/347-5773   ✳◆

G310
Unity-in-Diversity Council
7433 Madora Avenue
Canoga Park, CA 91306
213/998-7812   ✳◆

G311
Universal Great Brotherhood
P.O. Box 9154
St. Louis, MO 63117   ✳

G312
University of the Wilderness
P.O. Box 1687
Evergreen, CO 80439
303/674-9724

G313
Wainwright House
Center for Development of Human Resources
260 Stuyvesant Avenue
Rye, NY 10580
914/967-6080

G314
Washington Buddhist Vihara
5017 16th Street, N.W.
Washington, DC 20011
202/723-0773   ✳

G315
Watercourse Ways
139 Sycamore Avenue
Mill Valley, CA 94941

G316
Watershed Foundation: Poetry Recordings
North American Poetry Network
930 F Street, N.W., Suite 612
Washington, DC 20004
202/347-4823   ◆

G317
West Art
P.O. Box 1396
Auburn, CA 95603
916/885-0969   ✳

G318
**Whole Life Times: Northeast Journal for a
   Positive Future**
290 Massachusetts Avenue
Arlington, MA 02174
617/646-2251   ✳

G319
Willow: A Woman's Retreat
6517 Dry Creek Road
Napa, CA 94558
707/944-8173

G320
Windsurfer Magazine
Bay Windsurfing
P.O. Box 776
Menlo Park, CA 94025
415/595-2285   ✳

G321
**Women at the Helm: International Women's
   Sailing**
2210 Wilshire Boulevard, #533
Santa Monica, CA 90403
213/659-6967   ✳

G322
Women in the Wilderness
Fort Mason, Building 201
San Francisco, CA 94123
415/556-0560   ✳◆

G323
Women's Sports Foundation
195 Moulton Street
San Francisco, CA 94123
415/563-6266   ✳

G324
WomenSpirit Journal
P.O. Box 263
Wolf Creek, OR 97497   ✳

G325
WoodenBoat Magazine
P.O. Box 78
Brooklin, ME 04616
207/359-4651   ✳

G326
World Goodwill
866 United Nations Plaza, #566
New York, NY 10017   ✳

G327
World Monastic Council
c/o Center on Technology and Society
P.O. Box 38-206
Cambridge, MA 02138
617/491-1112

G328
World Union for Progressive Judaism
838 Fifth Avenue
New York, NY 10021
212/249-0100

G329
World University
P.O. Box 40638
New Speedway - University Sta.
Tucson, AZ 85717
602/622-2170

G330
Yes Educational Society
1035 31st Street, N.W.
Washington, DC 20007
202/338-7874 ◆✳

G331
Yoga Journal
2054 University Avenue
Berkeley, CA 94704
415/841-9200 ✳

G332
Zen Center of San Francisco
300 Page Street
San Francisco, CA 94102

G333
Zen Center of Sonoma Mountain
6367 Sonoma Mountain Road
Santa Rosa, CA 95804
707/545-8105

G334
Zygon: Journal of Religion and Science
Rollins College
Winter Park, FL 32789
305/646-2134 ✳

Evolving Networks: Global and Futures

Lo, soul, seest thou not God's purpose
from the first?
The earth to be spanned,
connected by network.

Walt Whitman
Passage to India

In the year 2001, the turning of a century and the turning of a millennium, our daughters will be 21 and 23.

Once, when we were the age they will be then, we tried to imagine what the future would be like. But no longer.

Rapid, transforming change is no longer an idea grasped by talking to grandparents about 5-cent cups of coffee or looking at old photographs of horseless carriages. Accelerating change is now measured by each of us at least yearly—20 percent interest rates, small cars from Detroit, gizmos the size of a small paperback that play master chess. Where our personal knowledge is greatest, related perhaps to work or a hobby, the pace of change seems faster still and may be measured in months, weeks, and even days. Without knowing what they will be, we do know that the changes from 1980 to 2000 will be more numerous and more astonishing than the changes between 1960 and 1980.

Yet our failure as parents to imagine the future that will greet our daughters as they step into their young adulthood is not simply a shrug of the shoulders and a mutter that no prediction can stand up to the pace of change. Rather, we have recognized that our children's future is, above all, a matter of our *choice*. Mirtala Bentov eloquently states this perception in a poem accompanying a photograph of her sculpture "The Ever-Present Past," in her book *Thought Forms*:

I know, my descendent,
your destiny depends
on my victories,
joys, and misfortunes,
on how I embroider
my days and years.

It is not the technological surprises, or shifting social patterns, or sudden political events that make it so difficult to forge a vision of the future. Rather, it is the degree of conscious choice that human beings have with regard to the path we take to the future. We know one path leads to Armageddon, and we know other paths lead to slow decline and death. Even forgetting the probabilities of catastrophe, we know that one person's idealized, squeaky-clean future, all white and shiny with spaceships and benevolent bureaucracies, is another person's image of ticky-tacky boxes and omnipresent Big Brother. Similarly, one person's appropriate life-style may be another person's version of the Dark Ages.

FUTURE MAKING

Glowing with the shining light of the finest intellectual achievement of the human mind, one small bomb the size of a human body fused the scales of atomic matter and global civilization, the microcosm and the macrocosm. When the Enola Gay released its deadly cargo over Japan in 1945, humankind suffered a loss of ignorance about unseen nature and a loss of innocence about our own evolution. Humankind is now many decades past the point of no-return in accepting the reins of its own destiny in the cosmos.

Mushroom clouds are the ultimate bogeymen of our time. It may be true, as Bertrand Russell said, that we humans have always enacted the follies of which we are capable. Such acts are generally laid at the feet of politicians, but it really was science, through its standard-bearer physics, that lost its purity in 1945. Nuclear knowledge and decision making, once the sole province of the princes of science, instantly went to the center of world political consciousness. It sits there still, dominating the great gray area between global war and peace.

Signals of dramatic change are not always so explosive as the Hiroshima and Nagasaki "demonstrations." Yet, turns in the course of human evolution still may arrive with astounding swiftness. Genetic engineering, a product of the 1970s, is one such example, made possible by discoveries made several decades earlier about the structure of DNA. In 1980, an infant company–in an untried field and still many months away from a commercial product–sold out its first stock offering within hours. The faculty and trustees of Harvard University wrestled with their academic consciences about whether to form a profit-making partnership with another company jumping into the same unknown waters. Although consequences are as yet unknown, no one–scientists, politicians, or just plain folks–doubts that genetic engineering will profoundly shape the human future.

Genetic engineering is a perfect example of how events poke holes into the very worldviews that give birth to them. A crowning achievement of experimental science dedicated to reducing complexity to elementary pieces, so literally exemplified in snipping and splicing units of life's own information code, genetic engineering brings the reality of evolutionary self-responsibility right to the heart of the human experience. Born of a scientific worldview that perceives evolution as a process of accidental mutations, competitive natural struggle, and very long time frames, genetic engineering itself constitutes an emergent shift in the biological evolutionary process that is totally outside the context of Darwinian explanation.

Men and women acquired powers in the 1970s that humans had always considered godlike. Evolutionary historians of the future will mark this decade as a biological watershed, the moment when humankind began to create life-forms that never before existed on earth. We are, starting right now, taking a hand in our own biological evolution.

As the human responsibility for our own evolution increases, we need perspectives that place humankind and our planet in a larger context. While we can never be certain of the nature of the larger system that includes us all, it is imperative that we persist in stretching our mental models beyond today's transient truths in order to better understand what we do know.

We are two people among four billion.

What does that mean?

Can a person grasp a planet? Can a planet know a person?

Stand with us here, in a field on a mountaintop in the Adirondacks, a spot where we feel particularly in tune with the universe, watching the weather boil over purple peaks. Close your eyes and step outward. Change your scale of perception with us, so that we may find a comfortable perspective in which to place our planet and ourselves.

Step outward to the Milky Way, the shimmering necklace of stars ringing the clear night sky. Quickly swing by the sun, pass the giant planets and the outer extremities of our solar system, pass Alpha Centauri and Sirius a few light-years away, and speed 30,000 light-years to our galactic center. Grow and adopt the perspective of a Starmaker, become the brilliant being that is the Milky Way, a spiraling association of 400 billion suns in a disk 100,000 light-years across.

See, close by, the mini-galaxies making up the Magellanic Clouds, and our neighboring galaxies Sculptor and Fornax, part of our little local group, which extends out about 2 million light-years to include the beautiful Andromeda. Play, then, as part of our local group, with other supergalaxies, such as nearby Virgo, Perseus, Coma, and Hydra.

Raise your gaze yet further, Starmaker, and look to the rims of Universe. Stretch your galactic mind to encompass your 100 billion brothers and sisters, each a bright being averaging 100 billion stars.

As ancient Hindu scripture says, it may be that our universe is but an atom in another universe, a mote in another god's eye. But we have gone far enough to recognize our Milky Way as an individual among other galaxies that together form groups in a larger environment of cosmic groups.

So now, returning to the dense core of our own galactic perspective, look outward across your gracefully spinning body, past the Sagittarius Arm, farther out to a back eddy nestled in the Carina-Cygnus Arm, and focus on the small, second-generation star that humans call "the Sun."

As we return our perspective and sense of scale back toward the human home, passing Altair and Procyon and finally Alpha Centauri once again, notice that it is the solar system as a whole that looms in the distance and takes on the appearance of individuality against the relative emptiness of intragalactic space. It is the whole system of star, planets, satellites, comets, and encompassing energies that is an entity in the galactic association of solar systems.

Parked outside Pluto's orbit, a Starmaker might wonder about the complexity of this integrated solar animal, 5 billion years old. A glance at the solar subsystems confirms the suspicion of intelligence indicated by the profusion of nonrandom radio signals filling the inner solar space and even now leaking into galactic space. As our perspective narrows to the source of these signals, we approach the third planet.

Although still young, the brain of the solar system, the earth, already has 4 billion neurons and is rapidly growing more. Remarkably, as we zoom in on the pulsing marbled orb that constitutes the seat of solar intelligence and examine one of the billions of elements of this emergent planetary brain, we enter yet another cosmos. Each planetary neuron—a person, a human being—has a brain with something like 10 billion neurons, each neuron capable of perhaps 50,000 connections.

You are home.

Right now the natural limits—smallest to largest—of human networking are at minimum one of us alone and at maximum all of us together—a range from one person to four-going-on-five billion people.

Certain large numbers are sometimes breathlessly advanced to illustrate "unimaginable" complexity: neurons in the brain, people on the planet, stars in the galaxies, galaxies in the universe—individuals and billions all. Using a third-grade-arithmetic trick, cancel out all the "billions" and review the cosmic journey:

Our universe has 100 galaxies,

> Our galaxy has 400 stars,
> Our star system has a brain with 4 people,
> Our body has a brain with 10 neurons.
> Can you hold it in your hand? Universe, sun, and self?

One pair of practiced, globe-holding hands belong to Robert Muller, Secretary of the United Nations Economic and Social Council. Muller once described his view of the world to an audience of systems theorists, which he recounts in "A Copernican View of World Cooperation":

> I visualized our globe hanging in the universe and saw it first in its relations with the sun. I viewed it then as an orange cut in half and saw its atmosphere, its crust and its thin layer of life or biosphere. Within the biosphere, I saw the seas, the oceans, the polar caps, the continents, the mountains, the rivers, the lakes, the soils, the deserts, the animals, the plants, and the humans. Within the crust of the Earth, I saw the depths of the oceans, the continental plates, the underground reservoirs of water, oil, minerals, and heat.
>
> Within the mass of four billion people, I saw the nations, the races, religions, cultures, languages, cities, industries, farms, professions, corporations, institutions, armies, families, down to that incredible cosmos, the human being. In the human person, I saw the rich miraculous system of body, mind, heart and spirit linked through the senses with the heavens and the Earth. I visualized that person from conception to death. I saw the 60 trillion cells of his body, the infinitely small, the atom, microbial life, the incredible world of genes, which embody and transmit the patterns of life.
>
> And all along this Copernican path, at each step, I ask myself the question: "Are humans cooperating on this subject? Are they trying to understand it, appraise it, to see it in relation with everything else?" . . . There is a pattern in all this, a response to a prodigious evolutionary march by the human species toward total consciousness. . . . Something gigantic is going on, a real turning point in evolution.
>
> [I saw us at] the beginning of an entirely new era of which international cooperation at the United Nations was only a first outward reflection. I had not seen it earlier, because it had come in a haphazard way, in response to specific events, needs, crises and perceptions by governments and individuals all over the planet. But the result was now clearly here, glorious and beautiful like Aphrodite emerging from the sea. This was the beginning of a new age, a gigantic step forward in evolution. This was unprecedented and full of immense hope for man's future on his planet. Perhaps after all, we would be able to achieve peace and harmony on Earth. This time, humankind would be forced to think out absolutely everything and to measure the totality of our planet's conditions and evolution in our solar system and in time. The games of glory, aggrandizement and domination by specific groups would soon find their limits. The great hour of truth had arrived for the human race.
>
> Suddenly an image came to my mind. It was the good person of U Thant. He too had foreseen a serene, enlightened world, a world of peace and understanding enriched by ethics, morality, spirituality and philosophy. I remembered the scene of a reception he had offered to the U.S. astronauts after the first moon landing. I was talking in a corner with one of the astronauts. The Secretary-General came near us and inquired what we were talking about. The astronaut answered:

"Your colleague is asking me what I thought when I saw for the first time the entire Earth from outer space."

"Oh, I see," said U Thant. "I am not surprised by his question. But I am afraid he is not expecting anything new from you. He just wants a confirmation, for he has been living on the moon long before you, looking down on Earth with his global eyes and trying to figure out what the human destiny will be."

Vanity of vanities! U Thant was reminding me to take all this with a grain of salt and to return to Earth. My Copernican scheme receded for a moment from my mind and there remained only his enigmatic and kind smile, while the systems analysts were pursuing a discussion which became more and more incomprehensible to me. . . .

Robert Muller was on the original short lists of networkers recommended to us by Robert A. Smith, III (see Chapter 12). It would have been necessary to begin this chapter with a cosmic image if only to embrace the scope of our interview with Muller, which follows as *global networking, global mind*. Muller's perspective sets up the individual/collective bounds of human networking and introduces the networks concerned with world order and global/futures issues–*toward humanitas*.

GLOBAL NETWORKING, GLOBAL MIND

We wrote to Dr. Muller, mentioning the referral from Bob Smith, explaining what we were up to and requesting information. He responded immediately by sending us a list of U.S.-based international groups associated with the United Nations (nongovernmental organizations, or NGO's). Another packet of materials arrived a few days later and yet another a week or so after that. Each packet had a note attached with some scribbled comments about networking, but the third one went on to say: "I think I have so much to say on 'networking' that I will never have time to put it on paper. Perhaps the best solution would be for you to let me know when you next come to New York and we will tape a conversation."

Several months later, we took Muller up on his offer and met him in his modest 29th-floor office at the United Nations. Although he is head of one of the three principal components of the UN, Muller's immediate staff and accommodations exude all the pomp of a small college dean's office. Muller is the rare kind of unprepossessing person who combines a moving humanity with a wealth of knowledge and a vigorous involvement with the world around him. His own life story, *Most of All, They Taught Me Happiness*, reflects his experiences as a child in Alsace-Lorraine, joining the French underground during the Second World War, being imprisoned, and finally coming to the United States in the late 1940s to work at the UN.

Muller was an extremely easy man for us to interview. He seemed to know exactly why we had come and precisely what we needed to know. He required no leading questions to go directly to the heart of the matter. In essence, his message is this: Humanity is evolving toward a coherent global form best described by the metaphor of a human brain; each person, young or old, able-bodied or handicapped, is an important neuron in the emerging planetary brain that is constituted by the myriad "networkings" among people.

"Networkings," the external connections between people that constitute the internal connections of the planetary whole, is Muller's word. Such phrasings and much of the flavor of his multilingual accent have been retained in this interview.

MULLER: "This old planet and the human species on it are advancing in time as some kind of a big brain whose neurons are multiplying incessantly, encompassing everything from the individual to the planet, to humanity and the universe, getting deeper and deeper into the past and further and further into the future. Of course, the mathematical interconnections are absolutely staggering. The world brain is already so complicated that you cannot describe it accurately. New interconnections are being created so rapidly that any description would be out of date. This is a new biological phenomenon, one of the most momentous ones in the earth's history. The human species is becoming something new. It is similar to the passage from the protozoa to the metazoa."

Like R. Buckminster Fuller, Muller totally rejects the Malthusian assumption that population growth is the root of human misery. In an evolutionary context, more people potentially means a more complex and more capable planetary brain.

MULLER: "We do not even have the faintest idea as to how many people should live on this planet. The question is not even being asked. We are still very primitive when it comes to a transcendence beyond our noses on this little planet and to looking at the mystery of life and what it means to be born and to have life in the immense universe. The fundamental question, the greatest task in being human, and, as a matter of fact, the end goal of all networking, is to try to determine what the laws of the universe are, the cosmic laws which we ought to obey in order to fulfill our lives on this planet and contribute to the further evolution the cosmos has in mind for us.

"The reason Kepler studied astronomy and astrology was to find the laws of the cosmos that would give him clues as to how human societies should live on this planet. The day this will be done, then we will have really entered the new age. We are doing it the hard way, with many mistakes and very partial views instead of having a universal view, not only a global view for the planet but of our total relationship with the universe.

"Now, when you speak about world government, many listeners think that you should have your head examined. When you speak about cosmic government, then you are ready for an asylum! And yet, this is the real, ultimate issue. The question whether we will be blown up in a nuclear holocaust is very much part of it. Did all our long cosmic evolution have as the sole purpose the triggering of an atomic war to assert the righteousness and supremacy of a one power on earth? So we have a very tall order in our lap."

Giving us a thumbnail sketch of the UN's history, Muller began with the golden era of industrialism, the end of the 19th century, a time when "dreamers like the steelmaker and pacifist Andrew Carnegie" envisioned a world order established on a totally rational, scientific, technological, and professional basis. In the original scheme, a league of professional associations was to be created on an equal footing with a league of nations, but this idea got lost in the shuffle after World War I. Of course, the "half-a-loaf" League of Nations never got off the ground, because of the absence of the United States. In Muller's words, this is how the current UN came about: "Humpty Dumpty went to the Second World War, after which the world union idea was revived, but the project for a league of professional associations was never really revived as a possible peoples' democracy at the world level. World organization became a government-owned affair."

Outside the UN's political and legal functions is Muller's realm, a fascinating collection of world agencies connected to a latticework of international networks.

MULLER: "I am Secretary of the Economic and Social Council, where everything economic and social is brought together. Under the Charter, we are instructed to have a total worldview: demography, health, education, standards of living, longevity, culture, employment, children, women, the elderly, the hungry, the oppressed, the discriminated, everything you can imagine. The UN is a system of central universal organs with functional and regional agencies hooked into it. People usually do not have the faintest idea what beginnings of a world system exist here. The UN's world conferences on population, on the environment, on energy, on water, on the deserts, and so forth are the big drums being used to give messages and global warnings to people. We are, of course, still living primarily in a rational, scientific age, and this is definitely reflected in the UN. But ethical, moral, and even spiritual considerations are becoming stronger every year. The new ethics of what is right and wrong for humanity, that is really the basic business of the UN behind all the politics and the bureaucracy. It is a very, very difficult task, but we must go through it and work it out. Just another new fundamental biological process.

"Everything good or bad until now has always been decided in terms of what is good or bad for a group or a nation and seldom from the point of view of what is good or bad for the entire humanity. This has become a central question because our survival depends on it. Ecology has recently taught us to ask the question 'What is good and what is bad for our planet?' At every step we must henceforth ask, 'What is good and what is bad for humanity?' A completely new ethic is being born, but it is very difficult, because interest groups cling to their advantages and views: The powerful want to remain armed, the rich want to remain rich, everybody wants more, and few are those who would be ready to give up something for the good of the planet and humanity."

Even as Muller paints pictures of thickening global webs on every issue and topic from avocados to asteroids, the conversation always returns to the emphatic statement that there is no networking, no global brain, no anything without the individual human being. Muller does not see the individual as the unfortunate lowest rung on the ladder of global organization. Rather, humans are the very source and prescient mirror of global complexity.

MULLER: "The Indian yogis tell us that each human being is a microcosm of the cosmos. It makes good sense. How could it be otherwise?

"Even a particle, or an amoeba or a hydra, is a self-contained entity, but at the same time it is part of the totality. It is this type of complex relationship, being a whole and a part together, which is again, networking, because all connections together make up the total reality. As an individual, you feel and are an absolutely unique being, never to be repeated exactly the same in all eternity. And yet, you are part of the total universe and total stream of time. As a matter of fact, this shows us the range of human happiness: We can be happy through concentration upon ourselves (know thyself), through networking with others and the wonders of our planet, or through networking with God or the Total-Absolute through spirituality, meditation, and prayer.

"From the moment you have recognized both your entity, and being part of the total human family and universe, from that time you will change and the world will change. But, again, this is a very tall order, one of the hardest philosophical problems of our time. It was a great musician and humanist, Pablo Casals, who gave it the best expression when, with tears in his eyes, he used to exclaim: 'I am a miracle that God or Nature has made. Could I kill? Could I kill someone? No, I can't. Or another human being who is a miracle like me, can he kill me?'

"And to be great and unique, you don't have to be in the newspapers. Networking, in my view is not necessarily only the need to 'fight for something,' a cause. It can be a serene, natural association of sorts, from the monk's association with God in his monastery to people who like to collect stamps. *Networking is a form of happiness.* A person can say, 'There are lots of other people like me,' and you become a little world of your own: Some like astronomy and others like collecting stamps. It is truly a fantastic life, a beautiful life on this planet which offers so many possibilities of happiness in every direction.

"If I were a head of state, I would support networking because it gives so many people a sense of purpose. Not everybody can be a mathematician, a scientist, or a philosopher. Many people are interested only in their little gardens. But to have one's garden may not be enough. So you order a gardening magazine and you join a gardening club. There you meet other people with the same interest, with whom you can talk about things you love and you derive much happiness from that network. We are four and a half billion people, on this planet and each wants to be recognized as 'somebody,' as an entity. Even, and especially, when you are limited or handicapped, you want to be 'recognized.'

"When I feel depressed I read Beethoven's Heiligenstadt Testament, in which he tells his brother that he is becoming completely deaf but that he is determined to give the world what he feels in himself. You tell this to handicapped people and it gives them courage. Did you know that the Taj Mahal, in India, was designed by a blind Persian architect, Ustad Isha? Perhaps someone with sight would have never been able to design it.

"Once, I was asked to give a graduation speech to a school for the blind. I asked them to recommend a book which would speak about the great blind people of this earth throughout history. I could not believe it when I learned that such a book did not exist. I exclaimed: 'You have all these blind children and you do not even have a book about Homer, Milton, Euler, Ustad Isha, and all other great blind people who have contributed so much to human civilization?' So here again is the need for a network among the handicapped, who need their heroes and recognition of their entity.

"But it is even more; it has to do with transcendence. I'm digressing, but—" Encouraged to follow his thought, Muller explained his experience of listening to a record of a lovingly crafted autobiographical story he had written called "Happy Even in Prison" (a chapter in his book *Most of All, They Taught Me Happiness*), made for blind people by the U.S. Library of Congress.

MULLER: "With my eyes closed, I listened to that story. I was in a completely different world. I remembered things in that prison that had gone forever. Suddenly I discovered that when your eyes are closed, your mind functions better when it is auditively impressed and I realized that blind people might derive a pride from the extra perception they have by being only auditive.

"As part of the 1981 International Year for the Disabled, I have recommended that each nation should honor its great handicapped. National committees federating all handicapped associations are being established in each country. There are 450 million handicapped people in the world, and the world must do something about such a sizable problem. So we decided to make a big noise about it, to launch an International Year. Each country will report on the problem to the UN and look into all aspects of it. The result is that the handicapped have been hooked in on a world scale through the UN. They represent a network of 450 million people.

"A remarkable thing is that we have been able in the UN to have governments work together on a whole gamut of human problems, from childhood to old age. There is UNICEF. We had an International Year for the Child. There were two world women's conferences. There was a world youth conference, several conferences to combat racism. In 1982, there is a world conference on the elderly. I am sure that within a few years there will be a UN conference on the problem of death. All these efforts are aimed at very sizable worldwide networks of people, each with its host of nongovernmental organizations.

"Then there are networks between these various groups, for instance between old people and young people. In Africa and Asia, the aged are the superiors, the wise people, the people to whom the young go for counsel. In the West we put them in old people's homes. I have written a lot about this subject because of my relations with my grandfather. He was such a wise and warm human being. He had no ax to grind, contrary to my father. I could believe my grandfather. He had nothing to lose, but all to offer: wisdom. Today in the West we cut off the elderly from the young, because promoters want to build old people's homes. Thus we prevent an important channel of transmission of wisdom of life to the young. Then the developing countries imitate the great ideas of the West and run into untold problems. As a result, the need for proper networking will never end.

"Networking is done by people who have no networks. That seems to be a fundamental law. Those who have the major networks don't want to engage with those who have new views about humanity. For example, the multinational corporations give the cold shoulder to the UN. Having power, they don't want to network with the international agencies. The big TV stations don't want to network with new-age groups. They have their own monopoly. The New York *Times* doesn't want to network with anyone.

"This is why the voiceless people have begun to find out about networking in order to assert themselves again. It is the old story of humanity: Those in power do not want to give up anything, and those who are left out want to organize to be heard. So the UN's greatest allies are generally those who have no great power: the little countries, the innumerable nongovernmental organizations represented by observers to the UN, and the religions. If the Pope had vast military forces he probably wouldn't come to the UN. He has only spiritual power, and this is why he is allying with a weak United Nations sharing the same objectives.

"It is the absence of certain vital networks which causes much of the trouble in this world. There is no real networking between heads of state, an area where it would be so vitally needed for the survival of our planet; there is no networking between the military, there is no networking between ministries of justice and the police forces of this planet. International terrorists are better-organized. Here is where the system breaks down. In order to keep their advantages, sovereignty, and primacy, the governments of the big nations generally refuse to network. Roosevelt was a man who knew how to network. He insisted on seeing Stalin, Churchill, and De Gaulle, and he saw them and communicated with them all the time. He created a world system of communications, including cooperation between the military, which broke down after his death with the policy of the Iron Curtain and the cold war."

In a paper he showed us, "Proposals for Better World Security," Muller recalls the words of Chou En-lai:

I will never forget a wise and melancholic remark made by Premier Chou En-lai during the visit of Secretary-General Waldheim to Peking in 1972: "I am sitting here surrounded by my advisers trying to figure out what they might be scheming against us in Moscow and in Washington. In Moscow, they are trying to figure out what Peking and Washington might be scheming against them. And they are doing the same in Washington. But perhaps in reality no one is scheming against anyone." And he concluded that the role of the Secretary-General as an intermediary between heads of states was extremely important. As I listened to him, I closed my eyes for a moment and visualized the day when in his large office in the People's Hall there will be an audio-TV set linked with the offices of his main partners in the administration of planet Earth.

MULLER: "I have worked with a number of Secretaries-General and I noticed that they all had their private networks. Hammarskjöld wrote to Albert Schweitzer, asking him to come up with a resounding statement with other scientists for the ban of atomic tests. He did it in a private capacity, without asking the authorization of governments. And it worked. U Thant was very interested in the UFO's. I never knew about it and later learned that he had a network of three people who informed him of everything that was going on in this field. I assume that people in high positions all have their private networks.

"Networking operates all the time. You do it as a private person, you work with people who are like-minded, and this is quite a force, because the power of ideas is enormous."

For Muller, networking is a way of being fully human.

MULLER: "There is more to the art of networking. You really have to live it, not just passing information on without it touching you or being touched by you. You are part of the totality, you are a seeker of truth, of what is good for the human race, of what will be our fate, of what will improve our fate. If you are not totally honest, people will not trust you, they will not believe you. It has to be deeply lived. Then you are a good networker, a useful neuron which will not be rejected by the new brain in formation. Most of the time, people listen to you with the brain, but often you will be able to convince them only if you speak with your heart to their heart."

As Muller caught his breath, we asked him one last question.

MULLER: "Who are the greatest networkers that I know? That is a difficult question. I believe that the greatest networkers are those who did it at the highest or deepest human, philosophical, moral, ethical, and spiritual levels–people like the Buddha, Jesus, Gandhi, Schweitzer, Teilhard de Chardin, Martin Luther King, Hammarskjöld, U Thant, people who really transcended races, nations, and groups, and networked at the all-human level, linking the heavens and the earth and showing us our prodigious worth and journey in the universe. People like Bach, Beethoven, Shakespeare, Goethe, who make us feel the greatness of life and again fuse the heavens with the earth. They have reached the pinnacle of networking, not the heads of government of today, who will be completely forgotten in a few years. Those great people were not networking during their own times only, but they continue to network over the centuries into our own times. Their dreams and thoughts and feelings are still alive today. The real networkers are those who go deepest and come closest to the mystery of life in the universe. Of course, these are my great networkers, because I work for the United Nations. For the Catholics probably the Pope is the greatest networker, and for the Rotarians and International Lions their current presidents are the greatest networkers.

"What is really needed today is a new philosophy of life within our global conditions, a new hope, a new vision of the future. And the strange, beautiful thing is that probably this time the vision will not be the product of any one person, but will be a collective product. It will be the creation of the new human species as a macroorganism, as a perfected neural system made up of thousands and thousands of networks. As we move towards the bimillennium, perhaps networking will become the new democracy, a new major element in the system of governance, a new way of living in the global, miraculous, complex conditions of our strange, wonderful, live planet spinning and circling in the prodigious universe at a crossroads of infinity and eternity."

TOWARD HUMANITAS

"Humanitas" is the sometime-in-the-future organic totality of humankind as a whole. Four brief examples are given of the thickening global soup of networks, connected or soon to be connected around every imaginable subject—a mere wetting of the toes in the primordial ocean of emerging planetary consciousness.

The international hub of the appropriate technology (A.T.) movement is a tiny village in the mountains of Maine, barely 20 miles from the Canadian border (See Chapter 5, Using, for more on appropriate technology). It is from Rangeley, Maine, that TRANET, the Transnational Network for Appropriate/Alternative Technologies, conducts its business.

TRANET got its start at the 1976 HABITAT Forum of the UN Conference on Human Settlements, in Vancouver, Canada, and has grown to be a membership organization of 500, exchanging information with nearly 200 magazines, newsletters, and journals, and maintaining files on 1500 A.T. or "new age" groups and 10,000 names and addresses of interested individuals. This organization is known primarily through its quarterly newsletter/directory, an excellent distillation of information about activities and articles relevant to its membership.

"A network has no center," TRANET coordinator/executive director William Ellis told us at the start of our conversation. Hence, a network does not need imposing facilities and urban amenities. "I inherited this house, where I was born, from my parents. And this is where our family is practicing self-reliant living. We grow our own food, cut our own wood, and have fitted our house with solar collectors. We feel that if we espouse self-reliance, we should practice it."

Having just returned from one of his frequent trips around the world, on which he had spent time with "UN and government bureaucrats who talk appropriate technology from their high-life-style penthouses," Ellis was nonetheless feeling very optimistic. "Five years ago, the Nepalese Government thought that 'appropriate technology' was really our second-hand stuff. Now they understand what A.T. is all about, and they're eager to learn what's happening in Guatemala, in Africa, wherever."

For Ellis, Rangeley, Maine, is a perfect spot from which to reach around the globe. "Most of our international work is done by telephone, and the communications system here, the phones and the mail, are excellent. In fact, the phone service and mail is probably better here than it is in New York," he explains.

While it may be difficult for frustrated American post office and telephone users to accept that our communications system is "excellent," in reality these services are good when compared with many other countries. Ellis, and others with a truly global perspective, as well as global *experience*, are able to recognize what does work in the United States, as well as what does not.

Beyond its valuable information services, TRANET is also developing and espousing a philosophy of transnationalism grounded in networking. "A.T. goes way beyond windmills and conservation and cutting your own wood, way beyond the hardware and the software," Ellis says. "A.T. has also to do with the way our world is organized, which is why we have formed a network" (see Chapter 10).

TRANET's unfolding ideas about our preparation as global people to leap beyond national boundaries are presented in the Fall 1979 newsletter in a short essay, "A Second Level of World Governance":

Nation-states have governed world affairs for only a very brief period of human history. These autonomous governmental bodies have divided the land of the earth into a crazy-quilt chess board with little concern for culture, languages, religions, races, or ecologies. Both within and between these meaningless boundaries weird games of politics are played with the resources and lives of people. It is time to ask to what extent this world governmental system is to be changed if we are to reach the full potential of human development. . . .

People in all parts of the world are recognizing that big business, big government, big technology, and other centralized organizations cannot alone solve local problems or develop local potentials, only the people themselves can. And, people in all parts of the world are recognizing not only that small is beautiful but also that small is possible and small is happening. There is a worldwide revival of human rights, human dignity, and individual initiative. . . . This decade may be hailed as the beginning of the future because people-to-people networks initiated a more creative approach to world welfare–a complementary alternative to the U.N.–a second level of world governance.

Toward which end TRANET is working. In 1981, TRANET initiated the first of its people-to-people exchanges through its Associates Program in which skilled technical people from A.T. groups in one part of the world make 3-month site visits to A.T. groups in another part of the world, an idea that Ellis believes has its long-time precedents in the international Sister Cities program (Boston and Tokyo, for example) and the Vermont-based Experiment in International Living, which sponsors high school student exchanges.

Even TRANET's governing-board structure reflects its philosophy. Its 25 board members come from five geographic regions: Africa (presently represented with directors from Ghana, Senegal, Nigeria, and Tanzania); Asia and the Pacific (India, Pakistan, Papua New Guinea, and Indonesia); Latin America (Colombia, Mexico, Ecuador, Guatemala, and Chile); Europe and the Middle East (the Netherlands, England, France, Iran, and Switzerland); and North America (United States and Canada). Further, the annual meetings are rotated among the continents as is the presidency.

The developing TRANET philosophy is somewhat reminiscent of the original vision proposed for world government, prior to Woodrow Wilson's League of Nations scheme. Early UN, or perhaps more accurately, world-union, ideas put professional associations (potentially representing the whole range of people's interests) on an equal footing with nation-state governments. Had this idea become reality, the world union might now be according equal importance to national governments and the worldwide nongovernmentally indentured networks of windmill builders, of midwives, of poets. A dream, perhaps, but . . . Don Quixote for Secretary General, anyone?

One important planetary network that has been established to address itself to women's issues is the Women's International Network (WIN). WIN works at the global level to gather, edit, and disseminate information about women around the world. WIN News is an unprecedented publication, an open participatory quarterly containing "all the news that is fit to print by, for, and about women." WIN News is the work of Fran P. Hosken, an architect and city planner who reads five languages and whose energetic execution of this important channel of communication is yet another testimony to the effect that a single individual can have on the world when interest and talent are coupled with dedication and determination.

Hosken developed the idea for a "women's communication channel" when preparing to attend the International Year of the Woman Conference in Mexico City, in 1975. "The international media and existing press do not address themselves to women's issues," Hosken says. Thus, in early 1975, she began to put out a newsletter that described how the UN-sponsored conference was to be organized. In the previous year, Hosken had researched and compiled an international directory of women's groups. As a result, she had the ready-made beginnings of a global network that could serve as the feed tubes for her new newsletter.

With an emphasis equally divided between women in industrialized nations and women in developing countries, Hosken's newsletter provides a forum for communication unlike any other, reporting every 3 months on women's issues and their connection with the United Nations, international affairs, job opportunities, development, health, media, and violence. Serving as the editor, Hosken receives news from women from around the globe, which she then reviews, selects, types, pastes up, and prepares for the printer herself.

Hosken is also responsible for bringing to the public the issue of female circumcision, a practice that is routine in many parts of the world. In her book *The Hosken Report: Genital/Sexual Mutilation of Females*, Hosken reports that millions of girls and women in Africa have been circumcised and that the surgery is inflicted widely in other countries as well. A separate network within *WIN News* devoted to the distribution of information about genital mutilation has evolved out of this research–prompting campaigns in many countries to bring an end to this practice.

The circumcision network offers a valuable insight into how the dissemination of information ultimately can influence policy and result in perceivable change. Until Hosken began her research, female circumcision had been one of the world's best-kept secrets. Since Hosken's documentation has been made public, female circumcision has become an issue of concern at a number of government ministries, as well as the subject of a conference sponsored by the World Health Organization in Khartoum in the fall of 1979.

In reflecting on the 5 years of *WIN News*'s existence, Hosken writes, "There can be no longer any doubt that the women's movement for human rights and justice is the most important world-wide revolution which is improving the quality of life everywhere on the earth. . . . This *woman-made* revolution is concerned with human development, education and peace. . . . It is truly a grass-roots movement which has started spontaneously in the most diverse communities and parts of the world . . . everywhere, men are joining our leadership for change."

Global Education Associates (GEA), a New Jersey-based group with associates in 41 countries in Africa, Asia, Europe, Latin America, and North America, is "a network of networks," Patricia Mische, who cofounded GEA with her husband Gerald, writes. "Our role is that of a catalyst. Our associates around the world work through networks of which they are a part to catalyze a multi-issue coalition of networks to advance a more humane world order."

In its overview, GEA states its purposes:

Underlying GEA's program is an analysis of the "straight-jacket" of national security mobilization which prevents all nations–rich and poor alike–from meeting the basic human needs of their people. This straight-jacket is the result of unregulated global competition over arms, balance-of-payments deficits and scarce resources.

The mobilization for this three-fold competition–whether reluctantly implemented by compassionate leaders or manipulated by vested interests–lowers the priority of person-centered goals and subordinates human/religious values to national security needs. World peace is increasingly jeopardized and the economic and social justice values which are its foundations are undermined.

Growing global interdependence demands the cooperation of all people and nations to break out of this straight-jacket to establish a just world order in which basic human needs will be the highest priority.

GEA's aim is to develop a broadly-based, multi-issue constituency of persons who:

• Understand that national and personal self-interest in our time are synonymous with world interest; and

• Wish to work together toward a just and humanizing world order.

This broad statement of purpose is based on the work of the Misches, coauthors of the book *Toward a Human World Order: Beyond the National Security Straitjacket.* In this internationally recognized work, the Misches offer both a comprehensive critique of the current political/economic situation and practical suggestions for initiating a grass-roots "world order movement." Using these ideas, GEA has established an active organization that conducts lectures, workshops, and seminars, and offers accredited course institutes; provides consulting services to groups and institutions that are looking to expand their programs to include global perspectives; publishes monographs, newsletters, and other educational materials; and operates a resource center with books, films, and curriculum outlines on justice, peace, and other issues of global concern.

What sets GEA apart from many other groups that have attempted to work on the issues of global peace and justice is its underlying philosophy, which has been carefully articulated without being ideological. A recent edition of *The Whole Earth Papers,* the group's monograph series, contains several of the most provocative pieces on world-order issues we have seen in our survey, including articles "that hold out a basis for hope at a time when images of pessimism and despair pervade."

Perhaps one of the most intriguing aspects of GEA is the influence of women in the organization, highly unusual among groups dealing with international policy, national security, and global issues, traditionally closely guarded subjects discussed only in the higher reaches of government and multinational corporations, staffed almost exclusively by men. One third of GEA's board of directors are women, and women's concerns are strongly reflected in the organization's activities and statements.

Working largely through religious organizations, members of GEA have made presentations to such global groups as the Pontifical Commission of Justice and Peace, the World Council of Churches, and the Pro Mundi Vita conference on human rights in Brussels, as well as to meetings in Kenya, India, the Philippines, Japan, and Indonesia (the Misches' book has been translated into Japanese, German, Spanish, Hindi, Korean, and Chinese).

GEA's decision to work largely through religious groups stems both from the religious background of many of its members and from the recognition that with a very few salient examples (such as the current leadership in Iran), religions are largely without power in today's world (an idea echoed by Muller in our interview).

During our discussion at the UN, Muller suddenly reached for a book that had an apparently permanent place on the edge of his desk, The Yearbook of International Organizations: "This is one of the best reference books we have. At one point it was done by the UN in the Economic and Social Council, but it became such a headache that we farmed it out to them, because they were able to be self-financed." "They" are the Union of International Organizations (UIO), which was founded in 1907 as a clearinghouse for information on international governmental and nongovernmental groups. Based in Brussels, the group has an extensive publishing program, including the annual directory of international organizations, which lists, describes, and cross-references 8200 groups with an international focus.

While the UIO directory is the guidebook to the thousands of groups who think "planet," its companion, the UIO Yearbook of World Problems and Human Potential, is the global source book for networking. It is "an exercise in the development of a framework to handle and interrelate diverse, and seemingly incompatible, categories of information [in the hope that it] will lead to a new type of 'network strategy' more capable of portraying and containing the network of problems as it is now believed to be evolving."

Nearly 1200 pages in length, and including a frontispiece that requires the use of 3-D glasses, the encyclopedic volume on world problems and human potential is as wide-ranging in scope as anything we have ever encountered between two covers. It offers "perceptions of interlinked networks" in topical categories of world problems, human values, intellectual disciplines and sciences, international periodicals and serials, human diseases, international agencies and associations, traded commodities and products, economic and industrial sectors, occupations, jobs and professions, multinational corporations, and multilateral treaties and agreements.

Among the many unique features of this unprecedented work are its two internal dictionary/thesaurus/encyclopedia sections, one of which, "Integrative Transdisciplinary Concepts," includes words and phrases "which in some way either integrate or interrelate concepts especially from different disciplines" (e.g., "emergent systems," "cultural relativity," and "harmony"); the other of which, "Human Development Concepts," presents ideas concerned with the "psycho-social development of the individual as a unique human being" (e.g., "planetary consciousness," "spiritual development," and "evolution of the human mind"). Together, these two reference pieces provide a new mapping of humanity's unfolding potential and the start of a common language for global discussion of human problems and potentials.

Along with Muller, Ellis, Hosken, and other global networkers, the Union of International Organizations recognizes the interconnectedness of all people on the planet, an idea that is reflected in a UIO appendix entitled "Network Organizational Strategy":

> The greatest unrecognized resource at this time is the vast uncharted network of organizations of every kind, with every kind of preoccupation and with every degree of effectiveness. It is not known either what this network could achieve if its processes were facilitated, or what is the nature of its synergistic potential. Just as there is a Third World of underdeveloped countries constituting the greater proportion of the world's population, so there is a Third World of underdeveloped organizations which could (and do in part) constitute the most vital resource for the solution of world problems.

The UIO also publishes a monthly journal, *Transnational Associations*, written alternately, from article to article, in French and English, and which includes directory updates of The Yearbook of International Organizations as well as thought-provoking articles on the forms and processes that international organizations can use to carry out their work. Within these pages, the global potentials for networking are being sketched out (in large part stimulated by Anthony J. N. Judge, an editor of the magazine whose approach to understanding networking sits at a crossroads between "social physics" and what futurist Gus Jaccaci calls "social architecture").

In a technical article, "Implementing Principles by Balancing Configurations of Functions," Judge suggests that an organization is capable of seeing the interrelated nature of all of its work, as opposed to the familiar fragmentation which arises out of dealing individually with priorities, projects, and/or recommendations, by applying Fuller's concepts of tensegrity (the interrelated dynamic of "tension" and "integrity"). Highly abstract in its presentation and sophisticated in its description, drawing on principles and tools that are largely foreign to the real world of networking (such as Venn diagrams, David Bohm's concept of "holocyclation," and circuit design), Judge's theory nonetheless represents one of the frontiers of network theory. These conceptual leaps are being generated by someone who is earning his daily bread and butter by using a transnational global perspective.

A practical side of Judge's work may be seen in his efforts to improve the quality of large group conferences, the subject of a conference he helped organize in Brussels in 1980. Four months before the meeting, Judge circulated a 100-page report explaining its projected focus and structure, in order to initiate discussion before the conference began. Within the report, Judge included a recent article of his, "Participant Interaction Messaging: Improving the Conference Process," which suggests that conference boredom and frustration can be relieved by designing an easy-to-use messaging process among attendees. As a veteran of hundreds of international conferences, Judge has made recommendations about how to facilitate the creative process in meetings of large numbers of people. And he tackles and proposes solutions for such details as precisely where to place message boxes, how to aggregate individual messages into a bulletin, how to translate messages from one language to another, and even how to deal with message "sabotage."

The idea of large-group, multicultural conferences is new among us as a species, an everyday sort of evolutionary development born out of high-speed mobility, mutuality of interests, and the awareness of the whole globe as one entity. Before airplanes and telephones, large group conferences were generally homogeneous and/or limited to local gatherings. Hence, a development in our ability to cross cultures, even from America East to America West, and "live together" in the temporary world of the conference represents an innovation in human interaction, a small but encouraging step toward what author William Irwin Thompson calls the "planetization" of our collective consciousness—itself just a small step toward reconfiguring our social, economic, and political structures.

Another step in the process of networking on the global level is to bring together people actively making connections on global issues, and introducing them to one another in a comprehensive context, perhaps utilizing the kinds of principles and procedures that Judge and his colleagues have developed. Visions of a planet at peace flicker through our fantasies as we mingle with the crowd of people involved with TRANET, Global Education Associates, Human Rights Internet, the Women's International Network, the Women's International Information and Communication Service (ISIS), Planetary Citizens, and Bucky Fuller's World Game, and hundreds more. Meetings like the World Future Society's First Global Conference on the Future, held in Toronto in July 1980, and the First Assembly of the Fourth World (broadly defined by Britain's *Resurgence* magazine as "the small nations and small groups of the world working against giantism . . . and for a human scale"), held in London in July 1981, signify the continuing effort to thicken the planetary network—*e pluribus unum.*

We are beginning to accept the idea that "the future" is not something that will "happen" to us. We make the future every moment we live, an ancient idea that is the very essence of "karma" and most readily understood in the West through the biblical passage "As you sow, so shall you reap."

Our future is born out of our transforming ideas, out of our original and most basic human attribute, which is the ability to create images of a world that has not yet existed, but may.

May there be peace on earth—all else follows.

Evolving Guide

E

The Evolving Guide includes groups that are primarily concerned with global and futures issues. Many of these groups also work on other issues.

Each group is identified by a letter/number code. The letter E stands for Evolving. Every group whose code begins with E is listed in the Evolving Guide.

The entry for each network whose code is lower than 100 includes a brief description. These representative networks are a cross-section of the initial groups we contacted in our research. Each network whose code is greater than 100 is listed with complete contact information. If the ✳ symbol, for publications, or the ◆ symbol, for materials, appears with a listing, consult the Title Guide under Evolving Titles.

The Evolving Guide includes groups that are concerned with computer conferencing, foreign policy, future studies, humanitarian relief efforts, human rights, the Middle East, peace, space travel, transnational efforts, the Third World, the United Nations . . . and a few others.

E001
Association for World Education
P.O. Box 589
Huntington, NY 11743   ✳

✳ *Journal of World Education (quarterly/$20)*

International network of educators concerned with global issues. Issues include population, peace and disarmament, environment, cross-cultural training, and women.

E002
Catholic Peace Fellowship
339 Lafayette Street
New York, NY 10012
212/673-8990   ✳

✳ *Catholic Peace Fellowship Bulletin*

Educational group devoted to furthering peace. Bases work on tradition of pacifism within Catholic Church. Sponsors speaking tours, maintains film and tape library, organizes workshops, and counsels conscientious objectors.

E003
Commission to Study the Organization of Peace
866 United Nations Plaza, #4045
New York, NY 10030
212/688-4665

Research group, focusing on peace, that started in 1939. Scholars and civic leaders prepare reports distributed primarily to people at the United Nations on human rights, arms control, the ocean, and the UN in the future.

E004
Congressional Clearinghouse on the Future
3565 House Annex #2
Washington, DC 20515
202/225-3153   ✳

✳ *What's Next (monthly/$10)*

Center for members of U.S. Congress concerned with raising "futures consciousness" and translating futures issues into policy. Coordinates network of futurists to provide testimony and meet members of Congress.

E005
Consortium on Peace Research, Education, and Development
Bethel College
North Newton, KS 67117
316/283-2500   ✳✳

✳ *Peace Chronicle (bimonthly/$15)*
✳ *Peace and Change*

Key node in the global-peace and social-justice networks. Conducts research; publishes newsletter, journal, and studies; sponsors conferences and workshops. Organized into six internal networks and two task forces.

E006
Friends of the Third World
611 West Wayne Street
Fort Wayne, IN 46802
219/422-6821   ✳

✳ *Friends of the Third World Newsletter ($25)*

Hub for a number of social-change and hunger-related activities: a printing cooperative, a network of groups marketing third-world crafts and commodities, and book-catalog service. Helps groups get started.

E007
Global Education Associates
552 Park Avenue
East Orange, NJ 07017
201/675-1409   ✳✳◆

✳ *Associates Newsletter (6 issues)*
✳ *Whole Earth Papers ($10)*
◆ *Toward a Human World Order*

Coalition of networks working to achieve more-humane world order based on peace, social justice, ecological balance, economic well-being, and participatory decision making. Conducts lectures, workshops, research, and resource center.

E008
Human Rights Internet
1502 Ogden Street, N.W.
Washington, DC 20010
202/462-4320   ✳

✳ *Human Rights Internet Newsletter*
   (9 issues/$25)

International communications network and clearinghouse on human rights with 700 members including organizations, scholars, activists, and policy makers. Publishes newsletter and directory.

E009
Hunger Project
1735 Franklin Street
San Francisco, CA 94109
415/775-8100   ✳

✳ *Shift in the Wind (quarterly)*

Educational effort to end hunger by 1997 through making people aware that individual actions can make a difference. Ran full-page ads in 10 major newspapers mobilizing action for Cambodian relief effort. Outgrowth of est.

E010
Institute for Alternative Futures
Antioch School of Law
1624 Crescent Place, N.W.
Washington, DC 20009
202/265-0346   ✳◆

✳ *Government Tomorrow*
◆ *Anticipatory Democracy: People in the Politics of the Future*

Futures-oriented think tank that promotes idea of "anticipatory democracy," Alvin Toffler's proposed antidote for "future shock." Conducts studies, prepares public testimony, and organizes seminars. Aimed at government.

E011
Institute for Food and Development Policy
2588 Mission Street
San Francisco, CA 94110
415/648-6090   ✳◆◆

✳ *News and Notes (quarterly/$15)*
◆ *Food First ($80 slides, $30 filmstrip)*
◆ *World Hunger: Ten Myths ($2.25)*

Research, documentation, and education center on food. Challenges popular myths about hunger "in a world of plenty" in reports and slide/tape shows. Cofounded by Frances Moore Lappe, it promotes networking among interested groups.

E012
International Network for Social Network Analysis
150 St. George Street
Toronto, Ontario
CANADA M5S 1A1   ✳✳

✳ *Connections: Social Network Analysis (3 issues/$8)*
✳ *Social Networks: Journal of Structural Analysis*

Professional association of academic social network analysts and others interested in such study. Publishes bulletin that serves as network information exchange point, including member directory.

E013
National Peace Academy Campaign
1625 I Street, N.W., #726
Washington, DC 20006
202/466-7670   ✳

✳ *National Peace Academy Campaign Update (quarterly/$25)*

Hub of effort to create a national center where peacemaking is researched and taught, including nonviolent conflict resolution, nonmilitary crisis intervention, and cross-cultural communication.

E014
North American Congress on Latin America
151 West 19th Street, 9th Floor
New York, NY 10011
212/989-8890   ✳◆◆

✳ *NACLA Report on the Americas (bimonthly/$13)*
◆ *NACLA Research Methodology Guide ($1.50)*
◆ *NACLA Handbook: The U.S. Military Apparatus ($1.75)*

Independent political research collective concerned with Latin American solidarity, human rights, and trade unions. Source of valuable research on power structures, U.S. investments abroad, and U.S. military.

E015
North American Nonviolence Training Network
4722 Baltimore Avenue
Philadelphia, PA 19143   ◆

◆ *Directory of Nonviolence Trainers ($2)*

Publishers of the Directory of Nonviolence Trainers, listing several hundred people in U.S. skilled in nonviolence and social action. Also lists organizations. Unusual resource.

E016
Oxfam America
302 Columbus Avenue
Boston, MA 02116
617/247-3304

American node in Oxfam International network. Provides critical financial support to self-help development projects in poorest parts of Asia, Africa, and Latin America. Programs range from gardening coops to famine relief.

E017
Participation Publishers
153 Jefferson Street, Box 2240
Wickenburg, AZ 85358
602/684-7861   ◆◆◆

◆ *Linkage (voluntary compendium)*
◆ *Beyond Despair (Theobald)*
◆ *We're Not Ready for That Yet (Theobald/$10)*

Launching pad for seminal thinking and innovative networking experiments of futurist Robert Theobald, organizer of the Linkage system. Major node in network of people developing techniques for computer conferencing.

E018
Participation Systems Incorporated
c/o Politechs
43 Myrtle Terrace
Winchester, MA 01890
617/729-1976   ✳◆◆

✳ *Netnotes ($12)*
✦ *The Networkbook ($100)*
✦ *Networking: Legitech Experiments ($10)*

Information firm that develops and maintains communications and data-retrieval systems for policy makers and people working in the public sector. Includes Politechs Network, Legitech, and Publitech. Available by mail or computer.

E019
Planetary Citizens
777 United Nations Plaza
New York, NY 10017
212/490-2766   ✳✳✦

✳ *One Family (quarterly/$15)*
✳ *Planet Earth (semiannual/$15)*
✦ *Earth, Space and Our Place*

Transnational group working for "planetary consciousness." Registers individuals as Planetary Citizens, now numbering 200,000 in 50 countries. Issues Planetary Passport.

E020
Satellite Video Exchange Society
261 Powell Street
Vancouver, British Columbia
CANADA V6A 1G3   ✳✦

✳ *Videoguide ($5)*
✦ *International Video Exchange Directory ($4)*

Publishers of annual international directory of nonprofit independent video producers. Enables producers from around the world to know of one another. Publishes summary of international "alternative television."

E021
The Source
Telecomputing Corporation of America
1616 Anderson Road
McLean, VA 22102
703/821-6660   ✳

✳ *Source World ($2 issue)*

Computer information system providing access to 2000 data bases. One of the first home computer services. Users with terminals can access news wire services, stock-market reports, airline schedules, computer games, etc.

E022
Transnational Network for Appropriate/ Alternative Technologies
P.O. Box 567
Rangeley, ME 04970
207/864-2252   ✳

✳ *TRANET (quarterly/$15)*

Global network of appropriate/alternative technology, "new age," and experimental groups and centers. Supports humanistic applications of technology. Serves as clearinghouse and matchmaker for A.T. projects.

E023
Union of International Associations
1 rue aux Laines
1000 Brussels
BELGIUM
02 511 83 96   ✳✦✦

✳ *Transnational Associations (bilingual, monthly/$25)*
✦ *Yearbook of International Organizations ($69)*
✦ *Yearbook of World Problems and Human Potential ($65)*

Key node in interlocking global network of nongovernmental organizations. Collects, processes, and reports on the work of international groups. Generates useful theory about networks. Publishes several invaluable, unique works.

E024
United Nations Economic & Social Council
United Nations, Room 2977
New York, NY 10017
212/754-5727

Crossroads for inventory of world resources at the United Nations. Seedbed for myriad humanistically oriented programs around globe. See Chapter 9, "Evolving," for interview with Robert Muller, Secretary of the ECOSOC.

E025
War Control Planners
P.O. Box 19127
Washington, DC 20036
202/785-0708   ✳

✳ *Checkpoint*

Long-standing initiative to bring about world peace. Started by Harriet and Howard Kurtz. Aimed at nations sharing space-age technology.

E026
Women's International Network
187 Grant Street
Lexington, MA 02173
617/862-9431   ✳✦

✳ *WIN News (quarterly/$15)*
✦ *Hosken Report: Genital/Sexual Mutilation of Females ($17)*

One of the few noninstitutionally based networks concerned with women's issues on global scale. Excellent journal includes news and references from around the world. Information about female genital mutilation.

E027
World Constitution and Parliament Association
1480 Hoyt Street, Suite 31
Lakewood, CO 80215
303/233-3548   ✳✦

✳ *Across Frontiers*
✦ *Constitution for the Federation of Earth ($5)*

Twenty-year-old effort to create a global constitution and parliament. Recognizes interrelated nature of global issues and need for world government leading to world disarmament. Working toward ratification of global constitution.

E028
World Future Society
4916 St. Elmo Avenue
Washington, DC 20014
301/656-8274   ✳✳

✳ *Futurist (bimonthly/$18)*
✳ *Future Times*

Membership organization serving as key node in network of futurists. Sponsors conferences, publishes journal, and has book and film service. Publishes membership directory that serves networking function.

E101
Aerial Phenomena Research Organization
3910 East Kleindale Road
Tucson, AZ 85712
602/323-1825   ✳

E102
Africa Fund
American Committee on Africa
198 Broadway
New York, NY 10038
212/962-1210   ✳✦

E103
Africa News Service
P.O. Box 3851
Durham, NC 27702
909/286-0747   ✳

E104
Afro-Asian Center
C.P.O. Box 871
Kingston, NY 12401
914/246-7828

E105
After Thought: Research and Education About the Future
1405 Krameria Street, #37a
Denver, CO 80220   ✳

E106
American Association for the Advancement of Science
1776 Massachusetts Avenue, N.W.
Washington, DC 20036
202/467-4485   ✳✳

E107
American Field Service
313 East 43rd Street
New York, NY 10017
212/661-4550

E108
American Public Health Association
1015 Fifteenth Street, N.W.
Washington, DC 20005
202/789-5600   ✳

E109
Americans for Middle East Understanding, Inc.
475 Riverside Drive, Room 771
New York, NY 10027
212/870-2053   ✳

E110
Analog: Science Fiction/Science Fact
380 Lexington Avenue
New York, NY 10017
212/557-9100   ✳

E111
Aquarian Age: Monthly for Space and Equality
355 West Olive Avenue
Sunnyvale, CA 94086
408/735-7754   ✳

E112
Arms Control Association
11 Dupont Circle, N.W.
Washington, DC 20036
202/797-6450   ✳✦✦

E113
Asia-Pacific Affairs Associates
580 College Avenue
Palo Alto, CA 94306
415/857-1336   ✳

E114
Association Eveil de la Conscience Planetaire
Groupe de Chamarande
91730 Chamarande
FRANCE
6/491.24.54

E115
Association for the Study of Man-Environment
   Relations
P.O. Box 57
Orangeburg, NY 10962
914/634-8221

E116
Astronomical League
P.O. Box 3332
Des Moines, IA 50316   ✳

E117
Australian Willing Workers on Organic Farms
7 Duncan Avenue
Boronia, Victoria 3155
AUSTRALIA   ◆

E118
Autrement
73, rue de Turbigo
75003 Paris
France

E119
Avaiation/Space Writers Association
Clifford Road
Chester, NJ 07930
201/879-5667   ✳

E120
Bulletin of Concerned Asian Scholars
P.O. Box W
Charlemont, MA 01339
413/625-2714   ✳

E121
Byte: The Small Systems Journal
70 Main Street
Peterborough, NH 03458
603/924-9281   ✳

E122
Center for Creative Studies
Sheridan College of Applied Arts &
   Technology
Oakville, Ontario
CANADA L6H 2L1
413/845-9430   ◆

E123
Center for Development Policy
225 4th Street, N.E.
Washington, DC 20002
202/547-1656   ✳✳

E124
Center for Interdisciplinary Creativity
Southern Connecticut State College
501 Crescent Street
New Haven, CT 06515
203/397-4471

E125
Center for International Policy
120 Maryland Avenue, N.E.
Washington, DC 20002
202/544-4666   ✳

E126
Center for Peace Studies
University of Akron
Akron, OH 44304
216/375-7008   ✳

E127
Center for Peace and Conflict Studies
Wayne State University
5229 Cass Avenue
Detroit, MI 48202
313/577-3468   ◆

E128
Center for Policy Alternatives
Massachusetts Institute of Technology
77 Massachusetts Avenue
Cambridge, MA 02139
617/253-1667

E129
Center for Teaching International Relations
University of Denver
Denver, CO 80208
303/753-3106   ✳

E130
Center for U.F.O. Studies
1609 Sherman Avenue, #207
Evanston, IL 60201
312/491-6666   ✳

E131
Center for War/Peace Studies
218 East 18th Street
New York, NY 10003
212/475-0850   ✳✳

E132
Center of Telecommunications for the Third
World
P.O. Box 4766
San Jose
COSTA RICA
23-80-01

E133
Centerpoint Community
Albany R.D.
North Island
NEW ZEALAND   ✳

E134
Centre Link
31 Grove End Road
London NW8 9LY
ENGLAND
01/286-4287

E135
Centre Monchanin
4917 St. Urbain
Montreal, Quebec
CANADA H2T 2W1   ✳

E136
Claustrophobia: Life Extension
5047 Southwest 26th Drive
Portland, OR 97201   ✳

E137
Coalition for a New Foreign and Military Policy
120 Maryland Avenue, N.E.
Washington, DC 20002
202/546-8400   ✳

E138
Coevolution
6, rue Regis
75006 Paris
FRANCE   ✳

E139
Collectiv MAD/Media Alternative
Developpement
5/7 Rue Villehardouin
75003 Paris
FRANCE   ✳

E140
Communes Network
Birchwood
Storridge, Worcestershire
ENGLAND

E141
CommuniTree Group
470 Castro Street, #207-3002
San Francisco, CA 94114
415/474-0933   ◆

E142
Community Computer
9498 Argonne Way
Forestville, CA 95436
707/887-9676

E143
Community Computers
2704 North Pershing Drive
Arlington, VA 22201
703/527-4600

E144
CompuServe
5000 Arlington Centre Boulevard
Columbus, OH 43220
614/457-8600

E145
Compute Magazine
900-02 Spring Garden Street
Greensboro, NC 27403   ✳

E146
Computer Faire
333 Swett Road
Woodside, CA 94062
415/851-7075   ✳

E147
Computer Information Exchange
P.O. Box 159
San Luis Rey, CA 92068
714/757-4849   ◆

E148
Computer Music Journal
The MIT Press
28 Carleton Street
Cambridge, MA 02142   ✳

E149
Comunidad
P.O. Box 15128
S10465 Stockholm
SWEDEN
8/710.99.07

E150
Coop's Satellite Digest
Satellite Television Technology
P.O. Box G
Arcadia, OK 73007   ✳

E151
Creative Computing
P.O. Box 789
Morristown, NJ 07960   ✳

E152
De Kleine Aarde (The Little Earth)
Munsel 17
5280A Boxtel
NETHERLANDS
04116-76901   ✳

E153
Die Gruenen (The Green Alliance)
Bundesgeschäftsstelle
5300 Bonn 1
WEST GERMANY

E154
Down to Earth Association
13-43 Victoria Street
Fitzroy, Melbourne
AUSTRALIA   ✳

E155
**Dr. Dobb's Journal of Computer Calisthenics and
    Orthodontia**
P.O. Box E
Menlo Park, CA 94025
415/323-3111

E156
**Earthrise: New Myths and Paradigms for
    Tomorrow**
P.O. Box 120, Annex Sta.
Providence, RI 02901
401/274-0011

E157
East-West Communication Institute
1777 East-West Road
Honolulu, HI 96848

E158
Evolution
5-7 rue du Simplon
1207 Geneva
SWITZERLAND
022/36.44.52   ✳

E159
Experiment in International Living
Putney, VT 05346

E160
Family Tree Network
P.O. Box 17104
Tampa, FL 33682   ◆◆

E161
Fellowship of Reconciliation
P.O. Box 271
Nyack, NY 10960
914/358-4601

E162
Findhorn Foundation
The Park
Forres, IV 36 OTZ
SCOTLAND

E163
First Earth Battalion Foundation
740 Galisteo Street, #2
Sante Fe, NM 87501
505/983-3042

E164
Friedrichshof
A2424 Zurndorf
Burgenland
AUSTRIA
02147/23930

E165
Friends of the Filipino People
110 Maryland Avenue, N.E.
Washington, DC 20002
202/543-1093   ✳

E166
Future Shack
286 Congress Street
Boston, MA 02210
617/426-8826

E167
Future Studies Centre
15 Kelso Road
Leeds, LS2 9PR
ENGLAND

E168
Futures Network
2325 Porter Street, N.W.
Washington, DC 20008
202/966-8776   ◆◆◆

E169
Genesa Foundation
P.O. Box 327
Bonsall, CA 92003
714/728-2822

E170
Global Perspectives in Education
218 East 18th Street
New York, NY 10003
212/475-0850   ✳✳

E171
Helsinki Watch
205 East 42nd Street
New York, NY 10017
212/867-7035   ◆

E172
Home Video
475 Park Avenue South
New York, NY 10016 ✳

E173
Human Systems Network
P.O. Box 66
West Newton, MA 02165

E174
Humanity Foundation
International Headquarters
Vancouver, British Columbia
CANADA V6K 1N7
604/736-2547

E175
IOC/MAB
Kuringersteenweg 35
3500 Hasselt
BELGIUM
011/25.23.41

E176
Info Alternativ
Rotensterngasse 26
1020 Vienna
AUSTRIA
0222/240205

E177
InfoWorld: The Newspaper for the
   Microcomputing Community
Popular Computing, Incorporated
530 Lytton Avenue
Palo Alto, CA 94301
415/328-4602 ✳

E178
Information Center on Children's Cultures
U.S. Committee for UNICEF
331 East 38th Street
New York, NY 10016
212/686-5522

E179
Information Industry Association
316 Pennsylvania Avenue, S.E.
Washington, DC 20003
202/544-1969

E180
Innovation et Reseaux pour le Developpement
Case 116, 3 Rue de Varembe
1211 Geneva 20
SWITZERLAND ✳

E181
Institut Rural d'Information
Gorodka
24200 Sarlat La Caneda
FRANCE
53-593238

E182
Institute for Information Society
Fujimura Building Z-15-29
Shinjuku Shinjukuku Tokyo
JAPAN
341-8515 ◆

E183
Institute for Policy Studies
1901 Q Street, N.W.
Washington, DC 20009 ✳✳✳

E184
Institute for World Order
777 United Nations Plaza
New York, NY 10017
212/490-0010 ✳◆◆

E185
Institute for the Study of Conscious Evolution
2418 Clement Street
San Francisco, CA 94121
415/221-9222

E186
Institute for the Study of the Human Future
2000 Center Street, #1362
Berkeley, CA 94704
415/527-6679 ✳

E187
Institute of Noetic Sciences
600 Stockton Street
San Francisco, CA 94108
415/434-0626 ◆✳

E188
Intercontinental Press/Inprecor
410 West Street
New York, NY 10014 ✳

E189
Interlink Press Service
229 Sullivan Street, Box 2B
New York, NY 10012
212/599-0867 ✳

E190
International Center for Integrative Studies
45 West 18th Street
New York, NY 10011
212/691-6161 ✳◆

E191
International Communes Network
c/o IOC/MAB, Kuringersteenweg 35
3500 Hasselt
BELGIUM
011/25.23.41

E192
International Council for Computers in Education
Department of Computers and Information Science
University of Oregon
Eugene, OR 97403   ✳

E193
International Herald Tribune
181 avenue Charles de Gaulle
92200 Neuilly-sur-Seine, Paris
FRANCE
7471265   ✳

E194
International Journal of General Systems
42 William IV Street
London, WC2
ENGLAND   ✳

E195
International Kirlian Research
411 East 7th Street
Brooklyn, NY 11218
212/854-5196   ✳

E196
International Union for Conservation of Nature and Resources
Avenue du Mont-Blanc
1196 Gland
SWITZERLAND
022/64 32 54   ◆✳

E197
International Voluntary Services
1717 Massachusetts Avenue, N.W.
Washington, DC 20036
202/387-5533   ✳

E198
International Women's Tribune Center
305 East 46th Street, 6th Floor
New York, NY 10017
212/421-5633   ✳◆

E199
Interreligious Taskforce on U.S. Food Policy
110 Maryland Avenue, N.E.
Washington, DC 20002
202/543-2800

E200
Johnson-Lenz
695 Fifth Street
Lake Oswego, OR 97034   ◆◆◆

E201
Journal of Developing Areas
Western Illinois University
900 West Adams Street
Macomb, IL 61455   ✳

E202
Kokov
Raadhusstraede 13
1366 Copenhagen K
DENMARK
01/15.52.53

E203
Kosmos Centre
142 Prins Hendrik Kade
Amsterdam
NETHERLANDS
020-230686

E204
L-5 Society
1620 North Park Avenue
Tucson, AZ 85719
602/622-6351   ✳

E205
Laurieston Hall
Castle Douglas
Kirkcudbrightshire
SCOTLAND

E206
Leading Edge: A Bulletin of Social Transformation
P.O. Box 42247
Los Angeles, CA 90042
213/258-7333   ✳◆

E207
Lighter than Air Society
1800 Tripplett Boulevard
Akron, OH 44306

E208
Magic Circle: The Native American Indian
Wholeman Institute
1106 Irving Avenue
Dayton, OH 45419
513/293-9088   ✳

E209
Maison du Nouvel Age
71, Chaussee de Charles le Roi
Bruxelles
BELGIUM
2/538.22.52

E210
Mandala Verlag
Postfach 60
D5429 Klingelbach
WEST GERMANY   ◆

E211
Maryland Alliance for Space Colonization
3112 Student Union Building
University of Maryland
College Park, MD 20742
301/454-4234   ✳

E212
Middle East Peace Project
339 Lafayette Street
New York, NY 10012
212/475-4300   ◆

E213
Middle East Research and Information Project
P.O. Box 3122
Washington, DC 20010   ✳

E214
**Mushroom: A Magazine for Living in New
    Zealand**
P.O. Box 6098
Dunedin North
NEW ZEALAND   ✳

E215
**National Network in Solidarity with the
    Nicaraguan People**
1718 20th Street, N.W.
Washington, DC 20009
202/223-2328   ✳

E216
National Space Institute
P.O. Box 1420
Arlington, VA 22210
703/525-3103   ✳

E217
Netswerk Selbsthilfe
Greisenaustrasse #2
1000 Berlin 61
WEST GERMANY
030/691.3072

E218
Network to Educate for World Security
777 United Nations Plaza
New York, NY 10017
212/490-0010   ◆

E219
New Era Technologies
2025 Eye Street, N.W., #922
Washington, DC 20006
202/887-5440   ◆

E220
New Humanity Journal
51a York Mansions, Prince of Wales
London, S.W. II
ENGLAND   ✳

E221
News from Guatemala
P.O. Box 335, Station R
Toronto, Ontario
CANADA M4G 4C3   ✳

E222
Next: A Look into the Future
708 Third Avenue
New York, NY 10017   ✳

E223
Nucleus Network
188 Old Street
London, EC1
ENGLAND
01/250-1219   ✳

E224
Nuestro Magazine
461 Park Avenue South
New York, NY 10016
212/684-5999   ✳

E225
Office of Tibet
801 Second Avenue
New York, NY 10017
212/867-8720

E226
Office on Global Education
Church World Service
28606 Phillips Street
Elkhart, IN 46515
219/264-3102

E227
Omega: Global Networking
University of Prince Edward Island
Charlottetown, P.E.I.
CANADA C1A 4P3
902/892-4121   ✳

E228
Omni Magazine
909 Third Avenue
New York, NY 10022
212/593-3301

E229
Open Systems
2041 Polk Street, Suite E
San Francisco, CA 94109
415/885-6006   ✳

E230
Organization for the Advancement of Space Industrialization
P.O. Box 704
Santa Monica, CA 90406

E231
Papier Mache Video Institute
133 Hamilton Street
New Haven, CT 06511
203/777-0906

E232
Partnership for Productivity
c/o Ministry of Education and Youth
Roseau
DOMINICA

E233
People's Computer Company
1263 El Camino Real, P.O. Box E
Menlo Park, CA 94025
415/232-3111   ✳◆

E234
People's Translation Service
4228 Telegraph Avenue
Oakland, CA 94609
415/654-6725   ✳✳

E235
Phebus: Integrating Wholes and Parts
32 bis avenue Rene Coty
7504 Paris
FRANCE

E236
Planetary Association for Clean Energy
100 Bronson Avenue, Suite 1001
Ottawa, Ontario
CANADA K1R 6G8
613/236-6265   ✳

E237
Planetary Society
P.O. Box 3599
Pasadena, CA 91103

E238
Plenty
The Farm
156 Drakes Lane
Summertown, TN 38483   ✳◆◆

E239
Population Action Council
110 Maryland Avenue, N.E.
Washington, DC 20002
202/544-3303   ✳

E240
Prometheus Society
102 Morris Drive
Laurel, MD 20810
301/498-9270

E241
Promoting Enduring Peace
P.O. Box 103
Woodmont, CT 06460
203/878-4769

E242
Purser's Magazine for Family Computers
P.O. Box 466
El Dorado, CA 95623   ✳

E243
Radical Perspectives Network
Trumbull Hill Road
Shaftsbury, VT 05262

E244
Radio Amateur Satellite Corporation (AMSAT)
P.O. Box 27
Washington, DC 20044
202/488-8649

E245
Religion and Ethics Network
Bethany Theological Seminary
Butterfield & Meyers Roads
Oak Brook, IL 60521

E246
Rescue Communication Network
5853 Lakehurst
Dallas, TX 75230

E247
Research Utilization Network
Department of Political Science
University of Wisconsin
Eau Claire, WI 54701

E248
Resource Center for Nonviolence
P.O. Box 2324
Santa Cruz, CA 95063   ✳

E249
Resurgence: Of Small Nations, Small Communities, & Human Spirit
Ford House, Hartland
Bideford, Devon
ENGLAND
(023 74) 293   ✳

E250
Review of International Broadcasting
University Radio WUOT
Knoxville, TN 37916   ✳

E251
Robotics Age: Journal of Intelligent Machines
P.O. Box 801
La Canada, CA 91011
213/352-7937 ✳

E252
Saharan Peoples Support Committee
217 East Lehr
Ada, OH 45810

E253
Science Digest
Hearst Corporation
224 West 57th Street
New York, NY 10019 ✳

E254
Science Fiction Writers of America
68 Countryside Apartments
Hackettstown, NJ 07840
201/852-8531 ✳

E255
Science News
Science Service
1719 N Street, N.W.
Washington, DC 20036
202/785-2255 ✳

E256
Shalom Network
P.O. Box 221
River Edge, NJ 07661 ✳

E257
Sierra Club International Earthcare Center
800 Second Avenue
New York, NY 10017
212/867-0080 ✳

E258
Society for General Systems Research
Systems Science Institute
University of Louisville
Louisville, KY 40208 ✳◆

E259
Sourcebook Project
P.O. Box 107
Glen Arm, MD 21057

E260
Southeast Asia Resource Center
P.O. Box 4000-D
Berkeley, CA 94704
415/548-2546 ✳

E261
Southern Africa Committee
17 West 17th Street, 8th Floor
New York, NY 10011
212/989-3557 ✳

E262
Teilhard Centre for the Future of Man
81 Cromwell Road
London, SW7
ENGLAND
01/370-6660

E263
Teilhard Foundation
2290 Emerald Road
Boulder, CO 80302
303/443-3647 ✳

E264
The Network: Starflight and Immortality
P.O. Box 317
Berkeley, CA 94701

E265
Triangles: Network of Light
866 United Nations Plaza, #566
New York, NY 10017

E266
Turning Point Newsletter/England
Spring Cottage, 9 New Road
Ironbridge, Shropshire TF8 7AU
ENGLAND
095/245 2224 ✳

E267
Twenty-first Century Media
606 Fifth Avenue
East Northport, NY 11731
516/368-2609

E268
U.S. Association for The Club of Rome
1735 De Sales Street, N.W.
Washington, DC 20036
202/638-1029 ◆

E269
**U.S. Committee for Justice to Latin American
    Political Prisoners**
200 Park Avenue South, Suite 812
New York, NY 10003
212/254-6062 ✳

E270
U.S.-China People's Friendship Association
635 South Westlake Avenue, #202
Los Angeles, CA 90057
213/483-5810 ✳

E271
Universite Verte
Groupe de Chamarande
91730 Chamarande
FRANCE
6/491.24.54

E272
University Peace Studies Network
Earlham College
Richmond, IN 47374
317/962-6561

E273
Verein Lebensdorf
Postfach 302
6540 Simmern
WEST GERMANY
061/368.7539   ◆

E274
Volunteers in Technical Assistance
3706 Rhode Island Avenue
Mt. Rainier, MD 20822

E275
Washington Office on Latin America
110 Maryland Avenue, N.E.
Washington, DC 20002
202/544-8045   ✳

E276
Women in World Areas Studies
6425 West 33rd Street
St. Louis Park, MN 55426
612/925-4300

E277
**Women's International Information &
   Communication Service (ISIS)**
Case Postale 301, 1227 Carouge
Geneva
SWITZERLAND   ✳◆

E278
**Women's International League for Peace and
   Freedom**
1213 Race Street
Philadelphia, PA 19107
215/LO3-7110   ✳

E279
**Women's International Resource Exchange
   Service**
2700 Broadway, Room 7
New York, NY 10025

E280
World Education Fellowship
2100 West Carlos Street
Alhambra, CA 91803
213/284-8773

E281
World Environment Center
300 East 42nd Street
New York, NY 10017
212/697-3232   ✳

E282
World Federalists Association
1011 Arlington Boulevard, #W219
Arlington, VA 22209
703/524-2141   ✳

E283
World Game of R. Buckminster Fuller
3500 Market Street
Philadelphia, PA 19104
215/387-5400   ◆◆◆

E284
World Hunger Education Service
2000 P Street, N.W., #205
Washington, DC 20036
202/223-2995   ✳◆

E285
**World Institute for Advanced Phenomenological
   Research**
348 Payson Road
Belmont, MA 02178

E286
World Peace News
777 United Nations Plaza, 11th
New York, NY 10017
212/686-1069   ✳

E287
World Peace Tax Fund
2111 Florida Avenue, N.W.
Washington, DC 20008
202/483-3751   ◆

E288
World Press Review
P.O. Box 915
Farmingdale, NY 11737
212/697-6162   ✳

E289
World Space Federation
P.O. Box 293
Grandview, MO 64030
816/966-8553   ✳

E290
World Union
Sri Aurobindo Ashram
Pondicherry - 605002
INDIA   ✳

E291
WorldPaper: The Global Community Newspaper
8 Arlington Street
Boston, MA 02116
617/536-3855   ✳

E292
Worldwatch Institute
1776 Massachusetts Avenue, N.W.
Washington, DC 20036
202/452-1999   ◆◆

10

What Is a Network?
A Model of Structure and Process

Constructing a theory about networks is very risky. For the most part, network theory has been based on physical systems that function as networks: communications, information, and transportation systems, just to name a few, all of which have their own theoretical heritages, primarily derived from engineering.

In the people-to-people/group-to-group networks that are the subject of this book, practice has preceded theory. Thus, we have used our personal knowledge and our interpretation of the experience of others to create a "model" of networks, briefly encapsulated in ten aspects or characteristics. We do not now have nor will we ever have the sole "correct" model of networks. What we have is *a* model that for us makes sense out of the mass of material we have assembled. With more time and information, our model of networks will inevitably change and improve.

Our model was not created in a vacuum, nor simply from our mail-order materials and personal experience. Some of our correspondents became collaborators in our struggle to understand networks. They wrote letters, sent articles, and recommended books that they thought might be helpful. One article in particular, by anthropologist Virginia Hine, was often mentioned by knowledgeable people, and a number of copies were sent to us. Indeed, Robert A. Smith, III (our original networker, see Chapter 12) had sent it to us shortly after its 1977 publication in *World Issues*, the magazine of the Center for the Study of Democratic Institutions. In this article, "The Basic Paradigm of a Future Socio-Cultural System," Hine, whose seminal work on networks has been done in conjunction with anthropologist Luther Gerlach, writes:

> Wherever people organize themselves to change some aspect of society, a non-bureaucratic but very effective form of organizational structure seems to emerge. We called the type of structure we were observing a "segmented polycephalous network."

In four breathtaking pages, Hine identifies three essential qualities of networks. They are (1) *segmented*, "composed of autonomous segments which are organizationally self-sufficient." Networks are (2) *decentralized*, connected by horizontal linkages such as overlapping membership and mobile leadership. And networks are held together through a fabric of (3) *shared values* and unifying ideas, an "ideological bond" that, in Hine's view, is the most important network characteristic. Shared values hold the decentralized segments of a network together in a dynamic pattern of interaction.

Challenging the assumption that bureaucracy and hierarchy are the only viable forms of organization for large numbers of people, Hine points to networks as another, and in many cases a more appropriate, form of large-scale organization. From her outpost on the social frontier, Hine sees networks growing most vigorously at the extreme ends of the scales of power and influence. Networks, she says, are emerging both among the global elite and the powerless everywhere.

> If this model of the emerging paradigm has any validity, the organizational structure of the future is already being created by the most as well as the least

powerful within the present paradigm. It is very clear, however, that the ideologies which inform [networks] at the two levels are diametrically opposed.

In this chapter we present a network model, elaborating upon the visible and invisible aspects of networking listed and briefly described in Chapter 1. Our ten-point model may be viewed as simply an extension of the Gerlach/Hine three-point model. We see the same network phenomena that they see, and that many others see. We suspect that most people will find that many of the network characteristics discussed here fit with their own images and ideas about networking.

A *model* is a package of ideas that we use to understand something about the world. A useful model contains a few interrelated and easy-to-remember concepts. A good model becomes a mental tool, one that requires learning and practice to use effectively, just as a physical tool such as a chisel or a telescope does. A new model, or mental tool, may seem somewhat strange at first, but if it is well designed, in time it will rest comfortably in the mind.

Our model of networks consists of ten characteristics, five of which describe a network's structure and five of which describe a network's process.

STRUCTURE	PROCESS
Wholeparts	Relationships
Levels	Fuzziness
Distributed	Nodes and Links
Fly-eyed	Me and We
Hydra-headed	Values

Each of the ten attributes represents one significant idea about networks and networking; all networks reflect at least one, if not several, of these aspects or characteristics. For us, the overall concept of networks includes all ten ideas working together, creating one general pattern that distinguishes networks from other types of organizations. In our minds, these concepts overlap and interweave into Bateson's pattern that connects.

THE STRUCTURE OF NETWORKS

(1) Wholeparts

All of life is made up of "whole" things that are also "part" of something else. A network is both a *whole* in and of itself, and a *part* of something larger than itself. A network participant is both a whole in and of it/him/herself and part of something larger—namely, a network. We use the coined word "wholeparts" to describe this interconnected attribute of the world around us.

Life abounds with examples of wholeparts. A person is both a whole individual *and* a part of a family. A family is a whole social unit of relatives *and* a part of a community. A community is a whole collection of individuals and families *and* a part of a country and a world. A person as a whole is also a macro-universe of his/her own, structured in another sequence of wholeparts: A whole body is an integration of many organ parts, human organs are wholes made up of cellular parts, and cells are wholes made up of molecular and atomic parts.

In networks of individuals, people are parts who are recognized as self-sufficient wholes capable of autonomous functioning. At the same time, a person participates—literally, "takes part"—in the "wholeness" of the network that arises from the work of many people. The same concept applies to networks that link groups and organizations: Each group is respected for its integrity and independent activities as a whole, while simultaneously being integrated as a part into the larger whole of the network. Judy Norsigian, for example, is a unique person who participates in the Boston Women's Health Book Collective. The Collective, in turn, is a part of the National Women's Health Network, composed of groups and individuals.

Virginia Hine uses the word *segmentation* to refer to the wholepart nature of networks. Describing a network as "a badly knotted fishnet," a web of links between self-reliant nodes, Hine considers segmentation to be one of the three key characteristics of a network. It is precisely this attribute of self-sustaining parts that gives the network form its remarkable resiliency and its adaptability to stress. Segmentation explains why, for example, underground political movements are so difficult to suppress. Squashing one node does little to impair the effectiveness of the net as a whole.

The independence of wholeparts in networks contrasts sharply with the standardized, synchronized, and precisely fitted parts of a bureaucracy that become more dependent as specialization and size increase. For example, while a person like Judy Norsigian can testify at a public health hearing without obtaining "clearance" from any "higher authority," an employee of a health insurance company does not enjoy such autonomy. Of course, no one in a network can be totally self-reliant, and, indeed, a network arises out of needs and visions that cannot be fulfilled in isolation. But by attributing respect to its own parts and supporting the independence of its participants, a network is encouraged to recognize the qualities of autonomy and interdependence at all levels of social interaction.

Because it treats its participants with respect, a network as a whole expects its voice to be treated with respect as it plays a part in a larger whole. Ultimately, the meaning of networks always comes back to people. The principle of wholeparts, of autonomy and respect for participants, is fundamentally a respect for people, a respect for one another's individuality and potential contribution to the whole.

(2) Levels

Mentioning hierarchy to a networker is like waving a red handkerchief at a bull. "We have no leader," the Great Atlantic Radio Conspiracy emphatically states. "We are all workers in an anti-hierarchical society." However, while networks are not hierarchies, they do reflect the pattern of levels. Just as everything is a wholepart, so does everything reflect the pattern of levels. A whole is one level and a part is another level. In the same way as atoms, molecules, cells, organs, and organisms are all levels within levels, so are people, groups, organizations, and societies levels within levels.

Levels are a useful tool for organizing complex structures, one we use every day to describe the world around us. Governments operate at the local, state, and national levels. Currency is composed of levels of values—cents in dimes in dollars. Measuring systems are made up of linear levels—inches in feet in miles. Time is counted in levels of seconds making up minutes which count hours in a day. Information systems are invariably organized in levels, from the Dewey Decimal codes at the local library to the parts of our telephone number (area code + local exchange + our phone). Computer hardware (the machine itself) is built up as a series of levels from simple on-off switches to highly complex "hardwired" logic. Computer software (the programs that tell the machine what to do) is designed in levels of increasingly general "languages"—machine languages, assembly languages, "higher" languages such as BASIC and FORTRAN, support and management utilities, and, finally, customized application procedures.

So, like everything else in the universe, networks are completely caught up in the pattern of levels. Networks are collectives of friends, organizations of members, coalitions of organizations, and alliances of coalitions. Networks form in neighborhoods to deal with community problems, in regions to deal with global problems, in transnational associations to deal with human problems. Networks are formed in every conceivable combination of social levels—from person to humankind.

Virtually every significant issue motivating the development of the networks of Another America has to do with the relations between levels of social organization—global, national, regional, state, local, grass-roots, family, individual. Whether the concern is with health care, ecology, energy, economics, power, personal growth, education, or communications, the networking approach invariably involves the rights, responsibilities, and interconnections of the many levels of social decision making. Jack Miller, of Anvil Press, expresses the sentiments of many networkers when he says, "We believe that forming networks is simply a natural outgrowth of our commitment to be responsible members of our community, region, nation, and world."

While networkers habitually dismiss the hierarchy model, they play freely with the concept of levels in their internal organization and external strategies. One example of the use of levels in networks is the antinuclear movement: Individuals belong to "affinity" groups that cooperate to form regional antinuclear organizations that, in turn, participate with other groups to plan, for example, a march on Washington. Each level—affinity group to national planning group—is seen as having integrity: "Smaller" levels are wholeparts included in "larger" levels that are also wholeparts. This abstraction translates into equal respect for all levels of human organization. We are attributing the pattern of "levels with respect for integrity" to networks without getting caught in the trap of authoritarian hierarchy.

A network is a whole made up of participant parts. In networks comprising individuals, each participant in turn is the hub of a personal network of family, friends, and contacts. Networks are composed of participants who have friends. This indistinct level of informally connected "friends" of participants is a rarely recognized but often crucial level for understanding the astonishing growth and influence that a small network might exert in a particular situation—an aspect of networking that politicians understand intuitively. Gerlach and Hine describe this as a process of "face-to-face recruitment along lines of pre-existing positive affect relationships." Hine translates from "social scientific-ese":

> Networks expand along these lines not because of media coverage or speeches by charismatic leaders. Too many networkers make the "old age" mistake (a costly one) of thinking they can attract numbers or spread ideas with mailings or flyers, when it is the one-to-one contact that is the basic growth mechanism of a network.

Networks also comprise groups (Gerlach and Hine define the "basic structure for sociocultural change" as a network made up of groups), and networks themselves may form networks. While new networks opening up new issues might think of themselves as alone in the world, many networks articulate important variations on the same general theme. For example, within the renewable-energy field, one network might concentrate on the whole spectrum of solar power, while another network might concentrate on passive solar devices, while still another network might concentrate on underground homes in the context of passive solar technologies. These networks of a feather often flock together as parts of a loosely seen "metanetwork"–a network of networks.

Like other types of organizations, networks reflect a level pattern. We see networks in terms of four levels: A group of *friends* (level 1) includes people who are *participants* (level 2) in a *network* (level 3) which is part of a larger *metanetwork* (level 4).

For the most part, the networks mentioned in this book are level 3 organizations. That is, the listed networks have some features of collective identity, including at least (a) a group name and (b) a mailing address. A level 3 network may also be identified by having a telephone number, a logo, stationery, flyers, publications, other media, products, offices, and/or a staff. In some cases, these groups operate in hierarchical fashion, with officers and traditional lines of authority, yet their interaction with other, similar groups makes them *nodes* (see below) in the larger network.

There are, of course, numerous level 2 networks, largely undocumentable, usually having a small membership but none or little of the level 3 group-identity paraphernalia. Examples of these would be groups of community, business, or professional friends who share experiences and exchange information. As for level 1, personal networks, most of us have a web of relationships that sustain us (or not) in our daily lives.

A few entries in this book are truly level 4 metanetworks, and there are many substantial fragments of metanetworks in most of the areas covered in our survey. It is our view that there is an increasingly choate metanetwork of shared values among all the extremely diverse networks we have identified as parts of Another America. Indeed, we hope that by putting such differing groups together we can help communicate the underlying pattern that connects them all and can contribute to the emergence of a globally/personally concerned metanetwork. Another America is a grand metanetwork, a pattern that connects us to a future of hope for ourselves and our children.

(3) Distributed

Although networks and bureaucracies both have level structure and are wholes with parts within wholes, networks and bureaucracies differ in how they structure the relationship between the whole and its parts. Bureaucracies tend to bring parts together through *centralized* control and to *maximize* the dependency of parts on the whole. Networks tend to bring parts together under *decentralized* cooperation and to *minimize* their dependency on the whole. Network parts are dispersed and flexibly connected, whereas bureaucratic parts are concentrated and rigidly connected.

Ideally, the forces of distribution and concentration can work together to maintain healthy parts and growing wholes. But in our time it is the tendency to centralization which has run rampant, and it is the process of decentralization which needs emphasis and development right now.

The statement of principles by TRANET, the Transnational Network for Appropriate/Alternative Technology, explains why they chose the term "network" to describe their organization.

> For governance, "network" implies a non-hierarchical system of equal, independent, self-sustaining members. Unlike a bureaucracy a network is dependent on no one of its parts. No organ performs a specialized task necessary for the function of the whole. A net has no center. It is made up of links between parts. TRANET's role [is] to strengthen these links. . . . The potentials for the future demand a humanization through decentralization.

TRANET is a whole: There are a name, an office in Rangeley, Maine, a staff, some files, and a vast collective memory bank of personal experience in its chosen field, appropriate technology (A.T.). Organizationally, TRANET resembles many of its member groups. Within the network, TRANET's role is not control but facilitation. Whereas a bureaucracy invariably has a controlling organ that serves as a decision maker, TRANET and other network hubs function to facilitate cooperative decision making.

A simple mental test can be used to judge whether a particular organization is predominantly centralized or decentralized. Just remove the individual or group that functions for the whole.

Imagine TRANET vanishing overnight. The international A.T. movement would certainly not collapse, nor would any of TRANET's members, although they would likely be somewhat inconvenienced and considerably saddened that a trusted channel of global communication had disappeared. Shortly thereafter, however, another international A.T. clearinghouse would certainly spring up, or perhaps several, particularly if TRANET happened to explode from internal dissension over goals and means.

By contrast, mentally remove "command central" from an industrial-age institution. The likely result is either paralysis or disintegration, or both. Imagine a bureaucractic army with its headquarters blown away: a helpless, headless, fragmenting giant. Now remember how many times United States aircraft "destroyed" the guerrilla headquarters of the "Viet Cong." The jungle network endured, and won.

According to the Gerlach/Hine model, decentralization (distribution) is the second major characteristic of networks, a concept that incorporates cooperation with independence. Networks strive for decentralization at every level, an idea that reflects a respect for the integrity and responsibility of people, each and every one of us. In networks, America now has many experiments in new forms of democratic cooperation.

(4) Fly-eyed

Like the fly whose "one" eye comprises thousands of individual eyes, networks "see" through many perspectives, although the unknowing observer may think they have only one point of view.

At times, a network seems to "see" with one eye and "speak" with one voice, testifying to consensus around an idea or a strategy. Such moments of unanimity are important, because they often reveal the essential common values and bonds that explain the unity among the diversity of network viewpoints.

At other times, a network may appear to be a babble of disconnected concerns and interests, or an arena of internecine warfare. Hine calls this trait "the 'fission-fusion' characteristic that confuses observers and leads the bureaucractically-minded to see networks as 'lacking' in organization." Networks not only tend to put up with disagreement, in many ways they depend upon it. The forthright independence of the members keeps the network as a whole from being dominated by any single node. Hine writes that while it is a shared vision that keeps a network together, "it is the conflicting concepts of goals-means that prevent any one segment from taking permanent control over all the others."

Reflecting a structure that requires relatively few people in authority, hierarchies are governed by rigid rules and codes, while bureaucracies keep order through standards and policies. The idea that there could be, or ought to be, one "correct" viewpoint, one authority who "knows best," is certainly consistent with the old-time physics, as well as the old-time religion. But just as the priestly ruler, from whom the word hierarchy is taken, is rapidly receding into history, so is the idea that there is *only one right* point of view.

Where once, b.e. (before einstein), educated folk knew for sure that the universe was governed by absolutes of space and time, right and wrong, now we all slip and slide around in a universe of relatives. Einstein shook off the blinders of his schooling in Newtonian mechanics and saw differently. He saw that the meaning of distance, speed, and time vary depending on your perspective.

Until the great triumphs of Copernicus, Kepler, and Galileo, the conventional wisdom had been that the earth was the center of the universe. Everything else in the heavens was explained from our God-given position on terra firma. Early scientists inaugurated a new age for humankind by establishing the sun as the "correct" and "true" center of at least our local heavens. Now even that view is seen as only one of many. The solar system may be understood with a point of reference on the sun, the earth, Pluto, the moon, an orbiting space station, or the star Alpha Centauri. All are valid perspectives.

R. Buckminster Fuller sometimes chides his audiences for being sunk in long-obsolete habits of thought, using the example of our conventional speech patterns, in which we say that "the sun goes down" at sunset and "the sun comes up" at sunrise. Surely we know, he says, that it is the earth which is moving. Yes, but conventional wisdom is correct at this time a.e. (after einstein). Relatively speaking, it is perfectly meaningful to regard ourselves as standing at the center of the universe to watch a sun coming up and going down and the stars circling around our heads like a cosmic halo.

The many perspectives of a network derive from the autonomy of its members. All have their own turf and agendas, yet they cooperate in the network because they also have some common values and visions. Just as the many points of reference of Einstein's universe are bound together by universal patterns of energy (such as the speed of light), so the many perspectives of a network are bound together by universal patterns of value.

An excellent example of this is manifest in the natural-childbirth movement—a loose network of parents, professionals, and health-care activists advocating a variety of alternatives to the routine maternity experience. While millions of people associate themselves in some way with the idea of "natural childbirth," sharp differences exist among those who favor medication-free births in the delivery room, those who advocate the use of in-hospital birthing rooms, and those who are working to establish out-of-hospital, freestanding birth centers, all of which are constituencies quite apart from those favoring midwife-attended home-births. Although these separate voices disagree as to which strategy will provide the best balance of risk, health, and meaningful experience for babies, mothers, and fathers, all are in agreement that the high-technology model of childbirth propounded by much of the medical profession must be changed and humanized.

(5) Hydra-headed

Networks, like all social organizations, need leadership, whether distributed or centralized. In networks, leadership is "polycephalous," to use Gerlach and Hine's term, which literally means "many-headed."

Ideally, all the participants in a network share in the leadership functions by taking responsibility for tasks and viewpoints related to the network as a whole. In practice, for the most part, network leadership is plural and porous, contrasting with hierarchies, in which leadership tends to become singular and closely held. A willingness to open mail and answer the phone is often the only ladder required or available for assuming a leadership role in a network.

As we pointed out above in the TRANET example, leadership in a network means facilitation, not control. An obvious and frequent problem that plagues contemporary networks is a confusion and conflict between cooperative leadership and singular control. In a telephone interview with us, James Gordon, a physician who is an energetic networker at the National Institute of Mental Health, remarked that the biggest problem in networks is power. Big egos. People losing spirit and falling into factionalism. It is hard, he said, to develop good leaders, and it is harder still to know how to deal with them. Hine comments:

> This factionalism, the ego-prickles of leaders, is one of the principal reasons for the spread of a network. Squabbles between leaders in a network often lead to splits so that two nodes appear in the place of one. I had many instances in my files . . . like the "eco-radical" who had a talent for inspiring a one-shot activity and collecting people who would then become a group around his leadership. Invariably, a dispute would arise as he tended to be very authoritarian. The group would fight with him. He would leave in a huff and start something else, leaving a trail of anger/bad vibes behind him but *also* six or eight *viable*, active nodes in the network. Leadership "problems" can be blessings in disguise though they never feel that way at the time.

The issue of leadership, cooperation conflicting with control, is not resolved in networks, as it can never be in any final sense. But in networks, contemporary society has experiments in many-headed leadership to offer as an alternative to the centuries of domination by singular, "top dog" leadership structures.

Polycephalous network leadership is not only cooperative and distributed, Hine points out, but it is also extremely mobile. People who are leaders in one segment of a network can easily serve a facilitating function in another segment of the same network or a different network. A "natural networker," particularly in the younger, "hobo" days, moves around from place to place, entering or starting networks at each stop, relating each new or newly discovered network to the ones encountered before.

The decade-long movement against the American war in Vietnam provides a dramatic example of mobile polycephalous leadership on a massive scale. Leadership sprouted everywhere, appearing and disappearing, incessantly moving, changing from moment to moment. Multiple leadership worked because there was a strong central core of values and assumptions that all members of the antiwar network shared either implicitly or explicitly.

In an active, dynamically growing network oriented to a change in the status quo, leadership may be even more than multiheaded and mobile. When a bureaucracy tries to suppress an unwelcome network, it may find itself confronting the second labor of Hercules. Each time one head was cut from the body of this multiheaded dragon of fable, two heads grew in its place. In multiple-leader networks, new leaders emerge in response to circumstance and need, and two heads will arise to fill a role left by the removal of any one head as needs demand.

THE PROCESS OF NETWORKING

(6) Relationships

Networks work because of the dynamic relationships that transpire among the people involved. We use the lunar analogy of "visible" and "invisible" faces of networks to underscore the shift required to understand the process of networking, a shift from thinking about *things* and the way they are built, to thinking about *relationships* and the way they behave.

Normally, through the conceptual glasses of substance and space, we are tuned to the things of the world, looking for solidity when we sit down and detouring around objects in our way. When we look at networks through the same materialistic glasses, they seem quite invisible. "Networks," writes Johnny Light from Detroit, "are quite invisible to the eye and difficult to document." But we all know, as futurist Robert Theobald says, "that much of the work in any system is done through informal and invisible networks, rather than through the formal visible authority structures."

Networks seem invisible because so much of the meaning of networks is bound up in relationships: the links, connections, communications, friendships, trusts, and values that give the network its life. In a network, the spatial furniture can be quite minimal: a phone, index cards, file drawers, a room in the basement. For a contrast, imagine taking a snapshot of a bureaucracy. Our picture is filled with offices, equipment, and parking lots. Now try using time-lapse photography magically tuned to the vibrations of human relationships. A network is revealed as having a richly diverse ecology of intertwining patterns and flows, while a bureaucracy appears in stiff, frozen tracks of controlled, habitual movement.

Another image of the visible and invisible worlds beneath our noses is suggested by a flight along the northeast corridor from Boston to Washington. In the morning, on the flight south, the structures and fixed patterns of the industrial world fill the window: roads, buildings, football fields, water towers. On the trip north, at night, a wondrous transformation has occurred. There are no asphalt parking lots, nor brick-and-mortar factories, nor geometrically plowed fields. Instead there are ribbons and clusters of light, myriad faint pinpricks in dark spaces between great shimmering seas of urban brilliance—a reality completely invisible to the daytime traveler.

Since networks are a type of organization, they have a form—a structure—that we have described in terms of wholeparts, levels, distribution, fly-eyed, and hydra-headed. There is also a process of networking, an activity of *doing* networking as well as *being* a network. Network processes are made up of relationships (the sixth characteristic we have identified), and the other four characteristics—(7) fuzziness, (8) nodes and links, (9) me and we, and (10) values—are all variations on the theme of relationships.

(7) Fuzziness

Now that you have tuned your mental vision to relationships, look again at the networks around you. If they still seem fuzzy, do not worry. Your relational glasses are not foggy, nor is your channel having technical difficulties. The boundaries of networks are often blurred and their activity often seems to turn on and off with no discernible regularity.

Think of your personal network. Can you clearly see who is in it and who is not? Is all of it always active with respect to you? Are your experiences with your friends always the same? If your networks are like our networks, the edges fade into an indistinct penumbra of relations and friends of friends. The personal network of Jack Eyerly, a "networker's networker" in Portland, Oregon (the "city of ash, roses, and rain"), "is a scattergun of affectations and affections, a universe of layered maps and diagrams, dark and bright, illuminated one by the others."

Hierarchies and bureaucracies are clearly bounded. You are either in or out. You are either a part of the royal family or you are not. You either work for General Motors or you do not. Within these institutions, a major subsystem serves as a boundary, like the skin of a body or the borders of a nation. While some networks do indeed have limited, carefully defined memberships, and may even be closed to outside interactions, most networks are quite open and have a very loosely defined participantship. People drop into and out of networks; network offices open, move, and close frequently; and network patterns ebb and flow according to the needs of the participants and consequences of external events.

In a note to us, Hine said that in her experience "no node in any network is aware of all the other nodes. It is the very nature of networks that they are fuzzily bounded if at all." Instead of being held together within a boundary, a network coheres from shared values, interests, goals, and objectives. A network is recognized by its clusters of interaction and channels of communication, rather than by a fixed boundary that includes and excludes.

It is shared values that establish the persisting identity of a network. Each person creates his or her own fuzzily bounded universe of interactions and values as members of many networks. For Eyerly:

> From the beginning I knew the little knots I tied into the tapestry had resonance; they reverberate still. Each new tying is with more skill, but the original tingle remains the final value.

(8) Nodes and Links

If you sat as a fly on our wall one day, you might have observed an exchange something like this:

> Robin in Toronto calls us in Boston. He wants to demonstrate the virtues of computer conferencing at his college; do we have any suggestions? We do. Call Barry at the University of Toronto. By the way, does Robin know of any networks in computer-aided art? He does. Robin suggests that we call Jackie at MIT in Cambridge or Ron in Los Angeles.

When we suggest that Robin call Barry, we are functioning as a link while treating Robin and Barry as nodes. When Robin suggests that we call Jackie and Ron, Robin is doing the linking and we are being a node.

In human networks, people are both nodes and links. It is people who set up relationships and it is people who are related. The roles are different but complementary, opposite but necessary for one another. As the above vignette illustrates, within one exchange a person may rapidly alternate between being a node and doing the linking.

Every participant of a network is potentially both a node and a link in the pattern of communication that constitutes the network as a whole. Each participant sometimes initiates or receives information as a node, and each participant sometimes acts as a link for other participants. At the level of personal networks, we daily experience this constant shifting back and forth between these two roles in communication.

In practice, in most established networks, some people and organizations will be nodes most of the time, while others will take on greater linking responsibilities. Indeed, the people we casually call "networkers" are the people who feel a personal calling to the task of setting up and maintaining relationships—links. Networks typically have a few participants who do most of the linking and many participants who are primarily nodes, but the possible combinations of these interrelationships are endless.

When modern physicists look at reality through their current models, they sometimes see a swarm of particles and they sometimes see a ripple of waves. Nodes and links are like particles and waves: Networks may appear to be assemblies of nodes or webs of links, depending upon the perspective chosen. As nodes, participants in a network are like "particles," single entries in a mailing list or phone directory. People are just so many pieces of mail when you are licking stamps. In linking, however, participants seem more like "waves" of interaction, spectra of interests, and diffraction patterns of meaning. When you are talking on the telephone to one of those pieces of mail, the feeling is very different.

(9) Me and We

In every area of networking we reached in creating this book, we encountered a deep concern with the relationship between individual people and the many levels of social organization that seem to encompass the person.

With respect to people, networkers do not choose between the one and the many; they affirm both. Many networks express their vision as simultaneously encompassing the integrity and significance of the individual and concerned with the importance of cooperation and collective interests. Like networks, people are wholeparts, autonomous individuals inevitably connected to other people by a variety of relationships. We are each simultaneously "me" and "we."

In the prevailing scientific models of evolution, both old and new, the track of progress seems to run from atoms to cells to organisms to societies. The place of the human individual and the development of consciousness are completely finessed, skipped over as if the question does not have its own unique meaning. On the one hand, people are seen as "special" organisms, and on the other hand people are regarded as simply units in societies. The implication of this viewpoint is that societies made up of people represent a more advanced stage of evolution than the individuals that compose them.

Recognizing a single track of evolution, we also perceive two interconnected rails on a spiraling track, like the double helix of DNA. One rail represents the successive development of more complex levels of individuality–amoebas to mollusks to apes to humans. The other rail represents the successive development of more complex levels of collectivity–mates to groups to tribes to civilizations. Our interpretation of evolution (see Chapter 11) is that the evolutionary development of individuals and their collective forms take place side by side.

Even without the framework of an evolutionary perspective, it is clear that in the worldview of the networkers of Another America the value of the individual and the value of the group are equivalent. Of course, within the context of a particular issue, either individual rights or collective interests might be emphasized to redress larger imbalances. Concern may shift from pole to pole within one issue.

When networkers hold self-interest and group-interest together, these values often appear conflicting and ambiguous, perhaps paradoxical. Much of this discomfort naturally comes from our shared conceptual habit of dualism, which encourages us to choose one or the other pole of apparent opposites. But just as a physicist looks first at waves and then at particles to understand the one reality of both together, so each of us daily alternates between group and individual viewpoints to grasp the meaning of our one life.

A remarkable example of a network (and culture) that sees the unity in complements, rather than irreconcilable opposites, is expressed in the statement of principles by the National Indian Youth Council (NIYC):

NIYC views individuals as part of their community and there is no distinction between the two. While NIYC is concerned with individualistic problems such as economic poverty, employment discrimination, health care and education, the approach to these problems includes the community as a whole.

Within the American Indian worldview, individuals and communities grow and change together.

In Another America, it is commonly recognized that social transformation cannot take place without personal transformation. Describing the common assumptions of the people in the Linkage network he has orchestrated, Theobald, for instance, says ". . . we accept that any effective pattern of action will require us to change both our personal values and the institutions which were formed in the industrial era." Expressing a similar understanding, the newsletter of the National Association for the Legal Support of Alternative Schools displays the following quotation from Kahlil Gibran (*The Prophet*) as a permanent feature of its masthead:

> If it is an unjust law you would abolish, that law was written with your own hand upon your own forehead. . . . And if it is a despot you would dethrone, see first that his throne erected within you is destroyed.

(10) Values

The context that gives coherence to a network is seen in values, not in objects. Network bonds tend to be subjective, rather than objective, more mental than physical, which is why, as we have said, networks seem so invisible to the object-trained eye.

Our human value heritage is deep and wide, rooted in the origin of the planet and life itself, blossoming over the past half billion years of births and deaths. With each new twist of evolution, life acquired new patterns of values to add to the values already established. The emergence of mortality and sex in simple cell groups, of instinct in reptiles and emotion in mammals, and of tools and speech in the far-distant human generations, have all contributed to our vast value heritage.

Strangely, among the values of the industrial age is the unfortunate paradox that human value is itself devalued. To the old-style scientific observer, measuring stick and rat cage in hand, values seemed mired in subjectivity. Values are "intangible" and cannot be registered on instrument dials; consequently, scientists have said, values must be "unreal." In contrast, among the values of the networks of Another America is the value of *valuing* itself. Human values are considered "real" in Another America, and a concern with value is seen as essential for humane organization and purpose.

The self-description of the Movement for a New Society (MNS) illustrates the entwined blend of values and networks.

> MNS is a network of autonomous groups committed to radical nonviolent social change. Together we are developing an analysis of the present system, a vision of a better world, and a sustained nonviolent struggle. . . . The values of the new society can become a part of our lives now as we build community and alternative institutions.

For members of the Southwest Research and Information Center, "one of the most important characteristics of the Center is the commitment of everyone connected with it." Networks cohere through the shared commitment of their participants to a cluster of values. Hine believes that the value bond is "perhaps the most significant aspect of the segmentary mode of organization. . . . The power of a unifying idea . . . lies in a deep commitment to a very few basic tenets shared by all."

Peter and Trudy Johnson-Lenz, two very experienced and very thoughtful networkers, feel that "integrity" is the essential value that guides the work of networkers in Another America. Integrity, for Johnson-Lenz, is explicitly Januslike, embracing both the person and the ecosystem/planet. Integrity is the value of a dynamic balance between the individual and the collective, between me and we.

Flowing from the integrity of wholeparts, person to planet, Johnson-Lenz perceive four broad values "at the heart of the networking movement":

(1) Self-reliance	(2) Interdependence
(3) Self-interest	(4) Collective interest

Noting the obvious contrasts represented in their observations, they write:

> At first glance, these values may seem to be in conflict: self-reliance with interdependence, and self-interest with collective interest. Yet from a broader perspective they can be seen as complementary opposites which when balanced together create a dynamic, workable whole.

The values of Another America do not present a consistent tableau of step-by-step precepts for behavior. A set of values that stresses collective interests over individual interests or the reverse implies that more of one means less of the other. In Another America, a healthy dose of self-interest is regarded as acceptable if a person also has a healthy measure of group-interest. Self-growth is good when balanced with a consciousness of collective-growth. The values of Another America are about people and planet together.

As we said at the outset of this book, it is not the network form or process which distinguishes a movement for social change from an elite breakfast club that runs an industry, nor is it bonds of values. The difference between *all* networks and the *particular* networks we selected to represent Another America lies in the values themselves.

Hine, Muller, and others have pointed out that networks are now most evident at the two extremes of power, but the ideologies in these sectors are utterly different. Since the life of a network lies in its values, then, says Hine:

> Perhaps one of the crucial tasks of the immediate future is to clarify and expose the underlying assumptions that provide the ideological "glue" for [networks] emerging at the various levels of the global social structure. The key to the future may very well be conceptual rather than organizational.

From the first day of our network project, we considered it a crucial task to clarify the values that connected the networks we were selecting for print. In the beginning, as we set off in every direction searching for networks, we could only hope that we would recognize a common fabric of values that would give shape to our growing collection. Fortunately, by the simple strategy of starting with one richly connected networker, following up recommendations, and letting one network lead us to others (see Chapter 12), a cluster of values has emerged.

We are now convinced that there is a vast metanetwork of individual and social change that, in the fuzzy way of networks, maps the territory of an emerging future in

America. Another America is a metanetwork, and its values are healing, sharing, using, valuing, learning, growing, and evolving. Three of these values (healing, learning, growing) are oriented to the individual. Three more (sharing, using, evolving) are oriented to the collective. The seventh (valuing) is oriented to the process of human valuing itself.

Most of our book consists of descriptions of networks and networking within the context of these values. To distinguish between networks and to facilitate your searching, we have listed networks under one of the value topics. In fact, networks and their participants usually reflect many or all of these values in some way. These values together, a pulsating mosaic of individual and collective dynamics, connects the myriad webs into the far-reaching metanetwork we perceive emerging out of the din of evolutionary transformation.

A letter from Mark Satin, author of *New Age Politics*, is a unique but typical example of the many pokes and prods we received from our collaborators to clarify, insofar as we were able, the larger vision that binds the whole.

> I'm glad [your book] is being done and I hope and trust that you'll do a good job. It can be an extremely important book, as you well know—if the networks seem to cohere, then people will understand that they make up fragments of a coherent social movement. People will be more willing to join our networks if they sense that all the networks fit together into a larger whole, a whole that is true to our larger visions and values, a whole that adds up to a different and more satisfying way of living our lives. So I hope you'll include a chapter on the deeper or larger network that all our partial networks seem to contribute to.

CHAPTER 11

What Does It Mean?
Evolution, Systems, and Networks

Most people have, at one moment or another in their lives, been led to the peak experience of asking the "big questions": Who are we? What are we doing here? Where are we going? Several millennia of recorded history indicate that these questions are eternal, questions that are addressed by every generation but ultimately and finally answered by none.

It is clear to many of us that now is a time when we must again collectively address the big questions and come up with viable means of meeting the awesome challenges and possibilities of the future. The hard work of acquiring a new "worldview," a new context of beliefs about what is real and what is possible, must be done by all of us in our own lives and work.

From our point of view, the most interesting and significant networks are those that manage to maintain an understanding of the larger context while coping with the minutiae of daily detail. For the Community Congress of San Diego, innovation is based on "caretaker" values, and it requires two abilities:

(1) An understanding of the "big picture," which [is] the ability to put suggestions or ideas into context or perspective—a world perspective, state perspective, local (county, city, neighborhood) perspective; and,

(2) An understanding of the very small, very specific operational details required to carry out a particular "big picture" or vision.

We have combined theory and practice, vision and detail, in our work and in our book. This book would have been impossible without countless hours of setting up files, skimming resources, writing letters, typing addresses, licking stamps, going to the post office, opening mail, and making innumerable small decisions. It also would have been impossible without a larger purpose and vision that guided our choices and led us through the many crises inevitable on any vision-quest. In the end, we could not have pulled together our voluminous and disparate universe of information about networks into a coherent whole without first articulating a theory and a vision that was at least satisfactory to ourselves.

Every person operates out of a mental framework of assumptions and images about the world even while going about the most ordinary of tasks. For most of us, most of the time, this worldview is not articulated.

Since the mental model that informs the networks of Another America differs in some fundamental ways from the established worldview, networkers often consider it necessary to set up some theoretical underpinnings for their work and to explicitly state their essential values. Networkers vary, of course, in their predisposition to articulate theory, and there are many "natural networkers" with great intuitive resources who act effectively from inner wisdom without ever consciously creating a theory to explain what they are doing.

For our purpose of mapping the emerging future through the networks of Another America, we found it necessary to establish a larger, more encompassing context for the map as a whole. As Johnny Light, of Guild Communications, reminded us early in our research:

Overview is crucial! In the great age of specialization where many brilliant people know everything about every insignificant thing, completely out of context with what all the other brilliant people know, we have created a magnificent deception of the whole of creation. Every camp or idea thinks it has the whole picture, when in reality the whole picture is created from a composite of all the camps, all the ideas, all the perspectives, all the knowledge of human and natural history, past, present, and future, information received through books, through the senses and direct experience, through the psychic realms, the unconscious, the dream states, the mind-body-spirit continuum.

The year was 1964. A housewife with an infant daughter, concerned with the quality of New York City's little corner of life-sustaining atmosphere, formed a small network called Citizens for Clean Air. Today, Hazel Henderson is a self-trained, internationally recognized economic theorist and visionary, a compelling speaker who delivered one of the keynote addresses at the 1980 First Global Conference on the Future.

Henderson is associated with the phrase "thinking globally, acting locally," and she is an important node in many networks. Her ideas reflect the integrity of her own hard-won understanding of a world radically different from the world she was taught to see, and she is an inspiring role model.

Henderson's 1978 book *Creating Alternative Futures: The End of Economics* is often discussed in the same breath as *Small Is Beautiful*, the legendary book by E. F. Schumacher (who contributed the foreword to the work by his younger colleague). In her book, Henderson establishes this context for networks:

NETWORKS: THE "UNORGANIZATIONS" OF TOMORROW

Out of all our current social ferment, organizations are slowly learning that if they and our society are to survive, they will need to reformulate their goals and restructure themselves along less pyramidal, hierarchical lines. Such participatory, flexible, organic, and cybernetic design is now mandatory in the face of cataclysmic changes. As Bennis points out, "Democracy becomes a functional necessity whenever a social system is competing for survival under conditions of chronic change." Adds Richard Cornuelle in *De-Managing America*, "People will no longer be used." He believes that their self-discovery and self-expression are now creating a final revolution and transformation of authority.

In fact, the ultimate organizational design is already visible to those whose perception is attuned. These new organizations already exist, although they are metaphysical. They are most often referred to as networks, and their participants describe themselves as "networkers." They have no headquarters, no leaders, and no chains of command. They are free-form and self-organizing, composed of hundreds of autonomous, self-actualizing individuals who share a similar worldview and similar values.

Few organizational theorists have yet studied networks because they are evanescent, ebbing and flowing around issues, ideas, and knowledge. It is impossible to guess how many of these networks exist today in the United States and other industrialized countries. The numbers certainly run into the many thousands in this country, and many hundreds exist transnationally. Their chief product is information processing, pattern recognition, and societal learning.

Networks are a combination of invisible college and a modern version of the Committees of Correspondence that our revolutionary forefathers used as vehicles for political change. Luckily, networks are linked by the mimeograph machine, the postal system, and the telephone—all decentralized technologies accessible to individual users with constitutional guarantees of privacy. Networks can now create a recognizable, media-reportable, national event expressing grass-roots interest in a political issue in a matter of hours. Even a nation as communications-rich as our own now requires this kind of instant political signaling system to its decision centers in order to overcome bureaucratic inertia and hardening of our political arteries.

Networking cross-hatches all existing structured institutions and links diverse participants who are in metaphysical harmony. Sociologists are beginning to evidence interest in studying networking. However, these spontaneous organic forms will elude such outside observers since they create "static" on the lines, and this is instantly picked up by networkers who then regroup, using alternative channels.

To try to analyze this new organizational form with traditional, reductionist social science approaches would be unfortunate; networking is the most vital, intelligent, integrative organizational mode on our turbulent social scene. Perhaps this self-organizing mode represents a new maturing of human intelligence. It may even augur the next evolutionary step in developing human consciousness, which is now necessary if we are to survive on spaceship Earth.

As we read this passage, Henderson's message is that networks cannot be grasped with the analytic, specialized tools of the industrial mind-set. Rather, she says, networks can be understood only in a context that includes evolution, the planet, and humankind as a whole.

Henderson writes from within a new "paradigm" (from the Greek word for pattern) of thought that has been developing since the early decades of the 20th century, and her message is either crystal-clear or quite confusing, depending on the attunement of the listener-reader to the assumptions of the emerging worldview. In this chapter we highlight some features of the new paradigm and outline an evolutionary context for human networks.

Summarizing the "big picture" is a tall order. Indeed, from the specialized point of view, it is an impossible order. Coincidentally, however, the same conceptual crises and influences that have led a few people to think about networks have led a few scientists to think about "general theory." There is an increasingly visible stream in modern science that flows out of the belief that the universe is both detailed and integrated, both infinitely diverse and richly patterned. This new stream has many contributing academic tributaries, from vaguely expressed "interdisciplinary interests" to clearly articulated approaches such as "general systems theory."

A "general" theory grows out of the recognition that many specialized theories may have something in common—perhaps a formula, or coefficient, or key concept. A general theory combines these similarities into a pattern and in doing so creates a transdisciplinary context for understanding the scientifically separated parts of the natural world. We believe that the tenets of general theory are precursors of a new philosophy about ourselves, our planet, and our universe. The "new science" provides a "new metaphysics" for reconstructing our shared worldview.

One idea that captures much of the new worldview is "transformation." Transformation means radical, fundamental change, usually occurring suddenly and out of chaos. The idea is not abstract. It is of the essence of our time.

TRANSFORMATION

In 1948, the English philosopher/physicist/banker Lancelot Law Whyte published *The Next Development in Man*, written during the years 1941-43, while he was immersed in the fire and rubble of war among the great industrial-scientific nations of the world. As part of the team developing the first jet for the Allies, Whyte was thoroughly involved in the war effort. Even so, Whyte was also peering through a new scientific lens of general theory, seeing the indicators of a great transformation in the development of the human species.

To think effectively about the plausibility and significance of a major evolutionary change in our time, a long view of the whole of human evolution is required. Whyte saw five important transformations in human history, beginning with the primordial transition of primate biology to symbolic consciousness and continuing to the now-occurring transition from the industrial European age to an age of global unity.

(1) *Circa 5-2 million b.c.* With an indistinct ancestry at least 2 million and perhaps 5 million years old, nomadic, hunter-gatherer "hominids" gradually developed the skills of symbol making, tool making, fire use, and speech. These hominids were the primate precursors of the modern human subspecies, *Homo sapiens sapiens*, who appeared around 40,000 b.c.

(2) *Circa 10,000 b.c.* Suddenly, where bands of 20 had roamed, settled agricultural communities of 200 now appeared, marking a shift that is often considered to be the ancient dawn of civilization. Within a millennium, agriculture had sprouted, flowered, and taken root, and religious tombs and temples multiplied, "inventions" that were to become the central pillars of the ancient era. By 5000 b.c., neolithic towns had grown to cities of 10,000 and the great theocracies of Egypt and Mesopotamia (an area now roughly described as Iraq) had started their ascent to splendor. Under stress resulting from multiple influences such as intercultural trade, the adoption of writing, savage war, and geological catastrophes, the towering but fragile hierarchies of ancient gods and priestly rulers began to disintegrate in the last two millennia b.c.

(3) *Circa 600 b.c.* Out of the confusion of multiple deities, a new voice in human consciousness emerged, an early self-conscious rationalism that was archetypified in the Golden Age of Greek thought, beginning with the Athenian lawmaker Solon and culminating in the twin wellsprings of Western worldviews, Plato and Aristotle. Often recognized as the dawn of Western civilization, this period is also the era of Gautama Siddhartha (Buddha), Lao-tse (the founder of Taoism), and Confucius (Kung Fu-tse), who represent a similar transition in the East.

(4) *Circa a.d. 1600.* Modern history begins with the shift to the scientific-industrial worldview, which developed out of the monastic ponderings of Bacon, the movable type of Gutenberg, the astrological reveries of Kepler, the telescope of Galileo, and the absolutes of Newton. This set of ideas, which reached its peak of certainty and influence at the end of the 19th century, still dominates the thinking of modern society.

(5) *Circa a.d. 1920.* The signs of the next great transformation in human development first became visible in the years following World War I. Predicting that the many threads of change would rapidly coalesce into a coherent worldview in the post-World War II years, Whyte said that this transition would probably be complete by the end of the 20th century. Or else, he felt, humankind would be in serious trouble.

In 1964, Kenneth Boulding, one of the first scientists to recognize the potential applicability of general systems theory, published *The Meaning of the Twentieth Century*. In this little book, Boulding proposed that within the broad sweep of human evolution two really important transitions are apparent: One happened roughly 12,000 years ago and the other is happening now. Boulding sees all human history, from the agricultural dawn of civilization to the beginning of the 20th century, as one huge epoch–that he calls simply "civilization," and that he sees as coming after several million years of "precivilization" hunting and gathering. The "meaning of the 20th century" is that *now* is the time of a second great transition in human evolution–to what Boulding calls "postcivilization."

In 1980, the futurist Alvin Toffler published a best seller, *The Third Wave*, which interprets human history in terms of three "waves of development." The First Wave on Toffler's calendar, which he characterizes as agricultural, begins after the earliest precivilization era and spans the period from 10,000 b.c. to the emergence of science in the 16th and 17th centuries a.d. The Second Wave, which he characterizes as industrial, is the worldview that dominated the globe until around 1955. For the past three decades, Toffler says, we have been hurtling into the future on the crest of a great Third Wave of human evolution.

Perhaps the most apocalyptic example of this viewpoint is the widely quoted remark by the biophysicist John Platt, who wrote: "The present generation is the hinge of history. . . . We may now be in the time of the most rapid change in the whole evolution of the human race, either past or to come."

Although they differ on the stages of human evolution, these writers have a common theme: We live in an evolutionarily significant moment, a period of confusion and instability that nevertheless carries the seeds for the emergence of the next level of human development, both personal and social.

EMERGENT EVOLUTION

Where do networks fit in on this scale? We believe that networking–people making connections between people–is as old as the first symbol-making hominids and has survived and changed over the several million years of crucial transitions in human development. Networks of tool makers, fire starters, cave painters, mammouth hunters, and sign speakers must have organized into various social support systems to cope with personal and collective survival during the first millions of years of human existence. Similarly, informal networks were undoubtedly important in the era of ancient civilization, dominated by the development of elaborate control hierarchies, when, for example, those rejecting the prevailing authority, such as the early Jews and Christians, survived and grew on the branches of their network tree.

Networks have certainly been important during the industrial-rational age. Operating within bureaucracies, this period's characteristic organizational form, is the so-called "old-boy network," a term that belies the real influence and power such a peer group holds. While informal networks of people with a common worldview have performed a crucial integrating function for established institutions, networks also have been the foundation for revolutions in this era–from the Committees of Correspondence of the American Revolution to the Spanish anarchists to the cells of the classical communist revolution to the many contemporary media voices and congregations of single-issue movements.

The idea of transformation on the largest scale is based on a radically revised view of evolution–a very charged word at the end of the 20th century, as evidenced by a 1981 court battle over what children should be taught about the origin of life. Unnoticed in the current political confusion surrounding the debate of "Creationists" versus "Neo-Darwinians" is a growing scientific underground that is merging Darwin's evolutionary theory into a new, more comprehensive model that is sometimes called *emergent evolution*. Emergent evolution is a simple term encompassing the many converging ideas of the past quarter century of anthropologists such as Gregory Bateson, biologists such as Ludwig von Bertalanffy, philosophers such as Lancelot Law Whyte, economists such as Kenneth Boulding, psychologists such as Abraham Maslow, and humanists such as Arthur Koestler.

Four ideas in the new paradigm of evolution are important to us in understanding contemporary change networks: emergence, inclusion, transition, and acceleration. The principle of *emergence* suggests that there are some qualities in networks that are clearly new in human history. The principle of *inclusion* suggests that earlier forms of human organization are carried into future forms. The principle of *transition* (including both periods of "chaos" and moments when the process seems to "step-back-to-leap-forward") explains the current period of confusion and also suggests that new networks are reaching back to earlier stages of human evolution in order to fashion a synthesis for the future. Finally, from our present vantage point in time, it appears that terrestrial evolution is a process of progressive *acceleration*. Each cycle of stability and transformation leading to a new level of organization is shorter than the cycle that went before–which explains why momentous evolutionary change is possible in our time.

(1) Emergence

For millions of years, hominids existed without fire. Then, suddenly (in terms of paleo-archaeological time scales), they discovered how to use and conserve fire. In evolutionary theory, this idea is called emergence, referring to the notion that evolution seems to proceed through cycles of long, slow swells of "horizontal" change followed by wind-whipped chops of rapid "vertical" change. This pattern is sometimes represented as a series of "steps," like a set of stairs, up a scale of progressive development. But the steps of evolution do not always march steadily up the slope of progress. Rather, they appear to zigzag their way toward greater complexity, with evolution sometimes appearing to be retreating, rather than advancing.

The Darwinian-industrial concept of evolution portrays a process of sluggish continual change: from slime to slug to reptile to ape to human. According to the conventional model, isolated, random mutations, which are recorded as genetic variations, have survived a natural competitive struggle (the survival of the fittest), slowly building up terrestrial complexity to human life–layer by sedimentary layer.

While natural selection is certainly a powerful process in evolution, the new paradigm of emergent evolution also recognizes another process, transformation, in which sudden and sharp discontinuities punctuate the progress of slow change. These rifts either signal a leap to a new, more complex level of life or they signal a devastating crash to some earlier level of life. Over the long haul, human life and civilization are testimony to the fact that, so far, life on this planet appears to have leaped more often than collapsed. The theory of emergence suggests that evolution does indeed generate "new things under the sun," that there is a creative principle of order operating together with the randomizing principle of disorder. There is a process of building up as well as a process of tearing down.

In the longest view, there have been two fundamental, sharp transformations in life on earth: between purely *physical* systems (such as atoms, minerals, and clocks) and *biological* forms (such as amoebas, reptiles, and rats); and between purely *biological* life and *human* life (such as us and you). The biologist Theodosius Dobzhansky has called these transitions the "quantum leaps" of evolution and the "points of evolutionary transcendence." An amoeba is as different from a rock as a person is from a dog.

Each of these major levels–physical, biological, and human–contains clearly identifiable levels of organization. Quarks, subatomic particles, atoms, and molecules are successive levels of physical organization; cells, organelles, organs, and organisms are levels of biological organization. What Whyte, Boulding, Toffler, and others are trying to perceive are the significant transitions that mark the evolutionary development of *humankind*, the levels and periods of emergent transformation in human psyches and societies.

(2) Inclusion

The theory of emergent evolution provides a context for understanding networking as both an extremely old and an entirely new human activity. Emergent evolution describes a process of long, slow change alternating with short, rapid change and sudden transformation. As a cumulative process, earlier levels of life are absorbed into later levels of life. In biological development, for example, the cell could not have coalesced without stable molecular structures; organs could not have arisen without preexisting cells; and complex organisms could not have appeared without the existence of specialized organs. Smaller worlds are subsumed into ever larger worlds.

Within the human world, we can see this process of successive inclusion at work in communications. The invention of the press on which this book is printed was only possible because writing was developed 3000 years before, itself an impossible invention had not the first spoken words been uttered several million years earlier. The telephone, television, and the computer all stand on the shoulders of speaking, writing, and printing, at the same time as these electromagnetic media possess qualities of speed, distibution, and flexibility that are entirely new in human experience. The concept of the computer includes the first symbol ever conceived and the first word ever spoken by our most distant human ancestors.

(3) Transition

In his now-classic essay *The Structure of Scientific Revolutions*, Thomas Kuhn brilliantly described the chaos that exists just prior to and during periods of transition between "old" and "new" scientific worldviews, a recurrent pattern in the evolution of scientific thought. Dominant scientific models reach a certain peak of success in being able "to explain everything" just when anomalies–odd fragments of experiments and theories that do not fit the prevailing view–become numerous and troublesome. Adherents of new viewpoints–generally younger, uncommitted scientists–attack the dominant model and promote a profusion of alternative models.

A "clash of worldviews" between scientific perspectives creates a period of confusion and tension that is suddenly resolved by the presentation of a new synthesis. The new paradigm invariably incorporates the now-apparent partial truths of the older model, provides consistent explanations for the precipitating anomalies, and opens up new territory for scientific exploration. In time, the "new synthesis" becomes the "established model" and begins to reach its exploratory limits, as a new cycle of challenge, chaos, and transformation ensues.

While many modern theorists have recognized that "chaos-in-transformation" is a natural part of the evolutionary pattern, some have gone farther and perceived that in major transitions there is also a distinct "step-back-to-leap forward." Kuhn, for example, suggests that new paradigms emerge not from established, successful, "mature" scientists but rather from newcomers who are "embryonic" scientists not locked into the old structure–like the young Swiss patent clerk Albert Einstein. What Kuhn and others have suggested is that when evolution gets "stuck" at a certain level of organization, it may revert to an earlier, more plastic level of order before the leap to a new synthesis is possible. This back-and-forth pattern also contributes to evolution's "zigzag" appearance. In our culture, the idea is encapsulated in the expression "one step back and two steps forward."

The author and systems theorist Arthur Koestler, who uses the French expression "reculer pour mieux sauter" to describe this pattern, has drawn a parallel between biological change and the process of human creativity in science, art, and humor. Koestler suggests that when a creative person has become consciously stuck on a problem, his/her mind retreats first to a lower level of consciousness in order to find the pathway to a creative solution. Below the level of full wakefulness, previously unrecognized associations crystallize, exploding in a sudden synthesis–a flash of insight. In a moment, the mind leaps over the problem to the solution, from the stuck place to a new level of understanding. Referring to the subtle part the unconscious plays in scientific creativity, one physicist cracked that all great discoveries are a product of the "three B's": Insights come while in Bed, in the Bath, or while waiting for a Bus.

Platt believes a new international order is developing in the retreat-to-advance pattern. We are stuck, he contends, at the nation-state level of human organization. World order is not emerging from alliances of nations, which are notoriously fragile and incomplete. Rather, he says, thousands of subnational organizations are forming multinational associations and creating an increasingly interdependent web of international corporate, institutional, and professional relationships that are not directly dependent on national governments. That is, we are not moving directly from national to international government but, rather, are detouring through earlier subnational stages in order to re-form at a higher transnational level.

(4) Acceleration

A popular view of evolution's vast time span is dramatized by Carl Sagan's use of a one-year calendar to represent the significant dates in cosmic-terrestrial development. Sagan's calendar begins with the Big Bang birth of the universe on January 1, shows the formation of the earth on September 14, the dinosaurs reigning around Christmas, and the first humans appearing on the last day, December 31. In the last minute of this last day, 11:59:20 p.m., to be precise, agriculture emerged along with gods and priests. All the rest of human history occupies only the last few seconds of this cosmic calendar.

Seeing human history as but a flash in the cosmic drama and the human home as but a mote in the vastness of the universe certainly rids us of our bloated sense of anthropocentric self-importance. Yet, minuteness also robs us of a sense of significance, the sense that we play some role in the drama that has meaning for the largest whole. Viewing the vastness of cosmic time, it is difficult to imagine significant evolutionary shifts happening in our lifetime–the equivalent of fractions of a second on the scale of Sagan's calendar. Transformation over a few generations is under-standable only when the accelerating pace of evolution is recognized. A quick review of "the big picture" illustrates this idea.

Life first appeared on earth a billion or so years after the planet's birth almost 5 billion years ago. The bacteria-based bioplanet developed slowly for more than 3 billion years (!) until life exploded in diversity with the coemergence of sex (male and female) and mortality (birth and death) 500 million years ago. Mammals became numerous 75 million years ago. Erect, tool-making primates appeared between 2 and 5 million years ago. Humans settled towns 12,000 years ago. The "ancient" cultures of Greece and Rome flourished 2500 years ago. The industrial era is less than 400 years old.

Galactic change is measured in billions and millions of years, biological change in millions and hundreds of thousands of years, and distant human change in thousands and hundreds of years. Billions, millions, millennia, centuries—today, change of evolutionary significance is measured in decades and years.

Textbook Darwinian theory portrays evolution as slow moving and incremental—a process that "takes a long time." Within that worldview it is difficult to imagine that evolution is accelerating, apt to suddenly shift direction, and may indeed be recognizable within the span of a single human life. Yet, through the mental lens of the new paradigm, our responsibility, right now, for the evolution of ourselves and the planet, is inescapable.

We can only wonder how long it will be before evolutionary changes will seem to approach "light speed," the recognition that it is the moments of spontaneous human creativity which are the pulsing tip of the evolutionary process unfolding on the terrestrial stage. Even when human history is seen as a flicker and flash in time, it is the *last* and *next* flash of earth's evolution, and it inherits the significance of all the earlier flashes.

GENERAL SYSTEMS

Holism—as in holistic health, holistic education, or holistic economics—is a popular expression of the perennial philosophy that the details of the world are all related in broad patterns and encompassing contexts. While the legends of science abound with the search for universal laws and logic, for the most part the practice of science has focused on specific details about how the world works and the search for general patterns has been neglected. Over the past half century, however, a new approach has been developing within science that combines the traditional concern for analysis with a renewed interest in patterns.

In the years between the First and Second World Wars, various thinkers suggested that there are some universal principles common to all the sciences: In South Africa, Smuts propounded "holism"; in Russia, Bogdanov developed "*tektologia*" (the general science of organization); in England, Whyte put forth his "unitary principles"; and in Germany, Von Bertalanffy called his approach to unifying science "general systems theory."

In the late 1940s, the ideas of general theory started to coalesce, becoming a visible, permanent part of the scientific community in December 1954, when the Society for General Systems Research (SGSR) was founded, under the aegis of the American Association for the Advancement of Science (AAAS)—an event that occurred at the dawn of the Third Wave in Toffler's evolutionary chronology. While general systems ideas have yet to be absorbed into the scientific mainstream, it is interesting to note that the first president of SGSR, a quarter century ago, Kenneth Boulding, was chairman of the board of AAAS in 1980.

The general systems idea is simple: It assumes that there are some organizational patterns common to all "systems," whether they be physical, biological, or human. Such patterns are inherent in the evolutionary process of the earth and humankind. A *system* may be generally defined as *a persisting identity of components and relationships*. Atoms, cells, organisms, people, nations, and galaxies are all examples of systems.

Using this definition, we can see that if everything with a patterned integrity is a system, then networks are systems. A *network* may be generally defined as *a persisting identity of nodes and links*. Examples of networks abound in this book. While saying that networks are a type of human organization, we can also say that networks are a type of system. Our network model is a systems model.

By defining a network as having a "persisting identity," we are saying that a network—a system—is a "whole" that encompasses a variety of "parts"—components and relationships. As we said in Chapter 10, wholeparts, such as networks and people, represent two levels: the level of the whole and the level of the parts. Human bodies are wholes of interrelated organs. Nations are wholes of interrelated institutions. Atoms are wholes of interrelated particles. Networks are wholes of interrelated participants.

Virtually every general evolutionary theory that attempts to span the complete spectrum of systems—physical, biological, and human—has described existence as a series of semiautonomous levels of organization. *Level* structure appears to be an inherent feature of all systems and thus of networks (see Chapter 10).

While most people are passingly familiar with the "building block" image of reality—atoms in cells in organisms in societies—people are less familiar with the idea that each level of a system maintains a substantial degree of autonomy within the context of larger systems. Governments, for example, are typically organized as national, regional, and local systems, each level being partially autonomous and partially dependent. Our city, Newton, functions both independently and interrelatedly within the Boston metropolitan area and the state of Massachusetts, which in turn functions in New England and as part of the United States of America. As citizens of Newton, Massachusetts, and the United States, we are also individuals who are autonomous yet dependent within families, which in turn are both autonomous and dependent within neighborhoods and communities. Every level is a wholepart.

The tension between autonomy and dependence is inherent in the idea of wholepart systems and networks. Since no system can be totally autonomous or totally dependent, forming and maintaining a "persisting identity" involves a dynamic balance between these two tendencies. The general name for this pattern of a balancing twosome is *complementarity*.

Complements are interrelated opposites. On the largest scale, evolution can be seen as a process of complementary tendencies to *order* and *disorder*. On the smallest scale, complementarity provides the explanatory vehicle for modern physics, the theory of quantum mechanics. In this model, reality is both *wave* like and *particle* like. Depending on your perspective, the "same" energy-matter may alternately appear as a wave and as a particle—a "now you see me, now you don't wavicle." Niels Bohr, the physicist who first propounded this model in the early decades of the 20th century, later adopted a coat of arms bearing the Chinese yin/yang symbol of complementarity and the Latin inscription "*Contraria sunt complementa*" (Contraries are complements).

Life grows between the scales of the very large and the very small. Early life vibrated to the complements of light and dark, hot and cold, acidity and alkalinity, activity and passivity. Later life exploded in diversity with the emergence of the complements male and female, and birth and death. The human mind seems to harbor a complementary nature based on two brains in one, a right-hemisphere/left-hemisphere functioning. Human social life is a complex balance between the complements of individual freedom and collective responsibility.

Levels and *complements* are the two great interrelated metapatterns of systems theory. *Complementary* processes of order and disorder generate *levels* of evolutionary complexity, each *level* reflecting *complementary* dynamics of autonomy and dependence. The snake swallows its tail in a spiral of emergence.

Bringing these abstractions back into our own lives, we are a man and a woman who are unique individuals at the same time as we are a couple who depend upon one another for love and nurturance while also being parents who give to our children and receive love and affection in return. In short, we are complementary opposites (male and female) who by commitment and marriage have formed into a couple (another level, another complement of husband and wife) that functions to raise a family (yet another level, yet another complement as parents and children). The same is true for you in your relations with others.

We all know the everyday analytic rule of thumb for thinking about complex matters: To understand something, we are taught to break it down. The essence of the classical scientific method is that changing one thing at a time works best. In school, we were given one tool to use for probing the unknown: analysis. *Take the problem apart*: First disassemble, then study the parts, breaking the parts down if necessary, and, finally, reassemble. In practice, the strategy is a good one for a car, and a poor one for a cat. While you can take a functioning car apart piece by piece and then put it back together again and drive away, you cannot do the same thing to a cat: Once disassembled, a cat will never purr again. Some things respond well to analysis; other things do not.

In a similar way, the old paradigm habitually pits opposites against one another, considering them "irreconcilable" and "contradictory." Matter is real and mind is not. Males are better than females. Disorder is the one universal one-way tendency. Objective is good, subjective is not. Black or white. The combinations are endless.

It is important to recognize that duals and opposites are as bound up in Western philosophy and culture as they are in the East. In the industrial West, however, the rule of thumb is that where there are two, one prevails. One is right, two is a disagreement.

In duals (and duels), one wins; in complements (and compliments), both dance.

New paradigms are supposed to subsume the old ones. Obviously, the "dominant-submissive" interpretation of opposites can be accommodated within the framework of complementarity, since paired opposites can take on a variety of balanced and unbalanced forms: Sex roles, for example, can be male-dominated, female-dominated, rigorously equal, or flexibly supportive. Similarly, traditional analysis, "breaking down," can certainly be done within the framework of levels simply by continually focusing on "lower" or "smaller" levels and ignoring "higher" or "larger" levels. Analysis and dualism are not "wrong," just limited.

Levels and complements can be useful abstractions, helping to translate experience into the new paradigm and serving as handy conceptual "rules of thumb." *Levels* and *complements* are conceptual tools that subsume and extend the old paradigm tools of *analysis* and *dualism*. As a rule of thumb, *levels* means looking at wholes as well as parts, seeing ever-more-encompassing contexts as well as seeing ever smaller pieces. As a rule of thumb, *complementarity* means looking at process as well as structure, of seeing interplay between contrasting tendencies as well as dominant trends of the moment.

When you are stuck at one level, look for an answer at another level; when you see one process, look for the "hidden face," the complementary process.

EMERGING NETWORKS

The big news of our time is evolution. Whereas the industrial worldview opened up the "New World" of the Americas and sent a terrestrial species on voyages into space, the new era has embarked on voyages into time. We are rapidly becoming conscious of the process of evolution in daily life. In *The Aquarian Conspiracy*, Marilyn Ferguson, an emerging philosopher of these changing times, writes:

> While most of our institutions are faltering, a twentieth-century version of the ancient tribe or kinship has appeared: the network, a tool for the next step in human evolution.

> Amplified by electronic communications, freed from the old restraints of family and culture, the network is the antidote to alienation. It generates power enough to remake society. It offers the individual emotional, intellectual, spiritual, and economic support. It is an invisible home, a powerful means of altering the course of institutions, especially government.

> Anyone who discovers the rapid proliferation of networks and understands their strength can see the impetus for worldwide transformation. The network is the institution of our time: an open system, a dissipative structure so richly coherent that it is in constant flux, poised for reordering, capable of endless transformation.

> This organic mode of social organization is more biologically adaptive, more efficient, and more "conscious" than the hierarchical structures of modern civilization. The network is plastic, flexible. In effect, each member is the center of the network.

> Networks are cooperative, not competitive. They are true grass roots: self-generating, self-organizing, sometimes even self-destructing. They represent a process, a journey, not a frozen structure.

Early in this chapter we presented a series of visions about the momentous transformation now underway that encompasses the whole of humankind and our planetary home. In shaping a broad conceptual vehicle for understanding networks, we have suggested the relevance of this form to understanding the two extremes of human history, the prehierarchical era and the postbureaucratic age.

Hierarchy developed in the theocratic, agricultural period of history, and is an earlier form of human organization than bureaucracy, which arose and was refined in the self-conscious industrial era. Following the principles of evolutionary inclusion outlined above, modern bureaucracies incorporate the characteristics of authoritarian control structures as well as the more primitive informal networks of cooperation (among the authoritarian "good old boys").

We believe that networks are simultaneously "very old" and "very new," an idea that is supported by common sense as well as abstract theory. During the several million years in which hominids walked erect, conceived of and made tools, utilized fire, and progressed from hunting calls to language, from banging things with clumsy hand axes to painting delicately drawn bison, *some* new social forms *must* have emerged. Between the extended families and hunting bands of primates and the settled town and temple life of early civilization is a long gap, a mystery time of social development at the dawn of symbol-based evolution.

Earlier patterns are included in later ones. Early patterns of human social interaction were essentially forms of small-group dynamics. What little evidence we have suggests that early hominids lived in groups of a few score members and were, of course, mobile as a social unit. These communities were not geographically rooted; the groups moved as the changing environmental conditions required.

While we can imagine that the primate social heritage of family and band was still extremely important in the emerging human social patterns, there nevertheless *must have been* some new twists based on the emergent symbolic capabilities. Generally speaking, words like local, kinship, tribe, neighborhood, friends, and community seem appropriate to this era.

If, indeed, humankind has a great reservoir of experience in small-group dynamics, then that evolutionary experience is available to every human being, since we are all members of that one species who came from a cave in the hills to a home in the valley.

Thus, networks are a "step back" and a "leap forward." In many respects, networks seem to involve a rediscovery of small-group interaction, a reaching back to more intimate forms of association before simple human relationships became obscured by hierarchy and bureaucracy. In other respects, networks reflect the leap forward, a form of organization with globe-encompassing capability that subsumes the enduring aspects of authority and bureaucracy. *Segmented polycephalous ideological networks*, what Gerlach and Hine call "SPINs," are simultaneously the natural form for organizing our communities and the natural form for organizing our planet.

Another America is a map, and we are early time cartographers charting the contemporary emerging future from the perspective of America in the 1980s. While the longer evolutionary context helps explain the seemingly paradoxical "oldness" and "newness" of networks, the description of contemporary networks is necessarily cast against the backdrop of the dominant industrial worldview, our immediate springboard to the future. It is the novelties and shades of contrast with the prevailing worldview that provide the distinct, specific descriptions of the future social forms among us. We who straddle this chaotic transition to the next level of human understanding and order must necessarily nurture an appreciation of both viewpoints. Reality—right now—is a dynamic composite of both worldviews.

12

The Art of Networking

Good networking is good guessing, you know.
It is an art, not a science.

Patricia Wagner and Leif Smith
The Networking Game

As we said in the Introduction, this book is actually two books in one. The twelve *chapters* of prose (Chapters 1-12) describe networks and networking. Five guides, one of which is interleaved with Chapters 3 through 9, and four of which follow this chapter, collectively constitute a *directory* of networks.

The directory is composed of a Topic Guide, an Organization Guide, a Location Guide, a Keyword Guide, and a Title Guide. Each is described in more detail below.

GUIDE BY GUIDE

(1) Topic Guide

The first guide is the seven-part Topic Guide. Each of the networks indexed in this book has been initially grouped into the one topic area we felt reflected its primary function. Each of the seven topical chapters (Healing, Sharing, Using, Valuing, Learning, Growing, and Evolving) is followed by its part of the Topic Guide.

Each part of the Topic Guide has two sections. The first section includes an average of about 33 networks that are further described by short annotations; the second section is a listing of an average of 185 additional networks with complete contact information. The annotations indicate the range and depth of work being done by networks in the topic area; the listings indicate the great variety of networks related to each area.

Annotated listings *do not* represent our recommendations, nor are they a registry of "special" or "important" networks. They are, in fact, a cross-section of our very earliest respondents and serve to provide an intermediate level of description (between the chapters and the directory) relevant to all the networks listed.

The Topic Guide enables you to find groups involved in various aspects of the issues described in the chapters that precede them. For example, the Healing Guide lists groups concerned with issues of health and the life cycle. Thus, the Boston Women's Health Book Collective is listed in the Healing Guide. So, too, are the Gray Panthers, who are concerned with issues of aging, clearly a part of the life cycle. Consult the Topic Guide to find groups working on aspects of the same general issue.

Each of the networks in this book has its own unique code, which is dictated by (a) the topical group it is in; (b) its alphabetic position in the topical group; and (c) whether it has an annotation. Each code begins with a letter and is followed by a number. All networks listed under Healing (Chapter 3) begin with **H**. All networks listed under Sharing (Chapter 4) begin with **S**. In the same way, networks in Using begin with **U**, Valuing with **V**, Learning with **L**, Growing with **G**, and Evolving with **E**. The number that follows the letter indicates whether a network has an annotation. All networks whose numbers are lower than 100 are annotated. All networks whose numbers are higher than 100 are not annotated. Thus, **E001**, the Association for World Education, is annotated. **E101**, the Aerial Phenomena Research Organization, is not.

In addition to providing the address and telephone number (where available), the Topic Guide also indicates whether we have listed publications (✳) or materials (♦)–what we call "titles"–produced by the network (see Title Guide, below).

The seven-part Topic Guide serves as the master reference section. All the other guides use only names of networks or titles of publications and materials that networks produce together with the appropriate code to refer you back to the complete topical listings where contact information is contained.

(2) Organization Guide

The second guide is the Organization Guide, which immediately follows this chapter. The Organization Guide is a combined, alphabetized list of all the networks included in the book.

All the names in the directory have been alphabetized according to the American Standard Code for Information Interchange (ASCII), which is the standard alphabetizing system recognized by most computers. The ASCII system is an internally consistent set of conventions that establishes an order that generally corresponds to what we recognize as alphabetical order, with some exceptions. According to the ASCII standard, most punctuation and common symbols (such as /, + , or ") precede numbers (0..9), which precede all the capital letters (A..Z), which precede all the lowercase letters (a..z). A capital "Z," therefore, precedes a lowercase "a." Thus, organizations or titles whose names are their acronyms, and are consequently made up of all capital letters, will be ordered first. Hence, SANE precedes Safe Energy Alternatives, while D.C. Gazette precedes Dakota Resource Council (because punctuation–"."–precedes small letters–"a").

Use the Organization Guide to see whether networks you know about are listed in this book. Note their code, then turn to their part of the Topic Guide (indicated by the first letter in the code–**H** for Healing, and so on) for complete contact information.

(3) Location Guide

The third guide is the Location Guide, following the Organization Guide. The Location Guide allows you to find where groups are situated geographically. The Location Guide is organized by state in alphabetic order, according to the two-letter post office symbol for each state, beginning with Alaska (AK) and continuing through Wyoming (WY). The District of Columbia (DC) is alphabetized as if it were a state. Listings for the United States are followed by Canadian listings, in alphabetic order by the Canadian provinces. The Canadian listings are followed by the listings not located in North America, alphabetized by country.

The Location Guide enables you to find groups near you. Copy down the identification codes for each of the networks whose zip code is near yours. Then locate the address for each network by finding its listing in its part of the Topic Guide. (Remember: Groups whose code begins with **H** can be found in Healing, and so on). You can also use the Location Guide to find groups in places you are planning to visit. Sometimes you can use the Location Guide to find groups you may know under a different name by checking the zip code.

(4) Keyword Guide

The fourth guide is the Keyword Guide, following the Location Guide. The Keyword Guide enables you to find networks that are concerned with your special areas of interest. Unless you've been living on the moon, some interest of yours is probably listed in the Keyword Guide (even if you have been on the moon, you'll find SPACE as a keyword). When you see a word that interests you, note the codes of the networks that have that keyword and look them up in the appropriate portion of the Topic Guide to get contact information. Remember: If the network's code number is lower than 100, an annotated description of the group's work is provided.

We have listed an average of two keywords for each network, with a maximum of four keywords—words that serve as keys to unlock one important aspect of a group's work. The words are arranged alphabetically in the Keyword Guide. We tried to choose words that are representative of a group's interests, particularly when those words appear in the group's name or in an associated phrase, such as a subtitle. Each keyword could have many, many more groups listed under it, and each group could have many, many more keywords associated with it. We used our judgment to create relatively limited and concise keyword listings.

In using the Keyword Guide, you will observe that not all networks with similar areas of concern are listed in the same topic area. For example, some of the bicycle groups are listed in Sharing, some in Using, and some in Growing. The reason for this is that while all are concerned with bicycles, each is concerned with a different aspect of bicycles: as a community resource (Sharing), as an alternative to engine-powered vehicles (Using), and as a recreational activity (Growing). Creating the Keyword Guide has enriched our understanding of how all the networks and their topics interweave, overlap, and ultimately cohere as one.

(5) Title Guide

The fifth and final guide is the Title Guide, which follows the Keyword Guide. In many cases, titles cited are only samples taken from long catalogs of offerings such as books, tapes, or films.

Each title listed is identified by the code number of the group that produces the title. We have listed an average of one title per network and as many as three titles for a network. These titles cover a range of *publications* (✳) produced by the networks in this book including newsletters, newspapers, journals, magazines, and other periodicals, as well as *materials* (◆) such as directories, reports, handbooks, books, films and tapes, and other products (for example, calendars, computer software programs, maps, and even in one case, jewelry).

Wherever possible, we have included prices for these items. Usually, the prices quoted are annual prices for publications and rental fees for audiovisual materials. However, many groups have elaborate pricing structures, including such variables as age, health, membership status, income, and institutional affiliation. To simplify the information, we have generally listed the price charged to individuals with no other considerations. Thus, the prices listed here may or may not apply to you. Consider the prices representative. We recommend that you *always inquire* when ordering materials. Accept the authority of the network to know its own prices. Please do not insist, "But, the Network Directory says . . . ." Also, do not expect anyone to send you free material. *Always send a self addressed stamped envelope* (SASE) when making an inquiry, and offer to pay for copying.

The Title Guide enables you to see what kinds of materials are available from networks in each topic area. This guide follows the organization of the seven topical areas, with each area further broken down by publication and material type. For example, you've just read Chapter 4, Sharing Networks: Cooperatives and Communities, and you would like to be able to receive regular information in this area, or perhaps read a book. Turn to the Title Guide, locate the Sharing Titles (the second grouping), find the headings "newsletter" and "book" and peruse those titles.

Remember that each title's code number is identical to the group that produces the materials. Every title listed within the topic is available from the group whose address is listed in the corresponding part of the Topic Guide. Conversely, you can tell whether a title has been provided for a particular network by the inclusion of ✳ (publication) and ✦ (material) symbols with that network's listing in the Topic Guide.

WHY THE NETWORKS THAT ARE HERE ARE HERE

This book has been created out of a process woven by choice and chance. From the time we began working on the book, we made one choice after another, mounting up to thousands of tiny choices, each also involving some amount of chance.

Our very first choice was to begin gathering names for our book by contacting one person whom we knew to be a richly connected networker. His story is an inspiration for every person who has ever networked or wanted to.

Every network name in this book has been generated from our contact with one unlikely person with an improbable name from a place no one has ever heard of. Robert A. Smith, III, a retired NASA organizational management official, from Pine Apple, Alabama, is one of the pioneers of the modern networking movement.

In the spirit of networking, which glorifies no leaders and elevates no heroes, Bob Smith has remained a backstage person, quietly forging connections among people of like interests and ideas for the past two decades.

We first met Smith on the telephone in the mid-1970s. Someone, somewhere, had mentioned to Smith that we were doing something of interest to him and, one day, he simply picked up the telephone and called us, and a lifelong friendship was born.

If anyone whom we know deserves to be called a "networker," Bob Smith does. We are but two of the many hundreds of people who have benefited from Smith's unique talent of connecting people.

Smith's personal story is exemplary of how one person without credentials, extensive education, or contacts "in high places" can make a difference in the world. Smith, whose name is among the most common of any, has used his own life canvas to nurture an important, meaningful one-person network that now reaches around the globe.

As the oldest of four children growing up in rural southern Alabama, Smith early on developed what he calls an "eiditic capacity," the ability to entertain himself. "We did not have kindergarten, and since we lived so far from town, my mother encouraged my imagination so that from the time I was very young, I could entertain myself," he recalls.

This self-motivating principle would serve him well later in life when, at the age of 43, in 1964, he suffered a nearly fatal heart attack, a brush with death that completely reshaped his life.

Smith's recuperation was long and slow, offering him an opportunity to sit for many hours each day, drinking in the beauty of his backyard garden, where one day he apperceived what he later understood to be a peak experience. "Suddenly, I became aware of how small I was in one sense, and how large I was in another sense," he explains. "I could feel my connection to the whole cosmos, and from there I was bolted into writing, writing that just came through me."

Smith's "automatic writing" took the form of a dialogue between the author Henry Miller and the transcendentalist Henry David Thoreau. "I felt that I was at Walden Pond," he says. "I could actually see the cabin."

Having transcended linear time and space in one transformative moment, Smith, like a spring pod in his lush garden, burst open, making himself open to many new experiences. In the summer of 1966, he spent two intense weeks at the National Training Laboratories in Bethel, Maine, where he both gained self-confidence and began to take his own thoughts seriously. "I began to read more. I studied Teilhard de Chardin, Goethe, and Jefferson, and developed the courage to dialogue with other people interested in the same ideas. And my wife, Dot, was very supportive of my emerging role change."

Smith's new path was unfolding at the same time that the government, where he was now working as head of a management research program at NASA, began using WATS (Wide Area Telephone Service) lines.

"I am a strong believer in synchronicity," Smith explains, "but people need to be connected to one another in order to form synergetic partnerships. So I started to use my WATS line to connect people. Some officials in government might say that I 'misused' my WATS line, but I believe that I put it to the very best use in a meaningful way. It was my global 'underground.' WATS lines can be used to create open processes, to open up ideas everywhere." Which is precisely what Smith did.

By the end of the 1960s, Smith was on a "first name basis" with people who were completely outside his early life and experiences, and he was nurturing a kind of human horticulture, companion-planting people with similar interests in each other's mental garden. "I started directing people with similar ideas to one another," he says, "Then people began to 'use' me, and by that I mean 'in' a very loving way, to find others with similar interests."

During his last years at NASA, before his retirement in 1977, Smith had made a practice of keeping a file of names and addresses, as well as pieces of literature written by people who were interested in the same things that he was. As his farewell gesture to his dearly departed WATS line, Smith distributed his own catalog of contacts called *Try It! The Invisible College Directory and Network of Robert A. Smith, III.* This concoction, totally devoid of any organizing principle other than Smith's own intuitive feeling for what is "good in the world," was a compendium that made public his personal network, photocopied and stapled together.

The Invisible College was a cut-and-paste networking scrapbook of names, addresses, letterheads, drawings, and quotes, complete with cutouts of book reviews, newspaper articles, photographs, brochures, and thought-provoking headlines. It included such diverse novelties as a picture of Stevie Wonder, a birthday announcement for a four-year-old in Pine Apple, Alabama, quotes from Dane Rudhyar and Sri Chinmoy, a recipe for peanut pie from Angie Stevens in Plains, Georgia, an ad for a meditation bench, a photograph of Sasquatch/Big Foot positioned next to a snapshot of *Whole Earth Catalog* publisher Stewart Brand. It was half typed, half written by hand and crossed out, and it concluded, on page 82, with these words penned in by Smith: "As Bob Dylan would probably put it, this directory is a concern with chaos, watermelons, collard greens, clocks, meditation, space travel, everything.' It may reveal how diversity does not necessarily lead to structured pluralism or fragmented separatism but rather a unity with a profound mosaic."

When the suggestion first was made that we write a book about networking, we knew just where to begin. We sat right down and wrote to our friend Bob Smith. His initial response, followed by literally scores more, set in motion the lines of contact, the many swirls, spirals, curlicues, parabolas, and ellipses by which choice and chance have woven together the patterns that appear as this book on networking.

A few days after we first wrote Smith, an encouraging and helpful letter returned from him suggesting nine people to contact, including an academic who had written several books on human service networks, an eclectic writer and thinker who has experimented with several forms of personal networks, a government bureaucrat whom Smith calls an "idea broker," a couple whose work together has involved designing advanced computer tools that simplify the process of networking, the editor of a continuous forum for discussion of societal trends and philosophical issues, a nonviolent-social-change organizer who has lived in several cultures and done scholarly research on governing by consensus, an author who had just completed a book that suggests the network form as the most appropriate for social transformation, and a humanistic psychologist who had organized a small peer-support network.

Following Smith's lead, we wrote letters to these people, saying that Smith suggested that we contact them and describing what we planned to do. Six of these nine people responded immediately with suggestions of more people to contact. (Smith, in the meantime, had made more contact suggestions and had also written to several people telling them of our plans, thus preparing an exceptionally receptive audience for our requests.) Within about two weeks, we had a list of 50 people to contact, and we again made some choices, eliminating a few people from the list because their work seemed to fall outside the scope of the way in which the book was developing. We wrote to everyone else.

Then chance had its first significant opportunity to intervene and put its unmistakable mark on the book. Some of the next group of people probably never received our letter; some no doubt read it and threw it away; a few probably put it aside with the intention of responding later, and the rest, quite a large number, wrote back. Now we had about 150 names to choose among, including quite a few contact lists that people had sent us, some already on mailing labels.

At this point, choice and chance joined hands. We combined intuition with judgment, personal suggestions with geography, and our own interests with others that we had never even considered in order to reach any group that seemed to be performing a networking function. During the following year, we spent hundreds of hours making choices about whom to write to and many hundreds more reading and absorbing the responses that people sent back. In all, we sent our basic letter of inquiry—which posed the simple question, "Are you a network or do you perform a significant networking function?"—to 4000 individuals and groups.

Many of the people we contacted wrote back enthusiastically saying that, yes, indeed, they considered themselves to be a network or part of a network and wanted to be included. Other people sent packets of information with the implicit or explicit suggestion that we use our judgment about their inclusion in the directory. A few people wrote back and said they thought they wanted to be included but needed more information before committing themselves. A very few people wrote back and said that while they thought the book was a good idea, they declined the offer to be included. And a handful of people wrote back saying that they didn't understand our question and had no interest in being included. (The quintessential response in this category came from the editor of a linguistic journal, who asked if, by "networking," we meant something like "coffeepotting," which she had done, and obviously outgrown, at the age of 3.)

We then found ourselves with a long list of names of people who indicated that they wanted to be included in the book. Nearly all those names are included here. Now choice enters in again. When we looked at the preponderance of respondents, we perceived an underlying coherence, a shared value system that threaded through the groups. In a few cases, we perceived something else, and relied upon our judgment *not* to include them.

Then we went back through the list again, reexamining the names of those who had not responded and found a few (about 100) more names that we felt belonged in the book, either because we knew the group and understood that if they had had the time to respond they would have, or because someone from the group had responded in an informal way that went unrecorded. All those groups have also been included in these pages.

The stray piece of mail, properly addressed and received, that somehow got mistakenly filed with the wrong group, or worse, buried in the bottom of our children's crayon drawer, obviously is not included here. The errors that we have tried not to make—by devising an information retrieval system that requires each of us seeing each entry many times over—have inevitably been made. Somewhere, someone reading this book will remember the long sincere letter s/he sent asking for inclusion which we somehow, in spite of our organization and good intentions, misplaced. In anticipation of all such omissions, we apologize and hope to do better the next time around.

So no matter how carefully we have chosen, inclusion finally gets left to chance. We know from our files that every name included here is representative of hundreds, if not thousands, more like itself.

ON NETWORKING WELL

Networking is something we do naturally. Each time we ask a question or answer one, we are networking at the very simplest level.

For some people, networking is an innate gift, one that allows them to communicate gracefully and effortlessly. For others, networking is a skill to be learned. For still others, networking grates against their very private souls.

Networking is a process that helps information flow, but it is not a universal panacea for all our social ills. Networks are appropriate sociology for certain kinds of activities, but they do not serve every need that human culture requires.

There are benefits to networks and networking—and there are pitfalls. Consider networking as an art, an aesthetic skill that must be cultivated with imagination, good taste, and bountiful sensitivity.

The Networking Game

In Denver, Colorado, philosopher Leif Smith and poet Patricia Wagner have designed and implemented a communications process for networking that they call the "office for Open Network" (see Chapter 7). In 1980, Smith and Wagner gathered together some of the wisdom they had gained from being the architects and principal users of the office for Open Network and published a powerful small handbook called *The Networking Game*, from which the quote at the beginning of this chapter is taken.

The Networking Game is a tool that people can use at conferences to keep track of the connections they are making. Dedicated to "everyone who asks friendly questions about anything," *The Networking Game* is also a cogent manual for remaining

afloat in the enormous sea of information around us. And it is a short, simple mani-
festo of good manners for communicating in depth with strangers who share your
interests but have yet to become friends.

Smith and Wagner set out five rules for "the networking game":

(1) Be useful.

(2) Don't be boring.

(3) Listen.

(4) Ask questions.

(5) Don't make assumptions.

Simple, practical advice. Powerful implications.

What Smith and Wagner propose is a kind of "voluntary simplicity" (see Duane
Elgin's book by that name) in the exchange of information. *The Networking Game*
suggests a sort of Spartan etiquette in exchanging information, one that allows
people to both give and receive without being exploited. Information is a natural
resource just as real as gold, silver, and oil—and just as valuable. People with information can be exploited by others who want it, and they can exploit people to obtain
it.

What follows are brief excerpts from each of Smith and Wagner's five points:

Rule Number One: Be Useful

You really don't have to remember everything and write it all down to be a
good networker (or as Leif has named such people, a good weaver). You simply
have to know how to tell your game partners where to find the information. Your
usefulness might be reduced by burdening yourself with too much information;
learn to travel light. . . . The Networking Game is not about convincing people or
getting them to agree; it is simply about being useful to people, one at a time. . . .

Rule Number Two: Don't Be Boring

We have noticed, in the course of managing our networking office, that three
contacts are often more useful than thirty. The quality of the information is the
most important factor, always. . . . The point is not to send a group of people out
into your personal information pool to leech off your friends and associates.
Very boring.

Rule Number Three: Listen

Networking magic takes advantage of differences among people by rearrang-
ing the world into shared patterns, which often are startling and exciting. These
patterns can open new possibilities. But unless you listen with all your power
and alertness you will never know what magic might have been found.

Rule Number Four: Ask Questions

A good question is sometimes more useful than a good answer. If you ask a
question before you offer advice, you might not have to offer anything more.

Rule Number Five: Don't Make Assumptions

The wild card is the idea that sets human networkers apart from computers. It leaps across logic and transforms strangers into friends, enemies into coworkers. It makes a changing world a challenge rather than a threat to the way we live our lives. It is a gamble, but there is very little to lose.

Networking can be a blessing and it can be a burden. Elegant networking is perhaps what Cooper Edens means when he writes of "the Great Rainbow Balancing Act," in *The Caretakers of Wonder.*

The Person Who Networks

Perhaps the most significant characteristic of people who network is their finely developed sense of intuition, the ability to *feel* what is going on around them. Intuition enables people to know where to go to get information, whom to trust, and in what way to share. Intuition allows people to make small connections that appear to be giant leaps. Sometimes networkers know precisely where to go to find the information they need; more often, they operate on hunches.

Practiced networkers move with delicacy and humility, knowing that waiting to be asked is more appropriate than imposing help where it is not wanted. In their cores, networkers are generous; they are able to give without keeping score. One vital exemplary network expresses this idea, as well as its attitude toward the world, in its one-word title: PLENTY.

In this nourishing role, networkers become like parents. In an impromptu interview with Hazel Henderson, she said, "Being a networker is just like being a mother. You're constantly giving out, sending things, making new matches, writing letters, increasing the size of your phone bill. But you don't count how many letters you've written or total up the hours that you spend networking. You just do it because it has to be done, just the way you do with children."

Like parents, networkers are easily overloaded with requests and demands, a problem that increases exponentially the more a person networks. Networker "burnout" is a malady that comes from what we might call "nodeness," the affliction that comes with being a node (a connection) in a network. In contacting people for this book, we found that sometimes the people whose names were suggested the *most* frequently as the *best* networkers were the people who had the *least* time to respond. This paradox, in which the act of networking can in fact render people incapable of networking can also create its own solution. Some overloaded networkers eventually cut the lines of access to themselves by setting up screening filters which allow them to be more selective about responding. Several frequently recommended people whom we wrote to early on in our book-writing responded to us through people who work with or for them. By distancing themselves from public accessibility, the original networkers actually help to endow their colleagues who take over the networking responsibilities and thus become networkers in their own right.

In the end, anyone who has the desire can become a networker. Networking has nothing to do with fame or credentials. It has to do with hard work and good intentions.

Some Networking Tips and Tools

(1) Devise some method for storing information that allows you to retrieve it when you need it.

(2) Keep it simple. Simplicity is the key to good networking. If you're feeling overloaded by networking, stop. Learn to say no. It's a shorter word than yes. You may

find yourself somewhat surprised to learn that if you don't do something, someone else might. If you're so swamped with information that you've lost your driver's license in the piles of paper stacked on every flat surface in your room, become more selective and prune and thin the information overgrowth.

(3) In general, use the telephone only for local networking. Otherwise use the mail. It's cheaper and less intrusive to people you don't know.

(4) Use postcards. Writing a postcard teaches you how little you really need to say.

(5) Recycle envelopes. A significant proportion of the envelopes we received had already been recycled once. Remember to open envelopes carefully. Otherwise, you may not be able to reuse them.

(6) Buy stamps. Save yourself the aggravation of writing to people and then never hearing from them because you forget to mail the letter. Buy stamps in bulk and alleviate this unnecessary guilt-provoking situation.

(7) About money. Most networks don't have any. Networking is often a voluntary, self-initiated effort. Stick with the basics and networking will not become confused with funding, budgets, overhead, and an endless cycle of proposal writing.

(8) Think big, act small. Very small. Overextension means sudden death to a network. But this does not mean that you can't fantasize, romanticize, and dream, all like fertilizers to the networking garden. Just don't try to do more within your network than is practical. Networks don't build hydroelectric plants; highly organized groups, with technical feasibility studies and considerable capital, do. When appropriate, network. When not, don't.

Ultimately, networking is very personal. It begins with one person, threads through many others, and returns to one person. Networking is not a mass communications process. It is a person-to-person process with each connection made with gentle skill and great caring.

In the end, think of networking as Leif Smith does, as a journey, as a quest, as a never-ending process of seeking, integrating, and seeking once again.

You are an explorer traveling a universe that has no map.

Ask directions and follow them. Then allow yourself to get lost.

Take both paths—impossible to do in space, infinitely possible over time.

Go in circles. You may find they are spirals.

Enjoy long visits with people—in letters, on the phone, and, best of all, in person.

Allow yourself to love the people you network with, and soon you will be networking with many.

Stay in touch—with others and with yourself.

Remember that you are the gateway to the networking universe.

Guides

Organization Guide

Location Guide

Keyword Guide

Title Guide

U101   Abalone Alliance
V101   Abortion Fund
L101   Academy for Educational Development
H101   Academy of Orthomolecular Psychiatry
V102   Accion/Micro Enterprise Development Corporation
S101   Acres, U.S.A: A Voice for Eco-Agriculture
H102   Action Coalition for Retirement with Dignity
L102   Action for Children's Television
G101   Actualizations
H103   Acupressure School of Massage Therapy
L103   Adult Education Association of the United States of America
H104   Advocates for Freedom in Mental Health
E101   Aerial Phenomena Research Organization
E102   Africa Fund
E103   Africa News Service
E104   Afro-Asian Center
E105   After Thought: Research and Education About the Future
V103   Agape Foundation: Fund for Nonviolent Social Change
S102   Agricultural Marketing Project
V104   Akwesasne Notes: For Native and Natural Peoples
U102   Alabama Solar Coalition
U103   Alaska Center for the Environment
S103   Alaska Youth Advocates
U104   Alaskan Conservation Foundation
H105   Aletheia Psycho-Physical Foundation
V001   Alliance Against Sexual Coercion
L104   Alliance for Citizen Education
U105   Alliance for Environmental Education
H106   Alliance for Perinatal Research and Services
H107   Alliance for the Liberation of Mental Patients
L105   Alliance of Information and Referral Services
S104   Alliance of Warehouse Federations
U106   Alternate Currents/SolarCity
U107   Alternate Energy Institute
L106   Alternate Media Center
L107   Alternative America: Directory of 5000 Groups and Organizations
U108   Alternative Directions in Energy and Economics
V002   Alternative Fund Federal Credit Union
H001   Alternative Medical Association
L108   Alternative Press Center
L109   Alternative Press Syndicate
L110   Alternative Schools Network
U001   Alternative Sources of Energy
G102   Alternatives Resource Center
L001   Alternatives in Education
V105   Alternatives to Violence Project
U109   Alternatives: Journal of Friends of the Earth, Canada
G103   Alternatives: Tools for Holistic Living
L111   Amateur Radio Research and Development
H108   American Academy of Husband-Coached Childbirth
H109   American Alliance for Health and Physical Education
S105   American Association for State and Local History
E106   American Association for the Advancement of Science
L112   American Association of University Women
G104   American Astrology
H110   American Conference of Therapeutic Selfhelp/Selfhealth
E107   American Field Service
U110   American Forestry Association
H111   American Healing Association

L113	American Historical Association
H112	American Holistic Medical Association
H113	American Holistic Nurses' Association
S106	American Homebrewers Association
G001	American Humanist Association
G105	American Institute of Buddhist Studies
E108	American Public Health Association
U111	American Rivers Conservation Council
L114	American Society for Training and Development
G106	American Spiritual Healing Association
V106	American Town Meetings Project
U112	American Wind Energy Association
E109	Americans for Middle East Understanding, Inc.
V107	Amnesty International
E110	Analog: Science Fiction/Science Fact
V108	Anarchist Association of the Americas
G107	Anima: An Experiential Journal
V109	Animal Rights Network
G108	Animal Town Cooperative Games
U113	Animal Welfare Institute
L002	Another America Networking
V110	Another Mother for Peace
G002	Another Place
S107	Antahkarana Circle
L003	Anthropology Resource Center
L115	Antioch University West
U002	Anvil Press
L116	Appalachia Educational Laboratory
U114	Appalachia Science in the Public Interest
L117	Appalachian Journal
G109	Appalachian Mountain Club
L118	Appalshop Films
U115	Applewood Journal
U116	Aprovecho Institute
E111	Aquarian Age: Monthly for Space and Equality
G110	Aquarian Minyan
G111	Aquarian Research Foundation
G112	Arcana Workshops
S108	Architecture 2001
U117	Arcosanti
U118	Arkansas Solar Action Coalition
V111	Armistice/Live Without Trident
E112	Arms Control Association
L119	Arton's Publishing: Fuse Magazine
S109	Arts Services Associates
E113	Asia-Pacific Affairs Associates
L120	Aspen Institute for Humanistic Studies
S110	Associated Cooperatives
L121	Associated Information Managers
E114	Association Eveil de la Conscience Planetaire
H114	Association for Childbirth at Home International
L004	Association for Experiential Education
L122	Association for Humanistic Education
G003	Association for Humanistic Psychology
G113	Association for Moral Education
G114	Association for Research and Enlightenment
H115	Association for Research and Enlightenment Clinic
V112	Association for Self-Management
G004	Association for Transpersonal Psychology
G115	Association for Unity, Research, and Awareness
E001	Association for World Education
H116	Association for the Preservation of Anti-Psychiatric Artifacts
E115	Association for the Study of Man-Environment Relations

V003	Association of Community Organizations for Reform Now
V113	Association of Libertarian Feminists
G116	Association of National Non-Profit Artists' Centers
V114	Association on American Indian Affairs
G117	Astro*Carto*Graphy
E116	Astronomical League
L123	Ateed Centre
L124	Atlanta Network: Teaching, Learning and Interest Sharing
G118	Auroville Association
H117	Austin Lay Midwives Association
E117	Australian Willing Workers on Organic Farms
E118	Autrement
E119	Aviation/Space Writers Association
V115	Back to the People: New Age Goods
G119	Baha'i International Community
U119	Banyan Tree Books
V004	Barter Project
S111	Basement Alliance
H118	Bay Area Coalition on Occupational Safety and Health
H119	Bay Area Committee for Alternatives to Psychiatry
V116	Bay Area Lawyers for the Arts
G120	Bear Tribe Medicine Society
L125	Bear's Guide to Non-Traditional College Degrees
H120	Beauty Without Cruelty
G005	Bed & Breakfast League
H121	Being Thin
L126	Berkeley Outreach Recreation Program
U003	Bicycle Network
S112	Bicyclist Federation of Pennsylvania
S113	Bikeways in Buffalo
S114	Birdsong Farm
H122	Birth and Life Bookstore
H123	Birthing Monthly Newsletter
G121	Black Bart Newsletter
G122	Black Hills Alliance
V117	Black Law Journal
G123	Blackberry Books
S115	Blooming Prairie Warehouse
S116	Bloomington Free Ryder: Biweekly Newspaper
L127	Book People
G124	Boomerang Newsletter
H124	Boston Area Childbirth Education
S117	Boston Building Materials Cooperative
H125	Boston Center for Psychosynthesis
U120	Boston Clamshell Coalition
V118	Boston INFACT
H126	Boston Self-Help
V119	Boston Study Group
S118	Boston Urban Gardens
G125	Boston Visionary Cell
H127	Boston Women's Health Book Collective
L128	Both Sides Now
S119	Boulder Women's Network
G126	Brain/Mind Bulletin
H128	Bread & Roses Women's Health Center
S120	Briarpatch Network
U121	British Columbia Energy Coalition
V120	Brown Committee
E120	Bulletin of Concerned Asian Scholars
V121	Bulletin of the Atomic Scientists
U122	Bullfrog Films
S121	Butterbrooke Farm Seed Co-op

U123	By Hand and Foot: Tools Dependent on Human Energy
E121	Byte: The Small Systems Journal
V122	California Agrarian Action Project
G127	California Association of Bicycle Organizations
S122	California Cooperative Federation
V123	California Housing Information and Action Network
S123	California Institute for Rural Studies
V005	California Newsreel
H129	California School of Herbal Studies
V124	California Tax Reform Association
V006	Cambridge Documentary Films
G006	Cambridge Zen Center
G128	Camp Winnarainbow
V007	Campaign for Economic Democracy
V125	Campaign for Political Rights
G129	Canada Quilts
L129	Canadian Alliance of Home Schoolers
U124	Canadian Coalition for Nuclear Responsibility
H130	Canadian Coordinating Council on Deafness
H131	Canadian Holistic Healing Association
L130	Canadian Information Sharing Service
U125	Canadian Renewable Energy News
G130	Canadian Sport Parachuting Association
H132	Cancer Counseling Center
H133	Cancer Counseling and Research Center
L131	Canyon Cinema Cooperative
H134	Cape Cod Health Care Coalition
H135	Carolina Brown Lung Association
S124	Carousel Press: Books for Parents
S125	Carrier Pigeon/Alyson Publications
U004	Cascadian Regional Library
V126	Catalyst National Network
U126	Catfish Alliance
E002	Catholic Peace Fellowship
V127	Caucus for a New Political Science
G131	Center for Arts Information
H002	Center for Attitudinal Healing
V128	Center for Auto Safety
L132	Center for Black Studies
S126	Center for Community Change
S127	Center for Community Economic Development
U127	Center for Community Technology
V129	Center for Conflict Resolution
V130	Center for Conflict Resolution
E122	Center for Creative Studies
V131	Center for Defense Information
E123	Center for Development Policy
H136	Center for Early Adolescence
U128	Center for Environmental Problem Solving
G132	Center for Esoteric Studies
H137	Center for Humane Options in the Childbirth Experience
H003	Center for Integral Medicine
E124	Center for Interdisciplinary Creativity
E125	Center for International Policy
L133	Center for Investigative Reporting
G007	Center for Leisure Guidance
H004	Center for Medical Consumers and Health Care Information
V132	Center for National Security Studies
S128	Center for Neighborhood Development
U005	Center for Neighborhood Technology
V133	Center for New National Security
L134	Center for New Schools

V134	Center for Nonprofit Organization
V135	Center for Nonviolent Persuasion
E126	Center for Peace Studies
E127	Center for Peace and Conflict Studies
E128	Center for Policy Alternatives
V136	Center for Popular Economics
V137	Center for Public Representation
V138	Center for Research on Criminal Justice
H005	Center for Science in the Public Interest
G133	Center for Studies of the Person
E129	Center for Teaching International Relations
E130	Center for U.F.O. Studies
E131	Center for War/Peace Studies
V139	Center for Women in Government
G134	Center for Women's Studies and Services
V140	Center for a Woman's Own Name
U129	Center for the Biology of Natural Systems
G135	Center for the History of American Needlework
L135	Center for the Study of Democratic Institutions
V141	Center for the Study of Responsive Law
E132	Center of Telecommunications for the Third World
G136	Center of the Light
V142	Center on Law and Pacifism
L005	Center on Technology and Society
E133	Centerpoint Community
V008	Central Committee for Conscientious Objectors
E134	Centre Link
E135	Centre Monchanin
H006	Cesarean Connection
H138	Cesareans/Support Education and Concern (C/SEC)
L136	Change in Liberal Education Network
U130	Charles Stewart Mott Foundation
G137	Chautauqua Institution
G138	Cherry Creek: A Theatre Company
U131	Chesapeake Energy Alliance
S129	Chicago Association of Neighborhood Development Organizations
S130	Chicago Men's Gathering Newsletter
G139	Chicago Mural Group
H139	Child Care Information Exchange
H140	Children in Hospitals
G140	Children's Art Foundation
L137	Children's Creative Response to Conflict Program
H141	Children's Defense Fund
H142	Children's Holistic Institute for Life Development
V143	Children's Legal Rights Information and Training Program
G008	Chimo: The Holistic Magazine for Our Times
H143	Choosing Healthy Options in Changing Environments
H144	Chrysalis
L138	Church Street Center for Community Education
G141	Churches Center for Theology and Public Policy
H145	Cinema Medica
S131	Circle Pines Center
S132	Circle of Light/Findhorn
V144	Citizen Action
V145	Citizen Alert
V146	Citizen Soldier
U006	Citizen/Labor Energy Coalition
V147	Citizens Commission on Police Repression
S001	Citizens Committee for New York City
U132	Citizens Energy Council
V009	Citizens Involvement Training Project
V148	Citizens Party
U133	Citizens United for Responsible Energy

U134	Citizens for Safe Power Transmission
U007	Citizens for a Better Environment
U135	Citizens' Energy Project
L139	City Lights Journal
S133	City Miner: Community/Personal Adventure/Aesthetics
S002	Civic Action Institute
V149	Civilian Congress
E136	Claustrophobia: Life Extension
S134	Cleareye Natural Foods
H146	Clearing Community and School of the Healing Arts
L140	Clearinghouse of Free-Standing Educational Institutions
U136	Clippings in Ecotopia
G142	Clown College
H147	Club SeneX
S003	CoEvolution Quarterly
L006	Coalition for Alternatives in Postsecondary Education
U137	Coalition for Direct Action at Seabrook
E137	Coalition for a New Foreign and Military Policy
H007	Coalition for the Medical Rights of Women
L141	Coalition to End Animal Suffering in Experiments
V150	Coalition to End Grand Jury Abuse
E138	Coevolution
E139	Collectiv MAD/Media Alternative Developpement
L142	College Media Journal
V151	Come Unity: An Alternative Independent Journal
G143	Coming Changes Newsletter
V010	Commission for the Advancement of Public Interest Organizations
E003	Commission to Study the Organization of Peace
V011	Committee Against Registration and the Draft
H008	Committee for Abortion Rights and Against Sterilization Abuse
V152	Committee for Action Research on the Intelligence Community
U008	Committee for Nuclear Responsibility
G144	Committee for the Game
L007	Committee of Small Magazine Editors and Publishers
V153	Committee on Native American Struggles
H148	Committee to End Violence Against the Next Generation
V154	Common Cause
L143	Common Ground
S135	Common Health Warehouse
U009	Commonweal
E140	Communes Network
E141	CommuniTree Group
S004	Communities: Journal of Cooperative Living
E142	Community Computer
E143	Community Computers
S005	Community Congress of San Diego
S136	Community Economics
L144	Community Education Cooperative
U138	Community Energy Action Network
L145	Community Information Center
S137	Community Jobs
L008	Community Memory Project
H149	Community Network Development Project
U139	Community Network for Appropriate Technologies
S138	Community Produce
S006	Community Self-Reliance
S139	Community Self-Reliance Center
S007	Community Service
S140	Community Service Restitution
G145	Community for Religious Research and Education
U140	Compost Science/Land Utilization
E144	CompuServe
E145	Compute Magazine

E146	Computer Faire
E147	Computer Information Exchange
E148	Computer Music Journal
E149	Comunidad
L146	Conditions: Writing by Women
E004	Congressional Clearinghouse on the Future
S141	Connecticut Citizen Action Group
V155	Conscience and Military Tax Campaign
G146	Consciousness Synthesis Clearing House
U141	Conservation Foundation
U142	Conservation and Renewable Energy Inquiry and Referral Service
S142	Consortium for Youth of South Central Connecticut
E005	Consortium on Peace Research, Education, and Development
V156	Constructive Citizen Participation
U143	Consumer Action Now
H009	Consumer Coalition for Health
S143	Consumer Coop Press Service
V157	Consumer Education Research Group
L147	Consumer Educational Resource Network
V158	Consumer Information Center
G147	Contact Quarterly: A Vehicle for Moving Ideas
U144	Continued Action on Transportation in the U.S.
E150	Coop's Satellite Digest
G009	Cooperative Communities of America
S008	Cooperative Directory Association
S144	Cooperative League of the USA
S145	Cooperative and Communal Living Network
H150	Coping with the Overall Pregnancy/Parenting Experience
U145	Cornerstones: Energy Efficient Housebuilding
G148	Cosmic Awareness Communications
L148	Council for Educational Development and Research
L009	Council for the Advancement of Experiential Learning
V012	Council on Economic Priorities
S146	Council on Foundations
G149	Council on International Educational Exchange
L149	Council on Interracial Books for Children
S147	Country Journal
S148	Countryside: The Magazine for Serious Homesteaders
S149	Crafts Fair Guide
V159	Crafts Report: Marketing and Management for Crafts Professionals
E151	Creative Computing
G150	Creative Education Foundation
S150	Creative Loafing in Atlanta
L150	Creative Women's Collective
G151	Creative Yoga Studio
U010	Critical Mass Energy Project
V160	Cultural Correspondence
L151	Cultural Survival
V161	Custody Action for Lesbian Mothers
L152	D.C. Gazette
U146	Dakota Resource Council
G152	Damage Magazine: Not for Everybody
S151	Dandelion Community Co-op
E152	De Kleine Aarde (The Little Earth)
S152	Delaware Friends of Bikecology
V162	Democratic Socialist Organizing Committee
S153	Densmore Discoveries
L153	Denver Free University
U147	Design Alternatives
G153	Dialogue House Library
G154	Diamond Sangha Center: Zen Buddhist Society
E153	Die Gruenen (The Green Alliance)

G155	Different Worlds: Magazine of Adventure Role-Playing Games
G156	Dimensional Mind Approach
L154	Direct Cinema Limited
V163	Disability Rights Center
V164	Displaced Homemakers Network
S154	Distributing Alliance of the Northcountry Cooperatives
H151	Do It Now Foundation
H152	Doctors Ought to Care
U148	Documentary Guild
G157	Dormant Brain Research and Development Laboratory
L155	Double Helix: Community Media
S155	Dovetail Press: Design for the Owner-Involved Builder
E154	Down to Earth Association
L156	Downtown Community Television Center
E155	Dr. Dobb's Journal of Computer Calisthenics and Orthodontia
S156	Draft Horse Journal
G010	Dromenon: Journal of New Ways of Being
G011	Dying Project
V165	ERAmerica
U149	Earth Cyclers
U150	Earth Lab Institute
L157	Earthbooks Lending Library/Allegheny Branch
L158	Earthenergy Media
U151	Earthmind: Energy Research, Education and Books
E156	Earthrise: New Myths and Paradigms for Tomorrow
U152	Earthtone: For People Tuned to the Earth
H153	East West Academy of Healing Arts
H010	East West Journal
E157	East-West Communication Institute
H154	East/West Center for Holistic Health
U153	Ecology Action of the Midpeninsula
L010	Education Exploration Center
L011	Education for Freedom of Choice in Ohio
L159	Educational Film Library Association
L160	Educational Futures
L161	Educational Resources Information Center
L162	Educomics
L012	Electronic Information Exchange System
V013	Emergency Land Fund
G012	Emissaries of Divine Light
G158	Encounter Four: Adventure Course for Youth in Trouble
H155	Endometriosis Association
U154	Energy Consumer
U155	Energy People
U156	Energy Probe
U157	Energy Task Force
V166	Engage/Social Action
U011	Environmental Action Foundation
U012	Environmental Action Inc.
U158	Environmental Action Reprint Service
U013	Environmental Defense Fund
U159	Environmental Policy Institute
V167	Equal Times: Boston's Newspaper for Working Women
G159	Esalen Institute
V168	Eschaton Foundation: Community Spirit Fund
G160	Essene Light Center
G161	Essentia Films
E158	Evolution
E159	Experiment in International Living
V169	Exploratory Project for Economic Alternatives
S157	F.A.R.O.G. Forum: Journal Bilingue

G162   Faithist Journal
S158   Family Connection
G163   Family Pastimes
E160   Family Tree Network
S159   Family of New Age Networkers
L163   Far West Laboratory
U160   Farallones Institute: Integral Urban House
U161   Farallones Institute: Rural Center
U162   Farming Uncle: For Natural People and Mother Nature Lovers
G164   Feathered Pipe Ranch
S160   Fed-Up Coop
V170   Federal Laboratory Consortium
S161   Federation of Co-ops
S009   Federation of Egalitarian Communities
S162   Federation of Ohio River Cooperatives
S163   Federation of Southern Cooperatives
S164   Fellowship House Farm
E161   Fellowship of Reconciliation
L164   Feminary: A Feminist Journal for the South
V171   Feminist Alliance Against Rape
U163   Feminist Resources on Energy and Ecology
L013   Feminist Writers' Guild
L014   Feminist Writers' Guild/New York
L165   Ferity: Hawaii's Feminist Newsjournal
S165   Film-Makers Cooperative
E162   Findhorn Foundation
L166   Fine Print: A Review for the Arts of the Book
G165   Fine Woodworking
L167   Fireworks: Feminist Journal of the John Dewey High School
E163   First Earth Battalion Foundation
H156   Flower Essence Society
L168   Flower Films
V172   Focus/Midwest
L015   FocusCreativity
G166   Focusing Institute
L016   Folk-School Association of America
S166   Food Conspiracy Cooperative
S010   Food Learning Center
U014   Food Monitor
U164   Food Research and Action Center
L169   Food for Thought Books
G167   Foundation for Inner Peace
G168   Foundation of Light
V173   Free For All
L017   Free University Network
S167   Free Venice Beachhead
V174   Freedom of Information Clearinghouse
E164   Friedrichshof
G169   Friends Journal
V175   Friends Peace Committee
U015   Friends of the Earth
E165   Friends of the Filipino People
U165   Friends of the Parks
E006   Friends of the Third World
U016   Friends of the Trees
G170   Front Range: Women in the Visual Arts
G171   Fund for Advancement of Camping
U166   Fund for Animals
E166   Future Shack
E167   Future Studies Centre
E168   Futures Network

G172   Games

S168	Gay Community News
S169	Gay Sunshine Press
U167	General Assembly to Stop the Powerline
U168	General Whale
E169	Genesa Foundation
S170	Gentle Strength Cooperative
U169	Georgia Solar Coalition
U170	Geothermal World Info Center
L170	Gifted Children Newsletter
V176	Give and Take Bartering Center
E007	Global Education Associates
E170	Global Perspectives in Education
S171	Goodfellow Catalog of Wonderful Things
V177	Government Institutes
V014	Grantsmanship Center
H011	Gray Panthers
L018	Great Atlantic Radio Conspiracy
G173	Great Expeditions: Real Travellers and Explorers
S172	Greater Illinois People's Cooperative
U017	Green Mountain Post Films
U171	Greenpeace Alaska
U172	Greenpeace Examiner
U018	Greenpeace Foundation
U173	Greenpeace Seattle
U174	Greenpeace/Vancouver
V178	Greensboro Justice Fund
S173	Grindstone Island Centre
L171	Guild Books and Periodicals
L019	Guild Communications Network
G174	Guild of American Luthiers
L172	Gulf of Maine Bookstore
L173	Hagborn: A Radical Feminist News Journal
V179	Halt: Americans for Legal Reform
U175	Hands-On: Guidebook to Appropriate Technology in Massachusetts
S174	Hanover Consumer Cooperative Society
G175	Hanuman Foundation Tape Library
G176	Hardscrabble Hill: Residential Retreat Center for Women
S175	Harmony Community
U176	Harrowsmith Magazine/Canada
S176	Hartford Food System
G177	Hartley Productions: Films for a New Age
V180	Harvest Publications
H157	Hawaii Health Network
G178	Healing Light Center
H158	Health Activation Network
H159	Health Link
H012	Health Policy Advisory Council
H160	Health Policy Council
H161	Health Writers
U177	Health and Energy Learning Project
H162	Health for the New Age
E171	Helsinki Watch
V015	Henry George School of Social Science
U178	Herb Quarterly
H163	Herbal Education Center
U179	High Country News: Natural Resources of the Rockies
G179	High Times
H164	Hippocrates Health Institute
H165	Holistic Health Organizing Committee
H166	Holistic Health Practitioners' Association
H167	Holistic Health Referrals
H168	Holistic Health Review

L174   Holistic Life University
H169   Holistic Psychotherapy and Medical Group
H170   Holmes Center for Research in Holistic Healing
L020   Holt Associates
V181   Home Equity Conversion Project
S177   Home Front: For Young Pregnant Women and their Families
S178   Home Ownership Development Program
L175   Home Study Exchange
E172   Home Video
H171   Home-Oriented Maternity Experience
H172   Homebirth
V182   Homemakers Organized for More Employment
H173   Homeopathic Educational Services
S179   Homesteaders News
L176   Homosexual Information Center
H013   Hospice Institute for Education Training and Research
H174   Hot Springs Information Network
U180   Hudson Valley Green
G180   Human Dimensions Institute and Center
H014   Human Ecology Action League
V183   Human Economy Center
U181   Human Environment Center
E008   Human Rights Internet
E173   Human Systems Network
U182   Humane Society of the United States
L021   Humanistic Psychology Institute
E174   Humanity Foundation
E009   Hunger Project
H015   Huxley Institute for Biosocial Research
L177   Hydra Book Company

G181   I Ching Sangha
E175   IOC/MAB
U183   Illinois South Project
V016   Illinois Women's Agenda
G182   Illuminations
V017   Indian Rights Association
S180   Indianapolis Mayor's Bicycle Task Force
V184   Indochina Curriculum Group
U184   Infinite Energy
G183   Infinite Odyssey: Wilderness Adventures
E176   Info Alternativ
E177   InfoWorld: The Newspaper for the Microcomputing Community
V185   Inform, Incorporated
E178   Information Center on Children's Cultures
E179   Information Industry Association
S181   Information Tree/San Francisco
L178   Information for People
H175   Informed Homebirth
U185   Inland Regional Council
V186   Inmate Legal Association
G184   Inner Paths: Eastern and Western Spiritual Thought
G185   Inner-Space Interpreters Services
E180   Innovation et Reseaux pour le Developpement
G186   Insight Meditation Society
G187   Insight Training Seminars
E181   Institut Rural d'Information
E010   Institute for Alternative Futures
S182   Institute for Community Economics
G188   Institute for Consciousness and Music
U186   Institute for Ecological Policies
H176   Institute for Family Research and Education
E011   Institute for Food and Development Policy

E182	Institute for Information Society
V187	Institute for Labor Education and Research
S011	Institute for Local Self-Reliance
S012	Institute for Non-Violent Education, Research, and Training
V188	Institute for Peace and Justice
E183	Institute for Policy Studies
L179	Institute for Responsive Education
V018	Institute for Social Justice
V189	Institute for Social Justice/Eastern Office
V190	Institute for Social Service Alternatives
V019	Institute for Southern Studies
L180	Institute for Wholistic Education
E184	Institute for World Order
G189	Institute for the Development of the Harmonious Human Being
G190	Institute for the New Age
E185	Institute for the Study of Conscious Evolution
E186	Institute for the Study of the Human Future
E187	Institute of Noetic Sciences
S013	Institute on Man and Science
H177	Integral Health Services
L022	Intercommunity Center for Justice and Peace
E188	Intercontinental Press/Inprecor
S183	Interest File
H178	Interface Foundation
V020	Interfaith Center on Corporate Responsibility
E189	Interlink Press Service
U187	Intermediate Technology
U188	International Biomass Institute
E190	International Center for Integrative Studies
H179	International Childbirth Education Association
G191	International Church of Ageless Wisdom
H180	International College of Applied Nutrition
E191	International Communes Network
S184	International Cooperative Community
E192	International Council for Computers in Education
U189	International Federation of Organic Agricultural Movements
H181	International Foundation for the Promotion of Homeopathy
E193	International Herald Tribune
G192	International Home Exchange Service
E194	International Journal of General Systems
E195	International Kirlian Research
E012	International Network for Social Network Analysis
G193	International New Thought Alliance
V191	International Seminars in Training for Nonviolent Action
L181	International Society for General Semantics
U190	International Solar Energy Society
U191	International Tree Crops Institute U.S.A.
E196	International Union for Conservation of Nature and Resources
E197	International Voluntary Services
E198	International Women's Tribune Center
E199	Interreligious Taskforce on U.S. Food Policy
G013	Intimate Talk: Journal of Expression
S185	Intra-Community Cooperative
U192	Izaak Walton League of America

V192	Jewish Peace Fellowship
E200	Johnson-Lenz
V193	Joint Center for Political Studies
E201	Journal of Developing Areas
H182	Journal of the Nutritional Academy
G194	Jump Cut: A Review of Contemporary Cinema
G195	Jungian-Senoi Dreamwork Institute

V194	Kapitalistate: Working Papers on the Capitalist State
G196	Karma Triyana Dharmachakra
L182	Kartemquin Films
H183	Ken Dychtwald & Associates
S014	Kerista Village
V195	King City Senior Barter Bank
G197	Kite Lines
V021	Know Feminist Publishers
E202	Kokov
E203	Kosmos Centre
G198	Kripalu Yoga Center
G199	Kripalu Yoga Fellowship/Toronto
G200	Kronos: Journal of Interdisciplinary Synthesis

E204	L-5 Society
H016	La Leche League International
G014	Lama Foundation
U193	Lamoureux Foundation: Home Energy Workshops
S186	Lancaster Independent Press
L183	Latino Institute
G201	Laughing Man Institute
E205	Laurieston Hall
E206	Leading Edge: A Bulletin of Social Transformation
V196	League for Ecological Democracy
G202	League of American Wheelmen
U194	League of Michigan Bicyclists
L184	Learning Connection
L185	Learning Exchange
L186	Learning Tools
L187	Learning Web
V197	Legal Services Corporation
H017	Lesbian Mothers National Defense Fund
L023	Liberation News Service
V198	Libertarian Review
G203	Life Systems Educational Foundation
G204	Life Understanding Foundation
H184	Life-Force Cancer Project
E207	Lighter than Air Society
G205	Lilith: The Jewish Women's Magazine
G206	Lindisfarne Association
L188	Link Learning Network
S187	Living Free: Personal Journal of Self-Liberation
S188	Logical Connection: Skillsharing for Private Practitioners
H185	Long Island Childbirth Alternatives
V199	Looking Left
G207	Lorian Association: Serving the Spirit of Wholeness
V200	Los Angeles Commission on Assaults Against Women
S189	Los Angeles Men's Collective
G208	Lost Music Network
S190	Love Family
G209	Love Project
G210	Love: A Journal
G211	Lucis Trust

G212	M. Gentle Men for Gender Justice
H186	Macrobiotic Health Information Center of New Jersey
H187	Macrobiotic: A Guide for Natural Living
H018	Madness Network News
E208	Magic Circle: The Native American Indian
G213	Magical Blend: A Magazine of Synergy
S191	Magnolia: Southeastern Confederation for Cooperation
U195	Maine Audubon Society
S192	Maine Bicycle Coalition

U196	Maine Organic Farmers and Gardeners Association
S193	Maine Times
E209	Maison du Nouvel Age
V201	Making It Legal: Primer for Craftmaker, Artist and Writer
L189	Manas: Journal of Independent Inquiry
E210	Mandala Verlag
G214	Many Hands: Guide to Holistic Health and Awareness
H188	Marion County Community Mental Health Center
L190	Martha Stuart Communications
E211	Maryland Alliance for Space Colonization
V202	Maryland Food Committee
H189	Massachusetts Coalition of Battered Women Service Groups
V203	Massachusetts Public Interest Research Group
H190	Massage and Bodywork
G015	Matagiri Sri Aurobindo Center
H191	Maternal and Child Health Center
H192	Maternity Center
L191	Math Science Network
G215	Maui Zendo
L192	Media Access Project
L193	Media Alliance
L194	MediaSense
S194	Mediaworks
H193	Medical Self-Care Magazine
S195	Men's Program Unit
S196	Men's Resource Center
G216	Menorah: Sparks of Jewish Renewal
V204	Mental Health Law Project
H194	Mental Patients Association
S197	Message Post
G217	Metamorphoses: Development in Canada
V205	Mexican American Legal Defense and Educational Fund
S198	Michigan Federation of Food Cooperatives
H195	Mid-Hudson Area Maternity Alternatives
E212	Middle East Peace Project
E213	Middle East Research and Information Project
S199	Midwest Academy
V206	Midwest Committee for Military Counseling
G218	Minnesota Zen Meditation Center
U197	Mississippi Solar Coalition
L195	Mix Recording Publications
V022	Mobilization for Survival
U198	Modern Energy & Technology Alternatives
G219	Modern Haiku
G220	Monroe Institute of Applied Sciences
L196	Mother Earth News
V207	Mother Jones
H019	Mothering Magazine
S200	Mothers and Others
U199	Mountain Bicyclists' Association
V023	Movement for Economic Justice
V024	Movement for a New Society
G221	Movement of Spiritual Inner Awareness
L197	Ms. Magazine
U200	Mudsharks Co-op
G222	Muktananda Meditation Center
L198	Museum of Holography
E214	Mushroom: A Magazine for Living in New Zealand
U201	Musicians United for Safe Energy
S201	Mutual Aid Project

H020	NAPSAC: Safe Alternatives in Childbirth
G223	Naropa Institute
V208	National Abortion Federation
V209	National Action Committee on the Status of Women
V210	National Action/Research on the Military Industrial Complex
H021	National Alliance for Optional Parenthood
H196	National Alliance for the Mentally Ill
U202	National Association for Gardening
L199	National Association for Gifted Children
L200	National Association for the Education of Young Children
S015	National Association of Housing Cooperatives
L024	National Association of Legal Services to Alternative Schools
S016	National Association of Neighborhoods
V025	National Association of Office Workers
U203	National Association of Railroad Passengers
U204	National Audubon Society
S017	National Catholic Rural Life Conference
U019	National Center for Appropriate Technology
S018	National Center for Citizen Involvement
L201	National Center for Educational Brokering
L202	National Center for Research in Vocational Education
L025	National Center for Service-Learning
L203	National Chicano Research Network
H022	National Citizens Coalition for Nursing Home Reform
H197	National Coalition Against Domestic Violence
U205	National Coalition Against the Misuse of Pesticides
L204	National Coalition of Alternative Community Schools
H198	National College of Naturopathic Medicine
S019	National Commission on Resources for Youth, Inc.
V026	National Committee Against Repressive Legislation
L205	National Committee for Citizens in Education
H199	National Committee for Prevention of Child Abuse
V211	National Committee for Responsive Philanthropy
S020	National Congress of Neighborhood Women
V212	National Consumer Cooperative Bank
V213	National Council of La Raza
H200	National Council on Alternative Health Care Policy
L206	National Diffusion Network
V214	National Economic Development and Law Center
S021	National Family Farm Coalition
L026	National Federation of Community Broadcasters
L207	National Federation of Local Cable Programmers
H201	National Feminist Therapists Association
V215	National Gay Task Force
H202	National Health Federation
S022	National Hispanic Coalition for Better Housing
L208	National Home Study Council
S202	National Hook-up of Black Women
H203	National Hospice Organization
V027	National Indian Youth Council
U206	National Intervenors
V216	National Lawyers Guild
S023	National Neighbors
E215	National Network in Solidarity with the Nicaraguan People
V217	National Network of Grantmakers
S024	National Network of Runaway and Youth Services
L209	National News Bureau
V218	National Organization for Women
V219	National Organization for an American Revolution
V220	National Organization for the Reform of Marijuana Laws
L210	National Organizations Advisory Council for Children
G224	National Outdoor Leadership School
E013	National Peace Academy Campaign

V221	National Prison Project
L211	National Radio Club
U207	National Recycling Coalition
V222	National Resistance Committee
S203	National Runaway Switchboard
S025	National Self-Help Clearinghouse
S026	National Self-Help Resource Center
L027	National Society for Internships and Experiential Education
E216	National Space Institute
L212	National Technical Information Service
S027	National Training and Information Center
S204	National Trust for Historic Preservation
H023	National Women's Health Network
U208	Nationwide Forest Planning Clearinghouse
U209	Natural Food Associates
S028	Natural Helping Networks Project
U020	Natural Resources Defense Council
U210	Nature Conservancy
G225	Nature Explorations
U211	Needmor Fund
S029	Neighborhood Information Sharing Exchange
S205	Neighborhood Organization Research Group
E217	Netswerk Selbsthilfe
H204	Network Against Psychiatric Assault
S206	Network Exchange News Service
L213	Network for Learning
E218	Network to Educate for World Security
V223	Network: A Catholic Social Justice Lobby
L214	Networking Group
V224	Nevada Elected Women's Network
G226	New Age Awareness Center
V225	New Age Caucus
S207	New Age Chicago
G227	New Age Gazette
G228	New Age Government
G016	New Age Information Service
G229	New Age Magazine
G230	New Age Mating
G231	New Age Music Network
G232	New Age Network of Colorado Springs
G233	New Age Resource Center
H205	New Age Wellness Center
H206	New Age in Austin
U212	New Alchemy Institute
V028	New American Movement
G234	New Art Examiner: Independent Voice of the Visual Arts
G235	New Atlantean Research Society
H207	New Beginnings Birth Center
S208	New Community Project
G236	New Dimensions Radio and Tapes
V226	New Directions for Women
V227	New Directions for Young Women
H024	New Directions in Psychology
U213	New England Coalition on Nuclear Pollution
V228	New England Cooperative Training Institute
S209	New England Food Cooperative Organization
V229	New England Free Press
V029	New England Human Rights Network
U214	New England Regional Energy Project
U215	New England Solar Energy Association
L215	New England Training Center for Community Organizers
U216	New Environment Association
E219	New Era Technologies

L216	New Front Films
G017	New Games Foundation
H025	New Hampshire Feminist Health Center
E220	New Humanity Journal
L028	New Jersey Unschoolers
U217	New Life Farm
G237	New Life Foundation for Holistic Health and Research
U218	New Mexico Solar Energy Association
G238	New Options for a Vital United States (NOVUS)
L217	New Orleans Video Access Center
L218	New Pages Press
G239	New Realities: Magazine of Body, Mind and Spirit
V230	New Seed Press Feminist Collective
S210	New Seeds Information Service
U219	New Times Films
G240	New Trust Network
V030	New Ways to Work
S211	New West Trails
V231	New World Alliance
V232	New World Review
V233	New York Public Interest Research Group
S212	New York State Coalition for Local Self Reliance
S030	New York Urban Coalition
E221	News from Guatemala
H208	Newtrition Outreach: Whole Foods Information
E222	Next: A Look into the Future
V234	Nine to Five (9 to 5)
U220	Non Nuclear Network
E014	North American Congress on Latin America
U221	North American Mycological Association
G241	North American Network of Women Runners
E015	North American Nonviolence Training Network
S031	North American Students of Cooperation
S213	North Carolina Anvil
U222	North Carolina Coalition for Renewable Energy Resources
H209	North Carolina Occupational Safety and Health Project
V235	North Country M.N.S. Organizing Collective
S214	North Oak Street Chowder and Marching Society
U223	Northcoast Environmental Center
U224	Northeast Appropriate Technology Network
L219	Northern California Open Network
L220	Northern California/Southern Oregon Resource Network
H210	Northern Pines: A Wholistic Health Retreat
U225	Northern Rockies Action Group
U226	Northern Sun Alliance
U227	Northwest Coalition for Alternatives to Pesticides
S215	Northwest Organic Herb Cooperative
S216	Northwest Provender Alliance
L029	Northwest Regional Educational Laboratory
S217	Northwest Regional Foundation
L221	Northwest Women in Educational Administration
U021	Nuclear Information and Resource Service
E223	Nucleus Network
E224	Nuestro Magazine
H211	Nurse Healers/Professional Associates Cooperative
H212	Nurses in Transition
H213	Nutritional and Preventive Medical Clinic
U228	Ocean Education Project
V236	Off Our Backs: A Women's News Journal
U229	Office of Appropriate Technology
E225	Office of Tibet
E226	Office on Global Education

L030	Ohio Coalition for Educational Alternatives Now
V237	Ohio Public Interest Campaign
S218	Old House Journal
S219	Older Women's Network
U230	Olympic Peninsula Citizens against Toxic Spray
G242	Omega Foundation
G018	Omega Institute for Holistic Studies
E227	Omega: Global Networking
H214	Omega: Program of Grief Assistance
E228	Omni Magazine
H215	On Our Own Network
V238	One Less Bomb Committee
H216	Ontario Patients' Self-Help Association
G243	Ontario Zen Center
L031	Open Network
V239	Open Road
E229	Open Systems
V240	Organization Resource Associates
E230	Organization for the Advancement of Space Industrialization
L032	Organizational Development Network
S220	Organize Training Center
G244	Ottawa Psychic Study Centre
G245	Outdoor Education for the Handicapped Project
G246	Outside: Magazine of the Great Outdoors
G247	Outward Bound
S221	Owner-Builder Publications
E016	Oxfam America
G248	Oz Projects: Retreat in the Redwoods
S222	Ozark Area Community Congress
U231	Ozark Institute
U232	Pacific Northwest Research Center
L222	Pacific Region Association of Alternative Schools
L223	Packard Manse Media Project
E231	Papier Mache Video Institute
G249	Parabola: Myth and the Quest for Meaning
H026	Parent Support-Group Project
S223	Parents Anonymous
L224	Parents Union for Public Schools
H217	Parents Without Partners
E017	Participation Publishers
E018	Participation Systems Incorporated
E232	Partnership for Productivity
H218	Pavillion Newsletter: Advocacy for the Disabled
G250	Pax Center
V241	Peace Project
V031	Peacework
V242	People's Business Commission
E233	People's Computer Company
H219	People's Doctor: Medical Newsletter for Consumers
E234	People's Translation Service
S224	Personal Freedom Network
U233	Personal Mobility Committee
E235	Phebus: Integrating Wholes and Parts
G251	PhenomeNEWS
V243	Physicians for Social Responsibility
L225	Pioneer Productions
U022	Planet Drum Foundation
E236	Planetary Association for Clean Energy
E019	Planetary Citizens
E237	Planetary Society
H220	Planned Parenthood
V032	Planner's Network

E238	Plenty
S225	Plexus: San Francisco Bay Area Women's Newspaper
G252	Poetry Project
U234	Pollution Probe Foundation
V244	Popular Economics Press
E239	Population Action Council
U235	Potomac Alliance
V245	Powder River Basin Resource Council
U236	Prairie Alliance
L226	Primary/Secondary Peace Education Network
G019	Prison Ashram Project
V246	Prisoners Union
V247	Privacy Journal
L227	Process: Networking Forum for Citizen Participation
V248	Productivity Group
G253	Progressive Utilization Theory Universal (Prout)
V249	Project Equality
U237	Project Jonah
S226	Project SHARE: Improving the Management of Human Services
V033	Project Work
S032	Project for Kibbutz Studies
L228	Project on the Status and Education of Women
E240	Prometheus Society
E241	Promoting Enduring Peace
G254	Protestant Committee on Urban Ministry
L229	Providence Learning Connection
G255	Providence Zen Center
H221	Psychiatric Inmates' Rights Collective
G020	Public Action Coalition on Toys
H222	Public Citizen Health Research Group
V250	Public Eye: A Journal Concerning Repression in America
L230	Public Media Center
H223	Pumpkin Hollow Farm
E242	Purser's Magazine for Family Computers
H224	Pyramid: Resource Sharing Network for Drug Abuse Prevention
G256	Quadrinity Center
L231	Quest: A Feminist Quarterly
S227	RFD: Country Journal for Gay Men Everywhere
U238	Rachel Carson Trust Fund for the Living Environment
V251	Radical Alliance of Social Service Workers
V252	Radical America
E243	Radical Perspectives Network
E244	Radio Amateur Satellite Corporation (AMSAT)
U023	Rain Community Resource Center
S228	Raisin Consciousness
G257	Rare Earth: Exotic Properties for Sale
G258	ReVision: A Journal of Knowledge and Consciousness
V253	Recon Publications
U239	Redwood City Seed Company
S229	Regional Young Adult Project
E245	Religion and Ethics Network
H225	Renaissance House
V034	Renewal Newsletter: New Values, New Politics
E246	Rescue Communication Network
E247	Research Utilization Network
L232	Research for Better Schools
U240	Resource Center Network
E248	Resource Center for Nonviolence
U241	Resources for the Future
E249	Resurgence: Of Small Nations, Small Communities, & Human Spirit
E250	Review of International Broadcasting

S033	Riptide/University Services Agency
G021	Rites of Passage
V254	Robert's Think Tank
E251	Robotics Age: Journal of Intelligent Machines
V255	Rocky Flats Nuclear Weapons Facilities Project
L233	Rodale Press
G259	Roues Libres: Association Cycliste
G260	Rowan Tree: Publishers of The Unicorn
G261	Rowe Conference Center
G262	Rudrananda Ashram
S034	Rural America
S230	Rural American Women
V035	SANE
G263	SYDA Foundation
U242	Safe Energy Alternatives Alliance
U243	Safe Energy Resources
L234	Sagamore Institute
U244	Saginaw Valley Nuclear Study Group
E252	Saharan Peoples Support Committee
L235	Salt Magazine
G264	Samisdat
U245	San Diego Center for Appropriate Technology
L236	San Francisco Bay Guardian
G265	San Francisco Mime Troupe
H226	San Francisco Young Adult Network
U246	San Luis Valley Solar Energy Association
G266	Sanatana Dharma Foundation
L237	Sandy River School
V256	Sanity Now!
S231	Santa Clara Valley Bicycle Association
H227	Sarasota School of Natural Healing Arts
U247	Saskatoon Environmental Society
E020	Satellite Video Exchange Society
S035	School of Living: Publishers of Green Revolution
E253	Science Digest
E254	Science Fiction Writers of America
E255	Science News
U248	Science for the People
U024	Scientists' Institute for Public Information
U249	Sea Shepherd Conservation Society
S232	Sealand: The Cheap Land Catalogue
V257	Second Wave: Magazine of the New Feminism
U250	Seed Savers Exchange
G267	Segue Foundation: Publishers of Books and Magazines
H228	Self Care Associates
H229	Seminars on Sexuality
G268	Shadybrook House
E256	Shalom Network
G269	Shambhala Booksellers
L238	Shambhala Publications
G270	Shanti Nilaya
S233	Share Foundation/Television Network
L239	Shelter Publications
S036	Shelterforce Collective
G271	Siddha Yoga Dham Ann Arbor
G272	Siddha Yoga Dham Boston
U251	Sierra Club
E257	Sierra Club International Earthcare Center
U252	Sierra Club Radioactive Waste Campaign
L240	Signs: Journal of Women and Culture in Society
G022	Sing Out! The Folk Song Magazine
G273	Sino-American Buddhist Association

L241	Sipapu: Newsletter for Librarians
G274	Sirius Community
V258	Sister Courage: Radical Feminist Newspaper
V036	SkillsBank
G275	Sluggo: Journal of Disturbing Clues
U253	Small Farm Energy Project
L242	Small Press Review
S037	Small Towns Institute
G276	Sobek Expeditions: Outdoor Adventure Rivers Specialists
V259	Social Advocates for Youth
U254	Society for Animal Rights
E258	Society for General Systems Research
G277	Society for Human and Spiritual Understanding
H230	Society for Occupational and Environmental Health
H231	Society for the Protection of the Unborn Through Nutrition
G278	Society of Folk Harpers and Craftsmen
S234	Society of Ontario Nut Growers
L243	Society of Scribes and Illuminators
V260	Sojourner: Northeast Women's Journal of News and the Arts
G279	Sojourners: Christian Renewal Community
U255	Solar Business Office
U256	Solar Energy Association of Northeast Colorado
U257	Solar Energy Digest
U258	Solar Energy Research Institute
U259	Solar Greenhouse Digest
U260	Solar Lobby
U261	Solar Times: News of the Solar Energy Industry
G280	Soluna: Creative Healing and Self-Exploration
G281	Sorting It Out: Support for Spiritual Leavetakers
H232	Soundiscoveries
E259	Sourcebook Project
V261	South Carolina Committee Against Hunger
V262	South Carolina Libertarian Party
E260	Southeast Asia Resource Center
E261	Southern Africa Committee
S235	Southern Appalachian Resource Catalog
L244	Southern California Open Network
V263	Southern Coalition on Jails and Prisons
S236	Southern Neighborhoods
U262	Southern Oregon Citizens Against Toxic Sprays
U263	Southern Oregon Living Lightly Association
V264	Southern Poverty Law Center
L245	Southern Progressive Periodicals Directory
S237	Southern Rural Development Center
U025	Southern Unity Network/Renewable Energy Project
L033	Southwest Educational Development Laboratory
L034	Southwest Research and Information Center
S238	Spectrum: Cooperative Newspaper for the Tallahassee Community
G023	Sphinx and Sword of Love Bookstore
G282	Spirals: Bridging the Gap Between Science and Mysticism
G024	Spiritual Community Guide
G283	Spiritual Emergency Network
G284	Spiritual Friends
G285	Spiritual Frontiers Fellowship
H233	Spring Hill: Community, Retreat and Counseling Center
G286	Sproing: Science Fiction and Fantasy
G287	Sri Aurobindo's Action Center
G025	Sri Chinmoy Centre
G288	St. Louis Unit of Service of World Goodwill
S239	Star Root: Fortnightly Newspaper
G289	Stash
H234	Statewide Comprehensive Health Education Coalition
L246	Stay Smart

U264	Stock Seed Farms
L247	Stony Hills: New England Alternative Press Review
L035	Student Press Law Center
U265	Sudbury 2001
G290	Sufi Order for the Esoteric Arts & Sciences
U266	Summit Coalition for Alternatives to Pesticides
G291	Summit Lighthouse
S240	Support Center: Management Assistance to Non-Profit Groups
G292	Survival Cards
H027	Survival Foundation
G293	Synergic Power Institute
U267	Synerjy: Directory of Energy Alternatives
V265	Syracuse Peace Council
G294	T'ai Chi
G295	Taeria Foundation Spiritual Community
H028	Tallahassee Feminist Women's Health Center
V266	Tarrytown Group
U026	Task Force Against Nuclear Pollution
V267	Tax Reform Research Group
V268	Taxation With Representation
G296	Tayu Institute
L248	Teachers' Centers Exchange
V269	Team for Justice
S241	Techqua Ikachi: Traditional Hopi Viewpoint
E262	Teilhard Centre for the Future of Man
E263	Teilhard Foundation
L249	Telecommunications Cooperative Network
G297	Temple of Understanding
H029	Terrap: Network for Agoraphobics
S242	Texas Observer: A Journal of Free Voices
U268	Texas Solar Energy Coalition
G298	Textile Artists' Newsletter: Review of Fiber Arts
G299	The Awakeners
G300	The Churchman
G301	The Farm
G302	The Loving Brotherhood
V270	The Militant: Socialist Newsweekly
L250	The Network: Educational Service and Research
E264	The Network: Starflight and Immortality
U269	The Plan: Community Food Tree Nurseries
L251	The Progressive
S243	The Smallholder: Ideas and Information for Country People
E021	The Source
V271	The Spokeswoman: Feminist News Digest
U270	The Sproutletter: Sprouts, Raw Foods, and Nutrition
G026	The Sun: A Magazine of Ideas
G303	Theatre-Action
G304	Theosophical Society of America
U271	Three Mile Island Alert
G305	Three-H-O Foundation (3HO)
U272	Tilth: Biological Agriculture in the Northwest
L252	Today News Service
V272	Toolbox Training and Skills-sharing Collective
V273	Toronto Association for Peace
U027	Total Environmental Action
H030	Touch for Health Foundation
G306	Trailhead Ventures
V274	Transaction Periodicals Consortium
G027	Transformation Project
E022	Transnational Network for Appropriate/Alternative Technologies
S244	Transportation Alternatives
G307	Travelers' Directory

U273	Tree People
H235	Tri-Self Clinic
E265	Triangles: Network of Light
V275	Tribal Sovereignty Program
U274	Trojan Decommissioning Alliance
S245	Trust for Public Land
E266	Turning Point Newsletter/England
H236	Turtle Island Holistic Health Community
E267	Twenty-first Century Media
E268	U.S. Association for The Club of Rome
E269	U.S. Committee for Justice to Latin American Political Prisoners
E270	U.S.-China People's Friendship Association
U275	Underground Space Center
L253	Uni-Ed Associates
G308	Unified States of Awareness Communications
L254	Unifilm
V276	Union Women's Alliance to Gain Equality
L036	Union for Experimenting Colleges and Universities
V277	Union for Radical Political Economics
V278	Union of Concerned Scientists
E023	Union of International Associations
L255	United Ministries in Education
E024	United Nations Economic & Social Council
S246	United Neighborhood Centers of America
G309	United States Parachute Association
G310	Unity-in-Diversity Council
G311	Universal Great Brotherhood
E271	Universite Verte
E272	University Peace Studies Network
G312	University of the Wilderness
S038	Urban Alternatives Group
S039	Urban Alternatives Group/Columbus
S247	Urban Planning Aid
L256	Urban Scientific & Educational Research
U276	Urban Solar Energy Association
U277	Valley Watch
V279	Vanguard Public Foundation
H237	Vanier Institute of the Family
S248	Vegetarian Society of D.C.
H238	Vegetarian Times
U278	Velo Quebec
E273	Verein Lebensdorf
V280	Vermont Alliance
U279	Vermont Yankee Decommissioning Alliance
V281	Veterans Education Project
V282	Vietnam Veterans Against the War
S249	Village of Anything Is Possible
V037	Vocations for Social Change
E274	Volunteers in Technical Assistance
G313	Wainwright House
E025	War Control Planners
S040	Warmlines: A Parent Network and Resource Center
S250	Washington Area Bicyclist Association
S251	Washington Blade: Gay Newspaper of the Nation's Capital
G314	Washington Buddhist Vihara
L257	Washington Community Video Center
V283	Washington Monthly
E275	Washington Office on Latin America
U028	Washington Small Farm Resources Network
V284	Washington Spectator & Between the Lines

H239	Washington State Midwifery Council
U280	Waste Watch
G315	Watercourse Ways
U281	Waterloo Public Interest Research Group
G316	Watershed Foundation: Poetry Recordings
V038	We-Know-Now Free Trade Exchange
G028	Well Being: A Network for Spiritual Journeyors
H240	Well-Being Magazine
H241	Wellness Associates
H242	Wellness Institute
G317	West Art
L258	Western Behavioral Sciences Institute
U282	Western Massachusetts Resource Network
U283	Western Massachusetts Solar Energy Association
L259	White Buffalo Multimedia
S252	Whiteaker Community Council
G318	Whole Life Times: Northeast Journal for a Positive Future
H243	Wholistic Health and Nutrition Institute
U284	Wilderness Society
G319	Willow: A Woman's Retreat
U285	Wind Power Digest: Access to Wind Energy Information
U029	Wind-Light Workshop
S253	Winds of Change
U286	Windstar Foundation: Educational, Research and Retreat Center
G320	Windsurfer Magazine
V285	Wisconsin Women's Network
S254	Wishing Well
V286	Woman Activist: Action Bulletin for Women's Rights
S255	Woman's Place
H244	Womancare: A Feminist Women's Health Center
L260	Womansplace Bookstore
V287	Women Against Violence Against Women
V288	Women Against Violence in Pornography and Media
H245	Women Healthsharing
G029	Women Outdoors
V039	Women U.S.A.
H246	Women and Health Roundtable
U287	Women and Life on Earth
U288	Women and Technology Project
G321	Women at the Helm: International Women's Sailing
L261	Women in Focus: Film Production and Distribution
U289	Women in Solar Energy
E276	Women in World Areas Studies
G322	Women in the Wilderness
V040	Women's Action Alliance
L262	Women's Educational Equity Communications Network
V289	Women's Enterprises of Boston
V290	Women's Equity Action League
H031	Women's Health Services
L263	Women's History Research Center
L264	Women's Information Exchange
S256	Women's Information, Referral and Education Service
L265	Women's Institute for Freedom of the Press
E277	Women's International Information & Communication Service (ISIS)
E278	Women's International League for Peace and Freedom
E026	Women's International Network
E279	Women's International Resource Exchange Service
V291	Women's Legal Defense Fund
V292	Women's Party for Survival
L266	Women's Press
L267	Women's Referral Service
G323	Women's Sports Foundation
V293	Women's Work Force Network

L268	Women: Journal of Liberation
L269	WomenSpace Women's Center
G324	WomenSpirit Journal
U290	Wood 'n Energy
G325	WoodenBoat Magazine
S257	Wool Gathering
V294	Working Papers for a New Society
V295	Working Women's Institute
H247	Working on Wife Abuse
L270	Workshop for Learning Things
U291	World Association for Solid-Waste Transfer and Exchange
E027	World Constitution and Parliament Association
E280	World Education Fellowship
E281	World Environment Center
E282	World Federalists Association
E028	World Future Society
E283	World Game of R. Buckminster Fuller
G326	World Goodwill
E284	World Hunger Education Service
U292	World Information Service on Energy
E285	World Institute for Advanced Phenomenological Research
G327	World Monastic Council
E286	World Peace News
E287	World Peace Tax Fund
E288	World Press Review
E289	World Space Federation
E290	World Union
G328	World Union for Progressive Judaism
G329	World University
E291	WorldPaper: The Global Community Newspaper
E292	Worldwatch Institute

G330	Yes Educational Society
S258	Yestermorrow: Design/Builder School
G331	Yoga Journal
V296	Youth International Party
L271	Youth Liberation Press
V297	Youth Project

G332	Zen Center of San Francisco
G333	Zen Center of Sonoma Mountain
U293	Zero Population Growth
L272	Zipporah Films
G334	Zygon: Journal of Religion and Science

Location Guide

ALASKA

AK	99501	S103	Alaska Youth Advocates
AK	99501	U103	Alaska Center for the Environment
AK	99501	U104	Alaskan Conservation Foundation
AK	99501	U171	Greenpeace Alaska

ALABAMA

AL	35209	U102	Alabama Solar Coalition
AL	35460	S163	Federation of Southern Cooperatives
AL	36101	V264	Southern Poverty Law Center

ARKANSAS

AR	72315	U118	Arkansas Solar Action Coalition
AR	72632	U231	Ozark Institute

ARIZONA

AZ	85008	L260	Womansplace Bookstore
AZ	85010	H151	Do It Now Foundation
AZ	85018	H115	Association for Research and Enlightenment Clinic
AZ	85064	L105	Alliance of Information and Referral Services
AZ	85251	G193	International New Thought Alliance
AZ	85252	G227	New Age Gazette
AZ	85253	U117	Arcosanti
AZ	85281	S170	Gentle Strength Cooperative
AZ	85358	E017	Participation Publishers
AZ	85701	V227	New Directions for Young Women
AZ	85705	S166	Food Conspiracy Cooperative
AZ	85712	G104	American Astrology
AZ	85712	E101	Aerial Phenomena Research Organization
AZ	85717	G329	World University
AZ	85719	S211	New West Trails
AZ	85719	E204	L-5 Society
AZ	86002	V201	Making It Legal: Primer for Craftmaker, Artist and Writer
AZ	86003	U259	Solar Greenhouse Digest
AZ	86030	S241	Techqua Ikachi: Traditional Hopi Viewpoint
AZ	86401	G162	Faithist Journal

CALIFORNIA

CA	90005	V120	Brown Committee
CA	90005	V123	California Housing Information and Action Network
CA	90005	V147	Citizens Commission on Police Repression
CA	90015	V014	Grantsmanship Center
CA	90017	H144	Chrysalis
CA	90018	G221	Movement of Spiritual Inner Awareness
CA	90019	S228	Raisin Consciousness
CA	90024	V117	Black Law Journal
CA	90025	S189	Los Angeles Men's Collective
CA	90025	V173	Free For All
CA	90025	V225	New Age Caucus
CA	90026	G294	T'ai Chi
CA	90028	H111	American Healing Association
CA	90028	L176	Homosexual Information Center
CA	90032	L189	Manas: Journal of Independent Inquiry
CA	90036	V200	Los Angeles Commission on Assaults Against Women
CA	90036	V287	Women Against Violence Against Women

CA	90042	G126	Brain/Mind Bulletin
CA	90042	E206	Leading Edge: A Bulletin of Social Transformation
CA	90057	E270	U.S.-China People's Friendship Association
CA	90069	L154	Direct Cinema Limited
CA	90075	H170	Holmes Center for Research in Holistic Healing
CA	90210	U273	Tree People
CA	90210	V110	Another Mother for Peace
CA	90210	G112	Arcana Workshops
CA	90211	H229	Seminars on Sexuality
CA	90272	H003	Center for Integral Medicine
CA	90277	G146	Consciousness Synthesis Clearing House
CA	90291	S167	Free Venice Beachhead
CA	90401	V007	Campaign for Economic Democracy
CA	90403	H184	Life-Force Cancer Project
CA	90403	G321	Women at the Helm: International Women's Sailing
CA	90406	E230	Organization for the Advancement of Space Industrialization
CA	90631	H180	International College of Applied Nutrition
CA	90701	H114	Association for Childbirth at Home International
CA	90733	V196	League for Ecological Democracy
CA	90733	L244	Southern California Open Network
CA	91011	E251	Robotics Age: Journal of Intelligent Machines
CA	91016	H202	National Health Federation
CA	91103	E237	Planetary Society
CA	91104	H030	Touch for Health Foundation
CA	91109	G291	Summit Lighthouse
CA	91206	G178	Healing Light Center
CA	91306	G310	Unity-in-Diversity Council
CA	91407	L267	Women's Referral Service
CA	91413	H108	American Academy of Husband-Coached Childbirth
CA	91507	G185	Inner-Space Interpreters Services
CA	91747	V256	Sanity Now!
CA	91803	E280	World Education Fellowship
CA	92003	E169	Genesa Foundation
CA	92024	H190	Massage and Bodywork
CA	92025	G270	Shanti Nilaya
CA	92037	G133	Center for Studies of the Person
CA	92038	L258	Western Behavioral Sciences Institute
CA	92048	G278	Society of Folk Harpers and Craftsmen
CA	92068	E147	Computer Information Exchange
CA	92101	G134	Center for Women's Studies and Services
CA	92103	H244	Womancare: A Feminist Women's Health Center
CA	92103	U138	Community Energy Action Network
CA	92107	H201	National Feminist Therapists Association
CA	92107	G209	Love Project
CA	92110	S005	Community Congress of San Diego
CA	92112	G284	Spiritual Friends
CA	92115	U245	San Diego Center for Appropriate Technology
CA	92117	U257	Solar Energy Digest
CA	93010	U170	Geothermal World Info Center
CA	93101	V180	Harvest Publications
CA	93102	L135	Center for the Study of Democratic Institutions
CA	93102	L158	Earthenergy Media
CA	93103	G132	Center for Esoteric Studies
CA	93105	G204	Life Understanding Foundation
CA	93111	S219	Older Women's Network
CA	93120	G108	Animal Town Cooperative Games
CA	93643	S221	Owner-Builder Publications
CA	93920	G159	Esalen Institute
CA	93920	G283	Spiritual Emergency Network
CA	94025	H029	Terrap: Network for Agoraphobics
CA	94025	U187	Intermediate Technology
CA	94025	G240	New Trust Network
CA	94025	G320	Windsurfer Magazine

CA	94025	E155	Dr. Dobb's Journal of Computer Calisthenics and Orthodontia
CA	94025	E233	People's Computer Company
CA	94062	E146	Computer Faire
CA	94064	U239	Redwood City Seed Company
CA	94086	E111	Aquarian Age: Monthly for Space and Equality
CA	94101	H018	Madness Network News
CA	94101	S014	Kerista Village
CA	94101	S181	Information Tree/San Francisco
CA	94101	U008	Committee for Nuclear Responsibility
CA	94101	V222	National Resistance Committee
CA	94101	L007	Committee of Small Magazine Editors and Publishers
CA	94101	G213	Magical Blend: A Magazine of Synergy
CA	94101	G230	New Age Mating
CA	94101	G275	Sluggo: Journal of Disturbing Clues
CA	94101	G296	Tayu Institute
CA	94102	H119	Bay Area Committee for Alternatives to Psychiatry
CA	94102	S120	Briarpatch Network
CA	94102	S220	Organize Training Center
CA	94102	S229	Regional Young Adult Project
CA	94102	U101	Abalone Alliance
CA	94102	V103	Agape Foundation: Fund for Nonviolent Social Change
CA	94102	G332	Zen Center of San Francisco
CA	94103	V005	California Newsreel
CA	94103	V015	Henry George School of Social Science
CA	94103	L163	Far West Laboratory
CA	94103	L206	National Diffusion Network
CA	94103	L248	Teachers' Centers Exchange
CA	94103	L262	Women's Educational Equity Communications Network
CA	94103	G003	Association for Humanistic Psychology
CA	94105	S245	Trust for Public Land
CA	94105	U015	Friends of the Earth
CA	94107	V207	Mother Jones
CA	94107	V246	Prisoners Union
CA	94107	L131	Canyon Cinema Cooperative
CA	94108	U251	Sierra Club
CA	94108	V205	Mexican American Legal Defense and Educational Fund
CA	94108	L115	Antioch University West
CA	94108	E187	Institute of Noetic Sciences
CA	94109	H226	San Francisco Young Adult Network
CA	94109	V259	Social Advocates for Youth
CA	94109	L222	Pacific Region Association of Alternative Schools
CA	94109	G239	New Realities: Magazine of Body, Mind and Spirit
CA	94109	E009	Hunger Project
CA	94109	E229	Open Systems
CA	94110	U108	Alternative Directions in Energy and Economics
CA	94110	V149	Civilian Congress
CA	94110	L236	San Francisco Bay Guardian
CA	94110	L264	Women's Information Exchange
CA	94110	G265	San Francisco Mime Troupe
CA	94110	E011	Institute for Food and Development Policy
CA	94114	H212	Nurses in Transition
CA	94114	V032	Planner's Network
CA	94114	V279	Vanguard Public Foundation
CA	94114	V288	Women Against Violence in Pornography and Media
CA	94114	G181	I Ching Sangha
CA	94114	G236	New Dimensions Radio and Tapes
CA	94114	E141	CommuniTree Group
CA	94117	H007	Coalition for the Medical Rights of Women
CA	94118	G101	Actualizations
CA	94119	G192	International Home Exchange Service
CA	94120	L166	Fine Print: A Review for the Arts of the Book
CA	94120	G017	New Games Foundation
CA	94121	E185	Institute for the Study of Conscious Evolution

CA	94122	L174	Holistic Life University
CA	94122	G117	Astro*Carto*Graphy
CA	94123	U018	Greenpeace Foundation
CA	94123	V116	Bay Area Lawyers for the Arts
CA	94123	L021	Humanistic Psychology Institute
CA	94123	L193	Media Alliance
CA	94123	G322	Women in the Wilderness
CA	94123	G323	Women's Sports Foundation
CA	94124	G256	Quadrinity Center
CA	94126	L181	International Society for General Semantics
CA	94126	G152	Damage Magazine: Not for Everybody
CA	94129	G282	Spirals: Bridging the Gap Between Science and Mysticism
CA	94131	H153	East West Academy of Healing Arts
CA	94131	U022	Planet Drum Foundation
CA	94131	L143	Common Ground
CA	94133	L139	City Lights Journal
CA	94133	L230	Public Media Center
CA	94140	S169	Gay Sunshine Press
CA	94140	U237	Project Jonah
CA	94140	V276	Union Women's Alliance to Gain Equality
CA	94140	L162	Educomics
CA	94301	V030	New Ways to Work
CA	94301	L170	Gifted Children Newsletter
CA	94301	G225	Nature Explorations
CA	94301	E177	InfoWorld: The Newspaper for the Microcomputing Community
CA	94305	V230	New Seed Press Feminist Collective
CA	94305	G004	Association for Transpersonal Psychology
CA	94306	U153	Ecology Action of the Midpeninsula
CA	94306	E113	Asia-Pacific Affairs Associates
CA	94501	U168	General Whale
CA	94516	G121	Black Bart Newsletter
CA	94538	S233	Share Foundation/Television Network
CA	94549	H224	Pyramid: Resource Sharing Network for Drug Abuse Prevention
CA	94558	G319	Willow: A Woman's Retreat
CA	94566	G127	California Association of Bicycle Organizations
CA	94574	G266	Sanatana Dharma Foundation
CA	94602	S188	Logical Connection: Skillsharing for Private Practitioners
CA	94605	S038	Urban Alternatives Group
CA	94606	S225	Plexus: San Francisco Bay Area Women's Newspaper
CA	94609	H118	Bay Area Coalition on Occupational Safety and Health
CA	94609	E234	People's Translation Service
CA	94610	H166	Holistic Health Practitioners' Association
CA	94612	S136	Community Economics
CA	94612	V198	Libertarian Review
CA	94612	L133	Center for Investigative Reporting
CA	94613	L191	Math Science Network
CA	94618	H173	Homeopathic Educational Services
CA	94618	G298	Textile Artists' Newsletter: Review of Fiber Arts
CA	94701	H165	Holistic Health Organizing Committee
CA	94701	S133	City Miner: Community/Personal Adventure/Aesthetics
CA	94701	U160	Farallones Institute: Integral Urban House
CA	94701	G013	Intimate Talk: Journal of Expression
CA	94701	G194	Jump Cut: A Review of Contemporary Cinema
CA	94701	E264	The Network: Starflight and Immortality
CA	94703	H169	Holistic Psychotherapy and Medical Group
CA	94703	H204	Network Against Psychiatric Assault
CA	94703	L008	Community Memory Project
CA	94703	G110	Aquarian Minyan
CA	94704	S171	Goodfellow Catalog of Wonderful Things
CA	94704	V138	Center for Research on Criminal Justice
CA	94704	V214	National Economic Development and Law Center
CA	94704	G269	Shambhala Booksellers
CA	94704	G331	Yoga Journal

CA	94704	E186	Institute for the Study of the Human Future
CA	94704	E260	Southeast Asia Resource Center
CA	94705	H183	Ken Dychtwald & Associates
CA	94705	S145	Cooperative and Communal Living Network
CA	94705	V194	Kapitalistate: Working Papers on the Capitalist State
CA	94706	S124	Carousel Press: Books for Parents
CA	94706	G155	Different Worlds: Magazine of Adventure Role-Playing Games
CA	94707	U119	Banyan Tree Books
CA	94708	H148	Committee to End Violence Against the Next Generation
CA	94708	L263	Women's History Research Center
CA	94709	H103	Acupressure School of Massage Therapy
CA	94709	L013	Feminist Writers' Guild
CA	94709	G145	Community for Religious Research and Education
CA	94709	G195	Jungian-Senoi Dreamwork Institute
CA	94709	G281	Sorting It Out: Support for Spiritual Leavetakers
CA	94709	G293	Synergic Power Institute
CA	94710	U150	Earth Lab Institute
CA	94710	L127	Book People
CA	94710	L195	Mix Recording Publications
CA	94720	L126	Berkeley Outreach Recreation Program
CA	94804	S110	Associated Cooperatives
CA	94902	G024	Spiritual Community Guide
CA	94902	G231	New Age Music Network
CA	94920	H002	Center for Attitudinal Healing
CA	94920	G167	Foundation for Inner Peace
CA	94922	S184	International Cooperative Community
CA	94924	U009	Commonweal
CA	94924	L239	Shelter Publications
CA	94930	G128	Camp Winnarainbow
CA	94937	H193	Medical Self-Care Magazine
CA	94941	H181	International Foundation for the Promotion of Homeopathy
CA	94941	H241	Wellness Associates
CA	94941	H243	Wholistic Health and Nutrition Institute
CA	94941	S149	Crafts Fair Guide
CA	94941	G027	Transformation Project
CA	94941	G315	Watercourse Ways
CA	94947	G021	Rites of Passage
CA	94948	S254	Wishing Well
CA	94956	U115	Applewood Journal
CA	94960	G028	Well Being: A Network for Spiritual Journeyors
CA	94965	S003	CoEvolution Quarterly
CA	94966	G257	Rare Earth: Exotic Properties for Sale
CA	95003	G118	Auroville Association
CA	95006	H228	Self Care Associates
CA	95030	S231	Santa Clara Valley Bicycle Association
CA	95060	S033	Riptide/University Services Agency
CA	95061	H221	Psychiatric Inmates' Rights Collective
CA	95061	U269	The Plan: Community Food Tree Nurseries
CA	95061	G175	Hanuman Foundation Tape Library
CA	95063	V168	Eschaton Foundation: Community Spirit Fund
CA	95063	G140	Children's Art Foundation
CA	95063	E248	Resource Center for Nonviolence
CA	95108	H200	National Council on Alternative Health Care Policy
CA	95222	G276	Sobek Expeditions: Outdoor Adventure Rivers Specialists
CA	95338	U151	Earthmind: Energy Research, Education and Books
CA	95401	U139	Community Network for Appropriate Technologies
CA	95422	G201	Laughing Man Institute
CA	95430	L168	Flower Films
CA	95436	V275	Tribal Sovereignty Program
CA	95436	E142	Community Computer
CA	95446	H129	California School of Herbal Studies
CA	95460	L125	Bear's Guide to Non-Traditional College Degrees
CA	95465	U161	Farallones Institute: Rural Center

CA	95468	G248	Oz Projects: Retreat in the Redwoods
CA	95481	G273	Sino-American Buddhist Association
CA	95521	U223	Northcoast Environmental Center
CA	95560	S239	Star Root: Fortnightly Newspaper
CA	95603	G317	West Art
CA	95616	S122	California Cooperative Federation
CA	95616	S123	California Institute for Rural Studies
CA	95616	V122	California Agrarian Action Project
CA	95623	E242	Purser's Magazine for Family Computers
CA	95694	S253	Winds of Change
CA	95694	U191	International Tree Crops Institute U.S.A.
CA	95694	L241	Sipapu: Newsletter for Librarians
CA	95804	G333	Zen Center of Sonoma Mountain
CA	95814	U229	Office of Appropriate Technology
CA	95814	U255	Solar Business Office
CA	95814	V124	California Tax Reform Association
CA	95841	L219	Northern California Open Network
CA	95959	H156	Flower Essence Society
CA	95959	G189	Institute for the Development of the Harmonious Human Being
CA	95969	L242	Small Press Review
CA	96067	L220	Northern California/Southern Oregon Resource Network

COLORADO

CO	80204	L004	Association for Experiential Education
CO	80206	L186	Learning Tools
CO	80206	G286	Sproing: Science Fiction and Fantasy
CO	80208	E129	Center for Teaching International Relations
CO	80215	E027	World Constitution and Parliament Association
CO	80217	U184	Infinite Energy
CO	80218	S153	Densmore Discoveries
CO	80218	U199	Mountain Bicyclists' Association
CO	80218	V255	Rocky Flats Nuclear Weapons Facilities Project
CO	80218	L031	Open Network
CO	80218	L153	Denver Free University
CO	80220	E105	After Thought: Research and Education About the Future
CO	80301	U128	Center for Environmental Problem Solving
CO	80302	S119	Boulder Women's Network
CO	80302	L194	MediaSense
CO	80302	G161	Essentia Films
CO	80302	G170	Front Range: Women in the Visual Arts
CO	80302	G223	Naropa Institute
CO	80302	E263	Teilhard Foundation
CO	80306	H175	Informed Homebirth
CO	80306	S106	American Homebrewers Association
CO	80306	S155	Dovetail Press: Design for the Owner-Involved Builder
CO	80306	S194	Mediaworks
CO	80306	L238	Shambhala Publications
CO	80306	G287	Sri Aurobindo's Action Center
CO	80401	H143	Choosing Healthy Options in Changing Environments
CO	80401	U258	Solar Energy Research Institute
CO	80422	G157	Dormant Brain Research and Development Laboratory
CO	80439	G312	University of the Wilderness
CO	80517	U107	Alternate Energy Institute
CO	80537	G012	Emissaries of Divine Light
CO	80537	G242	Omega Foundation
CO	80631	U256	Solar Energy Association of Northeast Colorado
CO	80901	V142	Center on Law and Pacifism
CO	80932	S224	Personal Freedom Network
CO	80934	G232	New Age Network of Colorado Springs
CO	81009	V158	Consumer Information Center
CO	81055	U158	Environmental Action Reprint Service
CO	81101	U246	San Luis Valley Solar Energy Association

CO	81211	**G306**	Trailhead Ventures
CO	81654	**U286**	Windstar Foundation: Educational, Research and Retreat Center

CONNECTICUT

CT	06064	**L211**	National Radio Club
CT	06106	**S141**	Connecticut Citizen Action Group
CT	06120	**S176**	Hartford Food System
CT	06260	**H177**	Integral Health Services
CT	06282	**H027**	Survival Foundation
CT	06410	**H235**	Tri-Self Clinic
CT	06443	**U261**	Solar Times: News of the Solar Energy Industry
CT	06460	**E241**	Promoting Enduring Peace
CT	06470	**G165**	Fine Woodworking
CT	06470	**G228**	New Age Government
CT	06483	**S121**	Butterbrooke Farm Seed Co-op
CT	06510	**V228**	New England Cooperative Training Institute
CT	06511	**H013**	Hospice Institute for Education Training and Research
CT	06511	**S142**	Consortium for Youth of South Central Connecticut
CT	06511	**E231**	Papier Mache Video Institute
CT	06515	**E124**	Center for Interdisciplinary Creativity
CT	06702	**U291**	World Association for Solid-Waste Transfer and Exchange
CT	06807	**G177**	Hartley Productions: Films for a New Age
CT	06830	**G247**	Outward Bound
CT	06880	**V109**	Animal Rights Network

DISTRICT OF COLUMBIA

DC	20001	**S202**	National Hook-up of Black Women
DC	20001	**U135**	Citizens' Energy Project
DC	20001	**V164**	Displaced Homemakers Network
DC	20001	**L026**	National Federation of Community Broadcasters
DC	20001	**L035**	Student Press Law Center
DC	20002	**U177**	Health and Energy Learning Project
DC	20002	**U206**	National Intervenors
DC	20002	**U228**	Ocean Education Project
DC	20002	**V011**	Committee Against Registration and the Draft
DC	20002	**V026**	National Committee Against Repressive Legislation
DC	20002	**V035**	SANE
DC	20002	**V125**	Campaign for Political Rights
DC	20002	**V131**	Center for Defense Information
DC	20002	**V150**	Coalition to End Grand Jury Abuse
DC	20002	**V166**	Engage/Social Action
DC	20002	**V179**	Halt: Americans for Legal Reform
DC	20002	**E123**	Center for Development Policy
DC	20002	**E125**	Center for International Policy
DC	20002	**E137**	Coalition for a New Foreign and Military Policy
DC	20002	**E165**	Friends of the Filipino People
DC	20002	**E199**	Interreligious Taskforce on U.S. Food Policy
DC	20002	**E239**	Population Action Council
DC	20002	**E275**	Washington Office on Latin America
DC	20003	**U111**	American Rivers Conservation Council
DC	20003	**U159**	Environmental Policy Institute
DC	20003	**U203**	National Association of Railroad Passengers
DC	20003	**V220**	National Organization for the Reform of Marijuana Laws
DC	20003	**V247**	Privacy Journal
DC	20003	**V267**	Tax Reform Research Group
DC	20003	**L113**	American Historical Association
DC	20003	**L121**	Associated Information Managers
DC	20003	**L231**	Quest: A Feminist Quarterly
DC	20003	**E179**	Information Industry Association
DC	20004	**H009**	Consumer Coalition for Health
DC	20004	**S021**	National Family Farm Coalition
DC	20004	**S251**	Washington Blade: Gay Newspaper of the Nation's Capital

DC	20004	U205	National Coalition Against the Misuse of Pesticides
DC	20004	V193	Joint Center for Political Studies
DC	20004	G316	Watershed Foundation: Poetry Recordings
DC	20005	H196	National Alliance for the Mentally Ill
DC	20005	S015	National Association of Housing Cooperatives
DC	20005	S023	National Neighbors
DC	20005	S230	Rural American Women
DC	20005	S250	Washington Area Bicyclist Association
DC	20005	U188	International Biomass Institute
DC	20005	U235	Potomac Alliance
DC	20005	V133	Center for New National Security
DC	20005	V165	ERAmerica
DC	20005	V197	Legal Services Corporation
DC	20005	V231	New World Alliance
DC	20005	V290	Women's Equity Action League
DC	20005	L148	Council for Educational Development and Research
DC	20005	G279	Sojourners: Christian Renewal Community
DC	20005	G309	United States Parachute Association
DC	20005	E108	American Public Health Association
DC	20006	H023	National Women's Health Network
DC	20006	S022	National Hispanic Coalition for Better Housing
DC	20006	S029	Neighborhood Information Sharing Exchange
DC	20006	U164	Food Research and Action Center
DC	20006	U284	Wilderness Society
DC	20006	V101	Abortion Fund
DC	20006	V211	National Committee for Responsive Philanthropy
DC	20006	V213	National Council of La Raza
DC	20006	V293	Women's Work Force Network
DC	20006	L027	National Society for Internships and Experiential Education
DC	20006	L103	Adult Education Association of the United States of America
DC	20006	E013	National Peace Academy Campaign
DC	20006	E219	New Era Technologies
DC	20007	H230	Society for Occupational and Environmental Health
DC	20007	S126	Center for Community Change
DC	20007	U113	Animal Welfare Institute
DC	20007	G330	Yes Educational Society
DC	20008	L265	Women's Institute for Freedom of the Press
DC	20008	E168	Futures Network
DC	20008	E287	World Peace Tax Fund
DC	20009	H005	Center for Science in the Public Interest
DC	20009	S011	Institute for Local Self-Reliance
DC	20009	S016	National Association of Neighborhoods
DC	20009	S026	National Self-Help Resource Center
DC	20009	S137	Community Jobs
DC	20009	S240	Support Center: Management Assistance to Non-Profit Groups
DC	20009	S248	Vegetarian Society of D.C.
DC	20009	U112	American Wind Energy Association
DC	20009	V010	Commission for the Advancement of Public Interest Organizations
DC	20009	V023	Movement for Economic Justice
DC	20009	V112	Association for Self-Management
DC	20009	V143	Children's Legal Rights Information and Training Program
DC	20009	V148	Citizens Party
DC	20009	V171	Feminist Alliance Against Rape
DC	20009	V212	National Consumer Cooperative Bank
DC	20009	V236	Off Our Backs: A Women's News Journal
DC	20009	V283	Washington Monthly
DC	20009	L140	Clearinghouse of Free-Standing Educational Institutions
DC	20009	L152	D.C. Gazette
DC	20009	L192	Media Access Project
DC	20009	L200	National Association for the Education of Young Children
DC	20009	L208	National Home Study Council
DC	20009	L228	Project on the Status and Education of Women
DC	20009	L257	Washington Community Video Center

DC	20009	G124	Boomerang Newsletter
DC	20009	G216	Menorah: Sparks of Jewish Renewal
DC	20009	E010	Institute for Alternative Futures
DC	20009	E183	Institute for Policy Studies
DC	20009	E215	National Network in Solidarity with the Nicaraguan People
DC	20010	E008	Human Rights Internet
DC	20010	E213	Middle East Research and Information Project
DC	20011	G314	Washington Buddhist Vihara
DC	20012	H171	Home-Oriented Maternity Experience
DC	20013	U010	Critical Mass Energy Project
DC	20013	U026	Task Force Against Nuclear Pollution
DC	20014	V177	Government Institutes
DC	20014	E028	World Future Society
DC	20015	U238	Rachel Carson Trust Fund for the Living Environment
DC	20016	G141	Churches Center for Theology and Public Policy
DC	20018	V223	Network: A Catholic Social Justice Lobby
DC	20024	G106	American Spiritual Healing Association
DC	20036	H021	National Alliance for Optional Parenthood
DC	20036	H022	National Citizens Coalition for Nursing Home Reform
DC	20036	H141	Children's Defense Fund
DC	20036	H197	National Coalition Against Domestic Violence
DC	20036	H222	Public Citizen Health Research Group
DC	20036	H246	Women and Health Roundtable
DC	20036	S002	Civic Action Institute
DC	20036	S018	National Center for Citizen Involvement
DC	20036	S024	National Network of Runaway and Youth Services
DC	20036	S034	Rural America
DC	20036	S127	Center for Community Economic Development
DC	20036	S144	Cooperative League of the USA
DC	20036	S146	Council on Foundations
DC	20036	S204	National Trust for Historic Preservation
DC	20036	U011	Environmental Action Foundation
DC	20036	U012	Environmental Action Inc.
DC	20036	U021	Nuclear Information and Resource Service
DC	20036	U105	Alliance for Environmental Education
DC	20036	U110	American Forestry Association
DC	20036	U141	Conservation Foundation
DC	20036	U181	Human Environment Center
DC	20036	U241	Resources for the Future
DC	20036	U260	Solar Lobby
DC	20036	U280	Waste Watch
DC	20036	U292	World Information Service on Energy
DC	20036	U293	Zero Population Growth
DC	20036	V004	Barter Project
DC	20036	V128	Center for Auto Safety
DC	20036	V141	Center for the Study of Responsive Law
DC	20036	V154	Common Cause
DC	20036	V163	Disability Rights Center
DC	20036	V169	Exploratory Project for Economic Alternatives
DC	20036	V174	Freedom of Information Clearinghouse
DC	20036	V204	Mental Health Law Project
DC	20036	V221	National Prison Project
DC	20036	V242	People's Business Commission
DC	20036	V281	Veterans Education Project
DC	20036	V291	Women's Legal Defense Fund
DC	20036	V297	Youth Project
DC	20036	L114	American Society for Training and Development
DC	20036	L147	Consumer Educational Resource Network
DC	20036	L201	National Center for Educational Brokering
DC	20036	L256	Urban Scientific & Educational Research
DC	20036	E025	War Control Planners
DC	20036	E106	American Association for the Advancement of Science
DC	20036	E112	Arms Control Association

DC	20036	E197	International Voluntary Services
DC	20036	E255	Science News
DC	20036	E268	U.S. Association for The Club of Rome
DC	20036	E284	World Hunger Education Service
DC	20036	E292	Worldwatch Institute
DC	20037	U182	Humane Society of the United States
DC	20037	L112	American Association of University Women
DC	20044	V108	Anarchist Association of the Americas
DC	20044	V152	Committee for Action Research on the Intelligence Community
DC	20044	V218	National Organization for Women
DC	20044	E244	Radio Amateur Satellite Corporation (AMSAT)
DC	20045	L252	Today News Service
DC	20208	L161	Educational Resources Information Center
DC	20515	E004	Congressional Clearinghouse on the Future
DC	20525	L025	National Center for Service-Learning
DC	20550	V170	Federal Laboratory Consortium
DC	20585	U154	Energy Consumer

DELAWARE

| DE | 19807 | S152 | Delaware Friends of Bikecology |
| DE | 19899 | V159 | Crafts Report: Marketing and Management for Crafts Professionals |

FLORIDA

FL	32303	H028	Tallahassee Feminist Women's Health Center
FL	32304	S191	Magnolia: Southeastern Confederation for Cooperation
FL	32304	S238	Spectrum: Cooperative Newspaper for the Tallahassee Community
FL	32304	U126	Catfish Alliance
FL	32604	L122	Association for Humanistic Education
FL	32789	G334	Zygon: Journal of Religion and Science
FL	33145	H147	Club SeneX
FL	33176	H205	New Age Wellness Center
FL	33577	H227	Sarasota School of Natural Healing Arts
FL	33578	G171	Fund for Advancement of Camping
FL	33595	G142	Clown College
FL	33612	H149	Community Network Development Project
FL	33682	E160	Family Tree Network
FL	33704	G300	The Churchman
FL	33710	V151	Come Unity: An Alternative Independent Journal
FL	33710	G235	New Atlantean Research Society

GEORGIA

GA	30032	S236	Southern Neighborhoods
GA	30050	G102	Alternatives Resource Center
GA	30305	U025	Southern Unity Network/Renewable Energy Project
GA	30305	U169	Georgia Solar Coalition
GA	30306	S150	Creative Loafing in Atlanta
GA	30310	V013	Emergency Land Fund
GA	30324	L124	Atlanta Network: Teaching, Learning and Interest Sharing

HAWAII

HI	96708	G215	Maui Zendo
HI	96753	S132	Circle of Light/Findhorn
HI	96816	H157	Hawaii Health Network
HI	96817	V241	Peace Project
HI	96822	L165	Ferity: Hawaii's Feminist Newsjournal
HI	96822	G154	Diamond Sangha Center: Zen Buddhist Society
HI	96848	E157	East-West Communication Institute

IOWA

IA	50316	E116	Astronomical League
IA	50322	S017	National Catholic Rural Life Conference
IA	50677	S156	Draft Horse Journal
IA	52240	H146	Clearing Community and School of the Healing Arts
IA	52240	S115	Blooming Prairie Warehouse
IA	52240	L188	Link Learning Network
IA	52342	H159	Health Link

ILLINOIS

IL	60010	V140	Center for a Woman's Own Name
IL	60131	H016	La Leche League International
IL	60187	G304	Theosophical Society of America
IL	60201	E130	Center for U.F.O. Studies
IL	60204	L185	Learning Exchange
IL	60509	H006	Cesarean Connection
IL	60521	E245	Religion and Ethics Network
IL	60602	H231	Society for the Protection of the Unborn Through Nutrition
IL	60603	S129	Chicago Association of Neighborhood Development Organizations
IL	60604	H199	National Committee for Prevention of Child Abuse
IL	60604	V016	Illinois Women's Agenda
IL	60604	V250	Public Eye: A Journal Concerning Repression in America
IL	60604	V271	The Spokeswoman: Feminist News Digest
IL	60605	U007	Citizens for a Better Environment
IL	60605	V206	Midwest Committee for Military Counseling
IL	60605	L134	Center for New Schools
IL	60606	U005	Center for Neighborhood Technology
IL	60607	S027	National Training and Information Center
IL	60607	S172	Greater Illinois People's Cooperative
IL	60611	H014	Human Ecology Action League
IL	60611	H219	People's Doctor: Medical Newsletter for Consumers
IL	60611	S130	Chicago Men's Gathering Newsletter
IL	60611	V217	National Network of Grantmakers
IL	60611	G234	New Art Examiner: Independent Voice of the Visual Arts
IL	60614	H152	Doctors Ought to Care
IL	60614	S199	Midwest Academy
IL	60614	S203	National Runaway Switchboard
IL	60614	U006	Citizen/Labor Energy Coalition
IL	60614	L171	Guild Books and Periodicals
IL	60614	G139	Chicago Mural Group
IL	60620	V282	Vietnam Veterans Against the War
IL	60625	H145	Cinema Medica
IL	60637	V121	Bulletin of the Atomic Scientists
IL	60637	G166	Focusing Institute
IL	60640	L110	Alternative Schools Network
IL	60651	G246	Outside: Magazine of the Great Outdoors
IL	60657	S207	New Age Chicago
IL	60657	V028	New American Movement
IL	60657	L182	Kartemquin Films
IL	60820	S195	Men's Program Unit
IL	61455	E201	Journal of Developing Areas
IL	61820	U236	Prairie Alliance
IL	62948	U183	Illinois South Project

INDIANA

IN	46208	S180	Indianapolis Mayor's Bicycle Task Force
IN	46515	E226	Office on Global Education
IN	46516	U285	Wind Power Digest: Access to Wind Energy Information
IN	46590	H123	Birthing Monthly Newsletter
IN	46802	E006	Friends of the Third World
IN	47374	E272	University Peace Studies Network

IN	47401	S116	Bloomington Free Ryder: Biweekly Newspaper
IN	47401	S205	Neighborhood Organization Research Group
IN	47401	G262	Rudrananda Ashram
IN	47402	G292	Survival Cards
IN	47714	U277	Valley Watch

KANSAS

KS	66044	V132	Center for National Security Studies
KS	66103	H104	Advocates for Freedom in Mental Health
KS	66502	L017	Free University Network
KS	67117	E005	Consortium on Peace Research, Education, and Development
KS	67901	S249	Village of Anything Is Possible

KENTUCKY

KY	40208	E258	Society for General Systems Research
KY	40408	L016	Folk-School Association of America
KY	40506	G245	Outdoor Education for the Handicapped Project
KY	40507	U114	Appalachia Science in the Public Interest
KY	40601	L006	Coalition for Alternatives in Postsecondary Education
KY	41858	L118	Appalshop Films

LOUISIANA

LA	70113	V003	Association of Community Organizations for Reform Now
LA	70113	V018	Institute for Social Justice
LA	70130	L217	New Orleans Video Access Center

MASSACHUSETTS

MA	01002	V136	Center for Popular Economics
MA	01002	L169	Food for Thought Books
MA	01002	L180	Institute for Wholistic Education
MA	01002	G105	American Institute of Buddhist Studies
MA	01002	G274	Sirius Community
MA	01003	U240	Resource Center Network
MA	01003	U283	Western Massachusetts Solar Energy Association
MA	01003	V009	Citizens Involvement Training Project
MA	01004	U287	Women and Life on Earth
MA	01004	V183	Human Economy Center
MA	01005	G186	Insight Meditation Society
MA	01007	U243	Safe Energy Resources
MA	01040	H215	On Our Own Network
MA	01059	U175	Hands-On: Guidebook to Appropriate Technology in Massachusetts
MA	01060	S006	Community Self-Reliance
MA	01060	G214	Many Hands: Guide to Holistic Health and Awareness
MA	01061	G147	Contact Quarterly: A Vehicle for Moving Ideas
MA	01096	U282	Western Massachusetts Resource Network
MA	01230	G136	Center of the Light
MA	01249	V292	Women's Party for Survival
MA	01266	G206	Lindisfarne Association
MA	01302	U224	Northeast Appropriate Technology Network
MA	01339	E120	Bulletin of Concerned Asian Scholars
MA	01340	U148	Documentary Guild
MA	01367	G261	Rowe Conference Center
MA	01376	U017	Green Mountain Post Films
MA	01431	H233	Spring Hill: Community, Retreat and Counseling Center
MA	01701	S200	Mothers and Others
MA	01742	V238	One Less Bomb Committee
MA	01810	L250	The Network: Educational Service and Research
MA	01890	E018	Participation Systems Incorporated
MA	02072	L223	Packard Manse Media Project
MA	02108	H026	Parent Support-Group Project
MA	02108	S168	Gay Community News

MA	02108	S177	Home Front: For Young Pregnant Women and their Families
MA	02108	G109	Appalachian Mountain Club
MA	02108	G125	Boston Visionary Cell
MA	02110	L272	Zipporah Films
MA	02111	L003	Anthropology Resource Center
MA	02112	V037	Vocations for Social Change
MA	02115	S118	Boston Urban Gardens
MA	02115	V189	Institute for Social Justice/Eastern Office
MA	02115	L225	Pioneer Productions
MA	02116	H150	Coping with the Overall Pregnancy/Parenting Experience
MA	02116	H164	Hippocrates Health Institute
MA	02116	H189	Massachusetts Coalition of Battered Women Service Groups
MA	02116	S182	Institute for Community Economics
MA	02116	S223	Parents Anonymous
MA	02116	S247	Urban Planning Aid
MA	02116	S256	Women's Information, Referral and Education Service
MA	02116	V167	Equal Times: Boston's Newspaper for Working Women
MA	02116	V203	Massachusetts Public Interest Research Group
MA	02116	V234	Nine to Five (9 to 5)
MA	02116	V289	Women's Enterprises of Boston
MA	02116	L020	Holt Associates
MA	02116	G183	Infinite Odyssey: Wilderness Adventures
MA	02116	E016	Oxfam America
MA	02116	E291	WorldPaper: The Global Community Newspaper
MA	02117	H232	Soundiscoveries
MA	02118	S117	Boston Building Materials Cooperative
MA	02127	V191	International Seminars in Training for Nonviolent Action
MA	02130	G290	Sufi Order for the Esoteric Arts & Sciences
MA	02131	S158	Family Connection
MA	02134	S208	New Community Project
MA	02134	V258	Sister Courage: Radical Feminist Newspaper
MA	02134	G006	Cambridge Zen Center
MA	02134	G229	New Age Magazine
MA	02138	H167	Holistic Health Referrals
MA	02138	S032	Project for Kibbutz Studies
MA	02138	V118	Boston INFACT
MA	02138	V184	Indochina Curriculum Group
MA	02138	V278	Union of Concerned Scientists
MA	02138	L005	Center on Technology and Society
MA	02138	L107	Alternative America: Directory of 5000 Groups and Organizations
MA	02138	L151	Cultural Survival
MA	02138	G023	Sphinx and Sword of Love Bookstore
MA	02138	G258	ReVision: A Journal of Knowledge and Consciousness
MA	02138	G305	Three-H-O Foundation (3HO)
MA	02138	G327	World Monastic Council
MA	02139	H247	Working on Wife Abuse
MA	02139	S183	Interest File
MA	02139	S209	New England Food Cooperative Organization
MA	02139	U120	Boston Clamshell Coalition
MA	02139	U137	Coalition for Direct Action at Seabrook
MA	02139	U248	Science for the People
MA	02139	V001	Alliance Against Sexual Coercion
MA	02139	V006	Cambridge Documentary Films
MA	02139	V257	Second Wave: Magazine of the New Feminism
MA	02139	V260	Sojourner: Northeast Women's Journal of News and the Arts
MA	02139	V294	Working Papers for a New Society
MA	02139	G007	Center for Leisure Guidance
MA	02139	G182	Illuminations
MA	02139	E128	Center for Policy Alternatives
MA	02140	H191	Maternal and Child Health Center
MA	02140	V029	New England Human Rights Network
MA	02140	V031	Peacework
MA	02142	E148	Computer Music Journal

MA	02143	H214	Omega: Program of Grief Assistance
MA	02143	V229	New England Free Press
MA	02143	V244	Popular Economics Press
MA	02143	V252	Radical America
MA	02144	H024	New Directions in Psychology
MA	02144	H127	Boston Women's Health Book Collective
MA	02145	U276	Urban Solar Energy Association
MA	02146	H010	East West Journal
MA	02146	H126	Boston Self-Help
MA	02146	H217	Parents Without Partners
MA	02146	S140	Community Service Restitution
MA	02146	G151	Creative Yoga Studio
MA	02146	G277	Society for Human and Spiritual Understanding
MA	02154	H138	Cesareans/Support Education and Concern (C/SEC)
MA	02155	G029	Women Outdoors
MA	02158	H121	Being Thin
MA	02158	S040	Warmlines: A Parent Network and Resource Center
MA	02159	H125	Boston Center for Psychosynthesis
MA	02160	L102	Action for Children's Television
MA	02161	H218	Pavillion Newsletter: Advocacy for the Disabled
MA	02165	L002	Another America Networking
MA	02165	E173	Human Systems Network
MA	02166	H178	Interface Foundation
MA	02167	V119	Boston Study Group
MA	02167	G272	Siddha Yoga Dham Boston
MA	02172	V243	Physicians for Social Responsibility
MA	02172	L270	Workshop for Learning Things
MA	02173	H124	Boston Area Childbirth Education
MA	02173	E026	Women's International Network
MA	02174	G318	Whole Life Times: Northeast Journal for a Positive Future
MA	02178	H139	Child Care Information Exchange
MA	02178	E285	World Institute for Advanced Phenomenological Research
MA	02192	H140	Children in Hospitals
MA	02208	S125	Carrier Pigeon/Alyson Publications
MA	02210	E166	Future Shack
MA	02215	H172	Homebirth
MA	02215	L179	Institute for Responsive Education
MA	02238	L141	Coalition to End Animal Suffering in Experiments
MA	02238	G156	Dimensional Mind Approach
MA	02536	U212	New Alchemy Institute
MA	02601	H134	Cape Cod Health Care Coalition

MARYLAND

MD	20034	G009	Cooperative Communities of America
MD	20742	L145	Community Information Center
MD	20742	E211	Maryland Alliance for Space Colonization
MD	20810	E240	Prometheus Society
MD	20822	E274	Volunteers in Technical Assistance
MD	20850	U142	Conservation and Renewable Energy Inquiry and Referral Service
MD	20852	S226	Project SHARE: Improving the Management of Human Services
MD	21044	L009	Council for the Advancement of Experiential Learning
MD	21044	L205	National Committee for Citizens in Education
MD	21057	E259	Sourcebook Project
MD	21201	V202	Maryland Food Committee
MD	21202	S178	Home Ownership Development Program
MD	21203	G202	League of American Wheelmen
MD	21204	H187	Macrobiotic: A Guide for Natural Living
MD	21207	G197	Kite Lines
MD	21212	G188	Institute for Consciousness and Music
MD	21218	U131	Chesapeake Energy Alliance
MD	21218	L018	Great Atlantic Radio Conspiracy
MD	21218	L108	Alternative Press Center

| MD | 21218 | **L268** | Women: Journal of Liberation |
| MD | 21771 | **V115** | Back to the People: New Age Goods |

MAINE

ME	03906	**S114**	Birdsong Farm
ME	04011	**U145**	Cornerstones: Energy Efficient Housebuilding
ME	04011	**L172**	Gulf of Maine Bookstore
ME	04011	**G123**	Blackberry Books
ME	04046	**L235**	Salt Magazine
ME	04071	**H210**	Northern Pines: A Wholistic Health Retreat
ME	04086	**S193**	Maine Times
ME	04105	**U195**	Maine Audubon Society
ME	04112	**S192**	Maine Bicycle Coalition
ME	04347	**U189**	International Federation of Organic Agricultural Movements
ME	04347	**U196**	Maine Organic Farmers and Gardeners Association
ME	04469	**S157**	F.A.R.O.G. Forum: Journal Bilingue
ME	04472	**V182**	Homemakers Organized for More Employment
ME	04472	**G176**	Hardscrabble Hill: Residential Retreat Center for Women
ME	04616	**G325**	WoodenBoat Magazine
ME	04912	**G237**	New Life Foundation for Holistic Health and Research
ME	04938	**L237**	Sandy River School
ME	04953	**S012**	Institute for Non-Violent Education, Research, and Training
ME	04955	**L247**	Stony Hills: New England Alternative Press Review
ME	04962	**S161**	Federation of Co-ops
ME	04967	**V102**	Accion/Micro Enterprise Development Corporation
ME	04970	**E022**	Transnational Network for Appropriate/Alternative Technologies

MICHIGAN

MI	48069	**G251**	PhenomeNEWS
MI	48077	**L019**	Guild Communications Network
MI	48103	**H208**	Newtrition Outreach: Whole Foods Information
MI	48104	**S198**	Michigan Federation of Food Cooperatives
MI	48104	**L203**	National Chicano Research Network
MI	48104	**L204**	National Coalition of Alternative Community Schools
MI	48104	**G271**	Siddha Yoga Dham Ann Arbor
MI	48105	**V106**	American Town Meetings Project
MI	48107	**S031**	North American Students of Cooperation
MI	48202	**L132**	Center for Black Studies
MI	48202	**E127**	Center for Peace and Conflict Studies
MI	48210	**G308**	Unified States of Awareness Communications
MI	48226	**V269**	Team for Justice
MI	48439	**L218**	New Pages Press
MI	48502	**U130**	Charles Stewart Mott Foundation
MI	48640	**U244**	Saginaw Valley Nuclear Study Group
MI	48901	**U194**	League of Michigan Bicyclists
MI	49046	**S131**	Circle Pines Center

MINNESOTA

MN	55097	**S010**	Food Learning Center
MN	55102	**H236**	Turtle Island Holistic Health Community
MN	55112	**L199**	National Association for Gifted Children
MN	55403	**L216**	New Front Films
MN	55404	**U226**	Northern Sun Alliance
MN	55407	**S143**	Consumer Coop Press Service
MN	55407	**L010**	Education Exploration Center
MN	55408	**G260**	Rowan Tree: Publishers of The Unicorn
MN	55414	**S104**	Alliance of Warehouse Federations
MN	55414	**S154**	Distributing Alliance of the Northcountry Cooperatives
MN	55414	**V235**	North Country M.N.S. Organizing Collective
MN	55414	**G254**	Protestant Committee on Urban Ministry
MN	55420	**H179**	International Childbirth Education Association

MN	55426	E276	Women in World Areas Studies
MN	55455	U275	Underground Space Center
MN	55808	G218	Minnesota Zen Meditation Center
MN	55957	U002	Anvil Press
MN	55987	V038	We-Know-Now Free Trade Exchange
MN	56082	G138	Cherry Creek: A Theatre Company
MN	56349	U167	General Assembly to Stop the Powerline
MN	56353	U001	Alternative Sources of Energy

MISSOURI

MO	63103	V188	Institute for Peace and Justice
MO	63105	G288	St. Louis Unit of Service of World Goodwill
MO	63108	L155	Double Helix: Community Media
MO	63117	G311	Universal Great Brotherhood
MO	63132	V172	Focus/Midwest
MO	63764	H020	NAPSAC: Safe Alternatives in Childbirth
MO	64030	E289	World Space Federation
MO	64052	G285	Spiritual Frontiers Fellowship
MO	64106	S128	Center for Neighborhood Development
MO	64110	L136	Change in Liberal Education Network
MO	64111	V249	Project Equality
MO	64133	S101	Acres, U.S.A: A Voice for Eco-Agriculture
MO	64673	U250	Seed Savers Exchange
MO	65102	H234	Statewide Comprehensive Health Education Coalition
MO	65626	S222	Ozark Area Community Congress
MO	65638	U217	New Life Farm
MO	65760	S009	Federation of Egalitarian Communities

MISSISSIPPI

| MS | 39211 | U197 | Mississippi Solar Coalition |
| MS | 39762 | S237 | Southern Rural Development Center |

MONTANA

MT	59601	U225	Northern Rockies Action Group
MT	59601	G164	Feathered Pipe Ranch
MT	59701	U019	National Center for Appropriate Technology
MT	59801	U288	Women and Technology Project

NEBRASKA

NB	68407	U264	Stock Seed Farms
NB	68503	G115	Association for Unity, Research, and Awareness
NB	68739	U253	Small Farm Energy Project

NORTH CAROLINA

NC	27314	G210	Love: A Journal
NC	27403	E145	Compute Magazine
NC	27510	H136	Center for Early Adolescence
NC	27514	V019	Institute for Southern Studies
NC	27514	L164	Feminary: A Feminist Journal for the South
NC	27514	G026	The Sun: A Magazine of Ideas
NC	27603	U222	North Carolina Coalition for Renewable Energy Resources
NC	27702	S213	North Carolina Anvil
NC	27702	E103	Africa News Service
NC	27705	H209	North Carolina Occupational Safety and Health Project
NC	27705	G019	Prison Ashram Project
NC	27870	H135	Carolina Brown Lung Association
NC	28215	G160	Essene Light Center
NC	28608	L117	Appalachian Journal
NC	28705	S227	RFD: Country Journal for Gay Men Everywhere
NC	28722	G180	Human Dimensions Institute and Center

| NC | 28739 | **L196** | Mother Earth News |
| NC | 28909 | **S235** | Southern Appalachian Resource Catalog |

NORTH DAKOTA

| ND | 58601 | **U146** | Dakota Resource Council |

NEW HAMPSHIRE

NH	03048	**G002**	Another Place
NH	03301	**H025**	New Hampshire Feminist Health Center
NH	03301	**U290**	Wood 'n Energy
NH	03450	**U027**	Total Environmental Action
NH	03458	**E121**	Byte: The Small Systems Journal
NH	03755	**S174**	Hanover Consumer Cooperative Society

NEW JERSEY

NJ	07017	**E007**	Global Education Associates
NJ	07018	**S036**	Shelterforce Collective
NJ	07042	**U242**	Safe Energy Alternatives Alliance
NJ	07052	**V157**	Consumer Education Research Group
NJ	07060	**L032**	Organizational Development Network
NJ	07102	**L012**	Electronic Information Exchange System
NJ	07105	**S108**	Architecture 2001
NJ	07109	**H186**	Macrobiotic Health Information Center of New Jersey
NJ	07401	**U132**	Citizens Energy Council
NJ	07461	**G302**	The Loving Brotherhood
NJ	07661	**E256**	Shalom Network
NJ	07675	**V226**	New Directions for Women
NJ	07727	**L028**	New Jersey Unschoolers
NJ	07740	**L253**	Uni-Ed Associates
NJ	07840	**E254**	Science Fiction Writers of America
NJ	07930	**E119**	Aviation/Space Writers Association
NJ	07960	**E151**	Creative Computing
NJ	08028	**G200**	Kronos: Journal of Interdisciplinary Synthesis
NJ	08540	**G005**	Bed & Breakfast League
NJ	08625	**V186**	Inmate Legal Association
NJ	08816	**G299**	The Awakeners
NJ	08903	**V274**	Transaction Periodicals Consortium

NEW MEXICO

NM	87103	**H019**	Mothering Magazine
NM	87106	**L034**	Southwest Research and Information Center
NM	87108	**V027**	National Indian Youth Council
NM	87196	**S008**	Cooperative Directory Association
NM	87197	**V153**	Committee on Native American Struggles
NM	87501	**H031**	Women's Health Services
NM	87501	**U029**	Wind-Light Workshop
NM	87501	**U218**	New Mexico Solar Energy Association
NM	87501	**L024**	National Association of Legal Services to Alternative Schools
NM	87501	**L175**	Home Study Exchange
NM	87501	**G011**	Dying Project
NM	87501	**E163**	First Earth Battalion Foundation
NM	87564	**G014**	Lama Foundation
NM	88301	**G295**	Taeria Foundation Spiritual Community

NEVADA

| NV | 89421 | **V224** | Nevada Elected Women's Network |
| NV | 89513 | **V145** | Citizen Alert |

NEW YORK

| NY | 10001 | **S001** | Citizens Committee for New York City |

NY	10001	L150	Creative Women's Collective
NY	10001	G010	Dromenon: Journal of New Ways of Being
NY	10003	H160	Health Policy Council
NY	10003	V105	Alternatives to Violence Project
NY	10003	V162	Democratic Socialist Organizing Committee
NY	10003	V178	Greensboro Justice Fund
NY	10003	V187	Institute for Labor Education and Research
NY	10003	V216	National Lawyers Guild
NY	10003	V277	Union for Radical Political Economics
NY	10003	L213	Network for Learning
NY	10003	G020	Public Action Coalition on Toys
NY	10003	G153	Dialogue House Library
NY	10003	G184	Inner Paths: Eastern and Western Spiritual Thought
NY	10003	G252	Poetry Project
NY	10003	E131	Center for War/Peace Studies
NY	10003	E170	Global Perspectives in Education
NY	10003	E269	U.S. Committee for Justice to Latin American Political Prisoners
NY	10004	V185	Inform, Incorporated
NY	10005	V039	Women U.S.A.
NY	10007	H012	Health Policy Advisory Council
NY	10007	S201	Mutual Aid Project
NY	10007	U024	Scientists' Institute for Public Information
NY	10010	H154	East/West Center for Holistic Health
NY	10010	U106	Alternate Currents/SolarCity
NY	10010	U157	Energy Task Force
NY	10010	V146	Citizen Soldier
NY	10010	V232	New World Review
NY	10010	L109	Alternative Press Syndicate
NY	10011	H168	Holistic Health Review
NY	10011	S111	Basement Alliance
NY	10011	U201	Musicians United for Safe Energy
NY	10011	V012	Council on Economic Priorities
NY	10011	V215	National Gay Task Force
NY	10011	L022	Intercommunity Center for Justice and Peace
NY	10011	L023	Liberation News Service
NY	10011	L226	Primary/Secondary Peace Education Network
NY	10011	G249	Parabola: Myth and the Quest for Meaning
NY	10011	E014	North American Congress on Latin America
NY	10011	E190	International Center for Integrative Studies
NY	10011	E261	Southern Africa Committee
NY	10012	H004	Center for Medical Consumers and Health Care Information
NY	10012	H120	Beauty Without Cruelty
NY	10012	L106	Alternate Media Center
NY	10012	G131	Center for Arts Information
NY	10012	G267	Segue Foundation: Publishers of Books and Magazines
NY	10012	E002	Catholic Peace Fellowship
NY	10012	E189	Interlink Press Service
NY	10012	E212	Middle East Peace Project
NY	10013	V296	Youth International Party
NY	10013	L156	Downtown Community Television Center
NY	10013	L198	Museum of Holography
NY	10014	H225	Renaissance House
NY	10014	V270	The Militant: Socialist Newsweekly
NY	10014	L014	Feminist Writers' Guild/New York
NY	10014	L190	Martha Stuart Communications
NY	10014	L254	Unifilm
NY	10014	E188	Intercontinental Press/Inprecor
NY	10016	H008	Committee for Abortion Rights and Against Sterilization Abuse
NY	10016	S165	Film-Makers Cooperative
NY	10016	S246	United Neighborhood Centers of America
NY	10016	U013	Environmental Defense Fund
NY	10016	V114	Association on American Indian Affairs
NY	10016	L210	National Organizations Advisory Council for Children

NY	10016	**E172**	Home Video
NY	10016	**E178**	Information Center on Children's Cultures
NY	10016	**E224**	Nuestro Magazine
NY	10017	**H238**	Vegetarian Times
NY	10017	**H240**	Well-Being Magazine
NY	10017	**U020**	Natural Resources Defense Council
NY	10017	**U143**	Consumer Action Now
NY	10017	**U267**	Synerjy: Directory of Energy Alternatives
NY	10017	**V040**	Women's Action Alliance
NY	10017	**L197**	Ms. Magazine
NY	10017	**L249**	Telecommunications Cooperative Network
NY	10017	**G119**	Baha'i International Community
NY	10017	**G149**	Council on International Educational Exchange
NY	10017	**G211**	Lucis Trust
NY	10017	**G326**	World Goodwill
NY	10017	**E019**	Planetary Citizens
NY	10017	**E024**	United Nations Economic & Social Council
NY	10017	**E107**	American Field Service
NY	10017	**E110**	Analog: Science Fiction/Science Fact
NY	10017	**E171**	Helsinki Watch
NY	10017	**E184**	Institute for World Order
NY	10017	**E198**	International Women's Tribune Center
NY	10017	**E218**	Network to Educate for World Security
NY	10017	**E222**	Next: A Look into the Future
NY	10017	**E225**	Office of Tibet
NY	10017	**E257**	Sierra Club International Earthcare Center
NY	10017	**E265**	Triangles: Network of Light
NY	10017	**E281**	World Environment Center
NY	10017	**E286**	World Peace News
NY	10018	**V113**	Association of Libertarian Feminists
NY	10018	**G022**	Sing Out! The Folk Song Magazine
NY	10019	**H220**	Planned Parenthood
NY	10019	**U166**	Fund for Animals
NY	10019	**V107**	Amnesty International
NY	10019	**L101**	Academy for Educational Development
NY	10019	**G205**	Lilith: The Jewish Women's Magazine
NY	10019	**E253**	Science Digest
NY	10021	**H015**	Huxley Institute for Biosocial Research
NY	10021	**U165**	Friends of the Parks
NY	10021	**V295**	Working Women's Institute
NY	10021	**G113**	Association for Moral Education
NY	10021	**G190**	Institute for the New Age
NY	10021	**G328**	World Union for Progressive Judaism
NY	10022	**S244**	Transportation Alternatives
NY	10022	**U204**	National Audubon Society
NY	10022	**V126**	Catalyst National Network
NY	10022	**V208**	National Abortion Federation
NY	10022	**L120**	Aspen Institute for Humanistic Studies
NY	10022	**G172**	Games
NY	10022	**E228**	Omni Magazine
NY	10023	**V134**	Center for Nonprofit Organization
NY	10023	**L149**	Council on Interracial Books for Children
NY	10023	**L159**	Educational Film Library Association
NY	10023	**G179**	High Times
NY	10024	**H142**	Children's Holistic Institute for Life Development
NY	10025	**V190**	Institute for Social Service Alternatives
NY	10025	**E279**	Women's International Resource Exchange Service
NY	10027	**V020**	Interfaith Center on Corporate Responsibility
NY	10027	**V033**	Project Work
NY	10027	**V127**	Caucus for a New Political Science
NY	10027	**L240**	Signs: Journal of Women and Culture in Society
NY	10027	**E109**	Americans for Middle East Understanding, Inc.
NY	10028	**V251**	Radical Alliance of Social Service Workers

NY	10030	E003	Commission to Study the Organization of Peace
NY	10036	S019	National Commission on Resources for Youth, Inc.
NY	10036	S025	National Self-Help Clearinghouse
NY	10036	S030	New York Urban Coalition
NY	10036	U219	New Times Films
NY	10038	V233	New York Public Interest Research Group
NY	10038	E102	Africa Fund
NY	10111	U207	National Recycling Coalition
NY	10573	H211	Nurse Healers/Professional Associates Cooperative
NY	10580	G297	Temple of Understanding
NY	10580	G313	Wainwright House
NY	10583	H132	Cancer Counseling Center
NY	10591	V266	Tarrytown Group
NY	10960	V192	Jewish Peace Fellowship
NY	10960	L137	Children's Creative Response to Conflict Program
NY	10960	E161	Fellowship of Reconciliation
NY	10962	E115	Association for the Study of Man-Environment Relations
NY	10974	H242	Wellness Institute
NY	11030	H101	Academy of Orthomolecular Psychiatry
NY	11211	S020	National Congress of Neighborhood Women
NY	11215	L146	Conditions: Writing by Women
NY	11215	L271	Youth Liberation Press
NY	11217	S218	Old House Journal
NY	11218	E195	International Kirlian Research
NY	11223	U136	Clippings in Ecotopia
NY	11223	L167	Fireworks: Feminist Journal of the John Dewey High School
NY	11361	H116	Association for the Preservation of Anti-Psychiatric Artifacts
NY	11367	U129	Center for the Biology of Natural Systems
NY	11435	G025	Sri Chinmoy Centre
NY	11510	L214	Networking Group
NY	11530	U014	Food Monitor
NY	11553	L184	Learning Connection
NY	11576	L142	College Media Journal
NY	11713	V155	Conscience and Military Tax Campaign
NY	11731	E267	Twenty-first Century Media
NY	11737	E288	World Press Review
NY	11743	E001	Association for World Education
NY	11786	H185	Long Island Childbirth Alternatives
NY	12125	G018	Omega Institute for Holistic Studies
NY	12147	S013	Institute on Man and Science
NY	12180	U144	Continued Action on Transportation in the U.S.
NY	12201	L173	Hagborn: A Radical Feminist News Journal
NY	12202	U193	Lamoureux Foundation: Home Energy Workshops
NY	12222	V139	Center for Women in Government
NY	12401	E104	Afro-Asian Center
NY	12457	G015	Matagiri Sri Aurobindo Center
NY	12498	L259	White Buffalo Multimedia
NY	12498	G196	Karma Triyana Dharmachakra
NY	12521	H223	Pumpkin Hollow Farm
NY	12571	U134	Citizens for Safe Power Transmission
NY	12571	U180	Hudson Valley Green
NY	12589	H195	Mid-Hudson Area Maternity Alternatives
NY	12754	U162	Farming Uncle: For Natural People and Mother Nature Lovers
NY	12779	G263	SYDA Foundation
NY	12810	S255	Woman's Place
NY	12866	L234	Sagamore Institute
NY	13146	S134	Cleareye Natural Foods
NY	13202	H102	Action Coalition for Retirement with Dignity
NY	13203	H110	American Conference of Therapeutic Selfhelp/Selfhealth
NY	13203	V265	Syracuse Peace Council
NY	13210	H176	Institute for Family Research and Education
NY	13217	S212	New York State Coalition for Local Self Reliance
NY	13217	U163	Feminist Resources on Energy and Ecology

NY	13224	U216	New Environment Association
NY	13683	V104	Akwesasne Notes: For Native and Natural Peoples
NY	13901	V199	Looking Left
NY	14214	U252	Sierra Club Radioactive Waste Campaign
NY	14222	S113	Bikeways in Buffalo
NY	14222	G150	Creative Education Foundation
NY	14223	S187	Living Free: Personal Journal of Self-Liberation
NY	14226	G001	American Humanist Association
NY	14722	G137	Chautauqua Institution
NY	14801	S179	Homesteaders News
NY	14850	S139	Community Self-Reliance Center
NY	14850	V002	Alternative Fund Federal Credit Union
NY	14850	L187	Learning Web
NY	14850	G168	Foundation of Light

OHIO

OH	43140	S214	North Oak Street Chowder and Marching Society
OH	43210	L202	National Center for Research in Vocational Education
OH	43214	S039	Urban Alternatives Group/Columbus
OH	43215	L030	Ohio Coalition for Educational Alternatives Now
OH	43220	E144	CompuServe
OH	43229	H137	Center for Humane Options in the Childbirth Experience
OH	43603	U211	Needmor Fund
OH	44017	V240	Organization Resource Associates
OH	44060	G268	Shadybrook House
OH	44114	V144	Citizen Action
OH	44114	V237	Ohio Public Interest Campaign
OH	44114	L011	Education for Freedom of Choice in Ohio
OH	44115	V025	National Association of Office Workers
OH	44115	L269	WomenSpace Women's Center
OH	44120	G241	North American Network of Women Runners
OH	44304	E126	Center for Peace Studies
OH	44306	E207	Lighter than Air Society
OH	45201	L036	Union for Experimenting Colleges and Universities
OH	45202	U233	Personal Mobility Committee
OH	45387	S007	Community Service
OH	45419	E208	Magic Circle: The Native American Indian
OH	45429	L207	National Federation of Local Cable Programmers
OH	45662	U221	North American Mycological Association
OH	45810	E252	Saharan Peoples Support Committee

OKLAHOMA

| OK | 73007 | E150 | Coop's Satellite Digest |
| OK | 73118 | U133 | Citizens United for Responsible Energy |

OREGON

OR	97034	E200	Johnson-Lenz
OR	97116	L177	Hydra Book Company
OR	97201	E136	Claustrophobia: Life Extension
OR	97204	H198	National College of Naturopathic Medicine
OR	97204	L029	Northwest Regional Educational Laboratory
OR	97207	S028	Natural Helping Networks Project
OR	97210	U023	Rain Community Resource Center
OR	97214	H188	Marion County Community Mental Health Center
OR	97214	S196	Men's Resource Center
OR	97215	H001	Alternative Medical Association
OR	97223	U152	Earthtone: For People Tuned to the Earth
OR	97228	U172	Greenpeace Examiner
OR	97326	U266	Summit Coalition for Alternatives to Pesticides
OR	97330	G016	New Age Information Service
OR	97330	G144	Committee for the Game

OR	97370	S197	Message Post
OR	97401	U274	Trojan Decommissioning Alliance
OR	97401	L221	Northwest Women in Educational Administration
OR	97402	H182	Journal of the Nutritional Academy
OR	97402	S252	Whiteaker Community Council
OR	97402	U116	Aprovecho Institute
OR	97403	U208	Nationwide Forest Planning Clearinghouse
OR	97403	U232	Pacific Northwest Research Center
OR	97403	E192	International Council for Computers in Education
OR	97405	S159	Family of New Age Networkers
OR	97424	U200	Mudsharks Co-op
OR	97440	S206	Network Exchange News Service
OR	97440	U004	Cascadian Regional Library
OR	97440	U227	Northwest Coalition for Alternatives to Pesticides
OR	97440	U270	The Sproutletter: Sprouts, Raw Foods, and Nutrition
OR	97440	L266	Women's Press
OR	97497	G324	WomenSpirit Journal
OR	97520	U263	Southern Oregon Living Lightly Association
OR	97520	V036	SkillsBank
OR	97526	H105	Aletheia Psycho-Physical Foundation
OR	97526	U262	Southern Oregon Citizens Against Toxic Sprays

PENNSYLVANIA

PA	15003	G135	Center for the History of American Needlework
PA	15221	V021	Know Feminist Publishers
PA	16001	G158	Encounter Four: Adventure Course for Youth in Trouble
PA	16037	L157	Earthbooks Lending Library/Allegheny Branch
PA	16503	G250	Pax Center
PA	17102	U271	Three Mile Island Alert
PA	17201	G107	Anima: An Experiential Journal
PA	17402	S035	School of Living: Publishers of Green Revolution
PA	17604	S186	Lancaster Independent Press
PA	17979	G198	Kripalu Yoga Center
PA	18049	U140	Compost Science/Land Utilization
PA	18049	L233	Rodale Press
PA	18078	L246	Stay Smart
PA	18411	U254	Society for Animal Rights
PA	18853	G191	International Church of Ageless Wisdom
PA	19034	S112	Bicyclist Federation of Pennsylvania
PA	19072	V161	Custody Action for Lesbian Mothers
PA	19096	G187	Insight Training Seminars
PA	19101	U003	Bicycle Network
PA	19102	H107	Alliance for the Liberation of Mental Patients
PA	19102	V017	Indian Rights Association
PA	19102	V175	Friends Peace Committee
PA	19102	V210	National Action/Research on the Military Industrial Complex
PA	19102	G169	Friends Journal
PA	19103	L160	Educational Futures
PA	19104	H011	Gray Panthers
PA	19104	V022	Mobilization for Survival
PA	19104	E283	World Game of R. Buckminster Fuller
PA	19107	L209	National News Bureau
PA	19107	L255	United Ministries in Education
PA	19107	E278	Women's International League for Peace and Freedom
PA	19108	L104	Alliance for Citizen Education
PA	19108	L224	Parents Union for Public Schools
PA	19123	L232	Research for Better Schools
PA	19134	V253	Recon Publications
PA	19142	V219	National Organization for an American Revolution
PA	19143	V024	Movement for a New Society
PA	19143	G253	Progressive Utilization Theory Universal (Prout)
PA	19143	E015	North American Nonviolence Training Network

PA	19144	**G111**	Aquarian Research Foundation
PA	19144	**G307**	Travelers' Directory
PA	19146	**V008**	Central Committee for Conscientious Objectors
PA	19464	**S164**	Fellowship House Farm
PA	19547	**U122**	Bullfrog Films

RHODE ISLAND

RI	02864	**G255**	Providence Zen Center
RI	02886	**H207**	New Beginnings Birth Center
RI	02901	**E156**	Earthrise: New Myths and Paradigms for Tomorrow
RI	02906	**V160**	Cultural Correspondence
RI	02906	**L229**	Providence Learning Connection
RI	02908	**L215**	New England Training Center for Community Organizers

SOUTH CAROLINA

| SC | 29201 | **V261** | South Carolina Committee Against Hunger |
| SC | 29503 | **V262** | South Carolina Libertarian Party |

SOUTH DAKOTA

| SD | 57701 | **G122** | Black Hills Alliance |

TENNESSEE

TN	37203	**S105**	American Association for State and Local History
TN	37203	**U155**	Energy People
TN	37204	**S102**	Agricultural Marketing Project
TN	37212	**V263**	Southern Coalition on Jails and Prisons
TN	37212	**L245**	Southern Progressive Periodicals Directory
TN	37916	**E250**	Review of International Broadcasting
TN	38111	**G233**	New Age Resource Center
TN	38383	**G301**	The Farm
TN	38483	**E238**	Plenty

TEXAS

TX	75080	**L015**	FocusCreativity
TX	75090	**V135**	Center for Nonviolent Persuasion
TX	75117	**H174**	Hot Springs Information Network
TX	75230	**E246**	Rescue Communication Network
TX	75551	**U209**	Natural Food Associates
TX	75704	**L128**	Both Sides Now
TX	75711	**G226**	New Age Awareness Center
TX	76102	**H133**	Cancer Counseling and Research Center
TX	76541	**U190**	International Solar Energy Society
TX	77006	**G222**	Muktananda Meditation Center
TX	77025	**H113**	American Holistic Nurses' Association
TX	77590	**L144**	Community Education Cooperative
TX	78616	**H206**	New Age in Austin
TX	78701	**S242**	Texas Observer: A Journal of Free Voices
TX	78701	**L033**	Southwest Educational Development Laboratory
TX	78704	**U268**	Texas Solar Energy Coalition
TX	78731	**V248**	Productivity Group
TX	78751	**H117**	Austin Lay Midwives Association
TX	79901	**H192**	Maternity Center

VIRGINIA

VA	22030	**V130**	Center for Conflict Resolution
VA	22031	**U186**	Institute for Ecological Policies
VA	22043	**V286**	Woman Activist: Action Bulletin for Women's Rights
VA	22090	**L183**	Latino Institute
VA	22091	**H109**	American Alliance for Health and Physical Education
VA	22101	**L111**	Amateur Radio Research and Development

VA	22102	E021	The Source
VA	22116	V284	Washington Spectator & Between the Lines
VA	22161	L212	National Technical Information Service
VA	22180	H158	Health Activation Network
VA	22180	H203	National Hospice Organization
VA	22201	U147	Design Alternatives
VA	22201	E143	Community Computers
VA	22209	U192	Izaak Walton League of America
VA	22209	U210	Nature Conservancy
VA	22209	G238	New Options for a Vital United States (NOVUS)
VA	22209	E282	World Federalists Association
VA	22210	E216	National Space Institute
VA	22213	V268	Taxation With Representation
VA	22314	H106	Alliance for Perinatal Research and Services
VA	22601	V034	Renewal Newsletter: New Values, New Politics
VA	22844	G103	Alternatives: Tools for Holistic Living
VA	22938	G220	Monroe Institute of Applied Sciences
VA	23093	S004	Communities: Journal of Cooperative Living
VA	23451	G114	Association for Research and Enlightenment

VERMONT

VT	05255	S147	Country Journal
VT	05262	E243	Radical Perspectives Network
VT	05301	U123	By Hand and Foot: Tools Dependent on Human Energy
VT	05301	U213	New England Coalition on Nuclear Pollution
VT	05301	U215	New England Solar Energy Association
VT	05301	U289	Women in Solar Energy
VT	05346	E159	Experiment in International Living
VT	05363	U178	Herb Quarterly
VT	05401	H163	Herbal Education Center
VT	05401	U202	National Association for Gardening
VT	05401	V176	Give and Take Bartering Center
VT	05401	L138	Church Street Center for Community Education
VT	05402	U214	New England Regional Energy Project
VT	05476	G264	Samisdat
VT	05602	U279	Vermont Yankee Decommissioning Alliance
VT	05602	V280	Vermont Alliance
VT	05674	S258	Yestermorrow: Design/Builder School

WASHINGTON

WA	98101	S138	Community Produce
WA	98102	V111	Armistice/Live Without Trident
WA	98104	V195	King City Senior Barter Bank
WA	98104	G203	Life Systems Educational Foundation
WA	98105	U173	Greenpeace Seattle
WA	98107	H122	Birth and Life Bookstore
WA	98111	H017	Lesbian Mothers National Defense Fund
WA	98112	V272	Toolbox Training and Skills-sharing Collective
WA	98119	S190	Love Family
WA	98122	S216	Northwest Provender Alliance
WA	98223	U272	Tilth: Biological Agriculture in the Northwest
WA	98227	V254	Robert's Think Tank
WA	98267	U198	Modern Energy & Technology Alternatives
WA	98305	U230	Olympic Peninsula Citizens against Toxic Spray
WA	98408	G174	Guild of American Luthiers
WA	98502	H239	Washington State Midwifery Council
WA	98507	G148	Cosmic Awareness Communications
WA	98507	G208	Lost Music Network
WA	98650	S215	Northwest Organic Herb Cooperative
WA	98844	S107	Antahkarana Circle
WA	98844	U016	Friends of the Trees
WA	98926	S037	Small Towns Institute

WA	99008	U149	Earth Cyclers
WA	99201	S217	Northwest Regional Foundation
WA	99209	G120	Bear Tribe Medicine Society
WA	99220	L178	Information for People
WA	99362	U028	Washington Small Farm Resources Network
WA	99403	U185	Inland Regional Council

WISCONSIN

WI	53202	S109	Arts Services Associates
WI	53203	H128	Bread & Roses Women's Health Center
WI	53203	H155	Endometriosis Association
WI	53562	G207	Lorian Association: Serving the Spirit of Wholeness
WI	53594	S148	Countryside: The Magazine for Serious Homesteaders
WI	53701	G219	Modern Haiku
WI	53703	V129	Center for Conflict Resolution
WI	53703	V137	Center for Public Representation
WI	53703	V181	Home Equity Conversion Project
WI	53703	V285	Wisconsin Women's Network
WI	53703	L251	The Progressive
WI	53703	G289	Stash
WI	53715	H161	Health Writers
WI	53715	S185	Intra-Community Cooperative
WI	53715	U127	Center for Community Technology
WI	53715	G212	M. Gentle Men for Gender Justice
WI	54115	G143	Coming Changes Newsletter
WI	54413	S257	Wool Gathering
WI	54601	H112	American Holistic Medical Association
WI	54701	E247	Research Utilization Network
WI	54880	S135	Common Health Warehouse

WEST VIRGINIA

WV	25325	L116	Appalachia Educational Laboratory
WV	26505	S162	Federation of Ohio River Cooperatives
WV	27276	L001	Alternatives in Education

WYOMING

WY	82520	U179	High Country News: Natural Resources of the Rockies
WY	82520	G224	National Outdoor Leadership School
WY	82801	V245	Powder River Basin Resource Council

_____ CANADA _____

BRITISH COLUMBIA

V0E 1X0	U121	British Columbia Energy Coalition
V0G 1B0	S243	The Smallholder: Ideas and Information for Country People
V0G 2J0	S210	New Seeds Information Service
V4V 1X5	H131	Canadian Holistic Healing Association
V5T 1A9	S160	Fed-Up Coop
V5T 3H7	L261	Women in Focus: Film Production and Distribution
V6A 1G3	E020	Satellite Video Exchange Society
V6J 1M5	U249	Sea Shepherd Conservation Society
V6K 1N7	E174	Humanity Foundation
V6K 1P8	U174	Greenpeace/Vancouver
V6K 3G7	H194	Mental Patients Association
V6R 4G5	V239	Open Road
V6R 4G7	G173	Great Expeditions: Real Travellers and Explorers

MANITOBA

| R3M 0R7 | S175 | Harmony Community |

ONTARIO

K0K 1J0	**U176**	Harrowsmith Magazine/Canada
K0K 1Z0	**S151**	Dandelion Community Co-op
K1L 8B9	**G130**	Canadian Sport Parachuting Association
K1N 8V3	**G303**	Theatre-Action
K1P 5H3	**H237**	Vanier Institute of the Family
K1P 6H8	**L227**	Process: Networking Forum for Citizen Participation
K1R 5K5	**G217**	Metamorphoses: Development in Canada
K1R 6G8	**E236**	Planetary Association for Clean Energy
K1S 5B4	**U125**	Canadian Renewable Energy News
K1Y 1E5	**H130**	Canadian Coordinating Council on Deafness
K1Y 4J3	**G244**	Ottawa Psychic Study Centre
K7H 3C6	**G163**	Family Pastimes
K9J 7B8	**U109**	Alternatives: Journal of Friends of the Earth, Canada
L0S 1J0	**S234**	Society of Ontario Nut Growers
L6H 2L1	**E122**	Center for Creative Studies
L6J 1B8	**V156**	Constructive Citizen Participation
M4E 2R5	**G243**	Ontario Zen Center
M4G 4C3	**E221**	News from Guatemala
M4P 2H4	**G199**	Kripalu Yoga Fellowship/Toronto
M4T 1M9	**V209**	National Action Committee on the Status of Women
M5C 2B1	**G008**	Chimo: The Holistic Magazine for Our Times
M5R 1V3	**L119**	Arton's Publishing: Fuse Magazine
M5R 2G3	**L130**	Canadian Information Sharing Service
M5R 2G5	**H213**	Nutritional and Preventive Medical Clinic
M5R 2S1	**U234**	Pollution Probe Foundation
M5S 1A1	**E012**	International Network for Social Network Analysis
M5S 1X7	**U220**	Non Nuclear Network
M5S 2C3	**U156**	Energy Probe
M5S 2S8	**L123**	Ateed Centre
M5S 2T1	**S173**	Grindstone Island Centre
M5V 1W2	**G116**	Association of National Non-Profit Artists' Centers
M5W 1X9	**H216**	Ontario Patients' Self-Help Association
M6H 4E1	**V273**	Toronto Association for Peace
M6S 4T3	**H245**	Women Healthsharing
N0A 1J0	**L129**	Canadian Alliance of Home Schoolers
N2L 3G1	**U281**	Waterloo Public Interest Research Group
P3E 2R8	**G129**	Canada Quilts
P3E 4S7	**U265**	Sudbury 2001

PRINCE EDWARD ISLAND

C1A 4P3	**E227**	Omega: Global Networking

QUEBEC

G1R 4S2	**G259**	Roues Libres: Association Cycliste
H2E 2Z7	**U278**	Velo Quebec
H2T 2W1	**E135**	Centre Monchanin
H3X 3T4	**U124**	Canadian Coalition for Nuclear Responsibility

SASKATCHEWAN

S7K 3N9	**U247**	Saskatoon Environmental Society

——————————————————— OTHER COUNTRIES ———————————————————

AUSTRALIA	E117	Australian Willing Workers on Organic Farms
AUSTRALIA	E154	Down to Earth Association
AUSTRIA	E164	Friedrichshof
AUSTRIA	E176	Info Alternativ

BELGIUM	E023	Union of International Associations
BELGIUM	E175	IOC/MAB
BELGIUM	E191	International Communes Network
BELGIUM	E209	Maison du Nouvel Age
COSTA RICA	E132	Center of Telecommunications for the Third World
DENMARK	E202	Kokov
DOMINICA	E232	Partnership for Productivity
ENGLAND	H162	Health for the New Age
ENGLAND	S232	Sealand: The Cheap Land Catalogue
ENGLAND	L243	Society of Scribes and Illuminators
ENGLAND	G280	Soluna: Creative Healing and Self-Exploration
ENGLAND	E134	Centre Link
ENGLAND	E140	Communes Network
ENGLAND	E167	Future Studies Centre
ENGLAND	E194	International Journal of General Systems
ENGLAND	E220	New Humanity Journal
ENGLAND	E223	Nucleus Network
ENGLAND	E249	Resurgence: Of Small Nations, Small Communities, & Human Spirit
ENGLAND	E262	Teilhard Centre for the Future of Man
ENGLAND	E266	Turning Point Newsletter/England
FRANCE	E114	Association Eveil de la Conscience Planetaire
FRANCE	E118	Autrement
FRANCE	E138	Coevolution
FRANCE	E139	Collectiv MAD/Media Alternative Developpement
FRANCE	E181	Institut Rural d'Information
FRANCE	E193	International Herald Tribune
FRANCE	E235	Phebus: Integrating Wholes and Parts
FRANCE	E271	Universite Verte
INDIA	E290	World Union
JAPAN	E182	Institute for Information Society
NETHERLANDS	E152	De Kleine Aarde (The Little Earth)
NETHERLANDS	E203	Kosmos Centre
NEW ZEALAND	E133	Centerpoint Community
NEW ZEALAND	E214	Mushroom: A Magazine for Living in New Zealand
SCOTLAND	E162	Findhorn Foundation
SCOTLAND	E205	Laurieston Hall
SWEDEN	E149	Comunidad
SWITZERLAND	E158	Evolution
SWITZERLAND	E180	Innovation et Reseaux pour le Developpement
SWITZERLAND	E196	International Union for Conservation of Nature and Resources
SWITZERLAND	E277	Women's International Information & Communication Service (ISIS)
WEST GERMANY	E153	Die Gruenen (The Green Alliance)
WEST GERMANY	E210	Mandala Verlag
WEST GERMANY	E217	Netswerk Selbsthilfe
WEST GERMANY	E273	Verein Lebensdorf

Keyword Guide

A.T.	S003	CoEvolution Quarterly.
A.T.	S111	Basement Alliance
A.T.	U001	Alternative Sources of Energy
A.T.	U004	Cascadian Regional Library
A.T.	U005	Center for Neighborhood Technology
A.T.	U019	National Center for Appropriate Technology
A.T.	U023	Rain Community Resource Center
A.T.	U025	Southern Unity Network/Renewable Energy Project
A.T.	U029	Wind-Light Workshop
A.T.	U112	American Wind Energy Association
A.T.	U115	Applewood Journal
A.T.	U116	Aprovecho Institute
A.T.	U123	By Hand and Foot: Tools Dependent on Human Energy
A.T.	U127	Center for Community Technology
A.T.	U139	Community Network for Appropriate Technologies
A.T.	U150	Earth Lab Institute
A.T.	U160	Farallones Institute: Integral Urban House
A.T.	U161	Farallones Institute: Rural Center
A.T.	U175	Hands-On: Guidebook to Appropriate Technology
A.T.	U187	Intermediate Technology
A.T.	U197	Mississippi Solar Coalition
A.T.	U212	New Alchemy Institute
A.T.	U217	New Life Farm
A.T.	U224	Northeast Appropriate Technology Network
A.T.	U229	Office of Appropriate Technology
A.T.	U231	Ozark Institute
A.T.	U245	San Diego Center for Appropriate Technology
A.T.	U265	Sudbury 2001
A.T.	U283	Western Massachusetts Solar Energy Association
A.T.	U285	Wind Power Digest: Access to Wind Energy Information
A.T.	U286	Windstar Foundation: Educational, Research and Retreat Center
A.T.	U287	Women and Life on Earth
A.T.	U288	Women and Technology Project
A.T.	L005	Center on Technology and Society
A.T.	E022	Transnational Network for Appropriate/Alternative Technologies
A.T.	E227	Omega: Global Networking
A.T.	E238	Plenty
A.T.	E274	Volunteers in Technical Assistance
ACADEMIC	S032	Project for Kibbutz Studies
ACADEMIC	U129	Center for the Biology of Natural Systems
ACADEMIC	V121	Bulletin of the Atomic Scientists
ACADEMIC	V193	Joint Center for Political Studies
ACADEMIC	V274	Transaction Periodicals Consortium
ACADEMIC	V277	Union for Radical Political Economics
ACADEMIC	L003	Anthropology Resource Center
ACADEMIC	L112	American Association of University Women
ACADEMIC	L120	Aspen Institute for Humanistic Studies
ACADEMIC	L132	Center for Black Studies
ACADEMIC	L136	Change in Liberal Education Network
ACADEMIC	L151	Cultural Survival
ACADEMIC	L181	International Society for General Semantics
ACADEMIC	L191	Math Science Network
ACADEMIC	L203	National Chicano Research Network
ACADEMIC	L206	National Diffusion Network
ACADEMIC	L228	Project on the Status and Education of Women
ACADEMIC	E012	International Network for Social Network Analysis
ACADEMIC	E106	American Association for the Advancement of Science
ACADEMIC	E120	Bulletin of Concerned Asian Scholars

ACADEMIC	E124	Center for Interdisciplinary Creativity
ACADEMIC	E126	Center for Peace Studies
ACADEMIC	E194	International Journal of General Systems
ACADEMIC	E258	Society for General Systems Research
ACADEMIC	E285	World Institute for Advanced Phenomenological Research
ACID RAIN	U281	Waterloo Public Interest Research Group
AFRICA	V005	California Newsreel
AFRICA	E102	Africa Fund
AFRICA	E103	Africa News Service
AFRICA	E104	Afro-Asian Center
AFRICA	E252	Saharan Peoples Support Committee
AFRICA	E261	Southern Africa Committee
AGENT ORANGE	V146	Citizen Soldier
AGENT ORANGE	V282	Vietnam Veterans Against the War
AGING	H011	Gray Panthers
AGING	H022	National Citizens Coalition for Nursing Home Reform
AGING	H102	Action Coalition for Retirement with Dignity
AGING	H147	Club SeneX
AGING	H183	Ken Dychtwald & Associates
AGING	S201	Mutual Aid Project
AGING	S219	Older Women's Network
AGING	V181	Home Equity Conversion Project
AGING	V195	King City Senior Barter Bank
AGING	G001	American Humanist Association
AGING	E136	Claustrophobia: Life Extension
AGORAPHOBIA	H029	Terrap: Network for Agoraphobics
AGRICULTURE	S035	School of Living: Publishers of Green Revolution
AGRICULTURE	S101	Acres, U.S.A: A Voice for Eco-Agriculture
AGRICULTURE	S102	Agricultural Marketing Project
AGRICULTURE	S147	Country Journal
AGRICULTURE	U001	Alternative Sources of Energy
AGRICULTURE	U005	Center for Neighborhood Technology
AGRICULTURE	U146	Dakota Resource Council
AGRICULTURE	U149	Earth Cyclers
AGRICULTURE	U188	International Biomass Institute
AGRICULTURE	U189	International Federation of Organic Agricultural Movements
AGRICULTURE	U212	New Alchemy Institute
AGRICULTURE	U231	Ozark Institute
AGRICULTURE	U239	Redwood City Seed Company
AGRICULTURE	U272	Tilth: Biological Agriculture in the Northwest
AGRICULTURE	V122	California Agrarian Action Project
AGRICULTURE	L034	Southwest Research and Information Center
AGRICULTURE	L216	New Front Films
ALLERGY	H014	Human Ecology Action League
AMNESTY	V107	Amnesty International
ANARCHIST	V108	Anarchist Association of the Americas
ANARCHIST	V239	Open Road
ANIMAL RIGHTS	U113	Animal Welfare Institute
ANIMAL RIGHTS	U166	Fund for Animals
ANIMAL RIGHTS	U182	Humane Society of the United States
ANIMAL RIGHTS	U204	National Audubon Society
ANIMAL RIGHTS	U254	Society for Animal Rights
ANIMAL RIGHTS	V109	Animal Rights Network

ANIMAL RIGHTS	L141	Coalition to End Animal Suffering in Experiments
ANIMAL RIGHTS	E196	International Union for Conservation of Nature and Resources
ANOMALIES	E259	Sourcebook Project
ANTHROPOLOGY	L003	Anthropology Resource Center
ANTHROPOLOGY	L151	Cultural Survival
ANTHROPOLOGY	G021	Rites of Passage
APPALACHIA	S235	Southern Appalachian Resource Catalog
APPALACHIA	U114	Appalachia Science in the Public Interest
APPALACHIA	L116	Appalachia Educational Laboratory
APPALACHIA	L117	Appalachian Journal
APPALACHIA	L118	Appalshop Films
ARCHITECTURE	S108	Architecture 2001
ARCHITECTURE	S221	Owner-Builder Publications
ARCHITECTURE	S258	Yestermorrow: Design/Builder School
ARCHITECTURE	U027	Total Environmental Action
ARCHITECTURE	U117	Arcosanti
ARCHITECTURE	U160	Farallones Institute: Integral Urban House
ARCHITECTURE	L160	Educational Futures
ARCHITECTURE	L239	Shelter Publications
ARCHITECTURE	E283	World Game of R. Buckminster Fuller
ARTS	H144	Chrysalis
ARTS	S109	Arts Services Associates
ARTS	S133	City Miner: Community/Personal Adventure/Aesthetics
ARTS	S149	Crafts Fair Guide
ARTS	S171	Goodfellow Catalog of Wonderful Things
ARTS	S213	North Carolina Anvil
ARTS	U201	Musicians United for Safe Energy
ARTS	V116	Bay Area Lawyers for the Arts
ARTS	V172	Focus/Midwest
ARTS	V201	Making It Legal: Primer for Craftmaker, Artist and Writer
ARTS	V213	National Council of La Raza
ARTS	V257	Second Wave: Magazine of the New Feminism
ARTS	V260	Sojourner: Northeast Women's Journal of News and the Arts
ARTS	L018	Great Atlantic Radio Conspiracy
ARTS	L150	Creative Women's Collective
ARTS	L166	Fine Print: A Review for the Arts of the Book
ARTS	L195	Mix Recording Publications
ARTS	L198	Museum of Holography
ARTS	G022	Sing Out! The Folk Song Magazine
ARTS	G025	Sri Chinmoy Centre
ARTS	G107	Anima: An Experiential Journal
ARTS	G116	Association of National Non-Profit Artists' Centers
ARTS	G125	Boston Visionary Cell
ARTS	G131	Center for Arts Information
ARTS	G134	Center for Women's Studies and Services
ARTS	G137	Chautauqua Institution
ARTS	G138	Cherry Creek: A Theatre Company
ARTS	G139	Chicago Mural Group
ARTS	G140	Children's Art Foundation
ARTS	G147	Contact Quarterly: A Vehicle for Moving Ideas
ARTS	G170	Front Range: Women in the Visual Arts
ARTS	G174	Guild of American Luthiers
ARTS	G182	Illuminations
ARTS	G194	Jump Cut: A Review of Contemporary Cinema
ARTS	G208	Lost Music Network
ARTS	G223	Naropa Institute
ARTS	G231	New Age Music Network
ARTS	G234	New Art Examiner: Independent Voice of the Visual Arts

ARTS	G252	Poetry Project
ARTS	G265	San Francisco Mime Troupe
ARTS	G278	Society of Folk Harpers and Craftsmen
ARTS	G298	Textile Artists' Newsletter: Review of Fiber Arts
ARTS	G303	Theatre-Action
ARTS	G317	West Art
ARTS	E148	Computer Music Journal
ASIA	V184	Indochina Curriculum Group
ASIA	E104	Afro-Asian Center
ASIA	E113	Asia-Pacific Affairs Associates
ASIA	E120	Bulletin of Concerned Asian Scholars
ASIA	E165	Friends of the Filipino People
ASIA	E260	Southeast Asia Resource Center
ASSOCIATIONS	L002	Another America Networking
ASSOCIATIONS	L107	Alternative America: Directory of 5000 Groups and Organizations
ASSOCIATIONS	E023	Union of International Associations
ASTROLOGY	G104	American Astrology
ASTROLOGY	G117	Astro*Carto*Graphy
AUDUBON	U195	Maine Audubon Society
AUDUBON	U204	National Audubon Society
AUTOS	V128	Center for Auto Safety
BABY-SITTING	H139	Child Care Information Exchange
BABY-SITTING	S124	Carousel Press: Books for Parents
BAHA'I	G119	Baha'i International Community
BANK	V002	Alternative Fund Federal Credit Union
BANK	V212	National Consumer Cooperative Bank
BARTER	S038	Urban Alternatives Group
BARTER	U016	Friends of the Trees
BARTER	V004	Barter Project
BARTER	V036	SkillsBank
BARTER	V038	We-Know-Now Free Trade Exchange
BARTER	V173	Free For All
BARTER	V176	Give and Take Bartering Center
BARTER	V195	King City Senior Barter Bank
BATTERED WOMEN	H189	Massachusetts Coalition of Battered Women Service Groups
BATTERED WOMEN	H247	Working on Wife Abuse
BATTERED WOMEN	V001	Alliance Against Sexual Coercion
BATTERED WOMEN	V171	Feminist Alliance Against Rape
BATTERED WOMEN	V285	Wisconsin Women's Network
BATTERED WOMEN	V287	Women Against Violence Against Women
BICYCLES	S112	Bicyclist Federation of Pennsylvania
BICYCLES	S113	Bikeways in Buffalo
BICYCLES	S152	Delaware Friends of Bikecology
BICYCLES	S180	Indianapolis Mayor's Bicycle Task Force
BICYCLES	S192	Maine Bicycle Coalition
BICYCLES	S231	Santa Clara Valley Bicycle Association
BICYCLES	S244	Transportation Alternatives
BICYCLES	S250	Washington Area Bicyclist Association
BICYCLES	U003	Bicycle Network
BICYCLES	U194	League of Michigan Bicyclists
BICYCLES	U199	Mountain Bicyclists' Association
BICYCLES	U233	Personal Mobility Committee

BICYCLES	U278	Velo Quebec
BICYCLES	G127	California Association of Bicycle Organizations
BICYCLES	G202	League of American Wheelmen
BICYCLES	G259	Roues Libres: Association Cycliste
BIOREGIONS	U022	Planet Drum Foundation
BIRTH CONTROL	H007	Coalition for the Medical Rights of Women
BIRTH CONTROL	H008	Committee for Abortion Rights and Against Sterilization Abuse
BIRTH CONTROL	H021	National Alliance for Optional Parenthood
BIRTH CONTROL	H025	New Hampshire Feminist Health Center
BIRTH CONTROL	H028	Tallahassee Feminist Women's Health Center
BIRTH CONTROL	H031	Women's Health Services
BIRTH CONTROL	H128	Bread & Roses Women's Health Center
BIRTH CONTROL	H220	Planned Parenthood
BIRTH CONTROL	U293	Zero Population Growth
BIRTH CONTROL	V028	New American Movement
BIRTH CONTROL	V101	Abortion Fund
BIRTH CONTROL	V208	National Abortion Federation
BIRTH CONTROL	V218	National Organization for Women
BIRTH CONTROL	L011	Education for Freedom of Choice in Ohio
BIRTH CONTROL	E239	Population Action Council
BLACKS	S202	National Hook-up of Black Women
BLACKS	V013	Emergency Land Fund
BLACKS	V117	Black Law Journal
BLACKS	L132	Center for Black Studies
BOATS	G320	Windsurfer Magazine
BOATS	G321	Women at the Helm: International Women's Sailing
BOATS	G325	WoodenBoat Magazine
BODY	H103	Acupressure School of Massage Therapy
BODY	H105	Aletheia Psycho-Physical Foundation
BODY	H109	American Alliance for Health and Physical Education
BODY	H121	Being Thin
BODY	H190	Massage and Bodywork
BODY	H191	Maternal and Child Health Center
BODY	S207	New Age Chicago
BODY	L239	Shelter Publications
BODY	G027	Transformation Project
BODY	G147	Contact Quarterly: A Vehicle for Moving Ideas
BODY	G151	Creative Yoga Studio
BODY	G198	Kripalu Yoga Center
BODY	G199	Kripalu Yoga Fellowship/Toronto
BODY	G241	North American Network of Women Runners
BODY	G294	T'ai Chi
BODY	G315	Watercourse Ways
BODY	G331	Yoga Journal
BOOKS	H122	Birth and Life Bookstore
BOOKS	S124	Carousel Press: Books for Parents
BOOKS	U119	Banyan Tree Books
BOOKS	V230	New Seed Press Feminist Collective
BOOKS	L127	Book People
BOOKS	L149	Council on Interracial Books for Children
BOOKS	L157	Earthbooks Lending Library/Allegheny Branch
BOOKS	L166	Fine Print: A Review for the Arts of the Book
BOOKS	L169	Food for Thought Books
BOOKS	L171	Guild Books and Periodicals
BOOKS	L172	Gulf of Maine Bookstore
BOOKS	L177	Hydra Book Company
BOOKS	L218	New Pages Press

BOOKS	L233	Rodale Press
BOOKS	L238	Shambhala Publications
BOOKS	L242	Small Press Review
BOOKS	L260	Womansplace Bookstore
BOOKS	G023	Sphinx and Sword of Love Bookstore
BOOKS	G120	Bear Tribe Medicine Society
BOOKS	G123	Blackberry Books
BOOKS	G233	New Age Resource Center
BOOKS	G269	Shambhala Booksellers
BOOKS	G330	Yes Educational Society
BOOMERANG	G124	Boomerang Newsletter
BRAIN	G126	Brain/Mind Bulletin
BRAIN	G157	Dormant Brain Research and Development Laboratory
BREAST-FEEDING	H016	La Leche League International
BREAST-FEEDING	H123	Birthing Monthly Newsletter
BREAST-FEEDING	V020	Interfaith Center on Corporate Responsibility
BREAST-FEEDING	V118	Boston INFACT
BROWN LUNG	H135	Carolina Brown Lung Association
BUDDHIST	G006	Cambridge Zen Center
BUDDHIST	G105	American Institute of Buddhist Studies
BUDDHIST	G154	Diamond Sangha Center: Zen Buddhist Society
BUDDHIST	G186	Insight Meditation Society
BUDDHIST	G196	Karma Triyana Dharmachakra
BUDDHIST	G215	Maui Zendo
BUDDHIST	G218	Minnesota Zen Meditation Center
BUDDHIST	G223	Naropa Institute
BUDDHIST	G243	Ontario Zen Center
BUDDHIST	G255	Providence Zen Center
BUDDHIST	G273	Sino-American Buddhist Association
BUDDHIST	G314	Washington Buddhist Vihara
BUDDHIST	G332	Zen Center of San Francisco
BUDDHIST	G333	Zen Center of Sonoma Mountain
BUSINESS	S033	Riptide/University Services Agency
BUSINESS	S120	Briarpatch Network
BUSINESS	S153	Densmore Discoveries
BUSINESS	S188	Logical Connection: Skillsharing for Private Practitioners
BUSINESS	S240	Support Center: Management Assistance to Non-Profit Groups
BUSINESS	U255	Solar Business Office
BUSINESS	U265	Sudbury 2001
BUSINESS	V020	Interfaith Center on Corporate Responsibility
BUSINESS	V033	Project Work
BUSINESS	V102	Accion/Micro Enterprise Development Corporation
BUSINESS	V112	Association for Self-Management
BUSINESS	V159	Crafts Report: Marketing and Management for Crafts
BUSINESS	V169	Exploratory Project for Economic Alternatives
BUSINESS	V185	Inform, Incorporaed
BUSINESS	V242	People's Business Commission
BUSINESS	V248	Productivity Group
BUSINESS	V266	Tarrytown Group
BUSINESS	V289	Women's Enterprises of Boston
BUSINESS	L015	FocusCreativity
BUSINESS	L032	Organizational Development Network
BUSINESS	L121	Associated Information Managers
BUSINESS	L258	Western Behavioral Sciences Institute
BUSINESS	E160	Family Tree Network
BUSINESS	E229	Open Systems

CABLE TELEVISION	L207	National Federation of Local Cable Programmers
CALLIGRAPHY	L243	Society of Scribes and Illuminators
CANCER	H004	Center for Medical Consumers and Health Care Information
CANCER	H132	Cancer Counseling Center
CANCER	H133	Cancer Counseling and Research Center
CANCER	H162	Health for the New Age
CANCER	H184	Life-Force Cancer Project
CANCER	G270	Shanti Nilaya
CATHOLIC	H214	Omega: Program of Grief Assistance
CATHOLIC	S017	National Catholic Rural Life Conference
CATHOLIC	V223	Network: A Catholic Social Justice Lobby
CATHOLIC	L022	Intercommunity Center for Justice and Peace
CATHOLIC	E002	Catholic Peace Fellowship
CATHOLIC	E161	Fellowship of Reconciliation
CELEBRATIONS	S107	Antahkarana Circle
CELEBRATIONS	L018	Great Atlantic Radio Conspiracy
CELEBRATIONS	G002	Another Place
CELEBRATIONS	G102	Alternatives Resource Center
CESAREANS	H006	Cesarean Connection
CESAREANS	H138	Cesareans/Support Education and Concern (C/SEC)
CHICANO	V205	Mexican American Legal Defense and Educational Fund
CHICANO	L203	National Chicano Research Network
CHILD CARE	H019	Mothering Magazine
CHILD CARE	H139	Child Care Information Exchange
CHILD CARE	S040	Warmlines: A Parent Network and Resource Center
CHILDBIRTH	H006	Cesarean Connection
CHILDBIRTH	H016	La Leche League International
CHILDBIRTH	H019	Mothering Magazine
CHILDBIRTH	H020	NAPSAC: Safe Alternatives in Childbirth
CHILDBIRTH	H106	Alliance for Perinatal Research and Services
CHILDBIRTH	H108	American Academy of Husband-Coached Childbirth
CHILDBIRTH	H114	Association for Childbirth at Home International
CHILDBIRTH	H122	Birth and Life Bookstore
CHILDBIRTH	H123	Birthing Monthly Newsletter
CHILDBIRTH	H124	Boston Area Childbirth Education
CHILDBIRTH	H137	Center for Humane Options in the Childbirth Experience
CHILDBIRTH	H138	Cesareans/Support Education and Concern (C/SEC)
CHILDBIRTH	H145	Cinema Medica
CHILDBIRTH	H169	Holistic Psychotherapy and Medical Group
CHILDBIRTH	H171	Home-Oriented Maternity Experience
CHILDBIRTH	H172	Homebirth
CHILDBIRTH	H175	Informed Homebirth
CHILDBIRTH	H179	International Childbirth Education Association
CHILDBIRTH	H185	Long Island Childbirth Alternatives
CHILDBIRTH	H191	Maternal and Child Health Center
CHILDBIRTH	H192	Maternity Center
CHILDBIRTH	H195	Mid-Hudson Area Maternity Alternatives
CHILDBIRTH	H207	New Beginnings Birth Center
CHILDBIRTH	H231	Society for the Protection of the Unborn Through Nutrition
CHILDBIRTH	H239	Washington State Midwifery Council
CHILDBIRTH	S177	Home Front: For Young Pregnant Women and their Families
CHILDBIRTH	G301	The Farm
CHILDREN	H002	Center for Attitudinal Healing
CHILDREN	H026	Parent Support-Group Project

CHILDREN	H136	Center for Early Adolescence
CHILDREN	H140	Children in Hospitals
CHILDREN	H141	Children's Defense Fund
CHILDREN	H142	Children's Holistic Institute for Life Development
CHILDREN	H199	National Committee for Prevention of Child Abuse
CHILDREN	H237	Vanier Institute of the Family
CHILDREN	V143	Children's Legal Rights Information and Training Program
CHILDREN	V230	New Seed Press Feminist Collective
CHILDREN	L020	Holt Associates
CHILDREN	L102	Action for Children's Television
CHILDREN	L137	Children's Creative Response to Conflict Program
CHILDREN	L149	Council on Interracial Books for Children
CHILDREN	L170	Gifted Children Newsletter
CHILDREN	L199	National Association for Gifted Children
CHILDREN	L200	National Association for the Education of Young Children
CHILDREN	L210	National Organizations Advisory Council for Children
CHILDREN	L253	Uni-Ed Associates
CHILDREN	G017	New Games Foundation
CHILDREN	G020	Public Action Coalition on Toys
CHILDREN	G108	Animal Town Cooperative Games
CHILDREN	G128	Camp Winnarainbow
CHILDREN	G140	Children's Art Foundation
CHILDREN	E127	Center for Peace and Conflict Studies
CHILDREN	E178	Information Center on Children's Cultures
CHINA	V006	Cambridge Documentary Films
CHINA	E270	U.S.-China People's Friendship Association
CITIZENS	H022	National Citizens Coalition for Nursing Home Reform
CITIZENS	H222	Public Citizen Health Research Group
CITIZENS	S001	Citizens Committee for New York City
CITIZENS	S002	Civic Action Institute
CITIZENS	S018	National Center for Citizen Involvement
CITIZENS	S029	Neighborhood Information Sharing Exchange
CITIZENS	S126	Center for Community Change
CITIZENS	S141	Connecticut Citizen Action Group
CITIZENS	S220	Organize Training Center
CITIZENS	U006	Citizen/Labor Energy Coalition
CITIZENS	U130	Charles Stewart Mott Foundation
CITIZENS	U132	Citizens Energy Council
CITIZENS	U133	Citizens United for Responsible Energy
CITIZENS	U135	Citizens' Energy Project
CITIZENS	U146	Dakota Resource Council
CITIZENS	U159	Environmental Policy Institute
CITIZENS	U251	Sierra Club
CITIZENS	U262	Southern Oregon Citizens Against Toxic Sprays
CITIZENS	V007	Campaign for Economic Democracy
CITIZENS	V009	Citizens Involvement Training Project
CITIZENS	V106	American Town Meetings Project
CITIZENS	V123	California Housing Information and Action Network
CITIZENS	V124	California Tax Reform Association
CITIZENS	V137	Center for Public Representation
CITIZENS	V141	Center for the Study of Responsive Law
CITIZENS	V144	Citizen Action
CITIZENS	V146	Citizen Soldier
CITIZENS	V147	Citizens Commission on Police Repression
CITIZENS	V148	Citizens Party
CITIZENS	V154	Common Cause
CITIZENS	V156	Constructive Citizen Participation
CITIZENS	V158	Consumer Information Center
CITIZENS	V203	Massachusetts Public Interest Research Group
CITIZENS	V225	New Age Caucus
CITIZENS	V233	New York Public Interest Research Group

CITIZENS	V237	Ohio Public Interest Campaign
CITIZENS	V267	Tax Reform Research Group
CITIZENS	L104	Alliance for Citizen Education
CITIZENS	L147	Consumer Educational Resource Network
CITIZENS	L179	Institute for Responsive Education
CITIZENS	L205	National Committee for Citizens in Education
CITIZENS	L227	Process: Networking Forum for Citizen Participation
CITIZENS	E010	Institute for Alternative Futures
CITIZENS	E019	Planetary Citizens
CITIZENS	E232	Partnership for Productivity
CLOWNS	G142	Clown College
COMICS	L162	Educomics
COMMON CAUSE	V154	Common Cause
COMMUNE	S004	Communities: Journal of Cooperative Living
COMMUNE	S014	Kerista Village
COMMUNE	S032	Project for Kibbutz Studies
COMMUNE	S145	Cooperative and Communal Living Network
COMMUNE	S190	Love Family
COMMUNE	S208	New Community Project
COMMUNE	E140	Communes Network
COMMUNE	E143	Community Computers
COMMUNE	E164	Friedrichshof
COMMUNE	E191	International Communes Network
COMMUNE	E202	Kokov
COMMUNITY	H149	Community Network Development Project
COMMUNITY	H188	Marion County Community Mental Health Center
COMMUNITY	S004	Communities: Journal of Cooperative Living
COMMUNITY	S005	Community Congress of San Diego
COMMUNITY	S007	Community Service
COMMUNITY	S009	Federation of Egalitarian Communities
COMMUNITY	S126	Center for Community Change
COMMUNITY	S127	Center for Community Economic Development
COMMUNITY	S136	Community Economics
COMMUNITY	S137	Community Jobs
COMMUNITY	S138	Community Produce
COMMUNITY	S139	Community Self-Reliance Center
COMMUNITY	S140	Community Service Restitution
COMMUNITY	S168	Gay Community News
COMMUNITY	S182	Institute for Community Economics
COMMUNITY	S222	Ozark Area Community Congress
COMMUNITY	S252	Whiteaker Community Council
COMMUNITY	U023	Rain Community Resource Center
COMMUNITY	U127	Center for Community Technology
COMMUNITY	U139	Community Network for Appropriate Technologies
COMMUNITY	V003	Association of Community Organizations for Reform Now
COMMUNITY	V168	Eschaton Foundation: Community Spirit Fund
COMMUNITY	L008	Community Memory Project
COMMUNITY	L026	National Federation of Community Broadcasters
COMMUNITY	L138	Church Street Center for Community Education
COMMUNITY	L145	Community Information Center
COMMUNITY	L155	Double Helix: Community Media
COMMUNITY	L156	Downtown Community Television Center
COMMUNITY	L204	National Coalition of Alternative Community Schools
COMMUNITY	L215	New England Training Center for Community Organizers
COMMUNITY	L257	Washington Community Video Center
COMMUNITY	G009	Cooperative Communities of America
COMMUNITY	G024	Spiritual Community Guide
COMMUNITY	G274	Sirius Community

COMMUNITY	G301	The Farm
COMMUNITY	E143	Community Computers
COMMUNITY	E149	Comunidad
COMPOST	U140	Compost Science/Land Utilization
COMPUTER	L008	Community Memory Project
COMPUTER	L012	Electronic Information Exchange System
COMPUTER	L031	Open Network
COMPUTER	L111	Amateur Radio Research and Development
COMPUTER	E018	Participation Systems Incorporated
COMPUTER	E021	The Source
COMPUTER	E121	Byte: The Small Systems Journal
COMPUTER	E122	Center for Creative Studies
COMPUTER	E141	CommuniTree Group
COMPUTER	E142	Community Computer
COMPUTER	E144	CompuServe
COMPUTER	E145	Compute Magazine
COMPUTER	E146	Computer Faire
COMPUTER	E147	Computer Information Exchange
COMPUTER	E148	Computer Music Journal
COMPUTER	E151	Creative Computing
COMPUTER	E155	Dr. Dobb's Journal of Computer Calisthenics and Orthodontia
COMPUTER	E166	Future Shack
COMPUTER	E177	InfoWorld: The Newspaper for the Microcomputing Community
COMPUTER	E182	Institute for Information Society
COMPUTER	E192	International Council for Computers in Education
COMPUTER	E219	New Era Technologies
COMPUTER	E229	Open Systems
COMPUTER	E233	People's Computer Company
COMPUTER	E242	Purser's Magazine for Family Computers
COMPUTER	E251	Robotics Age: Journal of Intelligent Machines
CONGRESS	V149	Civilian Congress
CONGRESS	E004	Congressional Clearinghouse on the Future
CONSCIOUSNESS	G004	Association for Transpersonal Psychology
CONSCIOUSNESS	G010	Dromenon: Journal of New Ways of Being
CONSCIOUSNESS	G126	Brain/Mind Bulletin
CONSCIOUSNESS	G146	Consciousness Synthesis Clearing House
CONSCIOUSNESS	G159	Esalen Institute
CONSCIOUSNESS	G184	Inner Paths: Eastern and Western Spiritual Thought
CONSCIOUSNESS	G185	Inner-Space Interpreters Services
CONSCIOUSNESS	G188	Institute for Consciousness and Music
CONSCIOUSNESS	G220	Monroe Institute of Applied Sciences
CONSCIOUSNESS	G258	ReVision: A Journal of Knowledge and Consciousness
CONSCIOUSNESS	G313	Wainwright House
CONSCIOUSNESS	E173	Human Systems Network
CONSCIOUSNESS	E185	Institute for the Study of Conscious Evolution
CONSCIOUSNESS	E187	Institute of Noetic Sciences
CONSCIOUSNESS	E235	Phebus: Integrating Wholes and Parts
CONSCIOUSNESS	E263	Teilhard Foundation
CONSERVATION	U104	Alaskan Conservation Foundation
CONSERVATION	U111	American Rivers Conservation Council
CONSERVATION	U141	Conservation Foundation
CONSERVATION	U142	Conservation and Renewable Energy Inquiry and Referral Service
CONSERVATION	U156	Energy Probe
CONSERVATION	U166	Fund for Animals
CONSERVATION	U192	Izaak Walton League of America
CONSERVATION	U210	Nature Conservancy
CONSERVATION	U249	Sea Shepherd Conservation Society
CONSERVATION	U251	Sierra Club

CONSERVATION	U273	Tree People
CONSERVATION	U284	Wilderness Society
CONSERVATION	E196	International Union for Conservation of Nature and Resources
CONSUMER	H004	Center for Medical Consumers and Health Care Information
CONSUMER	H009	Consumer Coalition for Health
CONSUMER	H120	Beauty Without Cruelty
CONSUMER	H219	People's Doctor: Medical Newsletter for Consumers
CONSUMER	U143	Consumer Action Now
CONSUMER	U154	Energy Consumer
CONSUMER	V128	Center for Auto Safety
CONSUMER	V157	Consumer Education Research Group
CONSUMER	V158	Consumer Information Center
CONSUMER	V212	National Consumer Cooperative Bank
CONSUMER	V249	Project Equality
CONSUMER	L147	Consumer Educational Resource Network
COOPERATIVES	S004	Communities: Journal of Cooperative Living
COOPERATIVES	S008	Cooperative Directory Association
COOPERATIVES	S010	Food Learning Center
COOPERATIVES	S015	National Association of Housing Cooperatives
COOPERATIVES	S031	North American Students of Cooperation
COOPERATIVES	S110	Associated Cooperatives
COOPERATIVES	S117	Boston Building Materials Cooperative
COOPERATIVES	S121	Butterbrooke Farm Seed Co-op
COOPERATIVES	S122	California Cooperative Federation
COOPERATIVES	S131	Circle Pines Center
COOPERATIVES	S135	Common Health Warehouse
COOPERATIVES	S143	Consumer Coop Press Service
COOPERATIVES	S144	Cooperative League of the USA
COOPERATIVES	S151	Dandelion Community Co-op
COOPERATIVES	S154	Distributing Alliance of the Northcountry Cooperatives
COOPERATIVES	S160	Fed-Up Coop
COOPERATIVES	S161	Federation of Co-ops
COOPERATIVES	S162	Federation of Ohio River Cooperatives
COOPERATIVES	S163	Federation of Southern Cooperatives
COOPERATIVES	S165	Film-Makers Cooperative
COOPERATIVES	S166	Food Conspiracy Cooperative
COOPERATIVES	S170	Gentle Strength Cooperative
COOPERATIVES	S172	Greater Illinois People's Cooperative
COOPERATIVES	S173	Grindstone Island Centre
COOPERATIVES	S174	Hanover Consumer Cooperative Society
COOPERATIVES	S184	International Cooperative Community
COOPERATIVES	S185	Intra-Community Cooperative
COOPERATIVES	S191	Magnolia: Southeastern Confederation for Cooperation
COOPERATIVES	S198	Michigan Federation of Food Cooperatives
COOPERATIVES	S209	New England Food Cooperative Organization
COOPERATIVES	S215	Northwest Organic Herb Cooperative
COOPERATIVES	S216	Northwest Provender Alliance
COOPERATIVES	S238	Spectrum: Cooperative Newspaper for Tallahassee
COOPERATIVES	U200	Mudsharks Co-op
COOPERATIVES	V212	National Consumer Cooperative Bank
COOPERATIVES	V228	New England Cooperative Training Institute
COOPERATIVES	L131	Canyon Cinema Cooperative
COOPERATIVES	L144	Community Education Cooperative
COOPERATIVES	L249	Telecommunications Cooperative Network
COOPERATIVES	G009	Cooperative Communities of America
CORPORATIONS	S229	Regional Young Adult Project
CORPORATIONS	V007	Campaign for Economic Democracy
CORPORATIONS	V012	Council on Economic Priorities
CORPORATIONS	V020	Interfaith Center on Corporate Responsibility
CORPORATIONS	V118	Boston INFACT

CORPORATIONS	V141	Center for the Study of Responsive Law
CORPORATIONS	V172	Focus/Midwest
CORPORATIONS	V185	Inform, Incorporated
CORPORATIONS	V210	National Action/Research on the Military Industrial Complex
CORPORATIONS	V242	People's Business Commission
CORPORATIONS	L192	Media Access Project
CORPORATIONS	E183	Institute for Policy Studies
COUPLES	H176	Institute for Family Research and Education
COUPLES	H229	Seminars on Sexuality
COUPLES	S223	Parents Anonymous
COUPLES	E185	Institute for the Study of Conscious Evolution
CRAFTS	H230	Society for Occupational and Environmental Health
CRAFTS	S009	Federation of Egalitarian Communities
CRAFTS	S149	Crafts Fair Guide
CRAFTS	S171	Goodfellow Catalog of Wonderful Things
CRAFTS	S235	Southern Appalachian Resource Catalog
CRAFTS	S257	Wool Gathering
CRAFTS	U117	Arcosanti
CRAFTS	V104	Akwesasne Notes: For Native and Natural Peoples
CRAFTS	V115	Back to the People: New Age Goods
CRAFTS	V159	Crafts Report: Marketing and Management for Crafts
CRAFTS	V201	Making It Legal: Primer for Craftmaker, Artist and Writer
CRAFTS	L118	Appalshop Films
CRAFTS	L243	Society of Scribes and Illuminators
CRAFTS	G015	Matagiri Sri Aurobindo Center
CRAFTS	G120	Bear Tribe Medicine Society
CRAFTS	G129	Canada Quilts
CRAFTS	G135	Center for the History of American Needlework
CRAFTS	G165	Fine Woodworking
CRAFTS	G298	Textile Artists' Newsletter: Review of Fiber Arts
CRAFTS	G325	WoodenBoat Magazine
CRAFTS	E006	Friends of the Third World
CREATIVITY	S153	Densmore Discoveries
CREATIVITY	U128	Center for Environmental Problem Solving
CREATIVITY	V266	Tarrytown Group
CREATIVITY	L015	FocusCreativity
CREATIVITY	L150	Creative Women's Collective
CREATIVITY	L170	Gifted Children Newsletter
CREATIVITY	L199	National Association for Gifted Children
CREATIVITY	L206	National Diffusion Network
CREATIVITY	L246	Stay Smart
CREATIVITY	G150	Creative Education Foundation
CREATIVITY	G153	Dialogue House Library
CREATIVITY	E122	Center for Creative Studies
CREATIVITY	E124	Center for Interdisciplinary Creativity
CREATIVITY	E160	Family Tree Network
CREATIVITY	E169	Genesa Foundation
CULTURES	S157	F.A.R.O.G. Forum: Journal Bilingue
CULTURES	L003	Anthropology Resource Center
CULTURES	L151	Cultural Survival
CULTURES	L240	Signs: Journal of Women and Culture in Society
CULTURES	E135	Centre Monchanin
CULTURES	E157	East-West Communication Institute
CULTURES	E178	Information Center on Children's Cultures
DALAI LAMA	G105	American Institute of Buddhist Studies
DALAI LAMA	E225	Office of Tibet
DANCE	H109	American Alliance for Health and Physical Education

DANCE	G147	Contact Quarterly: A Vehicle for Moving Ideas
DATA BASE	S029	Neighborhood Information Sharing Exchange
DATA BASE	U023	Rain Community Resource Center
DATA BASE	L002	Another America Networking
DATA BASE	L012	Electronic Information Exchange System
DATA BASE	L031	Open Network
DATA BASE	L107	Alternative America: Directory of 5000 Groups and Organizations
DATA BASE	L123	Ateed Centre
DATA BASE	L161	Educational Resources Information Center
DATA BASE	L203	National Chicano Research Network
DATA BASE	L212	National Technical Information Service
DATA BASE	E018	Participation Systems Incorporated
DATA BASE	E021	The Source
DATA BASE	E144	CompuServe
DATA BASE	E175	IOC/MAB
DATA BASE	E176	Info Alternativ
DATA BASE	E219	New Era Technologies
DATA BASE	E283	World Game of R. Buckminster Fuller
DECENTRALISM	S035	School of Living: Publishers of Green Revolution
DECENTRALISM	V024	Movement for a New Society
DECENTRALISM	V034	Renewal Newsletter: New Values, New Politics
DECENTRALISM	V231	New World Alliance
DECENTRALISM	E249	Resurgence
DEVELOPMENT	E011	Institute for Food and Development Policy
DEVELOPMENT	E026	Women's International Network
DEVELOPMENT	E123	Center for Development Policy
DEVELOPMENT	E201	Journal of Developing Areas
DISABLED	H126	Boston Self-Help
DISABLED	H130	Canadian Coordinating Council on Deafness
DISABLED	H218	Pavillion Newsletter: Advocacy for the Disabled
DISABLED	V163	Disability Rights Center
DISABLED	L126	Berkeley Outreach Recreation Program
DISABLED	G245	Outdoor Education for the Handicapped Project
DISARMAMENT	V035	SANE
DISARMAMENT	V132	Center for National Security Studies
DISARMAMENT	V238	One Less Bomb Committee
DISARMAMENT	V273	Toronto Association for Peace
DISARMAMENT	E001	Association for World Education
DISARMAMENT	E003	Commission to Study the Organization of Peace
DISARMAMENT	E027	World Constitution and Parliament Association
DISARMAMENT	E112	Arms Control Association
DISARMAMENT	E131	Center for War/Peace Studies
DISARMAMENT	E218	Network to Educate for World Security
DRAFT	V008	Central Committee for Conscientious Objectors
DRAFT	V011	Committee Against Registration and the Draft
DRAFT	V031	Peacework
DRAFT	V110	Another Mother for Peace
DRAFT	V151	Come Unity: An Alternative Independent Journal
DRAFT	V192	Jewish Peace Fellowship
DRAFT	V206	Midwest Committee for Military Counseling
DRAFT	V222	National Resistance Committee
DRAFT	V253	Recon Publications
DRAFT	E002	Catholic Peace Fellowship
DREAMS	G195	Jungian-Senoi Dreamwork Institute
DROP ZONE	G309	United States Parachute Association

DRUGS	H151	Do It Now Foundation
DRUGS	H224	Pyramid: Resource Sharing Network for Drug Abuse Prevention
DRUGS	V220	National Organization for the Reform of Marijuana Laws
DRUGS	G179	High Times
DRUGS	G289	Stash
DYING	H013	Hospice Institute for Education Training and Research
DYING	H203	National Hospice Organization
DYING	H214	Omega: Program of Grief Assistance
DYING	H233	Spring Hill: Community, Retreat and Counseling Center
DYING	G011	Dying Project
DYING	G270	Shanti Nilaya
EARTH	S003	CoEvolution Quarterly
EARTH	U022	Planet Drum Foundation
EARTH	U109	Alternatives: Journal of Friends of the Earth, Canada
EARTH	U129	Center for the Biology of Natural Systems
EARTH	U150	Earth Lab Institute
EARTH	U152	Earthtone: For People Tuned to the Earth
EARTH	L196	Mother Earth News
EARTH	G200	Kronos: Journal of Interdisciplinary Synthesis
EARTH	G206	Lindisfarne Association
EARTH	E019	Planetary Citizens
EARTH	E023	Union of International Associations
EARTH	E024	United Nations Economic & Social Council
EARTH	E027	World Constitution and Parliament Association
EARTH	E163	First Earth Battalion Foundation
EARTH	E227	Omega: Global Networking
EARTH	E257	Sierra Club International Earthcare Center
EARTH	E268	U.S. Association for The Club of Rome
EARTH	E281	World Environment Center
EARTH	E290	World Union
EARTH	E291	WorldPaper: The Global Community Newspaper
EARTH	E292	Worldwatch Institute
ECOLOGY	H014	Human Ecology Action League
ECOLOGY	U153	Ecology Action of the Midpeninsula
ECOLOGY	U163	Feminist Resources on Energy and Ecology
ECOLOGY	U186	Institute for Ecological Policies
ECOLOGY	V196	League for Ecological Democracy
ECONOMICS	S127	Center for Community Economic Development
ECONOMICS	S136	Community Economics
ECONOMICS	S182	Institute for Community Economics
ECONOMICS	U108	Alternative Directions in Energy and Economics
ECONOMICS	V007	Campaign for Economic Democracy
ECONOMICS	V012	Council on Economic Priorities
ECONOMICS	V023	Movement for Economic Justice
ECONOMICS	V136	Center for Popular Economics
ECONOMICS	V169	Exploratory Project for Economic Alternatives
ECONOMICS	V183	Human Economy Center
ECONOMICS	V214	National Economic Development and Law Center
ECONOMICS	V244	Popular Economics Press
ECONOMICS	V277	Union for Radical Political Economics
ECONOMICS	E024	United Nations Economic & Social Council
ECOTOPIA	U119	Banyan Tree Books
ECOTOPIA	U136	Clippings in Ecotopia
EDGAR CAYCE	G114	Association for Research and Enlightenment
EDUCATION	H234	Statewide Comprehensive Health Education Coalition
EDUCATION	U105	Alliance for Environmental Education

EDUCATION	U228	Ocean Education Project
EDUCATION	V187	Institute for Labor Education and Research
EDUCATION	V205	Mexican American Legal Defense and Educational Fund
EDUCATION	V281	Veterans Education Project
EDUCATION	L001	Alternatives in Education
EDUCATION	L004	Association for Experiential Education
EDUCATION	L006	Coalition for Alternatives in Postsecondary Education
EDUCATION	L010	Education Exploration Center
EDUCATION	L027	National Society for Internships and Experiential Education
EDUCATION	L030	Ohio Coalition for Educational Alternatives Now
EDUCATION	L101	Academy for Educational Development
EDUCATION	L103	Adult Education Association of the United States of America
EDUCATION	L104	Alliance for Citizen Education
EDUCATION	L122	Association for Humanistic Education
EDUCATION	L136	Change in Liberal Education Network
EDUCATION	L138	Church Street Center for Community Education
EDUCATION	L140	Clearinghouse of Free-Standing Educational Institutions
EDUCATION	L144	Community Education Cooperative
EDUCATION	L147	Consumer Educational Resource Network
EDUCATION	L159	Educational Film Library Association
EDUCATION	L160	Educational Futures
EDUCATION	L161	Educational Resources Information Center
EDUCATION	L179	Institute for Responsive Education
EDUCATION	L180	Institute for Wholistic Education
EDUCATION	L200	National Association for the Education of Young Children
EDUCATION	L201	National Center for Educational Brokering
EDUCATION	L202	National Center for Research in Vocational Education
EDUCATION	L205	National Committee for Citizens in Education
EDUCATION	L221	Northwest Women in Educational Administration
EDUCATION	L226	Primary/Secondary Peace Education Network
EDUCATION	L228	Project on the Status and Education of Women
EDUCATION	L255	United Ministries in Education
EDUCATION	L262	Women's Educational Equity Communications Network
EDUCATION	G113	Association for Moral Education
EDUCATION	G149	Council on International Educational Exchange
EDUCATION	G150	Creative Education Foundation
EDUCATION	G245	Outdoor Education for the Handicapped Project
EDUCATION	G330	Yes Educational Society
EDUCATION	E001	Association for World Education
EDUCATION	E005	Consortium on Peace Research, Education, and Development
EDUCATION	E007	Global Education Associates
EDUCATION	E105	After Thought: Research and Education About the Future
EDUCATION	E170	Global Perspectives in Education
EDUCATION	E192	International Council for Computers in Education
EDUCATION	E226	Office on Global Education
EDUCATION	E280	World Education Fellowship
EDUCATIONAL LAB	L029	Northwest Regional Educational Laboratory
EDUCATIONAL LAB	L033	Southwest Educational Development Laboratory
EDUCATIONAL LAB	L116	Appalachia Educational Laboratory
EDUCATIONAL LAB	L148	Council for Educational Development and Research
EDUCATIONAL LAB	L163	Far West Laboratory
EDUCATIONAL LAB	L206	National Diffusion Network
EDUCATIONAL LAB	L232	Research for Better Schools
EDUCATIONAL LAB	L250	The Network: Educational Service and Research
ENERGY	U001	Alternative Sources of Energy
ENERGY	U006	Citizen/Labor Energy Coalition
ENERGY	U010	Critical Mass Energy Project
ENERGY	U025	Southern Unity Network/Renewable Energy Project
ENERGY	U107	Alternate Energy Institute
ENERGY	U108	Alternative Directions in Energy and Economics
ENERGY	U112	American Wind Energy Association

ENERGY	U121	British Columbia Energy Coalition
ENERGY	U125	Canadian Renewable Energy News
ENERGY	U132	Citizens Energy Council
ENERGY	U133	Citizens United for Responsible Energy
ENERGY	U135	Citizens' Energy Project
ENERGY	U138	Community Energy Action Network
ENERGY	U142	Conservation and Renewable Energy Inquiry and Referral Service
ENERGY	U145	Cornerstones: Energy Efficient Housebuilding
ENERGY	U151	Earthmind: Energy Research, Education and Books
ENERGY	U154	Energy Consumer
ENERGY	U155	Energy People
ENERGY	U156	Energy Probe
ENERGY	U157	Energy Task Force
ENERGY	U163	Feminist Resources on Energy and Ecology
ENERGY	U177	Health and Energy Learning Project
ENERGY	U184	Infinite Energy
ENERGY	U190	International Solar Energy Society
ENERGY	U193	Lamoureux Foundation: Home Energy Workshops
ENERGY	U198	Modern Energy & Technology Alternatives
ENERGY	U201	Musicians United for Safe Energy
ENERGY	U214	New England Regional Energy Project
ENERGY	U215	New England Solar Energy Association
ENERGY	U218	New Mexico Solar Energy Association
ENERGY	U222	North Carolina Coalition for Renewable Energy Resources
ENERGY	U242	Safe Energy Alternatives Alliance
ENERGY	U243	Safe Energy Resources
ENERGY	U246	San Luis Valley Solar Energy Association
ENERGY	U253	Small Farm Energy Project
ENERGY	U256	Solar Energy Association of Northeast Colorado
ENERGY	U257	Solar Energy Digest
ENERGY	U258	Solar Energy Research Institute
ENERGY	U261	Solar Times: News of the Solar Energy Industry
ENERGY	U267	Synerjy: Directory of Energy Alternatives
ENERGY	U268	Texas Solar Energy Coalition
ENERGY	U276	Urban Solar Energy Association
ENERGY	U283	Western Massachusetts Solar Energy Association
ENERGY	U285	Wind Power Digest: Access to Wind Energy Information
ENERGY	U289	Women in Solar Energy
ENERGY	U292	World Information Service on Energy
ENERGY	E236	Planetary Association for Clean Energy
ENTROPY	V242	People's Business Commission
ENVIRONMENT	H143	Choosing Healthy Options in Changing Environments
ENVIRONMENT	H230	Society for Occupational and Environmental Health
ENVIRONMENT	U007	Citizens for a Better Environment
ENVIRONMENT	U011	Environmental Action Foundation
ENVIRONMENT	U012	Environmental Action Inc.
ENVIRONMENT	U013	Environmental Defense Fund
ENVIRONMENT	U027	Total Environmental Action
ENVIRONMENT	U103	Alaska Center for the Environment
ENVIRONMENT	U105	Alliance for Environmental Education
ENVIRONMENT	U128	Center for Environmental Problem Solving
ENVIRONMENT	U158	Environmental Action Reprint Service
ENVIRONMENT	U159	Environmental Policy Institute
ENVIRONMENT	U181	Human Environment Center
ENVIRONMENT	U216	New Environment Association
ENVIRONMENT	U223	Northcoast Environmental Center
ENVIRONMENT	U238	Rachel Carson Trust Fund for the Living Environment
ENVIRONMENT	U247	Saskatoon Environmental Society
ENVIRONMENT	E115	Association for the Study of Man-Environment Relations
ENVIRONMENT	E281	World Environment Center

ERA	V016	Illinois Women's Agenda
ERA	V021	Know Feminist Publishers
ERA	V039	Women U.S.A.
ERA	V165	ERAmerica
ERA	V218	National Organization for Women
ERA	V285	Wisconsin Women's Network
ERA	V286	Woman Activist: Action Bulletin for Women's Rights
ERA	V290	Women's Equity Action League
ESALEN	G027	Transformation Project
ESALEN	G159	Esalen Institute
ESALEN	G283	Spiritual Emergency Network
ESKIMO	V114	Association on American Indian Affairs
ESOTERIC	G114	Association for Research and Enlightenment
ESOTERIC	G132	Center for Esoteric Studies
ESOTERIC	G185	Inner-Space Interpreters Services
ESOTERIC	G191	International Church of Ageless Wisdom
ESOTERIC	G204	Life Understanding Foundation
ESOTERIC	G290	Sufi Order for the Esoteric Arts & Sciences
EST	E009	Hunger Project
EVOLUTION	S003	CoEvolution Quarterly
EVOLUTION	E138	Coevolution
EVOLUTION	E158	Evolution
EVOLUTION	E168	Futures Network
EVOLUTION	E173	Human Systems Network
EVOLUTION	E185	Institute for the Study of Conscious Evolution
EXPERIENTIAL	L004	Association for Experiential Education
EXPERIENTIAL	L009	Council for the Advancement of Experiential Learning
EXPERIENTIAL	L027	National Society for Internships and Experiential Education
FAMILY	H141	Children's Defense Fund
FAMILY	H176	Institute for Family Research and Education
FAMILY	H197	National Coalition Against Domestic Violence
FAMILY	H237	Vanier Institute of the Family
FAMILY	S015	National Association of Housing Cooperatives
FAMILY	S017	National Catholic Rural Life Conference
FAMILY	S021	National Family Farm Coalition
FAMILY	S158	Family Connection
FAMILY	G163	Family Pastimes
FARMS	S006	Community Self-Reliance
FARMS	S021	National Family Farm Coalition
FARMS	S034	Rural America
FARMS	S102	Agricultural Marketing Project
FARMS	S121	Butterbrooke Farm Seed Co-op
FARMS	S148	Countryside: The Magazine for Serious Homesteaders
FARMS	S156	Draft Horse Journal
FARMS	S163	Federation of Southern Cooperatives
FARMS	U028	Washington Small Farm Resources Network
FARMS	U149	Earth Cyclers
FARMS	U162	Farming Uncle: For Natural People and Mother Nature Lovers
FARMS	U183	Illinois South Project
FARMS	U188	International Biomass Institute
FARMS	U189	International Federation of Organic Agricultural Movements
FARMS	U196	Maine Organic Farmers and Gardeners Association
FARMS	U209	Natural Food Associates
FARMS	U217	New Life Farm
FARMS	U253	Small Farm Energy Project

FARMS	U272	Tilth: Biological Agriculture in the Northwest
FARMS	V013	Emergency Land Fund
FARMS	L196	Mother Earth News
FARMS	E117	Australian Willing Workers on Organic Farms
FEDERALISTS	E282	World Federalists Association
FEMINIST	H025	New Hampshire Feminist Health Center
FEMINIST	H028	Tallahassee Feminist Women's Health Center
FEMINIST	H031	Women's Health Services
FEMINIST	H127	Boston Women's Health Book Collective
FEMINIST	H128	Bread & Roses Women's Health Center
FEMINIST	H144	Chrysalis
FEMINIST	H201	National Feminist Therapists Association
FEMINIST	H244	Womancare: A Feminist Women's Health Center
FEMINIST	S125	Carrier Pigeon/Alyson Publications
FEMINIST	S255	Woman's Place
FEMINIST	U163	Feminist Resources on Energy and Ecology
FEMINIST	U287	Women and Life on Earth
FEMINIST	V021	Know Feminist Publishers
FEMINIST	V024	Movement for a New Society
FEMINIST	V028	New American Movement
FEMINIST	V040	Women's Action Alliance
FEMINIST	V113	Association of Libertarian Feminists
FEMINIST	V171	Feminist Alliance Against Rape
FEMINIST	V180	Harvest Publications
FEMINIST	V209	National Action Committee on the Status of Women
FEMINIST	V218	National Organization for Women
FEMINIST	V226	New Directions for Women
FEMINIST	V230	New Seed Press Feminist Collective
FEMINIST	V257	Second Wave: Magazine of the New Feminism
FEMINIST	V258	Sister Courage: Radical Feminist Newspaper
FEMINIST	V271	The Spokeswoman: Feminist News Digest
FEMINIST	L013	Feminist Writers' Guild
FEMINIST	L014	Feminist Writers' Guild/New York
FEMINIST	L164	Feminary: A Feminist Journal for the South
FEMINIST	L165	Ferity: Hawaii's Feminist Newsjournal
FEMINIST	L167	Fireworks: Feminist Journal of the John Dewey High School
FEMINIST	L173	Hagborn: A Radical Feminist News Journal
FEMINIST	L231	Quest: A Feminist Quarterly
FEMINIST	G107	Anima: An Experiential Journal
FEMINIST	G134	Center for Women's Studies and Services
FEMINIST	E234	People's Translation Service
FEMINIST	E277	Women's International Information & Communication (ISIS)
FICTION	H144	Chrysalis
FICTION	L139	City Lights Journal
FICTION	L146	Conditions: Writing by Women
FICTION	L268	Women: Journal of Liberation
FICTION	G026	The Sun: A Magazine of Ideas
FILMS	H145	Cinema Medica
FILMS	S165	Film-Makers Cooperative
FILMS	U017	Green Mountain Post Films
FILMS	U122	Bullfrog Films
FILMS	U219	New Times Films
FILMS	V005	California Newsreel
FILMS	V006	Cambridge Documentary Films
FILMS	L118	Appalshop Films
FILMS	L131	Canyon Cinema Cooperative
FILMS	L154	Direct Cinema Limited
FILMS	L159	Educational Film Library Association
FILMS	L168	Flower Films

FILMS	L182	Kartemquin Films
FILMS	L216	New Front Films
FILMS	L223	Packard Manse Media Project
FILMS	L225	Pioneer Productions
FILMS	L254	Unifilm
FILMS	L259	White Buffalo Multimedia
FILMS	L261	Women in Focus: Film Production and Distribution
FILMS	L272	Zipporah Films
FILMS	G161	Essentia Films
FILMS	G177	Hartley Productions: Films for a New Age
FILMS	G194	Jump Cut: A Review of Contemporary Cinema
FOLK	L016	Folk-School Association of America
FOLK	G022	Sing Out! The Folk Song Magazine
FOLK	G278	Society of Folk Harpers and Craftsmen
FOOD	H005	Center for Science in the Public Interest
FOOD	H010	East West Journal
FOOD	H186	Macrobiotic Health Information Center of New Jersey
FOOD	H187	Macrobiotic: A Guide for Natural Living
FOOD	H208	Newtrition Outreach: Whole Foods Information
FOOD	H231	Society for the Protection of the Unborn Through Nutrition
FOOD	H238	Vegetarian Times
FOOD	S006	Community Self-Reliance
FOOD	S008	Cooperative Directory Association
FOOD	S010	Food Learning Center
FOOD	S012	Institute for Non-Violent Education, Research, and Training
FOOD	S017	National Catholic Rural Life Conference
FOOD	S031	North American Students of Cooperation
FOOD	S033	Riptide/University Services Agency
FOOD	S102	Agricultural Marketing Project
FOOD	S104	Alliance of Warehouse Federations
FOOD	S115	Blooming Prairie Warehouse
FOOD	S118	Boston Urban Gardens
FOOD	S122	California Cooperative Federation
FOOD	S132	Circle of Light/Findhorn
FOOD	S134	Cleareye Natural Foods
FOOD	S135	Common Health Warehouse
FOOD	S138	Community Produce
FOOD	S139	Community Self-Reliance Center
FOOD	S154	Distributing Alliance of the Northcountry Cooperatives
FOOD	S160	Fed-Up Coop
FOOD	S161	Federation of Co-ops
FOOD	S166	Food Conspiracy Cooperative
FOOD	S170	Gentle Strength Cooperative
FOOD	S172	Greater Illinois People's Cooperative
FOOD	S176	Hartford Food System
FOOD	S191	Magnolia: Southeastern Confederation for Cooperation
FOOD	S198	Michigan Federation of Food Cooperatives
FOOD	S209	New England Food Cooperative Organization
FOOD	S211	New West Trails
FOOD	S216	Northwest Provender Alliance
FOOD	S228	Raisin Consciousness
FOOD	S234	Society of Ontario Nut Growers
FOOD	S248	Vegetarian Society of D.C.
FOOD	U009	Commonweal
FOOD	U014	Food Monitor
FOOD	U161	Farallones Institute: Rural Center
FOOD	U164	Food Research and Action Center
FOOD	U202	National Association for Gardening
FOOD	U209	Natural Food Associates
FOOD	U231	Ozark Institute
FOOD	U239	Redwood City Seed Company

FOOD	U269	The Plan: Community Food Tree Nurseries
FOOD	U270	The Sproutletter: Sprouts, Raw Foods, and Nutrition
FOOD	V157	Consumer Education Research Group
FOOD	V202	Maryland Food Committee
FOOD	L169	Food for Thought Books
FOOD	L233	Rodale Press
FOOD	G248	Oz Projects: Retreat in the Redwoods
FOOD	E009	Hunger Project
FOOD	E011	Institute for Food and Development Policy
FOOD	E016	Oxfam America
FOOD	E199	Interreligious Taskforce on U.S. Food Policy
FOOD	E238	Plenty
FOREIGN POLICY	V034	Renewal Newsletter: New Values, New Politics
FOREIGN POLICY	V232	New World Review
FOREIGN POLICY	E112	Arms Control Association
FOREIGN POLICY	E123	Center for Development Policy
FOREIGN POLICY	E125	Center for International Policy
FOREIGN POLICY	E129	Center for Teaching International Relations
FOREIGN POLICY	E137	Coalition for a New Foreign and Military Policy
FOREIGN POLICY	E183	Institute for Policy Studies
FOREIGN POLICY	E184	Institute for World Order
FOREIGN POLICY	E199	Interreligious Taskforce on U.S. Food Policy
FRANCO-AMERICAN	S157	F.A.R.O.G. Forum: Journal Bilingue
FREE PRESS	S116	Bloomington Free Ryder: Biweekly Newspaper
FREE PRESS	S213	North Carolina Anvil
FREE PRESS	S242	Texas Observer: A Journal of Free Voices
FREE PRESS	S253	Winds of Change
FREE PRESS	V229	New England Free Press
FREE TRADE	V038	We-Know-Now Free Trade Exchange
FREE UNIVERSITY	L017	Free University Network
FREE UNIVERSITY	L153	Denver Free University
FREE UNIVERSITY	E205	Laurieston Hall
FREE UNIVERSITY	E271	Universite Verte
FRIENDS	V175	Friends Peace Committee
FRIENDS	G169	Friends Journal
FUNDING	S146	Council on Foundations
FUNDING	S229	Regional Young Adult Project
FUNDING	U130	Charles Stewart Mott Foundation
FUNDING	U130	Charles Stewart Mott Foundation
FUNDING	U211	Needmor Fund
FUNDING	U282	Western Massachusetts Resource Network
FUNDING	V002	Alternative Fund Federal Credit Union
FUNDING	V014	Grantsmanship Center
FUNDING	V018	Institute for Social Justice
FUNDING	V103	Agape Foundation: Fund for Nonviolent Social Change
FUNDING	V134	Center for Nonprofit Organization
FUNDING	V211	National Committee for Responsive Philanthropy
FUNDING	V212	National Consumer Cooperative Bank
FUNDING	V217	National Network of Grantmakers
FUNDING	V279	Vanguard Public Foundation
FUNDING	V297	Youth Project
FUTURE	U241	Resources for the Future
FUTURE	L012	Electronic Information Exchange System
FUTURE	G125	Boston Visionary Cell
FUTURE	G318	Whole Life Times: Northeast Journal for a Positive Future

FUTURE	E004	Congressional Clearinghouse on the Future
FUTURE	E010	Institute for Alternative Futures
FUTURE	E017	Participation Publishers
FUTURE	E028	World Future Society
FUTURE	E105	After Thought: Research and Education About the Future
FUTURE	E160	Family Tree Network
FUTURE	E166	Future Shack
FUTURE	E167	Future Studies Centre
FUTURE	E168	Futures Network
FUTURE	E182	Institute for Information Society
FUTURE	E186	Institute for the Study of the Human Future
FUTURE	E211	Maryland Alliance for Space Colonization
FUTURE	E222	Next: A Look into the Future
FUTURE	E228	Omni Magazine
FUTURE	E251	Robotics Age: Journal of Intelligent Machines
FUTURE	E267	Twenty-first Century Media
FUTURE	E268	U.S. Association for The Club of Rome
GAMES	V175	Friends Peace Committee
GAMES	G017	New Games Foundation
GAMES	G020	Public Action Coalition on Toys
GAMES	G108	Animal Town Cooperative Games
GAMES	G144	Committee for the Game
GAMES	G155	Different Worlds: Magazine of Adventure Role-Playing Games
GAMES	G163	Family Pastimes
GAMES	G172	Games
GAMES	G286	Sproing: Science Fiction and Fantasy
GARDENS	S118	Boston Urban Gardens
GARDENS	U115	Applewood Journal
GARDENS	U153	Ecology Action of the Midpeninsula
GARDENS	U176	Harrowsmith Magazine/Canada
GARDENS	U178	Herb Quarterly
GARDENS	U189	International Federation of Organic Agricultural Movements
GARDENS	U196	Maine Organic Farmers and Gardeners Association
GARDENS	U202	National Association for Gardening
GARDENS	U223	Northcoast Environmental Center
GARDENS	U259	Solar Greenhouse Digest
GAY	H225	Renaissance House
GAY	S125	Carrier Pigeon/Alyson Publications
GAY	S168	Gay Community News
GAY	S169	Gay Sunshine Press
GAY	S227	RFD: Country Journal for Gay Men Everywhere
GAY	S251	Washington Blade: Gay Newspaper of the Nation's Capital
GAY	S254	Wishing Well
GAY	V215	National Gay Task Force
GAY	L176	Homosexual Information Center
GAY	G296	Tayu Institute
GAY	G302	The Loving Brotherhood
GENERAL SYSTEMS	L002	Another America Networking
GENERAL SYSTEMS	L163	Far West Laboratory
GENERAL SYSTEMS	G150	Creative Education Foundation
GENERAL SYSTEMS	E023	Union of International Associations
GENERAL SYSTEMS	E028	World Future Society
GENERAL SYSTEMS	E122	Center for Creative Studies
GENERAL SYSTEMS	E194	International Journal of General Systems
GENERAL SYSTEMS	E258	Society for General Systems Research
GEOTHERMAL	U170	Geothermal World Info Center
GODDESS	G324	WomenSpirit Journal

GOVERNMENT	S037	Small Towns Institute
GOVERNMENT	U229	Office of Appropriate Technology
GOVERNMENT	V026	National Committee Against Repressive Legislation
GOVERNMENT	V034	Renewal Newsletter: New Values, New Politics
GOVERNMENT	V039	Women U.S.A.
GOVERNMENT	V106	American Town Meetings Project
GOVERNMENT	V120	Brown Committee
GOVERNMENT	V127	Caucus for a New Political Science
GOVERNMENT	V139	Center for Women in Government
GOVERNMENT	V148	Citizens Party
GOVERNMENT	V149	Civilian Congress
GOVERNMENT	V154	Common Cause
GOVERNMENT	V174	Freedom of Information Clearinghouse
GOVERNMENT	V177	Government Institutes
GOVERNMENT	V193	Joint Center for Political Studies
GOVERNMENT	V196	League for Ecological Democracy
GOVERNMENT	V198	Libertarian Review
GOVERNMENT	V199	Looking Left
GOVERNMENT	V219	National Organization for an American Revolution
GOVERNMENT	V224	Nevada Elected Women's Network
GOVERNMENT	V225	New Age Caucus
GOVERNMENT	V231	New World Alliance
GOVERNMENT	V239	Open Road
GOVERNMENT	V247	Privacy Journal
GOVERNMENT	V250	Public Eye: A Journal Concerning Repression in America
GOVERNMENT	V252	Radical America
GOVERNMENT	V267	Tax Reform Research Group
GOVERNMENT	V274	Transaction Periodicals Consortium
GOVERNMENT	V284	Washington Spectator & Between the Lines
GOVERNMENT	V296	Youth International Party
GOVERNMENT	L135	Center for the Study of Democratic Institutions
GOVERNMENT	L227	Process: Networking Forum for Citizen Participation
GOVERNMENT	L251	The Progressive
GOVERNMENT	E004	Congressional Clearinghouse on the Future
GOVERNMENT	E010	Institute for Alternative Futures
GOVERNMENT	E018	Participation Systems Incorporated
GOVERNMENT	E019	Planetary Citizens
GOVERNMENT	E027	World Constitution and Parliament Association
GOVERNMENT	E184	Institute for World Order
GOVERNMENT	E206	Leading Edge: A Bulletin of Social Transformation
GOVERNMENT	E247	Research Utilization Network
GOVERNMENT	E282	World Federalists Association
GRAND JURY	V150	Coalition to End Grand Jury Abuse
GREENPEACE	U018	Greenpeace Foundation
GREENPEACE	U171	Greenpeace Alaska
GREENPEACE	U172	Greenpeace Examiner
GREENPEACE	U173	Greenpeace Seattle
GREENPEACE	U174	Greenpeace/Vancouver
GROUPWARE	E200	Johnson-Lenz
GUATEMALA	E221	News from Guatemala
HEALING	H002	Center for Attitudinal Healing
HEALING	H111	American Healing Association
HEALING	H131	Canadian Holistic Healing Association
HEALING	H146	Clearing Community and School of the Healing Arts
HEALING	H153	East West Academy of Healing Arts
HEALING	H211	Nurse Healers/Professional Associates Cooperative
HEALING	H227	Sarasota School of Natural Healing Arts
HEALING	G106	American Spiritual Healing Association

HEALING	G178	Healing Light Center
HEALING	G280	Soluna: Creative Healing and Self-Exploration
HEALTH	H004	Center for Medical Consumers and Health Care Information
HEALTH	H009	Consumer Coalition for Health
HEALTH	H023	National Women's Health Network
HEALTH	H025	New Hampshire Feminist Health Center
HEALTH	H028	Tallahassee Feminist Women's Health Center
HEALTH	H030	Touch for Health Foundation
HEALTH	H031	Women's Health Services
HEALTH	H109	American Alliance for Health and Physical Education
HEALTH	H118	Bay Area Coalition on Occupational Safety and Health
HEALTH	H127	Boston Women's Health Book Collective
HEALTH	H128	Bread & Roses Women's Health Center
HEALTH	H134	Cape Cod Health Care Coalition
HEALTH	H157	Hawaii Health Network
HEALTH	H158	Health Activation Network
HEALTH	H159	Health Link
HEALTH	H161	Health Writers
HEALTH	H162	Health for the New Age
HEALTH	H164	Hippocrates Health Institute
HEALTH	H177	Integral Health Services
HEALTH	H186	Macrobiotic Health Information Center of New Jersey
HEALTH	H191	Maternal and Child Health Center
HEALTH	H202	National Health Federation
HEALTH	H209	North Carolina Occupational Safety and Health Project
HEALTH	H222	Public Citizen Health Research Group
HEALTH	H234	Statewide Comprehensive Health Education Coalition
HEALTH	H244	Womancare: A Feminist Women's Health Center
HEALTH	H245	Women Healthsharing
HEALTH	H246	Women and Health Roundtable
HEALTH	U177	Health and Energy Learning Project
HEALTH	E108	American Public Health Association
HEALTH POLICY	H012	Health Policy Advisory Council
HEALTH POLICY	H160	Health Policy Council
HEALTH POLICY	H200	National Council on Alternative Health Care Policy
HENRY GEORGE	V015	Henry George School of Social Science
HERBS	H001	Alternative Medical Association
HERBS	H129	California School of Herbal Studies
HERBS	H163	Herbal Education Center
HERBS	S215	Northwest Organic Herb Cooperative
HERBS	U178	Herb Quarterly
HISPANIC	S022	National Hispanic Coalition for Better Housing
HISPANIC	V213	National Council of La Raza
HISTORY	S105	American Association for State and Local History
HISTORY	S204	National Trust for Historic Preservation
HISTORY	V180	Harvest Publications
HISTORY	L113	American Historical Association
HISTORY	L263	Women's History Research Center
HISTORY	E276	Women in World Areas Studies
HOLISTIC ADS	H206	New Age in Austin
HOLISTIC ADS	S207	New Age Chicago
HOLISTIC ADS	L143	Common Ground
HOLISTIC ADS	L152	D.C. Gazette
HOLISTIC ADS	G214	Many Hands: Guide to Holistic Health and Awareness
HOLISTIC ADS	G227	New Age Gazette
HOLISTIC ADS	G318	Whole Life Times: Northeast Journal for a Positive Future

HOLISTIC HEALTH	H001	Alternative Medical Association
HOLISTIC HEALTH	H003	Center for Integral Medicine
HOLISTIC HEALTH	H027	Survival Foundation
HOLISTIC HEALTH	H030	Touch for Health Foundation
HOLISTIC HEALTH	H103	Acupressure School of Massage Therapy
HOLISTIC HEALTH	H112	American Holistic Medical Association
HOLISTIC HEALTH	H113	American Holistic Nurses' Association
HOLISTIC HEALTH	H115	Association for Research and Enlightenment Clinic
HOLISTIC HEALTH	H131	Canadian Holistic Healing Association
HOLISTIC HEALTH	H133	Cancer Counseling and Research Center
HOLISTIC HEALTH	H142	Children's Holistic Institute for Life Development
HOLISTIC HEALTH	H143	Choosing Healthy Options in Changing Environments
HOLISTIC HEALTH	H154	East/West Center for Holistic Health
HOLISTIC HEALTH	H157	Hawaii Health Network
HOLISTIC HEALTH	H159	Health Link
HOLISTIC HEALTH	H160	Health Policy Council
HOLISTIC HEALTH	H162	Health for the New Age
HOLISTIC HEALTH	H165	Holistic Health Organizing Committee
HOLISTIC HEALTH	H166	Holistic Health Practitioners' Association
HOLISTIC HEALTH	H167	Holistic Health Referrals
HOLISTIC HEALTH	H168	Holistic Health Review
HOLISTIC HEALTH	H169	Holistic Psychotherapy and Medical Group
HOLISTIC HEALTH	H170	Holmes Center for Research in Holistic Healing
HOLISTIC HEALTH	H173	Homeopathic Educational Services
HOLISTIC HEALTH	H178	Interface Foundation
HOLISTIC HEALTH	H181	International Foundation for the Promotion of Homeopathy
HOLISTIC HEALTH	H182	Journal of the Nutritional Academy
HOLISTIC HEALTH	H198	National College of Naturopathic Medicine
HOLISTIC HEALTH	H202	National Health Federation
HOLISTIC HEALTH	H205	New Age Wellness Center
HOLISTIC HEALTH	H210	Northern Pines: A Wholistic Health Retreat
HOLISTIC HEALTH	H232	Soundiscoveries
HOLISTIC HEALTH	H233	Spring Hill: Community, Retreat and Counseling Center
HOLISTIC HEALTH	H235	Tri-Self Clinic
HOLISTIC HEALTH	H236	Turtle Island Holistic Health Community
HOLISTIC HEALTH	H240	Well-Being Magazine
HOLISTIC HEALTH	H241	Wellness Associates
HOLISTIC HEALTH	H242	Wellness Institute
HOLISTIC HEALTH	H243	Wholistic Health and Nutrition Institute
HOLISTIC HEALTH	G003	Association for Humanistic Psychology
HOLISTIC HEALTH	G008	Chimo: The Holistic Magazine for Our Times
HOLISTIC HEALTH	G115	Association for Unity, Research, and Awareness
HOLISTIC HEALTH	G136	Center of the Light
HOLISTIC HEALTH	G203	Life Systems Educational Foundation
HOLISTIC HEALTH	G214	Many Hands: Guide to Holistic Health and Awareness
HOLISTIC HEALTH	G237	New Life Foundation for Holistic Health and Research
HOLISTIC HEALTH	G251	PhenomeNEWS
HOLISTIC HEALTH	E187	Institute of Noetic Sciences
HOLISTIC STUDIES	H129	California School of Herbal Studies
HOLISTIC STUDIES	H178	Interface Foundation
HOLISTIC STUDIES	H223	Pumpkin Hollow Farm
HOLISTIC STUDIES	L174	Holistic Life University
HOLISTIC STUDIES	L180	Institute for Wholistic Education
HOLISTIC STUDIES	G014	Lama Foundation
HOLISTIC STUDIES	G018	Omega Institute for Holistic Studies
HOLISTIC STUDIES	G159	Esalen Institute
HOLISTIC STUDIES	G164	Feathered Pipe Ranch
HOLISTIC STUDIES	G203	Life Systems Educational Foundation
HOLISTIC STUDIES	G223	Naropa Institute
HOLISTIC STUDIES	G248	Oz Projects: Retreat in the Redwoods
HOLISTIC STUDIES	G313	Wainwright House

HOME BIRTH	H020	NAPSAC: Safe Alternatives in Childbirth
HOME BIRTH	H114	Association for Childbirth at Home International
HOME BIRTH	H117	Austin Lay Midwives Association
HOME BIRTH	H137	Center for Humane Options in the Childbirth Experience
HOME BIRTH	H171	Home-Oriented Maternity Experience
HOME BIRTH	H172	Homebirth
HOME BIRTH	H175	Informed Homebirth
HOME BREWERS	S106	American Homebrewers Association
HOME EXCHANGE	G192	International Home Exchange Service
HOME SCHOOLS	L001	Alternatives in Education
HOME SCHOOLS	L020	Holt Associates
HOME SCHOOLS	L024	National Association of Legal Services to Alternative Schools
HOME SCHOOLS	L028	New Jersey Unschoolers
HOME SCHOOLS	L030	Ohio Coalition for Educational Alternatives Now
HOME SCHOOLS	L110	Alternative Schools Network
HOME SCHOOLS	L129	Canadian Alliance of Home Schoolers
HOME SCHOOLS	L175	Home Study Exchange
HOME SCHOOLS	L204	National Coalition of Alternative Community Schools
HOME SCHOOLS	L208	National Home Study Council
HOMEMAKERS	V164	Displaced Homemakers Network
HOMEMAKERS	V182	Homemakers Organized for More Employment
HOMEMAKERS	V285	Wisconsin Women's Network
HOMEOPATHY	H166	Holistic Health Practitioners' Association
HOMEOPATHY	H173	Homeopathic Educational Services
HOMEOPATHY	H181	International Foundation for the Promotion of Homeopathy
HOMESTEADERS	S148	Countryside: The Magazine for Serious Homesteaders
HOMESTEADERS	S178	Home Ownership Development Program
HOMESTEADERS	S179	Homesteaders News
HOMESTEADERS	S210	New Seeds Information Service
HOMESTEADERS	U115	Applewood Journal
HOMESTEADERS	U153	Ecology Action of the Midpeninsula
HOMESTEADERS	L196	Mother Earth News
HOPI	S241	Techqua Ikachi: Traditional Hopi Viewpoint
HOSPICE	H013	Hospice Institute for Education Training and Research
HOSPICE	H203	National Hospice Organization
HOT SPRINGS	H174	Hot Springs Information Network
HOUSING	S015	National Association of Housing Cooperatives
HOUSING	S016	National Association of Neighborhoods
HOUSING	S020	National Congress of Neighborhood Women
HOUSING	S022	National Hispanic Coalition for Better Housing
HOUSING	S023	National Neighbors
HOUSING	S031	North American Students of Cooperation
HOUSING	S034	Rural America
HOUSING	S036	Shelterforce Collective
HOUSING	S038	Urban Alternatives Group
HOUSING	S108	Architecture 2001
HOUSING	S111	Basement Alliance
HOUSING	S117	Boston Building Materials Cooperative
HOUSING	S155	Dovetail Press: Design for the Owner-Involved Builder
HOUSING	S178	Home Ownership Development Program
HOUSING	S179	Homesteaders News
HOUSING	S204	National Trust for Historic Preservation
HOUSING	S217	Northwest Regional Foundation

HOUSING	S218	Old House Journal
HOUSING	S221	Owner-Builder Publications
HOUSING	S258	Yestermorrow: Design/Builder School
HOUSING	U005	Center for Neighborhood Technology
HOUSING	U116	Aprovecho Institute
HOUSING	U145	Cornerstones: Energy Efficient Housebuilding
HOUSING	U147	Design Alternatives
HOUSING	U150	Earth Lab Institute
HOUSING	U151	Earthmind: Energy Research, Education and Books
HOUSING	U160	Farallones Institute: Integral Urban House
HOUSING	U275	Underground Space Center
HOUSING	V028	New American Movement
HOUSING	V123	California Housing Information and Action Network
HOUSING	V157	Consumer Education Research Group
HOUSING	V172	Focus/Midwest
HOUSING	V181	Home Equity Conversion Project
HOUSING	L160	Educational Futures
HOUSING	L239	Shelter Publications
HOUSING	G192	International Home Exchange Service
HOUSING	G257	Rare Earth: Exotic Properties for Sale
HUMAN RIGHTS	U008	Committee for Nuclear Responsibility
HUMAN RIGHTS	V017	Indian Rights Association
HUMAN RIGHTS	V021	Know Feminist Publishers
HUMAN RIGHTS	V026	National Committee Against Repressive Legislation
HUMAN RIGHTS	V029	New England Human Rights Network
HUMAN RIGHTS	V104	Akwesasne Notes: For Native and Natural Peoples
HUMAN RIGHTS	V107	Amnesty International
HUMAN RIGHTS	V151	Come Unity: An Alternative Independent Journal
HUMAN RIGHTS	E003	Commission to Study the Organization of Peace
HUMAN RIGHTS	E007	Global Education Associates
HUMAN RIGHTS	E008	Human Rights Internet
HUMAN RIGHTS	E014	North American Congress on Latin America
HUMAN RIGHTS	E125	Center for International Policy
HUMAN RIGHTS	E165	Friends of the Filipino People
HUMAN RIGHTS	E171	Helsinki Watch
HUMAN RIGHTS	E183	Institute for Policy Studies
HUMAN RIGHTS	E208	Magic Circle: The Native American Indian
HUMAN RIGHTS	E246	Rescue Communication Network
HUMAN RIGHTS	E269	U.S. Committee for Justice to Latin American Political Prisoners
HUMAN RIGHTS	E278	Women's International League for Peace and Freedom
HUMAN SERVICES	H188	Marion County Community Mental Health Center
HUMAN SERVICES	H189	Massachusetts Coalition of Battered Women Service Groups
HUMAN SERVICES	H201	National Feminist Therapists Association
HUMAN SERVICES	H224	Pyramid: Resource Sharing Network for Drug Abuse Prevention
HUMAN SERVICES	H247	Working on Wife Abuse
HUMAN SERVICES	S005	Community Congress of San Diego
HUMAN SERVICES	S019	National Commission on Resources for Youth, Inc.
HUMAN SERVICES	S024	National Network of Runaway and Youth Services
HUMAN SERVICES	S025	National Self-Help Clearinghouse
HUMAN SERVICES	S028	Natural Helping Networks Project
HUMAN SERVICES	S103	Alaska Youth Advocates
HUMAN SERVICES	S217	Northwest Regional Foundation
HUMAN SERVICES	S226	Project SHARE: Improving the Management of Human Services
HUMAN SERVICES	V164	Displaced Homemakers Network
HUMAN SERVICES	V251	Radical Alliance of Social Service Workers
HUMAN SERVICES	V259	Social Advocates for Youth
HUMAN SYSTEMS	L021	Humanistic Psychology Institute
HUMAN SYSTEMS	E115	Association for the Study of Man-Environment Relations
HUMAN SYSTEMS	E124	Center for Interdisciplinary Creativity
HUMAN SYSTEMS	E173	Human Systems Network

HUMAN SYSTEMS	E190	International Center for Integrative Studies
HUMAN SYSTEMS	E200	Johnson-Lenz
HUMAN SYSTEMS	E235	Phebus: Integrating Wholes and Parts
HUMANIST	G001	American Humanist Association
HUMANISTIC	L021	Humanistic Psychology Institute
HUMANISTIC	L120	Aspen Institute for Humanistic Studies
HUMANISTIC	L122	Association for Humanistic Education
HUMANISTIC	G003	Association for Humanistic Psychology
HUMANISTIC	G010	Dromenon: Journal of New Ways of Being
HUMANISTIC	G159	Esalen Institute
HUMANISTIC	G293	Synergic Power Institute
HUMANISTIC	E206	Leading Edge: A Bulletin of Social Transformation
HUNGER	U014	Food Monitor
HUNGER	V202	Maryland Food Committee
HUNGER	V261	South Carolina Committee Against Hunger
HUNGER	E006	Friends of the Third World
HUNGER	E009	Hunger Project
HUNGER	E011	Institute for Food and Development Policy
HUNGER	E016	Oxfam America
HUNGER	E199	Interreligious Taskforce on U.S. Food Policy
HUNGER	E226	Office on Global Education
HUNGER	E238	Plenty
HUNGER	E246	Rescue Communication Network
HUNGER	E284	World Hunger Education Service
I CHING	G181	I Ching Sangha
INDIAN	S241	Techqua Ikachi: Traditional Hopi Viewpoint
INDIAN	V017	Indian Rights Association
INDIAN	V027	National Indian Youth Council
INDIAN	V104	Akwesasne Notes: For Native and Natural Peoples
INDIAN	V114	Association on American Indian Affairs
INDIAN	V153	Committee on Native American Struggles
INDIAN	V275	Tribal Sovereignty Program
INDIAN	V297	Youth Project
INDIAN	G120	Bear Tribe Medicine Society
INDIAN	G122	Black Hills Alliance
INDIAN	E208	Magic Circle: The Native American Indian
INDOCHINA	V184	Indochina Curriculum Group
INDOCHINA	E113	Asia-Pacific Affairs Associates
INDOCHINA	E260	Southeast Asia Resource Center
INFORMATION	S029	Neighborhood Information Sharing Exchange
INFORMATION	S159	Family of New Age Networkers
INFORMATION	S181	Information Tree/San Francisco
INFORMATION	S183	Interest File
INFORMATION	U023	Rain Community Resource Center
INFORMATION	U024	Scientists' Institute for Public Information
INFORMATION	U158.	Environmental Action Reprint Service
INFORMATION	V152	Committee for Action Research on the Intelligence Community
INFORMATION	V158	Consumer Information Center
INFORMATION	V174	Freedom of Information Clearinghouse
INFORMATION	V254	Robert's Think Tank
INFORMATION	L019	Guild Communications Network
INFORMATION	L034	Southwest Research and Information Center
INFORMATION	L105	Alliance of Information and Referral Services
INFORMATION	L107	Alternative America: Directory of 5000 Groups and Organizations
INFORMATION	L121	Associated Information Managers
INFORMATION	L130	Canadian Information Sharing Service

INFORMATION	L145	Community Information Center
INFORMATION	L161	Educational Resources Information Center
INFORMATION	L178	Information for People
INFORMATION	L212	National Technical Information Service
INFORMATION	L220	Northern California/Southern Oregon Resource Network
INFORMATION	G016	New Age Information Service
INFORMATION	E022	Transnational Network for Appropriate/Alternative Technologies
INFORMATION	E179	Information Industry Association
INFORMATION	E182	Institute for Information Society
INSULATION	S117	Boston Building Materials Cooperative
INSULATION	S221	Owner-Builder Publications
INSULATION	U118	Arkansas Solar Action Coalition
INSULATION	U139	Community Network for Appropriate Technologies
INSULATION	U142	Conservation and Renewable Energy Inquiry and Referral Service
INSULATION	U143	Consumer Action Now
INSULATION	U145	Cornerstones: Energy Efficient Housebuilding
INSULATION	U147	Design Alternatives
INSULATION	U151	Earthmind: Energy Research, Education and Books
INSULATION	U193	Lamoureux Foundation: Home Energy Workshops
JEWISH	S032	Project for Kibbutz Studies
JEWISH	V192	Jewish Peace Fellowship
JEWISH	G110	Aquarian Minyan
JEWISH	G205	Lilith: The Jewish Women's Magazine
JEWISH	G216	Menorah: Sparks of Jewish Renewal
JEWISH	G328	World Union for Progressive Judaism
JEWISH	E256	Shalom Network
JOBS	H118	Bay Area Coalition on Occupational Safety and Health
JOBS	H135	Carolina Brown Lung Association
JOBS	H230	Society for Occupational and Environmental Health
JOBS	S005	Community Congress of San Diego
JOBS	S020	National Congress of Neighborhood Women
JOBS	S119	Boulder Women's Network
JOBS	S137	Community Jobs
JOBS	U181	Human Environment Center
JOBS	V003	Association of Community Organizations for Reform Now
JOBS	V012	Council on Economic Priorities
JOBS	V025	National Association of Office Workers
JOBS	V030	New Ways to Work
JOBS	V033	Project Work
JOBS	V037	Vocations for Social Change
JOBS	V040	Women's Action Alliance
JOBS	V112	Association for Self-Management
JOBS	V126	Catalyst National Network
JOBS	V163	Disability Rights Center
JOBS	V164	Displaced Homemakers Network
JOBS	V169	Exploratory Project for Economic Alternatives
JOBS	V182	Homemakers Organized for More Employment
JOBS	V227	New Directions for Young Women
JOBS	V234	Nine to Five (9 to 5)
JOBS	V249	Project Equality
JOBS	V271	The Spokeswoman: Feminist News Digest
JOBS	V276	Union Women's Alliance to Gain Equality
JOBS	V289	Women's Enterprises of Boston
JOBS	V295	Working Women's Institute
JOBS	L004	Association for Experiential Education
JOBS	L202	National Center for Research in Vocational Education
JOBS	L262	Women's Educational Equity Communications Network
KIBBUTZ	S032	Project for Kibbutz Studies

KIRLIAN	E195	International Kirlian Research
KITES	G197	Kite Lines
KNITTING	S257	Wool Gathering
KNITTING	G135	Center for the History of American Needlework
KROPOTKIN	V038	We-Know-Now Free Trade Exchange
KUBLER-ROSS	G270	Shanti Nilaya
LABOR	H009	Consumer Coalition for Health
LABOR	U006	Citizen/Labor Energy Coalition
LABOR	V005	California Newsreel
LABOR	V037	Vocations for Social Change
LABOR	V160	Cultural Correspondence
LABOR	V187	Institute for Labor Education and Research
LABOR	V246	Prisoners Union
LABOR	V276	Union Women's Alliance to Gain Equality
LABOR	L104	Alliance for Citizen Education
LABOR	E014	North American Congress on Latin America
LAND	S007	Community Service
LAND	S035	School of Living: Publishers of Green Revolution
LAND	S232	Sealand: The Cheap Land Catalogue
LAND	S243	The Smallholder: Ideas and Information for Country People
LAND	S245	Trust for Public Land
LAND	U014	Food Monitor
LAND	U140	Compost Science/Land Utilization
LAND	U146	Dakota Resource Council
LAND	U284	Wilderness Society
LAND	V013	Emergency Land Fund
LAND	V015	Henry George School of Social Science
LAND	V245	Powder River Basin Resource Council
LAND	V275	Tribal Sovereignty Program
LAND	G122	Black Hills Alliance
LAND	G257	Rare Earth: Exotic Properties for Sale
LATIN AMERICA	V102	Accion/Micro Enterprise Development Corporation
LATIN AMERICA	E014	North American Congress on Latin America
LATIN AMERICA	E215	National Network in Solidarity with the Nicaraguan People
LATIN AMERICA	E221	News from Guatemala
LATIN AMERICA	E269	U.S. Committee for Justice to Latin American Political Prisoners
LATIN AMERICA	E275	Washington Office on Latin America
LEARNING	L009	Council for the Advancement of Experiential Learning
LEARNING	L025	National Center for Service-Learning
LEARNING	L124	Atlanta Network: Teaching, Learning and Interest Sharing
LEARNING	L184	Learning Connection
LEARNING	L185	Learning Exchange
LEARNING	L186	Learning Tools
LEARNING	L187	Learning Web
LEARNING	L188	Link Learning Network
LEARNING	L213	Network for Learning
LEARNING	L229	Providence Learning Connection
LEARNING	L270	Workshop for Learning Things
LEGAL	H017	Lesbian Mothers National Defense Fund
LEGAL	H141	Children's Defense Fund
LEGAL	U007	Citizens for a Better Environment
LEGAL	U013	Environmental Defense Fund
LEGAL	U020	Natural Resources Defense Council
LEGAL	V040	Women's Action Alliance

LEGAL	V116	Bay Area Lawyers for the Arts
LEGAL	V117	Black Law Journal
LEGAL	V140	Center for a Woman's Own Name
LEGAL	V141	Center for the Study of Responsive Law
LEGAL	V142	Center on Law and Pacifism
LEGAL	V143	Children's Legal Rights Information and Training Program
LEGAL	V150	Coalition to End Grand Jury Abuse
LEGAL	V153	Committee on Native American Struggles
LEGAL	V157	Consumer Education Research Group
LEGAL	V179	Halt: Americans for Legal Reform
LEGAL	V186	Inmate Legal Association
LEGAL	V197	Legal Services Corporation
LEGAL	V201	Making It Legal: Primer for Craftmaker, Artist and Writer
LEGAL	V204	Mental Health Law Project
LEGAL	V205	Mexican American Legal Defense and Educational Fund
LEGAL	V214	National Economic Development and Law Center
LEGAL	V216	National Lawyers Guild
LEGAL	V221	National Prison Project
LEGAL	V264	Southern Poverty Law Center
LEGAL	V281	Veterans Education Project
LEGAL	V290	Women's Equity Action League
LEGAL	V291	Women's Legal Defense Fund
LEGAL	L024	National Association of Legal Services to Alternative Schools
LEGAL	L026	National Federation of Community Broadcasters
LEGAL	L035	Student Press Law Center
LEGAL	L263	Women's History Research Center
LESBIAN	H017	Lesbian Mothers National Defense Fund
LESBIAN	V161	Custody Action for Lesbian Mothers
LESBIAN	L146	Conditions: Writing by Women
LESBIAN	L164	Feminary: A Feminist Journal for the South
LIBERTARIAN	V113	Association of Libertarian Feminists
LIBERTARIAN	V198	Libertarian Review
LIBERTARIAN	V262	South Carolina Libertarian Party
LIBRARY	U004	Cascadian Regional Library
LIBRARY	L108	Alternative Press Center
LIBRARY	L145	Community Information Center
LIBRARY	L157	Earthbooks Lending Library/Allegheny Branch
LIBRARY	L159	Educational Film Library Association
LIBRARY	L241	Sipapu: Newsletter for Librarians
LIBRARY	G175	Hanuman Foundation Tape Library
LIFE EXTENSION	E136	Claustrophobia: Life Extension
LIFE EXTENSION	E264	The Network: Starflight and Immortality
LIFE PASSAGES	G021	Rites of Passage
LIFE PASSAGES	G270	Shanti Nilaya
LINKAGE	E017	Participation Publishers
LOVE	H176	Institute for Family Research and Education
LOVE	S190	Love Family
LOVE	G209	Love Project
LOVE	G210	Love: A Journal
LUTHIERS	G174	Guild of American Luthiers
MACROBIOTIC	H010	East West Journal
MACROBIOTIC	H186	Macrobiotic Health Information Center of New Jersey
MACROBIOTIC	H187	Macrobiotic: A Guide for Natural Living

MAGIC	**G213**	Magical Blend: A Magazine of Synergy
MARIJUANA	**V220**	National Organization for the Reform of Marijuana Laws
MEDIA	**S194**	Mediaworks
MEDIA	**S247**	Urban Planning Aid
MEDIA	**V288**	Women Against Violence in Pornography and Media
MEDIA	**L018**	Great Atlantic Radio Conspiracy
MEDIA	**L102**	Action for Children's Television
MEDIA	**L106**	Alternate Media Center
MEDIA	**L142**	College Media Journal
MEDIA	**L154**	Direct Cinema Limited
MEDIA	**L155**	Double Helix: Community Media
MEDIA	**L158**	Earthenergy Media
MEDIA	**L192**	Media Access Project
MEDIA	**L193**	Media Alliance
MEDIA	**L194**	MediaSense
MEDIA	**L207**	National Federation of Local Cable Programmers
MEDIA	**L223**	Packard Manse Media Project
MEDIA	**L230**	Public Media Center
MEDIA	**L245**	Southern Progressive Periodicals Directory
MEDIA	**L249**	Telecommunications Cooperative Network
MEDIA	**L257**	Washington Community Video Center
MEDIA	**L259**	White Buffalo Multimedia
MEDIA	**L261**	Women in Focus: Film Production and Distribution
MEDIA	**G236**	New Dimensions Radio and Tapes
MEDIA	**E020**	Satellite Video Exchange Society
MEDIA	**E250**	Review of International Broadcasting
MEDIA	**E267**	Twenty-first Century Media
MEDICAL	**H003**	Center for Integral Medicine
MEDICAL	**H004**	Center for Medical Consumers and Health Care Information
MEDICAL	**H007**	Coalition for the Medical Rights of Women
MEDICAL	**H101**	Academy of Orthomolecular Psychiatry
MEDICAL	**H112**	American Holistic Medical Association
MEDICAL	**H145**	Cinema Medica
MEDICAL	**H152**	Doctors Ought to Care
MEDICAL	**H155**	Endometriosis Association
MEDICAL	**H169**	Holistic Psychotherapy and Medical Group
MEDICAL	**H193**	Medical Self-Care Magazine
MEDICAL	**H212**	Nurses in Transition
MEDICAL	**H213**	Nutritional and Preventive Medical Clinic
MEDICAL	**H219**	People's Doctor: Medical Newsletter for Consumers
MEDICAL	**V243**	Physicians for Social Responsibility
MEDITATION	**H002**	Center for Attitudinal Healing
MEDITATION	**G006**	Cambridge Zen Center
MEDITATION	**G011**	Dying Project
MEDITATION	**G014**	Lama Foundation
MEDITATION	**G019**	Prison Ashram Project
MEDITATION	**G025**	Sri Chinmoy Centre
MEDITATION	**G112**	Arcana Workshops
MEDITATION	**G115**	Association for Unity, Research, and Awareness
MEDITATION	**G154**	Diamond Sangha Center: Zen Buddhist Society
MEDITATION	**G186**	Insight Meditation Society
MEDITATION	**G196**	Karma Triyana Dharmachakra
MEDITATION	**G215**	Maui Zendo
MEDITATION	**G218**	Minnesota Zen Meditation Center
MEDITATION	**G222**	Muktananda Meditation Center
MEDITATION	**G255**	Providence Zen Center
MEDITATION	**G262**	Rudrananda Ashram
MEDITATION	**G263**	SYDA Foundation
MEDITATION	**G271**	Siddha Yoga Dham Ann Arbor

MEDITATION	G272	Siddha Yoga Dham Boston
MEDITATION	G273	Sino-American Buddhist Association
MEDITATION	G274	Sirius Community
MEDITATION	G283	Spiritual Emergency Network
MEDITATION	G294	T'ai Chi
MEDITATION	G332	Zen Center of San Francisco
MEDITATION	G333	Zen Center of Sonoma Mountain
MEDITATION	E208	Magic Circle: The Native American Indian
MEDITATION	E265	Triangles: Network of Light
MEN	H108	American Academy of Husband-Coached Childbirth
MEN	S130	Chicago Men's Gathering Newsletter
MEN	S189	Los Angeles Men's Collective
MEN	S195	Men's Program Unit
MEN	S196	Men's Resource Center
MEN	S227	RFD: Country Journal for Gay Men Everywhere
MEN	G212	M. Gentle Men for Gender Justice
MENTAL HEALTH	H015	Huxley Institute for Biosocial Research
MENTAL HEALTH	H018	Madness Network News
MENTAL HEALTH	H024	New Directions in Psychology
MENTAL HEALTH	H104	Advocates for Freedom in Mental Health
MENTAL HEALTH	H116	Association for the Preservation of Anti-Psychiatric Artifacts
MENTAL HEALTH	H119	Bay Area Committee for Alternatives to Psychiatry
MENTAL HEALTH	H149	Community Network Development Project
MENTAL HEALTH	H188	Marion County Community Mental Health Center
MENTAL HEALTH	H196	National Alliance for the Mentally Ill
MENTAL HEALTH	H204	Network Against Psychiatric Assault
MENTAL HEALTH	H215	On Our Own Network
MENTAL HEALTH	H221	Psychiatric Inmates' Rights Collective
MENTAL HEALTH	V204	Mental Health Law Project
MENTAL HEALTH	L272	Zipporah Films
MENTAL PATIENTS	H107	Alliance for the Liberation of Mental Patients
MENTAL PATIENTS	H194	Mental Patients Association
MENTAL PATIENTS	H216	Ontario Patients' Self-Help Association
MICROCOMPUTER	E121	Byte: The Small Systems Journal
MICROCOMPUTER	E141	CommuniTree Group
MICROCOMPUTER	E145	Compute Magazine
MICROCOMPUTER	E147	Computer Information Exchange
MICROCOMPUTER	E177	InfoWorld: The Newspaper for the Microcomputing Community
MICROCOMPUTER	E219	New Era Technologies
MICROCOMPUTER	E233	People's Computer Company
MICROCOMPUTER	E242	Purser's Magazine for Family Computers
MICRONET	E144	CompuServe
MIDDLE EAST	E109	Americans for Middle East Understanding, Inc.
MIDDLE EAST	E212	Middle East Peace Project
MIDDLE EAST	E213	Middle East Research and Information Project
MIDDLE EAST	E256	Shalom Network
MIDWIVES	H020	NAPSAC: Safe Alternatives in Childbirth
MIDWIVES	H117	Austin Lay Midwives Association
MIDWIVES	H123	Birthing Monthly Newsletter
MIDWIVES	H171	Home-Oriented Maternity Experience
MIDWIVES	H172	Homebirth
MIDWIVES	H175	Informed Homebirth
MIDWIVES	H192	Maternity Center
MIDWIVES	H239	Washington State Midwifery Council
MIDWIVES	G301	The Farm

MILITARY	U232	Pacific Northwest Research Center
MILITARY	V008	Central Committee for Conscientious Objectors
MILITARY	V011	Committee Against Registration and the Draft
MILITARY	V031	Peacework
MILITARY	V111	Armistice/Live Without Trident
MILITARY	V119	Boston Study Group
MILITARY	V131	Center for Defense Information
MILITARY	V132	Center for National Security Studies
MILITARY	V133	Center for New National Security
MILITARY	V145	Citizen Alert
MILITARY	V149	Civilian Congress
MILITARY	V155	Conscience and Military Tax Campaign
MILITARY	V179	Halt: Americans for Legal Reform
MILITARY	V206	Midwest Committee for Military Counseling
MILITARY	V210	National Action/Research on the Military Industrial Complex
MILITARY	V222	National Resistance Committee
MILITARY	V238	One Less Bomb Committee
MILITARY	V255	Rocky Flats Nuclear Weapons Facilities Project
MILITARY	V273	Toronto Association for Peace
MILITARY	E014	North American Congress on Latin America
MILITARY	E025	War Control Planners
MILITARY	E112	Arms Control Association
MILITARY	E131	Center for War/Peace Studies
MILITARY	E137	Coalition for a New Foreign and Military Policy
MILITARY	E163	First Earth Battalion Foundation
MILITARY	E218	Network to Educate for World Security
MIME	G265	San Francisco Mime Troupe
MIRACLES	G167	Foundation for Inner Peace
MIRACLES	G238	New Options for a Vital United States (NOVUS)
MOHAWK	V104	Akwesasne Notes: For Native and Natural Peoples
MOTHERS	H006	Cesarean Connection
MOTHERS	H016	La Leche League International
MOTHERS	H017	Lesbian Mothers National Defense Fund
MOTHERS	H019	Mothering Magazine
MOTHERS	S200	Mothers and Others
MOTHERS	V161	Custody Action for Lesbian Mothers
MUKTANANDA	G222	Muktananda Meditation Center
MUKTANANDA	G263	SYDA Foundation
MUKTANANDA	G271	Siddha Yoga Dham Ann Arbor
MUKTANANDA	G272	Siddha Yoga Dham Boston
MUSHROOMS	U221	North American Mycological Association
MUSIC	U201	Musicians United for Safe Energy
MUSIC	L168	Flower Films
MUSIC	L195	Mix Recording Publications
MUSIC	G022	Sing Out! The Folk Song Magazine
MUSIC	G023	Sphinx and Sword of Love Bookstore
MUSIC	G152	Damage Magazine: Not for Everybody
MUSIC	G174	Guild of American Luthiers
MUSIC	G188	Institute for Consciousness and Music
MUSIC	G208	Lost Music Network
MUSIC	G231	New Age Music Network
MUSIC	G278	Society of Folk Harpers and Craftsmen
MUSIC	E148	Computer Music Journal
MX	V035	SANE
MX	V145	Citizen Alert

MYTH	G249	Parabola: Myth and the Quest for Meaning
MYTH	G258	ReVision: A Journal of Knowledge and Consciousness
MYTH	G282	Spirals: Bridging the Gap Between Science and Mysticism
NATUROPATHY	H198	National College of Naturopathic Medicine
NEIGHBORHOOD	S001	Citizens Committee for New York City
NEIGHBORHOOD	S002	Civic Action Institute
NEIGHBORHOOD	S007	Community Service
NEIGHBORHOOD	S016	National Association of Neighborhoods
NEIGHBORHOOD	S020	National Congress of Neighborhood Women
NEIGHBORHOOD	S022	National Hispanic Coalition for Better Housing
NEIGHBORHOOD	S023	National Neighbors
NEIGHBORHOOD	S026	National Self-Help Resource Center
NEIGHBORHOOD	S027	National Training and Information Center
NEIGHBORHOOD	S029	Neighborhood Information Sharing Exchange
NEIGHBORHOOD	S030	New York Urban Coalition
NEIGHBORHOOD	S118	Boston Urban Gardens
NEIGHBORHOOD	S128	Center for Neighborhood Development
NEIGHBORHOOD	S129	Chicago Association of Neighborhood Organizations
NEIGHBORHOOD	S181	Information Tree/San Francisco
NEIGHBORHOOD	S204	National Trust for Historic Preservation
NEIGHBORHOOD	S205	Neighborhood Organization Research Group
NEIGHBORHOOD	S217	Northwest Regional Foundation
NEIGHBORHOOD	S236	Southern Neighborhoods
NEIGHBORHOOD	S246	United Neighborhood Centers of America
NEIGHBORHOOD	U005	Center for Neighborhood Technology
NEIGHBORHOOD	V004	Barter Project
NEIGHBORHOOD	G007	Center for Leisure Guidance
NEW TOWNS	S013	Institute on Man and Science
NEW TOWNS	U117	Arcosanti
NEW TOWNS	U216	New Environment Association
NEWS SERVICE	S143	Consumer Coop Press Service
NEWS SERVICE	S206	Network Exchange News Service
NEWS SERVICE	S247	Urban Planning Aid
NEWS SERVICE	L023	Liberation News Service
NEWS SERVICE	L109	Alternative Press Syndicate
NEWS SERVICE	L209	National News Bureau
NEWS SERVICE	L252	Today News Service
NEWS SERVICE	E103	Africa News Service
NEWS SERVICE	E189	Interlink Press Service
NICARAGUA	E215	National Network in Solidarity with the Nicaraguan People
NOETIC	E187	Institute of Noetic Sciences
NONVIOLENCE	S012	Institute for Non-Violent Education, Research, and Training
NONVIOLENCE	S199	Midwest Academy
NONVIOLENCE	V024	Movement for a New Society
NONVIOLENCE	V103	Agape Foundation: Fund for Nonviolent Social Change
NONVIOLENCE	V129	Center for Conflict Resolution
NONVIOLENCE	V130	Center for Conflict Resolution
NONVIOLENCE	V135	Center for Nonviolent Persuasion
NONVIOLENCE	V175	Friends Peace Committee
NONVIOLENCE	V191	International Seminars in Training for Nonviolent Action
NONVIOLENCE	V228	New England Cooperative Training Institute
NONVIOLENCE	V235	North Country M.N.S. Organizing Collective
NONVIOLENCE	L137	Children's Creative Response to Conflict Program
NONVIOLENCE	E013	National Peace Academy Campaign
NONVIOLENCE	E015	North American Nonviolence Training Network
NONVIOLENCE	E127	Center for Peace and Conflict Studies

NONVIOLENCE	E248	Resource Center for Nonviolence
NUCLEAR	S164	Fellowship House Farm
NUCLEAR	U002	Anvil Press
NUCLEAR	U008	Committee for Nuclear Responsibility
NUCLEAR	U010	Critical Mass Energy Project
NUCLEAR	U017	Green Mountain Post Films
NUCLEAR	U018	Greenpeace Foundation
NUCLEAR	U020	Natural Resources Defense Council
NUCLEAR	U021	Nuclear Information and Resource Service
NUCLEAR	U024	Scientists' Institute for Public Information
NUCLEAR	U025	Southern Unity Network/Renewable Energy Project
NUCLEAR	U026	Task Force Against Nuclear Pollution
NUCLEAR	U101	Abalone Alliance
NUCLEAR	U120	Boston Clamshell Coalition
NUCLEAR	U122	Bullfrog Films
NUCLEAR	U124	Canadian Coalition for Nuclear Responsibility
NUCLEAR	U126	Catfish Alliance
NUCLEAR	U131	Chesapeake Energy Alliance
NUCLEAR	U134	Citizens for Safe Power Transmission
NUCLEAR	U137	Coalition for Direct Action at Seabrook
NUCLEAR	U138	Community Energy Action Network
NUCLEAR	U148	Documentary Guild
NUCLEAR	U155	Energy People
NUCLEAR	U158	Environmental Action Reprint Service
NUCLEAR	U174	Greenpeace/Vancouver
NUCLEAR	U177	Health and Energy Learning Project
NUCLEAR	U180	Hudson Valley Green
NUCLEAR	U206	National Intervenors
NUCLEAR	U213	New England Coalition on Nuclear Pollution
NUCLEAR	U219	New Times Films
NUCLEAR	U220	Non Nuclear Network
NUCLEAR	U226	Northern Sun Alliance
NUCLEAR	U232	Pacific Northwest Research Center
NUCLEAR	U235	Potomac Alliance
NUCLEAR	U236	Prairie Alliance
NUCLEAR	U242	Safe Energy Alternatives Alliance
NUCLEAR	U244	Saginaw Valley Nuclear Study Group
NUCLEAR	U247	Saskatoon Environmental Society
NUCLEAR	U248	Science for the People
NUCLEAR	U252	Sierra Club Radioactive Waste Campaign
NUCLEAR	U271	Three Mile Island Alert
NUCLEAR	U274	Trojan Decommissioning Alliance
NUCLEAR	U279	Vermont Yankee Decommissioning Alliance
NUCLEAR	V012	Council on Economic Priorities
NUCLEAR	V020	Interfaith Center on Corporate Responsibility
NUCLEAR	V022	Mobilization for Survival
NUCLEAR	V024	Movement for a New Society
NUCLEAR	V027	National Indian Youth Council
NUCLEAR	V035	SANE
NUCLEAR	V110	Another Mother for Peace
NUCLEAR	V111	Armistice/Live Without Trident
NUCLEAR	V121	Bulletin of the Atomic Scientists
NUCLEAR	V131	Center for Defense Information
NUCLEAR	V151	Come Unity: An Alternative Independent Journal
NUCLEAR	V168	Eschaton Foundation: Community Spirit Fund
NUCLEAR	V238	One Less Bomb Committee
NUCLEAR	V243	Physicians for Social Responsibility
NUCLEAR	V255	Rocky Flats Nuclear Weapons Facilities Project
NUCLEAR	V278	Union of Concerned Scientists
NUCLEAR	V292	Women's Party for Survival
NUCLEAR	L010	Education Exploration Center
NUCLEAR	L034	Southwest Research and Information Center

NUCLEAR	L192	Media Access Project
NUCLEAR	L223	Packard Manse Media Project
NUCLEAR	G122	Black Hills Alliance
NUCLEAR	G229	New Age Magazine
NUCLEAR	G279	Sojourners: Christian Renewal Community
NUCLEAR	E123	Center for Development Policy
NUCLEAR	E236	Planetary Association for Clean Energy
NURSES	H012	Health Policy Advisory Council
NURSES	H113	American Holistic Nurses' Association
NURSES	H211	Nurse Healers/Professional Associates Cooperative
NURSES	H212	Nurses in Transition
NURSING HOMES	H011	Gray Panthers
NURSING HOMES	H022	National Citizens Coalition for Nursing Home Reform
NUTRITION	H005	Center for Science in the Public Interest
NUTRITION	H010	East West Journal
NUTRITION	H015	Huxley Institute for Biosocial Research
NUTRITION	H101	Academy of Orthomolecular Psychiatry
NUTRITION	H164	Hippocrates Health Institute
NUTRITION	H180	International College of Applied Nutrition
NUTRITION	H182	Journal of the Nutritional Academy
NUTRITION	H208	Newtrition Outreach: Whole Foods Information
NUTRITION	H213	Nutritional and Preventive Medical Clinic
NUTRITION	H231	Society for the Protection of the Unborn Through Nutrition
NUTRITION	H238	Vegetarian Times
NUTRITION	H243	Wholistic Health and Nutrition Institute
NUTRITION	S010	Food Learning Center
NUTRITION	S111	Basement Alliance
NUTRITION	S216	Northwest Provender Alliance
NUTRITION	S248	Vegetarian Society of D.C.
NUTRITION	U270	The Sproutletter: Sprouts, Raw Foods, and Nutrition
NUTRITION	V118	Boston INFACT
NUTRITION	V202	Maryland Food Committee
NUTRITION	G103	Alternatives: Tools for Holistic Living
NUTRITION	E011	Institute for Food and Development Policy
OCEANS	U168	General Whale
OCEANS	U174	Greenpeace/Vancouver
OCEANS	U212	New Alchemy Institute
OCEANS	U228	Ocean Education Project
OCEANS	U237	Project Jonah
OCEANS	U238	Rachel Carson Trust Fund for the Living Environment
OCEANS	U249	Sea Shepherd Conservation Society
OCEANS	E257	Sierra Club International Earthcare Center
OFFICE WORKERS	V025	National Association of Office Workers
OFFICE WORKERS	V234	Nine to Five (9 to 5)
OPEN NETWORK	L031	Open Network
OPEN NETWORK	L219	Northern California Open Network
OPEN NETWORK	L244	Southern California Open Network
ORGANIZING	S002	Civic Action Institute
ORGANIZING	S012	Institute for Non-Violent Education, Research, and Training
ORGANIZING	S018	National Center for Citizen Involvement
ORGANIZING	S036	Shelterforce Collective
ORGANIZING	S199	Midwest Academy
ORGANIZING	S220	Organize Training Center
ORGANIZING	U021	Nuclear Information and Resource Service
ORGANIZING	V009	Citizens Involvement Training Project
ORGANIZING	V018	Institute for Social Justice

ORGANIZING	**V235**	North Country M.N.S. Organizing Collective
ORGANIZING	**V252**	Radical America
ORGANIZING	**L215**	New England Training Center for Community Organizers
OUTDOORS	**U192**	Izaak Walton League of America
OUTDOORS	**U195**	Maine Audubon Society
OUTDOORS	**U221**	North American Mycological Association
OUTDOORS	**L004**	Association for Experiential Education
OUTDOORS	**G029**	Women Outdoors
OUTDOORS	**G158**	Encounter Four: Adventure Course for Youth in Trouble
OUTDOORS	**G171**	Fund for Advancement of Camping
OUTDOORS	**G173**	Great Expeditions: Real Travellers and Explorers
OUTDOORS	**G183**	Infinite Odyssey: Wilderness Adventures
OUTDOORS	**G224**	National Outdoor Leadership School
OUTDOORS	**G225**	Nature Explorations
OUTDOORS	**G245**	Outdoor Education for the Handicapped Project
OUTDOORS	**G246**	Outside: Magazine of the Great Outdoors
OUTDOORS	**G276**	Sobek Expeditions: Outdoor Adventure Rivers Specialists
OWN NAME	**V140**	Center for a Woman's Own Name
PARACHUTING	**G130**	Canadian Sport Parachuting Association
PARACHUTING	**G309**	United States Parachute Association
PARENTS	**H019**	Mothering Magazine
PARENTS	**H020**	NAPSAC: Safe Alternatives in Childbirth
PARENTS	**H021**	National Alliance for Optional Parenthood
PARENTS	**H026**	Parent Support-Group Project
PARENTS	**H106**	Alliance for Perinatal Research and Services
PARENTS	**H117**	Austin Lay Midwives Association
PARENTS	**H124**	Boston Area Childbirth Education
PARENTS	**H127**	Boston Women's Health Book Collective
PARENTS	**H150**	Coping with the Overall Pregnancy/Parenting Experience
PARENTS	**H179**	International Childbirth Education Association
PARENTS	**H207**	New Beginnings Birth Center
PARENTS	**H217**	Parents Without Partners
PARENTS	**H220**	Planned Parenthood
PARENTS	**H237**	Vanier Institute of the Family
PARENTS	**S040**	Warmlines: A Parent Network and Resource Center
PARENTS	**S124**	Carousel Press: Books for Parents
PARENTS	**S158**	Family Connection
PARENTS	**S223**	Parents Anonymous
PARENTS	**V188**	Institute for Peace and Justice
PARENTS	**L001**	Alternatives in Education
PARENTS	**L010**	Education Exploration Center
PARENTS	**L028**	New Jersey Unschoolers
PARENTS	**L162**	Educomics
PARENTS	**L205**	National Committee for Citizens in Education
PARENTS	**L224**	Parents Union for Public Schools
PARENTS	**G172**	Games
PEACE	**S164**	Fellowship House Farm
PEACE	**S173**	Grindstone Island Centre
PEACE	**V008**	Central Committee for Conscientious Objectors
PEACE	**V022**	Mobilization for Survival
PEACE	**V029**	New England Human Rights Network
PEACE	**V031**	Peacework
PEACE	**V035**	SANE
PEACE	**V110**	Another Mother for Peace
PEACE	**V111**	Armistice/Live Without Trident
PEACE	**V130**	Center for Conflict Resolution
PEACE	**V142**	Center on Law and Pacifism
PEACE	**V155**	Conscience and Military Tax Campaign

PEACE	V175	Friends Peace Committee
PEACE	V188	Institute for Peace and Justice
PEACE	V192	Jewish Peace Fellowship
PEACE	V238	One Less Bomb Committee
PEACE	V241	Peace Project
PEACE	V253	Recon Publications
PEACE	V255	Rocky Flats Nuclear Weapons Facilities Project
PEACE	V265	Syracuse Peace Council
PEACE	V273	Toronto Association for Peace
PEACE	L022	Intercommunity Center for Justice and Peace
PEACE	L226	Primary/Secondary Peace Education Network ness
PEACE	G209	Love Project
PEACE	G229	New Age Magazine
PEACE	G250	Pax Center
PEACE	G279	Sojourners: Christian Renewal Community
PEACE	E001	Association for World Education
PEACE	E002	Catholic Peace Fellowship
PEACE	E003	Commission to Study the Organization of Peace
PEACE	E005	Consortium on Peace Research, Education, and Development
PEACE	E007	Global Education Associates
PEACE	E013	National Peace Academy Campaign
PEACE	E015	North American Nonviolence Training Network
PEACE	E019	Planetary Citizens
PEACE	E025	War Control Planners
PEACE	E109	Americans for Middle East Understanding, Inc.
PEACE	E126	Center for Peace Studies
PEACE	E127	Center for Peace and Conflict Studies
PEACE	E131	Center for War/Peace Studies
PEACE	E161	Fellowship of Reconciliation
PEACE	E163	First Earth Battalion Foundation
PEACE	E184	Institute for World Order
PEACE	E212	Middle East Peace Project
PEACE	E213	Middle East Research and Information Project
PEACE	E218	Network to Educate for World Security
PEACE	E241	Promoting Enduring Peace
PEACE	E243	Radical Perspectives Network
PEACE	E247	Research Utilization Network
PEACE	E256	Shalom Network
PEACE	E272	University Peace Studies Network
PEACE	E278	Women's International League for Peace and Freedom
PEACE	E286	World Peace News
PEACE	E287	World Peace Tax Fund
PEACE	E290	World Union
PESTICIDES	U009	Commonweal
PESTICIDES	U185	Inland Regional Council
PESTICIDES	U205	National Coalition Against the Misuse of Pesticides
PESTICIDES	U227	Northwest Coalition for Alternatives to Pesticides
PESTICIDES	U266	Summit Coalition for Alternatives to Pesticides
PESTICIDES	V122	California Agrarian Action Project
PESTICIDES	E236	Planetary Association for Clean Energy
PHENOMENOLOGY	E285	World Institute for Advanced Phenomenological Research
PHILIPPINES	E165	Friends of the Filipino People
PHILOSOPHY	L031	Open Network
PHILOSOPHY	L189	Manas: Journal of Independent Inquiry
PHILOSOPHY	G001	American Humanist Association
PHILOSOPHY	G249	Parabola: Myth and the Quest for Meaning
PHILOSOPHY	G258	ReVision: A Journal of Knowledge and Consciousness
PHILOSOPHY	E190	International Center for Integrative Studies
PHILOSOPHY	E235	Phebus: Integrating Wholes and Parts

PHILOSOPHY	E285	World Institute for Advanced Phenomenological Research
PLANNERS	H012	Health Policy Advisory Council
PLANNERS	V032	Planner's Network
POETRY	H144	Chrysalis
POETRY	S133	City Miner: Community/Personal Adventure/Aesthetics
POETRY	L014	Feminist Writers' Guild/New York
POETRY	L139	City Lights Journal
POETRY	L146	Conditions: Writing by Women
POETRY	L247	Stony Hills: New England Alternative Press Review
POETRY	G026	The Sun: A Magazine of Ideas
POETRY	G123	Blackberry Books
POETRY	G134	Center for Women's Studies and Services
POETRY	G206	Lindisfarne Association
POETRY	G219	Modern Haiku
POETRY	G252	Poetry Project
POETRY	G264	Samisdat
POETRY	G267	Segue Foundation: Publishers of Books and Magazines
POETRY	G316	Watershed Foundation: Poetry Recordings
POLLUTION	U009	Commonweal
POLLUTION	U026	Task Force Against Nuclear Pollution
POLLUTION	U213	New England Coalition on Nuclear Pollution
POLLUTION	U228	Ocean Education Project
POLLUTION	U234	Pollution Probe Foundation
POLLUTION	U252	Sierra Club Radioactive Waste Campaign
POLLUTION	U277	Valley Watch
POLLUTION	U281	Waterloo Public Interest Research Group
POPULATION	H021	National Alliance for Optional Parenthood
POPULATION	U293	Zero Population Growth
POPULATION	E001	Association for World Education
POPULATION	E239	Population Action Council
POPULATION	E292	Worldwatch Institute
PORNOGRAPHY	V288	Women Against Violence in Pornography and Media
POSTSECONDARY	L006	Coalition for Alternatives in Postsecondary Education
POSTSECONDARY	L017	Free University Network
POSTSECONDARY	L021	Humanistic Psychology Institute
POSTSECONDARY	L036	Union for Experimenting Colleges and Universities
POSTSECONDARY	L112	American Association of University Women
POSTSECONDARY	L115	Antioch University West
POSTSECONDARY	L125	Bear's Guide to Non-Traditional College Degrees
POSTSECONDARY	L153	Denver Free University
POSTSECONDARY	L228	Project on the Status and Education of Women
POSTSECONDARY	G142	Clown College
POSTSECONDARY	E013	National Peace Academy Campaign
POSTSECONDARY	E122	Center for Creative Studies
POSTSECONDARY	E129	Center for Teaching International Relations
POSTSECONDARY	E272	University Peace Studies Network
POVERTY	S126	Center for Community Change
POVERTY	U157	Energy Task Force
POVERTY	U164	Food Research and Action Center
POVERTY	V003	Association of Community Organizations for Reform Now
POVERTY	V013	Emergency Land Fund
POVERTY	V023	Movement for Economic Justice
POVERTY	V202	Maryland Food Committee
POVERTY	V261	South Carolina Committee Against Hunger
POVERTY	V264	Southern Poverty Law Center
POVERTY	E197	International Voluntary Services

PREGNANCY	H106	Alliance for Perinatal Research and Services
PREGNANCY	H108	American Academy of Husband-Coached Childbirth
PREGNANCY	H117	Austin Lay Midwives Association
PREGNANCY	H124	Boston Area Childbirth Education
PREGNANCY	H150	Coping with the Overall Pregnancy/Parenting Experience
PREGNANCY	H179	International Childbirth Education Association
PREGNANCY	H191	Maternal and Child Health Center
PREGNANCY	H192	Maternity Center
PREGNANCY	H195	Mid-Hudson Area Maternity Alternatives
PREGNANCY	H207	New Beginnings Birth Center
PREGNANCY	H231	Society for the Protection of the Unborn Through Nutrition
PRESERVATION	S105	American Association for State and Local History
PRESERVATION	S204	National Trust for Historic Preservation
PRESERVATION	S218	Old House Journal
PRESERVATION	L113	American Historical Association
PRESS	S186	Lancaster Independent Press
PRESS	S225	Plexus: San Francisco Bay Area Women's Newspaper
PRESS	U002	Anvil Press
PRESS	V232	New World Review
PRESS	V236	Off Our Backs: A Women's News Journal
PRESS	L023	Liberation News Service
PRESS	L035	Student Press Law Center
PRESS	L108	Alternative Press Center
PRESS	L109	Alternative Press Syndicate
PRESS	L133	Center for Investigative Reporting
PRESS	L152	D.C. Gazette
PRESS	L166	Fine Print: A Review for the Arts of the Book
PRESS	L218	New Pages Press
PRESS	L236	San Francisco Bay Guardian
PRESS	L241	Sipapu: Newsletter for Librarians
PRESS	L242	Small Press Review
PRESS	L245	Southern Progressive Periodicals Directory
PRESS	L247	Stony Hills: New England Alternative Press Review
PRESS	L252	Today News Service
PRESS	L265	Women's Institute for Freedom of the Press
PRESS	L266	Women's Press
PRESS	L271	Youth Liberation Press
PRESS	E188	Intercontinental Press/Inprecor
PRESS	E189	Interlink Press Service
PRESS	E193	International Herald Tribune
PRESS	E234	People's Translation Service
PRESS	E288	World Press Review
PRESS	E291	WorldPaper: The Global Community Newspaper
PRISON	S140	Community Service Restitution
PRISON	V019	Institute for Southern Studies
PRISON	V105	Alternatives to Violence Project
PRISON	V107	Amnesty International
PRISON	V138	Center for Research on Criminal Justice
PRISON	V186	Inmate Legal Association
PRISON	V213	National Council of La Raza
PRISON	V221	National Prison Project
PRISON	V246	Prisoners Union
PRISON	V263	Southern Coalition on Jails and Prisons
PRISON	G019	Prison Ashram Project
PRISON	E269	U.S. Committee for Justice to Latin American Political Prisoners
PSI	G185	Inner-Space Interpreters Services
PSYCHIATRY	H015	Huxley Institute for Biosocial Research
PSYCHIATRY	H018	Madness Network News

PSYCHIATRY	H107	Alliance for the Liberation of Mental Patients
PSYCHIATRY	H116	Association for the Preservation of Anti-Psychiatric Artifacts
PSYCHIATRY	H119	Bay Area Committee for Alternatives to Psychiatry
PSYCHIATRY	H204	Network Against Psychiatric Assault
PSYCHIATRY	H221	Psychiatric Inmates' Rights Collective
PSYCHOLOGY	H024	New Directions in Psychology
PSYCHOLOGY	H105	Aletheia Psycho-Physical Foundation
PSYCHOLOGY	H125	Boston Center for Psychosynthesis
PSYCHOLOGY	H201	National Feminist Therapists Association
PSYCHOLOGY	L021	Humanistic Psychology Institute
PSYCHOLOGY	L189	Manas: Journal of Independent Inquiry
PSYCHOLOGY	G003	Association for Humanistic Psychology
PSYCHOLOGY	G004	Association for Transpersonal Psychology
PSYCHOLOGY	G103	Alternatives: Tools for Holistic Living
PSYCHOLOGY	G107	Anima: An Experiential Journal
PSYCHOLOGY	G133	Center for Studies of the Person
PSYCHOLOGY	G166	Focusing Institute
PSYCHOLOGY	G188	Institute for Consciousness and Music
PSYCHOLOGY	G195	Jungian-Senoi Dreamwork Institute
PSYCHOLOGY	G220	Monroe Institute of Applied Sciences
PUBLIC HEALTH	E108	American Public Health Association
PUBLIC INTEREST	H222	Public Citizen Health Research Group
PUBLIC INTEREST	S018	National Center for Citizen Involvement
PUBLIC INTEREST	S240	Support Center: Management Assistance to Non-Profit Groups
PUBLIC INTEREST	U010	Critical Mass Energy Project
PUBLIC INTEREST	U114	Appalachia Science in the Public Interest
PUBLIC INTEREST	U281	Waterloo Public Interest Research Group
PUBLIC INTEREST	V010	Commission for Advancement of Public Interest Organizations
PUBLIC INTEREST	V128	Center for Auto Safety
PUBLIC INTEREST	V134	Center for Nonprofit Organization
PUBLIC INTEREST	V141	Center for the Study of Responsive Law
PUBLIC INTEREST	V154	Common Cause
PUBLIC INTEREST	V185	Inform, Incorporated
PUBLIC INTEREST	V203	Massachusetts Public Interest Research Group
PUBLIC INTEREST	V233	New York Public Interest Research Group
PUBLIC INTEREST	V237	Ohio Public Interest Campaign
PUBLIC INTEREST	L230	Public Media Center
PUBLIC INTEREST	G116	Association of National Non-Profit Artists' Centers
PUBLISHING	S125	Carrier Pigeon/Alyson Publications
PUBLISHING	S194	Mediaworks
PUBLISHING	V229	New England Free Press
PUBLISHING	L007	Committee of Small Magazine Editors and Publishers
PUBLISHING	L013	Feminist Writers' Guild
PUBLISHING	L218	New Pages Press
PUBLISHING	L233	Rodale Press
PUBLISHING	L242	Small Press Review
PUBLISHING	G123	Blackberry Books
PUBLISHING	G267	Segue Foundation: Publishers of Books and Magazines
RADIO	L018	Great Atlantic Radio Conspiracy
RADIO	L026	National Federation of Community Broadcasters
RADIO	L111	Amateur Radio Research and Development
RADIO	L142	College Media Journal
RADIO	L211	National Radio Club
RADIO	G236	New Dimensions Radio and Tapes
RADIO	E132	Center of Telecommunications for the Third World
RADIO	E244	Radio Amateur Satellite Corporation (AMSAT)
RADIO	E250	Review of International Broadcasting

RAPE	H247	Working on Wife Abuse
RAPE	V001	Alliance Against Sexual Coercion
RAPE	V006	Cambridge Documentary Films
RAPE	V171	Feminist Alliance Against Rape
RAPE	V200	Los Angeles Commission on Assaults Against Women
RAPE	V287	Women Against Violence Against Women
RAW FOOD	H027	Survival Foundation
RAW FOOD	H164	Hippocrates Health Institute
RAW FOOD	U270	The Sproutletter: Sprouts, Raw Foods, and Nutrition
RECREATION	H109	American Alliance for Health and Physical Education
RECREATION	H147	Club SeneX
RECREATION	H174	Hot Springs Information Network
RECREATION	S124	Carousel Press: Books for Parents
RECREATION	S131	Circle Pines Center
RECREATION	S150	Creative Loafing in Atlanta
RECREATION	U199	Mountain Bicyclists' Association
RECREATION	L126	Berkeley Outreach Recreation Program
RECREATION	G005	Bed & Breakfast League
RECREATION	G007	Center for Leisure Guidance
RECREATION	G009	Cooperative Communities of America
RECREATION	G017	New Games Foundation
RECREATION	G020	Public Action Coalition on Toys
RECREATION	G109	Appalachian Mountain Club
RECREATION	G127	California Association of Bicycle Organizations
RECREATION	G130	Canadian Sport Parachuting Association
RECREATION	G137	Chautauqua Institution
RECREATION	G155	Different Worlds: Magazine of Adventure Role-Playing Games
RECREATION	G172	Games
RECREATION	G173	Great Expeditions: Real Travellers and Explorers
RECREATION	G183	Infinite Odyssey: Wilderness Adventures
RECREATION	G197	Kite Lines
RECREATION	G225	Nature Explorations
RECREATION	G241	North American Network of Women Runners
RECREATION	G246	Outside: Magazine of the Great Outdoors
RECREATION	G247	Outward Bound
RECREATION	G248	Oz Projects: Retreat in the Redwoods
RECREATION	G259	Roues Libres: Association Cycliste
RECREATION	G276	Sobek Expeditions: Outdoor Adventure Rivers Specialists
RECREATION	G306	Trailhead Ventures
RECREATION	G307	Travelers' Directory
RECREATION	G320	Windsurfer Magazine
RECREATION	G322	Women in the Wilderness
RECYCLING	U188	International Biomass Institute
RECYCLING	U207	National Recycling Coalition
RECYCLING	U280	Waste Watch
RECYCLING	U291	World Association for Solid-Waste Transfer and Exchange
REFERRAL	S256	Women's Information, Referral and Education Service
REFERRAL	L105	Alliance of Information and Referral Services
REFERRAL	L267	Women's Referral Service
RELIGIONS	L255	United Ministries in Education
RELIGIONS	G107	Anima: An Experiential Journal
RELIGIONS	G119	Baha'i International Community
RELIGIONS	G137	Chautauqua Institution
RELIGIONS	G141	Churches Center for Theology and Public Policy
RELIGIONS	G145	Community for Religious Research and Education
RELIGIONS	G184	Inner Paths: Eastern and Western Spiritual Thought
RELIGIONS	G201	Laughing Man Institute
RELIGIONS	G216	Menorah: Sparks of Jewish Renewal

RELIGIONS	G250	Pax Center
RELIGIONS	G254	Protestant Committee on Urban Ministry
RELIGIONS	G279	Sojourners: Christian Renewal Community
RELIGIONS	G281	Sorting It Out: Support for Spiritual Leavetakers
RELIGIONS	G297	Temple of Understanding
RELIGIONS	G327	World Monastic Council
RELIGIONS	G334	Zygon: Journal of Religion and Science
RELIGIONS	E199	Interreligious Taskforce on U.S. Food Policy
RELIGIONS	E225	Office of Tibet
RELIGIONS	E245	Religion and Ethics Network
REPORTERS	U024	Scientists' Institute for Public Information
REPORTERS	L133	Center for Investigative Reporting
REPORTERS	L181	International Society for General Semantics
REPORTERS	L193	Media Alliance
REPORTERS	L265	Women's Institute for Freedom of the Press
RESOURCES	U015	Friends of the Earth
RESOURCES	U020	Natural Resources Defense Council
RESOURCES	U022	Planet Drum Foundation
RESOURCES	U109	Alternatives: Journal of Friends of the Earth, Canada
RESOURCES	U110	American Forestry Association
RESOURCES	U111	American Rivers Conservation Council
RESOURCES	U125	Canadian Renewable Energy News
RESOURCES	U146	Dakota Resource Council
RESOURCES	U159	Environmental Policy Institute
RESOURCES	U170	Geothermal World Info Center
RESOURCES	U176	Harrowsmith Magazine/Canada
RESOURCES	U179	High Country News: Natural Resources of the Rockies
RESOURCES	U191	International Tree Crops Institute U.S.A.
RESOURCES	U222	North Carolina Coalition for Renewable Energy Resources
RESOURCES	U224	Northeast Appropriate Technology Network
RESOURCES	U225	Northern Rockies Action Group
RESOURCES	U240	Resource Center Network
RESOURCES	U241	Resources for the Future
RESOURCES	U251	Sierra Club
RESOURCES	U267	Synerjy: Directory of Energy Alternatives
RESOURCES	U277	Valley Watch
RESOURCES	U280	Waste Watch
RESOURCES	U282	Western Massachusetts Resource Network
RESOURCES	U290	Wood 'n Energy
RESOURCES	V114	Association on American Indian Affairs
RESOURCES	V210	National Action/Research on the Military Industrial Complex
RESOURCES	V245	Powder River Basin Resource Council
RESOURCES	V275	Tribal Sovereignty Program
RESOURCES	L034	Southwest Research and Information Center
RESOURCES	L118	Appalshop Films
RESOURCES	L216	New Front Films
RESOURCES	G122	Black Hills Alliance
RESOURCES	E028	World Future Society
RESOURCES	E196	International Union for Conservation of Nature and Resources
RESOURCES	E257	Sierra Club International Earthcare Center
RESOURCES	E268	U.S. Association for The Club of Rome
RESOURCES	E283	World Game of R. Buckminster Fuller
RESOURCES	E292	Worldwatch Institute
RETREAT	H210	Northern Pines: A Wholistic Health Retreat
RETREAT	H223	Pumpkin Hollow Farm
RETREAT	H233	Spring Hill: Community, Retreat and Counseling Center
RETREAT	S114	Birdsong Farm
RETREAT	S164	Fellowship House Farm
RETREAT	S173	Grindstone Island Centre
RETREAT	S255	Woman's Place

RETREAT	U286	Windstar Foundation: Educational, Research and Retreat Center
RETREAT	G002	Another Place
RETREAT	G014	Lama Foundation
RETREAT	G164	Feathered Pipe Ranch
RETREAT	G176	Hardscrabble Hill: Residential Retreat Center for Women
RETREAT	G196	Karma Triyana Dharmachakra
RETREAT	G215	Maui Zendo
RETREAT	G248	Oz Projects: Retreat in the Redwoods
RETREAT	G261	Rowe Conference Center
RETREAT	G268	Shadybrook House
RETREAT	G319	Willow: A Woman's Retreat
RIGHTS	H007	Coalition for the Medical Rights of Women
RIGHTS	H008	Committee for Abortion Rights and Against Sterilization Abuse
RIGHTS	H221	Psychiatric Inmates' Rights Collective
RIGHTS	U254	Society for Animal Rights
RIGHTS	V017	Indian Rights Association
RIGHTS	V029	New England Human Rights Network
RIGHTS	V109	Animal Rights Network
RIGHTS	V125	Campaign for Political Rights
RIGHTS	V143	Children's Legal Rights Information and Training Program
RIGHTS	V163	Disability Rights Center
RIGHTS	V286	Woman Activist: Action Bulletin for Women's Rights
RIGHTS	E008	Human Rights Internet
RITUAL	G021	Rites of Passage
RITUAL	G249	Parabola: Myth and the Quest for Meaning
ROBOTS	E251	Robotics Age: Journal of Intelligent Machines
RUNAWAY	S024	National Network of Runaway and Youth Services
RUNAWAY	S203	National Runaway Switchboard
RURAL	S013	Institute on Man and Science
RURAL	S017	National Catholic Rural Life Conference
RURAL	S034	Rural America
RURAL	S037	Small Towns Institute
RURAL	S101	Acres, U.S.A: A Voice for Eco-Agriculture
RURAL	S123	California Institute for Rural Studies
RURAL	S147	Country Journal
RURAL	S148	Countryside: The Magazine for Serious Homesteaders
RURAL	S163	Federation of Southern Cooperatives
RURAL	S179	Homesteaders News
RURAL	S193	Maine Times
RURAL	S230	Rural American Women
RURAL	S237	Southern Rural Development Center
RURAL	S239	Star Root: Fortnightly Newspaper
RURAL	S243	The Smallholder: Ideas and Information for Country People
RURAL	U028	Washington Small Farm Resources Network
RURAL	U161	Farallones Institute: Rural Center
RURAL	U253	Small Farm Energy Project
RURAL	V122	California Agrarian Action Project
RURAL	V261	South Carolina Committee Against Hunger
RURAL	L220	Northern California/Southern Oregon Resource Network
SAFETY	H118	Bay Area Coalition on Occupational Safety and Health
SAFETY	H135	Carolina Brown Lung Association
SAFETY	H209	North Carolina Occupational Safety and Health Project
SAFETY	H230	Society for Occupational and Environmental Health
SAHARA	E252	Saharan Peoples Support Committee
SATELLITE	L119	Arton's Publishing: Fuse Magazine

SATELLITE	L256	Urban Scientific & Educational Research
SATELLITE	E020	Satellite Video Exchange Society
SATELLITE	E150	Coop's Satellite Digest
SATELLITE	E244	Radio Amateur Satellite Corporation (AMSAT)
SCHOOLS	H148	Committee to End Violence Against the Next Generation
SCHOOLS	L016	Folk-School Association of America
SCHOOLS	L022	Intercommunity Center for Justice and Peace
SCHOOLS	L024	National Association of Legal Services to Alternative Schools
SCHOOLS	L110	Alternative Schools Network
SCHOOLS	L134	Center for New Schools
SCHOOLS	L167	Fireworks: Feminist Journal of the John Dewey High School
SCHOOLS	L204	National Coalition of Alternative Community Schools
SCHOOLS	L205	National Committee for Citizens in Education
SCHOOLS	L208	National Home Study Council
SCHOOLS	L222	Pacific Region Association of Alternative Schools
SCHOOLS	L224	Parents Union for Public Schools
SCHOOLS	L226	Primary/Secondary Peace Education Network
SCHOOLS	L232	Research for Better Schools
SCHOOLS	L237	Sandy River School
SCHOOLS	L246	Stay Smart
SCHOOLS	L248	Teachers' Centers Exchange
SCHOOLS	L270	Workshop for Learning Things
SCHOOLS	G247	Outward Bound
SCHOOLS	E159	Experiment in International Living
SCHUMACHER	U187	Intermediate Technology
SCIENCE	H005	Center for Science in the Public Interest
SCIENCE	U024	Scientists' Institute for Public Information
SCIENCE	U114	Appalachia Science in the Public Interest
SCIENCE	U248	Science for the People
SCIENCE	V121	Bulletin of the Atomic Scientists
SCIENCE	V127	Caucus for a New Political Science
SCIENCE	V170	Federal Laboratory Consortium
SCIENCE	V278	Union of Concerned Scientists
SCIENCE	L003	Anthropology Resource Center
SCIENCE	L141	Coalition to End Animal Suffering in Experiments
SCIENCE	L151	Cultural Survival
SCIENCE	L191	Math Science Network
SCIENCE	L212	National Technical Information Service
SCIENCE	L258	Western Behavioral Sciences Institute
SCIENCE	G200	Kronos: Journal of Interdisciplinary Synthesis
SCIENCE	G282	Spirals: Bridging the Gap Between Science and Mysticism
SCIENCE	G334	Zygon: Journal of Religion and Science
SCIENCE	E106	American Association for the Advancement of Science
SCIENCE	E195	International Kirlian Research
SCIENCE	E222	Next: A Look into the Future
SCIENCE	E237	Planetary Society
SCIENCE	E253	Science Digest
SCIENCE	E255	Science News
SCIENCE	E258	Society for General Systems Research
SCIENCE	E259	Sourcebook Project
SCIENCE FICTION	G286	Sproing: Science Fiction and Fantasy
SCIENCE FICTION	E110	Analog: Science Fiction/Science Fact
SCIENCE FICTION	E254	Science Fiction Writers of America
SEEDS	S121	Butterbrooke Farm Seed Co-op
SEEDS	U016	Friends of the Trees
SEEDS	U239	Redwood City Seed Company
SEEDS	U250	Seed Savers Exchange
SEEDS	U264	Stock Seed Farms

SEEDS	U272	Tilth: Biological Agriculture in the Northwest
SELF-CARE	H193	Medical Self-Care Magazine
SELF-CARE	H228	Self Care Associates
SELF-HELP	H002	Center for Attitudinal Healing
SELF-HELP	H014	Human Ecology Action League
SELF-HELP	H026	Parent Support-Group Project
SELF-HELP	H029	Terrap: Network for Agoraphobics
SELF-HELP	H110	American Conference of Therapeutic Selfhelp/Selfhealth
SELF-HELP	H126	Boston Self-Help
SELF-HELP	H158	Health Activation Network
SELF-HELP	H184	Life-Force Cancer Project
SELF-HELP	H214	Omega: Program of Grief Assistance
SELF-HELP	H216	Ontario Patients' Self-Help Association
SELF-HELP	H217	Parents Without Partners
SELF-HELP	S001	Citizens Committee for New York City
SELF-HELP	S025	National Self-Help Clearinghouse
SELF-HELP	S026	National Self-Help Resource Center
SELF-HELP	S028	Natural Helping Networks Project
SELF-HELP	S030	New York Urban Coalition
SELF-HELP	S039	Urban Alternatives Group/Columbus
SELF-HELP	S223	Parents Anonymous
SELF-HELP	E016	Oxfam America
SELF-MANAGEMENT	V033	Project Work
SELF-MANAGEMENT	V112	Association for Self-Management
SELF-RELIANCE	S006	Community Self-Reliance
SELF-RELIANCE	S011	Institute for Local Self-Reliance
SELF-RELIANCE	S033	Riptide/University Services Agency
SELF-RELIANCE	S139	Community Self-Reliance Center
SELF-RELIANCE	S148	Countryside: The Magazine for Serious Homesteaders
SELF-RELIANCE	S179	Homesteaders News
SELF-RELIANCE	S187	Living Free: Personal Journal of Self-Liberation
SELF-RELIANCE	S193	Maine Times
SELF-RELIANCE	S210	New Seeds Information Service
SELF-RELIANCE	S212	New York State Coalition for Local Self Reliance
SELF-RELIANCE	S243	The Smallholder: Ideas and Information for Country People
SELF-RELIANCE	U002	Anvil Press
SELF-RELIANCE	U115	Applewood Journal
SELF-RELIANCE	U152	Earthtone: For People Tuned to the Earth
SELF-RELIANCE	U176	Harrowsmith Magazine/Canada
SELF-RELIANCE	U224	Northeast Appropriate Technology Network
SELF-RELIANCE	U240	Resource Center Network
SELF-RELIANCE	V275	Tribal Sovereignty Program
SELF-RELIANCE	L157	Earthbooks Lending Library/Allegheny Branch
SELF-RELIANCE	L196	Mother Earth News
SELF-RELIANCE	L233	Rodale Press
SELF-RELIANCE	G120	Bear Tribe Medicine Society
SEMANTICS	L181	International Society for General Semantics
SKILLS	S183	Interest File
SKILLS	S188	Logical Connection: Skillsharing for Private Practitioners
SKILLS	V004	Barter Project
SKILLS	V036	SkillsBank
SKILLS	V272	Toolbox Training and Skills-sharing Collective
SOCIAL JUSTICE	S164	Fellowship House Farm
SOCIAL JUSTICE	V018	Institute for Social Justice
SOCIAL JUSTICE	V022	Mobilization for Survival
SOCIAL JUSTICE	V023	Movement for Economic Justice

SOCIAL JUSTICE	V138	Center for Research on Criminal Justice
SOCIAL JUSTICE	V166	Engage/Social Action
SOCIAL JUSTICE	V178	Greensboro Justice Fund
SOCIAL JUSTICE	V189	Institute for Social Justice/Eastern Office
SOCIAL JUSTICE	V213	National Council of La Raza
SOCIAL JUSTICE	V217	National Network of Grantmakers
SOCIAL JUSTICE	V223	Network: A Catholic Social Justice Lobby
SOCIAL JUSTICE	V265	Syracuse Peace Council
SOCIAL JUSTICE	V269	Team for Justice
SOCIAL JUSTICE	L022	Intercommunity Center for Justice and Peace
SOCIAL JUSTICE	L272	Zipporah Films
SOCIAL JUSTICE	E005	Consortium on Peace Research, Education, and Development
SOCIAL NETWORKS	E012	International Network for Social Network Analysis
SOCIAL SERVICES	V190	Institute for Social Service Alternatives
SOCIAL SERVICES	V251	Radical Alliance of Social Service Workers
SOCIALIST	V162	Democratic Socialist Organizing Committee
SOCIALIST	V190	Institute for Social Service Alternatives
SOCIALIST	V194	Kapitalistate: Working Papers on the Capitalist State
SOCIALIST	V256	Sanity Now!
SOCIALIST	V270	The Militant: Socialist Newsweekly
SOFT ENERGY	U015	Friends of the Earth
SOFTWARE	E147	Computer Information Exchange
SOFTWARE	E155	Dr. Dobb's Journal of Computer Calisthenics and Orthodontia
SOFTWARE	E200	Johnson-Lenz
SOFTWARE	E219	New Era Technologies
SOFTWARE	E233	People's Computer Company
SOFTWARE	E242	Purser's Magazine for Family Computers
SOLAR	S155	Dovetail Press: Design for the Owner-Involved Builder
SOLAR	U007	Citizens for a Better Environment
SOLAR	U025	Southern Unity Network/Renewable Energy Project
SOLAR	U027	Total Environmental Action
SOLAR	U029	Wind-Light Workshop
SOLAR	U102	Alabama Solar Coalition
SOLAR	U106	Alternate Currents/SolarCity
SOLAR	U107	Alternate Energy Institute
SOLAR	U116	Aprovecho Institute
SOLAR	U118	Arkansas Solar Action Coalition
SOLAR	U133	Citizens United for Responsible Energy
SOLAR	U139	Community Network for Appropriate Technologies
SOLAR	U142	Conservation and Renewable Energy Inquiry and Referral Service
SOLAR	U150	Earth Lab Institute
SOLAR	U161	Farallones Institute: Rural Center
SOLAR	U169	Georgia Solar Coalition
SOLAR	U184	Infinite Energy
SOLAR	U188	International Biomass Institute
SOLAR	U190	International Solar Energy Society
SOLAR	U193	Lamoureux Foundation: Home Energy Workshops
SOLAR	U197	Mississippi Solar Coalition
SOLAR	U212	New Alchemy Institute
SOLAR	U215	New England Solar Energy Association
SOLAR	U218	New Mexico Solar Energy Association
SOLAR	U231	Ozark Institute
SOLAR	U246	San Luis Valley Solar Energy Association
SOLAR	U255	Solar Business Office
SOLAR	U256	Solar Energy Association of Northeast Colorado
SOLAR	U257	Solar Energy Digest
SOLAR	U258	Solar Energy Research Institute

SOLAR	U259	Solar Greenhouse Digest
SOLAR	U260	Solar Lobby
SOLAR	U261	Solar Times: News of the Solar Energy Industry
SOLAR	U268	Texas Solar Energy Coalition
SOLAR	U276	Urban Solar Energy Association
SOLAR	U283	Western Massachusetts Solar Energy Association
SOLAR	U289	Women in Solar Energy
SOUTH AFRICA	E102	Africa Fund
SOUTH AFRICA	E183	Institute for Policy Studies
SOUTH AFRICA	E261	Southern Africa Committee
SPACE	S003	CoEvolution Quarterly
SPACE	E025	War Control Planners
SPACE	E101	Aerial Phenomena Research Organization
SPACE	E110	Analog: Science Fiction/Science Fact
SPACE	E111	Aquarian Age: Monthly for Space and Equality
SPACE	E116	Astronomical League
SPACE	E119	Aviation/Space Writers Association
SPACE	E130	Center for U.F.O. Studies
SPACE	E136	Claustrophobia: Life Extension
SPACE	E168	Futures Network
SPACE	E204	L-5 Society
SPACE	E211	Maryland Alliance for Space Colonization
SPACE	E216	National Space Institute
SPACE	E228	Omni Magazine
SPACE	E230	Organization for the Advancement of Space Industrialization
SPACE	E237	Planetary Society
SPACE	E240	Prometheus Society
SPACE	E264	The Network: Starflight and Immortality
SPACE	E289	World Space Federation
SPIRITUAL	S132	Circle of Light/Findhorn
SPIRITUAL	G008	Chimo: The Holistic Magazine for Our Times
SPIRITUAL	G012	Emissaries of Divine Light
SPIRITUAL	G014	Lama Foundation
SPIRITUAL	G015	Matagiri Sri Aurobindo Center
SPIRITUAL	G019	Prison Ashram Project
SPIRITUAL	G024	Spiritual Community Guide
SPIRITUAL	G025	Sri Chinmoy Centre
SPIRITUAL	G028	Well Being: A Network for Spiritual Journeyors
SPIRITUAL	G106	American Spiritual Healing Association
SPIRITUAL	G115	Association for Unity, Research, and Awareness
SPIRITUAL	G167	Foundation for Inner Peace
SPIRITUAL	G175	Hanuman Foundation Tape Library
SPIRITUAL	G184	Inner Paths: Eastern and Western Spiritual Thought
SPIRITUAL	G201	Laughing Man Institute
SPIRITUAL	G207	Lorian Association: Serving the Spirit of Wholeness
SPIRITUAL	G211	Lucis Trust
SPIRITUAL	G221	Movement of Spiritual Inner Awareness
SPIRITUAL	G222	Muktananda Meditation Center
SPIRITUAL	G223	Naropa Institute
SPIRITUAL	G229	New Age Magazine
SPIRITUAL	G238	New Options for a Vital United States (NOVUS)
SPIRITUAL	G269	Shambhala Booksellers
SPIRITUAL	G277	Society for Human and Spiritual Understanding
SPIRITUAL	G284	Spiritual Friends
SPIRITUAL	G285	Spiritual Frontiers Fellowship
SPIRITUAL	G287	Sri Aurobindo's Action Center
SPIRITUAL	G288	St. Louis Unit of Service of World Goodwill
SPIRITUAL	G295	Taeria Foundation Spiritual Community
SPIRITUAL	G297	Temple of Understanding
SPIRITUAL	G301	The Farm

SPIRITUAL	**G305**	Three-H-O Foundation (3HO)
SPIRITUAL	**G310**	Unity-in-Diversity Council
SPIRITUAL	**G326**	World Goodwill
SPIRITUAL	**E174**	Humanity Foundation
SPIRITUAL	**E209**	Maison du Nouvel Age
SPIRITUAL	**E265**	Triangles: Network of Light
SPIRITUAL	**E290**	World Union
SPIRITUAL CRISIS	**G281**	Sorting It Out: Support for Spiritual Leavetakers
SPIRITUAL CRISIS	**G283**	Spiritual Emergency Network
SPORTS	**V290**	Women's Equity Action League
SPORTS	**G027**	Transformation Project
SPORTS	**G124**	Boomerang Newsletter
SPORTS	**G130**	Canadian Sport Parachuting Association
SPORTS	**G197**	Kite Lines
SPORTS	**G241**	North American Network of Women Runners
SPORTS	**G247**	Outward Bound
SPORTS	**G309**	United States Parachute Association
SPORTS	**G323**	Women's Sports Foundation
SRI AUROBINDO	**G015**	Matagiri Sri Aurobindo Center
SRI AUROBINDO	**G118**	Auroville Association
SRI AUROBINDO	**G287**	Sri Aurobindo's Action Center
STUDENTS	**L035**	Student Press Law Center
STUDENTS	**L125**	Bear's Guide to Non-Traditional College Degrees
STUDENTS	**G149**	Council on International Educational Exchange
STUDENTS	**E107**	American Field Service
STUDENTS	**E159**	Experiment in International Living
SUFI	**G018**	Omega Institute for Holistic Studies
SUFI	**G189**	Institute for the Development of the Harmonious Human Being
SUFI	**G290**	Sufi Order for the Esoteric Arts & Sciences
SURVEILLANCE	**V026**	National Committee Against Repressive Legislation
SURVEILLANCE	**V110**	Another Mother for Peace
SURVEILLANCE	**V125**	Campaign for Political Rights
SURVEILLANCE	**V147**	Citizens Commission on Police Repression
SURVEILLANCE	**V152**	Committee for Action Research on the Intelligence Community
SURVEILLANCE	**V174**	Freedom of Information Clearinghouse
SURVEILLANCE	**V247**	Privacy Journal
SURVEILLANCE	**V250**	Public Eye: A Journal Concerning Repression in America
SURVIVAL	**H027**	Survival Foundation
SURVIVAL	**S159**	Family of New Age Networkers
SURVIVAL	**S187**	Living Free: Personal Journal of Self-Liberation
SURVIVAL	**V022**	Mobilization for Survival
SURVIVAL	**G292**	Survival Cards
SYNCON	**E168**	Futures Network
SYSTEMS	**U129**	Center for the Biology of Natural Systems
SYSTEMS	**E121**	Byte: The Small Systems Journal
SYSTEMS	**E169**	Genesa Foundation
SYSTEMS	**E173**	Human Systems Network
SYSTEMS	**E194**	International Journal of General Systems
SYSTEMS	**E229**	Open Systems
SYSTEMS	**E258**	Society for General Systems Research
T'AI CHI	**G294**	T'ai Chi
TAXES	**S220**	Organize Training Center

TAXES	V003	Association of Community Organizations for Reform Now
TAXES	V124	California Tax Reform Association
TAXES	V155	Conscience and Military Tax Campaign
TAXES	V267	Tax Reform Research Group
TAXES	V268	Taxation With Representation
TAXES	E287	World Peace Tax Fund
TECHNOLOGY	U187	Intermediate Technology
TECHNOLOGY	U198	Modern Energy & Technology Alternatives
TECHNOLOGY	U288	Women and Technology Project
TECHNOLOGY	L005	Center on Technology and Society
TECHNOLOGY	L212	National Technical Information Service
TECHNOLOGY	E022	Transnational Network for Appropriate/Alternative Technologies
TECHNOLOGY	E028	World Future Society
TECHNOLOGY	E128	Center for Policy Alternatives
TECHNOLOGY	E132	Center of Telecommunications for the Third World
TEENAGERS	H026	Parent Support-Group Project
TEENAGERS	H136	Center for Early Adolescence
TEENAGERS	H150	Coping with the Overall Pregnancy/Parenting Experience
TEENAGERS	H226	San Francisco Young Adult Network
TEENAGERS	S024	National Network of Runaway and Youth Services
TEENAGERS	S142	Consortium for Youth of South Central Connecticut
TEENAGERS	S158	Family Connection
TEENAGERS	S177	Home Front: For Young Pregnant Women and their Families
TEENAGERS	S203	National Runaway Switchboard
TEILHARD	E262	Teilhard Centre for the Future of Man
TEILHARD	E263	Teilhard Foundation
TELECONFERENCING	L008	Community Memory Project
TELECONFERENCING	L012	Electronic Information Exchange System
TELECONFERENCING	E017	Participation Publishers
TELECONFERENCING	E018	Participation Systems Incorporated
TELECONFERENCING	E021	The Source
TELECONFERENCING	E138	Coevolution
TELECONFERENCING	E141	CommuniTree Group
TELECONFERENCING	E144	CompuServe
TELECONFERENCING	E166	Future Shack
TELECONFERENCING	E182	Institute for Information Society
TELECONFERENCING	E229	Open Systems
TELECONFERENCING	E233	People's Computer Company
TELECONFERENCING	E267	Twenty-first Century Media
THEOSOPHY	G304	Theosophical Society of America
THIRD WORLD	U116	Aprovecho Institute
THIRD WORLD	U292	World Information Service on Energy
THIRD WORLD	V230	New Seed Press Feminist Collective
THIRD WORLD	V258	Sister Courage: Radical Feminist Newspaper
THIRD WORLD	L210	National Organizations Advisory Council for Children
THIRD WORLD	L223	Packard Manse Media Project
THIRD WORLD	G279	Sojourners: Christian Renewal Community
THIRD WORLD	E006	Friends of the Third World
THIRD WORLD	E016	Oxfam America
THIRD WORLD	E026	Women's International Network
THIRD WORLD	E132	Center of Telecommunications for the Third World
THIRD WORLD	E189	Interlink Press Service
THIRD WORLD	E197	International Voluntary Services
THIRD WORLD	E198	International Women's Tribune Center
THIRD WORLD	E201	Journal of Developing Areas
THIRD WORLD	E232	Partnership for Productivity
THIRD WORLD	E234	People's Translation Service

THIRD WORLD	**E238**	Plenty
THIRD WORLD	**E274**	Volunteers in Technical Assistance
TIBET	**E225**	Office of Tibet
TOXICS	**U007**	Citizens for a Better Environment
TOXICS	**U009**	Commonweal
TOXICS	**U020**	Natural Resources Defense Council
TOXICS	**U185**	Inland Regional Council
TOXICS	**U205**	National Coalition Against the Misuse of Pesticides
TOXICS	**U213**	New England Coalition on Nuclear Pollution
TOXICS	**U223**	Northcoast Environmental Center
TOXICS	**U227**	Northwest Coalition for Alternatives to Pesticides
TOXICS	**U230**	Olympic Peninsula Citizens against Toxic Spray
TOXICS	**U232**	Pacific Northwest Research Center
TOXICS	**U247**	Saskatoon Environmental Society
TOXICS	**U252**	Sierra Club Radioactive Waste Campaign
TOXICS	**U262**	Southern Oregon Citizens Against Toxic Sprays
TOXICS	**U280**	Waste Watch
TOXICS	**U281**	Waterloo Public Interest Research Group
TRAINING	**S027**	National Training and Information Center
TRAINING	**S163**	Federation of Southern Cooperatives
TRAINING	**V129**	Center for Conflict Resolution
TRAINING	**V191**	International Seminars in Training for Nonviolent Action
TRAINING	**V228**	New England Cooperative Training Institute
TRAINING	**V272**	Toolbox Training and Skills-sharing Collective
TRAINING	**L032**	Organizational Development Network
TRAINING	**L114**	American Society for Training and Development
TRAINING	**L215**	New England Training Center for Community Organizers
TRAINING	**G187**	Insight Training Seminars
TRAINING	**G224**	National Outdoor Leadership School
TRAINING	**E015**	North American Nonviolence Training Network
TRAINING	**E248**	Resource Center for Nonviolence
TRANSFORMATION	**V034**	Renewal Newsletter: New Values, New Politics
TRANSFORMATION	**V231**	New World Alliance
TRANSFORMATION	**L002**	Another America Networking
TRANSFORMATION	**G010**	Dromenon: Journal of New Ways of Being
TRANSFORMATION	**G023**	Sphinx and Sword of Love Bookstore
TRANSFORMATION	**G027**	Transformation Project
TRANSFORMATION	**G126**	Brain/Mind Bulletin
TRANSFORMATION	**G206**	Lindisfarne Association
TRANSFORMATION	**G207**	Lorian Association: Serving the Spirit of Wholeness
TRANSFORMATION	**G229**	New Age Magazine
TRANSFORMATION	**G236**	New Dimensions Radio and Tapes
TRANSFORMATION	**G239**	New Realities: Magazine of Body, Mind and Spirit
TRANSFORMATION	**G258**	ReVision: A Journal of Knowledge and Consciousness
TRANSFORMATION	**G297**	Temple of Understanding
TRANSFORMATION	**G330**	Yes Educational Society
TRANSFORMATION	**E138**	Coevolution
TRANSFORMATION	**E162**	Findhorn Foundation
TRANSFORMATION	**E185**	Institute for the Study of Conscious Evolution
TRANSFORMATION	**E190**	International Center for Integrative Studies
TRANSFORMATION	**E200**	Johnson-Lenz
TRANSFORMATION	**E206**	Leading Edge: A Bulletin of Social Transformation
TRANSFORMATION	**E220**	New Humanity Journal
TRANSFORMATION	**E223**	Nucleus Network
TRANSFORMATION	**E227**	Omega: Global Networking
TRANSFORMATION	**E235**	Phebus: Integrating Wholes and Parts
TRANSFORMATION	**E249**	Resurgence
TRANSFORMATION	**E262**	Teilhard Centre for the Future of Man
TRANSFORMATION	**E263**	Teilhard Foundation

TRANSNATIONAL	U189	International Federation of Organic Agricultural Movements
TRANSNATIONAL	E007	Global Education Associates
TRANSNATIONAL	E022	Transnational Network for Appropriate/Alternative Technologies
TRANSNATIONAL	E023	Union of International Associations
TRANSNATIONAL	E024	United Nations Economic & Social Council
TRANSNATIONAL	E026	Women's International Network
TRANSNATIONAL	E174	Humanity Foundation
TRANSNATIONAL	E193	International Herald Tribune
TRANSNATIONAL	E198	International Women's Tribune Center
TRANSNATIONAL	E277	Women's International Information & Communication (ISIS)
TRANSNATIONAL	E279	Women's International Resource Exchange Service
TRANSNATIONAL	E288	World Press Review
TRANSPERSONAL	G004	Association for Transpersonal Psychology
TRANSPORTATION	S113	Bikeways in Buffalo
TRANSPORTATION	S180	Indianapolis Mayor's Bicycle Task Force
TRANSPORTATION	S244	Transportation Alternatives
TRANSPORTATION	U003	Bicycle Network
TRANSPORTATION	U144	Continued Action on Transportation in the U.S.
TRANSPORTATION	U194	League of Michigan Bicyclists
TRANSPORTATION	U199	Mountain Bicyclists' Association
TRANSPORTATION	U203	National Association of Railroad Passengers
TRANSPORTATION	U233	Personal Mobility Committee
TRANSPORTATION	V128	Center for Auto Safety
TRANSPORTATION	G130	Canadian Sport Parachuting Association
TRANSPORTATION	G320	Windsurfer Magazine
TRANSPORTATION	G321	Women at the Helm: International Women's Sailing
TRANSPORTATION	E207	Lighter than Air Society
TRAVEL	S149	Crafts Fair Guide
TRAVEL	S197	Message Post
TRAVEL	G005	Bed & Breakfast League
TRAVEL	G009	Cooperative Communities of America
TRAVEL	G024	Spiritual Community Guide
TRAVEL	G149	Council on International Educational Exchange
TRAVEL	G171	Fund for Advancement of Camping
TRAVEL	G173	Great Expeditions: Real Travellers and Explorers
TRAVEL	G192	International Home Exchange Service
TRAVEL	G257	Rare Earth: Exotic Properties for Sale
TRAVEL	G307	Travelers' Directory
TRAVEL	E107	American Field Service
TRAVEL	E159	Experiment in International Living
TRAVEL	E270	U.S.-China People's Friendship Association
TREES	U016	Friends of the Trees
TREES	U110	American Forestry Association
TREES	U149	Earth Cyclers
TREES	U165	Friends of the Parks
TREES	U191	International Tree Crops Institute U.S.A.
TREES	U200	Mudsharks Co-op
TREES	U208	Nationwide Forest Planning Clearinghouse
TREES	U223	Northcoast Environmental Center
TREES	U269	The Plan: Community Food Tree Nurseries
TREES	U272	Tilth: Biological Agriculture in the Northwest
TREES	U273	Tree People
TREES	U290	Wood 'n Energy
U.F.O.	E101	Aerial Phenomena Research Organization
U.F.O.	E130	Center for U.F.O. Studies
UNDERGROUND	U275	Underground Space Center

UNITED NATIONS	**E024**	United Nations Economic & Social Council
URBAN	**S001**	Citizens Committee for New York City
URBAN	**S005**	Community Congress of San Diego
URBAN	**S011**	Institute for Local Self-Reliance
URBAN	**S030**	New York Urban Coalition
URBAN	**S038**	Urban Alternatives Group
URBAN	**S039**	Urban Alternatives Group/Columbus
URBAN	**S111**	Basement Alliance
URBAN	**S118**	Boston Urban Gardens
URBAN	**S178**	Home Ownership Development Program
URBAN	**S244**	Transportation Alternatives
URBAN	**S247**	Urban Planning Aid
URBAN	**U157**	Energy Task Force
URBAN	**U160**	Farallones Institute: Integral Urban House
URBAN	**U276**	Urban Solar Energy Association
URBAN	**V032**	Planner's Network
URBAN	**L256**	Urban Scientific & Educational Research
URBAN	**G254**	Protestant Committee on Urban Ministry
UTILITIES	**S027**	National Training and Information Center
UTILITIES	**U006**	Citizen/Labor Energy Coalition
UTILITIES	**U011**	Environmental Action Foundation
UTILITIES	**U120**	Boston Clamshell Coalition
UTILITIES	**U134**	Citizens for Safe Power Transmission
UTILITIES	**U167**	General Assembly to Stop the Powerline
UTILITIES	**U186**	Institute for Ecological Policies
UTILITIES	**U271**	Three Mile Island Alert
UTILITIES	**V019**	Institute for Southern Studies
UTILITIES	**V245**	Powder River Basin Resource Council
VEGETARIAN	**H238**	Vegetarian Times
VEGETARIAN	**S248**	Vegetarian Society of D.C.
VETERANS	**V146**	Citizen Soldier
VETERANS	**V151**	Come Unity: An Alternative Independent Journal
VETERANS	**V281**	Veterans Education Project
VETERANS	**V282**	Vietnam Veterans Against the War
VIDEO	**S233**	Share Foundation/Television Network
VIDEO	**U148**	Documentary Guild
VIDEO	**L102**	Action for Children's Television
VIDEO	**L106**	Alternate Media Center
VIDEO	**L119**	Arton's Publishing: Fuse Magazine
VIDEO	**L155**	Double Helix: Community Media
VIDEO	**L156**	Downtown Community Television Center
VIDEO	**L158**	Earthenergy Media
VIDEO	**L190**	Martha Stuart Communications
VIDEO	**L194**	MediaSense
VIDEO	**L207**	National Federation of Local Cable Programmers
VIDEO	**L217**	New Orleans Video Access Center
VIDEO	**L256**	Urban Scientific & Educational Research
VIDEO	**L257**	Washington Community Video Center
VIDEO	**E020**	Satellite Video Exchange Society
VIDEO	**E150**	Coop's Satellite Digest
VIDEO	**E172**	Home Video
VIDEO	**E231**	Papier Mache Video Institute
VIETNAM	**V184**	Indochina Curriculum Group
VIETNAM	**V282**	Vietnam Veterans Against the War
VIETNAM	**L010**	Education Exploration Center
VIOLENCE	**H148**	Committee to End Violence Against the Next Generation

VIOLENCE	H197	National Coalition Against Domestic Violence
VIOLENCE	H199	National Committee for Prevention of Child Abuse
VIOLENCE	H247	Working on Wife Abuse
VIOLENCE	V001	Alliance Against Sexual Coercion
VIOLENCE	V105	Alternatives to Violence Project
VIOLENCE	V171	Feminist Alliance Against Rape
VIOLENCE	V257	Second Wave: Magazine of the New Feminism
VIOLENCE	V287	Women Against Violence Against Women
VIOLENCE	V288	Women Against Violence in Pornography and Media
VISUALIZATION	H133	Cancer Counseling and Research Center
VISUALIZATION	H232	Soundiscoveries
VISUALIZATION	G188	Institute for Consciousness and Music
VOLUNTEER	S018	National Center for Citizen Involvement
VOLUNTEER	V009	Citizens Involvement Training Project
VOLUNTEER	L025	National Center for Service-Learning
VOLUNTEER	E197	International Voluntary Services
VOLUNTEER	E274	Volunteers in Technical Assistance
VOTING	V007	Campaign for Economic Democracy
VOTING	V125	Campaign for Political Rights
VOTING	V137	Center for Public Representation
VOTING	V144	Citizen Action
VOTING	V156	Constructive Citizen Participation
VOTING	V193	Joint Center for Political Studies
VOTING	V268	Taxation With Representation
VOTING	L192	Media Access Project
WAREHOUSES	S104	Alliance of Warehouse Federations
WAREHOUSES	S115	Blooming Prairie Warehouse
WAREHOUSES	S154	Distributing Alliance of the Northcountry Cooperatives
WAREHOUSES	S191	Magnolia: Southeastern Confederation for Cooperation
WELLNESS	H158	Health Activation Network
WELLNESS	H183	Ken Dychtwald & Associates
WELLNESS	H205	New Age Wellness Center
WELLNESS	H228	Self Care Associates
WELLNESS	H241	Wellness Associates
WELLNESS	H242	Wellness Institute
WHALES	U018	Greenpeace Foundation
WHALES	U168	General Whale
WHALES	U171	Greenpeace Alaska
WHALES	U172	Greenpeace Examiner
WHALES	U173	Greenpeace Seattle
WHALES	U174	Greenpeace/Vancouver
WHALES	U237	Project Jonah
WHALES	U249	Sea Shepherd Conservation Society
WILDERNESS	U015	Friends of the Earth
WILDERNESS	U104	Alaskan Conservation Foundation
WILDERNESS	U204	National Audubon Society
WILDERNESS	U251	Sierra Club
WILDERNESS	U284	Wilderness Society
WILDERNESS	G021	Rites of Passage
WILDERNESS	G109	Appalachian Mountain Club
WILDERNESS	G183	Infinite Odyssey: Wilderness Adventures
WILDERNESS	G247	Outward Bound
WILDERNESS	G292	Survival Cards
WILDERNESS	G306	Trailhead Ventures
WILDERNESS	G312	University of the Wilderness
WILDERNESS	G322	Women in the Wilderness

WILDLIFE	U013	Environmental Defense Fund
WILDLIFE	U015	Friends of the Earth
WILDLIFE	U166	Fund for Animals
WILDLIFE	U204	National Audubon Society
WILDLIFE	E196	International Union for Conservation of Nature and Resources
WIND	U029	Wind-Light Workshop
WIND	U112	American Wind Energy Association
WIND	U157	Energy Task Force
WIND	U285	Wind Power Digest: Access to Wind Energy Information
WINDSURFING	G320	Windsurfer Magazine
WOMEN	H007	Coalition for the Medical Rights of Women
WOMEN	H023	National Women's Health Network
WOMEN	H028	Tallahassee Feminist Women's Health Center
WOMEN	H031	Women's Health Services
WOMEN	H127	Boston Women's Health Book Collective
WOMEN	H128	Bread & Roses Women's Health Center
WOMEN	H189	Massachusetts Coalition of Battered Women Service Groups
WOMEN	H244	Womancare: A Feminist Women's Health Center
WOMEN	H245	Women Healthsharing
WOMEN	H246	Women and Health Roundtable
WOMEN	S020	National Congress of Neighborhood Women
WOMEN	S119	Boulder Women's Network
WOMEN	S202	National Hook-up of Black Women
WOMEN	S219	Older Women's Network
WOMEN	S225	Plexus: San Francisco Bay Area Women's Newspaper
WOMEN	S230	Rural American Women
WOMEN	S255	Woman's Place
WOMEN	S256	Women's Information, Referral and Education Service
WOMEN	U287	Women and Life on Earth
WOMEN	U288	Women and Technology Project
WOMEN	U289	Women in Solar Energy
WOMEN	V016	Illinois Women's Agenda
WOMEN	V025	National Association of Office Workers
WOMEN	V039	Women U.S.A.
WOMEN	V040	Women's Action Alliance
WOMEN	V139	Center for Women in Government
WOMEN	V140	Center for a Woman's Own Name
WOMEN	V165	ERAmerica
WOMEN	V167	Equal Times: Boston's Newspaper for Working Women
WOMEN	V200	Los Angeles Commission on Assaults Against Women
WOMEN	V209	National Action Committee on the Status of Women
WOMEN	V218	National Organization of Women
WOMEN	V224	Nevada Elected Women's Network
WOMEN	V226	New Directions for Women
WOMEN	V227	New Directions for Young Women
WOMEN	V234	Nine to Five (9 to 5)
WOMEN	V236	Off Our Backs: A Women's News Journal
WOMEN	V260	Sojourner: Northeast Women's Journal of News and the Arts
WOMEN	V276	Union Women's Alliance to Gain Equality
WOMEN	V285	Wisconsin Women's Network
WOMEN	V286	Woman Activist: Action Bulletin for Women's Rights
WOMEN	V287	Women Against Violence Against Women
WOMEN	V288	Women Against Violence in Pornography and Media
WOMEN	V289	Women's Enterprises of Boston
WOMEN	V290	Women's Equity Action League
WOMEN	V291	Women's Legal Defense Fund
WOMEN	V292	Women's Party for Survival
WOMEN	V293	Women's Work Force Network
WOMEN	V295	Working Women's Institute
WOMEN	L112	American Association of University Women

WOMEN	L150	Creative Women's Collective
WOMEN	L197	Ms. Magazine
WOMEN	L221	Northwest Women in Educational Administration
WOMEN	L228	Project on the Status and Education of Women
WOMEN	L240	Signs: Journal of Women and Culture in Society
WOMEN	L260	Womansplace Bookstore
WOMEN	L261	Women in Focus: Film Production and Distribution
WOMEN	L262	Women's Educational Equity Communications Network
WOMEN	L263	Women's History Research Center
WOMEN	L264	Women's Information Exchange
WOMEN	L265	Women's Institute for Freedom of the Press
WOMEN	L266	Women's Press
WOMEN	L267	Women's Referral Service
WOMEN	L268	Women: Journal of Liberation
WOMEN	L269	WomenSpace Women's Center
WOMEN	G029	Women Outdoors
WOMEN	G134	Center for Women's Studies and Services
WOMEN	G170	Front Range: Women in the Visual Arts
WOMEN	G176	Hardscrabble Hill: Residential Retreat Center for Women
WOMEN	G205	Lilith: The Jewish Women's Magazine
WOMEN	G241	North American Network of Women Runners
WOMEN	G319	Willow: A Woman's Retreat
WOMEN	G321	Women at the Helm: International Women's Sailing
WOMEN	G322	Women in the Wilderness
WOMEN	G323	Women's Sports Foundation
WOMEN	G324	WomenSpirit Journal
WOMEN	E026	Women's International Network
WOMEN	E198	International Women's Tribune Center
WOMEN	E276	Women in World Areas Studies
WOMEN	E277	Women's International Information & Communication (ISIS)
WOMEN	E278	Women's International League for Peace and Freedom
WOMEN	E279	Women's International Resource Exchange Service
WORK	H209	North Carolina Occupational Safety and Health Project
WORK	S031	North American Students of Cooperation
WORK	V005	California Newsreel
WORK	V006	Cambridge Documentary Films
WORK	V023	Movement for Economic Justice
WORK	V025	National Association of Office Workers
WORK	V030	New Ways to Work
WORK	V033	Project Work
WORK	V036	SkillsBank
WORK	V126	Catalyst National Network
WORK	V167	Equal Times: Boston's Newspaper for Working Women
WORK	V234	Nine to Five (9 to 5)
WORK	V293	Women's Work Force Network
WORK	V295	Working Women's Institute
WORK STUDY	L006	Coalition for Alternatives in Postsecondary Education
WORK STUDY	L009	Council for the Advancement of Experiential Learning
WORK STUDY	L036	Union for Experimenting Colleges and Universities
WORLD GAME	E283	World Game of R. Buckminster Fuller
WRITERS	H161	Health Writers
WRITERS	S133	City Miner: Community/Personal Adventure/Aesthetics
WRITERS	V201	Making It Legal: Primer for Craftmaker, Artist and Writer
WRITERS	L007	Committee of Small Magazine Editors and Publishers
WRITERS	L013	Feminist Writers' Guild
WRITERS	L014	Feminist Writers' Guild/New York
WRITERS	L146	Conditions: Writing by Women
WRITERS	L181	International Society for General Semantics
WRITERS	L193	Media Alliance

WRITERS	L235	Salt Magazine
WRITERS	L242	Small Press Review
WRITERS	L243	Society of Scribes and Illuminators
WRITERS	L265	Women's Institute for Freedom of the Press
WRITERS	G013	Intimate Talk: Journal of Expression
WRITERS	G153	Dialogue House Library
WRITERS	E119	Aviation/Space Writers Association
WRITERS	E254	Science Fiction Writers of America
YELLOW PAGES	S211	New West Trails
YELLOW PAGES	V002	Alternative Fund Federal Credit Union
YELLOW PAGES	V037	Vocations for Social Change
YOGA	G015	Matagiri Sri Aurobindo Center
YOGA	G019	Prison Ashram Project
YOGA	G151	Creative Yoga Studio
YOGA	G198	Kripalu Yoga Center
YOGA	G199	Kripalu Yoga Fellowship/Toronto
YOGA	G266	Sanatana Dharma Foundation
YOGA	G331	Yoga Journal
YOUTH	H136	Center for Early Adolescence
YOUTH	H200	National Council on Alternative Health Care Policy
YOUTH	H226	San Francisco Young Adult Network
YOUTH	S019	National Commission on Resources for Youth, Inc.
YOUTH	S024	National Network of Runaway and Youth Services
YOUTH	S103	Alaska Youth Advocates
YOUTH	S142	Consortium for Youth of South Central Connecticut
YOUTH	S203	National Runaway Switchboard
YOUTH	S229	Regional Young Adult Project
YOUTH	U181	Human Environment Center
YOUTH	V027	National Indian Youth Council
YOUTH	V227	New Directions for Young Women
YOUTH	V259	Social Advocates for Youth
YOUTH	V297	Youth Project
YOUTH	L271	Youth Liberation Press
YOUTH	G158	Encounter Four: Adventure Course for Youth in Trouble
YOUTH	G171	Fund for Advancement of Camping
YOUTH	E190	International Center for Integrative Studies
YOUTH	E232	Partnership for Productivity
ZEN	G006	Cambridge Zen Center
ZEN	G154	Diamond Sangha Center: Zen Buddhist Society
ZEN	G215	Maui Zendo
ZEN	G218	Minnesota Zen Meditation Center
ZEN	G243	Ontario Zen Center
ZEN	G255	Providence Zen Center
ZEN	G332	Zen Center of San Francisco
ZEN	G333	Zen Center of Sonoma Mountain

✳ NEWSLETTER

H004	Health Facts (bimonthly/$8.50)
H006	The Bulletin (12 issues/$12 year)
H007	Coalition News (bimonthly/$10)
H008	CARASA News (monthly/$5)
H009	CHAN–Consumer Health Action Network (bimonthly/$15)
H011	Gray Panther Network (bimonthly/$5)
H012	Health/PAC Bulletin (6 issues/$14)
H013	Kharis (3 issues)
H014	Human Ecologist (monthly/$12)
H016	La Leche League News (6 issues/$3)
H020	NAPSAC News (4 issues/$8)
H021	Optional Parenthood Today (6 issues/$20)
H022	Collation (8 issues/$15)
H023	Network News (bimonthly/$25)
H025	WomenWise (quarterly/$5)
H028	The Examiner
H029	Terrap Times (bimonthly/$10)
H030	TFH Newsletter (monthly)
H031	Hot Flash ($5)
H110	Constructive Action for Good Health (monthly/$6)
H113	Beginnings: American Holistic Nurses' Association (4/$8)
H114	Birth Notes ($15 year)
H115	Pathways to Health (quarterly/free)
H119	On the Edge (bimonthly/$6)
H123	Birthing Monthly Newsletter ($12 year)
H128	Irregular Periodical (3 issues/$3)
H130	Communication: Newsletter of CCCD (6 issues/$6)
H131	CHHA Newsletter (quarterly/donation)
H136	Common Focus: Early Adolescence (5 issues/$8)
H137	Choice Words (bimonthly/$4)
H138	C/SEC Newsletter (quarterly/$8)
H141	Children's Defense Fund Reports (monthly/$15)
H143	CHOICE Newsletter
H148	Last Resort (bimonthly/$10)
H155	Endometriosis Association Newsletter (monthly/$4)
H157	Ku'u Lono ($5)
H158	Wellness Experience (bimonthly/$7.50)
H160	Health Forecast (quarterly/$5)
H161	Health Newsletter: Consumers Help Themselves (monthly/$15)
H162	Health for the New Age Newsletter ($20 year)
H166	Holistic Health Review (quarterly/$12)
H170	Research Reporter (quarterly/$3)
H171	News from H.O.M.E. (quarterly/$8)
H172	Homebirth (quarterly/$5)
H174	Hot Springs Information Network (quarterly/$4)
H175	Special Delivery (bimonthly)
H181	I.F.P. Homeopathy Newsletter ($15)
H194	In A Nutshell (monthly/$4)
H195	M.A.M.A. Newsletter (monthly/$4)
H196	Newsletter of NAMI (bimonthly/$10)
H199	Caring ($2.50 issue)
H201	NFTA Newsletter (bimonthly)
H209	NCOSH Safety & Health News (bimonthly/$5)
H211	Cooperative Connection
H212	TLC–The Line of Communication (quarterly/$5)
H214	Omega Report (quarterly/donation)

H218	*Pavillion Newsletter: Advocacy for the Disabled (12/$2)*
H219	*People's Doctor: Medical Newsletter for Consumers (12/$18)*
H221	*PIRC Newsletter*
H226	*San Francisco Young Adult Network (monthly/$5)*
H231	*Pregnant Issue: Medicate or Educate? (bimonthly/$10)*
H242	*Wellness Newsletter (bimonthly/$8)*
H246	*Roundtable Report (monthly/$15)*

✳ NEWSPAPER

| H018 | *Madness Network News ($5)* |
| H151 | *Drug Survival News (bimonthly/$4)* |

✳ JOURNAL

H001	*Journal of the Alternative Medical Association ($7 year)*
H007	*Second Opinion (bimonthly)*
H024	*State and Mind (4 issues/$4)*
H109	*Journal of Physical Education, Recreation & Dance (12/$39)*
H144	*Chrysalis (quarterly/$10)*
H156	*Flower Essence Quarterly ($10)*
H182	*Journal of the Nutritional Academy (monthly/$10)*
H185	*Childbirth Alternatives Quarterly ($5)*
H187	*Macrobiotic Review (quarterly/$6)*
H198	*NCNM Review (bimonthly/$9)*
H202	*NHF Public Scrutiny (monthly/$12)*
H224	*Prevention Resources (quarterly)*
H228	*Health Promotion Review (quarterly/$30)*
H237	*Transitions: Vanier Institute of the Family (quarterly)*
H245	*Healthsharing (quarterly/$8)*

✳ MAGAZINE

H005	*Nutrition Action (monthly/$15)*
H010	*East West Journal (monthly/$12)*
H019	*Mothering ($8 year)*
H116	*Off the Shelf: Magazine of Progressive Delirium (6/$5)*
H139	*Child Care Information Exchange (bimonthly/$15)*
H193	*Medical Self-Care Magazine (quarterly/$10)*
H206	*New Age in Austin (quarterly)*
H216	*Phoenix Rising (quarterly/$5)*
H238	*Vegetarian Times (10 issues/$17)*
H240	*Well-Being (monthly/$14)*

✦ DIRECTORY

H020	*Directory of Alternative Birth Services ($3.50)*
H027	*New Age Directory ($4.95)*
H167	*Holistic Health Services in Eastern Massachusetts*
H190	*Massage and Bodywork Resource Guide ($6.95)*
H225	*Gayellow Pages ($8)*
H247	*Working on Wife Abuse ($5)*

✦ REPORT

H004	*Cancer Therapies ($1.50)*
H004	*Medical X-Rays ($1.50)*
H006	*How to Start a Cesarean Support Group ($1)*
H020	*NAPSAC Conference Proceedings ($6)*
H023	*Health Resource Guides*
H027	*Love Your Body (recipes, $2.50)*
H029	*Agoraphobia: Symptoms, Causes, and Treatment ($3)*
H138	*Frankly Speaking: Pamphlet for Cesarean Couples ($4)*
H176	*How Can You Tell If You're Really In Love? (comic, $.50)*
H199	*Networking: What's It All About? ($1.25)*
H237	*Health for People in the 1980s*

H237   *Varieties of Family Lifestyles: Selected Bibliography*

✦ HANDBOOK

H006   *Mother's Guide to Cesarean Childbirth*
H011   *Nursing Homes: A Citizen's Action Guide*
H011   *Paying Through the Ear: Report on Hearing Health Care*
H016   *Womanly Art of Breastfeeding ($3.95)*
H027   *Survival into the 21st Century ($12.95)*
H188   *It Makes Good Sense: Working with Natural Helpers*
H197   *NCADV Handbook on Emergency and Long Term Housing (free)*
H197   *State Domestic Violence Laws and How to Pass Them (free)*

✦ BOOK

H001   *People's Desk Reference: Traditional Herbal Formulas ($74)*
H002   *Love Is Letting Go of Fear (Jampolsky, $4.95)*
H002   *There is a Rainbow Behind Every Cloud ($5.95)*
H002   *To Give Is to Receive (Jampolsky, $5.95)*
H012   *American Health Empire: Power, Profits and Politics*
H012   *Prognosis Negative: Crisis in the Health Care System*
H016   *Mother's in the Kitchen ($4.95)*
H105   *Path of Action (Schwarz, $3.95)*
H105   *Voluntary Controls ($3.95)*
H106   *Father Book: Pregnancy and Beyond ($7.60)*
H127   *Nuestros Cuerpos, Nuestras Vidas ($2)*
H127   *Our Bodies, Ourselves ($6.95)*
H127   *Ourselves and Our Children ($6.95)*
H133   *Getting Well Again ($2.75)*
H159   *Health Link Anthology ($2)*
H164   *Naturama: Living Textbook ($12.95)*
H169   *Birthing Normally: A Personal Growth Approach ($10.95)*
H173   *Homeopathic Medicine at Home*
H191   *Essential Exercises for the Childbearing Year (Noble)*
H230   *Health Hazards in the Arts & Crafts ($16)*
H230   *Women and the Workplace ($16)*
H241   *Wellness Workbook (Travis)*

✦ AUDIOVISUAL

H133   *Psychological Factors, Stress and Cancer (audiotapes, $55)*
H145   *First Days of Life ($40)*
H145   *Midwife ($40)*
H145   *Nutrition in Pregnancy ($40)*
H183   *Wellness Series (Dychtwald, cassettes, $72)*
H232   *Relax and Rediscover Freedom from Smoking ($16.30)*
H232   *Relax and Rediscover the Beautiful You ($16.30)*
H232   *Relax and Reduce ($16.30)*

—————————————— SHARING TITLES ——————————————

✳ NEWSLETTER

S001   *Citizens Report (quarterly)*
S002   *Neighborhood Ideas (10 issues/$25)*
S005   *Congressional Record (monthly)*
S005   *The Bulletin (weekly)*
S007   *Community Service Newsletter (bimonthly/$10)*
S011   *Self-Reliance (bimonthly/$8)*
S012   *Maine Statewide Newsletter (12 issues/$4)*
S015   *Cooperative Housing Bulletin (monthly)*
S016   *NAN Bulletin ($10 year)*
S018   *Newsline (bimonthly)*
S019   *Resources for Youth (quarterly)*

S022   *Housing and Community Development Monthly Report*
S023   *Neighbors: A Publication on Interracial Living ($5 year)*
S024   *Network News (6 issues/$10)*
S025   *Self-Help Reporter (bimonthly/free)*
S026   *Network Notes (monthly/$10)*
S029   *Neighborhood Information Sharing Exchange*
S034   *RWA Reporter*
S034   *Rural CDBG Monitor (bimonthly)*
S035   *Green Revolution (monthly/$8)*
S040   *Local Connections ($5)*
S102   *Farm, Food, Land (bimonthly/$5)*
S111   *Basement Alliance Newsletter*
S121   *Butterbrooke Farm Newsletter (quarterly/$5)*
S122   *Jam Today (bimonthly/$10)*
S129   *Can Do Monthly Newsletter (12 issues/$25)*
S130   *Chicago Men's Gathering Newsletter (monthly/$5)*
S135   *Common Press: Newsletter of Common Health Warehouse*
S136   *Public Works (quarterly/$5)*
S141   *Connecticut Citizen Action Group Report (bimonthly/$15)*
S145   *Grapevine (monthly/$10)*
S151   *Pappus (4 issues/$3.50)*
S153   *News from Densmore Discoveries*
S154   *DANCe Floor (monthly)*
S166   *Food Conspiracy Newsletter (monthly/$6)*
S170   *Gentle Strength Cooperative Newsletter (monthly)*
S174   *Co-op News (monthly)*
S175   *Connections: New Age Community Newsletter (monthly)*
S183   *Interest File Newsletter*
S185   *News & Goods of the ICC Network (monthly)*
S187   *Living Free (bimonthly/$6)*
S195   *Machomania (monthly/$6)*
S197   *Message Post (quarterly/$2)*
S198   *Food for Thought: MFFC Newsletter (quarterly/$3)*
S198   *People's Business (monthly/$3)*
S204   *Conserve Neighborhoods (bimonthly)*
S205   *NORG News Bulletin (quarterly)*
S206   *Network Exchange Report (weekly/$52)*
S212   *Foundation Stones (bimonthly/$5)*
S215   *Northwest Organic Herb Cooperative Newsletter*
S219   *Our OWN (quarterly)*
S231   *Spinning Crank ($5 year)*
S232   *Sealand Bulletin ($25 year)*
S234   *Newsletter of the Society of Ontario Nut Growers (2/$3)*
S236   *Southern Neighborhoods (bimonthly/$3)*
S241   *Techqua Ikachi: Traditional Hopi Viewpoint (6/donation)*
S244   *New York City Cyclist (quarterly/$10)*
S247   *Community Press Features (monthly/$15)*
S248   *Vegetarian Voice (bimonthly/$6)*
S250   *Ride On! (bimonthly/$8)*
S254   *Wishing Well (quarterly/$16)*
S256   *Wire Service Bulletin*
S257   *Wool Gathering (semiannual/$2)*

✳ NEWSPAPER

S014   *Storefront Classroom: A Utopian Newspaper (bimonthly/free)*
S020   *Neighborhood Woman*
S027   *Disclosure ($9 year)*
S034   *RuralAmerica (monthly/$15)*
S036   *Shelterforce ($5)*
S101   *Acres, U.S.A. (monthly/$9)*
S116   *Bloomington Free Ryder*
S137   *Community Jobs (monthly/$8.88)*

S150   *Creative Loafing in Atlanta (weekly/$12)*
S157   *Le F.A.R.O.G. Forum (monthly/$6)*
S160   *The Catalist: Fed-Up Co-op Newspaper (10 issues/$6)*
S161   *Cultivator: Co-op Paper on Maine's Food Supply (12/$3.50)*
S162   *Lovin' FORCful (bimonthly/$5)*
S167   *Free Venice Beachhead (monthly/$5)*
S168   *Gay Community News (weekly/$25)*
S186   *Lancaster Independent Press (weekly/$10)*
S193   *Maine Times*
S204   *Preservation News (monthly)*
S209   *Food for Thought (bimonthly)*
S213   *North Carolina Anvil (weekly/$10.40)*
S225   *Plexus: San Francisco Bay Area Women's Newspaper (12/$6)*
S228   *Raisin Consciousness: Cooperative Warehouse (bimonthly/$5)*
S238   *Spectrum: Coop Newspaper for Tallahassee (10 issues/$5)*
S239   *Star Root (fortnightly/$7)*
S251   *Washington Blade: Gay Newspaper (biweekly/$10)*
S252   *Whiteaker News (monthly)*
S253   *Winds of Change (monthly/$10)*

✳ JOURNAL

S003   *CoEvolution Quarterly (4 issues/$12)*
S005   *C/O: Journal of Alternative Human Services (quarterly)*
S014   *Utopian Eyes: A Journal of Visionary Arts (quarterly/$6)*
S017   *Catholic Rural Life (monthly)*
S030   *Neighborhoods: The Journal for City Preservation (4/$12 yr)*
S104   *Moving Food: Cooperating Food Distribution (bimonthly/$20)*
S106   *Zymurgy: American Homebrewers Association (quarterly/$8)*
S127   *CCED Review (quarterly/$24)*
S139   *Sprouts (monthly/free)*
S156   *Draft Horse Journal (quarterly)*
S169   *Gay Sunshine (quarterly/$8)*
S218   *Old House Journal (monthly/$16)*
S227   *RFD: Country Journal for Gay Men (quarterly/$12)*
S230   *News Journal of Rural American Women (bimonthly/$8)*
S242   *Texas Observer: Journal of Free Voices (biweekly/$18)*

✳ MAGAZINE

S004   *Communities: Journal of Cooperative Living (5 issues/$7.50)*
S018   *Voluntary Action Leadership (quarterly/$9)*
S025   *Social Policy (5 issues/$15)*
S031   *Co-op Magazine (bimonthly/$10.50)*
S037   *Small Town (bimonthly/$15)*
S105   *History News (monthly/$20)*
S126   *Federal Programs Monitor (monthly/$15)*
S144   *In League (monthly/$10)*
S147   *Country Journal (monthly/$12)*
S148   *Countryside: For Serious Homesteaders (monthly/$12)*
S179   *Homesteaders News (8 issues/$8)*
S204   *Historic Preservation (bimonthly)*
S243   *The Smallholder: For Country People (monthly/$11)*

✳ OTHER PUBLICATION

S016   *National Neighborhood Platform ($2)*

✦ DIRECTORY

S003   *Next Whole Earth Catalog ($14)*
S004   *Guide to Cooperative Living ($5.95)*
S006   *Consumers Directory of Local Farmers ($1.50)*
S008   *Food Co-Op Directory ($5)*
S024   *Network of Runaway Services: A Nationwide Guide ($4.75)*

S032   *Project for Kibbutz Studies Monographs*
S110   *Co-op Resource Center Catalogue*
S149   *Crafts Fair Guide (10 issues/$20)*
S157   *Franco American Resource Inventory of New England ($3)*
S171   *Goodfellow Catalog of Wonderful Things ($10.70)*
S184   *Rainbow Nation: Cooperative Community Guide III ($3)*
S194   *New Periodicals Index ($45 annually)*
S207   *New Age Chicago: Resource Guide to Alternative Services ($2)*
S211   *People's Yellow Pages: Grassroots Guide to Tucson ($3.95)*
S218   *Old House Journal Catalog of Resources*
S229   *National Directory of Corporate Charity ($32)*
S235   *Southern Appalachian Resource Catalog ($5)*

✦ REPORT

S001   *Lend a Hand ($.25)*
S002   *Citizen Participation in Community Development ($3)*
S002   *Neighborhood Action Guides ($1 each)*
S010   *Co-op Food Facts*
S011   *Cities, Energy and Self-Reliance ($2)*
S016   *Neighborhood Economic Enterprises ($3.50)*
S024   *Community Response to Community Problems ($5.50)*
S176   *Hartford Food System: A Case Study ($1.50)*
S178   *Homesteading in Baltimore*
S210   *New Seeds Bibliography ($1.50)*
S220   *Why Proposition 13 Won and What It Means ($.50)*

✦ HANDBOOK

S001   *New York Self Help Handbook ($4.95)*
S018   *Nonprofit Organization Handbook ($29.95)*
S019   *What Kids Can Do: Forty Projects by Kids ($6)*
S019   *Youth Counsels Youth Manual ($5)*
S025   *How to Organize a Self-Help Group ($3)*
S026   *Community Resource Centers: The Notebook ($8)*
S028   *Networks for Helping ($5)*
S031   *Food Co-op Handbook ($5.95)*
S124   *How to Organize a Babysitting Cooperative ($3.95)*
S126   *Community Reinvestment Act ($2.50)*
S155   *Timber Frame Planning Book (Elliott, $16.50)*
S159   *Human Survival Insurance Policy ($1)*
S201   *Older Person's Handbook: Ideas and Resources for Action*
S208   *Communes, Law and Common Sense ($3.35)*
S221   *Owner-Built Home ($9.20)*
S221   *Owner-Built Homestead ($9.20)*
S229   *Small Change from Big Bucks ($6)*

✦ BOOK

S013   *Small Towns and Small Towners*
S026   *Uplift: What People Themselves Can Do ($6)*
S032   *Communal Future: The Kibbutz and the Utopian Dilemma ($28)*
S035   *Decentralism (Loomis, $5)*
S035   *Education and Living (Borsodi, $5)*
S105   *Historic Preservation in Small Towns ($8.95)*
S124   *Weekend Adventures for City-weary Families ($5.95)*
S133   *City Miner Anthology ($6.95)*
S155   *Timber Frame Raising (Elliott, $10.95)*

✦ AUDIOVISUAL

S031   *Wind Through the Pines: Co-op Slide Show ($30 rental)*
S165   *Film-makers' Cooperative Catalogue*

◆ **OTHER MATERIAL**

S003   *One Million Galaxies (map, $5)*
S011   *Urban Gardener (poster, $3)*
S155   *Timber Frame Blueprints ($50)*
S180   *Bicycle User Map ($1)*

────────────────── USING TITLES ──────────────────

✳ **NEWSLETTER**

U001   *Energy Digest (monthly/$6)*
U005   *Neighborhood News (biweekly/$25)*
U011   *Power Line (monthly/$15)*
U012   *Environmental Action (monthly/$15)*
U013   *EDF Letter ($20 year)*
U016   *Tree Leaflet ($3)*
U020   *NRDC Newsletter (bimonthly/$7)*
U024   *SIPIscope (6 issues/$25)*
U025   *SUN/REP (monthly)*
U026   *Task Force Against Nuclear Pollution Progress Report*
U028   *WSFRN News Release*
U103   *Alaska Center News ($15 year)*
U107   *Solar Utilization News (monthly/$10)*
U111   *American Rivers ($15)*
U113   *Information Report (quarterly/$5)*
U114   *Citizens' Appalachia*
U117   *News of Arcosanti*
U127   *Human Scale Newsletter (bimonthly/$5)*
U128   *Center for Environmental Problem Solving Forum (3 issues)*
U131   *Crab Sheet (monthly/$5)*
U132   *Energy News Digest (monthly/$10)*
U134   *Seven-sixty-five (765) Hotline (monthly/$3)*
U139   *Appropriate Technologies Gazette (quarterly/$6)*
U141   *Conservation Foundation Letter (monthly/$12)*
U144   *Rolling Resistance*
U146   *Dakota Counsel ($15 year)*
U159   *Washington Resource Report (monthly)*
U167   *Hold That Line (semimonthly/$5)*
U169   *Solar Collector (bimonthly/$10)*
U173   *Greenpeace Seattle Newsletter (quarterly/$15)*
U174   *Greenpeace Chronicles (monthly/$7)*
U180   *Green Times (10 issues/$5)*
U182   *Shelter Sense: Animal Sheltering (bimonthly/$5)*
U183   *Notes from Illinois South (5 issues/donation)*
U188   *Biotimes (bimonthly/$10)*
U189   *IFOAM Bulletin (quarterly/$7)*
U193   *Johnny Solarseed Newsletter*
U194   *Michigan Bicyclist (quarterly)*
U196   *Maine Organic Farmer and Gardener (bimonthly/$3)*
U199   *Colorado Bicyclist (monthly/$4.50)*
U203   *NARP News (monthly/$10)*
U204   *Audubon Leader (biweekly/$10)*
U205   *Pesticides and You (monthly)*
U207   *Recycling News (quarterly/$20)*
U212   *New Alchemy Newsletter (quarterly/$25)*
U213   *On the Watch (monthly/$10)*
U215   *Newsletter of the NE Solar Energy Association (6 issues/$16)*
U216   *New Environment Bulletin (monthly/$3.50)*
U217   *New Life Farm Sprouts (contribution)*
U218   *Sunpaper (monthly/$15)*
U221   *Mycophile (bimonthly/$8)*
U222   *NCCRER Newsletter (bimonthly/$10)*

U223   *Econews: Northcoast Environmental Center (monthly/$10)*
U228   *Soundings (bimonthly)*
U235   *Potomac Alliance Power Plant ($5 year)*
U236   *Prairie Alliance Newsletter (monthly)*
U241   *Resources for the Future*
U242   *SEA Alliance News (bimonthly/$5)*
U245   *San Diego Center for A.T. Newsletter (monthly/$10)*
U251   *Sierra Club National News Report (biweekly/$12)*
U252   *Waste Paper (quarterly/$6)*
U253   *Small Farm Energy Project Newsletter ($5)*
U254   *Society for Animal Rights Report (monthly)*
U256   *Solar News Collector (monthly/$7)*
U257   *Solar Energy Digest (monthly/$35)*
U259   *Solar Greenhouse Digest (bimonthly/$10)*
U260   *Sun Times (monthly)*
U269   *Fruition (bimonthly/$10)*
U270   *The Sproutletter: Sprouts, Raw Foods & Nutrition (6/$8)*
U271   *Island Updates: News Watch on the Harrisburg Area (12/$15)*
U273   *Seedling News (monthly/$15)*
U275   *Underline (bimonthly)*
U276   *USEA Newsletter (monthly/$10)*
U277   *Ohio Valley Environment Newsletter (monthly/$12)*
U293   *Zero Population Growth Reporter (monthly/$5.50)*

✴ NEWSPAPER

U015   *Not Man Apart (monthly/$25)*
U019   *Appropriate Technology (A.T.) Times*
U101   *It's About Times: Abalone Alliance Newspaper (10 issues/$8)*
U124   *Transitions (quarterly/$10)*
U125   *Canadian Renewable Energy News (monthly/$14)*
U179   *High Country News: Natural Resources (biweekly/$5)*
U226   *Northern Sun News (bimonthly/$6)*
U261   *Solar Times (monthly/$12.50)*

✴ JOURNAL

U004   *Cascade: Journal of the Northwest (10 issues/$10)*
U007   *CBE Environmental Review (6 issues/$15)*
U009   *Common Knowledge (quarterly/$10)*
U010   *Critical Mass Journal (monthly/$7.50)*
U015   *Soft Energy Notes (bimonthly/$25)*
U021   *Groundswell: An Energy Resource Journal (monthly/$15)*
U022   *Raise the Stakes! The Planet Drum Review ($10)*
U109   *Alternatives: Friends of the Earth, Canada (quarterly/$10)*
U115   *Applewood Journal (bimonthly/$10)*
U140   *Compost Science/Land Utilization (bimonthly/$20)*
U178   *Herb Quarterly*
U195   *Maine Audubon Quarterly (monthly/$15)*
U202   *Gardens for All News (quarterly/$10)*
U208   *Forest Planning (monthly/$4.80)*
U209   *Natural Food and Farming (monthly/$12)*
U212   *Journal of the New Alchemists ($25 year)*
U227   *NCAP News (quarterly)*
U247   *Environmental Probe (quarterly/$5)*
U248   *Science for the People (bimonthly/$9)*
U267   *Synerjy (bimonthly/$11)*
U272   *Tilth: Biological Agriculture in the Northwest (4/$10)*
U290   *Forest Notes (quarterly)*

✴ MAGAZINE

U001   *Alternative Sources of Energy (bimonthly/$15)*
U014   *Food Monitor (bimonthly/$10)*

U024	Environment (monthly/$12.75)
U027	Solar Age ($20 year)
U106	Alternate Currents (bimonthly/$6)
U152	Earthtone: For People Tuned to the Earth (bimonthly/$5)
U154	Energy Consumer
U162	Farming Uncle: Natural People & Mother Nature Lovers ($8)
U172	Greenpeace Examiner (quarterly/$3)
U176	Harrowsmith (8 issues/$12)
U182	Humane Education (quarterly/$10)
U182	Humane Society News (quarterly/$10)
U192	Outdoor America (bimonthly/$5)
U204	Audubon: The National Audubon Society (bimonthly/$13)
U210	Nature Conservancy News (bimonthly/$10)
U224	New Roots (bimonthly/$10)
U234	Probe Post (bimonthly/$20)
U246	Solar Flashes (monthly/$10)
U278	Velo Quebec (8 issues/$5)
U284	Living Wilderness Magazine ($20)
U285	Wind Power Digest: Access to Wind Energy Information (4/$8)
U292	WISE (bimonthly/$15)

✳ OTHER PUBLICATION

U026	Clean Energy Petition
U120	No Nuclear News (clipping service, monthly/$7.50)

◆ DIRECTORY

U023	Portland Book: A Guide to Community Resources
U104	Alaskan Conservation Directory
U135	Citizens' Energy Directory ($10)
U170	Geothermal World Directory ($50)
U187	Intermediate Technology Directory ($2)
U206	Energy Bibliography (annotated, $2)
U240	Resource Center Network Directory
U283	Western Massachusetts Solar Register
U288	Women and Technology Network Directory

◆ REPORT

U008	Irrevy: An Irreverent View of Nuclear Power ($3.95)
U011	Utility Action Guide
U023	Consumer Guide to Woodstoves ($2)
U138	Protest S.O.N.G.S. Report on Radiation
U153	Appropriate Agriculture ($2)
U153	Biodynamic Gardening ($2.25)
U181	Youth Conservation Employment (free)
U229	Appropriate Technology and State Government ($.75)
U231	Solar Greenhouse Guide ($2)
U232	History of Herbicide Usage by Bonneville Power
U236	Clinton Nuclear Power Plant Fact Sheet
U236	Prairie Alliance White Papers
U239	Redwood Seed Company Catalog of Useful Plants ($.50)
U265	Retrospect/Prospect: Sudbury Economic Development
U281	Acid Rain: The Silent Crisis
U287	Women and Life on Earth Conference Papers ($.10 each)
U288	Something Old ... Women and Appropriate Technology ($2.50)
U288	Women and Technology: Deciding What's Appropriate ($2.50)

◆ HANDBOOK

U007	Solar Water Heating in Chicago
U021	Nuclear Information Resource Guide ($3)
U022	Reinhabiting a Separate Country ($7)
U023	Rainbook: Resources for Appropriate Technology ($7.95)

U029   *Homebuilt, Wind-Generated Electricity Handbook ($8)*
U113   *Animals and Their Rights ($2)*
U123   *Splitting Firewood ($3.95)*
U137   *It Won't Be Built! Seabrook Occupation Handbook*
U142   *Solar Energy Information Locator (free)*
U143   *Women's Energy Tool Kit ($4.95)*
U147   *It's (Insulated) Curtains for You: Step-by-step ($15)*
U157   *Windmill Power for City People*
U159   *Strip Mine Handbook: Citizen's Guide ($5)*
U164   *Guide to Welfare Reform ($3)*
U185   *Toolkit: Copy It! (donation)*
U199   *Parking for Bicycles: Guide to Selection and Installation*
U218   *Building Your Solar Greenhouse ($6.95)*
U280   *Waste Watchers: Conserving Energy and Resources ($4.50)*

◆ BOOK

U002   *Primer on Nuclear Power ($2.50)*
U003   *Man Who Loved Bicycles ($7)*
U015   *Soft Energy Paths (Lovins, $3.95)*
U016   *True Fairy Tale ($4)*
U017   *Energy War: Reports from the Front ($6.95)*
U017   *No Nukes: Everyone's Guide to Nuclear Power ($9)*
U018   *Mind in the Waters ($9.95)*
U018   *To Save a Whale ($6.95)*
U027   *Solar Age Resource Book ($9.95)*
U027   *Solar Home Book ($9.50)*
U029   *Wind and Windspinners: A Nuts 'n Bolts Approach ($8)*
U117   *Bridge Between Matter and Spirit (Soleri)*
U119   *Ecotopia (Callenbach, $4.95)*
U123   *Scythe Book: Mowing, Cutting, & Harvesting ($6.95)*
U145   *From the Walls In ($9.95)*
U151   *At Home with Alternative Energy ($9.95)*
U156   *Conserver Solution: Blueprint for Conserver Society ($6.95)*
U160   *Integral Urban House: Self-Reliant City Living ($14.25)*
U168   *Wake of the Whale ($35)*
U168   *Whales: A Book for Children ($5.95)*
U191   *Permaculture One*
U212   *Book of the New Alchemists*
U231   *Uncertain Harvest: Family Farm in Arkansas ($10)*
U248   *Science and Liberation ($6.50)*
U249   *Shepherds of the Sea (Watson)*
U250   *Seed Savers Exchange Yearbook ($3)*

◆ AUDIOVISUAL

U017   *Lovejoy's Nuclear War ($65 rental)*
U117   *Soleri: Two Suns Arcology (slideshow/$100)*
U122   *Harrisburg ($25)*
U122   *Home Energy Conservation Series ($85 rental)*
U148   *Radiation Workers: Reprocessing (3/4" videotape)*
U219   *Appalachia ($50 rental)*
U219   *Paul Jacobs and the Nuclear Gang*

◆ OTHER MATERIAL

U003   *Cycle and Recycle (wall calendar/$3)*
U018   *Whale Jewelry ($5)*
U022   *Backbone: The Rockies ($3.50)*
U286   *Windstar Poster (Armstrong & Denver, $100)*
U287   *Women and Life on Earth Postcards ($.20 each)*

VALUING TITLES

✳ **NEWSLETTER**

V007	CED News ($15)
V008	Counter Pentagon (bimonthly)
V011	Anti-Draft (6 issues/$10)
V012	CEP Newsletter (monthly/$15)
V016	Illinois Women's Agenda Newsletter ($25 year)
V017	Indian Truth (bimonthly/$15)
V020	Corporate Examiner (12 issues/$25 year)
V021	KNOW News ($6 year)
V022	The Mobilizer (monthly/$10)
V024	Dandelion (quarterly/$3.50)
V025	Working Women Newsletter (bimonthly/$5)
V028	Reproductive Rights Newsletter (4 issues/$3)
V029	New England Human Rights Newsletter (12 issues/$5 year)
V030	New Ways to Work (4 issues/$5)
V031	Peacework (monthly/$5)
V032	Planners Network (bimonthly)
V033	Project Work Newsletter (6 issues/$5)
V034	Renewal: New Values, New Politics (triweekly/$15)
V035	SANE World (monthly/$4)
V036	SkillsBank Newsletter (6 issues/$10)
V037	What's Left in Boston (monthly/$5)
V038	Free Trade: News 'n Views (biweekly)
V105	Alternatives to Violence Project Newsletter (monthly)
V111	Armistice/Live Without Trident (monthly/$5)
V113	Libertarian Feminists News (monthly/$5)
V114	Indian Affairs (bimonthly/$15)
V116	Working Arts (quarterly/$15)
V122	California Agrarian Action Project Newsletter (monthly)
V124	Tax Back Talk (monthly/$5)
V125	Organizing Notes (8 issues/$10)
V128	Lemon Times: Center for Auto Safety (quarterly/$15)
V129	Center for Conflict Resolution Newsletter (semiannual/$3)
V131	Defense Monitor (monthly/$12)
V132	First Principles (monthly/$15)
V135	Newsletter from Soulmates ($10)
V137	The Public I (quarterly/$15)
V139	News on Women in Government
V141	Diffusion: Newsletter of Social Experiments (quarterly)
V141	Multinational Monitor
V142	Center Peace (bimonthly/$5)
V144	Citizen Action News (bimonthly)
V146	Citizen Soldier ($5 year)
V147	Rap Sheet (monthly)
V153	CONAS Newsletter (quarterly/$5)
V154	Common Cause Frontline (bimonthly)
V156	Constructive Citizen Participation (quarterly/$4)
V162	Democratic Left (monthly/$15)
V164	Homemakers Network News (bimonthly/$5)
V178	Greensboro Justice Fund Newsletter (bimonthly/$10)
V183	Human Economy Newsletter ($12)
V185	Inform Reports (bimonthly/$25)
V187	ILER Grapevine (monthly)
V188	National Parenting for Peace & Justice Network ($10)
V191	ISTNA Newsletter
V192	Shalom: The Jewish Peace Fellowship (quarterly/$10)
V196	Synthesis: Newsletter for Social Ecology (quarterly/$3.25)
V202	Food and Poverty News (monthly/$10)
V203	Masscitizen: Newsletter of MassPIRG (quarterly/$15)
V205	MALDEF Newsletter (quarterly/$15)
V208	NAF Quarterly (4 issues/$10)

V209   *Status of Women News ($12 year)*
V211   *Responsive Philanthrophy ($15)*
V215   *It's Time: National Gay Task Force (bimonthly/$3)*
V218   *NOW Times*
V220   *The Leaflet: NORML (monthly/$25)*
V223   *Network: Catholic Social Justice (bimonthly/$18)*
V224   *Nevada Elected Women's Network Newsletter (monthly)*
V225   *New Age Harmonist*
V243   *Physicians for Social Responsibility Newsletter (quarterly)*
V245   *Powder River Breaks (monthly)*
V254   *Robert's Telling Tales (monthly/$5)*
V256   *Sanity Now! (bimonthly/$1)*
V262   *Southern Libertarian Messenger ($15 year)*
V265   *Peace Newsletter: Anti-War/Social Justice (monthly/$6)*
V266   *Tarrytown Letter (monthly/$24)*
V268   *Taxation With Representation Newsletter (monthly/$1)*
V269   *Team for Justice (bimonthly)*
V271   *The Spokeswoman: Feminist News Digest (monthly/$12)*
V275   *Native Self-Sufficiency (monthly/$6)*
V277   *Dollars & Sense (monthly)*
V278   *Nucleus (quarterly)*
V281   *Discharge Upgrading Newsletter (bimonthly/$10)*
V282   *The Veteran (bimonthly/$3)*
V284   *Washington Spectator & Between the Lines (22 issues/$10)*
V285   *The Stateswoman (quarterly)*
V286   *Woman Activist (monthly/$12)*
V287   *Women Against Violence Against Women ($12.50)*
V288   *WAVPM News Page (monthly/$10)*
V289   *Connections: Women in Trade & Technical Jobs ($15 year)*
V290   *In the Running: Timely News on Women in Sports (quarterly)*
V290   *WEAL Washington Report (bimonthly/$20)*
V291   *Women's Legal Defense Fund Newsletter (quarterly/$5)*
V293   *Connections (bimonthly)*

✳ NEWSPAPER

V003   *USA–United States of Acorn ($6)*
V013   *Forty Acres and a Mule (monthly/$4)*
V019   *Facing South (syndicated news column)*
V027   *Americans Before Columbus (monthly/$8)*
V104   *Akwesasne Notes: For Native and Natural Peoples (5/$6)*
V108   *Emancipation (monthly/$3)*
V151   *Come Unity (monthly/$5)*
V159   *Crafts Report (monthly/$14.50)*
V167   *Equal Times: For Boston's Working Women (biweekly/$8)*
V199   *Susquehanna Current (quarterly/free)*
V216   *Guild Notes of National Lawyers Guild (bimonthly/$18)*
V226   *New Directions for Women (bimonthly/$6)*
V239   *Open Roads: English-language Anarchist (4 issues/2 days pay)*
V246   *Prisoners Union Journal (monthly/$4)*
V258   *Sister Courage: Radical Feminist Newspaper (monthly/$4)*
V263   *Southern Coalition Report on Jails and Prisons*
V267   *People & Taxes (monthly/$7.50)*
V270   *The Militant: Socialist Newsweekly (weekly/$24)*
V276   *Union W.A.G.E. (bimonthly/$4)*

✳ JOURNAL

V019   *Southern Exposure (quarterly/$10)*
V112   *Self-Management (quarterly/$20)*
V117   *Black Law Journal (3 issues/$12.50)*
V127   *New Political Science (quarterly/$15)*
V143   *Children's Legal Rights Journal (bimonthly/$23)*
V190   *Catalyst: Socialist Journal of Social Services (4/$12)*

V194   *Kapitalistate (quarterly/$12)*
V213   *Agenda: A Journal of Hispanic Ideas (bimonthly/$12)*
V214   *Economic Development and Law Center Report (quarterly/$8)*
V236   *Off Our Backs: A Women's News Journal (monthly/$7)*
V257   *Second Wave: Magazine of the New Feminism (quarterly/$4)*
V259   *Youth Advocacy News (monthly/$10)*
V260   *Sojourner: New England Women's Journal (monthly/$8)*
V294   *Working Papers for a New Society*

✳ MAGAZINE

V014   *Grantsmanship Center News (bimonthly/$20)*
V023   *Just Economics (bimonthly/$12)*
V028   *Moving On (bimonthly/$5)*
V120   *Cornerstones: The Brown Committee (bimonthly)*
V121   *Bulletin of the Atomic Scientists (10 issues/$10)*
V152   *CounterSpy: For People Who Need to Know (quarterly/$10)*
V157   *Caveat Emptor: Consumers Bulletin (monthly/$10)*
V166   *Engage/Social Action (11 issues/$6)*
V171   *Aegis: Organizing to Stop Violence Against Women (6/$10.50)*
V172   *Focus/Midwest (bimonthly/$8)*
V207   *Mother Jones: A Magazine for the Rest of Us (monthly/$15)*
V232   *New World Review (bimonthly/$5)*
V233   *Agenda for Citizen Involvement (bimonthly/$15)*
V250   *Public Eye: Concerning Repression in America (quarterly/$8)*
V252   *Radical America (bimonthly/$10)*
V268   *Tax Notes: The Weekly Tax Service (52 issues/$200)*
V274   *Society (bimonthly/$12)*
V283   *Washington Monthly (monthly/$21)*

✳ OTHER PUBLICATION

V231   *Transformation Platform: The Dialogue Begins ($4)*

✦ DIRECTORY

V002   *Ithaca People's Yellow Pages ($.75)*
V010   *Periodicals of Public Interest Organizations ($5)*
V037   *Boston People's Yellow Pages ($4.95)*
V040   *Women's Action Almanac ($7.95)*
V134   *Contacts: Clubs, Societies and Organizations ($9.95)*
V158   *Consumer Information Catalog*
V164   *Displaced Homemaker Program Directory ($1)*
V182   *H.O.M.E. Craft Catalog ($1)*
V184   *Vietnam Era ($5)*
V217   *Grantseekers Guide: For Social & Economic Justice ($5)*
V221   *Prisoners' Assistance Directory ($10)*
V249   *Buyer's Guide ($20)*

✦ REPORT

V005   *Planning Work: Resources for Labor Education ($3)*
V015   *Foundation of Economic Freedom*
V022   *Peace Resource Packet ($4)*
V024   *New Society Packet ($.70)*
V033   *Alternative Work in New York City*
V131   *Nuclear War Prevention Kit*
V140   *Women Who Wish to Determine Their Own Names ($2)*
V141   *Nuclear Plants: The More They Build, the More You Pay ($5)*
V146   *Self-Help Guide on Agent Orange ($.10)*
V149   *Civilian Congress Biannual Listing (free)*
V150   *So You're Going to be a Grand Juror? ($.50)*
V163   *How Well Do You Understand Disability? ($.50)*
V169   *Building a Democratic Economy (Alperovitz & Faux, $.25)*
V169   *Small Business ($5)*

V131   *War Without Winners (rental, $50)*
V210   *Sharing Global Resources: Toward a New Economic Order*

✦ OTHER MATERIAL

V104   *Akwesasne Notes Posters*

LEARNING TITLES

✳ NEWSLETTER

L001   *Alternatives in Education ($2)*
L003   *ARC Newsletter ($5)*
L004   *Jobs Clearinghouse Bulletin ($4 year)*
L007   *Independent Publisher (monthly/$35)*
L009   *CAEL Newsletter (bimonthly)*
L013   *Feminist Writers' Guild Newsletter (quarterly/$10)*
L015   *FOCUSCreativity (triweekly/$35)*
L016   *Options (quarterly/$3)*
L017   *Learning Connection (4 issues/$15)*
L020   *Growing Without Schooling (bimonthly/$10)*
L021   *Perspectives (3 issues/$5)*
L022   *Justice in the Schools*
L024   *Tidbits (4 issues/$20)*
L026   *Fast Forward (quarterly)*
L026   *NFCB Newsletter (monthly/$15)*
L027   *Experiential Education*
L028   *New Jersey Unschoolers Newsletter*
L030   *OCEAN News ($10)*
L032   *OD Practitioner ($30)*
L034   *Nuclear Waste News (bimonthly/$5)*
L101   *Academy News (quarterly)*
L104   *Citizen Education Bulletin (monthly)*
L105   *AIRS Newsletter (quarterly/$15)*
L107   *Resources Newsletter (monthly/$5)*
L111   *AMRAD Newsletter (monthly/$12)*
L120   *Aspen Institute Chronicle (monthly)*
L121   *AIM Network (biweekly)*
L123   *Ateed Newsletter*
L129   *Canadian Home Schooler ($5 year)*
L137   *Sharing Space (quarterly/$3)*
L140   *Clearinghouse Newsletter (quarterly/$5)*
L145   *Community Information Spotlight (quarterly)*
L149   *Interracial Books for Children Bulletin (8 issues/$10)*
L153   *Denver Free University Connection (quarterly)*
L170   *Gifted Children Newsletter (bimonthly/$24)*
L175   *Hostex News ($10 year)*
L179   *Citizen Action in Education (monthly/$5)*
L183   *Educacion Liberadora (monthly)*
L185   *Learning Exchange News (quarterly)*
L188   *Link Magazine*
L189   *Manas (weekly/$10)*
L191   *Math/Science Broadcast (quarterly/free)*
L193   *Media File (monthly/$10)*
L201   *NCEB Bulletin (monthly/$11)*
L203   *La Red/The Net (monthly)*
L204   *National Coalition News (5 issues/$10)*
L205   *Network (monthly/$8)*
L217   *Video Vibes (3 issues/$5)*
L227   *Process: Networking Forum for Citizen Participation*
L228   *Status and Education of Women Newsletter (quarterly)*
L241   *Sipapu: Newsletter for Librarians (2 issues/$4)*
L242   *Small Press Review (monthly/$10)*

L250	*Inside the Network (quarterly)*
L255	*Connexions (bimonthly/$2)*
L258	*Colorado Glance: Between East & West, Looking Both Ways*
L265	*Media Report to Women (monthly/$20)*
L269	*WomenSpace Newsletter*

✳ NEWSPAPER

L152	*D.C. Gazette (monthly/$5)*
L167	*Fireworks: Feminist Journal of John Dewey H.S. (5 issues)*
L173	*Hagborn: Radical Feminist News Journal (quarterly/$3)*
L236	*San Francisco Bay Guardian (weekly/$31.20)*
L266	*Women's Press (bimonthly/$4)*

✳ JOURNAL

L004	*Journal of Experiential Education (semiannual)*
L008	*Journal of Community Communications (quarterly/$9)*
L021	*Humanistic Psychology Institute Review ($4 copy)*
L025	*Synergist*
L035	*SPLC Report (3 issues/$10)*
L114	*Training and Development Journal (monthly/$10)*
L122	*Journal of Humanistic Education ($15 year)*
L129	*Natural Life: Journal of Natural Living*
L130	*Connexions (5 issues/$12)*
L139	*City Lights Journal*
L151	*Cultural Survival Quarterly (4 issues/$15)*
L159	*Sightlines: Educational Film Library (quarterly/$15)*
L161	*Resources in Education (monthly/$42.70)*
L164	*Feminary: Feminist Journal for the South (3 issues/$6.50)*
L165	*Ferity: Hawaii's Feminist Newsjournal (bimonthly/$5)*
L166	*Fine Print: Review for the Arts of the Book (quarterly/$24)*
L181	*Etc: Review of General Semantics (quarterly/$20)*
L200	*Young Children (bimonthly/$12)*
L231	*Quest: A Feminist Quarterly*
L240	*Signs: Journal of Women and Culture in Society (4/$12)*
L253	*CORE/PALS Journal (2 issues/$7.50)*
L268	*Women: Journal of Liberation (3 issues/$5)*

✳ MAGAZINE

L034	*Mine Talk (bimonthly/$18)*
L034	*The Workbook: Environmental, Social and Consumer (8/$10)*
L102	*RE:ACT (semiannual/$15)*
L103	*Lifelong Learning: The Adult Years (monthly/$20)*
L109	*Alternative Media Magazine (quarterly/$5)*
L112	*Graduate Women (bimonthly/$8)*
L119	*Fuse: Canadian Video (bimonthly/$12)*
L142	*CMJ Progressive Media (biweekly/$75)*
L146	*Conditions (3 issues/$11)*
L160	*Built Environmental Education (quarterly/$10)*
L195	*Mix: The Recording Industry Directory (monthly/$18)*
L196	*Mother Earth News (bimonthly/$15)*
L197	*Ms. (monthly/$10)*
L207	*Community Television Review (monthly/$15)*
L218	*New Pages: News for the Progressive Booktrade (4 issues/$15)*
L233	*New Shelter (9 issues/$9)*
L233	*Organic Gardening (monthly/$9)*
L233	*Prevention (monthly/$9)*
L235	*Salt Magazine*
L247	*Stony Hills: New England Alternative Press Review (3/$3)*
L251	*Progressive (monthly/$17)*
L257	*Televisions (quarterly/$10)*

✳ OTHER PUBLICATION

L012	*Chimo: Electronic Newsletter of EIES*
L019	*Networkers Package ($10)*
L023	*LNS ($240 year)*
L162	*Corporate Crime Comics ($1.25)*
L162	*Food Comics ($1)*
L162	*Mama! Dramas (comics, $1)*

✦ DIRECTORY

L017	*Directory of Free Universities and Learning Networks ($1)*
L026	*SOURCETAP: Directory of Program Resources for Radio ($35)*
L107	*Alternative America: 5000 Groups and Organizations ($4)*
L108	*Alternative Press Index (quarterly/$25)*
L111	*Computerized Bulletin Board Systems Directory ($1)*
L125	*Bear's Guide to Non-Traditional College Degrees ($20)*
L152	*Gazette Guide ($3)*
L159	*More Films Kids Like ($8.95)*
L176	*Directory of Homosexual Organizations & Publications ($3)*
L204	*There Ought to Be Free Choice: School Directory ($5)*
L206	*NDN State Facilitators Profiles*
L208	*Directory of Accredited Home Study Schools (free)*
L218	*New Pages Guide to Alternative Periodicals ($2.50)*
L222	*California Guide to Alternative Education ($5)*
L242	*International Directory of Little Magazines & Small Presses*
L245	*Southern Progressive Periodicals Directory ($1.50)*
L261	*Women in Focus*
L265	*Index/Directory of Women's Media ($8)*

✦ REPORT

L005	*Managing Our World: The United Nations in the 1980s*
L009	*New Directions Sourcebooks in Experiential Learning*
L133	*Investigative Reports ($6)*
L136	*Renewing Liberal Education: A Primer ($6.50)*
L140	*Coming Home: Community Based Education and Development*
L141	*Coalition to End Animal Suffering in Experiments Fact Sheet*
L151	*Cultural Survival Occasional Papers ($4)*
L151	*Indian Peoples of Paraguay (Maybury-Lewis & Howe)*
L169	*Food and Agriculture Books ($.25)*
L169	*Social Change Literature ($.25)*
L212	*NTIS Information Services Catalog*
L260	*Womansplace Booklist ($1)*

✦ HANDBOOK

L010	*Teaching Human Dignity ($8.95)*
L010	*Teaching the Vietnam War ($7.50)*
L031	*Networking Game (Wagner & Smith, $1.50)*
L137	*Friendly Classroom for a Small Planet ($6.95)*
L158	*Home Video Handbook*
L161	*How to Use ERIC*
L187	*Learning Web: Working to Liberate the Educational Process*
L192	*Citizen's Guide to the Nuclear Industry's Media Blitz ($.25)*
L230	*Workers' Rights Handbook ($2.50)*
L239	*Stretching (Anderson, $7.95)*
L271	*Children's Rights Handbook ($3.45)*

✦ BOOK

L002	*Holonomy: A Human Systems Theory (Stamps, $12)*
L002	*Networking: The First Report and Directory*
L012	*The Network Nation: Human Communication via Computer*
L020	*How Children Learn (Holt, $1)*
L020	*Instead of Education (Holt, $3.50)*

L024   *Cheez! Uncle Sam ($8.95)*
L110   *Literacy in 30 Hours: Paulo Freire's Process ($2.50)*
L120   *Einstein and Humanism ($12)*
L192   *Taking the Initiative: Corporate Control of Referendum ($10)*
L238   *Little Green Book: Guide to Self-Reliant Living ($5.95)*
L239   *Shelter II ($10)*
L242   *Intelligent Guide to Book Distribution ($5.95)*
L248   *Essays on Teachers' Centers ($10)*
L258   *Journeys: An Inquiry into Meaning and Value*

✦ AUDIOVISUAL

L018   *Great Atlantic Radio Series (tapes, $5)*
L118   *Oaksie: Basketmaker, Fiddler and Harp Player ($35 rental)*
L118   *Ourselves and That Promise: Four Kentuckians ($40 rental)*
L118   *Strip Mining: Energy, Environment & Economics ($75 rental)*
L131   *Canyon Cinema Catalog No. 4 ($2)*
L154   *Eight Minutes to Midnight: Helen Caldicott (Benjamin)*
L154   *Karl Hess: Toward Liberty ($40 rental)*
L168   *Garlic Is as Good as Ten Mothers (Blank)*
L168   *Love Songs of the Southwest (Les Blank)*
L182   *Chicago Maternity Center Study ($40)*
L182   *Taylor Chain: Story of a Local Union ($50)*
L190   *Are You Listening? (videotape series)*
L216   *Northern Lights: From the Agarian Movement ($350 rental)*
L216   *War at Home: The Other War of the 1960s ($350 rental)*
L223   *Holy Smoke: Biblical Reflections on the Energy Crisis*
L223   *Hopeful Revolution: Nicaragua (filmstrip, $24)*
L254   *Educational Film Catalog*
L263   *Herstory (film, $648)*
L263   *Women and Law (film, $1362)*
L272   *Juvenile Court (Wiseman, $95)*
L272   *Manoeuvre (Wiseman, $95)*
L272   *Titicut Follies (Wiseman, $95)*

✦ OTHER MATERIAL

L031   *Open Network Information Packet ($4)*

———————————— GROWING TITLES ————————————

✳ NEWSLETTER

G001   *Free Mind (bimonthly/$15)*
G003   *AHP Newsletter (monthly/$20)*
G004   *Association for Transpersonal Psychology Newsletter (4/$25)*
G009   *News from CCA ($5 year)*
G011   *Dying Project Newsletter (donation)*
G017   *New Games News/Letter (quarterly/$5)*
G019   *Prison Ashram Project (bimonthly/donation)*
G025   *Anahata Nada (bimonthly)*
G028   *Spiritual Journeys (monthly/$12 year)*
G029   *Good News (monthly/$3)*
G111   *Aquarian Research Foundation Newsletter (monthly/$12)*
G112   *Thoughtline: Arcana Workshops Newsletter (monthly)*
G115   *AURA Newsletter (bimonthly/$10)*
G121   *Black Bart Newsletter*
G124   *Boomerang Newsletter*
G126   *Brain/Mind Bulletin (triweekly/$15)*
G127   *CABO Newsletter (monthly)*
G134   *CWSS Feminist Bulletin (bimonthly/$8)*
G135   *Center for History of American Needlework (quarterly/$15)*
G138   *Theaterwork (bimonthly/$5)*
G141   *Center Circles (monthly/$1)*

G143   *Coming Changes Newsletter (bimonthly/$15)*
G148   *Revelations of Awareness (biweekly/$30)*
G154   *Blind Donkey (quarterly/$10)*
G175   *Hanuman Foundation Dying Project*
G196   *Densal ($4 year)*
G199   *Kripaluvani: The Voice of Kripalu/Toronto (quarterly)*
G204   *Pyramid Guide Newsletter (bimonthly/$9)*
G209   *Seeker Newsletter (quarterly/$15)*
G210   *Love (quarterly)*
G220   *Expansion: A Consciousness Publication (bimonthly/$12)*
G231   *New Age Music Network Newsletter*
G232   *New Age Network Newsletter (bimonthly)*
G237   *New Life Now (quarterly/$10)*
G238   *NOVUS Newsletter*
G241   *North American Network of Women Runners (quarterly)*
G252   *Poetry Project Newsletter (monthly/$5)*
G253   *Prout News (biweekly/free)*
G255   *Newsletter of the Providence Zen Center (monthly/$5)*
G257   *Rare Earth Report (bimonthly/$72)*
G260   *The Unicorn (8 issues/$6)*
G262   *Rudra: Shree Gurudev Rudrananda Ashram (monthly)*
G266   *Friend of the World: Sanatana Dharma Foundation*
G268   *Dimensions ($20 year)*
G277   *Human and Spiritual Understanding Newsletter (quarterly)*
G282   *Spirals (bimonthly/$3)*
G288   *Sharings: St. Louis Unit for Service (quarterly/$4)*
G290   *Tributaries: Newsletter of the Sufi Order (monthly/$15)*
G294   *T'ai Chi (bimonthly/$5)*
G295   *Taeria News (monthly)*
G298   *Textile Artists' Newsletter: Review of Textile Arts (4/$6)*
G300   *The Churchman (monthly/$6.50)*
G302   *Loving Brotherhood Newsletter (monthly/$15)*
G307   *Vagabond's Shoes: For the Independent Traveler (4/$15)*
G310   *Spectrum (monthly)*
G311   *New Community: Bulletin of UGB (monthly)*
G314   *Washington Buddhist (quarterly/$15)*
G320   *Windsurfer (4 issues/$10)*
G321   *Women at the Helm (quarterly/$10)*
G322   *Women in the Wilderness (quarterly/$10)*
G326   *World Goodwill Newsletter (quarterly)*

✳ NEWSPAPER

G134   *Longest Revolution: Views of Progressive Feminism (6/$6)*
G152   *Damage (monthly/$10)*
G198   *Kripalu Yoga Quest*
G221   *Movement of Spiritual Inner Awareness (monthly/$7.50)*
G234   *New Art Examiner: Voice of the Visual Arts (10 issues/$15)*
G317   *West Art (bimonthly/$8)*
G318   *Whole Life Times (bimonthly/$3)*
G330   *Pathways: A Guide to Conscious Living (quarterly)*

✦ JOURNAL

G003   *Journal of Humanistic Psychology (4 issues/$12)*
G004   *Journal of Transpersonal Psychology (2 issues/$15)*
G010   *Dromenon: A Journal of New Ways of Being (4 issues/$9)*
G015   *Collaboration (quarterly/$2)*
G025   *Jharna-Kala (art quarterly/$10 year)*
G107   *Anima: An Experiential Journal (semiannual/$8.50)*
G113   *Moral Education Forum (quarterly/$12)*
G123   *Salted in the Shell*
G145   *Radical Religion (quarterly/$12)*
G147   *Contact Quarterly: A Vehicle for Moving Ideas*

G150   *Journal of Creative Behavior (quarterly/$10)*
G154   *Kahawai: Journal of Women and Zen (quarterly)*
G162   *Faithist Journal (bimonthly/$7.50)*
G169   *Friends Journal (19 issues/$12)*
G191   *Aquarian Lights (quarterly/$9.50)*
G192   *International Home Exchange Service (quarterly/$60)*
G193   *New Thought: Dedicated to Spiritual Enlightenment (4/$7)*
G194   *Jump Cut: Review of Contemporary Cinema (quarterly/$6)*
G200   *Kronos: Journal of Interdisciplinary Synthesis (4/$15)*
G201   *Laughing Man (bimonthly/$20)*
G206   *Lindisfarne Letter (semiannual/$25)*
G212   *M. Gentle Men for Gender Justice (quarterl)*
G216   *Menorah: Sparks of Jewish Renewal (monthly/$15)*
G217   *Metamorphoses: Alternative Development in Canada (6/$10)*
G218   *Udumbara: A Journal of Zen Master Dogen (semiannual/$5)*
G219   *Modern Haiku (3 issues/$7.50)*
G227   *New Age Gazette (monthly/$6)*
G235   *New Atlantean Journal (quarterly/$5)*
G249   *Parabola: Myth and the Quest for Meaning (quarterly/$14)*
G258   *ReVision: Knowledge and Consciousness (biannual/$15)*
G264   *Samisdat (500 pages/$12)*
G273   *Vajra Bodhi Sea (monthly)*
G275   *Sluggo: Journal of Disturbing Clues (quarterly/$7)*
G278   *Folk Harp Journal (quarterly/$8)*
G279   *Sojourners (monthly/$12)*
G280   *Soluna (bimonthly/$9)*
G287   *Auroville Review (quarterly/$12)*
G289   *Journal of Psychedelic Drugs (quarterly/$30)*
G296   *Ganymede (quarterly/$5)*
G303   *Liaison: Revue Culturelle (monthly)*
G324   *WomenSpirit (quarterly/$6)*
G334   *Zygon: Journal of Religion and Science (quarterly/$18)*

✳ MAGAZINE

G001   *Humanist (monthly/$12)*
G008   *Chimo: The Holistic Magazine of Our Times (monthly/$12)*
G013   *Intimate Talk ($24 year)*
G022   *Sing Out! The Folk Song Magazine (bimonthly/$8.50)*
G025   *Aum Magazine (monthly/$5 year)*
G026   *The Sun (12 issues/$12)*
G103   *Alternatives: Tools for Holistic Living (bimonthly/$12)*
G104   *American Astrology (monthly)*
G116   *Parallelogramme (bimonthly)*
G120   *Many Smokes (quarterly/$4)*
G129   *Canada Quilts (5 issues/$8.05)*
G130   *Canpara: Canadian Parachutist (8 issues/$20)*
G132   *Esoteric Review (bimonthly/free)*
G140   *Stone Soup: The Magazine by Children (5 issues/$12)*
G155   *Different Worlds: Adventure Role-Playing Games (6/$10.50)*
G165   *Fine Woodworking (bimonthly/$14)*
G172   *Games (bimonthly/$7.97)*
G173   *Great Expeditions: Real Travelers & Explorers (6/$15)*
G179   *High Times (monthly/$21)*
G184   *Inner Paths: Eastern & Western Spiritual Thought (6/$7.50)*
G197   *Kite Lines (quarterly/$9)*
G202   *American Wheelmen (monthly/$15)*
G205   *Lilith: The Jewish Women's Magazine (quarterly/$12)*
G208   *Op: Magazine of the Lost Music Network (8 issues/$8)*
G213   *Magical Blend: A Magazine of Synergy (quarterly/$10)*
G229   *New Age Magazine (monthly/$15)*
G246   *Outside (monthly/$12)*
G250   *Erie Christian Witness (bimonthly/donation)*

G251   *PhenomeNEWS (monthly/$5)*
G286   *Pandora: Role-Expanding Science Fiction and Fantasy (4/$6)*
G297   *World - Faiths - Insight (semiannual)*
G304   *American Theosophist (monthly/$7)*
G309   *Parachutist (monthly/$18.50)*
G323   *Women's Sports (monthly/$9.95)*
G325   *WoodenBoat (bimonthly/$15)*
G331   *Yoga Journal (bimonthly/$10)*

✦ DIRECTORY

G003   *AHP Resource Directory ($6)*
G005   *Bed & Breakfast Directory*
G024   *Spiritual Community Guide ($5.95)*
G102   *Alternative Celebrations Catalogue ($5)*
G163   *Family Pastimes Catalog*
G170   *Front Range: Women in the Visual Arts ($2.50)*
G185   *International Guide to PSI Periodicals & Organizations ($4)*
G214   *Many Hands: Guide to Holistic Health and Awareness*
G307   *Travelers' Directory (quarterly/$12)*
G309   *United States Drop Zone Directory ($3)*
G310   *Directory for a New World ($4)*

✦ REPORT

G020   *Guidelines on Choosing Toys for Children ($1)*
G021   *Basic Paradigm of a Future Socio-Cultural System (Hine)*
G149   *Student Travel Catalog*
G171   *Alternatives for Youth-At-Risk ($.50)*
G201   *Four Fundamental Questions (Da Free John, $1.95)*

✦ HANDBOOK

G019   *Inside/Out: A Spiritual Manual for Prison Life (free)*
G024   *Pilgrim's Guide to Planet Earth ($8.95)*
G149   *Whole World Handbook: Student Work, Study, & Travel ($3.95)*
G167   *Course in Miracles (two volumes, $35)*
G207   *Conversations With John (Spangler, $1.75)*

✦ BOOK

G011   *Grist for the Mill (Ram Dass & Levine, $3.95)*
G012   *Spirit of Sunrise (by Michael Cecil et al.)*
G015   *Essential Aurobindo ($3.95)*
G015   *Practical Guide to Integral Yoga ($6)*
G017   *More New Games ($6.95)*
G017   *New Games Book ($4.95)*
G027   *Psychic Side of Sports (Murphy & White)*
G120   *Bear Tribe's Self-Reliance Book ($4.25)*
G120   *Medicine Wheel (Sun Bear & Wabun, $6.75)*
G123   *Gulf of Maine Reader   1 ($4.95)*
G123   *Wolf Driving Sled (Lawless, $3.50)*
G134   *Rainbow Snake: Contemporary Women Poets*
G135   *Domestic American Textiles: A Sourcebook ($14.95)*
G153   *At a Journal Workshop (Ira Progoff, $7.95)*
G153   *Practice of Process Meditation (Progoff, $7.95)*
G161   *Metaphoric Mind: A Celebration of Creative Consciousness*
G161   *Opening: A Primer on Self-Actualization*
G165   *Fine Woodworking Design Book Two ($15.95)*
G166   *Focusing (Gendlin, $3.50)*
G186   *Experience of Insight (Goldstein)*
G186   *Living Buddhist Masters (Kornfield)*
G189   *Autobiography of a Sufi (Gold, $4.95)*
G189   *Beyond Sex (Gold, $5.95)*
G189   *New American Book of the Dead ($7.95)*

G195   *Jungian-Senoi Dreamwork Manual ($14.95)*
G201   *Enlightenment of the Whole Body (Da Free John, $10.95)*
G206   *Earth's Answer: Explorations of Planetary Culture ($6.95)*
G206   *Passages About Earth (William Irwin Thompson)*
G207   *Revelation: Birth of a New Age (Spangler, $5.95)*
G242   *On the New Age Books ($4)*
G247   *Outward Bound: Schools of the Possible ($8.95)*
G256   *No One Is to Blame: Love Divorce from Mom and Dad ($5.95)*
G267   *Roof: Poetry Series ($10)*
G270   *Letter to a Child with Cancer (Kubler-Ross, $2.95)*
G270   *On Death and Dying (Kubler-Ross, $2.95)*
G293   *Synergic Power: Beyond Domination and Permissiveness ($4.95)*
G322   *Women in the Wilderness (Galland, $7.95)*
G330   *Inner Development ($9.95)*

✦ AUDIOVISUAL

G011   *Living/Dying Retreat (tape, $2.50)*
G236   *New Dimensions Audio Tapes*
G270   *Life, Death and Life After Death (Kubler-Ross, $7.95)*
G274   *Guided Meditation Series (tapes, $6 each)*
G274   *It Can't Be Described in Words (tape, $7.98)*
G316   *Black Box (audio cassette magazine, 4 issues/$16.75)*

✦ OTHER MATERIAL

G009   *Travelers Network ($10 year)*
G117   *Astro*Carto*Graphy Maps ($18 each)*
G135   *Ethnic Costume Embroidery (slides, $9)*
G182   *Illuminations Buttons ($1)*
G182   *Illuminations Transparencies ($1.25-$3.50)*
G182   *Illuminations Windows of Light ($12.95)*
G292   *Survival Cards ($2.75 set)*
G297   *Continuum Exhibit: The Immortality Principle*

EVOLVING TITLES

✳ NEWSLETTER

E002   *Catholic Peace Fellowship Bulletin*
E004   *What's Next (monthly/$10)*
E005   *Peace Chronicle (bimonthly/$15)*
E006   *Friends of the Third World Newsletter ($25)*
E007   *Associates Newsletter (6 issues)*
E008   *Human Rights Internet Newsletter (9 issues/$25)*
E010   *Government Tomorrow*
E011   *News and Notes (quarterly/$15)*
E012   *Connections: Social Network Analysis (3 issues/$8)*
E013   *National Peace Academy Campaign Update (quarterly/$25)*
E018   *Netnotes ($12)*
E019   *One Family (quarterly/$15)*
E022   *TRANET (quarterly/$15)*
E025   *Checkpoint*
E026   *WIN News (quarterly/$15)*
E027   *Across Frontiers*
E101   *APRO Bulletin (monthly)*
E103   *Africa News Service (weekly/$25)*
E108   *Salubritas (quarterly)*
E109   *The Link (bimonthly/$10)*
E111   *Aquarian Age: Monthly for Space and Equality (12 issues/$10)*
E112   *Arms Control Today ($20 year)*
E116   *Reflector: The Astronomical League (quarterly)*
E119   *Aviation/Space Writers Newsletter (bimonthly/$40)*
E123   *Nuclear Export Monitor*

E125	*Current Issues ($15)*
E126	*International Peace Studies Newsletter (quarterly/free)*
E129	*Global Issue (bimonthly)*
E130	*CUFOS Associate Newsletter (monthly/$25)*
E131	*Global Report (4 issues/$15)*
E133	*Centerpoint (bimonthly)*
E137	*Close-up (quarterly/$10)*
E139	*Mad'Gazette*
E146	*Faire Word (monthly)*
E165	*Friends of the Filipino People Bulletin (monthly/$10)*
E170	*Global Perspectives*
E180	*Innovation et Reseaux pour le Developpement Forum (4/$20)*
E184	*Macroscope*
E186	*Trajectories (8 issues/$8)*
E187	*Institute of Noetic Sciences Newsletter (quarterly/$25)*
E195	*Kirlian Communications (monthly/$12)*
E196	*IUCN Bulletin (bimonthly/$20)*
E198	*International Women's Tribune Newsletter (4 issues/$5)*
E199	*Hunger*
E204	*L-5 News (monthly)*
E206	*Leading Edge: Bulletin of Social Transformation (17/$15)*
E208	*Magic Circle: The Native American Indian (donation)*
E211	*Outlook: Maryland Alliance for Space Colonization ($5 year)*
E215	*National Network Newsletter (monthly/$5)*
E216	*Insight: National Space Institute (bimonthly)*
E221	*News from Guatemala (monthly/$6.80)*
E227	*Omega News (Von Dreger and McManus, $5)*
E229	*Open Systems (monthly/$95)*
E234	*Newsfront International (semimonthly/$22)*
E236	*Planetary Association for Clean Energy Newsletter (4/$10)*
E238	*Plenty News (quarterly/donation)*
E239	*Popline: Population Action Council Monthly (12 issues)*
E248	*Resource Center for Nonviolence Newsletter (bimonthly)*
E256	*Shalom Network Newsletter (monthly/$10)*
E257	*International Report of Sierra Club Earthcare (monthly/$10)*
E258	*General Systems Bulletin (3 issues/$6)*
E263	*Noosphere (quarterly/$12)*
E266	*Turning Point Newsletter (biannual/$5)*
E269	*USLA Reporter (monthly/$4)*
E275	*Update Latin America (bimonthly)*
E277	*ISIS International Bulletin (quarterly/$15)*
E278	*Peace and Freedom (monthly/$4)*
E281	*World Environment Report (biweekly/$179)*
E282	*World Federalist Newsletter (quarterly)*
E289	*World Space Federation Newsletter (quarterly/$10)*

✳ NEWSPAPER

E009	*Shift in the Wind (quarterly)*
E020	*Videoguide ($5)*
E028	*Future Times*
E131	*Disarmament Times ($5)*
E138	*Coevolution*
E158	*Evolution*
E177	*InfoWorld: Newspaper for Microcomputing (26 issues/$18)*
E183	*In These Times (weekly)*
E193	*International Herald Tribune (daily)*
E199	*Action (monthly)*
E286	*World Peace (monthly/$14)*
E291	*WorldPaper (monthly/$15)*

✳ JOURNAL

E001	*Journal of World Education (quarterly/$20)*

E005   *Peace and Change*
E007   *Whole Earth Papers ($10)*
E012   *Social Networks: Journal of Structural Analysis*
E014   *NACLA Report on the Americas (bimonthly/$13)*
E019   *Planet Earth (semiannual/$15)*
E023   *Transnational Associations (bilingual, monthly/$25)*
E028   *Futurist (bimonthly/$18)*
E102   *Southern Africa Perspectives Series (monthly/$5)*
E113   *Asia Record: East and Southeast Asian Affairs (monthly/$12)*
E120   *Bulletin of Concerned Asian Scholars (quarterly/$14)*
E123   *Development/Finance (10 issues/$50)*
E135   *Monchanin Revue/Journal: Cross-Cultural Understanding (4/$6)*
E148   *Computer Music Journal (quarterly/$20)*
E183   *Race and Class (quarterly)*
E192   *Computing Teacher (7 issues/$14.50)*
E194   *International Journal of General Systems*
E201   *Journal of Developing Areas (quarterly/$12)*
E213   *MERIP Reports (9 issues/$12)*
E220   *New Humanity Journal*
E223   *Transformation News: Journal of Synthesis (quarterly/$7)*
E249   *Resurgence (bimonthly/$17.50)*
E250   *Review of International Broadcasting (monthly/$15)*
E251   *Robotics Age: Journal of Intelligent Machines (6 issues/$10)*
E260   *Southeast Asia Chronicle (bimonthly/$10)*
E270   *US-China Review (bimonthly/$6)*
E284   *Hunger Notes (monthly/$10)*
E290   *World Union (monthly/$6)*

✳ MAGAZINE

E021   *Source World ($2 issue)*
E106   *Science '82 (10 issues/$15)*
E106   *Science (weekly/$38)*
E110   *Analog: Science Fiction/Science Fact (monthly/$10)*
E121   *Byte: The Small Systems Journal (monthly/$18)*
E136   *Claustrophobia: Boundary Resistance Combozine (monthly/$30)*
E145   *Compute Magazine*
E150   *Coop's Satellite Digest (monthly/$50)*
E151   *Creative Computing (monthly/$15)*
E152   *De Kleine Aarde (The Little Earth)*
E154   *Down to Earth Magazine (bimonthly/$4)*
E170   *Intercom (quarterly/$8)*
E172   *Home Video (monthly/$12)*
E183   *Working Papers for a New Society (monthly)*
E188   *Intercontinental Press/Inprecor (weekly/$35)*
E197   *Dialogue: International Voluntary Services*
E214   *Mushroom: Living in New Zealand (bimonthly/$8.10)*
E222   *Next: A Look into the Future (bimonthly/$12)*
E224   *Nuestro Magazine*
E233   *Recreational Computing (bimonthly/$15)*
E234   *Connexions: International Feminist Quarterly (4/$10)*
E242   *Purser's Magazine (quarterly/$12)*
E253   *Science Digest (monthly/$13.97)*
E254   *Bulletin of the Science Fiction Writers (quarterly/$10)*
E255   *Science News (weekly/$19.50)*
E261   *Southern Africa (monthly/$10)*
E288   *World Press Review (monthly/$16)*

✳ OTHER PUBLICATION

E105   *Apocalypse How? (survey)*
E189   *Interlink Press Service*
E190   *Forum for Correspondence and Contact (by invitation)*

✦ DIRECTORY

E015	*Directory of Nonviolence Trainers ($2)*
E017	*Linkage (voluntary compendium)*
E020	*International Video Exchange Directory ($4)*
E023	*Yearbook of International Organizations ($69)*
E023	*Yearbook of World Problems and Human Potential ($65)*
E112	*World Military and Social Expenditures ($3.50)*
E147	*CIE People's Software News*
E196	*Red Data Books of Endangered Species ($22-$60)*
E210	*Das Adressbuch Alternatives Projekte*
E277	*International Women and Health Resource Guide ($8)*
E284	*Who's Involved with Hunger: An Organization Guide ($3)*

✦ REPORT

E014	*NACLA Research Methodology Guide ($1.50)*
E117	*Australian Resource List ($2)*
E160	*Love over Mind over Matter (Jaccaci, $3)*
E160	*Social Change: A Developmental Journey (Jaccaci, $3)*
E171	*Prague Winter: Human Rights in Czechoslovakia (free)*
E190	*Learning Laboratory: A Center of Youth Alternatives*
E200	*Consider the Groupware: Electronic Group Work ($5)*
E200	*Speculations on Facilitating Network Structures ($5)*
E212	*Middle East Peace Project Information Packet ($40 year)*
E218	*Elements of a Network to Educate for World Security*
E292	*World Watch Paper ($2)*

✦ HANDBOOK

E014	*NACLA Handbook: The U.S. Military Apparatus ($1.75)*
E018	*Networking: Legitech Experiments ($10)*
E018	*The Networkbook ($100)*
E027	*Constitution for the Federation of Earth ($5)*
E127	*Rights of the Child ($1.50)*
E273	*Alternatives Adressbuch (yearly)*

✦ BOOK

E007	*Toward a Human World Order*
E010	*Anticipatory Democracy: People in the Politics of the Future*
E011	*World Hunger: Ten Myths ($2.25)*
E017	*Beyond Despair (Theobald)*
E017	*We're Not Ready for That Yet (Theobald/$10)*
E026	*Hosken Report: Genital/Sexual Mutilation of Females ($17)*
E112	*Dangers of Nuclear War ($4.95)*
E122	*General Systems Theory and the Creative Process (King)*
E168	*Evolutionary Journal ($7.95)*
E168	*Hunger of Eve: A Woman's Odyssey (Hubbard, $8.95)*
E182	*Information Society (Masuda)*
E184	*Study of Future Worlds (Falk, $6.95)*
E184	*True Worlds: A Transnational Perspective ($9.95)*
E187	*Health for the Whole Person ($12.95)*
E206	*Aquarian Conspiracy (Ferguson, $15)*
E238	*Spiritual Midwifery (Gaskin, $8.95)*
E258	*General Systems Yearbook ($28)*
E268	*Limits to Growth*
E283	*Energy, Earth and Everyone (Gabel, $10.95)*
E283	*Ho-Ping: Food for Everyone (Gabel, $9.95)*
E283	*Introduction to the World Game (R.B. Fuller, $3.50)*
E292	*Sisterhood of Man (Newland, $3.95)*

✦ AUDIOVISUAL

E011	*Food First ($80 slides, $30 filmstrip)*
E019	*Earth, Space and Our Place*

E102   *Children Under Apartheid (photo exhibit, $15)*
E198   *Caribbean Women Speak Out (slide/tape)*
E238   *The Plenty Band (tape, $4.50)*
E287   *Conscience and War Taxes (slides, $50)*

◆ OTHER MATERIAL

E141   *Info/Liberty Internet (computer conference, $30)*
E168   *Theatre of the Future (multimedia show)*
E200   *Visions & Tools Packet for Electronic Networking ($5)*
E219   *MIST: Networker's Electronic Toolchest (microsoftware)*
E233   *Personal Computer Network (PCNET, software)*